A GUIDE TO
Microsoft®
Exchange Server 5.5

Ed Tittel

Barry Shilmover

Tim Catura-Houser

COURSE
TECHNOLOGY

ONE MAIN STREET, CAMBRIDGE, MA 02142

an International Thomson Publishing company I**T**P®

Cambridge • Albany • Bonn • Boston • Cincinnati • London • Madrid • Melbourne • Mexico City
New York • Paris • San Francisco • Singapore • Tokyo • Toronto • Washington

A Guide to Microsoft® Exchange Server 5.5 is published by Course Technology.

Publisher:	Keith Weiskamp
Acquisitions Editor:	Shari Jo Hehr
Managing Editors:	Paula Kmetz, Kristen Duerr
Product Managers:	Jeff Kellum, Jennifer Normandin
Production Editors:	Kim Eoff, Roxanne Alexander
Technical Editing:	Richard Ingram
Composition House:	GEX, Inc.
Text Designer:	GEX, Inc.
Cover Designer:	Wendy J. Reifeiss
Marketing Specialist:	Cynthia Caldwell
Marketing Manager:	Tracy Foley

QA
76
.9
C55
T58
1999

© 1999 by Course Technology—I(T)P®

For more information contact:

Course Technology
One Main Street
Cambridge, MA 02142

ITP Europe
Berkshire House 168-173
High Holborn
London WCIV 7AA
England

Nelson ITP Australia
102 Dodds Street
South Melbourne, 3205
Victoria, Australia

ITP Nelson Canada
1120 Birchmount Road
Scarborough, Ontario
Canada M1K 5G4

International Thomson Editores
Seneca, 53
Colonia Polanco
11560 Mexico D.F. Mexico

ITP GmbH
Königswinterer Strasse 418
53227 Bonn
Germany

ITP Asia
60 Albert Street, #15-01
Albert Complex
Singapore 189969

ITP Japan
Hirakawacho Kyowa Building, 3F
2-2-1 Hirakawacho
Chiyoda-ku, Tokyo 102
Japan

Trademarks

Course Technology and the Open Book logo are registered trademarks and CourseKits is a trademark of Course Technology. Custom Edition is a registered trademark of International Thomson Publishing.

I(T)P® The ITP logo is a registered trademark of International Thomson Publishing.

Some of the product names and company names used in this book have been used for identification purposes only and may be trademarks or registered trademarks of their respective manufacturers and sellers.

Disclaimer

Course Technology reserves the right to revise this publication and make changes from time to time in its content without notice.

ISBN 0-7600-1143-5

Printed in Canada

1 2 3 4 5 6 7 8 9 WC 02 01 00 99 98

BRIEF TABLE OF CONTENTS

TABLE OF CONTENTS

PREFACE

Welcome to *A Guide to Microsoft Exchange Server 5.5!* This new book from Course Technology offers you real-world examples, interactive activities, and over 100 hands-on projects that reinforce key concepts and help you prepare for the Microsoft Certification Exam #70-081, Implementing and Supporting Microsoft Exchange Server 5.5. This book also features troubleshooting tips for solutions to common problems that you will encounter.

To aid you in fully understanding Exchange Server 5.5 concepts, there are many features in this book designed to help you logically work through and confidently prepare for the exam.

This book is filled with hands-on projects that cover every aspect of Microsoft Exchange Server 5.5. The projects are designed to make what you learn *come alive* by actually performing the tasks. In addition to the hands-on projects, each chapter offers case projects that put you in the position of a consultant working in a variety of situations to fulfill the needs of clients. Also, every chapter includes a range of practice questions to help you prepare for the Microsoft certification exam. All of these features are offered to reinforce your learning so you will feel confident in the knowledge you gain from each chapter.

Chapter 1, "Introduction to Microsoft Exchange Server 5.5," describes the history of Exchange Server, its components and features, and some basic messaging concepts environment. In Chapter 2, "Exchange Server Architecture," you are given a detailed look at how the Exchange Server fits into a Windows NT network and insight into how the Exchange Server components communicate with each other.

In Chapter 3, "Installing Exchange Server 5.5," you go through the steps to plan and install Exchange Server. Chapter 4, "Exchange Server Communication," describes the communication processes used by Exchange Server and discusses the Message Transfer Agent. In Chapter 5, "Managing Message Recipients," you are introduced to the object-oriented structure of Exchange Server and some key message recipient components including mailboxes, distribution lists, and custom recipients. Chapter 6, "Exchange Clients and Client Configuration," builds on the information in Chapter 5 and steps you through the installation and configuration of Exchange clients. The last chapter dealing with configuration is Chapter 7, "Exchange Server Configuration." In this chapter, you look at the various management tools, including the Exchange Administrator, and site configuration issues.

In Chapter 8, "Intersite Connectors," we look at a number of connectors available for Exchange Server, including the X.400, Internet Mail Service, and Dynamic RAS connectors. Chapter 9, "The Internet Mail Service," focuses on the IMS, it's protocols, and how it is used. Chapter 10, "Internet Mail Protocols," provides a detailed review of the protocols supported by Exchange Server 5.5 and their configurations.

Chapter 11, "Exchange Security," discusses one of the most important aspects of using Exchange Server: ensuring security by using public and private folders and the Key Manager. Chapter 12, "Monitoring and Maintaining Exchange Server," covers the use of Performance Monitor with Exchange Server, various database administration strategies, and remote server administration. Chapter 13, "Exchange Server Forms," discusses creating and using Exchange Server electronic forms and the sample forms included with Exchange Server 5.5.

Chapter 14, "Using Exchange with Other Systems," takes you through the steps necessary to configure your Exchange Server to pass messages between various other types of servers including cc:Mail and NetWare. Finally, Chapter 15, "Troubleshooting Exchange Server," focuses on various problems that may arise and their solutions. The glossary is a complete compendium of all of the acronyms and technical terms used in this book, with definitions.

This book is intended to be read in sequence, from beginning to end. Each chapter builds on the preceding chapters, to provide a solid understanding of internetworking with Exchange Server 5.5. After completing the chapters, you may find it useful to go back through the book, and use the review questions and projects to prepare for the Microsoft Certification Exam #70-081, Implementing and Supporting Microsoft Exchange Server 5.5. Readers are also encouraged to investigate the many pointers to online and printed sources of additional information that are cited throughout this book.

FEATURES

To aid you in fully understanding Exchange Server 5.5, there are many features in this book designed to improve its value.

- **Chapter Objectives** Each chapter in this book begins with a detailed list of the concepts to be mastered within that chapter. This list provides you with a quick reference to the contents of that chapter, as well as a useful study aid.

- **Illustrations and Tables** Numerous illustrations aid you in the visualization of common setups, theories, and architectures. In addition, many tables provide details and comparisons of both practical and theoretical information.

- **Chapter Summaries** Each chapter's text is followed by a summary of the concepts it has introduced. These summaries provide a helpful way to recap and revisit the ideas covered in each chapter.

- **Review Questions** End-of-chapter assessment begins with a set of review questions that reinforce the ideas introduced in each chapter. These questions not only ensure that you have mastered the concepts, but are written to help prepare you for the Microsoft certification examination.

- **Hands-on Projects** Although it is important to understand the theory behind the technology, nothing can improve upon real world experience. With the exception of those chapters that are purely theoretical, each chapter provides a series of exercises aimed at providing you with hands-on implementation experience.

- **Case Projects** Finally, each chapter closes with a section that proposes a certain real-world situation. You are asked to evaluate the situation and decide upon the course of action needed to remedy the problems described. This valuable tool helps the student sharpen decision-making and troubleshooting skills — important aspects of set-up and administration.

TEXT AND GRAPHIC CONVENTIONS USED IN THIS BOOK

Where appropriate, additional information and activities have been added to this book to help the reader better understand what is being discussed in the chapter. Icons throughout the text alert individuals to additional materials. The icons used in this textbook are described below.

Note icons present additional helpful material related to the subject.

Tip icons highlight suggestions on ways to attack problems you may encounter in a real-world situation. As experienced network administrators, the authors have practical experience with how networks work in real business situations.

Caution icons appear in the margin next to concepts or steps that often cause difficulty. Each caution anticipates a potential mistake and provides methods for avoiding the same problem in the future.

Hands-on project icons precede each hands-on activity in this book.

Case project icons are located at the end of each chapter. They mark a more involved, scenario-based project. In this extensive case example, you are asked to independently implement what you have learned.

INSTRUCTOR'S MATERIALS

The following supplemental materials are available when this book is used in a classroom setting. All of the supplements available with this book are provided to the instructor on a single CD-ROM.

Electronic Instructor's Manual. The Instructor's Manual that accompanies this textbook includes:

- Additional instructional material to assist in class preparation, including suggestions for lecture topics, suggested lab activities, tips on setting up a lab for the hands-on assignments, and alternative lab setup ideas in situations where lab resources are limited.

- Solutions to all end-of-chapter materials, including the Project and Case assignments.

Course Test Manager 1.1. Accompanying this book is a powerful assessment tool known as the Course Test Manager. This cutting-edge Windows-based testing software helps instructors design and administer tests and pretests. In addition to being able to generate tests that can be printed and administered, this full-featured program also has an online testing component that allows students to take tests at the computer and have their exams automatically graded.

PowerPoint presentations. This book comes with Microsoft PowerPoint slides for each chapter. These are included as a teaching aid for classroom presentation, to make available to students on the network for chapter review, or to be printed for classroom distribution. Instructors, please feel at liberty to add your own slides for additional topics you introduce to the class.

TRANSCENDER CERTIFICATION TEST PREP SOFTWARE

Bound into the back of this book is a disk containing Transcender Corporation's Implementing and Supporting Microsoft Exchange Server 5.5 certification exam preparation software with one full exam that simulates the Microsoft Certification Exam #70-081.

ACKNOWLEDGMENTS

Ed Tittel

Every now and then, a book comes along that proves to be a particular challenge. This book belongs to that category, but we're very pleased to say that our own staff, particularly myself, Dawn Rader, David Johnson, and Mary Burmeister, were able to rise to this challenge and produce a book that is both jammed with information and readable to boot. Of course, we couldn't have done it without the wonderful team at The Coriolis Group, including Keith Weiskamp, our publisher, Shari Jo Hehr, our acquisitions editor, Sandra Lassiter, editorial and production direction, Paula Kmetz, managing editor, Jeff Kellum, project editor, Kim Eoff, production coordinator, and Robert Clarfield, CD-ROM developer, not to mention our bold and able copyeditor, Mary Millhollon. Thanks also to Coriolis's outstanding sales staff, especially Jim Barnett, Tom Mayer, Neil Gudovitz, and Anne Tull for their efforts to make this book sell. And finally, we're also grateful to the interior and cover design staff at Coriolis, who make these books look so sharp, including April Nielsen and Anthony Stock.

The real credit for this book goes to its authors, who labored mightily to see it to completion. In addition to Barry Shilmover and Tim Catura-Houser, both of whom contributed the bulk of the material, we'd also like to thank Chris Waters and Ramesh Chandak for their contributions as well. The work in here reflects the abilities of its writers and developers. Thanks for being such a great team. We can hardly wait for Exchange 6 to come along!

Barry Shilmover

First, I would like to thank my wife, Shawna, for understanding the long hours I put into this book and for not serving me with divorce papers during the project. I would not have been able to complete this book without her help. You are the best! My son, Jory, for still knowing who I was even though he never saw me. To the entire LANWrights team; Ed Tittel — for giving me a chance to work with your team, DJ — for putting up with my strange and wonderful questions, Dawn Rader and Mary Burmeister — for making the transition into the world of books relatively painless. Thanks to my family for understanding when I could not make it over for get-togethers. To anyone I missed, thanks. And finally, to my ITP class for buying me a drink the day after I stayed up all night to meet a deadline.

Tim Catura-Houser

Without the fantastic assistance of several super people, I couldn't have gotten the concepts presented to print. Somehow, a mere mega-thanks doesn't seem enough for Marilyn, for letting me stack servers like firewood in the living room. Compaq Computer, for helping build the stack of servers. And most important of all, a very special thanks to Dawn, DJ, Mary, and Ed, all from LANWrights, for the patience in converting me (regardless of the pain and suffering it caused them) from a writer of newsletters to a writer of technical manuals. Without the invaluable assistance of all of these grand folks, I never would have made it.

PREPARING FOR MICROSOFT CERTIFICATION

Microsoft offers a program called the Microsoft Certified Professional (MCP) program. Becoming a Microsoft Certified Professional can open many doors for you. Whether you want to be a network engineer, product specialist, or software developer, obtaining the appropriate Microsoft Certified Professional credentials can provide a formal record of your skills to potential employers. Certification can be equally effective in helping you secure a raise or promotion.

The Microsoft Certified Professional program is made up of many courses in several different tracks. Combinations of individual courses can lead to certification in a specific track. Most tracks require a combination of required and elective courses. One of the most common tracks for beginners is the Microsoft Certified Product Specialist (MCPS). By obtaining this status, your credentials tell a potential employer that you are an expert in a specialized computing area such as personal computer operating systems on a specific product, like Microsoft Windows 95.

How Can Transcender's Test Prep Software Help?

To become a Microsoft Certified Professional, you must pass rigorous certification exams that provide a valid and reliable measure of technical proficiency and expertise. The disk contained in this book, Transcender Corporation's Limited Version certification exam preparation software, can be used in conjunction with the book to help you assess your progress in the event you choose to pursue Microsoft professional certification. The Transcender disk presents a series of questions that were expertly prepared to test your readiness for the official Microsoft certification examination on Implementing and Supporting Microsoft Exchange Server 5.5 (Exam #70-081). These questions were taken from a larger series of practice tests produced by the Transcender Corporation — practice tests that simulate the interface and format of the actual certification exams. Transcender's complete product also offers explanations for all questions. The rationale for each correct answer is carefully explained, and specific page references are given for Microsoft product documentation and Microsoft Press reference books. These page references enable you to study from additional sources.

Practice test questions from Transcender Corporation are acknowledged as the best available. In fact, with their full product, Transcender offers a money-back guarantee if you do not pass the exam. If you have trouble passing the practice examination included on the enclosed disk, you should consider purchasing the full product with additional practice tests and personalized feedback. Details and pricing information are available at the back of this book. A sample of the full Transcender product is on the enclosed disk, including remedial explanations.

The Transcender product is a great tool to help you prepare to become certified. If you experience technical problems with this product, please e-mail Transcender at *course@transcender.com* or call (615) 726-8779.

Want to Know More about Microsoft Certification?

There are many additional benefits to achieving Microsoft Certified Professional status. These benefits apply to you as well as to your potential employer. As a Microsoft Certified Professional (MCP), you will be recognized as an expert on Microsoft products, have access to ongoing technical information from Microsoft, and receive special invitations to Microsoft conferences and events. You can access a comprehensive, interactive tool that provides full details about the Microsoft Certified Professional program online at *www.microsoft.com/mcp/mktg/cert.htm*. For more information on texts at Course Technology that will help prepare you for certification exams, visit our site at *www.course.com*.

When you become a Microsoft Certified Product Specialist, Microsoft sends you a Welcome Kit that contains:

- An 8-½" × 11" Microsoft Certified Product Specialist wall certificate. Also, within a few weeks after you have passed any exam, Microsoft sends you a Microsoft Certified Professional transcript that shows which exams you have passed.

- A Microsoft Certified Professional program membership card.

- A Microsoft Certified Professional lapel pin.

- A license to use the Microsoft Certified Professional logo. You are licensed to use the logo in your advertisements, promotions, proposals, and other materials, including business cards, letterheads, advertising circulars, brochures, yellow page advertisements, mailings, banners, resumes, and invitations.

- A Microsoft Certified Professional logo sheet. Before using the camera-ready logo, you must agree to the terms of the licensing agreement.

- A Microsoft TechNet CD-ROM.

- A 50% discount toward a one-year membership in the Microsoft TechNet Technical Information Network, which provides valuable information via monthly CD-ROMs.

- Dedicated forums on CompuServe (GO MECFORUM) and The Microsoft Network, which enable Microsoft Certified Professionals to communicate directly with Microsoft and one another.

- A one-year subscription to Microsoft Certified Professional Magazine, a career and professional development magazine created especially for Microsoft Certified Professionals.

- A Certification Update subscription. Certification Update is a bimonthly newsletter from the Microsoft Certified Professional program that keeps you informed of changes and advances in the program and exams.

- Invitations to Microsoft conferences, technical training sessions, and special events.

- Eligibility to join the Network Professional Association, a worldwide association of computer professionals. Microsoft Certified Product Specialists are invited to join as associate members.

A Microsoft Certified Systems Engineer receives all the benefits mentioned above as well as the following additional benefits:

- Microsoft Certified Systems Engineer logos and other materials to help you identify yourself as a Microsoft Certified Systems Engineer to colleagues or clients.

- Ten free incidents with the Microsoft Support Network and a 25% discount on purchases of additional 10-packs of Priority Development and Desktop Support incidents.

- A one-year subscription to the Microsoft TechNet Technical Information Network.

- A one-year subscription to the Microsoft Beta Evaluation program. This benefit provides you with up to 12 free monthly beta software CDs for many new Microsoft software products. This enables you to become familiar with new versions of Microsoft products before they are generally available. This benefit also includes access to a private CompuServe forum where you can exchange information with other program members and find information from Microsoft on current beta issues and product information.

Certify Me!

So you are ready to become a Microsoft Certified Professional. The examinations are administered through Sylvan Prometric (formerly Drake Prometric) and are offered at more than 700 authorized testing centers around the world. Microsoft evaluates certification status based on current exam records. Your current exam record is the set of exams you have passed. To maintain Microsoft Certified Professional status, you must remain current on all the requirements for your certification.

Registering for an exam is easy. To register, contact Sylvan Prometric, 2601 West 88th Street, Bloomington, MN, 55431, at (800) 755-EXAM (3926). Dial (612) 896-7000 or (612) 820-5707 if you cannot place a call to an 800 number from your location. You must call to schedule the exam at least one day before you want to take the exam. Taking the exam automatically enrolls you in the Microsoft Certified Professional program; you do not need to submit an application to Microsoft Corporation.

When you call Sylvan Prometric, have the following information ready:

■   Your name, organization (if any), mailing address, and phone number.

■   A unique ID number (e.g., your Social Security number).

■   The number of the exam you wish to take (#70-081 for the Implementing and Supporting Microsoft Exchange Server 5.5 exam).

■   A payment method (e.g., credit card number). If you pay by check, payment is due before the examination can be scheduled. The fee to take each exam is currently $100.

READ THIS BEFORE YOU BEGIN

Individuals who wish to get the most from these materials should have access to a networked PC that is running Microsoft Windows 95, Windows NT Workstation 4.0, or Windows NT Server 4.0. If Internet access is also available, you should be able to complete all of the exercises in this book. The following table summarizes the requirements and recommendations (in parentheses) for each of these operating systems:

Item	Windows 95	NT Workstation 4.0	NT Server 4.0
MB RAM	16 (32)	12 (64)	16 (64)
MB Disk space	90 (200)	116 (400)	124 (1,000)
CPU	386/16 (486+)	486/33 (Pentium)	486/33 (Pentium)
Display type	VGA (SVGA)	VGA (SVGA)	VGA (SVGA)
Network	Yes	Yes	Yes

When it comes to any of these operating systems, it's better to meet the recommended configurations, rather than the minimum configurations. While the minimum configurations work, such systems may be slow and sometimes painful to use. In fact, it's nearly impossible to give any of these operating systems too much memory, disk space, or CPU power. These various Windows environments almost exemplify the notion that "more is better" when it comes to such things.

System Requirements for Transcender Corporation's Test Prep Software

- 8 MB RAM (16 MB recommended)

- VGA/256 Color display or better

- 3.5" disk drive

- Microsoft Windows 3.1, Windows for Workgroups 3.11, Windows NT 3.51, Windows NT 4.0, or Windows 95

Upgrade to the full version of ExchangeCert 5.5

What you get with the full version:

- Three full-length exams
- Detailed answer explanations for every question
     - *each explanation gives specific citations to common study references for easier study*

- Documentation that includes a study outline
- Money Back if You Don't Pass Guarantee
     - *see our website for guarantee details*

ExchangeCert 5.5 is one of an entire line of Microsoft exam simulations designed to help you attain Microsoft certification. Transcender offers simulations of exams for every certification – MCSE (Microsoft Certified Systems Engineer), MCSD (Solution Developer), MCPS (Product Specialist) and MCT (Trainer). See our website at **http://www.transcender.com** for detailed product information and to download product demos.

To order your upgrade, mail us:
The coupon below, filled out with your information (no reproductions or photocopies please)

A check or money order, made out to Transcender Corporation, for $129, plus $6 shipping ($25 outside U.S.)

Terms and Conditions:
Maximum one upgrade per person. Prepayment by check, money order, or credit card, payable to Transcender Corporation. For your own protection, do not send currency through the mail. Allow 4–6 weeks for delivery.

Send to: Upgrade Program
Transcender Corporation
242 Louise Avenue
Nashville, TN 37203

Please send me the ExchangeCert 5.5 Upgrade. Enclosed is my check or credit card number, payable to Transcender Corporation for $129 plus $6 ($25 outside U.S.). TN residents add $10.64 for sales tax.

Name _____ School_____

Address_____ Credit Card: VISA   MC   AMEX   DISC

City_____State _____ CC# _____

Zip _____Country _____ Expiration _____

Phone _____ Name on Card _____

E-Mail _____ Signature_____
                                            _____ CRS51098

Transcender Corporation
SINGLE-USER LICENSE AGREEMENT

This is a legal agreement between you, the end user, and Transcender Corporation. BY BREAKING THE SEAL ON THE ENVELOPE AT THE BACK OF THIS BOOK, YOU ARE AGREEING TO BE BOUND BY THE TERMS OF THIS AGREEMENT. IF YOU DO NOT AGREE TO THE TERMS OF THIS AGREEMENT, YOU MAY RETURN THE PRODUCT TO THE PLACE OF PURCHASE AND, UPON RECEIPT OF THE UNOPENED PACKAGE, THE PURCHASE PRICE WILL BE REFUNDED AS LONG AS NONE OF THE COMPONENTS ARE MISSING, ALTERED OR DAMAGED.

Transcender Corporation Software License

1. **Grant of Single-User License.** Transcender Corporation grants to you a **single-user**, non-exclusive, non-transferable license to use this copy of the enclosed Transcender Corporation product, *ExchangeCert 5.5* (the "Software"), on a single computer. You may not install this copy of the Software on a network server or allow multiple users. If you wish to put the Software on a network server or allow any other user or multiple users, you must purchase a network or multiple-user license for the Software.

2. **Copyright.** This product, including the program and the manual, is copyrighted. You may install the Software on your hard disk and/or make an archival copy by installing the Software on another floppy disk, but the program and manual may not, in whole or in part, be copied, photocopied, reproduced, translated or reduced to any medium, electronic or otherwise, or machine readable form without prior consent, in writing, from Transcender Corporation.

3. **No Transfer.** You may not sell, rent, lease, sublicense, disclose or otherwise transfer the Software or the documentation, in whole or in part, to any third party.

4. **Term.** The term of this Agreement and the license granted to you pursuant to this Agreement shall commence upon opening of this package and shall terminate after three years or upon your discontinuing the use of the software, whichever comes first.

5. **Title.** Title in and to the software and documentation remain exclusively in Transcender, subject to the express, limited and non-exclusive license granted to you pursuant to this Agreement.

6. **Governing Law.** This Agreement shall be construed, interpreted and governed by the laws of the State of Tennessee.

BY YOUR OPENING OF THIS SEALED PACKAGE, YOU ACKNOWLEDGE THAT YOU HAVE READ AND UNDERSTAND THE FOREGOING AND THAT YOU AGREE TO BE BOUND THEREBY.

INTRODUCTION TO
EXCHANGE SERVER 5.5

In this overview chapter, you'll be introduced to the origins of Microsoft messaging, and learn important key terms and concepts essential to a good understanding of Exchange Server. Then, you'll examine the client/server architecture as it applies to Microsoft Exchange Server. From there, you'll move on to review some of the newly integrated features of Exchange Server and how these features can enhance a messaging system.

AFTER READING THIS CHAPTER AND COMPLETING THE EXERCISES, YOU WILL BE ABLE TO:

- Explain the concepts of Exchange Server
- Understand several key components of Exchange Server
- Understand some of the database objects within Exchange Server
- Explain how Exchange connectors function
- Define several key terms associated with Exchange Server
- Understand Exchange client/server architecture
- Understand the new features of Exchange Server

MESSAGING INTRODUCTION

In 1972, Ray Tomlinson of the Bolt, Beranek, and Newman (BBN) Corporation developed the first email program, which utilized the Network Control Protocol (NCP). NCP was one of the first networking protocols, and was implemented in the Department of Defense's (DoD's) Advanced Research Projects Agency network (ARPAnet). The purpose of this program was to allow the exchange of messages between linked sites on the ARPAnet to create a faster way to communicate. A few years later, a group headed by Vinton Cerf, from Stanford, and Bob Kahn, from the Defense Advanced Research Projects Agency (DARPA), developed a new network protocol known as the Transmission Control Protocol/Internet Protocol (TCP/IP). This protocol allowed diverse computer networks to interconnect and communicate.

With the development and standardization of TCP/IP, the Internet was born, allowing vast networks to interconnect and communicate. Over the years, as the Internet began its metamorphosis, the first email standards, such as UUCP (Unix-to-Unix Copy), were developed to provide the ability to send text messages using the American Standard Code for Information Interchange (ASCII) character set. With these standards, messages couldn't use non-English symbols, such as accents and other diacritical marks. Additionally, these standards were incapable of transmitting files, such as images, sounds, and documents consisting of multiple fonts and text styles.

As the Internet grew, new standards were developed to accommodate the ever-growing need for seamless communication. Standards, such as UUEncode/UUDEcode, which were used to send non-ASCII files (such as executables and images), required a high level of expertise from their users. To solve these and other problems, the Multipurpose Internet Mail Extensions (MIME) standard was proposed in RFC 1521. MIME allows multiple character sets, embedded pictures, and binary documents (even sound and video) to be sent via most existing email systems.

Within the past six to eight years, the Internet has been commercialized and is now one of the fastest-growing resources for information. Government studies indicate that, by the year 2000, there will be over 500,000 host servers on the Internet. These studies also show that by that same year, there will be close to 5,000,000 intranet servers. Although the growth of the Internet is incredible, it is the underlying growth rate of intranets that drives the need for effective communication.

In their earliest stages, email programs were designed to provide basic communication. At that time, the need for sophisticated messaging systems had not yet emerged. The technology required to connect multiple systems was still in its developmental stages. However, internetworking technologies quickly improved, and allowed a multitude of hardware platforms as well as network operating systems to connect and interact.

As technology improved and more corporations began implementing intranets, the need to develop messaging systems that were capable of communicating within the intranet's confines, as well as with the Internet, began to develop. The need for messaging systems of greater capabilities was directly related to improvements in internetworking technologies. It is this ever-increasing need for communication that Microsoft has endeavored to meet, with a variety of products, the latest of which is MS Exchange.

In 1991, Microsoft purchased an electronic messaging product called Network Courier. Microsoft enhanced this product and released it under the name Microsoft Mail (MS Mail). Subsequently, it was the first email application released by Microsoft. As this messaging system began to gain popularity, the emphasis shifted to developing a more robust and secure messaging system. Overall, MS Mail was an adequate messaging system, but it suffered from a number of deficiencies, including relatively weak security, an inability to serve clients using different operating systems, and it also lacked a suite of administrative tools. These issues prompted Microsoft to develop a messaging system that included a suite of administrative tools that was more secure and robust.

MICROSOFT MESSAGING

As networks grew in size and complexity, Microsoft recognized the need for greater functionality and began engineering a new messaging system from the ground up, intended to replace MS Mail. Thus, today Microsoft offers its Exchange Server, perhaps one of the most powerful messaging systems in the industry, capable of servicing any business, regardless of its size. Likewise, Microsoft has replaced its original, underpowered MS Mail client software with a new generation of powerful, friendly Outlook email clients.

The continuing evolution of messaging systems has effectively changed the way we communicate. Factors, such as distance and transit times, are no longer a consideration. As email continues to increase in popularity and ease-of-use, it is becoming a preferred method for communication. Today, you can send an email message clear across the world within a few hours. You can post information on a server that can be viewed by everyone or specifically targeted audiences within your corporation. You now have the ability to effectively communicate with your colleagues in offices located in other cities, states, and countries. In the past few years, Microsoft has made strides in the software industry that have had a large impact on electronic commerce, making it more efficient, cost effective, and accurate.

During the development of Microsoft Exchange, one of the greatest concerns was the ability to provide a complete communications solution. Nowadays, it is rare to find a single operating system capable of encompassing all the functions of a single corporation. Typically, within a single large corporation you will find several operating systems, such as DOS, Windows 3.x, Windows 95, Windows NT Workstation, Macintosh, and some derivative of Unix. You might also find several network operating systems, such as NetWare, Banyan Vines, and Windows NT. Exchange Server is designed to communicate with all of these effectively.

Exchange Server uses a variety of *connectors* that enable you to connect the server to other messaging systems within your organization. One of Exchange Server's advantages is its ability to support external message connectors that can be plugged into it, thereby extending a server's capabilities. Due to its integration with Windows NT, the cumbersome task of administering the system is lessened. Many tasks that would generally require a change in both the messaging system and the server's operating system (such as adding a new user account and a mailbox for a user) may be accomplished simultaneously from within Exchange Server.

If your corporation has offices worldwide, Exchange Server supports many ways to connect to these sites. Exchange Server can use any wide area network (WAN) connectivity that supports TCP/IP, IPX/SPX (Internetwork Packet Exchange/Sequenced Packet Exchange), or NetBEUI (Network BIOS Extended User Interface) network protocols. You can configure Exchange to use Windows NT Server's Remote Access Service (RAS) to allow connectivity with remote users. Exchange Server also supports data encryption. It can be configured so users can encrypt messages using public keys, to make transmission of their messages more secure.

In the following sections, you'll explore the various features of Microsoft Exchange Server. This includes an in-depth look at the components that make up Exchange Server, how mail is sent and received through Exchange, and how to set up Exchange clients. In addition, you'll explore the client/server architecture upon which Exchange is based. Finally, we take a look at some of the features that are new to Exchange Server 5.5.

Exchange Server Concepts

Microsoft Exchange Server is a robust system that allows you to exchange information in the form of messages. These messages can include documents, graphics, audio files, and many other elements from almost any kind of application. Users can send these messages to individuals on the Internet or on other systems. Users can also post these messages in public folders where others may view them.

Exchange Server is made up of several components that create and manage objects within the system. These objects are the messaging system resources and can be servers, mailboxes, public folders, address books, and so forth. The way these objects are structured and organized is part of the Exchange architecture. Exchange is organized hierarchically, grouping objects and items by class, order, rank, and so on. Each of these objects is a member of the hierarchy tree: The highest-ranked object in the Exchange hierarchy sits at the top of the tree. This object represents the family patriarch. Below the patriarch are other objects that represent children, with their own children situated below them, and so forth.

The hierarchy tree shows relationships among the objects it contains. One of these relationships is called the *parent-child relationship*. In parent-child relationships, a child inherits traits from its parents. Additionally, child objects may also have other *child objects* beneath them, making them *parent objects* to those child objects below them. The example shown in Figure 1.1 represents a single organization, consisting of two sites, with multiple servers at each site.

The three objects that constitute the main structure in the Exchange hierarchy are:

- Organizations
- Sites
- Servers

Organizations

The highest object at the top of an Exchange hierarchy is called an *organization*. All other objects are contained within an organization. The organization is the parent for all the sites within it. This allows administrators to configure a system at the organization level and apply its parameters to all *sites* within an organization. Because an organization encompasses an entire Exchange system, each corporation should create only one organization.

Sites

Sites are groupings of one or more Exchange Servers. A single site can contain resources from several servers without reference to their locations. This grouping of resources makes use of resources easy through what is known as location transparency. For example, let's say a user's mailbox resides on a site server. This site server is called that mailbox's home server. All users sending mail to this mailbox need not know the location of a mailbox to send it mail. To those users, the mailbox simply appears within the site listing. This means that from a user's perspective, a site creates a transparent messaging environment. This also allows administrators to configure a site only once, and all site servers automatically inherit such configuration data. To create a site, two conditions must exist. First, a permanent high-speed connection must exist between the site servers, and, second, all the site servers must belong to the same *Windows NT domain*. Although it is recommended that all site servers should be in the same domain, it is not required, if they are in seperate NT domains then there must be a two-way trust between them.

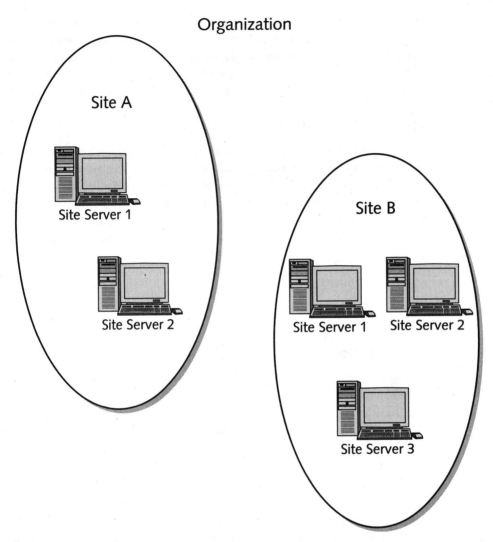

Figure 1.1   The three main objects within the Exchange hierarchy.

Servers

Exchange Servers are computers that run the Windows NT operating system and the Exchange Server software. Residing on these servers are the mailboxes, public and private folders, data, and other information that comprises a site. Each of the site's servers inherits configuration parameters from the site, while at the same time, each one can be configured individually. For example, recipients within a site can be administered at the site level; however, they may also be administered from their home servers (the server where their mail accounts were created).

In the sections that follow, you'll learn more about the core components that make up Exchange Server, and how they interoperate to handle message retrieval and delivery services.

EXCHANGE COMPONENTS

There are several vital components that provide functionality to Exchange Server. They are referred to as the core components and are files that take the form of executables (EXEs) and Dynamic Link Libraries (DLLs) files. These core components are sometimes called services, because many of them run as services on the Microsoft Windows NT Server operating system. The following elements are considered core components for Exchange Server:

- *Directory Service (DS)*
- *Information Store*
- *Message Transfer Agent (MTA)*
- *System Attendant (SA)*

Exchange Server is designed to utilize a series of objects, containers, and databases. An *object* is a messaging system resource, such as a server, mailbox, public folder, address book, and so forth. These objects are listed in the form of records within the system *directory*. The directory contains all objects within the Exchange Server system. This implies that, because an object is a record within the directory, the directory must be a database. In fact, Exchange Server stores information in several databases, and then manipulates these databases to send, receive, and store messages. The Exchange Server Administrator allows you to view the hierarchical relationship of these objects within your system.

A *container* is an object within Exchange Server that holds other objects. A good analogy is that of storing a number of small containers within a single larger container. For example, all mailbox objects are stored within a recipient's container. This means that the recipient's container is also an object, because it holds other objects. Containers, and all objects within them, operate according to the parent-child relationship within the Exchange environment, which defines a hierarchical structure among objects. This structure controls *permissions* for the objects in the hierarchy. Permissions are rules that determine which users may access which objects, and what rights those users have to such objects. Any permissions granted to a parent object are automatically inherited by all its children.

Directory Service

As listed earlier, one of the main components of Exchange is the Directory Service, sometimes called by its acronym, DS. The function of the Directory

Service is to create and manage storage of all objects within an organization. The database that stores all these objects within the system is called the *directory database*. The directory stores objects according to the hierarchical structure defined by the parent-child relationships among and between objects within the hierarchy.

The primary purpose of the directory is to provide a centralized location for objects within the Exchange environment. This allows users and administrators to locate a system's resources easily so that they may use or administer them. Objects stored in the Exchange directory have properties, also called attributes, which define characteristics for types of objects. For example, an object can be a user (such as John Smith) or an entire Exchange organization (Best); each type of object has a different collection of associated attributes. Furthermore, objects also have associated permissions, which determine their access characteristics. As shown in Figure 1.2, the object Marie Deloris can take properties such as first name, last name, job title, email address, and numerous others.

Information Store

The Information Store creates and manages the message database on an Exchange Server. This database stores information such as email messages, electronic forms, spreadsheets, word processor documents, graphics images, audio files, and many other items from almost any application. Users can access the information within the Information Store through their mailboxes and folders in their client applications. The Information Store is comprised of two main databases:

- **Public Information Store** The public Information Store database is contained in the file PUB.EDB. It contains the public folders on the server. Public folders are containers that can contain documents, messages, forms, and any other information your users want to distribute within the messaging system. Essentially, public folders act like public mailboxes.

- **Private Information Store** The private Information Store contains the users' mailboxes and private folders. The private Information Store database is contained in the file PRIV.EDB. Exchange uses the integrated security features within Microsoft Windows NT. This means that user mailboxes and folders will only be accessible by their respective owners and to others who have been granted access permission. These folders contain the users' private mailboxes. As such, users can keep any information they put into these folders private and inaccessible by other users.

Message Transfer Agent (MTA)

The Message Transfer Agent (MTA) handles routing for all messages, whether such messages are routed within the same site, between different sites, or to

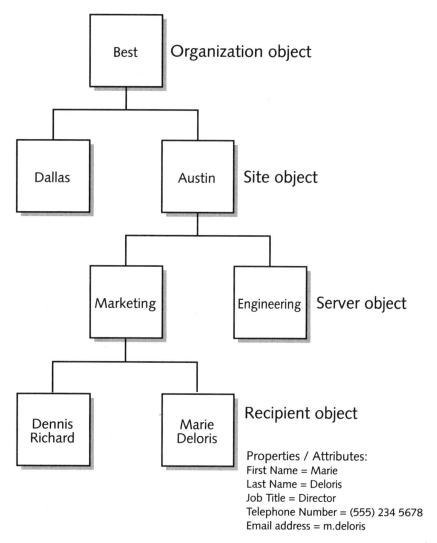

Figure 1.2 shown with labels: Best — Organization object; Dallas, Austin — Site object; Marketing, Engineering — Server object; Dennis Richard, Marie Deloris — Recipient object.

Properties / Attributes:
First Name = Marie
Last Name = Deloris
Job Title = Director
Telephone Number = (555) 234 5678
Email address = m.deloris

Figure 1.2   The Exchange hierarchy and some example properties of an object.

so-called foreign sites (which means that they're routed to non-Exchange servers). MTA does not get involved if the recipient's mailbox is on the same server. Additionally, the MTA uses components known as connectors. Connectors manage the actual connection to other systems as well as the transfer of data, and the MTA handles all routing functions. The primary functions of the MTA include:

- Originator/Recipient Addressing
- Message format translation
- Message routing

The MTA is modeled after the X.400 standard (which is discussed in the section entitled "Exchanging Mail" later in this chapter) and, as such, uses the Originator/Recipient Addressing scheme. If messages are routed to an X.400 messaging system, the MTA changes the format of such messages from the native Exchange format, known as the Microsoft Database Exchange Format (MDBEF), to a native X.400 format, known as the Interpersonal Message (IPM) format.

The ability to translate messages to the IPM format allows Exchange clients to exchange mail with X.400 mail users. When an MTA receives a message to be forwarded, it first determines the route that the message must travel to reach its destination. It then examines the message recipient's Distinguished Name (DN). If that address does not resolve the next route, it then examines the Originator/ Recipient Address. The MTA compares the address with the routing information contained within the Exchange Server's Gateway Address Routing Table (GWART). Because there may be several possible paths available, administrators can assign values to such different paths, where these values are called costs. Costs allow priorities to be assigned to different routes, and the MTA can be instructed to factor cost into its routing decisions.

Thus, when an MTA encounters multiple possible paths between a sending and a receiving server, it automatically chooses the path with the lowest cost. If the MTA cannot resolve the specified address, it sends the message originator a report known as a non-delivery report (NDR). This alerts the user or administrator who created the message that it is undeliverable, and provides valuable feedback when messages cannot be sent because of addressing or other reachability problems.

System Attendant (SA)

The System Attendant (SA) is an Exchange service that runs in the background. It monitors and logs most Exchange Server processes, and builds and maintains a routing table for the site to which it belongs. The SA logs information, such as tracking information that includes the routes that messages take, and indicates whether or not messages are received at their destinations. The SA also compiles the routing tables for the entire site. This is the table that the MTA uses when it determines which route to assign to outgoing messages.

In addition to these functions, the SA monitors the connection between servers, verifies such connections, and, at the same time, checks on Exchange services running on other servers. The SA sends test messages between itself and other servers to execute these checks. In addition, whenever new user accounts are created, the SA is responsible for generating their underlying email addresses.

In the following section, we put together all the various pieces of Exchange Server that we've discussed thus far. It is essential to understand these underlying components, and their interrelationships, to grasp the power of Exchange Server fully and completely.

EXCHANGING MAIL

The process of exchanging email resembles using the postal service to exchange letters. When users send email, the Exchange Server assumes the role of the post office. Exchange Server is responsible for processing end-user requests and routing mail to the appropriate destination. The only information end users must know is the destination address for their messages (unlike the post office, Exchange automatically knows each user's return address).

When a client uses Exchange Server to send a message, that message is first delivered to the Information Store, which holds all messages to be sent or received on an Exchange Server. The Information Store occupies a database that is the primary system database for Exchange (SYSTEM.EDB). The Information Store cannot be manipulated or directly accessed by users or administrators. Instead, the Information Store acts like the post office, and is comprised of two main components—a public Information Store and a private Information Store—which, as we discussed earlier, are also databases.

After the Information Store receives a message, it then decides where that message should be delivered. It does this by searching the directory. As mentioned earlier, the directory incorporates both a directory database and a Directory Service. The directory database (DIR.EDB) manages all objects in the organization and makes its information available to appropriate users, administrators, and system processes. The Directory Service manipulates information within the directory database. It also processes directory requests from users and other applications. In addition, the Directory Service also supports other important functions:

- It maintains the directory objects stored within the directory database and displays them in a hierarchical tree structure.

- It sends replication notifications to directories on other servers and receives directory replication notifications from other servers.

- It provides an interface between Exchange clients and the directory database.

- It enforces rules to control the structure and contents of the directory database.

After the directory has verified the necessary information, the message is handed off to the MTA, which is responsible for delivering that message. The MTA also ensures that the message is delivered to its destination successfully. Thus, the MTA is an object that routes messages within a system, as well as to gateways that connect to outside email systems. The MTA provides resolution for external addresses, and, if necessary, can even convert message formats to ensure compatibility with destination email services. The MTA uses four components to route data to other email systems and servers:

- Exchange Site Connector
- Remote Access Service (RAS) Connector
- X.400 Connector
- Internet Mail Connector

Each of these components is explained in the sections that follow.

Exchange Site Connector

The Exchange Site Connector connects two or more sites using a Microsoft interprocess communications interface called *Remote Procedure Calls (RPCs)* to permit Exchange servers to communicate and exchange data. For an Exchange Site Connector to establish a connection to a site, that site must be accessible through a permanent network connection of some kind (a dial-up connection will not work). Site Connectors are easy to configure, because they use the RPC protocol. When you use RPC, you do not need to worry about configuring a network transport. The connector uses an existing transport, which means that you can use multiple network operating systems and protocols to interconnect such sites.

Remote Access Service (RAS) Connector

The RAS Connector is used between sites that do not have a permanent connection between them. It provides a way to connect using asynchronous communications, such as a regular dial-up phone connection, ISDN, or X.25. It is this connector that allows remote servers and users to communicate with Exchange Server.

X.400 Connector

The Exchange Server X.400 Connector is based on the X.400 standard, developed by the International Telegraph and Telephone Consultative Committee (CCITT). X.400 is a set of standards related to the exchange of electronic messages. These messages can take the form of voice mail, faxes, telexes, or email. This standard was developed to enable the creation of a global electronic messaging network. The goal for electronic messaging through the X.400 standard is to make it possible to send an electronic message from anywhere in the world to almost anywhere in the world, just as you can place a phone call from almost anywhere, to almost anywhere. X.400 defines a series of protocols at the application level, and is dependent on other protocols, such as the X.25 protocol for actual physical transportation of data. X.400 standards are referred to by their year of official adoption, and by a specified color. To date, X.400 versions include the following:

- 1984 "Red Book"
- 1988 "Blue Book"
- 1992 "White Book"

As this standard applies to Exchange Server, the X.400 Connector connects sites that support only low bandwidth connections, or that use existing X.400 backbones (such as public X.400 systems). Exchange Server supports the following X.400 protocols, with the following related transports:

- Transport Protocol, Class 0 (TP0)/X.25
- Transport Protocol, Class 4 (TP4)/Connectionless Network Protocol (CLNP)
- Transmission Control Protocol/Internet Protocol (TCP/IP)

To achieve a global messaging system, a standard numbering system was created for X.400. This numbering system had to be capacious enough to accommodate the entire world's population. The address scheme that X.400 uses is called the Originator/Recipient Addressing (O/R Addressing) scheme. This scheme uses a hierarchical format and consists of countries, communication providers, corporations or organizations, and several other categories. These categories are called fields and are represented in Table 1.1.

The Originator/Recipient Address (see Figure 1.3) specifies an unambiguous path to a location within an X.400 network, where the recipient is located. It does not specify the path the message must take, only a path to where the recipient is located.

Table 1.1 X.400 O/R Addressing field examples.

Field	Abbreviation	Description
Country Code	c = USA	Country
Admin Mgmt. Domain (ADMD)	a = Sprint	Third-party network system (ATT, MCI, Sprint, and so forth)
Priv. Mgmt. Domain (PRMD)	p = BestNet	Subscriber service to the ADMD (company name)
Organization	o = Best	Company name or organization
Surname	s = Bogart	Last name
Given Name	g = Humphrey	First name

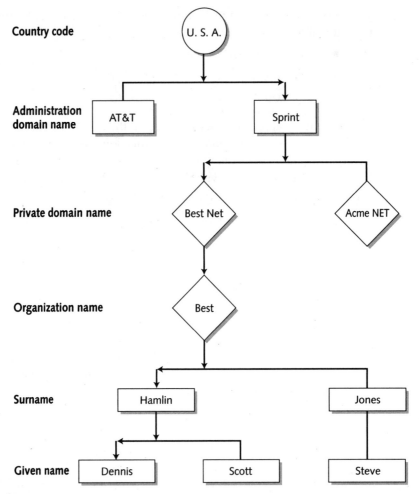

Figure 1.3 X.400 O/R Address example.

Internet Mail Service

The Internet Mail Service allows users to communicate with other users on the Internet. This occurs through the use of the Simple Mail Transfer Protocol (SMTP). Exchanging mail between such users is transparent to Exchange users, because the SMTP protocol is built into Exchange Server.

To ensure that the post office is working efficiently and that all email is being routed correctly, the System Attendant monitors the Information Stores. Additionally, it monitors connections between servers to make sure that messages sent from a sending server are received at the target server. The System Attendant is a service that must be running for Exchange messaging processes to run. In addition, the SA also performs several important functions:

1

- It creates email addresses for new message recipients to ensure that email gets to the correct mailbox on the correct server.
- If the messaging tracking feature is enabled, the SA logs the information needed to track messages.

As mentioned earlier, Exchange Server is based on a hierarchy of organizations and sites. To recap, an organization is one or more Exchange Servers that communicate with each other to provide messaging services for an entire group. For example, if you have a company located in a single building with all the computers connected via a local area network (LAN), you can have an Exchange Server as the organization that will service the entire enterprise (as shown in Figure 1.4).

The organization is at the top of the hierarchical structure in an *enterprise*. The term enterprise should be considered synonymous with the term corporation. An enterprise can consist of one organization or several organizations. Each organization can be comprised of a single site or several sites. (Recall that a site is one or more Exchange Servers that share the same directory information.) Changes in the directory information are automatically replicated to all Exchange Servers within the same site. Site servers must be connected via a permanent network, and they must belong to the same Windows NT domain.

For example, if you have a company that has multiple offices in two different locations, an Exchange Server at each location can service its own site. In this case, the two site servers represent the entire enterprise. The directory information on these servers is shared and can be replicated to the other sites. This provides accurate information for the entire enterprise. As shown in Figure 1.5, each site within an enterprise can have its own Exchange Server, which is managed locally. The directory on these servers contains the information for the entire enterprise, and it's automatically replicated between them.

Also, you may have offices in multiple locations yet use only one organization server for the entire enterprise. This is not the most efficient method, because all users at the second location must traverse a WAN link to access the Exchange Server. For example, you could have a company with multiple locations and only one Exchange Server located at one of its locations. This server would be the organization server by default. The users at any location other than the one where the organization server resides can still access this server, but they must traverse the WAN to do so. As shown in Figure 1.6, the organization is administrated from one server, even though there are multiple locations. This allows for centralized management and ease of administration, at the cost of communications efficiency and slower access for remote users.

Given this organizational division, Exchange Server is scalable and can accommodate both large and small companies. The hierarchical scalability of

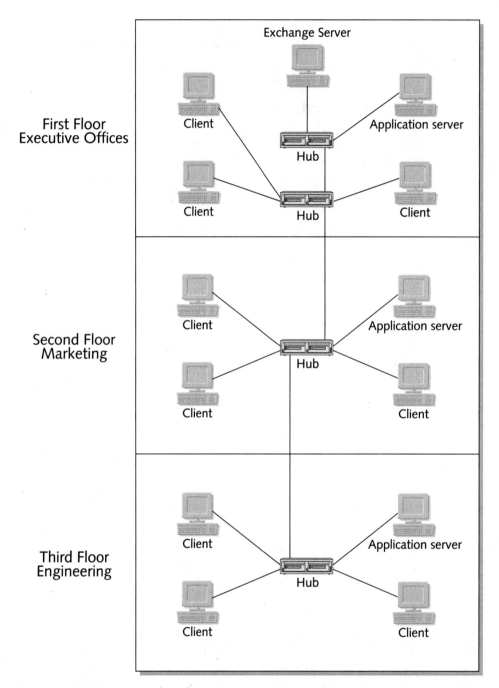

Figure 1.4   A typical configuration.

Exchange Server also simplifies the task of administration and centralizes client management.

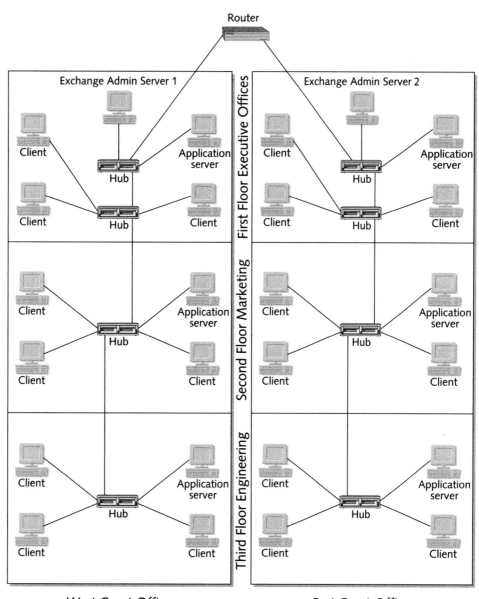

Figure 1.5   Exchange Server in an enterprise environment.

EXCHANGE CLIENTS

Exchange Server must run on a Windows NT Server computer; however, the network and clients can run on a variety of network operating systems, including Windows NT, NetWare, and Banyan Vines.

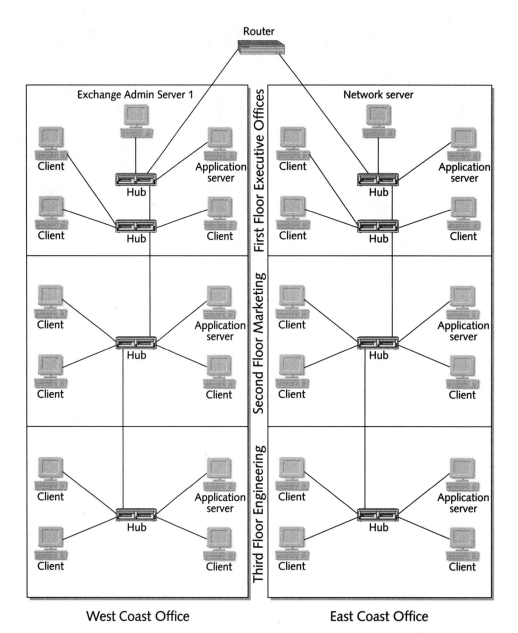

Figure 1.6 Centralized management with Exchange Server.

For Exchange Server to coexist in a Novell NetWare environment, the following requirements must be met:

- **The SAP agent must be installed.** The Service Access Point (SAP) must be running on the Exchange Server computer if you wish to integrate Novell NetWare clients and your Exchange Server computer is not on the same LAN segment as a NetWare server.

- **NetBIOS must be installed on the Exchange Server.** NetBIOS is a network interface. It supports the network basic input/output system, a necessary component for communicating on a NetWare network.

- **Ethernet frame types must be configured.** If you have multiple frame types configured for the Windows NT NWLink protocol or if you have more than one network card installed in a Microsoft Exchange Server computer, set the internal network number to a unique number other than zero.

- **Gateway and Client Services For NetWare (GSNW and CSNW) must be installed.** To optimize the performance of email delivery on Exchange Servers using the IPX/SPX protocol, you must install GSNW (on Windows NT Server installing GSNW also automatically installs CSNW).

- **File scan on NetWare servers must be enabled.** If you plan to store any email data on a NetWare server, you must enable file scan on that server. Because Microsoft Outlook does not support specific file operations for NetWare servers, file scan must be enabled on the shares where the data is stored to make them accessible.

Clients on a Banyan Vines network can also connect to an Exchange Server. To accomplish this, you must:

1. Make sure that the Banyan Vines protocol (ncacn_vns_spp) is the first protocol listed in the RPC binding order on the Microsoft Outlook computers. Any protocols not in use should be removed from the binding order.

2. Install the Banyan Vines redirector on the Exchange Server computer.

3. Set the Exchange Server computer name to match the Banyan Vines computer name exactly.

The preferred client software for use with Exchange Server is Microsoft Outlook (we discuss how to set up other Exchange clients in Chapter 6). Outlook is a desktop information manager that helps users organize and manage email, calendars, contacts, documents, and scheduling. Currently, you can install Outlook as the client for Microsoft Exchange Server on the following platforms:

- Microsoft Windows 3.x
- Microsoft Windows 95
- Microsoft Windows 98
- Microsoft Windows NT
- Apple Macintosh

EXCHANGE CLIENT/SERVER ARCHITECTURE

Microsoft Exchange Server is a client/server system. Client/server means that processing takes place on both client and server computers. This is a key advantage of the client/server architecture—which is sometimes called *distributed processing*. Here is an example of what occurs in distributed computer processing: A client sends a request to the server, then the server processes the request and returns some result to the client. Depending on the request a client makes, the server could also send data back to the client for processing. This occurs if the client request requires a local process to execute (such as moving email files from the server to a local directory, or from a local directory to the server). One disadvantage of a client/server model is that servers carry a disproportionate share of the processing load; this usually imposes greater requirements on the server hardware platform and related system components (such as RAM, disk space, network connections, and so forth).

There are two major components to a client/server architecture (see Figure 1.7) that Exchange Server refers to as the front end and back end. The front end is defined as the user or client computer. Exchange Server uses the front end to provide access to email, scheduling, and shared information. To clarify further, think of it this way: users log in to a Microsoft NT Server running Exchange Server. The Exchange client software, which resides on the users' systems, then logs in to the Exchange Server software on the server, and permits users to access their email. The back end consists of the main components of Microsoft Exchange Server, which run on a Windows NT computer. The back end also supports administrative tasks as well as basic messaging services.

Communications between front end and back end processes are also handled by RPCs, using a Microsoft-specific RPC protocol. This kind of protocol is specifically designed to support client/server communication between computers, and is independent of any underlying network protocols. This is important, because such RPCs can support communication between servers and clients that might be running different network protocols. A Remote Procedure Call enables procedures (instructions) issued from one computer to be transmitted over the network to another computer, where those instructions are executed. The transfer of the instructions is completely transparent to both the program that issues such instructions and to the user who may be running the program. In fact, it appears to the program that issues such instructions that these instructions are executed locally. Thus, the RPC protocol is a key component of the distributed processing that occurs within the client/server architecture.

When a user reads a message, the client program issues a *Messaging Application Programming Interface (MAPI)* instruction. The client-side RPC protocol transfers this instruction to the server where the message physically exists. The server-side RPC protocol receives the request, executes it, and sends the message

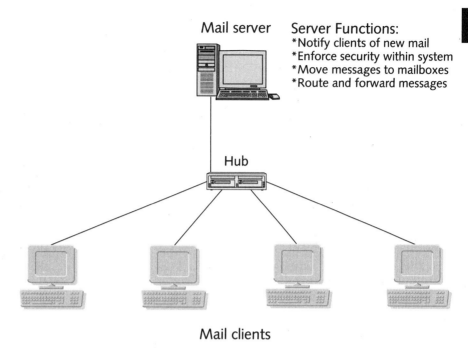

Mail server   Server Functions:
                *Notify clients of new mail
                *Enforce security within system
                *Move messages to mailboxes
                *Route and forward messages

Hub

Mail clients

Client Functions:
*Act as the interface for accessing messages
*Create messages
*Read messages
*Send messages
*Forward and reply messages

Figure 1.7   An illustrated example of the client/server messaging system.

back to the client (which is viewed on the screen). RPC clients make requests, and RPC servers make replies; hence, RPC is also known as a request/reply protocol.

Microsoft's MAPI provides a standard *application programming interface (API)* for client/server messaging interaction. To better understand MAPI, let's first go over what an API is. All programs include certain built-in functions. Other programs, through the use of specific instructions, can invoke these functions. Such specific instructions that permit one program to tell another program what to do define an API. Several years ago, most client/server messaging products included their own APIs to support client/server interaction. Unfortunately, this also meant that client applications would only work with whatever messaging system its API invoked. Likewise, if a user needed to connect to multiple messaging systems (such as Lotus Notes, Microsoft Exchange, cc:Mail, and so on), that user would have to install multiple client applications (see Figure 1.8) to gain access to all of them.

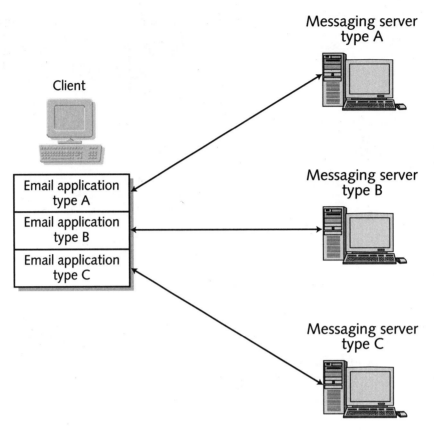

Figure 1.8   Multiple client programs to interact with multiple APIs.

Microsoft created a general purpose Messaging API, also known as MAPI, to reach two goals. First, MAPI provides a standard API for client/server interaction. As implied by its name, this standard applies only to client/server messaging. MAPI enables a single client application to interact with different messaging servers (see Figure 1.9).

MAPI's second goal was to standardize services for client messaging applications. These services would support the creation of universal address books, universal inboxes, and a method to store different types of message data in a single folder. Through the use of standardized transport mechanisms, MAPI allows a single client application to connect to different messaging systems.

Now that you have a firm understanding of the Exchange Server components and architecture, let's take a look at some of the features that are new to Exchange Server 5.5.

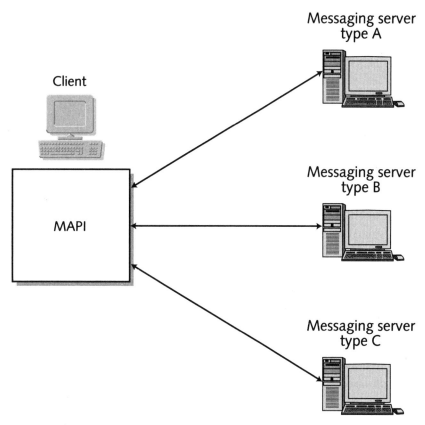

Figure 1.9   A single client interacting with different messaging servers through MAPI.

NEW FEATURES OF MICROSOFT EXCHANGE SERVER VERSION 5.5

The following items represent some of Exchange Server version 5.5's most noteworthy new features, including enhancements to some of the functionality delivered in Exchange Server version 5:

- **Microsoft Cluster Server**   MS Cluster Server provides fault tolerance for hardware in the event of a system failure. A cluster includes an active node and a secondary node. The active node acts as the primary mail server to processes and route messages on a network. Both active and secondary nodes monitor each other constantly. If the active node experiences a hardware failure, the secondary node assumes the role of the primary mail server without interrupting mail service or dropping client connections. MS Cluster Server is installed on the active node first, then on the secondary node. When the cluster is established, setup detects that Exchange Server is installed on the active node and adds the Exchange Server resources, such as the System Attendant, the directory, and the Information Store, to the secondary node. By doing so, this enables the active node to failover to the secondary node. Failover protection ensures that another server always remains available, and mail service need never be interrupted.

- **Enhanced security policies** Multiple password policies can be set to prevent changes to the Key Management Server without authorization from administrator(s). The Key Management Server provides data security and integrity as well as proof of origin for messages. It allows users to encrypt messages and to sign their messages digitally, raising overall confidentiality within an organization. By setting multiple password policies for the Key Management administrator's account, it reduces the chances of unauthorized changes being made to the Key Management Server configuration. To make a change in the Key Management Server configuration, an administrator must supply two valid passwords.

- **Trusted messages sent between organizations** This allows users to verify the source of messages sent from other organizations.

- **New database structure for the public Information Store, private Information Store, and directory** With the new database structure, the Information Store is limited only by your hardware's capacity. The database engine has been enhanced, and provides more robust data storage capabilities. Its enhancements include better caching schemes for quicker updates to transaction logs. Copying of the transaction logs into the database is performed sequentially and is more dynamic, and requires fewer threads to be spawned to carry out those copy commands. This increases overall performance and can be beneficial for balancing server loads.

- **Ability to set deleted item retention period for Information Stores, mailboxes, and public folders** If using Microsoft Outlook version 8.03 or later, users can retrieve deleted items in mailboxes and public folders by using the Recover Deleted Items command.

- **Incorporates ability to restrict users access to address book views** If you have multiple companies on a single Exchange Server, you can restrict users in one company from viewing the address book of another company.

- **Supports multiple and differential offline address books** This allows users to download differential entries in offline address books, so only the changes in the offline address books that have occurred since the last download will be downloaded.

1

- **Supports MIME Hypertext Markup Language (MHTML)** This enables the MIME encapsulation of aggregate documents, such as an HTML document with inline pictures.

- **Migration of Lotus cc: Mail DB8** The Lotus cc: Mail source extractor supports Lotus cc: Mail version 5.x (DB6), version 6, and version 8 (DB8).

- **Microsoft Exchange Chat service** Exchange Server now includes chat services that enable users to chat with each other online and in real time.

- **Supports Internet Message Access Protocol version 4 (IMAP4)** This is the email protocol that enables users to retrieve email messages from their Inbox and retrieve Microsoft Exchange public folder information.

All in all, these new capabilities add significantly to Exchange Server's capabilities, and also to user's abilities to exchange and interact with a broader variety of materials than ever before.

CHAPTER SUMMARY

In this chapter, we covered the beginning of the Internet and how its development and growth spawned the need for more effective methods of communication. Email has become one of the most effective and popular communication mediums today, and its widespread use continues to be a force that drives messaging systems to support ever-greater capabilities. After we reviewed the development and impact of email, we covered the history of Microsoft messaging systems, and how these systems have evolved into today's prime attraction—namely, Microsoft Exchange Server.

This chapter explored basic Exchange messaging system concepts as well as some of the innerworkings of Exchange Server. The main concepts presented in the latter part of the chapter include how Exchange Server works within network environments, interacts with operating systems, operates within a client/server architecture, and supports clients. Finally, there was a quick review of Exchange Server 5.5's new features.

By now, you should possess the basic building blocks necessary to build a firm foundation for the materials you will work your way through in the upcoming chapters.

KEY TERMS

- **application programming interface (API)**—A set of instructions that allow one program to invoke the functions of a second program.

- **child objects**—Objects located within parent objects. The permissions granted to a child object are inherited from its parent.

- **connector**—An object that sets the properties for a given connection. Every established connection uses connectors to communicate with the messaging system.

- **container**—An Exchange Server object that holds other objects. Mailbox objects are placed in a recipient's object. This means that the recipient's object is also a container.

- **directory**—Holds information about the organization's resources and users, such as servers, mailboxes, public folders, and distribution lists. The directory and its contents get replicated automatically to all servers within the same site.

- **directory database**—The database that contains all the information about the objects in your Exchange Server.

- **Directory Service**—The service that manipulates the information contained within the directory database. This service processes requests from users and applications.

- **distributed processing**—Computing activity that is distributed on both client and server computer systems, as clients make requests for services, and servers attempt to satisfy them.

- **enterprise**—The corporate organization.

- **Information Store**—Contains the messages in users' mailboxes and public folders. The Information Store's two main components are the public Information Store and the private Information Store.

- **Message Transfer Agent (MTA)**—The component responsible for routing messages to their destinations. The MTA provides addressing and routing information for sending messages.

- **Messaging Application Programming Interface (MAPI)**—A series of APIs designed specifically for messaging.

- **object**—A messaging system resource, such as a server, mailbox, public folder, or address book, that is listed in the directory.

- **organization**—The largest administrative unit in Microsoft Exchange Server, usually consisting of one or more sites. Organizations provide services for an entire group.

- **parent object**—An object that contains other objects. An object is a parent to all the objects within it; all objects contained within it are its child objects, or children.

- **parent–child relationship**—The relationship that exists between a parent object and a child object. The relationship is dictated by permissions, which are inherited from parent to child.

- **permissions**—A set of rules that controls access to objects, such as containers within a system. These rules dictate which users can access an object and how those users may manipulate it.

- **private Information Store**—The component of the Information Store that contains user mailboxes and messages.

- **public Information Store**—The component of the Information Store that contains public files, folders, and messages.

- **Remote Procedure Call (RPC)**—A protocol for starting programs on a different computer, feeding them input, and accepting their output. This allows computers to spread the processing load among a number of computers.

- **site**—A server or series of servers that communicate with each other using the same directory information.

- **System Attendant (SA)**—A service that must be running for messaging processes to run. The SA is a maintenance service that runs in the background.

- **Windows NT domain**—A grouping of network servers and other computers that share common security and user account information. Users log on to the domain, not individual servers in the domain. Once logged on to the domain, the user has access to the network resources within the domain.

REVIEW QUESTIONS

1. When a user sends a message using Exchange Server, where is the message first received for processing?
   a. Message Transfer Agent
   b. Information Store
   c. System Attendant
   d. Directory

2. Which of the following make up the Information Store? (Choose all that apply.)

   a. Key Management Server

   b. Private Information Store

   c. Directory Service

   d. Public Information Store

3. When you send a message using Exchange Server, what component is responsible for looking up the recipient information for routing the message?

   a. Public Information Store

   b. Private Information Store

   c. Directory Service

   d. Message Transfer Agent (MTA)

4. In which component are the user mailboxes and messages kept on an Exchange Server?

   a. Directory Service

   b. Public Information Store

   c. Information Stores

   d. Private Information Store

5. The System Attendant is a ———————— that monitors messaging processes and ensures email is getting routed correctly.

   a. Service

   b. Runtime

   c. Procedure call

   d. Process

6. Exchange Server is which type of messaging system?

   a. Front end/back end

   b. Application/client

   c. Client/server

7. What are the two major components of client/server architecture?

   a. High end

   b. Front end

   c. Low end

   d. Back end

8. The front end is loaded on the server system. True or False?

9. The back end provides the main administrative tasks, as well as basic messaging services. True or False?

1

10. What is the Remote Procedure Call (RPC) protocol?

    a. Protocol designed specifically for client/server communication.

    b. The interface the user interacts with.

    c. A protocol used specifically for Microsoft Networking.

    d. The process by which the System Attendant monitors the messaging system.

11. The directory consists of two main components: the _____ and the _____ .

12. On which network environments can Microsoft Exchange Server coexist? (Choose all that apply.)

    a. Banyan Vines

    b. Novell NetWare

    c. Windows NT

    d. Unix

13. On which platforms can you currently install the Outlook client? (Choose all that apply.)

    a. Apple Macintosh

    b. Windows 95, 3.x

    c. Windows NT 3.1, 3.51, 4

    d. Windows NT 3.51, 4

14. To achieve automatic directory replication, site servers that belong within the same organization musts also belong to the same _____ .

15. Which type of Exchange Server can control and manage other servers within the same enterprise?

    a. Site Server

    b. Administrative Server

    c. Exchange Server

    d. Primary Site Server

16. The component that allows Exchange Server to connect with other existing systems and acts as the translator between these systems is known as the

    _____ .

    a. Messaging Application Programming Interface (MAPI)

    b. Exchange Site Connector

    c. Remote Procedure Call

    d. Information Store

17. What is the purpose of the X.400 Standard?

    a. To develop a standard numbering system

    b. To develop a series of standardized transport protocols

    c. To create a global electronic messaging network

    d. To develop the Originator/Recipient Addressing scheme

18. Which of the following transports of the X.400 Connector does Exchange Server currently support? (Choose all that apply.)

    a. TP0/X.25

    b. TP1/X.25

    c. TP4/CLNP

    d. TCP/IP

19. Connectors do not have to be used with Exchange Server version 5.5. True or False?

20. The type of RPC being made depends on the network protocols being used. True or False?

 # CASE PROJECTS

1. Your company has two locations—London and New York. You want to implement Exchange Server as your messaging environment.

   Required result:

   Describe the best solution in which Exchange Server can provide service for each location, service for respective users, and maintain directory information for the entire organization.

   Optional desired result:

   Plan the configuration to allow all servers to replicate directory information automatically.

   Proposed solution:

   Configure an Exchange Server at each location as a site server, and configure the servers as members of their own separate domains. Then, using the Site Connector, connect the two sites. This provides automatic replication of all directory information.

   Which results does the proposed solution provide?

   a. The proposed solution provides the required result and the optional desired result.

   b. The proposed solution provides only the required result.

   c. The proposed solution does not provide the required result.

2. You have several employees in your corporation who will be traveling to a remote location and working there for an extended period of time. As such, they will be setting up a server at the remote location.

Required result:

Describe the communication method by which the Exchange Server at the remote site would be able to communicate with the organization.

Proposed solution:

Configure the remote site server to use the Windows NT Remote Access Service over a standard dial-up phone connection, such as a 56.6Kbps modem. The remote site server will dial up the organization's network server and establish a connection. Then, configure Exchange to use the Remote Access Service Connector to connect to the two Exchange Servers and replicate email for the remote site server. This will allow the remote users to log on to a local server, and send and retrieve email. Although this is not the most elegant solution, it will work if no faster means of communication is available, such as ISDN.

a. The proposed solution is a fair representation of Exchange Server's capabilities.

b. The proposed solution is not a fair representation of Exchange Server's capabilities.

EXCHANGE SERVER ARCHITECTURE

In this chapter, you'll examine the Exchange Server architecture at a moderate level of detail. Throughout this chapter, you'll explore the various parts of Exchange Server, so you can better understand its innerworkings. Likewise, this chapter creates a foundation that you'll need to understand complex messaging systems. Finally, you'll explore several client-side elements that should round out your appreciation for Exchange Server's architecture and built-in capabilities. This chapter presents a more or less theoretical overview of Exchange Server, but builds on the materials presented in Chapter 1.

AFTER READING THIS CHAPTER AND COMPLETING THE EXERCISES, YOU WILL BE ABLE TO:

- Understand Exchange Server architecture
- Configure Exchange Server in different environments
- Understand the different routines that create Exchange Server

How Exchange Works

Exchange follows a fundamental concept—namely, object orientation—that drives the design of modern operating systems like Windows NT and database query languages like SQL. An object-oriented program is similar in form to a collection of nested Chinese boxes. One box fits inside another, which may in turn have one or more boxes that fit inside it, and so on. When it comes to object-oriented programs, these boxes are usually called containers.

For Exchange, the largest container is your *organization*. Within that container, you place a *site* and at least one server. In Microsoft Exchange, servers talk to other servers constantly, but clients communicate only with a single server. By contrast, Windows 95 Post Office creates a messaging environment wherein all clients talk to a single email server. Because this creates an environment that does not scale well, the Peer-to-Peer Post Office available in Windows 95 no longer exists in Windows 98.

Exchange can be configured in a variety of ways, depending on factors such as the size of your organization, the number of users in an area, and other mail systems that Exchange must communicate with, such as the Internet or Lotus Notes. Other factors include a message's priority setting, the distance between groups, and the cost of delivering messages. Just as there is no one best way to run a company, there is no single best way to design an Exchange organization. Also, please recall that all Exchange-to-Exchange communication is performed using *Remote Procedure Call (RPC)* protocols, as discussed in Chapter 1, and that such RPC connections must be permanent. The slang term commonly used in the field is that such connections are nailed up.

Throughout this book, we use the word email. This word was chosen to keep the concepts easy to relate to what you already know. Perhaps a better term is emessaging, because Exchange can deliver so much more than textual email. Using *Object Linking and Embedding (OLE)*, an email can incorporate a spreadsheet or a complex form, created using Visual Basic.

In the sections that follow, you will learn about the system requirements for an Exchange Server, and examine a more or less typical multi-site Exchange installation. You will also revisit the key Exchange components in some detail, including mailboxes, connectors, the *Exchange Directory Service (DS)*, the *Information Store*, the *Message Transfer Agent (MTA)*, and the *System Attendant (SA)*. You will also learn more about Exchange *log files* and the Exchange Optimizer, as well as what's involved in performing an upgrade to Exchange 5.5 from earlier versions.

SYSTEM REQUIREMENTS

According to Microsoft, the system requirements for installing Microsoft Exchange on a standard server are as follows for various types of systems. Both platforms require Microsoft Windows NT Server 4.0 service pak 3 or later.

For Intel and compatible systems:

- Intel Pentium 60 or faster processor (Pentium 133 recommended)
- 24MB RAM (32MB recommended)
- 250MB of available hard-disk space (500MB recommended)

For RISC-based systems:

- Alpha processor
- 32MB RAM (48MB recommended)
- 300MB of available hard disk space (500MB recommended)
- Microsoft Windows NT Server version 4 and Windows NT Server version 4 Service Pack 3 or later
- CD-ROM drive
- Enterprise Server

Older versions of NT do not work with Exchange 5.5; this restriction is new to this version of Exchange.

Now that you've observed the hardware requirements for Exchange Server, let's examine the kind of typical Exchange environment you're likely to encounter when evaluating a usage scenario for this technology.

EXCHANGE IN THE REAL WORLD

Let's look at an example of an Exchange system: You are the email master of a large multinational corporation, known as Widgets, Inc. Widgets has offices in Seattle, WA; Redmond, WA; New York, NY; and Paris, France.

The entire scope of your mail system combines all of these offices, to which you give an organizational name of Widget-Mail. Because Seattle and Redmond are so close together, you set up a high-speed microwave link between the two areas, and, therefore, bandwidth is not a problem. Given this, you create one site for both areas and call it Northwest. Because of your high-speed link, you only require one server for the site. However, you can have a server in both Seattle and Redmond, or multiple servers in both Seattle and Redmond.

The offices in New York and Paris have no nearby offices, so they become sites of their own. You name them East, for the New York office, and Europe, for the

Paris office. Your New York office has a large number of users, owing to your company's stunning success at exporting widgets. To keep performance up, there are three Windows NT Servers in the New York office. Experience has taught you to use logical descriptive server names, so you name them Accounting-NY, Sales-NY, and Logistics-NY. Of course, you also have different servers in your Northwest site, as well, with their own self-documenting names (see Figure 2.1).

Sending a message from an Exchange Server in Seattle to a server in New York by mapping one server directly to another might not only be confusing, but it could cost extra time, money, and energy. Here's why: To move mail from Northwest to New York, for example, you might send multiple copies of the same message to multiple individual servers in New York. This creates unnecessary traffic on the link between the two offices, because the same information is sent several times.

It would be more efficient, for example, to route all mail from Northwest to a bridgehead server in New York, which could then expand the mail at that site. If the CEO in the Northwest site creates a message to schedule a conference with all employees, a single copy of the message could be sent to the server you designate as a bridgehead in the East site. In turn, this server would expand that

Figure 2.1   Example of an Exchange organization with three sites.

2

message to reach all designated users on all servers in the East site. For this reason, this expansion process is also sometimes called message fan-out, because it takes a single message and re-creates it as many times as are necessary to reach an audience on multiple servers, on the remote side of a wide area network (WAN) connection.

This message expansion process is memory-intensive; thus, choosing an expansion server carefully is important. Remember also that any site may have multiple servers. For clarity's sake, we have only drilled down to the site level at East in this example (in reality, it would have to create copies for all three servers that we know operate at this site).

Each site must support a minimum of one connection to other Exchange sites. You may even create more than one connection between any two servers, and assign a cost to each connection (or each type of connection, when costs are equivalent). The lowest-cost route(s) will be attempted first, then the server will move up the cost scale, when an attempt to use a lower-cost previous connection fails.

Ultimately, all Exchange messages must be delivered to a storage area associated with a named user or group account. This storage area is known as a mailbox, and is the subject of the section that follows next.

MAILBOXES

To use Exchange, a user must have a mailbox. Commonly, mailboxes contain the following:

- **First name** A maximum of 16 characters
- **Last name** A maximum of 40 characters
- **Alias name** A maximum of 64 characters; used for non-Exchange systems
- **Display name** A maximum of 256 characters
- **Directory name** A maximum of 64 characters; used to route mail, and cannot be changed

In addition, users may be identified using Exchange Directory Services. Mailbox configurations provide the ultimate level of control, because individual mailbox settings can override site-level configuration data. Finally, when the storage limit for a mailbox is reached, you can configure a warning message followed by a message stating that it is forbidden to send mail owing to storage limitations.

In Exchange version 5.5, you can now block mailboxes that have reached their storage limits from receiving new mail!

Now that you have an overall view of how Exchange handles the big picture, let's drill down to a single server and see what a client/server mail system can do. To start this investigation, you'll examine the role that connectors play in the Exchange environment.

Connectors

Life would be much easier if we only had to deal with one type of mail service. In the real world, juggling different types of mail is commonplace. For Exchange, a special software component called a *connector* manages links with foreign email systems and converts incoming messages to a format that Exchange can use, while sometimes converting outgoing messages to specific formats required for other systems.

Exchange supports a variety of built-in connectors, and third-party connectors are also available. Microsoft's connectors can even track messages, and record such tracking information to a log file located in the \Exchsrvr\Tracking.log subdirectory. On the other hand, Microsoft's *Messaging API (MAPI)* makes it possible to use third-party connectors. Because such third-party connections usually provide application-level links between incompatible email systems, these connectors may also be called *gateways*.

The list of Microsoft-provided connectors includes:

- **Lotus Notes** Supports rich text, OLE, Document Links, and DirSync. DirSync support is new to Exchange 5.5.
- **Lotus cc:Mail** Supports Export version 5.14, Import/Export versions 5.15 and 5.16, and Post Office Database versions 6 and 8.
- **Internet Mail Service (IMS)** Supports *Simple Mail Transfer Protocol (SMTP), Internet Mail Access Protocol version 4 (IMAP4), ETRN, Lightweight Directory Access Protocol (LDAP), Secure Multipurpose Mail Extensions (S/MPME), Secure Sockets Layer (SSL) and SASL.* Prior to Exchange 5.0, this connector was named the Internet Mail Connector. IMS was renamed to emphasize its improved and expanded features.
- **Microsoft Mail Connector, Connector Interchange** Enables routing to and from Microsoft Mail.
- **Microsoft Mail Connector, MTA, PC** Transfers mail to Microsoft Mail on PCs.
- **Microsoft Mail Connector, MTA, AppleTalk** Transfers mail to Microsoft Mail on Macintosh computers (AppleTalk).
- **NNTP Connector** Serves as a newsgroup connector that works with the *Network News Transfer Protocol (NNTP)* for access to Usenet and other NNTP-based newsgroups.
- **X.400 Connector** An international standard for global messaging that supports a wide variety of message-handling capabilities, defined by the ITU (International Telecommunications Union).

Other connectors are available (usually for a fee) from Microsoft and third parties. These connectors support other widely used messaging systems (such as IBM PROFS) but also provide access to fax services and telephone voice mail as well. When connectors that support such enriched services are available, incoming faxes and voice mail messages show up in the same inbox that announces the arrival of file-based email messages. In general, such service-oriented connectors use the MAPI interface, which helps to make the term "universal" in what Microsoft calls its Universal Inbox live up to its claim.

DIRECTORY SERVICE (DS)

The Directory Service (DS) houses a structure called a *Global Address List (GAL)*, which incorporates names for distribution lists, mailboxes, and servers. In addition, the DS holds data for mapped addresses, aliases, and routing information. This information is replicated (copied) to other Exchange servers. DS installs the Lightweight Directory Access Protocol (LDAP) within a site by default to convey this kind of information between Exchange servers. LDAP is configured through the Protocols icon in the Exchange Administrator.

In the course of performing its functions, the DS communicates with the following Exchange components:

- **Administrator program** Permits authorized users to modify connectors, servers, and so forth; to create new items (objects); and to view and modify the GAL. The Administrator program has many interconnecting services, and it's where you will "live" for the most part, when working with Exchange.

- **Connectors** Uses the DS to look up addresses, configuration, and replication information.

- **Directory Synchronization** Looks up recipients, and controls custom recipients. Frequently abbreviated to DirSync.

- **Exchange Clients** Finds (usually in Outlook clients) addresses; modifies distribution lists (if allowed by the Administrator program); and views (and perhaps modifies) the GAL, *Personal Address Book (PAB)*, and Outlook Web Access (OWA).

- **Information Store** Gets data about mailboxes, stores messages, and can create directories for public folders and configuration data.

- **Message Transfer Agent (MTA)** Finds configuration and addresses from the DS. Also, handles notification for inbound and outbound mail from other directories.

- **Microsoft Mail Connector** Handles configuration information and address lookup for older MS Mail servers.

- **Other directories** Talks to other Directory Services within the same site to replicate Directory Service data.

- **System Attendant (SA)** Verifies directory information, looks up addresses, supplies configuration data, and generates routing tables.

LDAP is an industry standard protocol for Directory Service applications of all kinds, including Exchange DS, and is itself a subset of the full-blown Directory Access Protocol (DAP). Clients with permission to use LDAP can add, delete, or modify within this X.500-compliant service. Users can search for specific information using any application that supports LDAP. Exchange Server 5.5 supports LDAP version 2 and most version 3 requests, but LDAP is only supported when using TCP/IP as a transport protocol (because LDAP is TCP/IP-based).

There are a total of eight directory-related requests and eight matching responses in Exchange version 5.5. Permission authentication can come from basic (clear text), basic (clear text) using SSL, NT Challenge/Response, NT Challenge/Response using SSL, or the Microsoft Commercial Internet System (MCIS) Membership system. MCIS is based on NT Challenge/Response but has been optimized for Internet use.

When configuring LDAP, you can allow or disallow anonymous users, configure search options, specify referral servers, and adjust or disable idle time-out settings. Once you've mastered the locator service provided by the Exchange DS, it's time to grapple with the way Exchange messages and data may be represented and stored. That's where the Information Store comes in, and is the subject of the next section.

INFORMATION STORE

Assuming an Exchange message is delivered successfully, it lives on in the Information Store. Two different databases reside in the Information Store—public and private. Rather than route a message created for delivery to a user on the same server to the Message Transfer Agent (MTA), the Information Store handles local delivery internally. Each of the other major Exchange components also has a relationship with the Information Store, as follows:

- **Administrator program** Provides information about folder sizes, logged on users, resources, and so on.

- **Connectors** Sends messages to and from foreign systems.

- **Directory Services (DS)** Looks up addresses and data on user mailboxes. Allows creation of public folders (if permitted by administrative rules).

- **Exchange Clients** Sends and receives messages from Outlook or other client-side software.

- **Message Transfer Agent (MTA)** Handles new mail. Incoming and outgoing mail is handed off to the MTA by the Information Store.

- **System Attendant (SA)** When instructed, creates log entries to track Information Store activity.

Thus, the Information Store plays a pivotal role in storing incoming email messages for their intended recipients, and in providing temporary storage for outbound email messages before they are sent. It works most closely with the MTA when handling inbound and outbound traffic; the MTA is the focus of the section that follows.

Message Transfer Agent (MTA)

The Message Transfer Agent (MTA) tells the System Attendant (SA) that it is about to send to or receive messages from other systems or sites. The MTA supplies the base functionality to enable communications within Exchange. This subsystem provides the vehicle for communication with other servers, sites, and systems. In some cases (such as Microsoft Mail), the MTA also performs format conversion. In addition, the MTA maps and routes delivery points. Because the MTA is involved in moving messages, it talks to other components of Exchange, such as:

- **Administrator program** An access program used to manage messages.

- **Directory Service (DS)** A database that contains user names and addresses, that acts almost like a type of phonebook.

- **Directory Synchronization** Like a Directory Service, but for databases on foreign messaging services.

- **Information Store** A service that sends messages for outbound delivery and receives new mail from the MTA.

- **Microsoft Mail Connector** A service that informs the MTA when new mail needs to be delivered.

- **System Attendant (SA)** A service that responds to MTA requests that it log each message transfer.

In its role as the primary handler of all incoming and outgoing messages, the MTA can rightly be considered the pivot point for any Exchange Server. No less important, however, is the System Attendant, which provides the administrative interface for any Exchange Server; it is the focus of the next section.

System Attendant (SA)

The management module for Exchange Server is the System Attendant (SA). You can think of the SA as the control center for any Exchange Server. This digital servant does things like:

- Gather information about services running on each server in a site.
- Check messaging links between servers (in one site, within a site, between two different sites, and between two different systems).
- Check directory-replication information and correct whatever inconsistencies it discovers.
- Log information about messages sent while tracking messages.
- Build routing tables for a site.
- Generate email addresses for new recipients.
- Help enable or disable added security measures, such as digital signatures or encryption.

The System Attendant may be accessed directly by Exchange administrators, or through applications written to its specific interface. Although it is responsible for some advanced security features, particularly those related to message encryption and digital signatures, most security measures that apply to Exchange result from its operation on a Windows NT Server. This provides the subject for the section that follows next.

Security And Safety

Exchange is tightly integrated with the Windows NT Server operating system. Thus, many security functions available in Exchange derive from native Windows NT security mechanisms. This includes the ability to create a special administrative group purely for Exchange administrators to use, to control who may access the SA and other Exchange configuration controls. It also includes use of standard NT access controls, such as setting file permissions for message stores, application directories, and other key Exchange assets, so that only authorized Exchange administrators can access and manipulate their contents. In general, it's wise to use built-in NT security mechanisms to help protect Exchange as much as possible.

Exchange does add a few options to the User Manager For Domains that enable mailbox creation when creating new users on an NT domain controller. Exchange also includes a modified version of the built-in NTBACKUP.EXE program, which can back up the Exchange Information Store without requiring you to stop Exchange services. This makes it much easier to leave Exchange running, yet still make complete system backups.

Always make online backups of any Exchange server, because this allows the server to operate uninterrupted. It is also possible to move data from one Exchange Server to another when restoring from a backup, which provides a handy way to migrate a DS and an Information Store from one server to another.

Because email is so important, protecting Exchange assets is an important task. Managing security and ensuring data availability both play important roles in this process. In a similar vein, Exchange also supports a logging mechanism that can permit its activities to be recorded and analyzed; this serves as the subject for the section that follows.

LOG FILES

Before a message is sent to the Information Store database, it is written to a log file. This prevents Exchange from slowing down during peak usage periods. Some time after a message is logged, it will then be written to the database, depending on system activity levels. Microsoft's technique for updating the database is called "lazy commit," and works like "lazy write" for disk updates in that the log file acts like a kind of cache where new messages can be stored short-term, until the server has sufficient idle CPU cycles to update the underlying database. Because Exchange log files are written contiguously, rather than in random access order—which is the norm for the Exchange Information Store—the log file can often absorb new messages far more quickly than the database itself. Furthermore, this technique works equally well for both NTFS and FAT partitions.

Once a group of messages is written to the database, and the write operation completes successfully, a special mark called a checkpoint is entered into the log file. In the event of a power outage, or some other system failure, Exchange will examine the log for the most recent checkpoint, and continue to write messages into the database from the log from that point forward. This way, it is far less likely that any messages will be lost because only one message—the one being written to the log when the system fails—is ever likely to be completely lost.

For the same reason, log files are permitted to grow to only 5MB in size, at which point the current log file is closed and saved and a new one is created. Even if media failures cause a log file to become corrupted, it is unlikely that more than one log file would be affected by such a failure beyond the point of recoverability.

Thus, message logging plays a key role in maintaining message integrity in the Exchange environment. But because message applications invariably create large numbers of files, including logs, the Exchange Optimizer tool plays an equally important role in keeping track of available file space and in ensuring best placement of Exchange mailboxes (where user and group message files are apt to proliferate in great numbers). The Optimizer defines the focus for the section that follows next.

Optimizer

The Optimizer scans the Exchange Server's hardware configuration for items that include the following:

- Amount of memory
- Number of drives
- Space available on drives
- Throughput of disk subsystems

Once this information is obtained, an optimizing wizard will make suggestions for placement of mailboxes, log files, and other Exchange-related objects. Once the wizard presents its suggestions, simply press OK in the Wizard dialog box to reconfigure Exchange.

 Do *not* run the Optimizer for Back Office—Small Business Server (SBS) version 4 or 4.01. This version of the Optimizer does not know about the 25-user limit that applies to SBS, and actually increases the memory needed!

Once you've installed Exchange and lived with it for a while, the Optimizer can prove to be an effective tool in helping you and your users get the most out of the software. At many sites, this tool quickly becomes a part of the Exchange administrator's regular maintenance routine. But beyond regular maintenance, there is the occasional need to upgrade Exchange software from one version to the next; this serves as the topic for the next section.

Upgrading

To upgrade from a previous version of Exchange to the current version, you can use either a one- or a two-step process. The specific requirements for each process are spelled out in the release notes that accompany new software from Microsoft. As these notes proclaim, they "contain information not available in the Microsoft Exchange Server documentation and information about changes that occurred after publication," which you must review carefully before upgrading.

In a nutshell, upgrading to Exchange Server 5.5 means that you must first install NT 4, then Service Pack 3, then Active Server Pages, then Internet Explorer 4.01, and the roll-up, in that order. (The roll-up is a collection of patches that

2

follow the most recent service pack—which, at the time of this writing, is Service Pack 3.) Only then can the real upgrade process begin. Also, be sure to check the release notes for sections labeled "General Server Notes" and "Known Problems," because these can alert you to potential difficulties that you may otherwise be unable to avoid.

EXCHANGE ON THE CLIENT-SIDE

Microsoft created a great deal of public confusion by using the word Exchange used to designate its Exchange Server product, but by releasing a Windows 95 email client package with the same name. For this reason, many people who use Windows 95 believe they have Exchange, the server, when they have only a 32-bit mail client package.

Microsoft has corrected this situation—as far as Microsoft is concerned, Exchange refers only to Exchange Server. The client side has been renamed Outlook, and is bundled with current versions of both Windows 95 and Windows 98.

But because Exchange includes client-side software, as well as server-side components, be aware that the first release of Exchange 5.5 contains Outlook version 8.0.x. Close examination of Outlook 98 (which ships with Windows 98 but also runs on Windows 95) shows that it is designated as version 8.5.x to identify its revision status. If you own Exchange Server 5.5, you are automatically entitled to use whichever version of Outlook you like, up to the number of client licenses assigned to that Exchange Server.

For road warriors with under-powered notebooks, Microsoft offers the Outlook Web Access (OWA). This is a browser-based Exchange client, with less capability, but also with lower system requirements that is well-suited for laptop use (or on older, less well-equipped desktop systems).

CHAPTER SUMMARY

In this chapter, you got a good overview of Exchange Server's architecture, and a short lesson on how this collection of components does its many jobs. We discussed both core and optional components of Exchange Server and briefly reviewed the client side. (Chapter 6 presents an in-depth look at Exchange clients.) This chapter is still quite abstract and theoretical; however, it should assist you greatly in understanding the inner workings of Exchange, as you investigate the rest of this book.

KEY TERMS

- **connector**—A type of mail service used by the MTA.

- **Directory Service (DS)**—Similar to a phonebook.

- **ETRN**—An ISP email transmission service for both SMTP and POP3 or IMAP4. ETRN is an Extended Simple Mail Transfer Protocol (ESMTP) command. (For more information, see Request For Comments 1985.)

- **gateway**—Moves mail out one type of service into a different one (for example, Exchange to Lotus Notes).

- **Global Address List (GAL)**—An address book that is generally available to all users. It can have restrictions in what a user can see. This allows views to be sorted by property.

- **Information Store**—A database where all a user's mail is stored.

- **Internet Message Access Protocol version 4 (IMAP4)**—A new format for email. Unlike POP3, IMAP4 can connect to multiple mailboxes and public folders. IMAP4 support is new to Exchange 5.5.

- **Internet Message Service (IMS)**—This is new to Exchange version 5.5. Formerly known as the IMC (Internet Mail Connector), IMS was renamed to demonstrate an improved feature set.

- **Lightweight Directory Access Protocol (LDAP)**—An electronic version of the phonebook white pages, for email addresses.

- **log file**—A to-do list for Exchange that records pending messages to be sent, before such messages are committed to the Information Store; sometimes called a transaction log.

- **Message Transfer Agent (MTA)**—The Exchange component program that actually moves the mail.

- **Messaging Application Programming Interface (MAPI)**—A Microsoft-supplied method to extend a program's functionality, used to invoke a variety of messaging services.

- **Network News Transfer Protocol (NNTP)**—The format for information stored on Usenet sites. Usenet is similar to a Bulletin Board System (BBS). One person posts a message that others can read and respond to publicly.

- **Object Linking and Embedding (OLE)**—A Microsoft technology that may be used to insert information from one document into another, where a change to the original document will propagate into the document that includes the insertion.

- **organization**—The entire company within the Exchange system. It is the top-level container.

- **Personal Address Book (PAB)**—A grouping of contact information, for a person, as opposed to a global or public list.
- **Remote Procedure Call (RPC)**—A message-passing facility that allows an application to call services on other machines on a network, as if caller and called were operating within one single, logical, distributed program.
- **Secure MIME (S/MIME)**—A form of MIME wherein mail attachments are encrypted to protect their contents from snooping.
- **Secure Sockets Layer (SSL)**—A protocol that creates secure communications by using public key cryptography and bulk data encryption.
- **Simple Mail Transfer Protocol (SMTP)**—A protocol for sending outgoing email.
- **site**—A subset of the organization. A site fits inside the organization, when thinking in an object fashion.
- **System Attendant (SA)**—An Exchange component used to performs general maintenance tasks.

REVIEW QUESTIONS

1. You decide to create multiple ways of connecting Exchange sites. In what order will the connections be made?
   a. The order in which you install them.
   b. The fastest connection type first.
   c. Any connection that is already open.
   d. Least cost, first, where you assigned the costs.
2. What are the proper version of NT Server, RAM requirement, and available hard-drive space for an Intel-based machine?
   a. NT 3.51 SP 5, Pentium 60, 24MB RAM, 250MB available hard-drive space
   b. NT 3.51 SP 5, Pentium 133, 32MB RAM, 500MB available hard-drive space
   c. NT 4 SP 3, Pentium 60, 24MB RAM, 250MB available hard-drive space
   d. NT 4 SP 3, Pentium 133, 32MB RAM, 500MB available hard-drive space
3. The IMS replaced the IMC. True or False?
4. When creating redundant site links, which considerations should you

include? (Choose all that apply.)

    a. Amount of RAM in the server

    b. Network bandwidth

    c. Distance between sites

    d. Cost of connection

5. Which of the following site connectors are included with Exchange 5.5? (Choose all that apply.)

    a. X.400

    b. MS Mail

    c. Internet Mail Service (IMS)

    d. Internet Mail Connector (IMC)

6. Which of the following is a characteristic of a bridgehead server?

    a. Acts as a "traffic cop" for the organization

    b. Takes a single piece of mail, and replicates it to all users

    c. Takes a single instance of mail, and replicates it to all intended users

    d. None of the above

7. Which authentication options are used by LDAP?

    a. Basic (clear text)

    b. Basic (clear text) using SSL

    c. MCIS

    d. All of the above

8. At what level does LDAP work?

    a. Organization

    b. Site

    c. Server

    d. All of the above

9. A user has not been performing maintenance on his mailbox and has ignored the warning messages you have configured. What can you configure as the next step to force maintenance?

    a. Forbid sending of mail

    b. Forbid receiving of mail

    c. All of the above

    d. None of the above

10. What is a site a subdivision of?

    a. Mailboxes

    b. Server

    c. Organization

    d. All of the above

11. Which of the following Exchange services does RPC need to work?
    (Choose all that apply.)

    a. A dial-up modem to be available at all times

    b. A list of other organizations to be able to communicate with them

    c. At the very least, a 64K permanent connection

    d. None of the above

12. A backup Exchange Server can be used on Windows 98, but for emergency use. It will be slow and cannot be done on Windows 95. True or False?

13. What is the meaning of the following statement? Exchange Server is based on MAPI.

    a. Mailboxes are usable by competing products, such as Lotus Notes

    b. Exchange has robust server security

    c. Other companies have a method to extend the capabilities of Exchange

    d. All of the above

14. What is OWA an acronym for?

    a. Overview of Windows Architecture

    b. Outlook Web Access

    c. Over Wan Architecture

    d. None of the above

15. How is it possible to share a single instance of data with other users?

    a. OWA

    b. OLE

    c. MAPI

    d. RPC

CASE PROJECTS

1. You have accepted a position at a company to improve the electronic communication among employees. The firm has a great deal of data to manage. Most of the information is of a sensitive nature. What can you do to provide both availability and security?

2. You have a security problem with your email system. It has been discovered that copies of confidential mail messages have been sent to your competitors and you have been asked to look at the system to find out how and stop it. You are using Exchange Server 5.5 and Outlook. What steps can you take, or protocols can you use, to improve the confidentiality of email in this environment?

EXCHANGE SERVER INSTALLATION

In this chapter, you'll explore Exchange Server installation. You'll learn what you need to know to install Exchange, be it the first server in an organization, a server at a new site, or simply adding another Exchange Server to an existing site. Because there's a lot involved in laying out a well-designed email system, you may be surprised by the amount of thought that must occur before you start popping CDs into drives and driving your mouse through any setup screens!

That's why any good installation starts with pencil and paper, as you work your way through the planning process so necessary to a successful installation experience. It's also a good idea to make sure the Windows NT Server where Exchange Server will reside is properly configured and ready to take on the task of hosting this incredibly demanding service. Only then will you be ready to tackle the ins and outs of an Exchange installation.

AFTER READING THIS CHAPTER AND COMPLETING THE EXERCISES, YOU WILL BE ABLE TO:

- Understand Exchange installation options for an organization, site, or server
- Install Exchange Server as the first server in an organization or as a server in a site
- Configure Exchange to communicate with other Exchange sites or other mail systems

You'll also examine foreign mail systems—which are non-Exchange mail servers, such as mail from the Internet—so you can better understand how Exchange works with other email systems and servers. To help you understand how to interconnect Exchange Servers or to link Exchange Servers to foreign mail systems, we'll also examine the installation process for a mail connector. Finally, you'll proceed through an actual Exchange Server installation, step-by-step.

PLANNING YOUR INSTALLATION

Before you even think about installing Microsoft Exchange Server, there are a number of things you must take into consideration. First and foremost, you must formulate a set of plans and designs that include everything from a naming convention for Exchange Servers and mailboxes, to a firm understanding of what kind of security you want to apply to your Exchange Servers. In the same vein, you'll want to decide which administrators will be allowed to operate on those servers, and you'll probably want to create a global group named something like Exchange Administrators to establish who's in and who's out of this elite administrative group.

The following list presents a few planning tips you should heed during this process:

- Within a *site*, all Exchange Servers need the same security context. Among other things, this means that while it is possible to span multiple domains, it is recommended that all exchange servers belong to the same Windows NT domain.

- Make a site as large as you can from the very start. You will learn that it is far easier to split overly large Exchange sites than it is to merge Exchange sites that are too small.

- Create a list that names your *organization*, all the sites within the organization, and all the Exchange Servers you intend to install.

- Create a list of all the users who will be sending and receiving email; develop a naming convention that will help you distinguish between the Bob Smith in Accounting, and the Bob Smith in Sales.

- Remember that replication is more bandwidth-intensive between servers within a site than between sites. This may mean upgrading the backbone to which servers are attached, or planning the physical layout of your network to consolidate server-to-server traffic on the backbone, rather than on local cable segments that ordinary users also access.

- The minimum net available bandwidth (NAB) between servers within a site is 64Kbps, but 128Kbps represents a more practical minimum. The higher the message traffic, the greater the NAB value should be.

- Any connection to another Exchange site must be permanent, not a dial-up connection. Dial-up connections only work for remote users, and don't support ongoing directory synchronization or regular message exchanges.

- Exchange may be installed on a Primary Domain Controller (PDC), a Backup Domain Controller (BDC), or a member server. A member server is best, because hardware resources are not consumed in verifying login rights (as is the case with any kind of *domain controller*, be it a PDC or a BDC). Understanding NT domains is essential to installing an effective Exchange organization.

When planning your Exchange rollout, map server locations, names, and container structures as closely as possible to your firm's political and geographical organization. Throughout this chapter, we'll build on the example in Chapter 2, in which the organization named Widgets operated a site in New York named East. Recall that the East site has Exchange Servers situated in the Accounting, Logistics, and Sales departments.

 The following is a list of points that will help you to ensure a successful Exchange installation experience in a production environment:

- Be sure to increase the size of the NT Server's pagefile by at least 100MB (some experts recommend pagefiles that are two to three times the size of the RAM installed in a machine, disk space permitting).

- Exchange Server requires NT4 Service Pack 3; it won't install unless this is already in place.

- Internet Information Server, version 3—or a newer version—is required if you wish to use Outlook Web Access.

- Exchange performs better when on a member server, not a domain controller, because it can get more ready access to the CPU.

- Keep your eyes peeled for Exchange Service Packs; for Exchange 5.5, Service Packs appear to be released about every 90 days.

All this planning pays off handsomely when you create your first Exchange Server. Because all other servers within an Exchange site use the configuration information established for the first server, it's absolutely essential to get things right the first time. Otherwise, alas, it may be time to do things over! But, for good or ill, that installation is what we tackle next.

INSTALLATION

Before you click SETUP.EXE on your Exchange CD-ROM, a little NT pre-configuration can save a lot of grief later on. Failure to follow the steps outlined in the following section will leave you with an Exchange installation that appears to work, at first, because you're installing from an Administrator account. Once you log off, however, Exchange has no way to validate itself and will fail miserably.

Therefore, the first pre-configuration step when installing Exchange is to create a service account. We explain how to do this in the section that follows.

SERVICE ACCOUNT CREATION

To create a service account using the User Manager For Domains, pick a unique, self-documenting account name (such as ExchgSvc). Make sure to grant this account the Log On As A Service permission. Likewise, be sure to select a secure, unguessable password, and store that password in a safe place.

Choose each Exchange Server's name carefully—you cannot rename an Exchange Server once it's installed without reinstalling the Exchange software. (You can, however, change the password later if you must.) This account information will be used if you create other Exchange Servers within the site. Remember also that the Exchange service account must belong to the same Windows NT domain as the Exchange Server itself. With these items carefully considered and addressed, here's how to create the service account, step-by-step:

1. Click Start | Programs | Administrative Tools (Common) | User Manager For Domains.
2. Select New User from the User menu.
3. Enter a name and password for the service account.
4. Enable (check) the User Cannot Change Password and the Password Never Expires checkboxes.
5. Disable (uncheck) the User Must Change Password At Next Logon and the Account Disabled checkboxes.
6. Click the Add button to add this new user definition.
7. Click the X-shaped close button in the upper right-hand corner of the User Manager For Domains window to exit the application.

The next step is to create an Exchange Administrator group (see Figure 3.1). This global group has full control of Exchange, and represents the group to which all Exchange Administrators should belong.

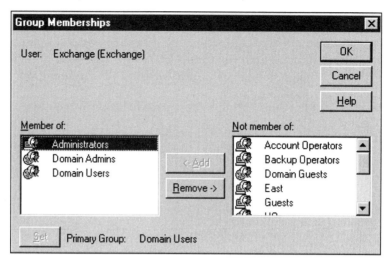

Figure 3.1   Creating the Exchange Administrator group.

To create this group:

1. Log on to the domain with administrative rights.

2. Click Start | Programs | Administrative Tools (Common) | User Manager For Domains | User | New Global Group.

3. Provide a name and description for the new global group.

4. Click Add.

5. Click the X-shaped close button in the upper right-hand corner of the User Manager for Domains window to exit the application.

Review your goals. Do you plan to use features such as Outlook Web Access (OWA)? If so, Internet Information Server (IIS) version 3 or later must be installed first. In fact, if you have a choice, we recommend installing IIS version 4.

This concludes the preinstallation NT configuration work that will help to ensure a successful Exchange installation. Now, it's finally time to install Exchange itself.

INSTALLING EXCHANGE

To install Exchange Server, perform the following steps:

1. Using an account with administrative privileges, log on to the NT Server where Exchange is to be installed.

2. Insert the Exchange CD-ROM and click Start | Explore.

3. Scroll down to the i386 or Alpha directories, depending on the type of CPU in your server, and click Setup. Otherwise, enter Setup using this command: D:\Setup\i386 (or whatever directory letter your CD-ROM drive uses).

4. Accept the licensing agreement, and choose an installation type. For Exchange, the installation types include Typical, Minimum, and Complete/Custom:

   ■ **Typical** Installs the four Exchange components—Directory Service, System Attendant, Information Store, and *Message Transfer Agent* (*MTA*)—and the Exchange Administrator.

   ■ **Minimum** Installs the four Exchange components only.

   ■ **Complete/Custom** Offers the following options (shown in Figure 3.2):

      ■ **Default installation directory** Allows you to change the default installation directory and offers the choice of MS Mail Connector, cc:Mail Connector, X.400 Connector, and Exchange Event Service.

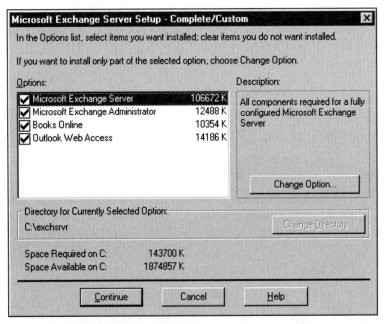

Figure 3.2 A Compete/Custom installation gives you all the choices shown here.

3

- **Microsoft Exchange Administrator** This software may be installed onto any NT machine (Server or Workstation) that will be used for Exchange administration. Exchange Administrator does not work on Windows 95 or Windows 98.

- **Books Online** This option provides access to online Exchange documentation. Books Online can be useful, but it also consumes about 135MB of disk space.

- **Internet Mail** This installs a connector that permits access to Internet-based mail services. Note that Internet Mail will not migrate some routing information.

- **Outlook Web Access** A lightweight method to obtain HTML-based email access using a Web browser or an Exchange client. Invoking this option requires that IIS version 3 or later be installed on the Exchange Server machine.

If you don't see all the options described in the preceding list, it is because you don't have enough disk space to accommodate them. A complete installation (without data) uses about 114MB of disk space. We don't recommend installing Exchange on a drive that has less than 500MB free, to leave room for data as well.

5. Choose the Add Licenses button.

6. In the Per Server box, type the number of Microsoft Exchange Server licenses you own, then choose Continue.

7. When a dialog box appears confirming that you are licensed for however many clients, select the I Agree That checkbox.

8. In the Choose Licensing Mode dialog box, choose Continue.

9. Enter the organization and site information. If this is an initial site, you will be asked: Are You Sure You Want To Create A New Site? Choose Yes if you are creating a new site. Otherwise, choose Join An Existing Site.

10. Enter the information in the Service Account and Password fields. Without a separate service account, Exchange cannot validate and will not run.

11. Confirm that rights have been granted, and click OK.

12. Click OK to begin installation.

13. As a final step you may click Run Optimizer. However, Optimizer may be run later, after mailbox creation.

Do not use Optimizer with BackOffice SBS.

EXCHANGE ADMINISTRATOR

The Exchange Administrator program is where you'll spend most of your time configuring Exchange. Be careful when making changes to an Exchange system. Also, be aware that the default mode for Exchange Administrator is to operate at the site level. Because Exchange uses a container concept, a change at the organization level will affect mail for your entire company! A change at the site level affects all servers within the site, but a change at the server level affects only the server. Be sure you're working in the right container before you start making changes!

In other words, Exchange inherits configurations from higher-level containers, unless you specify otherwise. A field tip from experienced Exchange administrators is that you should create an NT group called Exchange Administrators and assign it the role of Permissions Admin. Then, you can simply add the people who administer the servers to this group. This works nicely if you have frequent staff turnover, because you'll only need to modify the members of this group rather than visit all the places in the Exchange Administrator program where administrators are designated to make similar, but repeated, changes.

There are three main sections in the Admin program where you set the permission roles:

- Organization container (top level in the tree)
- Site container
- Configuration container within the site

The organization is the topmost level. Within the organization is the site. A site has configuration data and servers. Another container is the *recipients* (users) container. To simplify administration efforts, you can create multiple recipient containers. Pay attention when assigning permissions; permissions follow only as far as a boundary.

RECIPIENT CONTAINERS

Remember how well you planned your Exchange organization earlier in this chapter? Now, you can use the list you created to assist you in the creation of recipient containers. You should organize your containers in a logical order. For example, by geography and/or job function. A recipient container can contain another container. Using the Widgets example, the East site can have a recipient container, which has Accounting, Logistics, and Sales subcontainers. To create a new container:

1. Select the site or recipient container.
2. Click File|New Other|Recipients Container.
3. Give your new container a logical name.

Three types of recipients are available: custom, distribution lists, and mailboxes. Each of these is explored in the following sections.

Custom

Custom recipients are called custom because they are not part of your Exchange Server. Usually, custom recipient information represents an Internet address. Given that custom recipients are not part of your Exchange organization, they do not appear in the Directory Service (DS) list by default. Thus, custom recipient address data must be added to the DS database manually. To create a custom address that can appear in a DS, follow these steps:

1. Pick a container.
2. Choose File | New Custom Recipient.
3. Select the type of mail address (Internet Address, X.400, and so forth).
4. Enter the address.

Distribution Lists

The concept of distribution lists is similar to user groups in NT. Distribution lists may be used to create logical groupings of recipients who may be reached through a single address, rather than requiring repeated use of the same set of mailbox or custom recipient addresses. For example, Sales And Marketing might represent distribution lists that include all members of their respective departments; such lists make a great way to reach entire groups with a single address.

To create a distribution list follow these steps:

1. Pick a recipient container.
2. Pick File | New Distribution. (You will see six tabs on the list; click on the General tab.)
3. Enter a display name (remember to choose a logical name) and alias, and assign an owner. Ideally, the owner should not be an Exchange administrator. That way, someone else can manage some of the workload using Outlook, as opposed to requiring rights to the Exchange Administrators group.

A critical part of this process is to go to Properties and select your expansion server. Remember, an expansion server takes one copy of an email (and attachment, if it has one) and makes copies to all the mailboxes listed for distribution. This places quite a load on the RAM in an expansion server.

Mailboxes

User mailboxes represent the third type of recipients.

There are several ways to create mailboxes. You can use the Exchange Administrator's Extract and Import utilities, or you can create a mailbox in User Manager For Domains. To create a new mailbox in Exchange Administrator, follow these steps:

1. Pick a container listed in the Exchange Administrator.

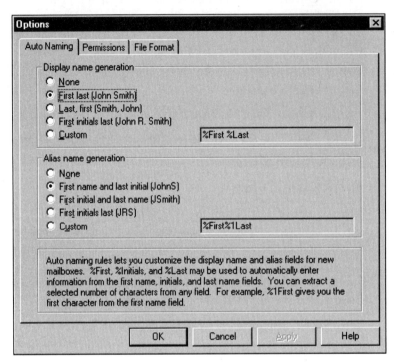

Figure 3.3 The Auto Naming tab.

2. At the toolbar, select File|New Mailbox.

If you are adding a new user to NT, and Exchange is already installed, the easiest method to add a user to Exchange is to select Exchange while in the User Manager For Domains. To create a new user in the User Manager For Domains, follow these steps:

1. From the User menu in the Windows NT User Manager For Domain, choose New User.

2. Type the account information, and then choose Add.

3. In the Connect To Server dialog box, type the name of the Microsoft Exchange Server where you want to create the mailbox.

The Extract and Import utilities are most useful when you need to set up a large number of users. To extract and import in Exchange Administrator, follow these steps:

1. From the Tools menu, choose to either extract from an NT domain or a NetWare (3.x or 4.x) server (as shown in Figure 3.4).

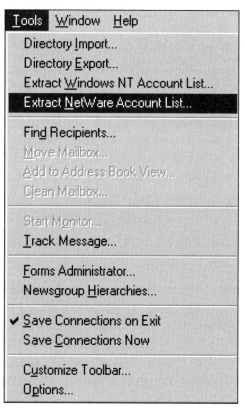

Figure 3.4 Exchange offers several import options.

2. Import the domain of choice into Exchange.

3. While importing, choose which recipient container you wish to import to and declare an existing mailbox as a template to set permissions; you may at your option also define an error log to monitor your success (or failure).

SITES

Stepping back from the user level, let's focus on sites and their properties. If you're not clear on what constitutes an Exchange site and its associated properties, please refer back to "How Exchange Works" in Chapter 2. Remember that Exchange uses a concept not unlike a box within a box. When configuring properties, choose your containers carefully: Any properties that you configure at the site level affect all servers within the site. If you expand the view of a site, you can adjust the properties of a particular server to override configuration settings at the site level. In the sections that follow, you'll learn more about the details involved in site configuration, starting with site addressing in the section that follows next.

SITE ADDRESSING

When dealing with site addressing, you configure the address properties for a default name for your site. You can pick a mail format, such as IMS, and click the Edit button. Be sure to recalculate the routing table in the Routing tab; otherwise, your mail delivery will fail. Also, keep in mind that in the Routing tab (see Figure 3.5), you can configure additional mail-routing choices, should a primary or low-cost connection ever fail. Remember, Exchange 5.5 always attempts to use the lowest-cost routes first.

When you've handled site addressing and routing, it's time to set the characteristics for a site's Message Transfer Agent (MTA). This is the topic of the next section.

MTA Configuration

Within your configuration container, you will find the Message Transfer Agent (MTA). The MTA allows you to configure simple items, such as Retry and Timeout values. Types of connections relevant to the MTA include the following:

- **Internet Mail Service (IMS)** Renamed in Exchange 5.0, the IMS was previously called the Internet Mail Connector (IMC). This new name reflects its added functionality, which includes support for LDAP and IMAP4.

Figure 3.5   The Routing tab.

- **Lotus cc:Mail** The "father" of Notes, cc:Mail is a popular email system that competed with MS Mail.

- **Lotus Notes** IBM/Lotus's competitor to Exchange.

- **Microsoft Mail** The "father" of Exchange, MS Mail is an older Microsoft email application. For best results, you might want to migrate existing users from MS Mail to Exchange.

- **Remote Access Service (RAS)** RAS is a secure method for Dial-Up Networking. Think of RAS as a way to extend the network, using a *very* long and *very* slow network connection from the server to the client.

- **Site Connector** A tool that connects sites within a local area network (LAN) or a wide area network (WAN).

- **X.400** Integrated with the MTA, X.400 can be configured to connect sites within Microsoft Exchange Server or to route messages to foreign X.400 systems. When handling communication between Microsoft Exchange Server and foreign X.400 systems, the connector maps addresses and converts Microsoft Exchange Server messages to native X.400 messages and vice versa.

It should be obvious now that when dealing with MTA configuration, you must deal with the kinds of connections with which the MTA will interact. The various mail connectors under its control help manage these connections. When this work is done, it's time to establish necessary parameters for the Information Store where Exchange keeps its inbound and outbound messages and other data. This is covered in the next section.

Information Store

The Information Store is where actual data is stored for individual mailboxes as well as for public folders. If you're careful, you can save yourself future headaches by understanding default behaviors of the Information Store.

For example, Information Store configuration options specify who may create new public folders. Because the default is to permit members of the Everyone group (all users, in other words) to create such folders, if you tighten up this option early on, you can avoid cleaning up a mess of public folders later on. At a bare minimum, you would want to restrict this privilege to the Exchange Administrators. Or, for better user service, you could create another NT user group called Exchange Operators, grant this group rights to create new user folders, and then add individuals from within the departments to this group. That way, each department has a representative who cannot only create folders on request, but who can also be made responsible for keeping chaos under control.

Other options include the ability to configure storage warning and public folder replication. All these features can help you control your users and to limit how much disk space they can consume on your Exchange Server. Use them often, but wisely.

 Remember, in Exchange 5.5, you can now refuse to accept mail in a mailbox after the threshold you set has been reached. Previously, you could only block the sending of mail as a control method.

The Information Store is where you configure storage warnings and limits, age limits for public folders, and DS listings. Another important tab on the Information Store is the Diagnostics Logging tab. Because diagnostics logging can be turned on at will, and reports exhaustively on all Information Store activity and errors, this can be a great troubleshooting aid when users report problems such as slow response time or are unable to access or send email.

Beyond the controls associated with the Information Store and diagnostics logging, it is also possible to monitor message traffic and activity on an Exchange Server. This, too, can be an important tool for troubleshooting, and serves as the topic for the following section.

3

Message Tracking

Tracking is a critical part of keeping messages flowing, but it is also critical for finding out why they aren't. Use the Exchange Administrator to configure tracking. Tracking configuration is handled in two key Exchange components: the Information Store and the MTA.

Here's how to decide where to begin your tracking efforts. If the sender and receiver for a message both reside within a single site, that message never leaves Exchange, so it may be tracked entirely within the Information Store. But if a message destination resides outside the site, it will pass through MTA, and must be tracked through that component.

Message tracking creates a log file, which resides in the ExchSrvr\tracking subdirectory. The System Attendant component creates this log file; the file name takes a format of *YYYYMMDD*.LOG. Thus, a log file recording on June 6, 1998, would be named 19980606.log (here, the first 06 stands for June, and the second 06 stands for the sixth day of that month).

FOREIGN MAIL SYSTEMS

Any system that is not part of the Exchange mail environment is considered a foreign system. To swap messages and attachments with a foreign mail system, two key ingredients are required: a network link from Exchange to the foreign system and a way to convert data between Exchange formats to something that the foreign system can understand (which is almost always matched by the reverse conversion, to change foreign formats into something that Exchange can understand).

 Microsoft provides a wizard (the Internet Mail Service Wizard) to help you configure the Internet Mail Service (IMS) with Exchange. You should know about any new Exchange features, such as this new wizard. The best source of such information is the Release Notes that ship with the product, or the Microsoft Exchange Web page, located at **http://www.microsoft.com/exchange**. When you use the IMS Wizard, you install and configure TCP/IP so that IMS can talk to the Internet. Also, you must have access to a DNS server, whether it be a local DNS server that you control or a DNS server available at or through an Internet Service Provider (ISP). Within DNS, both the A record (host) and the Mail Exchanger must be configured. You may handle this yourself, or ask your ISP to do it, depending on where your DNS server resides. (BackOffice SBS almost always uses an ISP's DNS server.)

Because access to foreign mail systems requires some common networking protocol to be available to Exchange as well, the next issue is to configure the protocols necessary to support whatever connections your site may need. This is covered in the next section.

Protocols

Hypertext Transfer Protocol (HTTP) with Active Server Pages (ASP) requires IIS to be installed somewhere where it can make a Remote Procedure Call (RPC) request. Access to ASP also requires the Challenge Handshake Authentication Protocol (CHAP) authentication protocol. CHAP permits Exchange to be accessed using a Web browser, such as the Outlook Web Access (which is covered in Chapter 6).

Other protocols available in Exchange include:

- **Lightweight Directory Access Protocol (LDAP)** LDAP is used to query a DS to find email addresses. Users can choose an internal LDAP server to find someone within their own organization or use a public server, such as Four11 or BigFoot, to locate external addresses.

- **Network News Transfer Protocol (NNTP)** NNTP is used to access any public newsgroups directly from the Internet, or to select newfeeds for delivery to an Exchange Server, where incoming newsgroups may be placed in public folder(s). Support for NNTP is new to Exchange 5.

- **Post Office Protocol version 3 (POP3)** POP3 is used to bring in mail from the Internet. Currently, POP3 is the most popular way to process incoming mail for desktop clients.

- **Internet Message Access Protocol version 4 (IMAP4)** IMAP4 is a successor to POP3, designed to improve efficiency for users who access email remotely. IMAP4 permits users to examine headers on the server side, and select only those messages they wish to download to their machines (unlike POP3, which is an all-or-nothing proposition in this regard). Support for IMAP4 is new to Exchange 5.5.

In the sections that follow, you'll learn more about the most common Exchange *connectors* that you're likely to encounter when configuring access to foreign mail systems. These connectors include the Lotus cc:Mail Connector, the Microsoft Mail Connector, the Site Connector, and the X.400 Connector, in that order.

Lotus cc:Mail Connector

The Lotus cc:Mail Connector connects Exchange to cc:Mail versions 5.15 and 6. This is useful if you need to connect and transfer mail to or from any cc:Mail servers.

Within the cc:Mail Connector, you must specify the address for a cc:Mail post office. You can also control how messages flow from the cc:Mail Connector to that cc:Mail post office, and how messages flow from the Connector Store (a storage area for inbound or outbound messages that pass through this connector) to the Exchange Information Store. These controls help to regulate traffic between the two mail systems, and thereby ensure reliable delivery.

3

Microsoft Mail Connector

The Microsoft Mail Connector is used to facilitate migration from or co-existence with older MS Mail programs and Exchange Server. In the real world, most Exchange administrators consider Microsoft Mail a technology dinosaur. Nevertheless, the product is still in wide use, especially on older PCs (80386 and older CPUs) that simply can't run Outlook or other, more modern email clients.

To connect to MS Mail, follow these steps:

1. Click Connections|Container.
2. Select MS Mail Connector|File|Properties.
3. On the Interchange tab, select an account for the Administrator. (The Maximize MS Mail Compatibility setting stores OLE objects in an older format compatible with MS Mail and the current format that's compatible with Exchange.)
4. On the Local Postoffice tab, identify the MS Mail post office where the mail interchange will occur.
5. Select your connection type.
6. On the Connector MTA tab, define the MTA for each Post Office.
7. On the General tab, define size limits.
8. On the Address tab, define which addresses that the MS Mail Connector should use. You can load balance across multiple addresses by selecting different connectors for different mail sites (remember, MS Mail handles both PC and AppleTalk clients).

Site Connector

The Site Connector is the easiest and fastest connector to configure because it links multiple Exchange sites together; therefore, no conversion is needed. To configure the Site Connector, follow these steps:

1. Click File|New Other|Site Connector.
2. Enter the name of the other site (which can be a bridgehead server).

X.400

Lotus Notes relies on the X.400 format. To be truly proficient with Exchange, it's important to know how to connect Exchange to other systems. Given the huge install base for Notes, you should be familiar with the X.400 Connector.

A configuration of an X.400 Connector might look something like this:

```
c=US;A=MCI;p=EXORG1;o=EXSITE2;s=Catura-Houser;g=Tim
```

Here's an element-by-element explanation of this cryptic notation, where each element is separated by a semicolon:

- **c=US** c equals the country (United States in this case).
- **A=MCI** A equals the central message, or backbone, carrier (MCI in this case).
- **p=EXORG1** p is your private management domain (here, it is your Exchange organization).
- **o=EXSITE2** o is the organization (the Exchange site for the designated mailbox).
- **s=Catura-Houser** s equals the recipient's surname (Catura-Houser in this case).
- **g=Tim** g equals the recipient's given (first) name (Tim in this case).

X.400 supports the MTA, RAS, TP4, TCP/IP, and X.25 protocols. This gives it a truly global reach, as it was designed to provide. The X.400 Connector is the most generic of all connectors, but its generality also helps explain why it's often much slower than the Exchange Site Connector.

In addition to the protocols that convey message data between Exchange Servers, and to and from foreign mail systems, numerous activities occur between Exchange Servers, especially among servers that all belong to the same site or that share specific DS relationships. One such activity is *directory replication*, which is the subject of the section that follows next.

Replication

Replication may be understood best as a kind of information cloning process, where a master copy of data drives duplicate copies, so that any change to the master is reflected relatively quickly in all its duplicates. To explain why replication makes sense, imagine that you have created a Global Address List (GAL) that includes addresses for everyone in your multinational company, but that addresses reside only on the servers at the sites where those users reside. Any time a user in Redmond, WA, wants to find the address for a coworker based in New York, that user would have to cross the network link from Redmond to New York to look up the address. This process might be repeated many times a day, increasing long-distance network traffic and costs for only a small benefit to the users.

On the other hand, if you were to replicate address lists and other data, such as public folders, users could look this information up locally. Long-distance network traffic would drop, thereby reducing costs. Local lookup happens much faster than wide-area lookup, which also improves performance. In a nutshell, this explains why replication for shared, widely accessed information—such as for DS databases and public folders—is a good idea.

For that reason, Exchange provides a Directory Replication Connector. You can use this connector's General Property page to establish local and remote bridgehead servers. You can also add an administrative note to explain the configuration and usage properties of the connector (note that administrative notes are visible only to administrators).

Using the Directory Replication Connector employs the same process that updates the directories for all Microsoft Exchange Server computers within a site to deliver updated information between sites. Within a site, directory replication is automatic for Exchange Servers. Between sites, you can configure directory replication to deliver all updates across the link, or configure it so that only necessary information replicates to other sites. To conserve bandwidth, most Exchange administrators opt for the latter, even though it involves extra work.

To set up directory replication between sites, you must create and configure a Directory Replication Connector, which provides bidirectional replication connection between two sites. You must designate and schedule one server at each site to request updated directory information from the other site. At these scheduled times, the local server requests directory updates from the remote server. To configure replication, perform the following sequence of actions:

1. Select the Configuration container.

2. Install the Directory Replication Connector.

3. Select File|New Other|Directory Replication (see Figure 3.6).

4. Schedule the time when replication should occur (choose a time when network traffic is low; when changes on one side require immediate replication to the other, you can temporarily override this setting with a different time—such as two minutes from now).

Replication normally applies to propagating updates among like systems. Exchange can also propagate or accept updates from foreign mail systems. When this activity occurs, it's called synchronization. This is the subject of the next section.

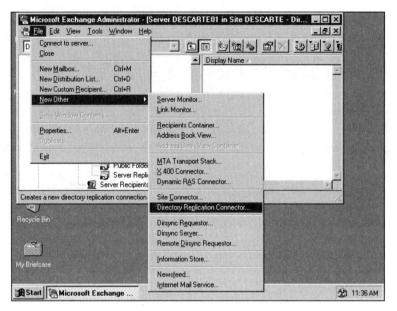

Figure 3.6 Configuring directory replication.

Synchronization

Synchronization describes a sharing of information between Exchange and other systems, such as MS Mail, to keep their directories and other commonly held information in substantial agreement. Synchronization is an efficient process because only changed data is transferred between servers.

Exchange supports this optional step with any system that supports the MS Mail For PC Networks version 3 directory synchronization protocol. This protocol is usually called *DirSync*, and underlies the process involved in synchronizing two dissimilar directories. The DirSync process consists of three steps.

1. DirSync requestors send changes to a DirSync server.

2. The DirSync server creates a master copy of all updates.

3. The master copy is transmitted to all DirSync requestors.

Exchange can be a requestor or a server in this relationship. When MS Mail is in the picture, MS Mail should already have its own DirSync server running, so Exchange will be a requestor. As always, remember that MS Mail supports Apple-Talk and choose your transports and connections accordingly.

To configure synchronization, perform the following steps:

1. Click File|New Other|DirSync Server.

2. Configure times for the DirSync master copy and the DirSync requestors and click OK.

3. Click Start|Settings|Control Panel|Services|Start DirSync Service.

4. On the MS Mail Server(s), select File|New Other|DirSync Remote Requestor.

5. While at the MS Mail post office, run ADMIN.EXE to send DirSync messages to the shadow post office of the Exchange Server.

6. In the Exchange Server, click File|New Other|DirSync Requestor.

7. Set the time for DirSync requestors to send changes to the DirSync server.

8. Click Start|Settings|Control Panel|Services|Start DirSync Service.

Directory synchronization messages are normally sent at the beginning of each hour as selected in the Schedule property page. You can, however, force the directory synchronization process to start manually. To do this, you must add a value to the Windows NT Server Registry. Pausing the Microsoft Exchange Directory Synchronization service will yield an error message, which you can safely ignore. This process forces the directory synchronization process to occur.

As hands-on experience with Exchange will quickly illustrate—especially when migration from another email system comes into play—there's more data than directories and public folders that has to pass between foreign mail systems and Exchange. This is where Exchange's import functions come into play. These import functions are discussed in the next section.

Importing Data

Importing mail into Exchange can save a great deal of time and aggravation during any migration process. True, it takes work to create an import process and to create connections so that you can run two mail systems while you test your mail migration tools. But because the alternative is to enter all user data manually, and to experience interruptions in mail service to your users, the pain also provides some gain.

Given the ability to avoid re-creating user and distribution list information from scratch, importing lists of users is a much better option. The Microsoft Exchange Migration Wizard is included with Exchange (see Figure 3.7) to facilitate this process. In addition to its data translation capabilities, the wizard also supports a phased implementation of Exchange and allows you to run an old mail system in tandem with Exchange for a while. Your other option is to import all the data at once, and then to do away with the old system immediately. Because unforeseen difficulties attend nearly every system migration, we don't recommend that you take this latter approach.

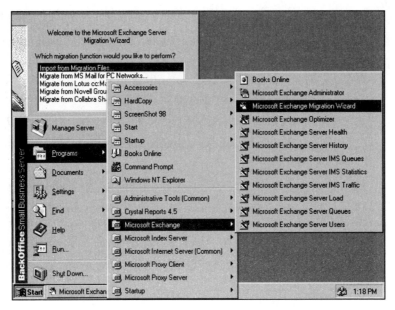

Figure 3.7 Accessing the Microsoft Exchange Migration Wizard.

The Migration Wizard can import messages and other data from:

- Collabra Share
- Lotus cc:Mail
- MS Mail
- Novell GroupWise

Importing can be a one-step or a two-step process. The one-step process extracts data from the foreign mail system and immediately imports it into Exchange. The two-step process stores the exported data in an intermediate form as the first step so that it can be investigated and massaged if necessary. The second step is to import this data into Exchange, usually following some manual intervention, manipulation, and cleaning up.

Wise administrators usually choose the two-step process. These steps involve an export process first and an import process second. Many experienced Exchange administrators use Access or Excel to reorder, reconfigure, and clean up the exported data before importing it into Exchange. This is particularly useful for Internet alias lists. (An alias is a valid substitute name address for another name. In this context, it usually refers to the username that so often accompanies a standard Internet email name that takes the name that makes sense only within the confines of some particular organization and takes the form *user@anyorg.com*.)

For example, the mail name **Tcat@descarte.descarte.com** only works internally within the Descarte organization. The corresponding alias, **tcat@usa.net**, is what is broadcast to the outside world. Keep in mind that Exchange also uses an alias to communicate to people who are not on your Exchange system. That explains why the address that shows up on the headers of messages that pass through the Internet Mail Service may differ from your internal Exchange address.

In addition to its import and export capabilities, and its directory synchronization and replication processes, Exchange also supports replication at the folder level. This provides the topic for our next section.

Folder Replication

Public folders are created on the client side. The important concept to remember when it comes to data replication is that Exchange creates only one copy of any data set per server on each server. You may configure replication between servers or between sites. You may set up folder replication by configuring a public folder's properties page (see Chapter 6 for details on how to create and replicate public folders).

For now, it suffices to say that this provides a handy technique to make local copies of all kinds of useful documents and templates available at every site (and perhaps, at every server) while maintaining only one master set of such data.

CHAPTER SUMMARY

In this chapter, we examined how important it is to plan names, structures, and locations for your organization, sites, and servers before installing Microsoft Exchange Server. We also explained how to configure Windows NT Server 4 properly to accommodate a successful Exchange installation. Then, we showed how to install Exchange 5.5 as an initial server, as well as an addition to an existing Exchange configuration environment.

We also examined the critical role that mail connectors play in an environment where multiple mail systems must interact, and explored the basics of the most commonly used mail connectors. Finally, we showed you how synchronization and replication can simplify administrative tasks, and about various methods to migrate from foreign mail systems into the Exchange environment.

KEY TERMS

- **connectors**—Used to create paths for messages to be sent outside a site. Such paths are represented by one or more address spaces, where multiple address spaces may be used to balance the messaging load when you use multiple connectors.

- **custom recipient**—A recipient in a foreign (non-Exchange) mail system whose address is in the Address Book.

- **directory replication**—The process of updating all Microsoft Exchange Server directories within a site and between sites, with the same information. Within a site, directory replication is automatic. Between sites, you can configure directory replication so that only desired information is replicated to other sites.

- **DirSync**—The directory synchronization object that imports and exports information outside a single Windows NT domain (to other domains or to foreign mail systems) during directory synchronization.

- **domain controller**—The Windows NT Server computer that maintains the security database for all user accounts in a domain. Windows NT Server domains can have one Primary Domain Controller (PDC) and one or more Backup Domain Controllers (BDCs).

- **Internet Message Access Protocol version 4 (IMAP4)**—Enables users with any IMAP4 client (which is compliant with RFC 2060) to access mail in a Microsoft Exchange Server mailbox. IMAP4 may also be used to read and post messages to public folders or to access another user's mailbox, if the proper access rights are granted.

- **Lightweight Directory Access Protocol (LDAP)**—An Internet protocol that allows access to directory information. Clients can use LDAP to browse, read, and search directory listings in the Microsoft Exchange Server 5.5 directory. For example, a user can view department name and location information, using any application that supports the LDAP protocol. LDAP requires a TCP/IP connection.

- **Message Transfer Agent (MTA)**—Like a postal service, the MTA routes messages to other Microsoft Exchange Server MTAs or gateways, Information Stores, or X.400 MTAs in foreign systems. It also maps addresses, routes messages, and converts message formats.

- **Network News Transfer Protocol (NNTP)**—The Internet protocol and service that supports Usenet and other public newsgroup distribution services. One or more servers or hosts running NNTP make up a Usenet site. Each Usenet site receiving a newsfeed can be configured to accept and generate an NNTP connection and newsfeed.

- **organization**—The root, or top-level object or starting point, of the Microsoft Exchange Server directory. All other directory objects are subordinate to the organization. When setting up Microsoft Exchange Server, you name the organization. This is the directory name used in addressing and cannot be changed.

- **recipient**—An object in the directory that can receive messages and information. Exchange Server recipients are mailboxes, distribution lists, public folders, and custom recipients.

- **site**—One or more Microsoft Exchange Server computers generally corresponding to a single geographical location that share the same directory information (mailboxes, distribution lists, routing tables). All servers in a site must be able to communicate with each other through synchronous Remote Procedure Calls (RPCs).

- **X.400**—An internationally recognized message-handling system.

REVIEW QUESTIONS

1. What is the service that routes information between servers in a single site?
   a. Directory Service
   b. System Attendant
   c. Information Store
   d. Windows NT
   e. Message Transfer Agent

2. On what version of Windows can Exchange 5.5 be run?
   a. Windows 95
   b. Windows NT 3.5x
   c. Windows NT 4
   d. All of the above

3. If you want to stop all Exchange services, which of the following would you stop?
   a. Server service
   b. NT
   c. Information Store
   d. System Attendant

4. The SMTP address is set for a site at:
   a. The site Addressing tab in Configuration
   b. Address page of a mailbox
   c. User Manager For Domains
   d. Address properties of IMS

5. You would like to have addresses for outside consultants available to you in your Directory Services. Can you do this? Yes or No?

6. You have MS Mail running, and you're looking to upgrade to Exchange. How many steps can you migrate in?

   a. Single step

   b. Two steps

   c. Both

   d. Not possible

7. You began your Exchange install while logged into NT with the account name Administrator. This means:

   a. Nothing. All will work fine.

   b. It won't work. You must reinstall.

   c. It will appear to work just fine, for a while.

   d. Not possible.

8. You have just completed an Exchange installation. When is it desirable to run the Optimizer? (Choose all that apply.)

   a. After installation of Exchange

   b. After a hardware change

   c. After a major software configuration change

   d. After the addition of many new users

9. The X.400 Connector will allow:

   a. Exchange to send and receive mail between another site supporting X.400.

   b. Removal of the dirty words filter, which the FCC recommends to prevent children from reading adult messages.

   c. You to send and receive mail from another Exchange site, within your company.

   d. All of the above.

10. Your next project is to create users in your freshly installed Exchange Server. How can you do this?

    a. By using User Manager For Domains

    b. Entering them via Exchange Administrator

    c. Exporting from another system, and importing into Exchange

    d. All of the above

11. Which of the following is the recommended minimum hardware for Exchange 5.5 (according to Microsoft)?

    a. P133 MHz, 32MB RAM

    b. P133 MHz, 32MB RAM, 100MB pagefile

    c. P60 MHz, 24MB RAM

    d. P60 MHz, 24MB RAM, 100MB pagefile

12. All servers within a single site share a single service account. True or False?

13. What type of computers can the Exchange Administrator be installed on without a full copy of Exchange? (Choose all that apply.)

    a. NT Servers

    b. NT Workstations

    c. Windows 95 or Windows 98

    d. All of the above

14. Exchange can talk directly to other Exchange Servers within its site using which of the following?

    a. Challenge Handshake Authentication Protocol (CHAP)

    b. InterProcess Communications (IPC)

    c. Remote Access Service (RAS)

    d. Remote Procedure Call (RPC)

15. What is the storage space limitation for the Information Store in Exchange version 5.5?

    a. Depends on the version of NT

    b. 16GB plus transaction logs

    c. 16GB with transaction logs

    d. No effective limit

16. Exchange can use third-party connectors, because it was designed around Microsoft Application Programming Interface. True or False?

HANDS-ON PROJECTS

The IP addresses mentioned in the first project belong to a set of so-called "private IP addresses" reserved for intranet use according to the dictates of RFC 1918. These private IP addresses are safe to use for experiments, because most routers will refuse to pass them on to the Internet, even if an Internet link is accidentally created. This choice was deliberate to prevent your DNS activities from producing unwanted side effects. The second project is far more mundane, but incredibly relevant to everyday Exchange Server administration, because it focuses on creating a user account with administrative access to Exchange.

PROJECT 3.1

For this hands-on project, it is assumed that you have Windows NT installed and configured according to the requirements listed in Chapter 2. The DNS server service should also be installed.

A good private address for TCP/IP for your servers is 10.0.0.x subnet mask 255.0.0.0. Configure DNS by performing the following steps:

1. Start|Programs|Administrative Tools (Common)|DNS Manager.
2. In the Primary Zone, enter either the name of the server or its IP address. Choose the icon on the left pane, and add the zone "TEST.com" and the zone file "test.com.dns." (be sure to include the period).
3. For the new zone, add records by clicking File|New Record. Add TEST and the IP address.
4. Add the MX record for the TEST.com domain. Set the preference value.
5. Repeat this on the second server, being mindful of the different names required and IP address for the second server.
6. Create the service account in User Manager For Domains on both servers. Check Password Never Expires, and deselect User Must Change Password At Next Login. Create several new users on both sites.

   Next, you need to install Exchange 5.5.
7. Create a new site. Name your organization and site.
8. Enter your service account or use the Browse button. Choose the Complete/Custom.
9. Run the Optimizer.
10. Repeat Steps 6 through 9 for the other server.

PROJECT 3.2

Create an Exchange user with administrative rights by performing the following steps:

1. Log in to one of your servers, using an account with administrator rights.
2. Select Start|Programs|Exchange|Exchange Administrator.
3. Select a server. Expand your view by clicking all the plus sign buttons.
4. Select Organization, and press Alt+Enter.
5. Select Permissions|Add.
6. Add a user account with Admin rights.

7. Log off, and log in with the new user you just created for the organization.

8. Repeat Steps 1 through 7 for the other servers.

CASE PROJECTS

3

1. You have accepted a position at the XYZ Corporation to improve the electronic communication among employees. You have decided to install Exchange Server to support your messaging environment. Describe the planning steps you should take, and the questions you should ask management and department heads about your organization to help you design the right kind of email system.

2. After you've completed your planning exercise at XYZ, what steps should you take on the Windows NT Server machine where you plan to install the first Exchange Server for your organization? Should this machine be a domain controller or a member server? List all necessary steps involved.

3. XYZ Corporation has several MS Mail servers and post offices in operation, left over from a previous implementation. Some of these post offices and their clients are still in daily use. Explain the pros and cons of a one-step versus a two-step migration, and discuss why a two-step migration may make more sense where Internet alias names come into play.

EXCHANGE SERVER COMMUNICATIONS

In this chapter, you'll explore *Message Transfer Agents* (MTAs), those critical components in Exchange that manage message transfer between multiple Exchange servers, and between Exchange and non-Exchange mail systems. Here, you'll learn how to make MTAs work for you, starting from the planning stages through establishing *connectors*, handling information transfer, message routing, and other key issues. In addition, you'll take an in-depth look at foreign mail systems and the role that MTAs play in connecting to non-Exchange mail servers, such as Lotus Notes. Finally, you'll work step-by-step through the creation of MTA connections.

AFTER READING THIS CHAPTER AND COMPLETING THE EXERCISES, YOU WILL BE ABLE TO:

- Understand the available Message Transfer Agent (MTA) options
- Describe the components that allow intrasite communication between Exchange Servers
- Explain the impact of Remote Procedure Calls (RPC) on network traffic
- Install Exchange MTAs within an Exchange Server

PLANNING YOUR MTAs

Before you install your first Message Transfer Agent (MTA), you need to determine which other mail systems will connect to Exchange. Exchange includes several built-in MTAs, which we'll explore throughout this chapter. Keep in mind that Exchange was created to work with the Messaging Application Program Interface (MAPI), which means that you need not be limited to MTAs provided by Microsoft.

Third-party developers have also created enhancements for Exchange, to provide access to systems as diverse as telephone voice mail systems and fax services. Regardless of who developed your MTA, you should familiarize yourself with the following facts about Exchange:

- Within a site, all servers communicate using RPC.

- Servers belonging to a single site communicate amongst themselves using what's called intrasite server communications.

- Replication is more network bandwidth intensive between servers within a site than between sites (because bandwidth within a site is usually cheaper than between sites).

- The minimum net available bandwidth (NAB) between servers within a site is 64Kbps, with 128Kbps a more practical minimum.

- Connections between Exchange Servers must be permanent. A common slang term for this is nailed up.

Exchange also goes to extraordinary lengths to ensure message delivery. If mail cannot be delivered, it stays on the server where the mail originated until the destination server becomes available, or until a timeout threshold is exceeded. If the wait exceeds the configured timeout threshold, such messages are returned to their senders.

In the section that follows next, we cover Exchange's requirements for information transfer.

INFORMATION TRANSFER

Exchange requires two components to transfer mail—the MTA and the *Directory Service (DS)*. Exchange is able to transfer many different kinds of information between servers, from plain text messages to video teleconferences, audio streams, and other forms of rich data, to a variety of information exchanges necessary to keep the Exchange environment synchronized and running properly. Table 4.1 shows the corresponding service for a variety of information types.

Table 4.1 Exchange information types and corresponding services.

Information Type	Service
Directory replication	Directory Service: Keeps multiple Exchange directories in agreement
Directory synchronization messages	Directory Synchronization: Keeps Exchange and foreign mail directories in agreement
Link Monitor messages	System Attendant by using the Information Store: Keeps track of active, working links between servers
Mail messages	Private Information Store: Transfers messages from one Information Store to another
Public folder hierarchy changes	Public Information Store: Maintains consistent file structures across multiple public folder instances
Public folder replication changes	Public Information Store: Maintains consistency across multiple public folder instances

The many types of information that move between Exchange servers (and to and from foreign mail services, where appropriate) require a delivery mechanism. For Exchange server-to-server communications, as well as for connector-to-server communications, that mechanism is a *Remote Procedure Call (RPC)*. This provides the topic for the next section.

REMOTE PROCEDURE CALLS

Remote Procedure Call (RPC) mechanisms permit programs running on one computer on a network to intercommunicate more or less directly. Microsoft's RPC technology is based on standard Unix RPC mechanisms, but is more or less limited to interconnecting Windows NT processes with one another across the network. RPC provides the basic information transfer mechanism between pairs of Exchange servers (among other roles).

Because RPC is a form of program-to-program communications, where Exchange is concerned, this mechanism involves programs on one server that generate requests to another server elsewhere on the network. This kind of communications can generate heavy network traffic that can easily flood a network. That's why a 64K connection is the bare minimum connection for use with Exchange, and why 128K represents more realistic minimum link bandwidth between Exchange servers.

Now that we've established the underlying requirements for MTA, we can move on to the examination of MTAs—and their behavior—in detail. This provides the discussion in the sections that follow.

MTA ROLES AND CAPABILITIES

Any information moved between two MTAs always takes the form of a message (see Figure 4.1). If the data is not initially in message form, it is placed within a message and then sent as such.

To perform any message transfer (be it normal message traffic or other data put into message form), an MTA performs the following steps:

1. The MTA looks up the recipient's server destination in the DS.

2. The MTA determines if following the delivery route requires leaving the site.

3. The sending MTA opens an RPC session by using NT's system service user account (this account must be created prior to installing Exchange Server, then referenced during its installation). Microsoft refers to this as an association.

4. Using the open RPC, the message is sent.

5. After the message is delivered successfully, the MTA on the receiving end uses the local DS to determine if the message needs to be passed on to another server. In a single site, the receiving MTA is invariably its final destination.

6. The MTA queues up the message and informs the Information Store of the new message.

In the section that follows, we explore the concept of Message Transfer Agent associations in more detail.

HOW MTA ASSOCIATIONS BEHAVE

If a message is intended for delivery to multiple recipients on multiple servers, the MTA creates a message for each server and sends only a single copy of that message to each remote MTA. By sending a single instance of a message to each server, Exchange reduces network traffic. The subsequent expansion of the message for delivery takes place on the other end of the network connection, at the destination server. This means that copying takes place only within the local *Information Store* (and creates no duplicate network traffic). This process is known as message fan-out.

Furthermore, the most common configuration is to create only a single connection from a source Exchange Server to each destination server. If such connections must ferry heavy message traffic, you may instead create multiple associations between a source server and a destination server. Multiple associations help to reduce the message backlog that can sometimes occur when only a single connection exists between Exchange Servers.

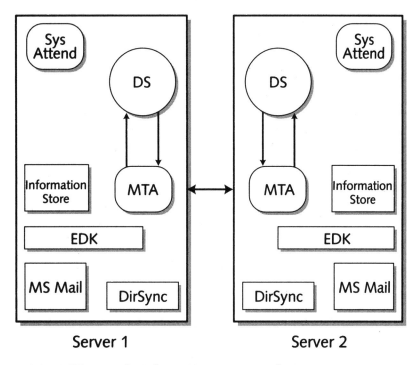

Server 1   **Server 2**

Figure 4.1 MTAs transfer information in message format.

The Exchange Optimizer utility analyzes server-to-server traffic, and determines the proper number of MTAs to create between servers. Exchange supports anywhere from a minimum of 20 to a maximum of 240 MTAs between servers, depending on the system where Exchange is installed and the bandwidth available on the link between any 2 servers. The default number of connections between servers is 40.

 Because of the high number of possible connections, it should be obvious why a high-speed link between Exchange Servers is so often desirable.

When an association is established and ready to use, all pending messages between both servers in the pair are delivered and received at the same time. This is called a two-way association. Also, any active RPC session is always delayed for five minutes before it's permitted to close. This delay leaves ample time for a local MTA to receive a notice that it needs to use the connection before it's shut down.

If five minutes is not an appropriate time-out delay, the RPC time-out delay setting may be configured in the MTA Site Configuration menu or by selecting the Advanced tab for any specific connector.

In the section that follows, we explain how MTAs identify a message's sender and intended recipients.

NAME IDENTIFICATION

Exchange uses a subset of the *X.400* standard to identify recipients. The naming can be in the format of either the *X.500* distinguished name (DN) or the X.400 Originator/Recipient (O/R) address.

With X.500, DN contains attributes that identify a recipient within an organization. DN has a specific path throughout the Exchange system. Within the DN, there is also a relative distinguished name (RDN), typically found as the last attribute in the DN. As an example, Tom Smith could have an RDN of *Toms* or perhaps *TomS*.

In X.400, the X.400 O/R name and address identify both the recipient and the originator. Here are some key points worth remembering about distinguished names and originator/recipient (O/R) addresses:

- Distinguished names based on X.500. Relative Distinguished Names typically occupy the last part of the DN (or appear as its final attribute).
- O/R names are based on X.400. O/R is similar but not identical to DN
- Exchange uses either DN and O/R for routing through an MTA.

Most commonly, Exchange Server uses distinguished names to address users. When you select a person from the address book, Exchange uses the corresponding distinguished name.

Exchange uses originator recipient addresses when a message comes in from an outside MTA X.400 sender. When the message arrives, if a distinguished name is available, the DN replaces the X.400 name. If this is not possible, X.400 is used to deliver the mail. When a user needs to send mail to an X.400 recipient, he or she can enter an O/R address manually by using a one-off address template.

One-off addresses are addresses for messages to mailboxes that do not appear in a Global Address List or in a user's personal address book. The term one-off is meant to indicate that such addresses serve to send a single message off to an address and are unlikely to be reused. One-off messages can traverse the Exchange message connector either from a Microsoft Outlook to a foreign mail system client, or from a foreign mail system client to an Outlook mailbox.

To access a one-off address template in Microsoft Outlook, follow one of these two approaches:

1. Open the Address Book, choose New Entry from the File menu, select an address type, then click OK.

2. Compose a new message (File|New|Message), choose To, choose New in the Address Book, select an address type, then click OK.

Although you may look at one-off address templates in the Exchange Administrator, you cannot modify them. Here's how to get to the One-Off Address Templates property page:

1. In the Administrator window, choose Configuration, choose One-Off Address Templates, and then select one of the language containers.

2. Double-click the specific template you want to view.

3. Select the Templates tab.

One-off addresses will come in handy for reaching out to foreign email systems, so it is worth making yourself familiar with the addressing requirements on the client side for such addresses, and with corresponding templates on the Exchange Administrator side.

Be they distinguished names, originator recipient names, one-off addresses, or native Exchange mailbox names, addresses play a key role in enabling MTAs to send and receive mail. In the section that follows, we explain how the MTA uses recipient addresses to manage message routing and delivery.

ROUTING WITH THE MTA

As mentioned earlier, the MTA looks at a message's recipient address to determine its destination. The routing process begins when another MTA, a connector, or a user sends a message to some particular MTA.

After a message is sent, the MTA compares the site name to the local site name. If this does not match, routing follows standard multisite procedures. If the address has an O/R address that does not match, the MTA confirms the validity of the O/R address. If it is not a valid address, the message is returned to the sender with a message that indicates that it is undeliverable because the address cannot be resolved.

If the DN or O/R address matches the local site, the next step that the MTA must take is to determine how to deliver that message:

- For DN and O/R addresses that are part of a distribution list, the distribution list is expanded, and the routing process repeats and processes address information for each member of the distribution list.

- For custom recipients, the MTA gets all recipients' DN addresses from the Directory Service, and the process is repeated using the new addresses based on distinguished names.

- For users on the local server, the MTA passes the message to the local Information Store for delivery to designated users' mailboxes.

- For recipients on other computers in the same site, the MTA forwards the mail to the recipients' home MTAs for delivery.

Any time an MTA cannot transfer a message, the MTA retries until one of two conditions is met: either message delivery eventually succeeds or the time-out period is exceeded, whichever comes first. Figure 4.2 illustrates the decision points for any incoming message. The default time-out setting is one day. If the time-out period elapses without a successful delivery, the mail is returned to its sender as undeliverable.

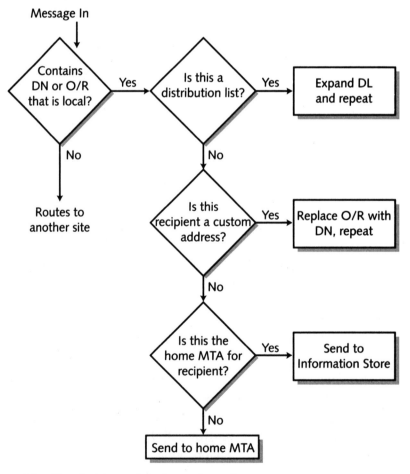

Figure 4.2 The decision points for an incoming message.

Message transfers within a single server represent the simplest kind of job that the MTA must perform: Basically, this consists of instructing the Information Store to copy a message from the sender's Outbox to the recipient's Inbox. As the number of sites increases, or foreign mail services come into play, the MTA's job gets progressively more complex. In the section that follows, you'll learn more about what's involved when transferring messages between Exchange sites.

INTRASITE SERVICE COMMUNICATIONS

All services within Exchange, with the exception of the DS, move data through email messages. If an Exchange service is not able to package its service requests in message format, the Information Store can normally perform this function.

Because all messages in Exchange must originate from some mailbox, Exchange uses its own special, internal, hidden mailboxes to handle this task. Remember, a hidden mailbox is one that exists in the Exchange environment, but which does not appear in DS lists of available mailboxes. Nevertheless, such hidden mailboxes can send and receive messages, as long as the sender knows a hidden mailbox's address. Because Exchange uses these special hidden mailboxes for its own purposes, the knowledge needed to address these mailboxes is built into the application itself.

The Information Store, the *System Attendant*, all message connectors, and MS Mail DirSync represent the most important Exchange services that use hidden mailboxes to transfer information between themselves on various Exchange servers. The messages involved are related to each such service's specific functions. Thus, for the Information Store, such messages carry folder and file replication messages. For the System Attendant, they carry configuration and status information. For the connectors, they carry messages and status data, and for the MS Mail DirSync (and other DirSyncs as well), they carry the information needed to synchronize DS with a foreign directory, and vice-versa.

Exchange Directory Services take a slightly different approach to data transfer. Rather than moving data through email messages, as most other services do, they use a replication technique to deliver updates from one DS to another on the network. A design known as the multimaster model replicates data from each individual DS to other Exchange servers in a site.

The contrasting model is a typical master/slave database relationship, as with the domain database maintained by a Primary Domain Controller (PDC) in Windows NT: the PDC database is the only copy that may be updated directly, and all updates replicate from the PDC to all Backup Domain Controllers (BDCs) in that environment. The multimaster model and the master/slave model both provide fault tolerance, but the multimaster model can reduce network traffic because each copy only needs to field those updates that differ from its database.

When a change is applied to a DS database, updates do not occur instantly. By default, there is a five-minute delay to introduce what is known as replication latency. When the replication latency expires, the local DS notifies all known servers, one at a time, and waits 30 seconds for changes to occur before calling the next server.

 Please consult KB Q137203 Microsoft Knowledge Base Article number Q137203 for all the details; if you don't have access to a local copy on TechNet, you can visit the online version at **http://www.microsoft.com/kb/**.

This prevents addresses that change two or more times within the latency period from causing multiple, overlapping updates to be sent across the network in quick succession, and provides another mechanism to reduce the impact of DS updates on network traffic.

When an update arrives at a remote Exchange Server, it also checks a unique number to establish a time stamp for its last update activity. This time stamp is compared to update time stamps in the database, to help the server determine which database values have changed since the last update occurred. The remote DS then requests all changes that are more recent than its last checkpoint.

When the update request from the receiving server is fielded, the sending DS with more recent updates to deliver connects to the remote DS (using RPC) and updates that receiving server, which in turn updates its local directory database. Within a single site, the Information Store sends this data directly to the MTA, which passes it from the sending to the receiving server. This provides a quick, efficient replication mechanism that helps to keep DS databases more or less in synchronization with one another (give or take five minutes, owing to the replication latency).

With Exchange sites, the Information Store helps to route all kinds of key information, including messages, DS updates, and other internal data, in much the same way that the MTA manages general message transfer, especially between sites and between Exchange and foreign mail services. In the sections that follow, we examine the role of the Information Store in Exchange in more detail.

INFORMATION STORES

Exchange supports two kinds of storage within each Information Store:

- **Private Information Store** Provides storage for messages, configuration data, and other information items to which access must be restricted on a user ID basis.

- **Public Information Store** Provides storage for public folders and their contents, and supports public access to a broad collection of materials intended for sharing, or for which security is not a concern.

The private Information Store exists primarily for individual end users to store their messages and other information delivered via Exchange. When a message is sent to a user whose mailbox resides on a different server, the MTA locates the destination server and queues the message up for delivery to that location. The MTA obtains messages that require delivery from the Information Store, then connects to the destination server's MTA (using RPC). As before with the directory replication time-out, the MTA holds the connection open for five minutes after the last pending message is sent, waiting for activity, then closes.

A public Information Store supports folders, so two types of information are involved—a public folder hierarchy and a set of public folder replicas. A public folder hierarchy is a collection of folders that must be displayed to all clients, because some data (that is, folders and the files or folders within them) might not reside on every single server. Thus, the public folder hierarchy is treated as a separate data structure, and is stored on every Exchange Server. Even though some copies of data might be replicated on every server anyway, maintaining a copy on every server ensures that public folder data sets that aren't fully replicated will remain accessible to all users. This explains why the public folder hierarchy is replicated independently of the public folders themselves.

Public folder replicas represent copies of data that reside on some given server, where Exchange replicates that data from one server to other servers, and keeps all copies more or less synchronized. When either the public folder hierarchy or the public folder replicas change, the Information Store informs the MTA so that the MTA can initiate and handle the necessary synchronization activity with other Exchange Servers, where necessary.

The System Attendant is an important nerve center for Exchange that monitors and manages server-to-server connections, and supports remote management capabilities. In the next section, you'll learn more about this essential Exchange element.

SYSTEM ATTENDANT

The System Attendant has several functions. One function is to check Link Monitor services. In other words, the System Attendant tests the availability and performance of connections between the servers, primarily by sending test messages and monitoring the results.

A System Attendant can also create a message destined for a System Attendant on a remote server. These messages generally relate to the remote server's configuration, time-out settings, and other server controls. This mechanism provides a form of remote management that can reach from one Exchange Server to another fairly transparently. But if the remote server is foreign, the System Attendant creates an auto responder that can respond to queries from a foreign message system, or initiate queries (depending on how the messaging environment is configured).

Finally, the System Attendant also manages the message tracking log that serves as a form of "fast cache" storage for Exchange messages before they are written to the Information Store. This approach is coupled with a checkpointing mechanism, as explained in Chapter 3, to permit Exchange to recover from system failures with minimal loss of data. The tracking log is written to disk by default every five minutes; should a system failure ever occur, the database can be rolled forward from its last backup by replaying all tracking logs up to the one that was written last before the system failed. This guarantees that no more than five minutes' worth of messages will ever be lost.

Connectors represent another key Exchange component—namely, the software element that manages the connection between any two Exchange Servers, and between any Exchange Server and any foreign mail system. In the section that follows, you'll learn more about these components that provide the glue that binds multiple messaging systems together in an Exchange environment.

CONNECTORS

Numerous connectors are included with Exchange itself, and even more third-party connectors are available for purchase. Although connectors may be properly considered the software elements that bind multiple messaging servers together, be they Exchange or foreign messaging systems, connectors can function at several levels of links for Exchange environments:

- Between Exchange Servers at the same site (called a server link)
- Between Exchange Servers at different sites (called a site link)
- Between an Exchange Server and a foreign mail system (called an external or gateway link)

Microsoft's Exchange Development Kit (EDK) includes the following connectors:

- Internet Mail Service
- Lotus cc:Mail
- Lotus Notes
- Third party

Such connectors behave in much the same way as the System Attendant. For local messages, the SA uses the Information Store to copy messages from the sender's mailbox into the recipient's mailbox, and no network activity is involved. On the other hand, the SA hands all remote mail off to the MTA. If the recipient is not an Exchange client, a custom recipient can be addressed. This process is known as backboning. Most Exchange connectors, including those mentioned in the preceding list, have the same relationship with the Information Store and the MTA as the System Attendant. That is, connectors check to see if a recipient is local first, and let the Information Store handle such deliveries. Also, they only interact with other Exchange servers or custom recipients if the need arises.

The MSMail Connector works differently than the System Attendant and most connectors. It is the only connector that passes messages directly to the MTA, whether the message has a local recipient or a recipient on another server. If the mail is destined for delivery to a recipient who is local to the server, the MTA forwards the message to the Information Store. If the message is destined for delivery to a recipient on some other server, the message is passed to the MTA. This is the only connector that interacts directly with the MTA. Please note, however, that the MTA considers the built-in Exchange Site and X.400 Connectors to be part of the MTA itself, and does not treat them as separate connectors. Rather, they represent the MTA's two primary methods for message delivery, where the Site connector handles Exchange-to-Exchange deliveries, and the X.400 Connector handles all other messages that are not explicitly routed to some other connector.

Because it provides services to synchronize the Exchange Directory Service database with other Exchange sites, or with directories under the purview of foreign mail systems, DirSync is a frequent user of Exchange connectors. In particular, DirSync maintains information for both MS Mail types—namely, PC and AppleTalk. DirSync is also responsible for foreign mail. In the event that DirSync must communicate with a remote server, it communicates using the services of the MTA.

All services, such as the Information Store (both public and private), the System Attendant, and the DirSync for MS Mail communicate through messages routed through the MTA. As mentioned earlier, the only exception to this practice is the Exchange Directory Service, which talks directly to other Directory Services through a special replication process.

Thus, reliable communication among all servers within a site is critical to the proper functioning of Exchange. As your site grows, you will have to add a server to a site at some point. Directory replication helps to ensure reliable communication, and provides the key ingredient necessary to add a new Exchange server to an existing site—namely, a copy of the site's DS database. To do these jobs, Exchange uses the *Knowledge Consistency Checker (KCC)*. In the section that follows, the process of adding a server to a site is explained further.

ADDING A SERVER TO A SITE

When you add an Exchange Server to an existing site, that server needs to know what to do. To add a server, you must first identify some other Exchange Server that is already active within the site, which then provides the data that the new server needs to become part of the site. The steps involved in adding a new server are as follows:

1. During the Exchange installation process, the new server adds itself to the directory on the existing server through an appropriate exchange of messages.

2. Next, the new server then copies the data in the directory on the existing server through the Directory Service in a specific order. All containers, with the exception of Recipients, are copied to the new server.

3. Using this newly acquired data, the new server tells other servers in the site to commence directory replication. This ensures that the new server's directory database matches the contents of the databases for all other servers. Because the initial database must be as accurate as possible, this replication task occurs immediately (rather than waiting for the usual five minutes).

In the sections that follow, you'll learn more about what's involved in re-creating a directory database on a new Exchange Server as it joins an existing site. This involves a fascinating bit of software, and some genuine software sleight of hand, where a virtual directory helps speed the creation of a real directory.

THE KNOWLEDGE CONSISTENCY CHECKER

Within any Exchange site, the Knowledge Consistency Checker (KCC) acts as a built-in integrity management mechanism for all Exchange Servers. This software component runs on each Exchange Server. Its job is to make sure that the contents of all directory databases on the servers in an Exchange site remain constantly in substantial agreement with one another.

In general, the KCC performs the following functions:

1. Attaches to a remote server.

2. Asks that server to report about all other servers in the site.

3. Using this information about other servers, connects to another remote server, gathers server information, and compares that data to the information from the first server.

4. Updates any differences among the servers. This process continues until the entire site is checked.

The KCC runs every three hours, by default. If you wish to perform a manual check, click the Directory Service object, which is located inside the local server container.

When a new server joins an Exchange site, extraordinary measures are required to construct a new directory in its entirety. This is covered in the next section.

HOW A BRAND-NEW DIRECTORY IS BUILT

4

When a new Exchange Server joins an existing site, the KCC uses a stub directory, which functions as a kind of "virtual directory" on the new server. This stub directory helps speed up the joining process by supplying the bare minimum of directory information that's needed to make a new server's directory database functional, with the idea that its directory can be fully fleshed out once initial installation is complete.

If Exchange didn't have a stub directory, the entire directory would have to be replicated before setup could complete. By using only a stub directory, setup can complete quickly, and the new server can take part in regular replication and message transfers. This permits installation to take place in a reasonable amount of time, and allows the new directory database to be fully populated within a reasonable amount of time after installation.

Other than when a new server joins a site, there is seldom a need to build a copy of the directory database in its entirety. In most cases, directory replication occurs piecemeal, and includes only recent updates between replication partners. In the section that follows, the replication mechanism is explained in greater detail.

REPLICATION LISTS AND MAINTENANCE BEHAVIOR

A replication link creates a Directory Service relationship between pairs of Exchange Servers. Two lists maintain this link—Reps-To (which stands for "replicates to," and indicates the sending partner in the relationship) and Reps-From (which stands for "replicates from" and indicates the receiving partner in the relationship).

Whenever a new server joins a site, that server will appear in both of these lists soon thereafter. Because each server knows about all the other servers in a site, each list is unique for each server. A unique list cannot be replicated to other servers, so a special synchronization mechanism (not replication) is used to maintain these lists—namely, the KCC.

Once the two replication lists are taken care of, actual directory replication may then occur. The next section addresses how this happens, and what Exchange mechanisms exist to support directory replication.

DIRECTORY MANAGEMENT

When any directory replication occurs, a unique number is assigned to that replication event. This unique number is known as the *Update Sequence Number (USN)*. Each time a replication occurs, the USN increments by one. This way, each server can query all the other servers to confirm directory changes and directory status. Note that if multiple changes occur on multiple servers for the same object, conflicting updates can occur. Exchange avoids inconsistencies by recognizing only the last, most recent changes are recorded (those with the highest USN).

A local DS finds changes by requesting a USN number from a remote server, which sends its most recent value. If the remote USN is higher, the local DS copies all changes made from the previous USN. The USN is then updated on the local server to match that on the remote server.

CHAPTER SUMMARY

In this chapter, you examined Message Transfer Agents (MTAs) and learned how to make efficient use of their capabilities. In particular, you learned about the differences between transferring messages on a single server, across a site, and between sites or with a foreign mail system. You also explored how connectors broker the connection to foreign mail systems and examined the roles that RPCs play in message transfer and network requirements.

Next, you looked at those Exchange components that allow a site to operate. You explored the components that make communication between servers possible within a site and investigated the crucial roles that the Directory Service, the Information Store, and connectors play in enabling such communication. In this process, you learned how various Exchange components cooperate to exchange non-mail data (usually in the form of special mail messages to hidden mailboxes, except for Directory Services, which uses a different mechanism called replication).

Finally, you examined how directory information is maintained and replicated between servers, including the roles of replication partners and replication lists. You explored what's involved when a new server joins an existing site, to understand directory replication in action when an entire new directory must be re-created from scratch. This latter activity represents an interesting compromise between installation speed and directory completeness, and relies on a stub directory to help bring the new server up as quickly as possible (after which its directory can be fully populated using normal Exchange directory replication mechanisms).

Key Terms

- **connector**—A type of mail service used by the MTA.

- **Directory Service (DS)**—A database of user names and related email addresses that's similar to the way a phone book maps names to addresses and phone numbers.

- **distinguished name (DN)**—Presentation of an X.500 name.

- **Information Store**—The Exchange component that's responsible for storing messages and other data; actually, Exchange has two Information Stores: private and public.

- **Knowledge Consistency Checker (KCC)**—An Exchange software component whose job is to ensure that all the Exchange Servers within a site have the same directory and server name data.

- **Message Transfer Agent (MTA)**—The program that actually moves the mail from a sending server to some recipient (often, another Exchange server).

- **Remote Procedure Call (RPC)**—A message-passing facility that allows a distributed application to call services on other machines within a network.

- **System Attendant (SA)**—The Exchange service that performs general maintenance tasks, including message logging (called message tracking by Microsoft) and link checking (to verify that inter-server links are working properly).

- **Update Sequence Number (USN)**—A unique, sequential number, used to identify the last time an update was made to a directory entry.

- **X.400**—An International Standards Organization (ISO/OSI) standard for electronic messaging; also refers to an Exchange connector used instead of an MTA. Although the X.400 Connector is slower than an Exchange MTA, it is generic and can deliver to many mail systems, including Exchange and foreign mail systems.

- **X.500**—The ISO/OSI standard for directory and authentication services. X.500 was designed specifically to permit different information systems to communicate addresses and access control data.

Review Questions

1. What form of communication must be used when two MTAs communicate?

   a. A message

   b. A USN value

   c. A disguised name

   d. A relative distinguished name

2. What is USN an abbreviation for?
   a. United States Navy
   b. Unique Serial Number
   c. Update Sequence Number
   d. All of the above

3. By default, Exchange creates ————————— associations.
   a. 1
   b. 20
   c. 40
   d. 240

4. Which two services transfer all mail within an Exchange site?
   a. Information Store
   b. Directory Service
   c. Remote Procedure Call
   d. Message Transfer Agent

5. Replication lists are used to send and receive updates from other servers. What are the names for these lists? (Choose all that apply.)
   a. Reps-For
   b. Reps-To
   c. Reps-By
   d. Reps-From

6. Which of the following software components references the Exchange replication lists ?
   a. Global Address List
   b. Stub directory
   c. Knowledge Consistency Checker
   d. Information Store

7. Which of the following performs link monitoring?
   a. Message Transfer Agent
   b. Information Store
   c. System Attendant
   d. All of the above

8. Which of the following is the only exception to the rule that Exchange Server service requests are sent as mail messages?
   a. Directory Service
   b. System Attendant
   c. DirSync
   d. Distribution list

9. EDK-based connectors include:

  a. Internet Mail Server

  b. Third-party connectors

  c. Lotus connectors for cc:Mail and Notes

  d. All of the above

10. Before changes are made to an object, such as a Distribution List (DL), there is a five-minute delay. What is this delay called?

  a. Copy delay

  b. Directory delay

  c. Replication delay

  d. Replication latency

11. Numerous Exchange activities, including connector deactivation and directory replication, are subject to a five-minute delay, called time-out. In Exchange, time-out values may not be altered. True or False?

12. Of the following, which represent the types of data that may be replicated in the public Information Store? (Choose all that apply.)

  a. Public folder hierarchy

  b. Public folders (and their contents)

  c. Directory lists

  d. Global Address Lists

13. Which type(s) of public Information Store data may an Exchange Server send? (Choose all that apply.)

  a. USN

  b. Public folder hierarchy

  c. Transaction logs

  d. Public folder replicas

14. Servers within a site use the _____ interface.

  a. IPC

  b. MTA

  c. RPC

  d. RAS

15. When working with Exchange Servers within a single site, no special connectors are required. True or False?

16. A client has sent a message to a distribution list. This message will route directly to each recipient, without expansion, because the distribution list is maintained on each Exchange Server. True or False?

17. Which of the following is the best definition for a directory stub?

   a. A minimal directory used to bootstrap the Exchange installation process when a new server joins an existing site.

   b. A virtual Exchange directory that permits any server to request a complete directory update when needed.

   c. A damaged Exchange directory that contains only a subset of the information required for completeness.

   d. None of the above.

18. The Knowledge Consistency Checker makes sure that all Exchange servers in a site are represented in the replication lists. True or False?

19. By default, how frequently does the Knowledge Consistency Checker run?

   a. Every five minutes

   b. Every hour

   c. Every two hours

   d. Every three hours

20. Of the following choices, which connector interacts directly with the MTA?

   a. Exchange Site Connector

   b. X.400 Connector

   c. MS Mail Connector

   d. cc:Mail Connector

HANDS-ON PROJECTS

Working with Exchange means that understanding the role and configuration of the Message Transfer Agent is essential. To that end, the hands-on project for this chapter takes you through the steps necessary to examine the configuration of an already-installed MTA.

PROJECT 4.1

 This hands-on project assumes that you have Windows NT installed and configured according to the requirements, and that you have installed Exchange 5.5.

You want to check the MTA configuration. You do this by performing the following steps:

1. Select Start|Programs|Exchange|Exchange Administrator.

2. Select Connect To Server, and choose the server you wish to connect to.

3. Click Configuration.

4. In the right-hand pane, find and select MTA Site Configuration.

5. Notice that the General tab displays. In the General tab, click the Enable Message Tracking checkbox.

6. Click the Permissions tab. Add the NT service account that you created when you set up NT.

7. Click the Messaging Defaults tab.

8. Observe the right-hand side of the chart. You can use this tab to configure time-outs. By selecting the field for a particular value, and clicking on the up arrow to the right of the field, you can increase the time-out for messages.

Notice that you can configure other parameters in this chart as well, such as set the size of a checkpoint file.

9. Click Apply, and click OK.

CASE PROJECTS

1. You are managing an Exchange site in New York. You wish to create two-way associations between the servers within that site. One of the servers has a slow link between itself and the other servers within that site. How can you modify the MTA site configuration from the default five-minute pause before disconnecting the server with the slower link from the rest of the site?

2. You have two LANs connected by a WAN. Currently, you have an RPC connection between the two LANs. What problems can this setup cause, and how can you reconfigure Exchange to modify its current behavior?

3. You have accepted a position as the Exchange administrator at a company. Currently, the firm is using MS Mail (PC and AppleTalk) for its messaging. You have been asked to upgrade the system to a system based on Exchange. It is imperative that you do not disrupt the current MS Mail system, because it is carrying day-to-day traffic for the firm. How can you leave the current MS Mail system in place, while adding Exchange Server's?

MANAGING MESSAGE RECIPIENTS

In this chapter, we'll examine the objects that can receive messages and other information. These objects are called recipients. As we examine the four types of recipients for Microsoft Exchange Server, we'll explore mailboxes and the information that can be contained within them, such as email messages and file attachments. In addition, we'll take a look at distribution lists, custom recipients, and public folders. Finally, we conclude the chapter with a discussion that covers how to manage and control recipient objects.

AFTER READING THIS CHAPTER AND COMPLETING THE EXERCISES, YOU WILL BE ABLE TO:

- Understand the differences between mailboxes, distribution lists, and custom recipients
- Configure mailboxes, distribution lists, and custom recipients
- Explore the different recipient object property pages
- Understand how to manage recipient objects

RECIPIENT OBJECTS EXPLORED AND EXPLAINED

A *recipient* is any object that can receive a message. One of the most important roles of an Exchange administrator is the creation and management of recipient objects. Such recipients include *mailboxes*, *distribution lists*, *custom recipients*, and *public folders*:

- **Mailboxes** A mailbox is where mail is delivered on the Exchange Server. Each user who is to receive messages through Exchange must have a mailbox.

- **Distribution lists** A distribution list (DL) is a logical grouping of recipients created to ease mass mailings, and to reach selected audiences through a single address.

- **Custom recipients** A custom recipient is a pointer to a foreign address or recipient outside an Exchange organization.

- **Public folders** A public folder is a repository for many types of information that can be shared by many users. Public folders make custom applications, such as customer trading systems, possible.

WORKING WITH MAILBOXES

The mailbox in Microsoft Exchange Server is where messages and attachments are stored and organized. Mailboxes can contain messages created by users and sent from users from within or outside of the organization. The mailbox resides on the Exchange Server; however, the user must use a client email application, such as Microsoft Outlook, to access mailbox information. Normally, a mailbox only has one user associated with it, but you can assign multiple users to a single mailbox.

CREATING MAILBOXES

As a general rule, all users who access your Microsoft Exchange Server require a mailbox. There are several ways to create mailboxes. You can use:

- Windows NT User Manager For Domains
- Microsoft Exchange Administrator program
- Microsoft Exchange extraction and import tools

Using User Manager For Domains

When the Microsoft Exchange Server is installed, it installs a User Manager For Domains extension called MAILUMX.DLL. This is a Dynamic Link Library (DLL). It links the Mailbox Properties page of the Exchange Administrator program to the User Manager For Domains. Any time an account is created with User Manager For Domains, a mailbox can also be created. When deleting a user account, the corresponding mailbox can be deleted.

 When you create a new NT user account, you will be prompted to connect to an Exchange Server that will create the mailbox for the user.

Using The Exchange Administrator Program

When you create a new Microsoft Exchange mailbox, you need to associate it with one or more NT user accounts. These accounts can be existing accounts (from the current or a trusted domain) or can be new accounts created by the Exchange Administrator program.

The Exchange Administrator program has the ability to create NT user accounts by directly accessing the NT domain Security Accounts Manager (SAM).

Using The Exchange Extraction And Import Tools

The Exchange extraction and import tools work in tandem to create mailboxes. The extraction tools gather information about the user accounts, and the import tools use this extracted information to create the mailboxes.

The two mail extraction tools available with Microsoft Exchange are:

- **Extract Windows NT Account List** This tool extracts user account information from existing Windows NT Servers and prepares this data for the creation of Exchange objects. To execute this command, you must be logged in to the NT domain from which the user account information is to be extracted. This tool is available from the Administrator program by selecting the Extract Windows NT Account List option from the Tools menu or from the command line.

- **Extract NetWare Account List** This tool extracts user account information from existing Novell NetWare 2.x, 3.x, or 4.x servers (as long as the NetWare server is running binary emulation). To use this tool, you must be logged in to the NetWare server with supervisor rights. This tool is available from the Administrator program by selecting the Extract NetWare Account List option from the Tools menu.

After one of the extraction tools is executed, the import tool can create Exchange recipients using the extracted data. Access the import tool by selecting the Directory Import option from the Tools menu. The import tool can also be used to modify existing recipients.

To make a major change (such as changing an area code in the entire Exchange site), you must export the directory, search and replace the area code in the text file, and import the directory back into Exchange.

MAILBOX PROPERTIES

Mailboxes, like objects, have properties. These properties can be viewed and configured through the mailbox's Properties pages (also referred to as tabs). The properties can be accessed in one of two ways. You can highlight the mailbox to be configured and select the Properties option from the File menu, or you can double-click the desired mailbox. Many of the object properties are straightforward and do not require any explanation (such as Address).

General

Within the General Properties page (shown in Figure 5.1), you can configure basic user information, such as the user's name and location. You can also assign the primary Windows NT user account to be used with the mailbox.

The following is important information found on the General Properties page:

- **Display** This is the name that appears in the Administrator windows and the Address Book. By default, this is generated automatically by combining the first name and the last name of the user. For example, if the user has the first name *Joe* and the last name *Smith*, the Display will

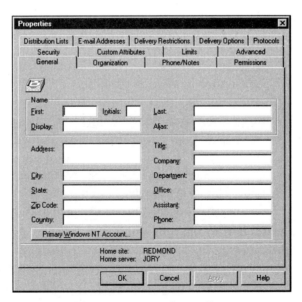

Figure 5.1   The General Properties page of a mailbox.

be *Joe Smith*. This can be changed manually by the administrator. Also, there is a limit of 256 characters in the Display field.

- **Alias** This is another name used to identify the mailbox that is usually used to generate foreign email addresses for the mailbox. By default, the alias name is automatically generated by combining the user's first name and the first initial of the user's last name. For example, the user mentioned in the previous paragraph would have an alias of *JoeS*. This can also be changed manually by the administrator, and it has a limit of 64 characters in the field.

- **Primary Windows NT Account** This is the NT domain account that is associated with this mailbox. You will be given the option to choose an existing user account or have a new user account created.

Organization

Within the Organization Properties page, you can record information about a mailbox's owners. You can also report the name of the user's manager or any staff members who report directly to the owner of the mailbox (also known as direct reports).

Phone/Notes

Detailed telephone information (business, fax, mobile, pager, and so forth) and optional notes for the mailbox are configured from the Phone/Notes Properties page. The information on this Properties page is optional.

Permissions

The Permissions Properties page allows you to specify which users and/or groups may have permission to access the mailbox. Sometimes, it makes sense to have one mailbox owned by multiple users. For example, all sales department members might want access to a single Sales mailbox. You can assign special roles for the mailbox to individual users, so that only certain users are able to create public folders, whereas all users can read their contents, for example.

Custom Attributes

The Custom Attributes Properties page allows you to enter custom information, such as employee numbers and birthdays, or other specialized information.

The Custom Attributes page contains 10 unique attribute fields that you can customize. These fields are in the Custom Attributes Properties page of the DS Site Configuration object.

Limits

The Limits Properties page (shown in Figure 5.2) allows you to set limits on message storage and the size of incoming and outgoing messages. A new feature in Microsoft Exchange Server 5.5 supports what is called *deleted message retention*, which may also be configured on this page. This feature allows users to recover messages they may have accidentally deleted from a mailbox, as long as they don't wait too long after the fact to do so (over time, retained deleted messages are flushed from the system, as available space and age of deleted messages dictate). The important information found on the Limits Properties page includes the following:

- **Deleted Item Retention Time** Microsoft Exchange Server can be configured to retain messages deleted from mailboxes for a specified amount of time before such messages are deleted permanently. When a user deletes messages, those items are marked as hidden until they are deleted permanently from the private Information Store (assuming that a deleted item retention period has been set). Users can recover deleted messages by selecting the Recover Deleted Items command (using Microsoft Outlook version 8.03 or higher) and then moving the messages to a different location. You can set retention periods for deleted items for both public and private Information Stores and for individual mailboxes or public folders. Deleted item retention periods set on individual mailboxes supersede the settings on the private Information Store.

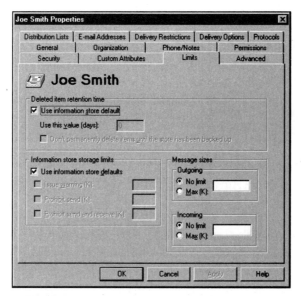

Figure 5.2   The Limits Properties page of a mailbox.

- **Information Store Storage Limits** You can set storage limits on how much space a mailbox can consume on a server. You can issue warnings, prohibit send (which means you can stop users from sending messages when other consumption thresholds are crossed), or prohibit send and receive (which means you can shut down all mail activity when a maximum consumption level is exceeded) as certain levels of consumption are reached.

The Prohibit Send option is not used when messages are sent by *Post Office Protocol version 3* or *Internet Message Access Protocol version 4 (IMAP4)* protocols. These protocols do not support this capability.

- **Message Sizes** You can specify a size limit on all incoming or outgoing messages for a mailbox. By default, there is no limit on message size.

Distribution Lists

The Distribution Lists Properties page specifies to which distribution lists a mailbox belongs. This lets you check membership in such lists on a mailbox by mailbox basis.

Email Address

When a mailbox is created, several non–Exchange mail addresses are created (also known as proxy or foreign addresses). The Email Address Properties page allows Exchange to communicate with foreign mail systems. By default, Exchange generates mail addresses for the following foreign systems automatically:

- Lotus cc:Mail
- Microsoft Mail
- Internet Mail (SMTP)
- X.400

Likewise, if other mail connectors are installed and configured on an Exchange Server, it will also generate mail messages for other foreign mail systems that may thereby become accessible.

Delivery Restrictions

The Delivery Restrictions Properties page allows you to accept or reject messages from any sender listed in the Exchange Server directory. By default, messages are accepted from everyone (All) and rejected from nobody (None).

Delivery Options

The Delivery Options Properties page allows you to give users a send "on behalf of" right for the mailbox. Essentially, this means that one user may send a message for other users (on their behalf, as it were). You may also specify an alternate recipient for messages. This alternate recipient may be configured to receive mail instead of the originally designated mailbox or in addition to that mailbox. This feature is especially useful when a user's original email address must change for some reason, because it permits mail directed to the original address to be delivered to the new address.

Protocols

The Protocols Properties page allows you to enable Internet protocols for individual mailboxes. You can specify different protocols and character sets on a per mailbox basis. Some of the related configuration options include:

- **IMAP4** IMAP supports a variety of message encoding formats. Within Exchange, the Message Encoding setting for IMAP determines what format Exchange Server messages will take when retrieved by an IMAP4 client. By default, Exchange enables public folders to be listed for all clients. Clearing the Include All Public Folders When A Folder List Is Requested box can improve performance for clients who have problems listing public folders. You may delegate a user to access another user's mailbox to view personal folders in the other user's mailbox, if necessary.

- **NNTP and POP3** Allows you to select either MIME or UUENCODE protocols for encoding mail messages.

Advanced

Within the Advanced Properties page (shown in Figure 5.3), you can set a simple display name, trust levels for directory synchronization, and hide the mailbox from the Address Book. To be more specific, the following advanced properties may be set on this page:

- **Simple Display Name** This name is used by non-Exchange mail systems that cannot recognize all characters used in an Exchange mailbox name, such as spaces and foreign characters (non-ANSI).

- **Directory Name** The name used to distinguish a mailbox in the Directory Service. This is a read-only field.

- **Trust Level** Used to specify whether a mailbox is to be replicated to other servers during directory synchronization. If the trust level set for the mailbox is higher than that set for the container, then the mailbox information will not be replicated during directory synchronization. Trust levels range from 0 through 100. (Note that the Hide From Address Book checkbox must be cleared to use this option.)

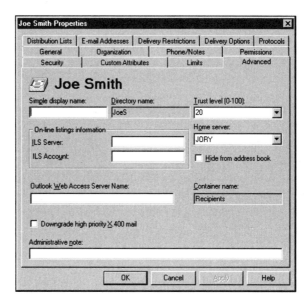

Figure 5.3   The Advanced Properties page of a mailbox.

- **Online Listing Information** If your organization uses Microsoft NetMeeting, you can specify *Internet Locator Server (ILS)* information for individual mailboxes. This enables NetMeeting users to locate mailbox owners and set up online meetings.

- **Home Server** The *home server* is the Exchange Server where the mailbox is physically located. After a mailbox is created, you can move that mailbox to another server by using the Move Mailbox option from the Tools menu.

- **Hide From Address Book** By checking this box, you can hide a mailbox from the Global Address List. However, even if the mailbox is hidden from the Address Book, you can still send messages to the mailbox if you know its email address.

- **Outlook Web Access Server Name** If an Outlook Web Access (OWA) server is specified, the user can employ a POP3 or IMAP4 client for email access, and also use the Outlook Web interface for calendaring or custom forms. Meeting requests and custom forms are received in a user's mailbox as messages that contain the URL where the request or forms reside. By default, if the Outlook Web Access server is not specified for a given mailbox, the Outlook Web Access server specified in the private Information Store is used. Messages that contain URLs for meeting requests and custom forms will not be sent if this field is left blank.

- **Container Name** This is the name of the container where a mailbox resides. This is a read-only field.
- **Downgrade High Priority X.400 Mail** Check this box to downgrade all X.400 messages marked as high priority and send them at normal priority. By default, X.400 messages marked as high priority are sent as such; overuse of this setting can cause message delivery to bog down.

MAILBOX ROLES

As mentioned earlier, you can assign users to mailboxes with specific *mailbox roles*. The Permissions tab is not shown, because it is set to be hidden within the Exchange Administrator by default. To view this tab, select Options from the Tools menu, and check the Show Permissions Page For All Objects box under the Permissions tab (as shown in Figure 5.4).

The Permissions Properties page has two fields. The first field shows which NT accounts have inherited rights to this mailbox. This is a read-only field. The second field shows which NT accounts have permissions to the mailbox and allows you to edit these accounts and their associated permissions. You assign permissions to a user or a group by giving them a role. Roles are predetermined sets of permissions that specify what activities can be performed on a mailbox. These roles are as follows:

- **Admin** Permits a user to manage any aspect of Exchange configuration.

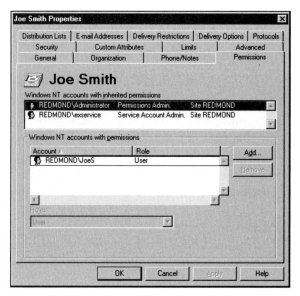

Figure 5.4 The Permissions Properties page of a mailbox.

- **Permissions Admin** Permits a user to manage access rights and permissions for Exchange objects (and resembles the Change right associated with NTFS files and folders).

- **Search** Permits a user to search the contents of an Information Store (public and private) on one or more Exchange Servers, depending on whether the role is granted on a per-server, per-site, or per-organization basis.

- **Send As** Permits a user to send an email message as if he or she were logged in as another user.

- **User** Permits users to access only those objects for which they have explicit access rights. This is the most restrictive of all Exchange user roles.

Each role represents a combination of Exchange permissions, where the permissions involved are as follows:

- **Add Child** Creates objects below the selected object in the directory hierarchy.

- **Modify User Attributes** Modifies user-level attributes associated with an object.

- **Modify Admin Attributes** Modifies administrator-level attributes associated with an object.

- **Modify Permissions** Modifies permissions on existing objects.

- **Delete** Enables users to delete objects.

- **Send As** Enables users to send messages with the sender's return address. This permission is also granted for server objects in the directory of the service account. This lets directory service processes send messages to each other.

- **Mailbox Owner** Enables users to read and delete messages in this mailbox. This permission is also granted for server objects in the directory to the service account. This lets directory processes send messages to each other.

- **Logon Rights** Enables users and services to access the directory. Users need this permission to use the Administrator program. Services also need this permission.

- **Replication** Enables users and services to replicate directory information with other servers. This permission is required by the Microsoft Exchange Server service account to replicate with other servers.

- **Search** Enables the selected user account to view the contents of the container. This permission is most useful for restricting access to Address Book View containers.

The relationship between Exchange roles and directory permissions is documented in Table 5.1.

Table 5.1   Directory permissions and roles.

Permission	Admin.	Permissions	Search	Send As	User
Add Child	X	X			
Modify User Attributes	X	X	X		X
Modify Admin Attributes	X	X			
Delete	X	X			
Logon	X	X			
Modify Permission		X			
Replication					
Mailbox Owner					X
Send As				X	X
Search		X			

WORKING WITH DISTRIBUTION LISTS

A distribution list is a logical grouping of recipients created to expedite the mass mailing of messages and other information. A message sent to a distribution list will be sent to all members of the distribution list.

CREATING A DISTRIBUTION LIST

Creating a distribution list is easy. In the Microsoft Exchange Administrator program, select the New Distribution List option from the File menu (or Ctrl+D). This action displays the Properties pages (similar to the ones for mailbox configuration) that you can use to configure a distribution list.

DISTRIBUTION LIST PROPERTIES

Many of the Properties pages have been covered in the previous sections. Two of the Properties pages deserve more explanation—the General and Advanced Properties pages.

The distribution list General Properties page (shown in Figure 5.5) is used to specify a new distribution list, modify the distribution list owner and name, and change the membership of the distribution list. The elements within this page are described in the list that follows next:

Figure 5.5   The General Properties page of a distribution list.

- **Display Name** This is the name (up to 256 characters) that will be seen in the Administrator program window and in the Address Book.

- **Alias Name** A shorter name given to the distribution list (up to 64 characters).

- **Owner** The owner of a distribution list. The owner is the primary contact for the list. The owner receives any notifications about the distribution list (for example, non-delivery reports). The owner also has the ability to change the name and membership of the distribution list. This is all done through the Microsoft Outlook client.

- **Expansion Server** When a message is sent to a distribution list, the Microsoft Exchange Server must expand the list, resolve the names of all the recipients in the list, and find the most efficient route for the message. With a large distribution list, the task of expanding the list can be very processor-intensive. This option allows you to specify a server to expand the distribution list, hence taking the load off the main server. The default is that any Exchange Server within the site where the distribution list is located can be used as the expansion server.

- **Notes** Allows you to enter additional information about the distribution list (up to 256 characters).

- **Members** This is the list of the recipients who are part of this distribution list. All distribution list members, which can include mailboxes, public folders, other distribution lists, and custom recipients, receive any message sent to the distribution list.

The Advanced Properties page (shown in Figure 5.6) is used to provide a simple display name, set message transfer limits, specify a trust level for directory synchronization, and determine whether the distribution list is hidden from the Address Book. The elements of this page are discussed in the list that follows:

- **Simple Display Name** The simple display name is a name used within foreign mail systems that cannot handle the Exchange non-ANSI characters.

- **Directory Name** The name used to distinguish the mailbox in the Directory Service. This is a read-only field.

- **Trust Level** The trust level determines whether information about the distribution list is replicated to other sites during directory synchronization. If the trust level set for the distribution is higher than that set for the directory synchronization requestor, the distribution list information will not be replicated during directory synchronization. Trust levels range from 0 through 100.

- **Message Size** You can set the size limit of messages sent to and from the distribution list. By default, there is no size limit for messages.

- **Distribution List Options** You can set several options on this Properties page, including enabling out-of-office messages and hiding the distribution list or distribution list membership from the Address Book. The options that pertain to distribution lists are as follows:

Figure 5.6   The Advanced Properties page of a distribution list.

- **Report To Distribution List Owner** If selected (by default, it is not selected), this option sends the distribution list owner notification reports when a message sent to the distribution list has requested a return receipt or is undeliverable.

- **Report To Message Originator** If selected (the default setting), this option sends to the message originator notification reports that indicate the delivery status for each member of the distribution list. When this option is not selected, the message originator receives reports from the list, not notification for each member.

- **Allow Out-Of-Office Messages To Originator** The out-of-office option is a mailbox mechanism that allows the mailbox owner to notify senders that they are unavailable to read the messages. If selected (by default, it is not selected), this option sends out-of-office messages from members of the distribution list to the originator on behalf of any member who has enabled his or her out-of-office option. It is not a good idea to activate this option for large distribution lists.

- **Hide From Address Book** If selected (by default, it is not selected), this option hides this distribution list from the Address Book. However, even if the mailbox is hidden from the Address Book, you can send messages to the mailbox if you know the email address.

- **Hide Membership From Address Book** If selected (by default, it is not selected), this option hides the recipients that are the members of this distribution list from the Address Book, but it does not hide the distribution list.

- **Container Name** This is the name of the container where the mailbox resides. This is a read-only field.

WORKING WITH CUSTOM RECIPIENTS

A custom recipient is a recipient that resides outside a site, organization, or post office (an example would be an Internet SMTP recipient). When a custom recipient is created, it appears in the Address Book and can receive messages just like any other recipient. A custom recipient does not, however, have a mailbox on the local Exchange Server. You can create a custom recipient in one of two ways: You can use the Exchange Administrator program or you can use the directory import feature to import custom recipients from other mail systems.

CREATING CUSTOM RECIPIENTS

A custom recipient can be created from the Exchange Administrator program by selecting the New Custom Recipient option from the File menu (or Ctrl+R).

You are then prompted to select the type of foreign email address to create and its address. The types of foreign email addresses available are:

- cc:Mail
- Microsoft Mail
- MacMail
- Internet Mail
- X.400
- Other address

CUSTOM RECIPIENT PROPERTIES

The properties for a custom recipient are very similar to those of a standard mailbox. The main difference is that you are prompted for the foreign mail address of the custom recipient. The format of this foreign mail address depends on the foreign mail system.

The General Properties page (shown in Figure 5.7) for a custom recipient is the same as that for a mailbox, except that you can change the custom recipient's email address.

The Advanced Properties page (shown in Figure 5.8) for a custom recipient is the same as that for a mailbox, except for the following:

- **Directory Name** This option is not read-only. You can modify it.

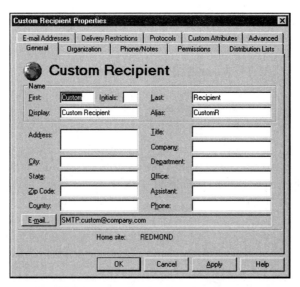

Figure 5.7   The General Properties page of a custom recipient.

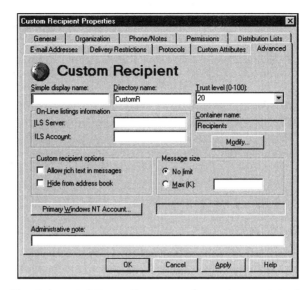

Figure 5.8   The Advanced Properties page of a custom recipient.

- **Container Name**   This option is not read-only. You can select a different container by clicking on the Modify button and selecting the desired container.

- **Custom Recipient Options**   You can select Allow Rich Text In Messages.

- **Primary Windows NT Account**   This is the NT domain account that is associated with the mailbox. You can either choose an existing user account or have a new user account created.

USING THE IMPORT FEATURE

The Microsoft Exchange Administrator program can automatically generate custom recipients based on information provided in an import file. This capability applies primarily to SMTP clients, where a certain collection of minimum custom recipient attributes is required to automatically import custom recipients. These attributes are as follows:

- **Obj-Class**   Maps to the type of recipient involved, be it a mailbox, a distribution list, and so forth.

- **First Name**   Maps to the user's first name.

- **Last Name**   Maps to the user's surname.

- **Display Name**   Maps to a typical Exchange display name that takes the format *last name, first name* based on the preceding values.

- **Alias Name**   Maps to the SMTP name for the recipient object.

- **Directory Name** Maps the Exchange DS entry to a foreign email system directory entry,
- **Email Address** Maps an SMTP email address to an Exchange email address.

The HEADER.EXE program included in the *Microsoft Exchange Resource Kit* might be used to create an import file to supply the foregoing information. The same data could also be manually entered into a file, using a simple text editor, such as Notepad. This provides a valuable alternative to the New Custom Recipient menu entry from the Exchange Administrator File menu when more than one SMTP custom recipient must be created.

MANAGING RECIPIENT OBJECTS

Because recipient objects provide the primary focus for message activity in the Exchange environment, managing such objects is an important part of the maintenance process for any Exchange Server. In general, this means managing mailboxes, distribution lists, and custom recipients to match changes in connections to foreign email systems or other Exchange Servers, changes in personnel, or changes in organizational structure.

In this section, we cover some typical recipient object management tasks, many of which will become commonplace for Exchange administrators as part of their daily routines:

- Using templates for mailbox creation
- Finding a recipient
- Moving a mailbox
- Cleaning a mailbox

USING TEMPLATES FOR MAILBOX CREATION

A template is a mailbox constructed for the purpose of creating new mailboxes. In other words, its configuration information can be used to create new mailboxes. You can use the Migration Wizard, the Directory Import command, or the Duplicate command to create new mailboxes. (Duplicating a template mailbox can create a single mailbox or a number of mailboxes.)

Any mailbox can be used as a template mailbox; however, several configuration items are not copied to the new mailbox or mailboxes. These items are:

- First name
- Last name
- Display name

- Alias name
- Directory name
- Email address

The template should be named something that clearly states the nature of the mailbox it will be used to create. For example, you might want to create a template for the users in sales. You could call the template *Sales* and use it to create a new mailbox for new users in the Sales department. You might also want to place a pound sign (#) as the first character of the template's name. This causes the templates to be listed at the top of the recipient's list. For example, you would name the Sales template #*Sales*. The templates can be hidden from the Address Book so that mail is not accidentally sent to the mailboxes associated with them.

FINDING A RECIPIENT

The Exchange Administrator program has a function that can search for recipients anywhere within the organization. This command is accessed by selecting the Find Recipients option in the Tools menu (see Figure 5.9). You can search for recipients based on several search criteria, including first, last, or display name; department; assistants; and so on.

MOVING A MAILBOX

Although a mailbox physically resides on a specific server, it is possible to move it to another server within the site. To do this, highlight the desired mailbox in the

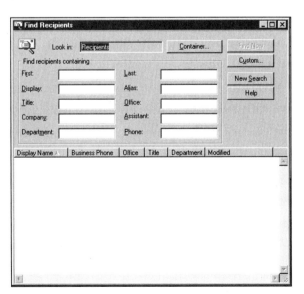

Figure 5.9   The Find Recipients page.

contents pane (the right window pane), and then select the Move Mailbox option from the Tools menu. Any time a user is moved, the associated client profile is updated automatically to point to its location on a different server.

When moving mailboxes to a new home server, the size of the mailbox contents on the destination server might increase. When a message is sent to multiple mailboxes on the same server, a single copy of the message is stored, and each recipient on that server receives a pointer to that single copy. This is called single-instance storage. When a mailbox is moved to a new server, the pointer must be replaced with a copy of the message, because pointers do not operate between servers. For example, if you moved 5 mailboxes from one server to another (each containing 10MB of messages and a pointer to 4 single-instance messages of 1MB each) the size of the private Information Store on the new home server would increase by 70MB (5 mailboxes, 14MB in each mailbox). On the original home server, this would take up 54MB of storage (5 mailboxes with 10MB of messages each and 4 single-instance messages of 1MB each).

Mailboxes can also be moved using the Home Server field on the Advanced Properties page of the user's mailbox.

 To select multiple mailboxes to be moved, hold the Shift key while clicking on contiguous users, or press the Ctrl key while clicking on noncontiguous users.

CLEANING A MAILBOX

Cleaning a mailbox is the task of deleting certain messages stored in a mailbox. To clean a mailbox, select the mailbox to be cleaned (in the Contents pane), then select the Clean Mailbox option from the Tools menu (shown in Figure 5.10). The administrator can select predefined criteria for cleaning a mailbox. Some of these criteria include:

- All messages older than a certain number of days
- All messages larger that a certain size (in kilobytes)
- Normal, personal, private, and confidential messages
- Read and unread messages

Regular application of this option helps keep the Information Store from becoming overly cluttered with outdated, unneeded, or irrelevant messages.

As the administrator, you also have the option to delete messages immediately or to move them to the Deleted Items folder. When in doubt, select the latter option, unless you have a recent backup to cover yourself against user backlash.

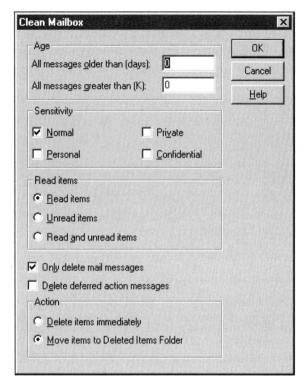

Figure 5.10   The Clean Mailbox dialog box.

CHAPTER SUMMARY

Recipients are objects that can receive messages and other information. There are four main types of recipients:

- **Mailboxes** A mailbox is a storage location on an Exchange Server, called the home server, that allows information to be sent, received, and stored. Email messages, file attachments, and forms are some common types of information that can be sent to a mailbox.

- **Distribution lists** A distribution list is a logical grouping of recipients. A distribution list allows for easy mass mailing of messages. All the members of a distribution list will receive any messages sent to that distribution list.

- **Custom recipients** A custom recipient is a non–Exchange email address that Exchange clients can send mail messages to.

- **Public folders** A public folder is an information container that can hold files, messages, and forms that many users can access. It is similar to a public mailbox.

In addition, you also learned about what's involved in managing recipient objects, from creating new mailboxes to cleaning up unwanted (or unneeded) messages and files.

KEY TERMS

- **custom recipient**—A pointer to a foreign address or recipient outside the organization.

- **deleted message retention**—The amount of time that deleted messages are kept before being permanently deleted.

- **distribution list**—A logical grouping of recipients created to ease mass mailing of messages.

- **expansion server**—A server used to expand distribution lists.

- **home server**—The server where a mailbox is physically located.

- **Internet Locator Server (ILS)**—A server that allows Microsoft NetMeeting users to locate mailboxes to set up online meetings.

- **Internet Message Access Protocol version 4 (IMAP4)**—An Internet client protocol used to access mail messages.

- **mailbox**—The location on the Exchange Server where mail is delivered.

- **mailbox roles**—A predefined set of mailbox rights.

- **online listing information**—See Internet Locator Server.

- **Post Office Protocol version 3 (POP3)**—An Internet client protocol used to access mail messages.

- **public folder**—A repository for many types of information, such as files, that can be shared by many users.

- **recipient**—An Exchange object that can have messages sent to it.

- **simple display name**—A name used for foreign messaging systems that cannot handle non-ANSI characters.

- **trust level**—A numerical value assigned to an object to specify whether the object will be replicated during directory synchronization.

REVIEW QUESTIONS

1. You must create a Windows NT account before you can create a corresponding mailbox. True or False?

2. You do not require a Windows NT account to have a mailbox on an Exchange Server. True or False?

3. Which of the following is an object that can receive, store, and organize messages?

   a. A distribution list

   b. A mailbox

   c. A custom recipient

   d. A POP3 account

4. Which of the following advanced mailbox properties are not configurable by the administrator?

   a. Simple display name

   b. Directory name

   c. Trust level

   d. Home server

5. Which of the following controls determine whether an object will be replicated during directory synchronization?

   a. Trust relationship

   b. Object trust

   c. Synchronization level

   d. Trust level

6. Which of the following is not an example of a mailbox attribute?

   a. Expansion server

   b. Alias

   c. Primary Windows NT account

   d. Country

7. Which of the following controls mailbox permissions?

   a. NT permissions

   b. NT groups

   c. Distribution lists

   d. Roles

8. Any mailbox can be used as a mailbox template. True or False?

9. A mailbox cannot have more than one user assigned to it. True or False?

10. What is the Internet Location Server used for?

    a. Locating users for online meetings

    b. Locating users for Microsoft Chat

    c. Locating users for Microsoft NetShow

    d. Locating users' email addresses in the site

5

11. Which recipient object would you use to allow for mass mailing to a single address?

    a. A distribution list

    b. An NT user group

    c. A mailbox with multiple users

    d. A custom recipient

12. You can move mailboxes from one server to another. True or False?

13. To allow another Exchange Server to deal with distribution lists, what do you set?

    a. A home server

    b. A SQL server

    c. An expansion server

    d. A distribution list server

14. What does a custom recipient allow you to do?

    a. Create a second name for an existing Exchange mailbox

    b. Have one message sent to the custom recipient be delivered to all its members

    c. Have Exchange communicate with foreign mail systems

    d. Define a custom mailbox role

15. To selectively delete messages from a mailbox, which of the following would you choose?

    a. Move mailbox

    b. Clean mailbox

    c. Delete mailbox

    d. Rename mailbox

16. Which program would you use to create mailboxes for NetWare users?

    a. The NetWare Extract tool

    b. Gateway Service For NetWare

    c. Directory synchronization

    d. Cannot be done

17. It is impossible to automate the location of Exchange recipients. True or False?

18. Distribution lists can be created with the User Manager For Domains. True or False?

19. If a user deletes a message, when is it possible for the user to recover the deleted message?

    a. Whenever the user wants. This is an automatic feature of Exchange.

    b. When the user is part of the Backup Operators NT group.

    c. When the administrator sets Deleted Message Retention period.

    d. Never.

20. If a distribution list is hidden from the Address Book, users cannot send email messages to the distribution list. True or False?

HANDS-ON PROJECTS

PROJECT 5.1

To create and configure a mailbox using the Exchange Administrator program:

1. From the Start Menu, select Programs | Microsoft Exchange | Microsoft Exchange Administrator.

2. Select the Recipients container in the left pane.

3. Select New Mailbox from the File menu (or select the mailbox icon). A Properties window should appear with several tabs.

4. Enter the name "Bill" in the First field. Enter the name "Bates" in the Last field. Notice that the Display and Alias fields are automatically created.

5. Enter any other information (such as address, title, company, and so forth).

6. Click the Primary Windows NT Account button. A window should appear with two radio buttons. Select the second radio button—Create A New Windows NT Account. The dialog box in Figure 5.11 should appear. Select the NT domain in which you would like to create the account. You can also change the default account name. When you are finished, click OK.

7. A dialog box should appear stating The Windows NT Account You Just Created Was Given A Blank Password. The user will be required to change the password upon first logon. Click OK.

8. Click the various Properties tabs to familiarize yourself with the configuration options available.

PROJECT 5.2

To create and configure a mailbox using the User Manager For Domains program:

1. From the Start Menu, select Programs | Administrative Tools (Common) | User Manager For Domains.

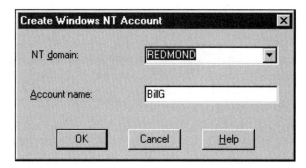

Figure 5.11   The Create Windows NT Account dialog box.

2. Within User Manager For Domains, select the New User option from the User menu. The New User dialog box should appear, allowing you to enter information specific to the user.

3. Only one piece of information is required, and that is the username. In the Username field, enter the name "JohnD". In the Full Name field, enter the name "John Doe". Click Add.

4. The next dialog box you will see should be either the one in Figure 5.12 or the Exchange Properties page for JohnD's mailbox. If you see Figure 5.12, click Browse, and select the Exchange Server you would like as the home server to this mailbox. Click OK. Now, the Exchange Properties page for JohnD's mailbox should appear.

5. Enter "John" in the First field and "Doe" in the Last field. Notice that the Display and Alias fields are automatically generated, as is the Primary Windows NT Account.

6. Click OK. You are now back to the User Manager For Domains program. Click Close.

PROJECT 5.3

To create and configure a distribution list:

1. From the Exchange Administrator program, select the File | New Distribution, or you can select the New Distribution list icon (the one with the two people on it). A Properties window should appear with several tabs.

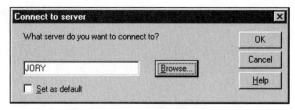

Figure 5.12   The Connect To Server dialog box.

2. Enter "Managers" in the Display field. Enter the same information in the Alias field.

3. Click Modify in the Members field. The left list box contains a listing of the Exchange recipients available. Choose some recipients. You can select them individually by clicking the name and then clicking Add, or you can select multiple recipients by holding down the Control key while selecting the recipients, and then click Add. Click OK to finish.

4. From the Expansion Server drop-down menu, either select a specific Exchange Server to act as the expansion server or leave the default, Any Server In Site.

5. Click OK to complete the distribution list configuration.

 PROJECT 5.4

To create and configure a custom recipient:

1. From the Exchange Administrator program, select File | New Custom Recipient (or select the world icon). A Properties window should appear with several tabs.

2. The New Email Address dialog box should appear (shown in Figure 5.13). Select the Internet Address option, then click OK.

3. The Internet Address Properties screen should appear. Type in an Internet address, such as "maryjane@company.com".

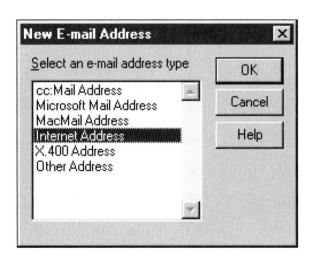

Figure 5.13   The New Email Address dialog box.

4. Click OK.

5. The Properties dialog box should appear next. Select the General Properties tab. Here, the only fields that are required are the Display and Alias fields. Type "Maryjane James" for the Display field and "maryjane@company.com" for the Alias field.

6. Click OK.

CASE PROJECTS

1. You work for an Internet Service Provider (ISP). You use Microsoft Exchange Server 5.5 to store your users' mailboxes. You have been tasked with creating 45 mailboxes for a client.

   Required result:

   Create the mailboxes as quickly and easily as possible.

   Optional desired results:

   The client would like to send one message that will be delivered to all 45 mailboxes. You do not want your Exchange Server to be impacted by messages sent to all 45 mailboxes.

   Proposed solution:

   Create a template named *Client*. Use this template to create all 45 mailboxes.

   Which results does the proposed solution provide?

   a. The proposed solution provides the required result and the optional desired results.

   b. The proposed solution provides only the required result.

   c. The proposed solution does not provide the required result.

2. You work for an ISP. You use Microsoft Exchange Server 5.5 to store your user's mailboxes. You have been tasked with creating 45 mailboxes for a client.

   Required result:

   Create the mailboxes as quickly and easily as possible.

   Optional desired results:

   The client would like to send one message that will be delivered to all 45 mailboxes. You do not want your Exchange Server to be impacted by messages sent to all 45 mailboxes.

   Proposed solution:

   Create a template named *Client*. Use this template to create all 45 mailboxes. Create a distribution list with all 45 mailboxes as the members.

Which results does the proposed solution provide?

   a. The proposed solution provides the required result and the optional desired results.

   b. The proposed solution provides only the required result.

   c. The proposed solution does not provide the required result.

3. You work for an ISP. You use Microsoft Exchange Server 5.5 to store your user's mailboxes. You have been tasked with creating 45 mailboxes for a client.

Required result:

Create the mailboxes as quickly and easily as possible.

Optional desired results:

The client would like to send one message that will be delivered to all 45 mailboxes. You do not want your Exchange Server to be impacted by messages sent to all 45 mailboxes.

Proposed solution:

Create a template named *Client*. Use this template to create all 45 mailboxes. Create a distribution list with all 45 mailboxes as the members. Specify a different Exchange Server as the expansion server.

Which results does the proposed solution provide?

   a. The proposed solution provides the required result and both optional desired results.

   b. The proposed solution provides the required result and one optional desired result.

   c. The proposed solution provides only the required result.

   d. The proposed solution does not provide the required result.

5

EXCHANGE CLIENTS AND CLIENT CONFIGURATIONS

O n the server side, the importance and capabilities of Exchange are undeniable. The U.S. Department of Defense recently announced that it plans to service over two million users through Exchange, and organizations like Boeing Aerospace already handle user populations as large as 140,000 using Exchange today. But there's more to email than just the server side of the equation: clients need email software, too. In this chapter, we set our sights on Microsoft's current email client packages, and explain their ins and outs, and whys and wherefores. Remember: you can't operate a client/server environment without both clients and servers!

That's why we'll explore both Outlook and the Outlook Web Access in this chapter. We'll explain how to install each of these packages and how to configure them to make them work their best for you. We'll also tell you what you need to know to make efficient use of Outlook views. In addition, you'll learn about Outlook's Calendar and Remote mail capabilities. Finally, we'll take you on a step-by-step walk through a Microsoft Outlook 98 installation and create a rule to sort incoming mail.

AFTER READING THIS CHAPTER AND COMPLETING THE EXERCISES, YOU WILL BE ABLE TO:

- Understand the options available to you from Outlook and Outlook Web Access

- Describe the installation process for Outlook and Outlook Web Access

- Comprehend the advantages and disadvantages of using Outlook's Personal folders

- Understand the concept and operation of offline storage

INSTALLING OUTLOOK

Just like with Exchange on the server side, a little planning goes a long way toward making Outlook work for you successfully. That's why you should consider the following issues before you install Outlook:

- Will users be able to configure their own settings or will you pre-configure, or lock down, those settings instead?

- How are you going to install Outlook—from a CD-ROM, across the network, or from a Web download?

- Will Outlook be installed locally on individuals' machines, or will its files reside on a server?

A server-based installation may be performed by copying the Outlook files from the CD-ROM to a hard drive, or by sharing the Outlook CD at the server and running SETUP.EXE. There is less chance for misconfiguration with a server-based installation. However, because the files must move across the network, a server-based installation requires a reliable network and can increase network traffic dramatically. If Outlook is already installed as a part of Office 97, before Exchange entered the network, Outlook will not know about Exchange and must be reconfigured manually.

 Microsoft recently released Outlook 98 (version numbers start with V.8.5x). The previous version of Outlook was V.8.0.3x. There are a number of changes between Outlook and Outlook 98. Because Microsoft is heavily marketing Outlook 98, expect much of your client-side messaging to be Outlook 98-based. To that end, this chapter focuses on Outlook 98. Please note also that Outlook 98 is different from Outlook Express, which is a subset of Outlook 98 that Microsoft bundles for free with Windows 98.

In the sections that follow, we'll explain Microsoft's system requirements for Outlook 98, and discuss Outlook file formats and related file extensions. You'll also learn about Outlook's support for views, which provide a way to limit what appears on screen when you interact with the program, and about Outlook's calendaring, scheduling, and appointment book capabilities. This section concludes with a discussion of Outlook's personal information management capabilities, which permit you to manage contact and address information for any number of individuals. In the next section, we begin this overview with a discussion of Outlook 98's system requirements.

SYSTEM REQUIREMENTS

Microsoft's stated minimum requirements for Outlook 98 are as follows:

- **Processor** 486/66

- **Memory Requirements** 8MB RAM for Windows 95, and 16MB RAM for Windows 98 or Windows NT 4.

- **Operating System** Windows 95, Windows 98, or Windows NT 4 with Service Pack 3 installed.

- **Browser** Internet Explorer 4.01 must be installed, but it doesn't have to be the default browser.

Outlook 98 offers three installation options:

- **Minimum** Installs core Outlook 98 files, including Internet Explorer 4.01, Microsoft VM for Java, and multimedia enhancements

- **Standard** Installs everything included in the Minimum installation, plus the Outlook Help files. This is the recommended installation option.

- **Full** Installs everything included with the Standard installation, plus Database Converters, Development Tools, Microsoft NetMeeting, and Outlook enhancements (such as Office sounds, animated cursors, and Lotus Organizer converter).

Disk space requirements vary, depending on the installation type. See Tables 6.1 through 6.3 for more details.

Assuming your machine meets the system requirements and has sufficient unused disk space available, installation should proceed without a hitch. But before you install the program, you should also understand Outlook's use of file extensions and on-disk folders. This is the subject of the next section.

CLIENT DATA

By default, Outlook 98 uses a file extension whenever it creates files that contain personal information. For Outlook 98, the .PST extension at the end of a file name denotes that an individual's folders and messages are stored within that file. Thus, for example, a file named BOBS.PST would contain Bob Smith's mail folders and all the messages within them. When mail folders and messages are stored locally and user profiles are in effect, the PST file is stored in each user's

Table 6.1 Minimum installation.

What's In Your Computer?	Size (If Downloading)	Installed Disk Size (Footprint)	Free Space Needed
IE 4.01 and Outlook 97	15MB	22MB	34MB
IE 4.01 only	15MB	39MB	55MB
Neither IE nor Outlook	26MB	65MB	102MB

Table 6.2   Standard installation.

What's In Your Computer?	Size (If Downloading)	Installed Disk Size (Footprint)	Free Space Needed
IE 4.01 and Outlook 97	16MB	22MB	37MB
IE 4.01 only	16MB	41MB	57MB
Neither IE nor Outlook	28MB	68MB	104MB

Table 6.3   Full installation.

What's In Your Computer?	Size (If Downloading)	Installed Disk Size (Footprint)	Free Space Needed
IE 4.01 and Outlook 97	21MB	32MB	52MB
IE 4.01 only	21MB	53MB	75MB
Neither IE nor Outlook	33MB	81MB	121MB

profile subdirectory. For example, if Bob Smith works on a Windows NT machine, and user profiles are in effect, his PST file will reside in the D:\WINNT\Profiles\Bobs\Application Data\Microsoft\Office\8.5\Outlook directory.

Most experienced Exchange administrators consider it a bad practice to store mail in a PST file. That's because this approach leaves it up to clients to back up their personal folders and messages. If personal folders and messages reside on the server, however, it should be subject to regular and reliable backup, which will then protect each user's folders and their messages.

There are two other Outlook file extensions that you are likely to encounter: .PAB (which represents a file used for Personal Address Book storage) and .SCD (which represents a file used for Schedule+ information, such as alerts, reminders, appointments, and other calendaring and scheduling data). Because these files are also important, you should remind your users that they are best stored on a server where they, too, can be regularly backed up. For these files, users can simply map to a server drive, and keep them in their personal directories on a file server somewhere on the network.

Because multiple users may need to share a single machine, or because a single user may have multiple email accounts, Outlook supports multiple mail profiles. This permits individual settings, views, newsgroups, and other elements to be customized on a per-profile basis. This provides the subject for the next section.

PROFILES

Outlook provides mail profiles for two reasons:

- To permit multiple users to share a single machine, with a single copy of Outlook installed. In this set of circumstances, each user would have his own separate profile, and would use it when launching Outlook to gain access to his mail.

- To permit a single user to operate multiple email accounts, where a different mail server, ISP, or login information is required for each account. As before, each external account would have its own separate profile, which would be used to access the mail associated with that account.

It is also possible to combine multiple users, where individual users have multiple accounts on a single machine as well. To create a new mail profile, do so by clicking Start | Settings | Control Panel | Mail, or within Outlook, click Tools | Accounts. The Internet Connection Wizard should appear as shown in Figure 6.1.

The options for each separate mail profile in Outlook include the ability to work through a local area network (LAN) or from a dial-up connection (see Figure 6.2). Dial-up connections are easy to misconfigure, so proceed with caution (and double-check all settings) when a profile requires dial-up access. You may also configure Outlook to try a LAN connection first, and if one is unavailable, to then try a dial-up connection. This approach is especially useful when configuring a laptop that operates in a network-connected docking station when its owner is in the office, but that must dial up a connection when its owner is away from the office.

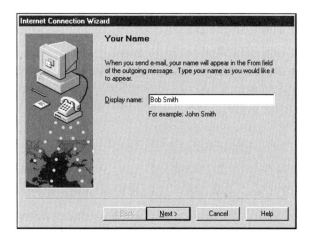

Figure 6.1   The Internet Connection Wizard assists you in creating a new profile.

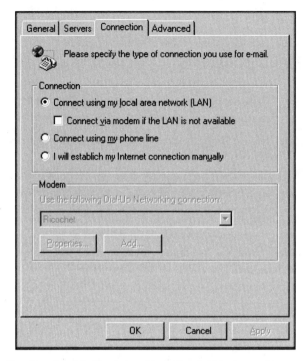

Figure 6.2 Configuring Outlook to attempt a LAN connection, or to use a dial-up connection if the LAN is unavailable.

In the next section, we deal with another aspect of how users away from the network deal with mail—namely the role that offline folders play in allowing disconnected users to read and reply to their email messages.

OFFLINE FOLDERS

Users often read and reply to messages when they have no active network connection, especially when they work on laptops. For this reason, Outlook includes support for local offline folders so that users can access messages from those folders and place replies into those folders without requiring a live connection.

To create an offline folder, follow these steps:

1. Go to Start|Settings|Control Panel, then double-click the Mail icon.

2. Choose a profile you want to configure for the offline folder.

3. Select the Services tab, choose Exchange Server, and click Properties.

4. Select the Advanced tab, and click the Offline Folder file settings button.

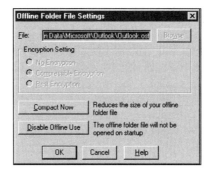

Figure 6.3 Configuring an offline folder.

5. In the file box (see Figure 6.3), enter a path and a file name for your folder.

6. Click OK.

Because users may deal with different sets of folders and tools when they're working in the office or away from the office, or because they may simply want to change their focus within Outlook, no matter where they're working, Outlook supports a view mechanism. This is the topic for the next section.

OUTLOOK WITH A VIEW

In the most general computing sense, a view represents a subset of all the data that's available to an application, usually one that's been carefully selected to meet a specific set of needs. Although this terminology is most often associated with databases, where views are used to restrict the data that users can see depending on the role they play in an organization, Outlook supports a similar mechanism. Outlook views are provided more as a convenience, however, and permit users to select for themselves the composition of their screens when they run the program.

In fact, Outlook's view options permit users to exercise a great deal of control over both screen layout and screen contents. A quick look at Figure 6.4 shows that the Outlook Folder List on the left side of the window contains a number of folders. In turn, each folder on display can contain subfolders within it. If you select a folder (the folder for the msexchange mailing list is shown in Figure 6.4) that selection causes the folder's contents to appear in the upper-right pane. In the same vein, selecting a message in that pane causes the lower-right pane to display the contents of the selected message. Panes may be added or deleted, moved or resized. This gives users tremendous flexibility.

The icons that appear in the Outlook Shortcuts icon bar (also known as the Outlook bar) on the left-hand side of the screen provide access to the program's

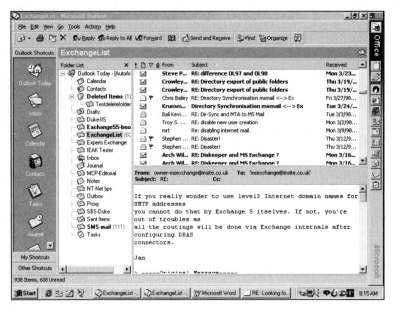

Figure 6.4   A simple view of Outlook hides numerous configuration options.

major areas of functionality. These icons are named and explained in the order in which they appear:

- **Outlook today**   All pending items for the day are listed here.

- **Inbox**   Where all incoming messages are stored (unless filtered out by a rule wizard).

- **Calendar**   Manages your daily, weekly, and monthly schedules.

- **Contacts**   Stores information similar to Rolodex card data, including how to reach people and organizations.

- **Tasks**   Tasks are specified in a form that resembles a To Do list, with the ability to define and sort tasks by type, description, or due date. Completed tasks may be checked off, and pending tasks may be associated with alerts and reminders. This interfaces very well with Outlook Today.

- **Journal**   A tool that permits users to record activities automatically or manually, to track activities over time, to use journal entries as shortcuts (to make it easy to return to or reactivate recurrent tasks), and to find files directly from journal entries, without having to remember paths. As shown in Figure 6.5, tracking is turned off by default in Outlook 98, but it can be a valuable feature.

- **Notes**   Notes are the Outlook equivalent of Post-It notes. Use notes to record questions, ideas, reminders, or anything else you wish to remember. Notes can also be useful to store information you might

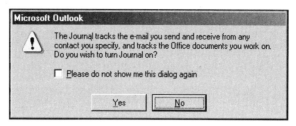

Figure 6.5   By default, tracking is turned off.

need again, such as accounts and passwords, directions, ISP phone numbers, and other small but important items.

- **Drafts** Holds mail that you are working on or saving to send at a later time.

- **Sent Items** Contains sent messages; these will be retained unless deleted manually, or removed by application of a rule.

- **Deleted Items** Stores deleted mail items until they are permanently deleted, either by aging out of the system or manual deletion from this area.

To the right of the Outlook bar is another vertical pane called the Folder List. Here, both default and user-created folders appear in a hierarchical list. The default folders have some interesting capabilities, too, and in some cases are tied to the icons in the Outlook Shortcuts bar. Here's what appears by default in this list, from top to bottom (notice that, except for Outlook Today, which always appears at the top of this list, all remaining items are listed in alphabetical order):

- **Outlook Today** Shows all pending items for today's date (as set for the computer), including tasks, mail, and so forth. This feature is new to Outlook 98. You can also fill text into the Find A Contact text box to search your Contacts database.

- **Calendar** Shows a view of the day's activities and tasks, with a miniature calendar for the current month in the upper right-hand corner of the display area. If you're familiar with personal planning tools and organizers, this looks just like an electronic version of one of their page-per-day layouts. This corresponds exactly to the Calendar icon in the Outlook bar.

- **Contacts** Lists the contents of the current user's Contacts database in alphabetical order by last name. On the far right of the display area, a series of buttons by first letter, number, or symbol permits users to change focus easily to the right part of the alphabet to find what they're looking for. This data corresponds to the information entered using the Contacts icon in the Outlook bar.

- **Deleted Items** Lists all items deleted from other folders but not yet permanently deleted from Outlook. Any item that shows up here can be restored to its original location, saved as a file, or moved into another folder. Corresponds exactly to the same entry in the Outlook bar.

- **Drafts** Includes all items that have been created but not yet sent; it's a form of pending storage. To send a draft item, you must move it into the Outbox folder, or use the Tools | Send menu entries.

- **Inbox** Stores all incoming messages until deleted or moved to another folder. The People and Projects subfolders are created by default to create suggested ways of sorting incoming mail (by sender in the People folder, and by project in the Projects folder).

- **Journal** Lists all current journal settings and journal entries; ties into the same data created using the Journal icon from the Outlook bar.

- **Notes** Lists all currently defined notes; ties into the same data created using the Notes icon from the Outlook bar.

- **Outbox** Stores all messages pending delivery (which may be instigated at any time through the Tools | Send menu entries).

- **Sent Items** Stores all sent messages for later review or deletion; ties into the same data available through the Sent Items icon in the Outlook bar.

- **Tasks** Stores all pending task information; ties into the same data available through the Tasks icon in the Outlook bar.

As new folders are created, they too will appear in the Folder List pane. Where elements match between the Outlook bar and the Folder List pane, it's a matter of personal preference which way you go to get to the related data—for both approaches, the results will be the same. In fact, you will notice that folders become highlighted if you pick their related icons.

All other folders that appear in your Folder List are custom creations that may be used to store incoming mail manually (you can right-click on any message in the Inbox, then select the Move To Folder entry from the pop-up menu to make this switch). You may also apply the Rules Wizard to incoming mail to direct such mail into appropriate folders (or delete it if you so choose). When new mail arrives, the names of the folders where new messages reside appear in boldface. Thus, you can tell at a glance where new mail has been deposited.

In Figure 6.4, the Outlook bar not only includes icons, but also Outlook Shortcuts, My Shortcuts, and Other Shortcuts buttons. Whenever you create a new folder, Outlook asks if you want to create a shortcut for the Outlook bar. The default is No. Nevertheless, you have the ability to customize the Outlook bar to your heart's content.

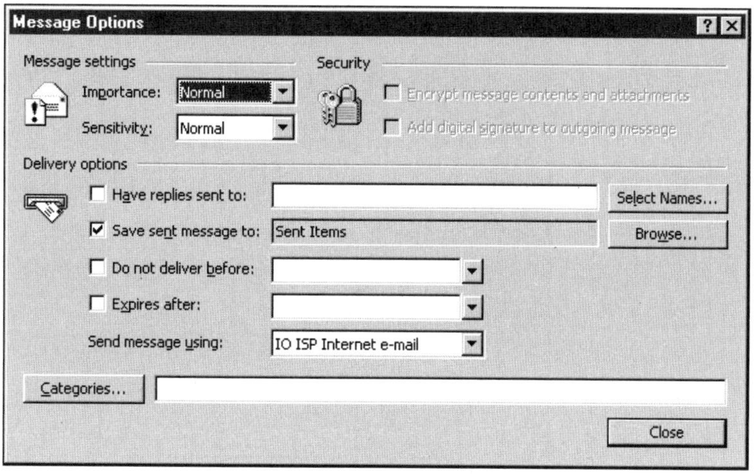

Figure 6.6   The Message Options dialog box.

Note that as you drill down in Outlook 98, many "hidden" features will surprise you. As shown in Figure 6.6, delivery of a message to a group was delayed until September. Clicking on the down arrow to the right of the date brings up a mini-calendar, allowing point-and-click selection. To elicit the Message Options dialog box, you must use the View|Options menu entries in the view that appears when you're creating a new email message.

Among its many capabilities, Outlook supports an appointment-minding mechanism as part of the Calendar view. This provides the topic for the next section.

APPOINTMENTS

To create an appointment in Outlook, open the Calendar view, then select the start date. Click on a date on the calendar in the upper right-hand corner of the display area if it's not for today. Next, right-click on a time bar in the time display on the left-hand side of the display area. This produces a pop-up menu that includes a New Appointment entry. If selected, this entry produces an appointment creation dialog box where you can provide the particulars for any given appointment. If you check the Reminder checkbox, your computer will warn you 15 minutes before the appointment is to occur, but this lead-time setting is easy to adjust.

Notice that you can invite other members of your workgroup (taken from your contacts database or a distribution list), schedule recurring meetings, and even interface with NetMeeting for an online discussion (see Figure 6.7). If you have to change a meeting time, you can either drag-and-drop the appointment to another time that day, or to another day on the calendar in the upper right-hand

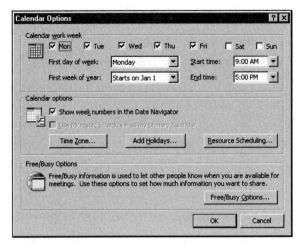

Figure 6.7   Group scheduling can include having Exchange Server reserve a meeting room, in addition to informing other users of the meeting.

corner of the display area. Alternatively, you may simply double-click an appointment to change its time manually. It is possible to inform Outlook about differences in time zones either for yourself, while you are traveling, or if someone you have a meeting with is in a different time zone. To set your Calendar options, select Tools | Options in the Calendar view.

Following the Calendar icon/folder, and its support for appointments and meetings, there's the Contacts icon/folder, with its database of information about individuals and their vital statistics. Contacts is the subject of the section that follows next.

CONTACTS

Like the rest of Outlook, Contacts can be organized by view. A sample of views includes: address cards, detailed address cards (choose View | Current View | Detailed Address Cards), phone lists, location, and category (see Figure 6.8).

Outlook 98 has a much easier-to-follow interface for organizing contacts than its predecessors. In the previous version, it was possible but difficult to describe and use alternate methods of contact. Notice in Figure 6.8 that there are still two contacts for Archell, Douglas J. This is a holdover from a previous version of Outlook. With Outlook 98, selecting a different physical address is never more than a click away.

This concludes our discussion of Outlook's icons and folders, which deliver an amazing array of functionality that goes well beyond mere email.

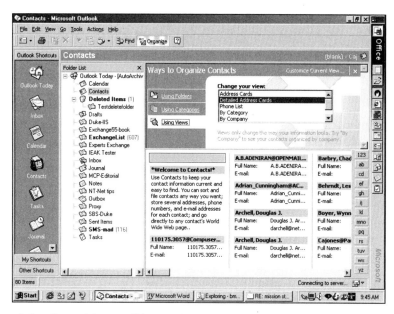

Figure 6.8   Organizing mail by contact.

OUTLOOK'S ADVANCED FEATURES

As you have seen, the clean look of Outlook 98 is one of its strong features. For example, we looked at the Organize feature while in Contacts in the preceding sections. Now, let's look at the Organize feature while in a mail folder.

As an example of what Outlook can do, we'd like to discuss the contents of one of our custom folders called ExchangeList (you probably won't have this one in your Outlook bar or Folder List, but you could build one just like it quite easily). We created this folder to hold mail that originated on an Exchange listserv, which is a busy mailing list devoted entirely to the discussion of Exchange-related technical matters.

A mailing list may be loosely defined as a self-selecting group of individuals who subscribe for daily deliveries of email messages on some specific topic or another. Individuals post questions or comments to mailing lists, to which other individuals may respond, which may provoke further questions or comments, and so forth.

A listserv is a special-purpose piece of software that collects messages from subscribers who want to post a message to the list, and then broadcasts those messages to all subscribers. There are several mailing lists on MCSE study topics that readers of this book might find interesting (for more information check the "More Resources" link at **http://www.lanw.com/examcram**).

If you looked at this folder on our machines, you would notice that it contains nearly 600 messages. Although this is an enormous amount of email, 95 percent of it is directly related to technical matters related to Exchange 5 and Exchange 5.5 that we have decided are worth keeping on our hard disks. The average daily message traffic from this listserv is in excess of 100 messages a day, so even 600 retained messages represent only a small fraction of a month's message traffic.

To simplify sorting through these messages, we used the Organize feature to sort them by topic. Here's how we did this:

1. Highlight ExchangeList in the Folder List.

2. Click Organize.

3. Click Using Views.

4. Select By Conversation Topic (see Figure 6.9).

Notice that the thread selected for expansion in Figure 6.9 displays two messages. The earlier message looks like it was unread. The newer reply has an action flag and has been read. What really happened was that the first message was short enough to permit us to use the preview pane to scan that message, so we never had to open it to read it in its entirety. This organization tool works quite well to permit us to scan our messages by topic, but Outlook also supports a variety of search tools that we often use to search for specific bits of text to help us find items of particular interest to certain topics at hand.

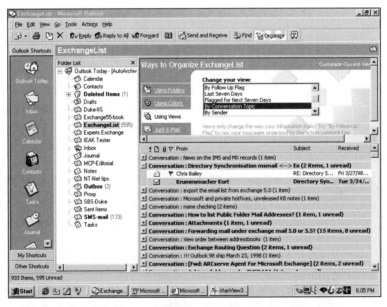

Figure 6.9   As soon as By Conversation Topic is selected, Outlook 98 organizes all messages by their subject lines.

In the sections that follow, we'll investigate other advanced features available in Outlook 98. These include its shortcut creation capabilities, its junk mail handling facilities, its import and export functions, its ability to recover deleted items, and its Rules Wizard, among other such features. We tackle shortcuts in the section that follows next.

ADVANCED SHORTCUTS

Whenever you create a new mail folder, Outlook 98 asks if you want to create a shortcut (remember, the default is No). Shortcuts are much more than simply ways to launch a view or some single advanced Outlook feature. We provide an example that adds a shortcut to the Outlook bar, which shows what shortcuts can do.

6

When we wrote this chapter, we launched a screen capture program to capture the screens that appear herein. This particular screen capture program captures screens in a bitmap file format (.BMP). After a screen has been captured, we must convert that file to a tagged image file format (.TIF), and save it on a server to upload along with this chapter, which was created in Microsoft Word. Switching from Word to Outlook to the screen capture program to the conversion tool and back again is a pain. That's why we created a shortcut to automate switching to the server directory where we can run the conversion tool (and ultimately grab the final screen shots). Here's how we did it:

1. Click on Other Shortcuts on the Outlook bar.

2. Right-click and select Outlook Bar Shortcut.

3. The default is to look in Outlook. Select, instead, File System (see Figure 6.10).

4. Click OK, and you have a new shortcut.

A final note on Outlook 98's advanced features: If you need entire groups besides the few that Outlook 98 offers, instead of right-clicking on the Outlook Shortcut Bar, right-click and select Add New Group to create a new group.

JUNK EMAIL

Today, junk email is a fact of life; unfortunately, so is *spamming*. Spamming is a phenomenon that occurs when some particular users (or group of users) inundate a mailbox with incoming messages to the point where it becomes completely choked, thereby blocking receipt of incoming messages. Whether they be unwanted messages from many sources (junk email) or numerous unwanted messages from a single source (spam), dealing with electronic trash in one's mailbox is now part of participating in the age of digital communications.

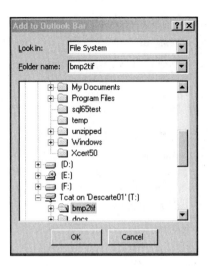

Figure 6.10   Shortcuts are not limited to Outlook. In this case, a shortcut to a folder on the server is set up.

Fortunately, Outlook 98 includes several methods for handling spam. Here again, we return to the Organizer utility. Highlight the Inbox folder, and select Organize. There are two types of junk email that Outlook can recognize—plain old junk and adult content (see Figure 6.11). Junk and Adult Content filters identify messages by looking for key words. It is possible to manually adjust these filter lists, but we have found Outlook's built-in filters to be reasonably usable (by which we mean, they haven't removed too many messages we really wanted to read).

For this example, we select Adult Content and configure Outlook to automatically move adult-content messages to the Deleted Items folder.

This provides a reasonably convincing demonstration of how easy it is to establish filters using the Organizer. We cover the Rules Wizard, which offers a broader range of filter types and mechanisms in a later section. In the next section, we change focus to using the Import And Export Wizard.

IMPORTING AND EXPORTING

Importing and exporting contact and schedule information is performed by using the Import And Export Wizard. If you need help, the Office Assistant can provide detailed assistance. Also, note the large number of methods offered to you for importing and exporting, as shown in Figure 6.12. As you select options from the Choose An Action To Perform list in the upper part of the window, corresponding details appear in the description below. These can provide some useful details about what each export or import action can do.

By selecting Import From Another Program Or File from the Choose An Action To Perform list, Outlook 98 can import directly from other *personal*

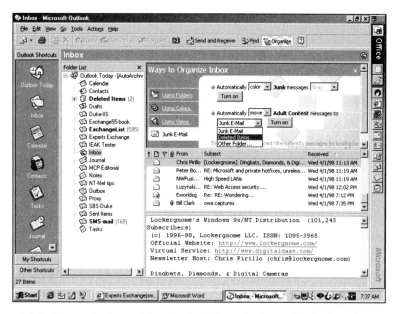

Figure 6.11   Unwanted email is a fact of life—dealing with it piece-by-piece needn't be.

information managers (PIMs) or text files. Microsoft's latest PIM will import with invisible conversion from legacy offerings. Some legacy programs supported by Outlook's Import And Export Wizard include: Act, ECCO, Lotus Organizer, and SideKick.

Outlook makes it equally painless to import data from other Microsoft programs, such as Outlook Express and Schedule+. Of course, Outlook can also import data from other Internet-based applications, such as Eudora (Lite and Pro), MS Internet Mail and News, and Netscape (Mail and Messenger).

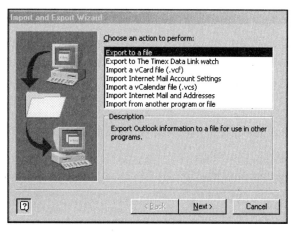

Figure 6.12   Importing and exporting data is widely supported in Outlook 98.

Also notice that you can export data to a variety of Microsoft programs, such as Access, Excel, and FoxPro, as well as export your data for other purposes, such as to update personal folders (.PST), import data into dBASE programs, or create mail-merge documents in MS Word.

Import works well when you're migrating to Outlook 98 from another email package or a PIM. Export comes in handy when feeding data into databases or creating mail-merge documents. Both capabilities are useful additions to Outlook's base messaging functionality. In the next section, we change our focus to investigate Outlook's abilities to recover deleted items before they're permanently expunged from a system.

DELETED ITEM RECOVERY

Just as Exchange 5.5 has improved its abilities to recover deleted items as compared to version 5, Outlook 98 offers similar improvements when compared to Outlook 97. To recover a deleted item in Outlook 98, follow these steps:

1. On the Outlook bar, click Outlook Shortcuts.
2. Click Deleted Items.
3. Select the items you want to retrieve in the right pane.
4. Right-click, and then select Move To Folder on the shortcut menu.
5. In the Move Items box, click the folder to which you want to move the items.

Although there's not much to this operation, it can be a real lifesaver whenever a user accidentally deletes a message he wanted to keep. This makes it simple and straightforward to recover from such accidents with aplomb. In the section that follows next, we tackle a somewhat murkier subject—namely, how to define and apply filtering rules to incoming email messages.

INBOX RULES

Inbox rules are a big gotcha in Outlook 98. To begin with, they are incompatible with previous versions of Outlook. Furthermore, both server- and client-based rules can apply to messages. This split may not be an issue for desktop computers that always connect to an Exchange Server, but separate sets of rules for clients and servers can cause grief for notebook users who sometimes connect directly to an Exchange Server and who use *Post Office Protocol (POP)* or *Internet Message Access Protocol (IMAP)* over the Internet at other times while traveling.

Among the unwanted effects that can sometimes result from a rules mismatch, the most frustrating is delivery of unwanted email just when it's least wanted—namely, when users dial in to retrieve email over a slow connection. Likewise, rules mismatches can sometimes prevent delivery of mail that's truly wanted when badly defined client-side rules come into play when users dial in for email, or when overly restrictive server-side rules are invoked when users grab their email across a network. There are no easy solutions to any of these problems at the time of this writing.

The good news is that creating rules is much easier than before. In previous versions, creating a rule was not a challenge, but creating a rule that actually worked was. To create a rule, select Tools|Rules Wizard, then click the New button on the right-hand side of the window.

If you have already created rules, you will find them displayed here. It is not advisable to write rules using the wizard until you have at least investigated the logic inherent in the Junk Email rules that may be created using the Organize button. A certain appreciation for the syntax, and for the exact meaning of the kind of operations that the wizard can apply, is required to make rules behave as intended. This is a topic that requires repeated experiments to grasp, and should be attacked with patience and determination.

The next topic changes gears from Outlook 98 to examine the Outlook Web Assistant, an HTML-based, lightweight alternative to Outlook 98.

OUTLOOK WEB ACCESS

Outlook Web Access (OWA) combines Exchange Server with HTML. This allows Exchange services, such as scheduling and messaging, to be available across an Internet link. To enable OWA, you must have numerous elements installed on your client machine, or available on your Exchange Server. These include *Active Desktop* (client), *Active Server* (IIS with Active Server Pages; server), and *ActiveX* (client and server). Given these elements, it is possible to run OWA from a system based on Windows (16 or 32 bit), Unix, or Macintosh. Access is granted to messages, public folders, the Global Address List (GAL), and calendars. For added functionality, clients must also install support for frames and JavaScript (both are included with IE 3.02 and newer versions).

When implementing OWA, if you do not use Challenge Handshake Authentication Protocol (CHAP) authentication, you must assure security by taking other measures. You can allow anonymous connections if you must, but it is difficult to find valid business reasons to ignore security completely, except to provide access to public folders. In this case, *self-registration* provides all required login information needed to post messages or other information anonymously.

IIS communicates with Exchange Server using Microsoft's Remote Procedure Call (RPC) mechanisms, which permits the two systems to interchange information directly. RPC essentially allows a procedure running in one program (in this case, Exchange Server) to call services from another program (in this case, IIS). For example, when you start Outlook up immediately after installation, a Web page from Microsoft Outlook appears in the Inbox entitled "Welcome to Microsoft Outlook 98." Although this document installs with the software, it represents the kind of functionality and access that the RPC link between Exchange and IIS can deliver. Remember too, that for Exchange 5.5 and OWA, Service Pack 3 (or later) and NT Server 4 are required. You must also install OWA using the Exchange Server Setup utility.

One option with OWA is to use the Secure Sockets Layer (SSL), a secure, encrypted alternative to standard Windows Sockets (also known as WinSock). When you choose to use SSL, the port used for Web communications moves from the standard port 80, for *HTTP* (the *Hypertext Transfer Protocol* is the default protocol used to move Web pages and related documents), to port 995 instead.

Using OWA, it is also possible to access public folders, to find names for message recipients in the Exchange Address Book, and to configure an auto-reply (to use when you are out of the office). Finally, OWA makes it possible to access Exchange to create appointments or edit your meeting planner.

OWA is compatible with Outlook. But this compatibility comes at a price: all OWA-related communications occur through HTTP. This is wonderful for accessing Exchange data using non-Exchange clients, such as a Web terminal at an airport or even a Windows CE-based handheld computer, but HTTP is not a speedy transport method. In the real world, it is not wise to depend on OWA for speedy communications. This may change as HTTP standards improve, but for now, OWA is a slower, less capable substitute for Outlook, even though it permits remote access from a variety of clients, and works well (best, in fact) over slow links.

In the final analysis, OWA provides a crucial link between Exchange and the Web, which permits clients to access messages, calendars, contact lists, and so forth, across the Internet. Although OWA is an add-in, it supplies the interface between the Exchange Server and Internet Information Server. With this "missing link" supplied, any browser that supports HTTP can act as a basic interface to Exchange.

CHAPTER SUMMARY

In this chapter, we examined some of Outlook 98's features, including Outlook's import and export capabilities. Although Outlook 98 maintains a simple appearance, it presents a staggering range of options and capabilities. Outlook 98 consists of a sizable family of programs that range from message handling to contact management to a full-fledged calendaring program. All this functionality can impose a heavy load on client machines, which in turn, requires attention to its RAM and disk space requirements.

Outlook also provides flexible folder creation and management features, with added functionality found in its Organize feature. In this chapter, you learned how mail profiles may be used, as well as Contacts, Notes, and the Journal. You learned how to recover deleted items, and investigated some of Outlook 98's advanced features, such as junk email controls and shortcut mechanisms. You also learned about deleted item recovery in Outlook and about working with the Rules Wizard, and some of its shortcomings.

Finally, you learned that the Outlook Web Assistant may be used on platforms where Outlook 98 cannot run, such as on a Macintosh client. OWA essentially acts as a software link between Exchange Server and IIS to permit a special Web add-on to access Exchange through an IIS Web server.

6

KEY TERMS

- **Active Desktop**—A Microsoft creation in which an icon layer exposes the desktop shortcuts and a background HTML layer hosts Web-like desktop components.

- **Active Server**—The server component of Active Platform. Delivers server-side, script-based processes.

- **ActiveX**—The core technology for networked object interconnection.

- **Hypertext Markup Language (HTML)**—An industry standard markup language used in Web documents. HTML is designed to be vendor-neutral and platform-independent. The current version of HTML is 4, and its specification may be downloaded from the W3C at **http://www.w3.org/ TR/REC-html40/**.

- **Internet Message Access Protocol (IMAP)**—A message format and delivery protocol. IMAP is the successor to POP. Unlike POP, IMAP allows messages to be stored on the server, where they can be backed up. IMAP also permits remote users to download message headers, and then use this information to selectively download message bodies (POP does not support this capability, which is especially useful for remote users).

- **Internet Mail Service (IMS)**—Prior to Exchange version 5, this was the IMC, or Internet Mail Connector. It was renamed to reflect new functionality added with Exchange 5.5, which includes IMAP support among a variety of other enhancements.

- **Outlook Web Access (OWA)**—An HTTP-based Exchange client that runs on different platforms and uses less resources than Outlook 98.

- **personal information manager (PIM)**—Client software that manages daily tasks and communications.

- **Post Office Protocol (POP)**—An Internet standard for incoming mail.

- **self-registration**—The ability to gain access to Exchange public folders, without a named account.

- **Secure/Multipurpose Internet Mail Extensions (S/MIME)**—A large collection of file types, used to identify attachments to email messages and file types for Web documents. S/MIME represents a secure, encrypted implementation of MIME that prevents anyone who does not possess the necessary decryption keys from being able to examine the contents of such files. Exchange version 5.5 supports S/MIME in the IMS.

- **spamming**—Technically, any email messaging that is unsolicited. Usually, spam refers to bulk email in which an individual or organization is attempting to sell something.

REVIEW QUESTIONS

1. You have Exchange version 5.5 running on NT4 with Service Pack 3. Internet Information Server with Active Server Pages is installed. You would like to install Outlook Web Access on the sales team's laptops. The laptops are running Windows 98. What do you need to do to complete your objective?

   a. Ensure that you have installed OWA on Exchange Server by running SETUP.EXE, and see if OWA support is installed. If not, install it.

   b. Install Personal Web Services on each laptop.

   c. Install OWA on each laptop.

   d. All of the above.

   e. None of the above.

2. Your company wants to have public folder access available to all users so they can easily post questions to your technical support group. What must you do?

   a. Create a folder shortcut for each folder you want to make public.

   b. Order the self-registration CD kit (MS Part # 288-0561616).

   c. Assign each user an Exchange mailbox when he or she sends in the registration card.

   d. All of the above.

   e. None of the above.

3. A new employee is using Outlook 98. You cannot find a way for Outlook to access Exchange. Why?

   a. Outlook 98 is not used with Exchange.

    b. The installation of Outlook 98 is incomplete. Rerun setup from the Outlook Setup folder.

    c. The user needs to use Outlook Web Access.

    d. None of the above.

4. After you configure an offline folder, you cannot synchronize with the sever. True or False?

5. Of the following choices, which represent valid ways to change a meeting time for an event that is already created in Outlook? (Choose all that apply.)

    a. Double-click the meeting entry, and change the time manually.

    b. Select the meeting entry in the Calendar view, then click the Edit menu entry, select "Change time," and make the necessary changes.

    c. Drag the meeting from its current time slot in the Calendar to its new time slot elsewhere in the Calendar.

    d. Delete the current Meeting entry, and create a new one at the proper date and time.

6. If it is to work properly, which of the following elements does Outlook 98 require to be installed? (Choose all that apply.)

    a. Outlook Express

    b. Outlook 98

    c. Internet Explorer 3.02

    d. Internet Explorer 4.01

    e. Service Pack 3, if the client is on NT

7. Of the following choices, which represent valid ways to create rules for mail processing?

    a. Select the junk mail tab in the Organizer.

    b. With the inbox selected, use the Rules Wizard in the Tools menu.

    c. Use the Rules Wizard from the Tools menu from any view.

    d. None of the above.

8. When using the Organize feature, which of the following types of junk email are listed? (Choose all that apply.)

    a. Junk messages

    b. Spam

    c. Adult Content messages

    d. Unwanted email

9. Which of the following does Outlook Web Access use to communicate between the user and the Exchange Server?

    a. Internet Mail Service

    b. Third-party connectors

6

    c. HTTP

    d. All of the above

10. You have a high volume of mail that comes in from a listserv. Finding the information you need is difficult. You wish to organize this information by topic. You select the folder for this group, then you click on the Organize feature. What selection should you make after selecting Organize?

    a. Using Folders

    b. Using Colors

    c. Using Views

    d. Junk Email

11. Which of the following would you select to create a profile for Outlook 98?

    a. Tools | Options

    b. View | Profiles

    c. Other Shortcuts | Profiles

    d. Start | Settings | Control Panel | Mail

12. It is possible to create a Secure Sockets Layer connection for secure access to Outlook Web Access. True or False?

13. It is possible to import a list of contact information from an old mainframe computer. True or False?

14. The Organize button changes its context, depending on which view is displayed in Outlook. True or False?

15. Which of the following selections allows you to create a new folder?

    a. File | New | Folder

    b. File | Create | Folder

    c. Right-clicking in the Outlook bar with the Shortcuts

    d. All of the above

16. S/MIME is only available to Exchange users within a site. True or False?

17. Of the following Outlook utilities, which one would you use to track messages or message activity?

    a. Calendar

    b. Journal

    c. Notes

    d. Tasks

18. Of the following Outlook utilities, which one would you use to maintain a to-do list and track unfinished work?

    a. Calendar

    b. Journal

    c. Notes

    d. Tasks

19. Of the following Outlook utilities, which one would you use to store useful bits of information?

 a. Calendar

 b. Journal

 c. Notes

 d. Tasks

20. The Contact list in Outlook is maintained on a per-user basis. True or False?

HANDS-ON PROJECTS

6

 PROJECT 6.1

To Install Outlook 98:

 1. Install Outlook 98, taking care to select Corporate or Workgroup mode. Be aware of system and disk space requirements.

 2. Restart, and log on with Administrator privileges. At this point, do not launch Outlook 98. Select Start|Settings|Control Panel|Mail (or Mail And Fax).

 3. In the General tab, select Add to create a profile.

 4. Remove all options except Exchange Server support. Click Next.

 5. Select a name for your profile, such as Admin. Click Next.

 6. Enter the name of your Exchange Server and the name of your mailbox. Click Next.

 7. Indicate that this computer is not roaming (traveling).

 8. Accept the location for the personal address book, and change the name to ADMIN.PAB. Click Next.

 9. Do not allow Outlook to be part of the Startup group. Click Next, then click Finish.

 10. Test the connection. Log in with your account, and open Outlook '98. Select File|New|Mail Message. Create a message for a known good account.

 PROJECT 6.2

To create a rule for sorting incoming mail:

 1. In the Outlook Folder List, right-click, then select New Folder.

2. Name your new folder Test Rule Folder. Click OK.

3. Leave the Folder Contains option set to Mail Items.

4. Choose where you want your folder to appear. If you want it at the first level, choose Outlook Today. If you want the folder to be a subset of another folder, select the first level folder. Choose No for creating an Outlook bar shortcut (the default).

5. Confirm the creation of your new folder. You may have to click on a plus key (+) to see it.

6. Click on the Inbox.

7. Choose a mail item that belongs in your new folder.

8. Click Organize.

9. Choose Create A Rule To Move Messages From (notice that by default, Outlook 98 inserts the From option and a name based on the mail item you selected).

10. Select your new folder by clicking on the arrow on the right side.

11. Click Create.

CASE PROJECTS

1. Your company uses a mix of desktop computers for the office staff and notebooks for sales professionals in the field. How can you set up Exchange so that both groups of workers can access Exchange?

2. Your Exchange Server receives a large volume of technically oriented email. The information is valuable; however, the large volume prevents your users from being able to find the data in an efficient manner. How can you organize the chaos?

3. You have accepted a position at a large law firm. Currently, the lawyers track their projects using the program, Timeslips Deluxe. What could you do to increase the efficiency of the law firm?

4. A user has a notebook computer with Outlook 98 installed on it. The user downloaded the program directly from the Microsoft Web site. You add a PC card Ethernet adapter and attempt to bring it online using Exchange. You learn that this is not an option. What can you do?

CHAPTER SEVEN

EXCHANGE SERVER MANAGEMENT

Microsoft Exchange is a complex product that contains many features and options. At times, the sheer number and variety of settings and options may seem overwhelming. The key to using Microsoft Exchange successfully is knowing how to configure and manage it properly. This chapter discusses Microsoft Exchange's various configuration and management options, with a special emphasis on Exchange Administrator as the control center for this powerful messaging service.

AFTER READING THIS CHAPTER AND COMPLETING THE EXERCISES, YOU WILL BE ABLE TO:

- Understand the Exchange Administrator utility
- Interact with the Exchange hierarchy as it appears in Exchange Administrator
- Grasp relationships among common objects in Exchange Administrator
- Navigate Exchange Administrator menus and functions

EXCHANGE SERVER MANAGEMENT OVERVIEW

During day-to-day administration of a Microsoft Exchange organization, you'll need to add mailboxes, set up address book views, establish connections to other sites, establish connections to the Internet, set up directory replication between sites, and more. To do all of this, you'll use the *Exchange Administrator* utility.

The Microsoft Exchange Administrator is, in effect, the control panel for Microsoft Exchange. From within this tool, you can manage an entire Microsoft Exchange organization. Its configuration capabilities extend to provide control over sites, servers, connections, protocols, and more.

The Exchange Administrator also provides status information for Information Stores, monitors, connectors, protocols, services, directory synchronization, and recipients. However, this versatility comes at a price—Exchange Administrator's many menus and dialogs can be confusing and overwhelming for new users. At first, the interface might seem a bit unwieldy, but once you get used to it, you'll appreciate what a good job Exchange Administrator does at presenting its treasure trove of information.

STARTING EXCHANGE ADMINISTRATOR

To launch the Exchange Administrator, follow these steps:

1. Select Exchange Server from the Start|Programs|Exchange|Exchange Administrator menu item.

   This is a shortcut to *ADMIN.EXE*, which is located in the \ExchSrvr\Bin directory (where Microsoft Exchange is installed). What you must do immediately after starting Exchange Administrator for the first time is to connect to an Exchange Server.

2. If you have not yet specified an Exchange Server, the Connect To Server dialog box should appear as shown in Figure 7.1. Enter the name of the Exchange Server to which you wish to connect. You may click the Browse button to display a graphical listing of the Exchange Servers in your organization, and select a server from that list, if you prefer.

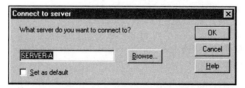

Figure 7.1   The Connect To Server dialog box.

You can control and configure multiple Exchange Servers from the Exchange Administrator; however, you must always be connected to at least one Exchange Server.

3. Once you've selected an Exchange Server, you may check the Set As Default checkbox to designate the chosen server as your default connection. Then, you will no longer be prompted to select a server when you launch the Exchange Administrator.

4. After making your selection, click OK.

The Exchange Administrator program attempts to connect to whatever server you specify. If this connection attempt completes successfully, the Exchange Administrator interface appears.

The Exchange Administrator Interface

7

As it appears in Figure 7.2, the initial Exchange Administrator interface displays your entire Microsoft Exchange organization. By selecting and expanding objects, you can view your organization at whatever level of detail you choose.

The Exchange Administrator title bar reveals the server name, site name, and the name of the currently selected object. The left-hand pane of the Exchange Administrator window shows your Exchange hierarchy, and can display every object within your Exchange organization. At the same time, the right-hand pane of the Exchange Administrator window displays details about whatever container object is currently selected on the left side of the window.

The Exchange hierarchy appears as a collection of component objects (that is, sites, servers, connectors, protocols, recipients, and so on) in a folder-like format quite reminiscent of the Windows NT Explorer. Every object displayed in the Exchange Administrator has an associated icon. Like the file directory hierarchy presented in Windows Explorer, many of these component objects contain additional objects themselves.

Plus and minus signs appear to the left of most objects in the hierarchy, to indicate that an object contains other objects. An object that lacks a plus or a minus sign indicates that it contains no additional objects. Clicking a plus sign expands the associated object, whereas clicking a minus sign collapses an already-expanded associated object.

When you select an object in the left-hand pane, all objects contained within or associated with that object appear in the right-hand pane, in much the same way that nested folders and files appear in the right-hand pane when a folder is selected using the Windows NT Explorer.

As Figure 7.2 shows, the top item in the Exchange hierarchy is your organization's name, as entered when Exchange was installed. To collapse the

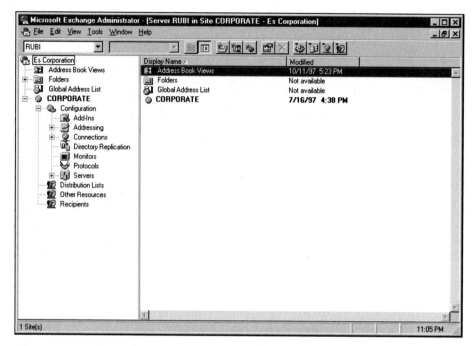

Figure 7.2   The Exchange Administrator interface.

view of the entire organization, simply double-click the organization's name. This allows you to navigate the hierarchy from the top down.

If this is your organization's first Exchange Server, or you have not yet established connections to the Exchange Server you've selected, only a small number of objects will appear in the hierarchy. After you've added connectors and other objects, however, you'll be able to navigate the Exchange Administrator to see the results upon your Exchange hierarchy.

THE EXCHANGE OBJECT HIERARCHY

Figure 7.3 shows the basic object hierarchy as it appears in Exchange Administrator, from the highest level down to the lowest. The following list describes this object hierarchy in some detail:

- **<Organization Name>** There is only one Organization object in any Microsoft Exchange installation, and it always appears at the top of the hierarchy. All other objects are secondary to the Organization object. The organization name is used for message addressing, and it may not be changed after installation.

- **<Organization Name>/Folders** The Folders object is the parent container for all organization folder information. The information

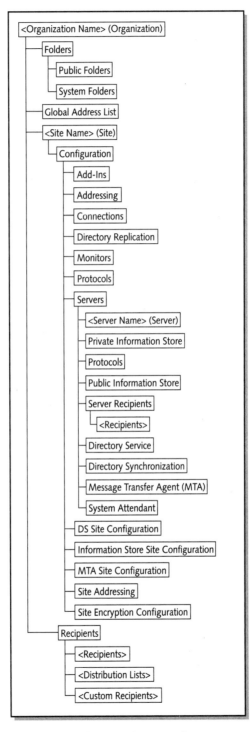

Figure 7.3   Object hierarchy of the Exchange Administrator.

7

displayed here is common to all sites within an organization. Two types of objects appear beneath the Folders object: Public Folders and System Folders.

- **<Organization Name>/Folders/Public Folders** The Public Folders object contains configuration information for all public folders in the organization. When a public folder is changed, the information contained in the Public Folders object causes that change to be copied to every replica of that folder throughout your organization. Selecting the Public Folders object displays your organization's public folders and their replicas.

- **<Organization Name>/Folders/System Folders** The System Folders object is a parent container for the following objects: Eforms Registry, Offline Address Book, and Schedule+ Free/Busy.

- **<Organization Name>/Folders/System Folders/Eforms Registry** This folder contains all the organization forms that have been created in your organization. It is a parent container for the following objects: Organization Forms Library, Events Root, and the EventConfig_Server.

- **<Organization Name>/Folders/System Folders/Eforms Registry/Organization Forms Library** The Organization Forms Library object is a public folder containing electronic forms. By default, when a form is saved to a public folder, it is made available to all Microsoft Exchange users.

- **<Organization Name>/Folders/System Folders/Eforms Registry/Events Root** This object contains folders that maintain event configuration information for all Exchange Servers in your organization.

- **<Organization Name>/Folders/System Folders/Eforms Registry/EventConfig_Server** The EventConfig_Server object contains folders that house event configuration information for specific Exchange Servers in your organization.

- **<Organization Name>/Folders/System Folders/Offline Address Book** This object contains lists of recipients to whom remote users can address messages. It is a parent container for multiple offline address books. Each site in an organization appears as an Offline Address Book object. Remote users can download offline address books and use them to send mail to any recipient in the Exchange organization.

- **<Organization Name>/Folders/System Folders/Schedule+ Free/Busy** This is a parent container for Schedule+ Free/Busy folders. Each site is represented by a Schedule+ Free/Busy folder. Every new mailbox results in an entry in the Schedule+ Free/Busy Information public folder for the current Exchange site and for the associated Windows NT account. Every time a change is made to a user's schedule, the appropriate site's Schedule+ Free/Busy folder is updated automatically. Through Microsoft Schedule+, users may set permissions for their free/busy information to prevent others from publishing it.

- **<Organization Name>/Global Address List** This object lists all your organization's mailboxes, distribution lists, public folders, and custom recipients.

- **<Organization Name>/<Site Name>** The Site object (and below) is where you'll spend most of your time when using the Exchange Administrator. There is one *Site object* for each site in your Exchange organization. The first site is added to the hierarchy when you install the first Exchange Server in your organization. A site is comprised of one or more Exchange Servers that have been grouped together. Each defined site has its own Site object. The Site object is a parent container for the following objects: Configuration and Recipients.

- **<Organization Name>/<Site Name>/Configuration Container** The *Configuration container object* contains configuration information about a specific site. This object is a parent container for the following objects: Add-Ins, Addressing, Connections, Directory Replication, Monitors, Protocols, Servers, DS Site Configuration, Information Store Site Configuration, MTA Site Configuration, Site Addressing, and Site Encryption Configuration.

- **<Organization Name>/<Site Name>/Configuration Container/Add-Ins** The Add-Ins object is a container for any third-party services that don't require mailboxes. The AppleTalk interchange is an example of such a third-party service.

- **<Organization Name>/<Site Name>/Configuration Container/Addressing** This object is for all directory entries dealing with Microsoft Exchange address generation. The Addressing object is a parent container for the following objects: Details Templates, E-Mail Address Generator, and One-Off Address Templates.

- **<Organization Name>/<Site Name>/Configuration Container/Addressing/Details Templates** This object maintains localized templates (by language and country) that specify how recipient object details are displayed.

7

- **<Organization Name>/<Site Name>/Configuration Container/Addressing/E-Mail Address Generator** This is a container for email generators. Email generators automatically generate email addresses for newly created Exchange recipients. The following email generators are contained in this object: cc:Mail Email Address Generator, Internet Email Address Generator, Microsoft Mail Address Generator, and X.400 Email Address Generator.

- **<Organization Name>/<Site Name>/Configuration Container/Addressing/One-Off Address Templates** This object maintains localized templates (by language and country) used to determine the format of new email addresses entered by a user when the email address is not in the Global Address List or Personal Address Book.

- **<Organization Name>/<Site Name>/Configuration Container/Connections Container** The *Connections container object* contains all connectors used to link Exchange sites with other Exchange sites, Microsoft Mail systems, or other foreign messaging systems. This is a very important object if you have connections to any of these systems. The Connections Container object is a parent container for the following objects: cc:Mail Connector, Internet Mail Service, Microsoft Mail Connector, Site Connector, X.400 Connector, Microsoft Mail Connector for AppleTalk Networks (Quarterdeck Mail), Dynamic RAS Connector, Directory Exchange Requestor, Directory Exchange Server, DirSync Server, and Remote DirSync Requestor.

- **<Organization Name>/<Site Name>/Configuration Container/Connections Container/cc:Mail Connector** The cc:Mail Connector object configures message transfer with Lotus cc:Mail systems. Chapter 14 discusses this object in detail.

- **<Organization Name>/<Site Name>/Configuration Container/Connections Container/Internet Mail Service** This object configures message transfer with Simple Mail Transfer Protocol (SMTP) based messaging systems. Chapter 14 discusses this object in detail.

- **<Organization Name>/<Site Name>/Configuration Container/Connections Container/Microsoft Mail Connector** This object configures message transfer with Microsoft Mail for PC Networks, Microsoft Mail for AppleTalk Networks, and Microsoft Mail For PC Networks gateways. Chapter 14 discusses this object in detail.

- **<Organization Name>/<Site Name>/Configuration Container/Connections Container/Site Connector** The Site connector object is used to create a link between Microsoft Exchange sites on the same network. Chapter 14 discusses site connectors in detail.

- **<Organization Name>/<Site Name>/Configuration Container/Connections Container/X.400 Connector** The X.400 Connector object is used to create a link between Microsoft Exchange sites over an X.400 network. It is also used to establish a link to a foreign X.400 messaging system.

- **<Organization Name>/<Site Name>/Configuration Container/Connections Container/Microsoft Mail Connector For AppleTalk Networks (Quarterdeck Mail)** This connector is used to configure message transfer with AppleTalk networks.

- **<Organization Name>/<Site Name>/Configuration Container/Connections Container/Dynamic RAS Connector** This connector object is used to create a link between Microsoft Exchange sites over a Windows NT RAS connection. Chapter 14 discusses this connector in detail.

- **<Organization Name>/<Site Name>/Configuration Container/Connections Container/Directory Exchange Requestor** This object is used by an Exchange Server to request directory information from other email systems (for example, Microsoft Mail).

- **<Organization Name>/<Site Name>/Configuration Container/Connections Container/Directory Exchange Server** This object is used by an Exchange Server to perform directory synchronization with external messaging systems.

- **<Organization Name>/<Site Name>/Configuration Container/Connections Container/DirSync Server** This object processes inbound updates from directory requestors and adds the updates into its own directory as custom recipient objects.

- **<Organization Name>/<Site Name>/Configuration Container/ Connections Container/Remote DirSync Requestor** This object is used by remote directory requestors to authenticate and respond to directory requestors during directory exchange.

- **<Organization Name>/<Site Name>/Configuration Container/Directory Replication** This object contains all directory replication connectors for Microsoft Exchange. These connectors result in a two-way exchange of directory updates. The Directory Replication

7

object is a parent container for the Directory Replication Connector object, which is used for the sharing of recipient information between sites.

- **<Organization Name>/<Site Name>/Configuration Container/Monitors** This object contains tools that monitor an Exchange organization's servers and the links between the servers. It is a parent container for the following objects: Server Monitors and Link Monitors.

- **<Organization Name>/<Site Name>/Configuration Container/Monitors/Server Monitors** This object monitors the status of an Exchange Server's services, providing warnings and alerts if an error occurs. Chapter 12 discusses Server Monitors in detail.

- **<Organization Name>/<Site Name>/Configuration Container/Monitors/Link Monitors** This object monitors the status of messaging connections. It does this by monitoring the amount of time it takes for messages to bounce between Exchange Servers. Administrative users can be alerted if the amount of time is longer than expected. Chapter 12 also covers Link Monitors in detail.

- **<Organization Name>/<Site Name>/Configuration Container/Protocols** This object contains the Internet protocols supported by Microsoft Exchange. It is a parent container for the following objects: IMAP4, HTTP, LDAP, NNTP, and POP3.

- **<Organization Name>/<Site Name>/Configuration Container/Protocols/IMAP4** IMAP4 stands for the Internet Message Access Protocol version 4. Users with an IMAP4 client can access mail in their Exchange Server mailboxes using this object. Such a client can also read and post messages to public folders, as well as access other users' mailboxes to which the user has been granted permission.

- **<Organization Name>/<Site Name>/Configuration Container/Protocols/HTTP** HTTP stands for Hypertext Transfer Protocol. When used with Windows NT's Active Server components, this connector allows users to access their Exchange Server mailboxes using most Internet browsers.

- **<Organization Name>/<Site Name>/Configuration Container/Protocols/LDAP** LDAP stands for Lightweight Directory Access Protocol, an Internet directory protocol. With this object, clients with appropriate security permissions can use LDAP-enabled programs to browse, read, and search directories. This object can be configured to specify authentication forms, permit anonymous access, permit searching, and more.

- **<Organization Name>/<Site Name>/Configuration Container/Protocols/NNTP** NNTP stands for Network News Transfer Protocol, an Internet protocol used for newsgroup support. With this connector, you can configure site defaults, message content, time-out options, and so forth.

- **<Organization Name>/<Site Name>/Configuration Container/Protocols/POP3** POP3 stands for Post Office Protocol version 3. This connector enables users with POP3 clients to retrieve their messages from their Exchange Server mailbox.

- **<Organization Name>/<Site Name>/Configuration Container/Servers** This object contains a list of all of the Exchange Servers in the parent site.

- **<Organization Name>/<Site Name>/Configuration Container/Servers/<Server Name>** The *Server object* represents a specific server in the server list. Each server is itself a parent container for the following objects: Private Information Store, Protocols, Public Information Store, Server Recipients, Directory Service, Directory Synchronization, Message Transfer Agent (MTA), and System Attendant.

- **<Organization Name>/<Site Name>/Configuration Container/Servers/<Server Name>/Private Information Store** This object stores all messages sent to individual mailboxes. The Private Information Store object is a parent container for the following objects: Logons and Mailbox Resources.

- **<Organization Name>/<Site Name>/Configuration Container/Servers/<Server Name>/Private Information Store/Logons** This object displays information about who is currently logged on to mailboxes.

- **<Organization Name>/<Site Name>/Configuration Container/Servers/<Server Name>/Private Information Store/ Mailbox Resources** This object displays detailed resource usage information about each mailbox. For example, from this object, you can see how much disk space an individual user's mailbox is taking up.

- **<Organization Name>/<Site Name>/Configuration Container/Servers/<Server Name>/Protocols** This object contains configuration dialogs for the Internet protocols discussed earlier in the Site/Configuration Container/Protocols object. This object is a parent container for the following objects: IMAP4, LDAP, NNTP, and POP3.

- **\<Organization Name\>/\<Site Name\>/Configuration Container/Servers/\<Server Name\>/Public Information Store/Server Replication Status** This object stores all messages posted to public folders. The Public Information Store object is a parent container for the following objects: Folder Replication Status, Logons, and Public Folder Resources.

- **\<Organization Name\>/\<Site Name\>/Configuration Container/Servers/\<Server Name\>/Public Information Store/Folder Replication Status** This object displays the status of public folder replication within the selected site.

- **\<Organization Name\>/\<Site Name\>/Configuration Container/Servers/\<Server Name\>/Public Information Store/Logons** This object displays information about who is currently logged on to public folders.

- **\<Organization Name\>/\<Site Name\>/Configuration Container/Servers/\<Server Name\>/Public Information Store/Public Folder Resources** This object displays detailed information about resource usage for each public folder. For example, from this object, you can see how much disk space an individual public folder is using.

- **\<Organization Name\>/\<Site Name\>/Configuration Container/Servers/\<Server Name\>/Server Recipients** The *Server Recipients container object* is a parent container for all Exchange recipients whose mailbox is housed on this server.

- **\<Organization Name\>/\<Site Name\>/Configuration Container/Servers/\<Server Name\>/Server Recipients/ \<recipients\>** The Recipients object contains a list of individual recipients whose mailboxes are contained on one of the Exchange Servers in the current site.

- **\<Organization Name\>/\<Site Name\>/Configuration Container/Servers/\<Server Name\>/Directory Service** This object contains configuration information about directory handling within the server's site.

- **\<Organization Name\>/\<Site Name\>/Configuration Container/Servers/\<Server Name\>/Directory Synchronization** This object contains general properties for Exchange directory synchronization. Also called the Exchange DXA.

- **\<Organization Name\>/\<Site Name\>/Configuration Container/Servers/\<Server Name\>/Message Transfer Agent (MTA)** This object transfers messages from one server to another or to external connectors.

- **<Organization Name>/<Site Name>/Configuration Container/Servers/<Server Name>/System Attendant** This object configures the Microsoft Exchange service that is responsible for managing log files. The System Attendant service starts all other Microsoft Exchange services.

- **<Organization Name>/<Site Name>/Configuration Container/DS Site Configuration** This object contains general Directory Service properties for the server and the server's site.

- **<Organization Name>/<Site Name>/Configuration Container/ Information Store Site Configuration** This object contains general properties for all the Information Stores within the server's site.

- **<Organization Name>/<Site Name>/Configuration Container/MTA Site Configuration** This object contains general properties for all of the Message Transfer Agents in the server's site.

- **<Organization Name>/<Site Name>/Configuration Container/Site Addressing** This object contains general site addressing information used during message routing.

- **<Organization Name>/<Site Name>/Configuration Container/Site Encryption Configuration** This object can be used to configure site encryption. Advanced security features can be configured by accessing the properties of this object. Chapter 11 covers the Site Encryption Configuration object in detail.

- **<Organization Name>/<Site Name>/Recipients/Mailbox** The Mailbox object is a private container that stores messaging data.

- **<Organization Name>/<Site Name>/Recipients/Distribution Lists** This object is made up of a group of individual recipients. Email can be sent to the group addressed as a single recipient or email address.

- **<Organization Name>/<Site Name>/Recipients/Custom Recipients** This object is for foreign recipients whose mailboxes are not contained on an Exchange Server.

- **<Organization Name>/<Site Name>/Recipients/Microsoft Schedule+ Free/Busy Connector** This object transfers free/busy scheduling information with Schedule+ for Microsoft Mail. Chapter 14 discusses this object in further detail.

THE EXCHANGE ADMINISTRATOR MENUS

The Exchange Administrator contains six items on its main menu: File, Edit, View, Tools, Window, and Help. A configurable toolbar appears below the main menu, from which you may access menu items quickly.

THE FILE MENU

As shown in Figure 7.4, the File menu may be used for many tasks. From it, you can connect to other servers, create new connections and objects, and modify and view object properties.

The File menu contains the following menu items:

- Connect To Server
- Close
- New Mailbox
- New Distribution List
- New Custom Recipient
- New Other
- Save Window Contents
- Properties
- Duplicate
- Exit

All of these menu items are covered in detail in the following list:

- **File | Connect To Server** Choose this menu item to connect to another Exchange Server. You'll be presented with the Connect To Server dialog box (shown earlier in Figure 7.1) where you can type in the name of the Exchange Server to connect to. Clicking the Browse button will display a list of Exchange Servers in your organization. Select the desired Exchange Server, and click OK. This fills in the name of the server in the Connect To Server dialog box for you. Once you are connected to an Exchange Server, the view will change to present the Exchange hierarchy as seen from that particular Exchange Server. The view differs because of settings, objects, and connectors that may be specific only to the chosen Exchange Server.

Figure 7.4   The File menu.

You can connect to multiple servers while in the Exchange Administrator. Note that each Exchange Server that you connect to is presented in its own window; therefore, only one connection may be in the foreground at any one time.

If you are connected to more than one Exchange Server, objects are created on the current (that is, foreground) server. Therefore, make sure that you are working with the correct server when creating objects.

- **File | Close** Select this menu item to close the connection to the current Exchange Server. If you are still connected to another Exchange Server, the view will change to display a window for that Exchange Server. After all connections to Exchange Servers are closed, no Exchange hierarchy views are displayed. The Exchange Administrator remains open (to connect to an Exchange Server) but only with limited menu options.

- **File | New Mailbox** Select the New Mailbox menu item to add a new mailbox to the currently selected site. If you do not have a site selected, select one before adding a mailbox. To add a mailbox, the site should be expanded, and the Recipients container selected. If you fail to select the Recipient container, however, the Exchange Administrator politely alerts you and offers to automatically expand the site and select the container for you. Next, the new mailbox dialog displays (see Figure 7.5). Fill in the appropriate information, select the corresponding Windows NT account (by clicking the Primary Windows NT Account button), and then click OK.

- **File | New Distribution List** Choose this menu item to create a new distribution list recipient. Like the New Mailbox menu item, distribution lists must be created in the Recipients container. Next, the new distribution list dialog displays (see Figure 7.6). Fill in the appropriate information, and click OK.

- **File | New Custom Recipient** Choose this menu item to create a Recipient object for a mailbox located in a foreign messaging system, such as cc:Mail, Microsoft Mail, or SMTP.

- **File | New Other** Selecting this menu item opens a submenu (see Figure 7.7), providing you the ability to create other types of Microsoft Exchange objects. The following items appear in the submenu, representing other objects that can be created: Server Monitor, Link Monitor, Recipients Container, Address Book View, Address Book View Container, MTA Transport Stack, X.400 Connector, Dynamic RAS Connector, Site Connector, Directory Replication Connector,

7

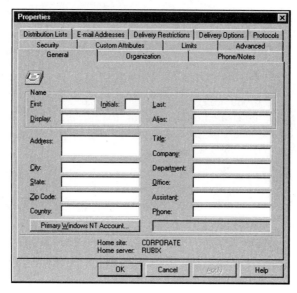

Figure 7.5   The new mailbox dialog box.

DirSync Requestor, DirSync Server, Remote DirSync Requestor, Information Store, Newsfeed, and Internet Mail Service. A brief description of each of these objects follows:

- **File | New Other | Server Monitor** Select this item to create an object that monitors the condition of one or more servers. Server Monitors can be configured to produce alerts when certain problems occur. Chapter 12 discusses Server Monitor objects in detail.

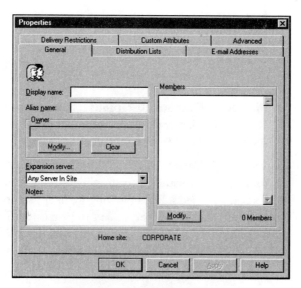

Figure 7.6   The new distribution list dialog box.

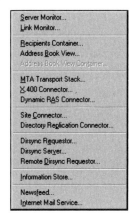

Figure 7.7   The New Other menu.

7

- **File | New Other | Link Monitor** Select this item to create an object that monitors messaging connections between Exchange Server sites and servers. Like Server Monitors, Link Monitors can be configured to generate alerts when certain problems occur. Chapter 12 discusses Link Monitor objects in detail.

- **File | New Other | Recipients Container** Choose this item to create custom recipient containers to hold recipients of your choosing. For example, you might add an Internet recipients container to hold the SMTP addresses of custom recipients.

- **File | New Other | Address Book View** Choose this menu item to configure the view of the Address Book.

- **File | New Other | Address Book View Container** Select this menu item to modify the configuration of the Address Book View Container.

- **File | New Other | MTA Transport Stack** Choose this menu item to define the transport protocol for newly created Dynamic RAS Connectors or X.400 Connectors. Before selecting this menu item, verify that you have all the necessary transport software properly configured in Windows NT.

- **File | New Other | X.400 Connector** Choose this menu item to define an X.400 connection to another Microsoft Exchange site or to a foreign system. An MTA transport stack must be defined before installing an X.400 Connector.

- **File | New Other | Dynamic RAS Connector** Select this menu item to establish a transitory remote access connection between Exchange Servers. A dynamic RAS connection can be made over a modem, ISDN, or X.25 system—assuming the appropriate MTA transport stack is installed.

- **File | New Other | Site Connector** Select this menu item to establish a connection between two Microsoft Exchange sites, where the two sites are on the same network.

- **File | New Other | Directory Replication** Connector Choose this menu item to share directories between two Microsoft Exchange sites.

- **File | New Other | DirSync Requestor** Choose this menu item to set up a directory synchronization requestor compatible with messaging systems supporting the MS Mail 3.x directory synchronization protocol. Directory Requestors are usually used by a messaging server to request updates from an MS Mail Post Office configured as a directory synchronization server. See Chapter 14 for more information.

- **File | New Other | DirSync Server** Select this menu item to set up a directory synchronization server compatible with the MS Mail 3.x directory synchronization protocol. See Chapter 14 for details.

- **File | New Other | Remote DirSync Requestor** Select this menu item to specify that a foreign messaging system will make directory requests from the selected Exchange Server DirSync server. See Chapter 14 for more information.

- **File | New Other | Information Store** Choose this menu item to create a public or private Information Store. Note that an Information Store can only be created if the selected Exchange Server does not already have an Information Store.

- **File | New Other | Newsfeed** Choosing this menu item starts a wizard designed to set up an NNTP newsfeed. Before selecting this menu item, get your ISP's Usenet site name, the names (or IP addresses) of your ISP's host servers, and the username and password your Exchange Server will use to log on to your ISP.

- **File | New Other | Internet Mail Service** Selecting this menu item launches a wizard designed to configure the Internet Mail Service to send and receive messages from the Internet. See Chapter 9 for details.

- **File | Save Window Contents** Select this menu item to save the contents of the object window to a *comma-separated text file (CSV)*. This might be useful for organizational documentation purposes.

- **File | Properties** Select this menu item to view (and optionally change) the properties of a particular Microsoft Exchange object or container. Often, double-clicking an object or container also brings up the properties.

- **File | Duplicate** After highlighting a recipient or distribution list, choose this menu item to make a copy of that object. The copy will be created in the recipients container holding the original object.

- **File | Exit** Selecting this menu item closes your Exchange Server connections and exits the Exchange Administrator.

THE EDIT MENU

From the Edit menu, you can do the standard Windows editing tasks. The Edit menu contains the following menu items:

- **Edit | Undo** After cutting, copying, or pasting text, select this menu item to undo text commands. Because most text operations in the Exchange Administrator occur within a dialog box, however, this menu item is not accessible. Press Ctrl+Z to undo when in a dialog box.

- **Edit | Cut, Copy, and Paste** Select these menu items to perform the standard Windows editing actions.

- **Edit | Delete** Select this menu item to delete the currently selected object from the Exchange hierarchy. Be careful, after an object is deleted, the action cannot be undone.

- **Edit | Select All** When viewing a recipient container's objects, select this menu item to select all the objects that are in that recipient container.

THE VIEW MENU

The View menu (see Figure 7.8) is used to filter and sort recipient containers' objects for viewing in the Exchange Administrator. This can be helpful, because as your Exchange organization grows, it can become difficult to find a particular recipient. The View menu contains the following menu items: Mailboxes, Distribution Lists, Custom Recipients, Public Folders, All, Hidden Recipients, Columns, Sort By, Font, Move Split Bar, Toolbar, and Status Bar. All of these menu items are discussed in detail in the following list:

- **View | Mailboxes, Distribution Lists, Custom Recipients, Public Folders, and All** These menu items are used to filter the displayed

Figure 7.8   The View menu.

recipient objects. Select the type of filtering you desire. A check mark will appear next to the current filter type. Select All to view all objects in the recipient container.

- **View | Hidden Recipients** Some recipients are designated as hidden and, therefore, don't show up in the Global Address List. Select this menu item to display hidden recipients in addition to the non-hidden recipients.

- **View | Columns** Choose this menu item to change the columns that appear in the right side of the Exchange Administrator. A dialog box appears, whereby you can add and remove columns for display (see Figure 7.9). Column widths can also be adjusted using this dialog box, although you might find it easier to change column widths by using your mouse in the Exchange Administrator.

- **View | Sort By** Select this menu item to sort the objects displayed in the right side of the Exchange Administrator. A submenu appears, whereby you can opt to sort by Display Name or by Last Modified Date.

- **View | Font** Choosing this menu item brings up a Font dialog box, from which you can select a font to display object information in the Exchange Administrator. This is particularly useful when viewing the Exchange Administrator output from a distance—from a video projector, for example.

- **View | Move Split Bar** Select this menu item to adjust the location of the dividing line between the left and right sides of the Exchange Administrator. You will likely find it easier to simply use your mouse to move the split bar.

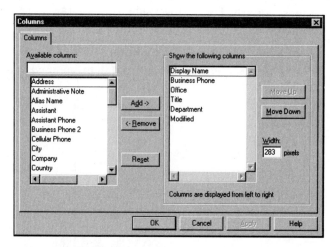

Figure 7.9   The Columns dialog box.

- **View | Status Bar** This menu item is used to toggle the status bar (at the bottom of the Exchange Administrator) on and off. The status bar displays useful information (object counts, for instance), so you'll probably want to keep the status bar on.

- **View | Toolbar** By default, the toolbar appears directly below the menus. This menu item toggles the toolbar on and off.

THE TOOLS MENU

The Tools menu (see Figure 7.10) is used to perform various administrative functions. After the File menu, the Tools menu is used most often. The Tools menu contains the following menu items: Directory Import, Directory Export, Extract Windows NT Account List, Extract NetWare Account List, Find Recipients, Move Mailbox, Add To Address Book View, Clean Mailbox, Start Monitor, Track Message, Forms Administrator, News Group Hierarchies, Save Connections On Exit, Save Connections Now, Customize Toolbar, and Options. All of these menu items are discussed in detail in the following list:

- **Tools | Directory Import** The Exchange Administrator can create or modify recipients from a comma-separated text file. The Directory Import menu item displays a dialog box from which you can specify the file and appropriate options (see Figure 7.11). You can create comma-delimited files using the Microsoft Exchange Migration Wizard or by using directory export tools in other messaging systems.

- **Tools | Directory Export** Choose this menu item to create a text file of the current site's directory information. This information can be imported into other messaging systems.

- **Tools | Extract Windows NT Account List** Select the Extract Windows NT Account List menu item to bring up a dialog box

Figure 7.10   The Tools menu.

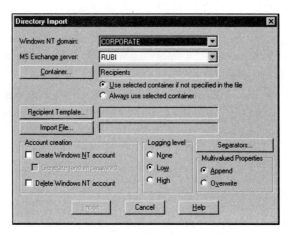

Figure 7.11 The Directory Import dialog box.

(see Figure 7.12) from which you can produce a comma-separated file (CSV), containing user information from a Windows NT domain user list. The contents of this file can then be imported into Microsoft Exchange (using the aforementioned Directory Import menu item) to create Exchange recipients.

- **Tools | Extract NetWare Account List** Choose the Extract NetWare Account List menu item to display a dialog box (see Figure 7.13) from which you can produce a comma-separated file (CSV), containing user information from a Novell NetWare account list. The contents of this file can then be imported into Microsoft Exchange (using the aforementioned Directory Import menu item) to create Exchange recipients. Chapter 14 addresses NetWare issues in relation to Exchange Server.

- **Tools | Find Recipients** Select this menu item to search your entire organization for a particular recipient. The criteria are entered using the Find Recipients dialog box (see Figure 7.14).

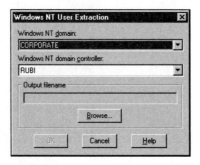

Figure 7.12 The Windows NT User Extraction dialog box.

Figure 7.13   The NetWare User Extraction dialog box.

7

- **Tools | Move Mailbox**   Select this menu item to move the selected mailbox from its current server to another server within the same Exchange site.

- **Tools | Add To Address Book View**   Choose this menu item to add the selected recipient to an Address Book view.

- **Tools | Clean Mailbox**   Select this menu item to delete messages in the selected recipient's mailbox. The criteria for deletion are entered using the Clean Mailbox dialog box.

- **Tools | Start Monitor**   After selecting a Server Monitor or Link Monitor, selecting this menu item starts the monitor.

- **Tools | Track Message**   Select this menu item to bring up the Message Tracking Center—a tool for tracking message routing as it

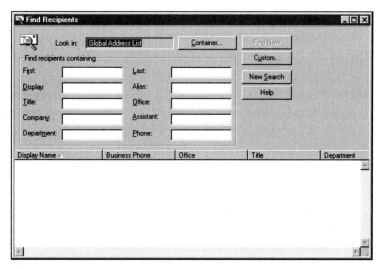

Figure 7.14   The Find Recipients dialog box.

travels through an Exchange organization. Chapter 12 discusses message tracking.

■ **Tools | Forms Administrator** Choose this menu item to bring up the Organization Forms Library Administrator. This dialog box lets you manage forms that were created using the Exchange Client's (or Outlook's) form designer tool.

■ **Tools | NewsGroup Hierarchies** Select this menu item to convert an existing Exchange public folder scheme into a hierarchy of newsgroup public folders.

■ **Tools | Save Connections On Exit** Select this menu item to specify that you want information about your current Exchange Server connections to be saved when you exit the Exchange Administrator. The next time you start the Exchange Administrator, the saved connection information will be used to try and reestablish connections to the Exchange Servers you were connected to earlier.

■ **Tools | Save Connections Now** Choose this menu item to save current Exchange Server connection information.

■ **Tools | Customize Toolbar** Select this menu item to modify the icons that appear on the toolbar. This is helpful if you want to add or remove icons for your own preferences.

■ **Tools | Options** Choose this menu item to bring up a dialog box of options that affect what information is displayed in the various dialog boxes, as well as how it is displayed (see Figure 7.15). The Auto Naming tab is used to specify the format for your display and alias names. The Permissions tab is used to specify object-related permission information. The File Format tab is used to specify the default file settings for directory import and export functions.

THE WINDOW MENU

The Window menu is the standard Window menu you are used to. The Refresh menu item is particularly useful, because it requests updated information from the Exchange Server and updates information that is currently displayed in the Exchange Administrator.

THE HELP MENU

This, too, is a standard Windows menu. The Microsoft Exchange Server Help Topics menu item brings up the standard help information for Microsoft Exchange. The Books Online menu item launches your Web browser and opens the official Microsoft Exchange documentation. The About Microsoft Exchange Server menu item displays version and copyright information. A System Info

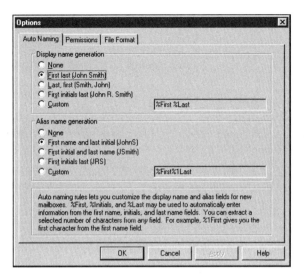

Figure 7.15   The Options dialog box.

button can be clicked to obtain detailed information about the Windows NT computer you are currently using.

CHAPTER SUMMARY

A key to using Microsoft Exchange successfully is knowing how to configure and manage the product properly. During the day-to-day administration of your Microsoft Exchange organization, you'll use the Exchange Administrator to manage an entire Microsoft Exchange organization, including configuring sites, servers, connections, and protocols. The Exchange Administrator also provides status information for Information Stores, monitors, connectors, protocols, services, synchronization, and recipients. You can control and configure multiple Exchange Servers from the Exchange Administrator; however, you are always connected to at least one Exchange Server. The first time you start the Exchange Administrator, the Connect To Server dialog box appears.

The Exchange Administrator interface displays your entire Microsoft Exchange organization. By selecting and expanding objects, you can view your organization at any level of detail you desire. The left side of the Exchange Administrator window shows your Exchange hierarchy, displaying every object that is in your Exchange organization. The right side of the Exchange Administrator window displays in detail the container object currently selected on the left side of the window.

The Exchange hierarchy displays component objects (sites, servers, connectors, protocols, recipients, and so forth) in a directory/subdirectory format. When you select an object in the left side of the window, the objects associated with that object appear in the right side of the window.

There is only one Organization object in a Microsoft Exchange installation, and it is always at the top of the Exchange hierarchy. All other objects are secondary to the organization object. There is one Site object for each site in your Exchange organization. The first site is added to the hierarchy when you install the first Exchange Server in your organization. A site is one or more Exchange Servers that have been grouped together. Each defined site has its own Site object. The Configuration container object contains configuration information about a specific site.

The Exchange Administrator contains six items on the menu: File, Edit, View, Tools, Window, and Help. From the File menu, you can connect to other servers, create new connections and objects, and modify and view object properties. The View menu is used to filter and sort recipient containers' objects for viewing in the Exchange Administrator. The Tools menu is used to perform various administrative functions and includes commands such as Directory Import, Extract Windows NT Account List, Extract NetWare Account List, Move Mailbox, Clean Mailbox, Start Monitor, and Track Message. The Extract Windows NT Account List menu item is used to produce a comma-separated file (CSV) containing user information from a Windows NT domain user list. The Extract NetWare Account List menu item is used to produce a CSV file containing user information from a Novell NetWare account list. The contents of these files can then be imported into Microsoft Exchange to create Exchange recipients.

KEY TERMS

- **ADMIN.EXE**—The file name of the Exchange Administrator program.

- **comma-separated text file (CSV)**—A text file containing data in a standard, easy-to-read format. Used for exporting and importing user information.

- **Configuration container object**—The object that maintains configuration information about a specific site.

- **Connect To Server dialog box**—Displays the first time you start the Exchange Administrator as well as when you opt to connect to another server. Used to enter the name of the Exchange Server that you want to connect to.

- **Connections container object**—The object that maintains all connectors used to link Microsoft Exchange with other Exchange sites, Microsoft Mail systems, or other foreign messaging systems.

- **Directory Import menu item**—Used to create or modify recipients from a comma-separated text file.

- **Exchange Administrator**—The control panel for Microsoft Exchange. From the Exchange Administrator, you can manage an entire Microsoft Exchange organization.

- **Extract NetWare Account List menu item**—Used to produce a comma-separated file (CSV) containing user information from a NetWare account list.

- **Extract Windows NT Account List menu item**—Used to produce a comma-separated file (CSV) containing user information from a Windows NT domain user list.

- **Organization object**—The top-most object in the Exchange hierarchy. All other objects are secondary to the organization object.

- **Server object**—Represents a specific Exchange Server in the server list. The Server object is a parent container.

- **Server Recipients container object**—Contains a list of recipient objects whose mailboxes are stored on the server.

- **Site object**—One or more Exchange Servers that have been grouped together. There is one Site object for each site in your Exchange organization.

REVIEW QUESTIONS

1. Which of the following tools are used to manage Exchange Server?
   a. DHCP Manager
   b. Exchange Administrator
   c. User Manager For Domains
   d. WINS Manager
   e. All of the above

2. Microsoft Exchange can be managed from a Windows 95 computer. True or False?

3. Which of the following objects can be created in the Exchange Administrator? (Choose all that apply.)
   a. Users
   b. Mailboxes
   c. Distribution lists
   d. Custom recipients
   e. All of the above

4. What is the file name of the Exchange Administrator?
   a. EXCHADMN.EXE
   b. EXCHANGE.EXE
   c. EXCHANGE32.EXE
   d. ADMIN.EXE
   e. None of the above

5. When is the Connect To Server dialog box displayed? (Choose all that apply.)
   a. The first time the Exchange Administrator is run.
   b. Every time the Exchange Administrator is run.
   c. When the File|Connect To Server menu item is selected.
   d. All of the above.

6. You can be connected to multiple Exchange Servers when in the Exchange Administrator. True or False?

7. Which of the following are objects (or object containers) in the Exchange hierarchy? (Choose all that apply.)
   a. Sites
   b. Servers
   c. Users
   d. Protocols
   e. All of the above

8. The Site object is the top item of the Exchange hierarchy. True or False?

9. Which object contains all the organization forms that are potentially available to all users in the organization?
   a. Eforms Registry object
   b. Public Folders object
   c. Site object
   d. Server object
   e. None of the above

10. How many site objects are there in the Exchange hierarchy?
   a. 1
   b. 10
   c. As many sites as have been defined
   d. None of the above

11. A site is one or more Exchange Servers that are grouped together. True or False?

12. What are some objects contained in the Configuration container? (Choose all that apply.)

    a. Global Address List

    b. Connections

    c. Servers

    d. Recipients

    e. All of the above

13. The Connections container object contains which objects? (Choose all that apply.)

    a. Lotus Notes Connector

    b. cc:Mail Connector

    c. Microsoft Mail Connector

    d. GroupWise Connector

    e. All of the above

14. The Protocols container object contains which objects?

    a. IMAP4

    b. HTTP

    c. LDAP

    d. NNTP

    e. POP3

    f. All of the above

15. The Server object represents a specific server in a site. True or False?

16. Which object can reveal how much space an individual user's mailbox is taking up?

    a. Logons

    b. Private Information Store/Mailbox Resources

    c. Servers

    d. Public Information Store/Mailbox Resources

    e. User mailbox usage cannot be determined in the Exchange Administrator.

17. The Private Information Store/Logons object contains a list of all users who have ever logged on to a mailbox. True or False?

18. You do not have to manually select the Recipients container before adding a user to a site. True or False?

19. What type of mailboxes would typically be added to the Custom Recipients object? (Choose all that apply.)

    a. cc:Mail

    b. Other Microsoft Exchange site users

    c. SMTP

    d. MS Mail

    e. All of the above

20. What is one way column widths can be adjusted in the Exchange Administrator?

    a. Column widths cannot be adjusted.

    b. From the View | Window Properties menu item.

    c. By using your mouse.

    d. None of the above.

21. After using the Exchange Administrator to connect to an Exchange Server for the first time, there are no sites displayed in the Exchange hierarchy. True or False?

22. What file formats can be imported to generate Microsoft Exchange recipients?

    a. Tab-delimited

    b. Comma-separated (CSV)

    c. EBCDIC

    d. Word 6.0/95

    e. All of the above

23. From where can the Exchange Administrator extract user lists? (Choose all that apply.)

    a. Windows NT

    b. NetWare 3.x

    c. SendMail

    d. Lantastic Messaging System

    e. All of the above

24. Although a group of mailboxes can be moved to another server, individual mailboxes cannot. True or False?

25. How can the official Microsoft Exchange documentation be accessed online?

    a. Insert the Microsoft Exchange CD, and run DOCS.EXE.

    b. From the Help | Official Documentation menu item.

    c. It can't—documentation is not available in electronic format.

    d. Insert Microsoft Exchange Clients CD, and select the Help | CD Help menu.

    e. None of the above.

HANDS-ON PROJECTS

The following projects illustrate some common Microsoft Exchange Server administrative tasks. You do not need any additional resources to perform these projects.

 PROJECT 7.1

To search for a recipient:

1. Start the Exchange Administrator program.
2. Select the Tools menu, then select the Find Recipients menu item. The Find Recipients dialog box should open.
3. Click the Container button to select the scope of your search.
4. To search your entire Microsoft Exchange organization, select Global Address List.
5. To search a specific site or server, click the plus and minus signs to select your choice.
6. Click OK to return to the Find Recipients dialog box.
7. In the Last text box, enter the last name of the recipient you want to search for.
8. Enter any additional criteria to narrow down the search.
9. To search custom attributes, click the Custom button, enter criteria for the 10 custom attributes, then click OK to return to the Find Recipients dialog box.
10. Click the Find Now button to begin the search.
11. All recipients matching your scope and criteria are displayed in the window below the criteria information.
12. To bring up the properties for a matching recipient, double-click the recipient. Make any changes to the properties, then click OK to return to the Find Recipients dialog box.
13. Close the Find Recipients dialog box to return to the Exchange Administrator.

 PROJECT 7.2

To add a new recipient container:

1. Start the Exchange Administrator program.
2. Select the File menu, select the New Other menu item, then select the Recipients Container menu item. The Properties dialog box should open.

Depending on which object was selected when the menu item was chosen, an interim dialog box might appear telling you that recipient containers cannot be created in the selected container. The dialog box will also ask if you want to switch to the proper container. Click OK.

3. Select the General tab, if it is not already selected.

4. In the Display Name text box, enter the display name of the recipient container. This is the name that will appear to users when they list recipient containers. Type "Conference Rooms".

5. In the Directory Name text box, enter the directory name of the recipient container. This is the internal name of the directory. Type the same value that you entered for the display name.

6. In the Administrative text box, enter any descriptive comments you desire. Type "This is a list of conference rooms that users can schedule for use".

7. Permissions can be assigned on the Permissions tab. The default permissions are usually sufficient, so accept the default permissions.

8. Click OK to create the recipient container and return to the Exchange Administrator. The new recipient container will appear in the left side of the window under the site it was created in. New recipients (Conference Rooms, in this case) can be added to this recipient container. The new recipient container will show up when users view the Global Address List.

PROJECT 7.3

To extract a NetWare account list:

1. Start the Exchange Administrator program.

2. Select the Tools menu, then select Extract NetWare Account List menu item. The NetWare User Extraction dialog box should open.

3. In the NetWare Server Name text box, enter the name of the NetWare server containing the user data you want to extract.

4. In the NetWare User text box, enter the username of a NetWare user with rights to access user data.

5. In the NetWare User Password text box, enter the password of the NetWare user that was entered in Step 4.

6. Click the Browse button to specify an output file name for the NetWare account list. The Microsoft Exchange Administrator (Save File) dialog box should appear.

7. Enter the name of the file that is to contain the NetWare account list. Click the Save button to return to the NetWare User Extraction dialog box. The file name will be listed in the Output File Name text box.

8. Click OK to start the extraction process. When the process is complete, use Notepad (or another file viewer) to examine the contents of the output file.

 PROJECT 7.4

To import a user directory list:

1. Start the Exchange Administrator program.
2. Select the Tools menu, then select the Directory Import menu item. The Directory Import dialog box should open.
3. In the Windows NT domain combo box, select the name of the domain where new user accounts will be created.
4. In the MS Exchange Server combo box, select the Exchange Server where you want to import directory information.
5. Click the Containers button to bring up the Directory Import Container dialog box. Select the container where directory information will be imported, then click OK.
6. Click the Import File button to bring up the Directory Import File dialog box. Select the file containing the directory information you want to import, then click the Open button. This returns you to the Directory Import dialog box. The file name will be listed next to the Import File button.
7. If these users do not have accounts on the specified domain, select the Create Windows NT Account checkbox. This will create an NT account for every new mailbox that is created. Selecting the Generate Random Password option results in random passwords being created and assigned to each created NT account. The passwords are written to the \ExchSrvr \Bin\Bimport.psw file and must be distributed to users before they can log on to Windows NT with their new account. If Generate Random Password is not selected, new Windows NT accounts are created with a password based on their account name.
8. Click the Import button to begin the directory import process. When the process is complete, use User Manager For Domains to verify that NT user accounts were created. In addition, use the Exchange Administrator to verify that the mailboxes were created and that the associated Windows NT user account matches.

7

CASE PROJECTS

1. Suppose the following situation exists:

   You are the administrator of your company's Windows NT Server (the Primary Domain Controller). You are also responsible for a Microsoft Exchange Server, version 5.5. Your company is migrating from NetWare to Windows NT, and you have been tasked with the responsibility to create mailboxes for each existing NetWare user account—so each NetWare user will have a mailbox on Microsoft Exchange as well as a corresponding Windows NT user account.

   Required result:

   Successfully create Exchange Server mailboxes for NetWare user accounts.

   Optional desired results:

   Create Windows NT accounts for each of the NetWare user accounts. Use the highest logging level to make sure that no errors occurred.

   Proposed solution:

   Use the Exchange Administrator's Extract NetWare Account List dialog box to generate a file containing NetWare directory information. Use the Exchange Administrator's Directory Import dialog box to select the appropriate Windows NT domain. Select the MS Exchange Server to select the appropriate server. Select the appropriate recipient container to create mailboxes in. Specify the file containing the NetWare directory information. Select High Logging level. Click the Import button to create the mailboxes.

   Which results does the proposed solution provide?

   a. The proposed solution produces the required result and both optional desired results.

   b. The proposed solution produces the required result and only one optional desired result.

   c. The proposed solution produces only the required result.

   d. The proposed solution does not provide the required result.

2. Suppose the following situation exists:

   You are responsible for your company's Microsoft Exchange Server 5.5. Among your many responsibilities, you have to create new mailboxes and distribution lists. Your Exchange organization currently has over 20,000 mailboxes. You have been given a list of new mailboxes to create. While casually looking the list over, you come across a mailbox that you are sure you have already created—but it is associated with a different Windows NT user account. A quick look through the various recipient containers does not reveal the mailbox. You want to know whether the mailbox has already been created.

Required result:

Determine if the mailbox exists.

Optional desired results:

Determine which Windows NT user account is associated with the mailbox. Correct the associated Windows NT user account.

Proposed solution:

Use the Find Recipient feature of the Exchange Administrator to locate the mailbox. Double-click the matching mailbox to display the properties for the mailbox. Click the Primary Windows NT Account button. Assign the correct Windows NT user account to this mailbox. Click OK.

Which results does the proposed solution provide?

a. The proposed solution produces the required result and both optional desired results.

b. The proposed solution produces the required result and only one optional desired result.

c. The proposed solution produces only the required result.

d. The proposed solution does not provide the required result.

7

INTERSITE CONNECTORS

In this chapter, you'll examine how an Exchange Server communicates between sites, and learn how to configure that server for optimal performance. In addition, you'll explore the X.400 Connector and how it may be used to communicate between sites. From there, you'll move on to configuring the Internet Mail Service, the Dynamic RAS Connector, and Exchange routing across the various connectors covered in this chapter. Finally, you'll work step-by-step through installations of a Site Connector, an X.400 Connector, a Dynamic RAS Connector, and a directory replication connector. By the time you've finished, working with Exchange connectors should be quite familiar.

AFTER READING THIS CHAPTER AND COMPLETING THE EXERCISES, YOU WILL BE ABLE TO:

- Understand how Exchange communicates between sites
- Configure the Site Connector between two sites
- Understand when to use the X.400 Connector to communicate between sites
- Explain the configuration options available for the Internet Mail Service
- Establish a connection between two remote sites using the Dynamic RAS Connector
- Understand how Exchange routes messages across multiple connectors

INTERSITE COMMUNICATIONS: EXPLORED AND EXPLAINED

It is not uncommon for organizations to have networks that span multiple sites. This is often due to geographic locations, network infrastructure, or administrative needs. Such organizations invariably require message connectivity among all sites, including remote sites. When two Exchange sites are connected and information is transferred between them, this is known as *intersite communication*. Communication between sites is somewhat different from communication within a single site, which is called *intrasite communication*.

With intrasite communication, servers communicate with each other directly using either the *Message Transfer Agent (MTA)* or the Directory Service (DS). Messages are delivered through MTA-to-MTA communication, and directory information is delivered through DS-to-DS communication (primarily directory replication). Both of these software components use the Remote Procedure Call (RPC) protocol to communicate, and all intrasite configuration is performed automatically by the Exchange Servers that are involved. Within a site, it is assumed that availability and speed of the network is high, and that servers can communicate directly with each other whenever they like.

On the other hand, intersite communication is more complex and requires some manual configuration effort. High-speed connections between these sites are not required, nor assumed to be available. An Exchange component, called a connector, must be installed at each site to enable information to pass between the sites. In a multiple-site situation, the MTA transfers all information, regardless of the type of data involved. Thus, when it comes to moving directory-related information from the DS in one site directly to the DS in another site, it places the directory-related information in a mail message and uses the MTA to deliver the data.

There are two types of connectors: messaging connectors and directory replication connectors. As the name is meant to connote, a messaging connector is primarily responsible for handling incoming and outgoing email messages through the connection that it oversees. Within MS Exchange Server, you will find four major messaging connectors:

- *Site Connector*
- *X.400 Connector*
- *Internet Mail Service*
- *Dynamic RAS Connector*

The directory replication connector transfers directory information between sites. The directory replication connector is different, not only because of the kind of information it handles, but also because it can use any messaging connector to relay directory information between servers.

Certain messaging connectors serve primarily to enable communications between Exchange and foreign mail systems. Some examples of this type of connector include the Internet Mail Service and the X.400 Connector. When used in this way, a connector takes Exchange messages and translates them into a format native to the foreign system so that foreign clients may read those messages. Likewise, the connector translates incoming messages from foreign mail formats into a format native to Exchange so Exchange clients may read such messages.

Now that you've learned about the basic capabilities of the various Exchange connectors, it's time to delve more deeply into their innerworkings. In the section that follows, you'll start to learn more about connector properties by examining those properties that all Exchange connectors have in common.

COMMON CONNECTOR PROPERTIES

Two fundamental connector properties are common to all Exchange connectors—namely, an address space and a connector cost. For this reason, these properties warrant detailed discussion.

Connector Address Space

Each connector has a property called an *address space*. When a connector is created outside a site, a logical path must also be defined to allow an MTA to determine how to get messages aimed at a connector to their final destinations. This logical path is what the address space represents, where addresses within the space must be unique for each different recipient.

A connector must have at least one address space entry to operate properly. The format for an address space depends on the address format native to the foreign messaging system. Thus, if you send a message to an SMTP network, the SMTP address space must be referenced to ensure its proper delivery.

A connector doesn't require an address space only for its messaging system, either. In fact, one connector may include multiple address space entries where each one is aimed at a different foreign messaging system. For example, the X.400 Connector may be used to send messages to a remote Internet mail system as well as to one or more remote X.400 mail systems. But a separate address space must be defined in the connector for each separate mail system that the X.400 connector is expected to be able to reach.

In Table 8.1, sample address space entries for X.400, MS Mail, and the Internet Mail Service (IMS) appear. Notice that each address space has a different format, and that individual recipient addresses elaborate on that format.

Table 8.1   Sample address space entries.

System	Address	Address Space
X.400	g=Bill;s=Gates;p=microsoft;c=us	c=us;p=microsoft...
MS Mail	MS:Microsoft/Redmond/Bgates	Microsoft/Redmond
IMS	bgates@microsoft.com	microsoft.com

Thus, the address space for X.400 specifies that the country is the United States (c=us) and that the private address space within the United States is named microsoft. Defining Bill Gates' individual address only requires adding an entry for his given name (g=Bill) and his surname (s=Gates) within the Microsoft X.400 address space (c=us,p=microsoft).

Likewise, for MS Mail Microsoft/Redmond represents its address space, and adding the /Bgates cognomen to the address space name simply names which mailbox within the space where a message should be delivered (the MS: occurs at the beginning of the Address string to identify which connector should handle the message).

Finally, the Internet Mail Service entry consists of a domain name, microsoft.com, that identifies the address space for Microsoft. Here, the bgates@ entry that is prefixed to the domain name identifies the recipient within the Microsoft domain to whom a message might be addressed. In each of these cases, the connector knows how to interpret and package addresses for outbound messages, and how to communicate this information to some foreign mail system. Going the other way, the connector also knows how to convert between foreign or external addresses for inbound messages into Exchange address formats, and how to deliver such messages to their intended recipients.

In the section that follows next, our focus shifts from how connectors handle addresses to the number and kind of connectors that may be created between sites.

Connector Cost

Within the Exchange environment, you can create multiple connectors between two sites. This requires that the MTA recognize the existence of multiple connectors, and that it choose some connector to handle a message when it wants to effect a message transfer or to accept an incoming message.

When multiple connectors between sites exist, these connectors may be of the same type (that is, both may be IMS Connectors) or of different types (that is, an IMS Connector and an X.400 Connector). You can use multiple connectors to balance the load between sites (by moving messages across both connectors where appropriate) and to increase fault tolerance in your Exchange organization (by permitting one connector to step in for another, when the other connector is unavailable for some reason). As long as one of the connectors between the sites is up and running, messages can be delivered between those two sites.

When choosing which connector to use, the MTA always checks the cost associated with each connector. When configuring a connector, you specify a cost value that ranges from 1 through 100, as shown in Figure 8.1. The lower its cost, the more frequently the MTA will use that connector.

For example, you can install a Site Connector with a cost of 1, for everyday use, and a Dynamic RAS Connector with a cost of 50, for fault tolerance. The cost equation between the two is such that if the MTA cannot send messages using

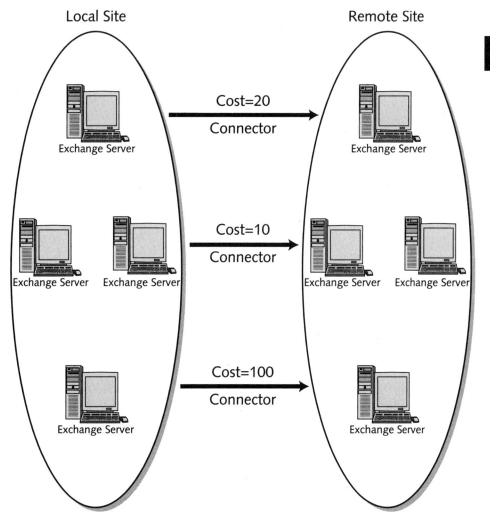

Figure 8.1 Connector costs.

the Site Connector, it will attempt to use the Dynamic RAS Connector. If these sites are in different geographic locations, you would not want to use the Dynamic RAS Connector all the time anyway, because of the long-distance charges involved. Assigning any one connector a higher cost than other connectors guarantees that the higher-cost connector will only be used when the lower-cost alternative is unavailable.

 To perform load balancing across multiple connectors, all must be assigned the same cost. To use one connector as a backup to another primary connector, assign the backup connector a higher cost than the primary connector.

Now that you've learned about the properties that are common to all Exchange connectors, you will begin an odyssey that will take you through all the major connectors included with Exchange, starting with the Site Connector in the section that follows next.

THE SITE CONNECTOR

The Site Connector is the easiest way to configure two sites to communicate. The Site Connector tells the MTA component of Exchange how to transfer messages to a remote site. With the Site Connector installed, the MTA can handle intersite as well as intrasite communication. The Site Connector maintains a list of *target servers* at the remote site. A target server (shown in Figure 8.2) is a server at the remote site that the local MTA can target to receive intersite messages. Any server within the remote site can be used as a target server.

When the local MTA needs to transfer a message to a remote site, it selects a target server from its target list and delivers the message to that server. The remote server is not necessarily the final destination for the message. In fact, the target server might need to transfer the message to another server at the remote site. This occurs until the message is delivered to its final destination. There is a maximum of one intersite hop allowed for any message being delivered to a remote site, but any number of intrasite transfers can occur thereafter.

You can also configure the Site Connector to work with *messaging bridgehead servers* (shown in Figure 8.3). A messaging bridgehead server receives mail from servers within a site and then delivers those messages, either to a messaging bridgehead server or a target server at the remote site. This permits Exchange administrators to specify which servers are used for intersite communications, and can offload some message transfer processing to other servers. Thus, it's appropriate to think of a messaging bridgehead server as a gateway for a site. It's

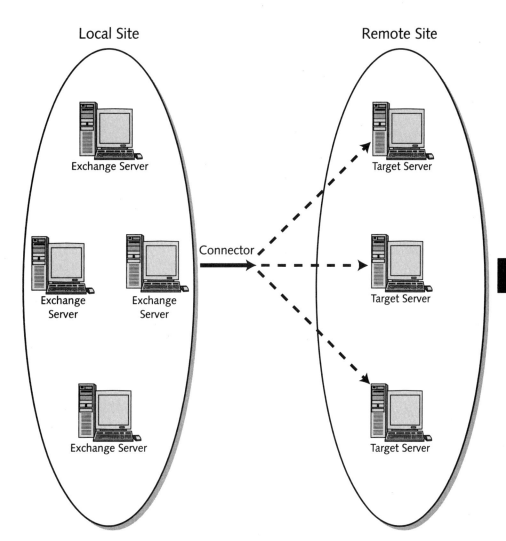

Local Site

Remote Site

8

Figure 8.2 The Site Connector target servers.

also the case that the larger the number of Exchange Servers at any specific site, the more likely it is to find one or more bridgehead servers in use, primarily because larger sites usually include more specialized servers than smaller ones.

The Site Connector uses RPC for intersite communications. For this reason, the Site Connector requires a permanent, high-speed connection between the sites it connects (at least 128K ISDN, if not a higher bandwidth connection, such as a fractional or a full T1 link, is recommended). The Site Connector can use any network protocol that supports RPCs, which includes NetBEUI, TCP/IP, or IPX/SPX (known as NWLink in the Windows NT environment).

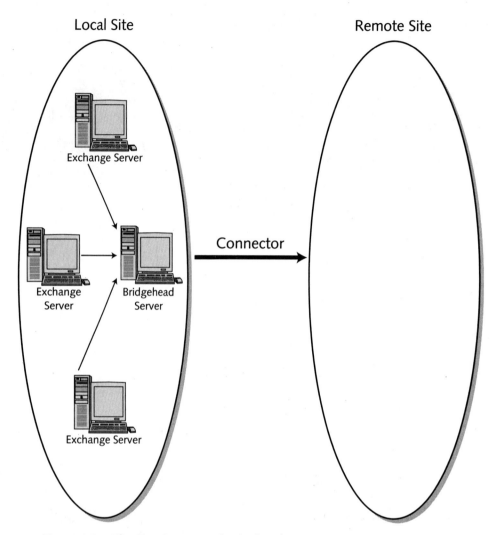

Figure 8.3   The Site Connector bridgehead servers.

To transfer messages to a remote site, the local MTA must authenticate itself on the remote site server. To do this, it uses a *Service account*. The account that is used for this process depends on the configuration of the two sites. Some common configurations include the following arrangements:

- **A single account in a single domain or two domains with a two-way trust.** If both Exchange sites belong to the same Windows NT domain, both sites can use the same service account. If the two sites belong to different Windows NT domains, then the service account from one domain may only be used in the other domain if a two-way trust relationship between the two domains is in place.

- **A single account in two domains with a one-way trust.** If two sites belong to different Windows NT domains, you can create a remote account with the same permissions as the service account in the local site. But then, the local site must trust the remote site's Windows NT domain. This represents a one-way trust where the local site trusts the remote site.

- **A specific remote service account in two domains without trust.** Using the Override page, you can specify a remote service account to be used in a remote Windows NT domain. You should do this if you do not want to set up trust relationships between the domains.

The Site Connector is also the most efficient connector that ships with Microsoft Exchange. The Site Connector is approximately 20 percent faster than the X.400 Connector. This is because message translation is not required when transferring messages from a local Exchange site to a remote Exchange site, because both sites use the same types of address spaces and message formats. Another nice feature of the Site Connector is that it provides automatic configuration for the remote side of any connection that it bridges.

8

There are five tabs on the Properties page for the Site Connector. They are as follows:

- **General** Identifies the target site, and allows you to specify a connection cost for the connector. You can also specify either any server, or some specific server as the local messaging bridgehead server. If a specific server is not selected as the messaging bridgehead, then any server in the local site can send messages to the remote site using the Site Connector.

- **Permissions** These settings control who may access the configuration information for the Site Connector, and what kinds of configuration changes they may make. You set permissions on the Site Connector the same way you set any other object permissions for Windows NT. You must have sufficient rights to set permissions; usually, this means you must be a member of the Exchange Administrators global group for the domain in which the Exchange Server resides.

- **Target Servers** Identifies which servers will receive the incoming messages to the site and the cost associated with each server. Costs can be used for load balancing or fault tolerance. The server with the lowest cost receives all the mail, unless it is unavailable.

- **Address Space** Identifies the X.400 address for the remote site. You also have the ability to add, edit, or remove any address. A different cost can be specified for each address space to allow for the selection of the address space to use.

- **Override** Allows you to enter information about the service account of the remote site. You use this property page if the service account in the remote site is different from the service account in the local site.

Each target server can be assigned a cost. The cost assigned to the target servers is different than the cost assigned to a Site Connector. When Exchange transfers information between sites, the lowest-cost connector is always used. The cost assigned to target servers acts more like a load-balancing option. For target servers, cost values may range from 0 through 100, where a value of 0 means that the server will be used 100 percent of the time and a value of 100 means that the server will be used only if no other paths are available.

Next to the Site Connector, the X.400 Connector is probably the most widely used of all Exchange messaging connectors. Consequently, it's covered in the section that follows next.

THE X.400 CONNECTOR

The X.400 Connector is based on the CCITT X.400 standard. It is similar to the Site Connector in that it may also use messaging bridgehead servers to route mail traffic. The X.400 Connector cannot, however, use target servers. Therefore, the X.400 Connector (shown in Figure 8.4) always uses messaging bridgehead servers for its message transfers.

The X.400 Connector allows you, as the administrator, to restrict times when the connector may operate. It also permits you to specify which users may send mail to the remote site.

Using a Site Connector, the MTA at the local site connects with the MTA at the remote site to transfer the information. With an X.400 Connector, each server must pass its information to a messaging bridgehead server. The messaging bridgehead server then connects to its partner bridgehead server at the remote site and transfers the information. Finally, the remote messaging bridgehead server will pass the inbound information to its final destination, if necessary.

The X.400 Connector requires less bandwidth than the Site Connector (low to medium bandwidth). Because all information must be converted to messages before information transfers may occur, this tends to slow the connector down. The X.400 Connector is also more complicated to configure than the Site Connector—the X.400 Connector's Properties page includes eight tabs as compared to the Site Connector's five tabs. Because all mail that traverses the X.400 Connector must also flow through messaging bridgehead servers, messaging bottlenecks can sometimes occur, which may in turn bog down intersite communications.

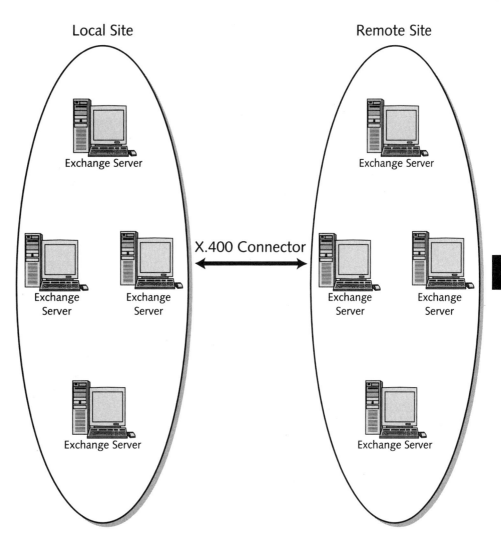

Figure 8.4   The X.400 Connector.

Performance considerations notwithstanding, there are certain benefits that pertain to the X.400 Connector:

- It is the most generic Exchange connector, and can link to a variety of mail systems.

- It may be used to connect to any X.400 system.

- It allows you to restrict message sizes and to control which users may access its services.

As mentioned earlier, an X.400 Connector requires more configuration than a Site Connector. You must perform two steps to install the X.400 Connector— that is, you must install the MTA transport stack and the X.400 Connector itself.

The MTA transport stack configures Microsoft Exchange to use the network transport used by the Windows NT Server. Thus, you must first configure one of the appropriate network transports before the connector may be configured. The available network transports that work with the X.400 Connector include the following:

- **TCP/IP** The Exchange Server uses the Windows NT TCP/IP services. The MTA uses port 102 to communicate.

- **TP4/CLNP** The Exchange Server includes an interface that permits it to operate using the Windows NT TP4 driver. This interface is used to communicate with remote systems that use the ISO/OSI TP4 protocol for message transport. Using the Connectionless Networking Protocol (CLNP) atop TP4, data is transferred without requiring a connection request. TP4 is also designed for transport use on a connectionless network. The server that runs the transport stack supplies the necessary TP4 network address information.

- **TP0/X.25** TP0/X.25 provides both dial-up and direct communications. To use this option, X.25 network software must be installed and operational on the server before installing the MTA transport stack. Multiple X.25 transport stacks may be installed on a server, and you can install multiple X.25 port adapters on a single server. Be aware that a separate MTA transport stack is required for each X.25 port on an adapter.

The X.400 Connector Properties tabs are explained in the following list:

- **General** Allows you to change the display name (the name displayed in the Administrator program), remote MTA name, and password (the same as the information specified in the MTA General property page in the other site). It also allows you to switch from the currently installed transport stack to another transport stack, as long as it is already installed on the server.

- **Schedule** Enables you to configure connector communications to occur at one of these preset intervals: Never, Always, or at Selected Times (which may be up to 15-minute intervals). This schedule only affects outgoing messages. It does not affect incoming messages from a remote site.

- **Stack** Allows you to specify additional address information. All the information on this page must match the transport stack's configuration at the remote site. The information available on this property page is based on whatever MTA transport stack you installed to use with the X.400 Connector.

- **Override** Allows you to override default MTA attributes for this specific X.400 Connector.

- **Connected Sites** Displays all sites that are directly connected. This setting is used to ensure that directory replication can occur.

- **Address Space** Allows you to add, edit, or remove address spaces used with this connector. You can also associate a cost with each address space on this tab.

- **Advanced** Enables you to specify X.400 message format and transfer information when sending messages to a remote site. This information does not affect the type of information that the local Exchange Server can receive from the remote site.

It is also important to note that you must configure each "side" of the X.400 Connector separately, before a connection between the two sites on either side of the connection can be made.

After the X.400 Connector, the Internet Mail Service (IMS) is by far the most popular foreign mail system connector for Exchange. IMS serves as the topic for the section that follows next.

8

USING INTERNET MAIL SERVICE

The Internet Mail Service (IMS) (shown in Figure 8.5) is a service that can be installed within Microsoft Exchange to provide the server the ability to send and receive mail from computers that use the Simple Mail Transfer Protocol (SMTP). Many of today's Internet mail systems use SMTP, and installing it almost guarantees a connection between your network and the Internet.

SMTP is a universal protocol that specifies the procedure for transferring mail between two computers running the TCP/IP protocol stack. For IMS to work, TCP/IP must be installed and configured on the Windows NT Server running Microsoft Exchange. An Internet connection, probably through some ISP, is also required to create the necessary link, but it is also possible to use IMS to connect to private SMTP-based mail servers that aren't part of the Internet per se.

The IMS includes many of the same property pages as the other connectors, including address space, connector costs, and delivery restrictions. But there are some disadvantages to using the IMS to link two Exchange sites together. All data must be translated from the Exchange message format to the SMTP format for delivery, then translated back from SMTP format to Exchange format on the remote side of the connector. Such data translations can slow down performance of the Exchange Server. Also, IMS only supports the scheduling of connections if you use a dial-up connection. Chapter 9 covers the Internet Mail Service in greater detail.

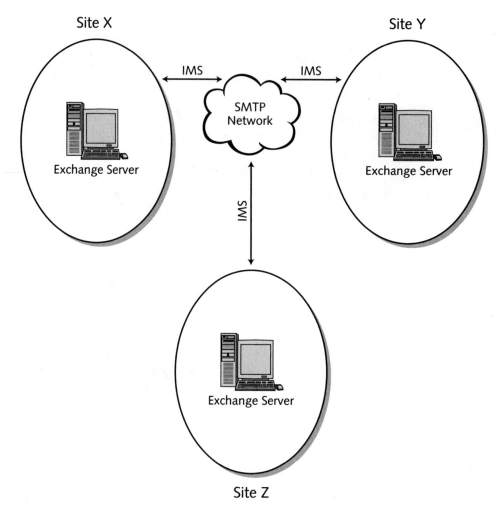

Figure 8.5   The Internet Mail Service.

When dial-up connections are needed in the Windows NT environment, the Remote Access Service (RAS) often comes into play. Even Exchange can use RAS as a connector, as you'll learn in the section that follows next.

THE DYNAMIC RAS CONNECTOR

The Dynamic RAS Connector uses Microsoft's Remote Access Service (RAS) for message transport between sites that have no permanent connection. RAS supports modem connections over normal telephone lines, ISDN, and X.25. The Dynamic RAS Connector can be set up to automatically activate a RAS connection on a scheduled basis or on demand. Before a RAS connection can be used, the following should be configured:

- The RAS network software, installed and configured on the Exchange Server computer.
- The service account or a Windows NT account with Send As and Mailbox Owner permissions for the Servers or Configuration containers in the remote site.
- The name to use for the MTA transport stack.
- The name of the remote server.
- The phone book entry for the remote server, including the name of the server and the phone number.
- The name you want to use for the Dynamic RAS Connector.

Like the X.400 Connector, you need to install the MTA transport stack (for RAS) before installing the Dynamic RAS Connector (as shown in Figure 8.6).

Because RAS connections may require additional processing to answer calls and handle communications, you might want to configure a calling server to dial a dedicated RAS server instead of using the Exchange Server to deal with these connections. The Dynamic RAS Connector also uses the concept of a messaging bridgehead server to concentrate traffic between two remote sites. This allows you to only require one RAS connection between any two sites. If this were not true, you would have to configure multiple modems, multiple RAS entries, and multiple phone lines, thereby making the connector quite inefficient.

The Dynamic RAS Connector includes many of the same features as the Site Connector and the X.400 Connector, including *address space* and *connector cost*. The Dynamic RAS Connector also has the ability (much like the X.400 Connector) to restrict those users permitted to access the connector.

For added security, the Dynamic RAS Connector includes a feature called *MTA callback*. If you enable this feature, the local server initiates a RAS connection to the remote server. When the remote server answers the call, the local server terminates the connection and waits for the remote server to call back. The remote server uses the phone number specified in the MTA callback number field. To use this option, RAS callback must be enabled on the RAS server.

Having now examined the primary connectors individually, you will now examine them when used together, in a variety of combinations. This provides the topic for the sections that follow next.

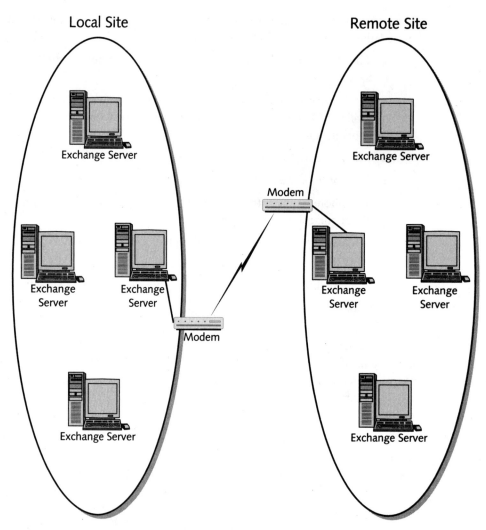

Figure 8.6   The Dynamic RAS Connector.

WORKING WITH MULTIPLE CONNECTORS

You have the ability to install multiple connectors between sites. You can use this method to provide load balancing as well as redundancy. The connectors you install can be of the same type (if you use a single transport) or they can be different types (if you have multiple transports installed and available). For example, you might want to configure an X.400 Connector as the main transport between two sites and then configure a Dynamic RAS Connector as a backup in case the X.400 Connector fails.

You can assign a number to each connector known as a cost. This allows you to control the importance of the message connectors. The cost value ranges from 1 through 100. The connector with the lowest cost will always be used over other connectors (with higher costs). You can use these costs to identify the primary and backup paths for message transfer to occur. It is common to assign the cost based on the real cost of the connection. If the Dynamic RAS Connector in the previous example requires connecting over a long-distance phone line, you would want to limit how often this connector is used.

The service responsible for delivery of all messages to recipients on any Exchange Server (excluding the server where the sender is located) is the Microsoft Exchange MTA. When the MTA receives a message for delivery to a recipient outside of the site, it must determine how to deliver that message to its final destination. It does this by using a process known as *message routing*, and it uses this process to determine how to deal with mail sent by the MTA to some MTA in a remote site by using one of the following Exchange connectors:

■ Site Connector

■ Dynamic RAS Connector

■ X.400 Connector

■ External connectors, such as the IMS or the Microsoft Mail Connector

It is important to note that the MTA always performs message routing independent of the number of connectors between the two sites.

Every connector has an associated address space (or spaces), that represents the set of addresses that may be reached through this connector. The System Attendant collects this address space information from all connectors and creates a route table known as the *Gateway Address Routing Table (GWART)*. Each Exchange Server has its own GWART. When the MTA needs to send a message to a remote site, it compares the recipient of the message with the GWART to determine which connectors might be able to deliver the message. This search provides the MTA with a list of connectors that it can use to deliver the message, and the MTA then selects a connector from that list based on the lowest cost value. If more than one connector has that lowest cost value, the MTA can balance the load across multiple connectors.

There are three major sections to the GWART. Each section is associated with an address type that Exchange may use to send mail. The different address types that can appear in the GWART are shown in Table 8.2.

Table 8.2   GWART address types.

Address	Description
Distinguished Name (DN)	The native Exchange address format. Type EX.
Domain Defined Attribute (DDA)	The format used for custom recipient storage. Type MS or SMTP.
Originator/Recipient (O/R) address	The native X.400 format. Type X.400.

The GWART is stored in a text file in the Exchsrvr\mtadata directory. When a server's routing information is updated, the GWART is also updated, and a single backup copy is kept in reserve. The most recent copy of the GWART is stored in the gwart0.mta file and the previous GWART is stored in the gwart1.mta file. If you should ever need to, you may use a regular text editor to edit these files.

Now that you've covered the important messaging connectors, it's time to turn our focus to another essential connection—that is, the directory replication connector used to synchronize Exchange directories across multiple sites. This is the topic of the next section.

THE ROLE OF DIRECTORY REPLICATION

Once you configure a messaging connector between two sites (Site Connector, X.400 Connector, Dynamic RAS Connector, and so on), you can also configure a directory replication connector as well. This connector replicates directory information between local and remote sites.

When you configure a directory replication connector between two sites, you need to specify one server to control the replication for that connector. This server is known as the directory *replication bridgehead*. You may have multiple directory replication bridgeheads within a site, but you may only have one bridgehead responsible for any connection to a remote site. Also, a site cannot have two directory replication paths to a remote site (see Figure 8.7).

In Figure 8.7, all three connectors are valid, but all three cannot be combined at one time because this would create more than one path for directory replication to take (that is, Site X can connect to Site Z directly or through Site Y, as shown in Table 8.3).

The directory replication bridgeheads always request the directory replication information. This information is never pushed (delivered without a request to initiate delivery); directly replication information must be requested explicitly. The directory replication bridgehead requests this information based on a replication schedule. When a change is made in the directory, a notification message is sent out notifying the replication bridgeheads of the changes. The directory replication bridgeheads then request changes be sent.

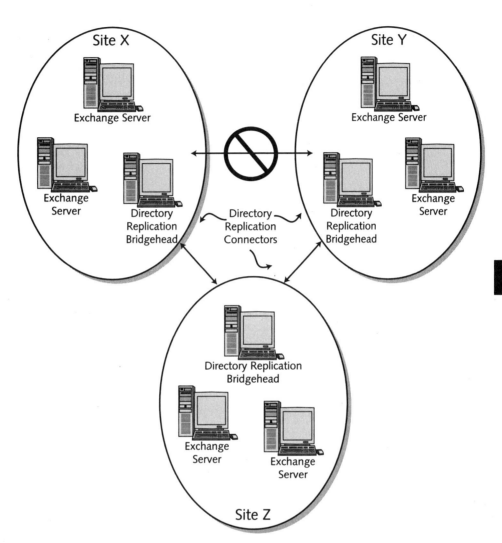

Figure 8.7   The directory replication bridgehead.

Table 8.3   Multiple directory replication bridgeheads.

Connector	From	To
A	Site X	Site Z
B	Site Z	Site Y
C	Site Y	Site X

When there are three sites joined with two connectors and directory replication is configured between them, the connection between the two most distant sites is said to be transitive. For example, in Figure 8.8, Site X and Site Z are connected, and Site Y and Site Z are connected. Due to this connection, Site X has a transitive connection to Site Y (through Site Z).

Transitive connections permit multiple sites to exchange updates without requiring the kinds of contortions that multiple domains and trust relationships require. This can be a tremendous boon for organizations with several major sites, and a large number of satellite sites.

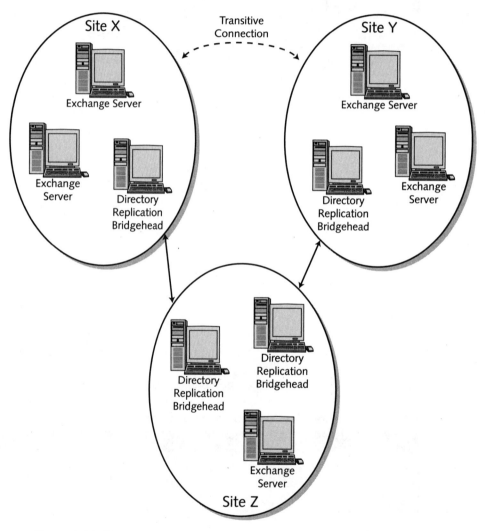

Figure 8.8   Transitive connections.

CHAPTER SUMMARY

In this chapter, you've learned about the role that Exchange messaging connectors play in binding sites together. To begin with, you explored the distinction between intrasite and intersite connections: where the former are based on the assumption of easy access and relatively high bandwidth, the latter require more configuration, planning, and pathways to transport messages from "here" to "there," wherever here and there may happen to be.

Our examination of the key roles that messaging connectors can play started with an exploration of the common properties that all connectors share: the address spaces that they can access on either side of a link and the cost factors associated with using such a link. If you recall, Exchange invariably picks the connector with the least cost, which means that connectors with equal and lowest costs can be used to balance message loads across multiple connectors, but also means that higher-cost connectors may be defined to provide fault tolerance when lower-cost connectors fail or are otherwise unavailable.

Following your examination of what Exchange connectors have in common, you explored the capabilities of the most popular and widely used connectors. Starting with the Site Connector, which may be used to handle intersite connections between Exchange Server sites, you learned that a permanent network connection is necessary for Site Connectors to function. Next, you learned about the X.400 Connector and its generic abilities to interconnect a variety of messaging systems (including Exchange systems, when the performance penalty associated with two-way translation is tolerable) for message exchange.

Following the X.400 Connector, you explored the Internet Mail Service (IMS) and its abilities to connect to any of a variety of SMTP-based messaging systems, including the Internet. Next, you investigated the capabilities of the Dynamic RAS Connector, which can provide dial-up–based message transfer services between sites on demand, or at regularly scheduled intervals. This latter connector is especially useful for smaller satellite operations where permanent, nailed-up connections may simply be too expensive to justify.

After your journey through the most common Exchange connectors and their capabilities, you examined what's involved in working with multiple connectors, be they present to share the message traffic for load-balancing, or simply available as a failsafe when fault tolerance is important. In fact, many commercial sites combine both abilities, and define a pool of low-cost connectors for load balancing, but also a higher-cost connector as a failsafe should the lower-cost connections become unavailable for some reason or another.

8

You concluded the chapter with a look at the ways that directory replication works, between two sites or among pairs of sites where transitive replication relationships permit a single site to propagate its changes through intermediate sites to outlying ones. This kind of flexibility gives the Exchange directory services capabilities that Windows NT domain services cannot currently match.

KEY TERMS

- **address space**—The path for messages to be sent outside a site.

- **address space cost**—A numerical value (from 1 through 100) that is used to assign a cost to a specific address space.

- **connector cost**—A numerical value (from 1 through 100) that is used to assign a cost to a specific connector.

- **Directory Replication Connector**—A connector used to replicate the Exchange directory between remote sites.

- **Dynamic RAS Connector**—A connector used to connect two remote sites via regular phone lines, ISDN, or X.25.

- **Gateway Address Routing Table (GWART)**—A list of all the address space information for all the connectors within a site.

- **Internet Mail Service (IMS)**—A connector used to connect a Microsoft Exchange site to either an SMTP mail system or a remote Microsoft Exchange site.

- **intersite communication**—Communication between two Exchange sites.

- **intrasite communication**—Communication between two Exchange Servers within a single site.

- **message routing**—The act of sending messages to remote Exchange sites.

- **Message Transfer Agent (MTA)**—Provides the addressing and routing information for sending messages.

- **messaging bridgehead server**—A server that sends messages to remote networks on behalf of the entire Exchange site.

- **MTA callback**—A security feature of the Dynamic RAS Connector that forces the remote site to dial the local site back before making a RAS connection.

- **Remote Access Service (RAS)**—A Windows NT service that allows the server to connect to a remote server using a temporary connection.

- **replication bridgehead**—A server that sends replication messages to remote networks on behalf of the entire Exchange site.

- **Service account**—A Windows NT account used to access Exchange information on the Windows NT server running Microsoft Exchange.

- **Site Connector**—The most efficient connector available to Microsoft Exchange.

- **target server**—A server in the remote site that can receive messages from the local site.

- **X.400 Connector**—A generic Exchange connector used to connect an Exchange Server to either an X.400 mail system or a remote Exchange site.

REVIEW QUESTIONS

1. You must establish a connection between the Microsoft Exchange Server computer in your company's main office and multiple Unix SMTP hosts in remote branches. Which type of connector would you use?

   a. Dynamic RAS Connector

   b. Internet Mail Service (IMS)

   c. Site Connector

   d. X.400 Connector

2. A Dynamic RAS Connector connects two of your sites. How can you maintain a continuous dial-up connection?

   a. Edit the Dial-Up Networking phone book entry for the connection.

   b. Can only be done with an X.400 Connector.

   c. Change the connector to IMS.

   d. Create a schedule for the Dynamic RAS Connector.

3. You have several connectors installed between two of your sites. You would like the Site Connector to always be used, unless it is unavailable. What must you do?

   a. Assign it a cost of 1 and the other connectors a cost of 100.

   b. Assign it a cost of 100 and the other connectors a cost of 1.

   c. Do not assign it a cost.

   d. Assign all the connectors a cost of 1.

4. You would like to connect two of your sites together. They are on the same high-speed LAN. Which connector would you use?

   a. Dynamic RAS Connector

   b. Internet Mail Service (IMS)

   c. Site Connector

   d. X.400 Connector

8

5. You have a Site Connector installed. You would like to install a backup connector that will use a modem to connect to the remote site. Which connector would you use?

   a. Dynamic RAS Connector

   b. Internet Mail Service (IMS)

   c. Site Connector

   d. X.400 Connector

6. Your server's GWART is corrupt. How would you recover it?

   a. You can't. You must reinstall.

   b. Copy the gwart0.mta from another Exchange Server.

   c. Copy the gwart1.mta from another Exchange Server.

   d. Copy the gwart1.mta to gwart0.mta on the server where the GWART is corrupt.

7. Why would you configure multiple connectors between two sites? (Choose all that apply.)

   a. For fault-tolerance reasons.

   b. There is no benefit to using multiple connectors.

   c. For load-balancing reasons.

   d. None of the above.

8. You cannot have multiple address spaces assigned to one connector. True or False?

9. You can have multiple replication bridgehead servers in a site. True or False?

10. Which of the following is true about the X.400 Connector? (Choose all that apply.)

    a. It is the fastest connector.

    b. You can limit which users can use it.

    c. You can limit the message size sent by it.

    d. You can configure the remote side of the connector automatically.

11. Which Exchange component makes all routing decisions?

    a. MTA

    b. DS

    c. RAS

    d. SA

12. The Site Connector uses the Exchange message format with no conversion necessary. True or False?

13. Which of the following statements are true for the Site Connector?

    a. It can schedule connections.

    b. You can limit which users can use it.

    c. You can limit the message size sent by it.

    d. You can auto-configure the remote side of the connector.

14. A messaging bridgehead server *must* communicate with another bridgehead server in the remote site. True or False?

15. The directory replication connector is used to replicate user directories between Windows NT Servers. True or False?

16. The only way a higher-cost connector will ever be used in an Exchange environment where two sites are linked by multiple connectors is if the lower-cost connector fails or is otherwise unavailable. True or False?

17. Which of the following reasons account for the possibility of performance delays when using the X.400 Connector? (Choose all that apply.)

    a. Translating from native Exchange to X.400 formats takes time.

    b. X.400 is a complex, and therefore inherently slow, messaging environment.

    c. Because all mail that traverses the X.400 Connector must also flow through messaging bridgehead servers, messaging bottlenecks can sometimes occur.

    d. Converting from the Exchange address space to the X.400 address space is unduly complex, and adds significantly to the transit time through an X.400 Connector.

18. When intersite communication is involved, even directory replication information must travel in the form of mail messages. True or False?

19. Of the following configuration settings, which are common to both the X.400 Connector and the Dynamic RAS Connector? (Choose all that apply.)

    a. Each connector has an associated cost.

    b. Each connector has an associated address space.

    c. Each connector can connect with multiple message systems.

    d. Each connector may limit the users who can access its services.

20. If Site A replicates directory information to Site B, and Site B replicates directory information to Site C, what kind of relationship does Site A have to Site C?

    a. Commutative

    b. Distributive

    c. Identity

    d. Transitive

8

HANDS-ON PROJECTS

These hands-on projects will help you understand the topics discussed throughout this chapter. Projects 8.1 through 8.4 explain how to install a Site Connector for Exchange, an X.400 Connector, a Dynamic RAS Connector, and a directory replication connector, respectively.

 ## PROJECT 8.1

To install a Site Connector:

1. In the Administrator window, select Connections.
2. From the File menu, select New Other, and then select Site Connector.
3. Type the name of the server in the target site, and click OK.

 ## PROJECT 8.2

To install an X.400 Connector:

1. First, you need to install the MTA transport stack. In the Administrator window, select a server in your organization.
2. From the File menu, select New Other, and then select MTA Transport Stack.
3. In the Type box, select the stack to be used. Now, you can install the X.400 Connector.
4. In the Administrator window, select a site in your organization.
5. Select Connections.
6. From the File menu, select New Other, and then select X.400 Connector.
7. In the Type box, select the type of MTA transport stack to use for the X.400 Connector.

 ## PROJECT 8.3

To install a Dynamic RAS Connector:

1. First, you must install the MTA transport stack. In the Administrator window, select Servers, and then select a server.
2. From the File menu, select New Other, and then select MTA Transport Stack.

3. In the Type box, select RAS MTA Transport Stack.

   Now, you can install the Dynamic RAS Connector.

4. Select the Connections object for the local site.

5. From the File menu, select New Other, and then select Dynamic RAS Connector.

PROJECT 8.4

To install a directory replication connector for a site:

1. In the Administrator window, select Directory Replication.

2. From the File menu, select New Other, and then select Directory Replication Connector.

3. In the Server in remote site box, type the name of the server in the remote site.

4. If the remote site is on the same network, select Yes, The Remote Site Is Available On This Network. If the remote site is not on the same network, select No, The Remote Site Is Not Available On This Network.

5. Select Configure Both Sites to create and configure a directory replication connector in the remote site automatically.

6. Click OK.

8

CASE PROJECTS

1. Your company has two Microsoft Exchange sites—one in London and one in New York. Both locations have dedicated connections to the Internet.

   Required result:

   Connect the two sites using the existing Internet connections.

   Optional desired results:

   Configure the sites so that there is a backup if the Internet connections get disconnected.

   Make sure that the backup connection is only used in emergency situations.

   Proposed solution:

   Use the Internet Mail Service to connect the two sites.

   Which results does the proposed solution provide?

   a. The proposed solution provides the required result and the optional desired results.

   b. The proposed solution provides only the required result.

   c. The proposed solution does not provide the required result.

2. Your company has two Microsoft Exchange sites—one in London and one in New York. Both locations have dedicated connections to the Internet.

Required result:

Connect the two sites using the existing Internet connections.

Optional desired results:

Configure the sites so that there is a backup if the Internet connections get disconnected.

Make sure that the backup connection is only used in emergency situations.

Proposed solution:

Use the Internet Mail Service to connect the two sites. Configure a Dynamic RAS Connector between the London and the New York sites. Assign both the IMS and the Dynamic RAS Connector a cost of 10.

Which results does the proposed solution provide?

   a. The proposed solution provides the required result and both optional desired results.

   b. The proposed solution provides the required result and one optional desired result.

   c. The proposed solution provides only the required result.

   d. The proposed solution does not provide the required result.

3. Your company has two Microsoft Exchange sites—one in London and one in New York. Both locations have dedicated connections to the Internet.

Required result:

Connect the two sites using the existing Internet connections.

Optional desired results:

Configure the sites so that there is a backup if the Internet connections get disconnected.

Make sure that the backup connection is only used in emergency situations.

Proposed solution:

Use the Internet Mail Service to connect the two sites. Configure a Dynamic RAS Connector between the London and the New York sites. Assign the IMS a cost of 1 and the Dynamic RAS Connector a cost of 10.

Which results does the proposed solution provide?

   a. The proposed solution provides the required result and both optional desired results.

   b. The proposed solution provides the required result and one optional desired result.

   c. The proposed solution provides only the required result.

   d. The proposed solution does not provide the required result.

THE INTERNET MAIL SERVICE

The Internet has become part of everyday life for network administrators. Many businesses now rely on the Internet for commerce, product delivery, advertising, and, most importantly, messaging. The Internet allows you to communicate with individuals and businesses that you might never have been able to reach so directly in the past. For example, you can purchase products easily and securely from anywhere in the world without actually talking to a real person.

Microsoft developed Exchange to meet a growing need to connect to the Internet. Microsoft Exchange Server with the *Internet Mail Service (IMS)* Connector allows you to connect your site to literally millions of other sites and users. This chapter goes into the details involved in installing and configuring the IMS connector for Microsoft Exchange Server.

AFTER READING THIS CHAPTER AND COMPLETING THE EXERCISES, YOU WILL BE ABLE TO:

- Understand how the Domain Name System (DNS) and the Simple Mail Transfer Protocol (SMTP) work
- Use the Internet Mail Service (IMS) Wizard
- Install and configure IMS
- Understand the features and options available from IMS
- Schedule the IMS to receive mail messages from remote sites using RAS connections

IMS: EXPLORED AND EXPLAINED

The Internet Mail Service is an integrated Microsoft Exchange component that uses the *Simple Mail Transfer Protocol (SMTP)*, the TCP/IP protocol suite, and the *Domain Name System (DNS)* to route messages to the Internet or direct them to an SMTP host. SMTP is a protocol that specifies the procedure for transferring mail messages between two systems by specifying the message format and the method to be used in delivering the message from the sending host to the receiving host.

The Windows NT TCP/IP suite must be installed and configured on a system running Microsoft Exchange so that IMS can function. TCP/IP and SMTP work in tandem to handle transmission of messages across the Internet or between SMTP hosts. IMS is a Windows NT service that may be installed as an option on an Exchange Server computer, and allows an Exchange Server to function as an SMTP server. That is, an Exchange Server with IMS installed functions like any other SMTP server, and can therefore send and receive SMTP messages from any mail server that supports SMTP (see Figure 9.1).

To function properly, IMS relies on two IP-based services—namely the Domain Name System (DNS) and the Simple Mail Transfer Protocol (SMTP). These components are discussed in detail in the following sections.

DOMAIN NAME SYSTEM

In a TCP/IP environment, every computer requires a unique numerical identifier that takes the form of an IP address. For example, 206.224.95.1 represents a typical IP address, expressed in numerical form. When using TCP/IP, if a user wishes to communicate with a server on a network, that server's IP address must somehow be supplied.

On a small network, it is fairly easy to remember a few IP addresses. On larger networks, however, this is a difficult, if not impossible, task. For this reason, each computer on the network may also be assigned a symbolic computer name that is easy to remember. For example, **www.lanw.com** is the name of the Web server at LANWrights, Inc. (the company that helped to put this book together).

The Domain Name System (DNS) is a distributed database that provides a hierarchical naming system to identify systems on the Internet or an intranet. DNS consists of two components: a server and a client. The server component of DNS maintains a database of domain and computer names. The client component, also known as a *resolver*, generates the DNS queries against the DNS database on the server that supply a numeric IP address when a symbolic name is proffered in a name resolution request.

9

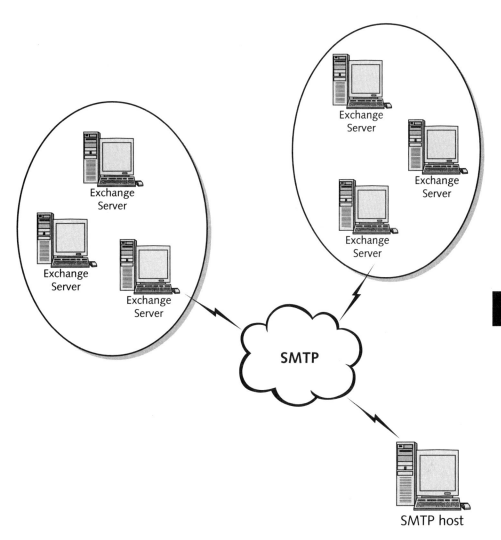

Figure 9.1   The Microsoft Exchange Server in an SMTP environment.

The DNS database is a hierarchical tree structure called the *domain name space* (in Exchange terms, you could think of this entire space as the collection of all address spaces within the DNS hierarchy). Each node in the tree structure is known as a *domain*, and each node below that is known as a subdomain. To better understand this, compare the DNS hierarchy to a file system. A file system begins at a root folder that may contain subfolders, and, like a file system, the root of the DNS hierarchy is at the top and is known as the *root* (or *top-level*) *domain*. Figure 9.2 illustrates the similarities between a DNS hierarchy and a file-system tree.

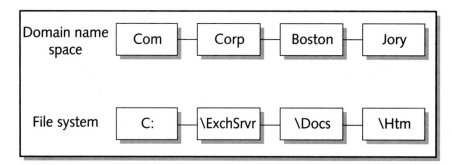

Figure 9.2   A comparison of the DNS tree and a file-system tree.

Examples of top-level domains on the Internet include .edu, used for educational institutions; .gov, used for government sites; and .com, which designates commercial sites. A complete domain name (from bottom to top) is called a *fully qualified domain name (FQDN)*. In the domain name space shown in Figure 9.3, jory.boston.corp.com is an FQDN.

The main function of DNS is *name resolution,* which means that it can translate from FQDNs to IP addresses, and from IP addresses to FQDNs (this latter procedure is known as a reverse lookup). For DNS, the name resolution process works as follows:

1. A client passes a query to a local name server (either IP-to-FQDN or FQDN-to-IP). If the query can be satisfied from the local server's database or its name cache (a list of name to IP address translations that DNS servers keep in memory to reflect recently requested translations), then the server will reply with the requested information.

2. If the local name server does not possess the required information, it will take the part of the client and query a remote name server for the name on the client's behalf. It will also forward the results of its query to the client when they are received.

3. If necessary, the local name server will start at the very top of the DNS hierarchy, and query one of the root name servers until it finds an appropriate tree, and then work its way through the hierarchy until all requested data is found. The local name server then forwards its results to the original client that requested name resolution services.

Now that you've learned the basics about the Domain Name System used to convert symbolic to numeric addresses, it's time to tackle the underpinnings of Internet email—namely, SMTP. This combination IP protocol and service provides the topic for the section that follows next.

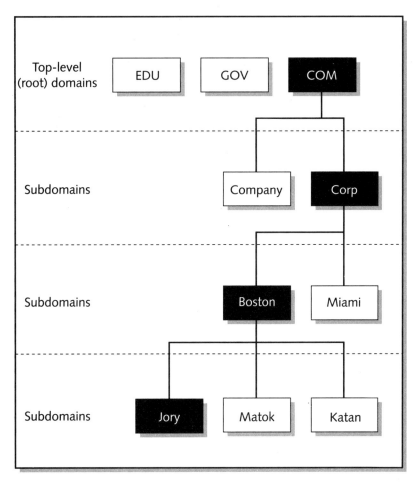

Figure 9.3 An example of a domain name space.

SIMPLE MAIL TRANSFER PROTOCOL

The Simple Mail Transfer Protocol is used to send messages from one host on the Internet to another using Transmission Control Protocol (TCP) port 25. When one host sends a mail message to another, the process works as follows:

1. The SMTP sender (client) establishes a connection to an SMTP receiver (server). The client requests an SMTP session by sending a **HELO** command. Before the client can continue, the server must send back an OK message indicating that it will accept the session request.

2. The client then informs the server that it's sending a message using the **MAIL FROM** command. The server returns an OK message if the user is authorized to send mail to it.

3. The client sends the server a list of the recipients of the message using the **RCPT TO** command. A **RCPT TO** command is issued for each recipient separately. The server must acknowledge the command by returning an OK message.

4. The client requests to send the actual message body by using the **DATA** command. The server must reply with an "OK to send message" before the client sends the message body to the server.

5. When the message has been sent successfully, the client sends a **QUIT** command to close the connection. The client can send another message by repeating Steps 2 through 4 before issuing the **QUIT** command.

In a nutshell, this explains how email is sent from a client to a server. The remainder of the delivery process consists of a series of server-to-server transfers, until the designated mail server for the target domain specified in the IP address for the recipient is reached. This explains why DNS also includes a so-called MX (mail exchange) record in its database for each domain—this record designates which SMTP server should receive the inbound email message for the intended recipient (or recipients).

Now that you've covered the basics of DNS and SMTP, it's time to explore the capabilities of the Exchange Internet Mail Service (IMS). This is the subject of the section that follows next.

INSTALLING IMS

Before you install IMS, be sure that TCP/IP is installed and configured on the Windows NT Server running Exchange and IMS. To install TCP/IP, follow these steps:

1. Right-click the Network Neighborhood icon, and select Properties from the drop-down menu.

2. Select the Protocol tab, click the Add button, select TCP/IP Protocol from the list, and click OK.

3. Enter your TCP/IP address, subnet mask, and default gateway.

4. Select the DNS tab.

5. Enter the host and domain names of the computer. Together, these represent a system's FQDN.

6. Enter one or more IP addresses for the DNS servers you wish to use for name resolution services (note that the list of servers represents the order in which resolution requests will be sent; you should always put local DNS servers higher in this list than remote DNS servers, because this produces the fastest name lookup behavior overall).

Microsoft Exchange 5.5 includes an Internet Mail Wizard for installing IMS (as shown in Figure 9.4). You may access the Internet Mail Wizard by selecting New | Other, and then selecting Internet Mail Service from the resulting set of menu selections.

Microsoft recommends that you review the items on the following list to ensure that your Exchange system is configured correctly before you install IMS:

- For improved security and performance, run IMS on a Windows NT Server using the Windows NT File System (NTFS) rather than a File Allocation Table (FAT) file system. This provides file-level security, and represents the best way to protect message files and other critical information resources related to IMS.

- Know the addressing scheme for your organization. This includes the domain name structure, as well as the IP address ranges involved.

- Determine the SMTP address for the site.

- Determine the address space that the Internet Mail Service will handle.

- Identify a recipient who is to receive notifications if the Internet Mail Service fails. (This recipient is known as a postmaster in Internet parlance.)

- Obtain the host name and domain name for the computer where the Internet Mail Service will be installed.

- Determine whether DNS will be used to provide host and domain name-to-Internet Protocol (IP) address resolution.

- Obtain the IP address of DNS servers or the SMTP hosts that will interact with the Internet Mail Service.

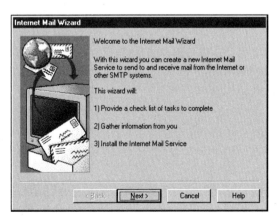

Figure 9.4   The IMS Internet Mail Wizard.

Check the "Hands-On Project" section later in this chapter for detailed instructions on installing IMS.

Once you've researched and collected all this information, you will be ready to configure the IMS. This makes the next section of this chapter a logical successor to the current one.

CONFIGURING INTERNET MAIL SERVICE: PROPERTIES PAGES

You may configure the Internet Mail Service using various tabs on its Properties page. Be aware that you must stop and then restart the IMS before any changes will actually take effect. To access the IMS Properties page, select the Connections option in the left pane of Exchange Administrator and then double-click the IMS to be modified in the right pane. You will learn all the details for each of the IMS Properties pages in the sections that follow next.

GENERAL

Within the General Properties page (shown in Figure 9.5), you can view the computer name (this is a read-only field) and enter an administrative note to distinguish this IMS connector from other IMS connectors installed on your system. You may also limit the maximum message size that this connector will handle to a specified number of kilobytes.

Figure 9.5   The IMS General Properties page.

PERMISSIONS

The Permissions Properties page (see Figure 9.6) includes two sections. The first section is a read-only section that lists those users with inherited rights to the connector, and the second section allows you to assign specific roles and rights to individual users and/or groups to the connector. You may assign any or all of the following roles:

- Admin
- Permissions Admin
- Search

You may also assign one or more rights to individuals designated for specific roles with the IMS. These include the following:

- Modify User Attributes
- Modify Admin Attributes
- Delete
- Modify Permissions
- Search

For more information on user roles and rights, refer to Chapter 5.

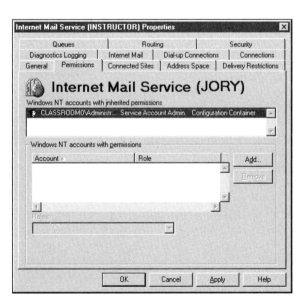

Figure 9.6   The IMS Permissions Properties page.

CONNECTED SITES

Within the Connected Sites Properties page (see Figure 9.7), you can specify connections to existing Microsoft Exchange Server sites. This information is important if you want to make sure that directory replication will take place and that other connectors in the organization may be accessed.

When you click the New button, you will see a dialog box similar to the one shown in Figure 9.8 (your organization's name will of course be different). The Connected Sites Properties dialog box has two tabs: General and Routing Address. Under the General tab, you are required to enter the organization name and the name of the site that will be connected. Under the Routing Address tab, you are required to enter the type of address to be used (such as SMTP), the routing cost involved with the connection, and the email address to use for the site on the other side of the connection.

ADDRESS SPACE

When a connector is created outside a site, a logical path must be created on the Address Space Properties page (see Figure 9.9) to allow the Message Transfer Agent (MTA) to determine how to deliver messages to their final destinations. This logical path, the address space, must be unique for each recipient. A connector must have at least one address space entry to operate properly. The format of the address space depends on the format of the remote messaging system. For example, if you are sending a message to an SMTP network, the SMTP address space must be used.

Figure 9.7   The IMS Connected Sites Properties page.

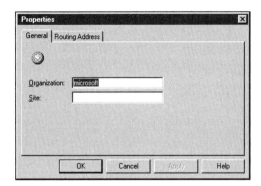

Figure 9.8   Adding a connected site.

If you create multiple routes to a single destination, in keeping with normal Exchange connector behavior, the IMS uses only the lowest cost route(s). The only time that IMS will use a route with a higher cost is when a lower cost route is unavailable. You may use MX records in your DNS server to override this feature and allow the forwarding of incoming mail to a secondary route. You may also create multiple routes with identical costs between two sites to provide load-balancing across all routes that share the same cost.

Figure 9.9   The IMS Address Space Properties page.

DELIVERY RESTRICTIONS

You can use the Delivery Restrictions Properties page (shown in Figure 9.10) to either accept or reject outbound messages from any recipient within the Microsoft Exchange site. If a recipient is listed in the Reject Messages box or is not listed in the Accept Messages From box, any messages such users address to the IMS will be returned to their originators. Please note, however, that you cannot control inbound messages using this Properties page, only outbound messages.

QUEUES

The Queues Properties page (see Figure 9.11) allows you to view important information about messages in their queues. You may view details about specific queued messages and delete problem messages; however, you cannot reorder messages in their queues. You may also use the Queues Properties page to determine the number of messages in any given queue. From within the Queues Properties page four distinct queues may be viewed:

- **Inbound messages awaiting conversion** Queues any incoming messages that need either to be converted to Exchange formats, or rerouted to the IMS, and then delivered to the Information Store.

- **Inbound messages awaiting delivery** Queues any converted incoming messages that remain to be delivered to their Exchange recipients.

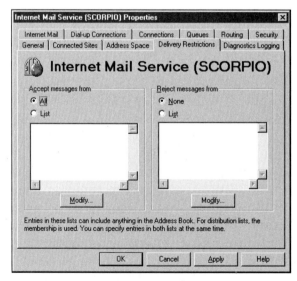

Figure 9.10   The IMS Delivery Restrictions Properties page.

Figure 9.11   The IMS Queues Properties page.

- **Outbound messages awaiting conversion** Queues any outgoing messages received by the IMS from the MTA that are waiting to be converted to an SMTP format by the IMS.

- **Outbound messages awaiting delivery** Queues any converted outgoing messages that remain to be delivered by the IMS scheduler.

Outbound messages are received by the MTA (which deposits them in the Exchsrvr\imcdata\out folder) and placed into the Internet Mail Service's MTS-OUT queue in the Information Store. The IMS then converts these messages into SMTP format, and moves them into the Out queue until they are transmitted. When inbound Internet messages arrive, the IMS stores them in its In queue (they are stored in the Exchsrvr\imcdata\in folder) until these messages may be converted and then moved into the MTS-IN queue in the Information Store.

You can view additional details about messages stored in one of the four IMS queues by either double-clicking a message, or selecting it and then clicking the Details button. The message detail information includes the following kinds of data:

- **Originator** The address of the user that sent the message.

- **MTS-ID** A unique identifier that includes the originating server's name, the date and time the message was sent, and a hexadecimal identifier. This field is not available (it's left blank) in the In and Out queues.

- **Message ID** A unique identifier given to a message by the Exchange Server that remains with the message from start to finish. This field is not available (it's blank) in the MTS-OUT queue.

- **Destination Host** The name of the server where the message is to be delivered.

- **Submit Time** The time the message arrived in the queue.

- **Size** The size of the message (in bytes).

- **Next Retry Time** The next scheduled time to resend the message. (This is available only if previous attempts to send were unsuccessful.)

- **Retries** The number of times IMS has tried to deliver the message.

- **Expiration** The time at which message retries will be stopped and a *non-delivery report (NDR)* will be sent to the originator.

- **Recipients** The addresses to which the message is to be delivered, including the status for attempts made to deliver the message.

There are several other options available to you on the Queues Properties page. Be aware that the information in the Queues windows represents the status of the queues when you accessed the Queues Properties page. This information is static, not dynamic. You can, however, refresh a queue's status information by clicking the Refresh button. You may also delete messages by highlighting the message and clicking the Delete button. You can delete messages in all the queues except for the MTS-IN queue. Finally, you can force IMS to try resending any outbound message. This comes in handy if you have made configuration changes to try to solve a problem and want to know if your changes actually work. To do this, select a message in one of the outbound queues, then click the Retry Now button.

ROUTING

Use the Routing Properties page (shown in Figure 9.12) to intercept any inbound messages from SMTP hosts, POP3, and IMAP4 clients, and reroute these messages to other SMTP hosts before the Internet Mail Service processes them.

You have the option of:

- Not rerouting incoming SMTP mail.
- Rerouting incoming SMTP mail (required for POP3/IMAP4 support).

When you add a routing address, you may specify whether addresses should be accepted as inbound or should be rerouted to a specific domain.

SECURITY

Use the Security Properties page (see Figure 9.13) to enable security on outbound connections to other mail systems. You can also encrypt or authenticate message transfers from a Microsoft Exchange Server to a remote

Figure 9.12   The Routing Properties page.

9

SMTP host. There are three security options available for connections to other systems in the Security Properties page:

- **Simple Authentication And Security Layer (SASL)** This is an Internet standard for handling user authentication and encryption of passwords and data payloads.

- **Secure Sockets Layer (SSL)** This is probably the most popular IP interface for applications of all kinds; SSL adds authentication and encryption services to the normal sockets interface but otherwise behaves the same as WinSock.

- **Windows NT Security** This option typically applies only when sender and receiver are both Windows NT machines, but it too offers increased password and message payload security.

The security options are:

- **No Authentication Or Encryption** No security features enabled.

- **SASL Authentication/SSL Encryption** Allows you to choose SASL/AUTH, SSL encryption, or both.

- **SASL/AUTH Clear Text Password Authentication** Sends the clear text account and password information on outbound connections using the AUTH LOGIN ESMTP extension.

- **SSL Encryption** Uses SSL encryption.

Figure 9.13   The IMS Security Properties page.

■ **Windows NT Challenge/Response Authentication And
Encryption** Uses Windows NT Challenge/Response authentication
to encrypt account and password information.

DIAGNOSTICS LOGGING

You can set the following logging levels for this connector using the Diagnostics
Logging Properties page (shown in Figure 9.14):

- Initialization/Termination
- Addressing
- Message Transfer
- SMTP Interface Events
- Internal Processing
- SMTP Protocol Logs
- Message Archival

You can select the following four levels to log:

■ **None** Only critical or error events and events with a logging level of
zero are logged. This is the default level.

■ **Minimum** Events with a logging level of 1 or lower are logged.

■ **Medium** Events with a logging level of 3 or lower are logged.

■ **Maximum** Events with a logging level of 5 or lower are logged.

Figure 9.14   The IMS Diagnostics Logging Properties page.

9

INTERNET MAIL

The Internet Mail Properties page (see Figure 9.15) allows you to configure the administrator's mailbox, message content, and message tracking.

The administrator's mailbox will receive any error notifications sent out by IMS as well as any messages sent to the postmaster. Select a recipient to act as the administrator for an IMS by clicking the Change button and selecting a

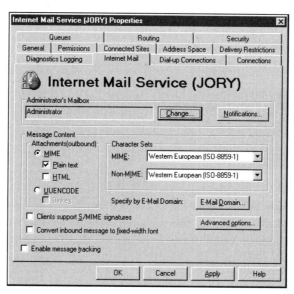

Figure 9.15   The Internet Mail Properties page.

recipient from the list. You can select either an individual recipient or a distribution list.

You can configure the circumstances under which IMS will notify the administrator when NDRs are generated by clicking the Notifications button. Notifications may be configured to always send notifications, or only to send notifications for specific types of NDRs, including the following:

- Email address could not be found.

- Multiple matches for an email occurred.

- Destination host could not be found.

- Protocol error occurred.

- Message time-out exceeded.

The remaining configuration options include the following settings:

- **Attachments (Outbound)** Allows you to specify either MIME (plain text or HTML) or UUEncoded (.UUE or .HQX, also known as binhex) attachments.

- **Character Sets** Allows you to specify a default character set for either MIME or non-MIME messages.

- **Email Domain** Allows you to choose different encoding methods, character sets, and message sizes for each domain hosted on your Microsoft Exchange Server. For example, you might want to use the MIME encoding method for your domain corp.com and the UUEncoded method for the boston.corp.com subdomain. To do this, you are required to list the subdomain before the domain.

- **Advanced** Allows you to set the following options: Disable Out Of Office Responses To The Internet, Disable Automatic Replies To The Internet, and Disable Sending Display Names To The Internet.

- **Message Tracking** Prompts the MTA to create a daily log file that contains all routing information about all the processed messages. You can use this log file to track specific messages using the Message Tracking Center.

DIAL-UP CONNECTIONS

You can use the Dial-up Connections Properties page (see Figure 9.16) to configure connection and schedule information. IMS can be configured to use the Windows NT *Remote Access Service (RAS)* to connect to an *Internet Service Provider (ISP)* or to a remote Microsoft Exchange site. You can use a dial-up connection with IMS if a permanent link does not exist or for fault tolerance should a permanent connection go down.

Figure 9.16   The Dial-up Connections Properties page.

To add dial-up connections to IMS, you must first configure one or more RAS entries in the RAS Phonebook. If you have multiple RAS entries in the Phonebook, only those entries selected in the Available Connections window will be used.

Some ISPs require your system to issue a command to identify itself to the provider and to notify the provider that messages are available to be sent. Using the Mail Retrieval dialog box (shown in Figure 9.17), you may configure your system to:

- Use ETRN, an SMTP extension that causes the remote host to send stored messages.
- Use TURN, an SMTP extension that causes the remote host to send stored messages requiring authentication.
- Issue a custom command.
- Not send any retrieval messages.

You can also specify a default time-out period (in minutes, indicating how long to keep the RAS connection open), the logon information for your ISP, and either a daily or weekly schedule to specify how frequently IMS should connect to the remote host to receive email.

CONNECTIONS

Within the Connections Properties page (see Figure 9.18), you can configure transfer mode, message delivery, connection acceptance, service message queue information, and security features.

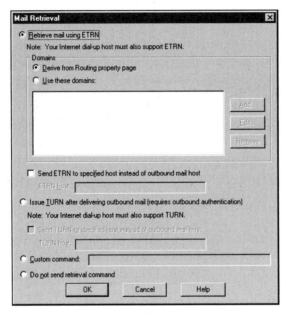

Figure 9.17   The Mail Retrieval dialog box.

Transfer Mode

The Transfer Mode feature allows you to set restrictions on how messages will be received and sent. You can use these options in the Transfer Mode feature:

- **Inbound & Outbound** Accept inbound messages, and send outbound messages.

Figure 9.18   The Connections Properties page.

- **Inbound Only** Accept only inbound messages.
- **Outbound Only** Send only outbound messages.
- **None (Flush Queues)** Do not accept inbound or outbound messages.
- **Advanced** Specify the maximum number of inbound connections, outbound connections, connections to a single host, and messages in a connection.

Message Delivery

The Message Delivery feature provides options for message receipt and delivery to remote recipients. You can set these options in the Message Delivery Feature:

- **Use Domain Name Service (DNS)** Use DNS to resolve all remote domains.
- **Forward All Messages To Host** Use a specific host to resolve and deliver all remote mail.
- **Dial Using** Use a RAS connection to connect to a remote host.
- **Email Domain** Use to specify how different domains will deliver their messages.

Accept Connections

The Accept Connections feature provides settings for what types of messages will be accepted. You can set these options in the Accept Connections feature:

- **From Any Host (Secure Or Nonsecure)** Messages from any host not explicitly listed will be accepted.
- **Only From Hosts Using** Specify whether the connection will use authentication, encryption, or both.
- **Hosts** Allows you to override the default for specific hosts.

Service Message Queues

The Service Message Queues feature is where you configure retries and time-outs. You can send these options in the Service Message Queues feature:

- **Retry Interval (Hrs)** Specifies the amount of time in hours that IMS will attempt to reconnect to a remote host if the initial connection failed. You can specify different intervals by separating them with commas. For example, to try after 15 minutes, then 1 hour, and then 5 hours, you would enter: .25, 1, 5.
- **Time-outs** Allows you to specify different time-outs for urgent, normal, or non-urgent messages.

9

Client Requirements

The following two features describe client requirements:

- **Clients Can Only Submit If Homed On This Server** Allows a client to submit messages only if they have a mailbox on the Microsoft Exchange Server where the IMS is located.

- **Clients Can Only Submit If Authentication Account Matches Submission Address** Allows a client to submit messages only if his Windows NT account matches the information in the From field in the message.

CHAPTER SUMMARY

Microsoft Exchange Server and the Internet Mail Service (IMS) use the Simple Mail Transfer Protocol to communicate between the server and a remote host. The TCP/IP protocol stack must be installed for IMS to function.

IMS also uses the Domain Name System protocol, which creates a hierarchical database of domain names and their IP address information. This allows IMS to resolve the domain names that you commonly use in your mail messages to the IP addresses that computers use to communicate.

SMTP is a method used by applications to send and receive mail messages. SMTP uses built-in commands to communicate between a client and a server. The IMS acts as an SMTP client when it sends messages and as an SMTP server when it receives messages.

Configuring IMS means interacting with any of its many Properties pages. Covering these consumed the bulk of this chapter, and included the following elements:

- **General Properties** Use this to examine the server name and to set maximum message sizes.

- **Permissions** Use this to set and examine permissions to change IMS configuration and to manipulate its various folders and queues.

- **Connected Sites** Use this to specify connections to existing Microsoft Exchange Server sites.

- **Address Space** Use this to specify the type of address space that the IMS connector will access; normally, this is an SMTP address space.

- **Delivery Restrictions** Use this to either accept or reject outbound messages from any recipient within the Microsoft Exchange site.

- **Queues** Use this to manage the inbound and outbound queues (which contain converted and unconverted messages for each direction) under the control of the IMS.

- **Routing** Use this to intercept any inbound messages from SMTP hosts, POP3, and IMAP4 clients, and reroute these messages to other SMTP hosts before the IMS processes them.

- **Security** Use this to set any of a number of Internet (SASL and SSL) or NT-specific security measures for SMTP message traffic.

- **Diagnostics Logging** Use this to set one of five levels of progressively more verbose activity logging for traffic through the IMS connector.

- **Internet Mail** Use this to configure the administrator's mailbox, message content, and message tracking.

- **Dial-up Connections** Use this to control how IMS uses dial-up (RAS) connections to schedule and establish links with sites or ISPs that are not permanently connected to the Exchange Server.

- **Connections** Use this to configure transfer mode, message delivery, connection acceptance, service message queue information, and security features.

Familiarity with these Properties pages is essential to a complete understanding of the IMS. Be sure to spend some time working with these Properties pages on a test server to make sure you are comfortable with each one, and its capabilities and controls.

KEY TERMS

- **domain name space**—The DNS database hierarchical tree structure.

- **Domain Name System (DNS)**—The hierarchical database of domain name to IP address relationships.

- **fully qualified domain name (FQDN)**—The full DNS path of an Internet host.

- **Internet Mail Service (IMS)**—A connector used to connect a Microsoft Exchange site to either an SMTP mail system or a remote Microsoft Exchange site.

- **Internet Service Provider (ISP)**—A third party that offers Internet connectivity to individuals and businesses.

- **name resolution**—The process that DNS uses to map a domain name to an IP address.

- **non-delivery report (NDR)**—A report sent out to a recipient or distribution list that informs the user or users of message delivery problems.

- **Remote Access Service (RAS)**—A Windows NT service that allows you to connect your server to another remote location using a dial-up connection.

- **resolver**—The client software that queries the DNS to convert a domain name to its IP address.

- **root domain**—The top domain in the hierarchical DNS tree. For example, .com or .org.

- **Simple Authentication And Security Layer (SASL) authentication**—A method that uses clear text to authenticate connections.

- **Simple Mail Transfer Protocol (SMTP)**—The mail protocol used to connect two hosts running the TCP/IP protocol.

- **Secure Sockets Layer (SSL) encryption**—A method to encrypt information between hosts.

- **subdomain**—Any domain listed below the top-level, or *root*, domain.

- **top-level domain**—See root domain.

- **Windows NT Challenge/Response authentication and encryption**—A method for authentication and encryption that is available to the Windows NT operating system.

REVIEW QUESTIONS

1. Your company hosts several domains for its clients. Some of the clients complain that they cannot see any of the attachments that are sent to them. What is going on?

    a. IMS does not route attachments.

    b. The clients must upgrade their client software to handle your attachment type.

    c. The clients need to change the attachment type for their domain in the IMS Properties pages.

    d. The clients are using an Apple Macintosh and cannot read your attachments.

2. How many Internet Mail Service connectors can you have installed on a single Microsoft Exchange Server?

    a. Depends on the bandwidth you have to the Internet

    b. Only one connector per server

    c. Only one connector per site

    d. An unlimited number of connectors

3. A client informs you that she can send email to your Exchange Server by using the IP address only, not the FQDN. Why?

   a. Your DNS entry is incorrect.

   b. She has the wrong IP address/FQDN combination.

   c. Your client's DNS is configured incorrectly.

   d. Your connection to the Internet is down.

4. You send a message through IMS to a colleague on a Unix host. He complains that the message is garbled. How would you fix the problem?

   a. Change the attachment encoding for the recipient's domain.

   b. Have your colleague change the attachment encoding for his messages.

   c. Change the attachment encoding in your client software.

   d. IMS cannot communicate with a Unix host.

5. What is the top-level domain for the following FQDN?

   jory.boston.corp.com

   a. jory

   b. boston

   c. corp

   d. com

6. DNS provides translation from FQDNs to numeric IP addresses and also from numeric IP addresses to FQDNs. True or False?

7. IMS can act as both an SMTP client and an SMTP server. True or False?

8. You make a configuration change to the IMS. What should you do next?

   a. Shut down and restart the Exchange Server computer.

   b. Stop and restart the Internet Mail Service.

   c. Stop and restart the SMTP service.

   d. Pause and restart the Internet Mail Service.

9. SMTP is a universally recognized messaging protocol. True or False?

10. You cannot schedule when IMS will connect to an ISP to receive messages. True or False?

11. What client component would you use to resolve a domain name to an IP address?

   a. A resolver program

   b. DNS

   c. IMS

   d. Microsoft Outlook

9

12. If you want IMS to connect to the Internet using a modem, what must be installed?

    a. RAS must be installed.

    b. A RAS Phonebook entry must be configured.

    c. NetBEUI must be installed.

    d. Both a and b.

13. You must use the IMS Wizard to install IMS. True or False?

14. What is the default Exchange domain naming convention?

    a. organization.site.com

    b. site.organization.com

    c. com.site.organization

    d. com.organization.site

15. The TCP/IP protocol does not need to be installed before IMS is installed. True or False?

16. You must use a DNS server for the IMS to function. True or False?

17. Which of the following IMS Properties pages would you use to set maximum message size for a message to be passed through the connector?

    a. General Properties

    b. Delivery Restrictions Properties

    c. Security Properties

    d. Internet Mail Properties

18. To establish and manage administrative controls over the IMS, which of the following properties pages should you use?

    a. General Properties

    b. Permissions Properties

    c. Security Properties

    d. Connections Properties

19. Of the following list of elements, which may be managed using the Connections Properties page? (Choose all correct answers.)

    a. Transfer mode

    b. Message delivery options

    c. Accept connections

    d. Client-side configuration

20. As the level of Diagnostics Logging increases from 1 to 5, the verbosity of the logs increases at the same time. True or False?

HANDS-ON PROJECTS

PROJECT 9.1

To install the Internet Mail Service:

1. In the Administrator window, select Connections.
2. From the File menu, select New | Other, and then Internet Mail Service.
3. Click the Next button on the first screen of the Internet Mail Wizard (see Figure 9.19).
4. Click the Next button.
5. Select the Microsoft Exchange Server on which you would like to install the Internet Mail Service (see Figure 9.20). You can optionally check the Allow Internet Mail Through A Dial-up Connection box. Click the Next button.
6. Select either Use Domain Name System (DNS) To Send Mail (the default) or Route All Messages Through A Single Host (see Figure 9.21). Routing all messages through a single host allows you to specify one or more hosts (separate host names with a comma) to handle the actual delivery of the message to the final destination. Click the Next button.
7. Select either All Internet Mail Addresses (Typical) or Only Mail Destined For A Particular Set Of Addresses, as shown in Figure 9.22. Click the Next button.
8. Enter the site address to use in the email addresses (see Figure 9.23). If you select @corp.com, the email will be user@corp.com. However, if you select @site.corp.com, the email will be user@site.corp.com. Click the Next button.

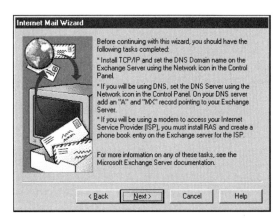

Figure 9.19   The Internet Mail Wizard welcome screen.

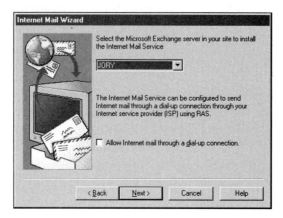

Figure 9.20   Selecting the server.

9. Select either to use (or create) an administrator mailbox for NDRs or use an existing recipient or distribution list for NDRs (see Figure 9.24). Click the Next button.

10. Enter the password for the Microsoft Exchange service account on the server where IMS is being installed (see Figure 9.25). Click the Next button.

11. Click the Finish button (see Figure 9.26).

12. At this time, the IMS Wizard will register the IMS and start all the necessary services. When it has completed this process, the window shown in Figure 9.27 will appear stating that you should run the Microsoft Exchange Performance Optimizer on the Microsoft Exchange Server where IMS has been installed.

13. Click the OK button.

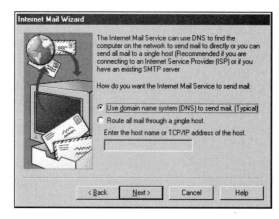

Figure 9.21   Selecting how to send mail.

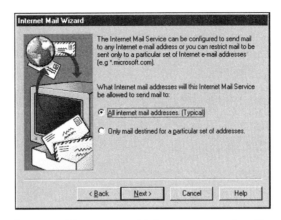

Figure 9.22   Selecting addresses to which you can send mail.

  CASE PROJECTS

9

1. Suppose the following situation exists:

Your company would like to connect several of its branch offices. It is your job as the senior system administrator to make sure that this is done correctly.

Required result:

Connect the offices together using the Internet.

Optional desired results:

Make sure that all connections to the Internet are protected.

Make sure that only mail messages are going to be delivered to/from the Internet.

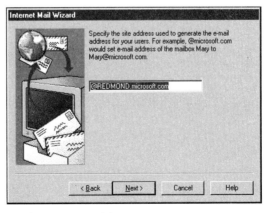

Figure 9.23   Specifying a site address.

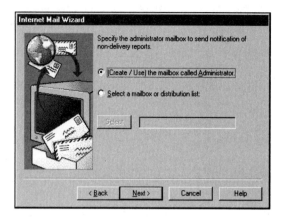

Figure 9.24   Specifying an administrator mailbox.

Proposed solution:

Use the Internet Mail Service to connect the remote sites.

Which results does the proposed solution provide?

a. The proposed solution provides the required result and both optional desired results.

b. The proposed solution provides the required result and one optional desired result.

c. The proposed solution provides only the required result.

d. The proposed solution does not provide the required result.

2. Your company would like to connect several of its branch offices. It is your job as the senior system administrator to make sure that this is done correctly.

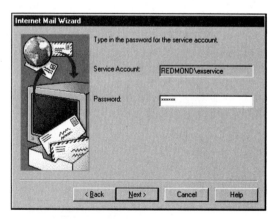

Figure 9.25   Selecting a password.

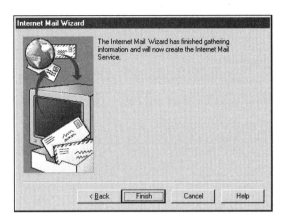

Figure 9.26   The Internet Mail Wizard.

Required result:

Connect the offices using the Internet.

Optional desired results:

Make sure that all connections to the Internet are protected.

Make sure that only mail messages are going to be delivered to/from the Internet.

Proposed solution:

Use the Internet Mail Service to connect the remote sites. Install a firewall, and block all TCP ports.

Which results does the proposed solution provide?

a. The proposed solution provides the required result and both optional desired results.

b. The proposed solution provides the required result and one optional desired result.

c. The proposed solution provides only the required result.

d. The proposed solution does not provide the required result.

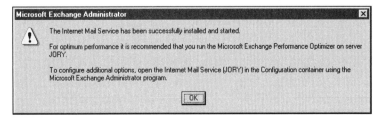

Figure 9.27   The final screen of the Internet Mail Wizard.

3. Your company would like to connect several of its branch offices. It is your job as the senior system administrator to make sure that this is done correctly.

Required result:

Connect the offices using the Internet.

Optional desired results:

Make sure that all connections to the Internet are protected.

Make sure that only mail messages are going to be delivered to/from the Internet.

Proposed solution:

Use the Internet Mail Service to connect the remote sites. Install a firewall, and block all TCP ports except port 25.

Which results does the proposed solution provide?

a. The proposed solution provides the required result and both optional desired results.

b. The proposed solution provides the required result and one optional desired result.

c. The proposed solution provides only the required result.

d. The proposed solution does not provide the required result.

CHAPTER TEN

INTERNET MAIL PROTOCOLS

Microsoft Exchange Server incorporates all of the most popular Internet protocols to provide a broad range of options to connect your users to the Internet and to Exchange Server. These include the email protocols, *Post Office Protocol version 3 (POP3)* and *Internet Message Access Protocol version 4 (IMAP4)*; the *Lightweight Directory Access Protocol (LDAP)*; the *Usenet Network News Transfer Protocol (NNTP)*; and the *Hypertext Transfer Protocol (HTTP)*.

Both POP3 and IMAP4 allow users to connect to Exchange Server to access their mailboxes remotely, be it from home or anywhere on the Internet. IMAP4 also allows users to read from and post to public folders located on an Exchange Server. LDAP allows you to share your Microsoft Exchange Address Book information with your remote users or with anonymous Internet users.

AFTER READING THIS CHAPTER AND COMPLETING THE EXERCISES, YOU WILL BE ABLE TO:

- Configure the Post Office Protocol version 3
- Configure the Internet Message Access Protocol version 4
- Configure the Lightweight Directory Access Protocol
- Configure the Network News Transfer Protocol
- Configure Microsoft Outlook Web Access

Using NNTP, you can connect your Microsoft Exchange Server to Usenet and receive or publish Usenet information. Finally, HTTP allows your users to gain complete access to their mailboxes, public folders, and schedules. HTTP also grants anonymous users access to specific public folders that you would like to share.

In the following sections, we explore the various Internet mail protocols that Exchange can use for communication, including:

- Transmission Control Protocol/Internet Protocol (TCP/IP)
- *Simple Mail Transfer Protocol (SMTP)*
- Post Office Protocol version 3 (POP3)
- Internet Message Access Protocol version 4 (IMAP4)
- Lightweight Directory Access Protocol (LDAP)
- Network News Transfer Protocol (NNTP)
- Hypertext Transfer Protocol (HTTP)

Proper installation and configuration of these protocols is imperative for successful Exchange Server deployment and communication. Because Internet access has moved past the point of "gee-whiz" technology to strategic business value, working with these protocols represents some of the most important topics that Exchange administrators must master.

OVERVIEW OF IP MESSAGING PROTOCOLS

The Internet is a network of networks that communicate using a common language that takes the form of a complex and powerful collection of networking protocols, called a protocol suite. This protocol suite is the Transmission Control Protocol/Internet Protocol (TCP/IP). An Internet protocol is a set of standards or rules designed to enable one computer on the Internet to communicate and exchange information with another.

TCP/IP was designed from its very inception to facilitate communication and information exchange between different types of computer platforms (for example, Windows NT Server and a Unix server). The Internet itself, with its millions of hosts and tens of millions of users, represents a stunning demonstration of what TCP/IP can do, and this technology has created a truly global online community.

Within Exchange, all associated protocols are managed in its Protocols container; this serves as the subject for the section that follows next.

THE PROTOCOLS CONTAINER

Each Exchange site and server includes an associated container called Protocols. Among the other protocols it supports, this container also stores configuration objects for each of the Internet protocols. You may configure the default settings that apply to all the protocols in a site, using the site's Protocols container. You may also configure settings that apply only to individual servers. If you configure default settings for protocols at the site level, those settings apply to all the servers in the site, but they do not replicate to other sites. Figure 10.1 shows the Internet protocol objects in the site and server containers.

All protocol objects, with the exception of the HTTP protocol, may be controlled at three levels: the site level, the server level, and the mailbox level. The HTTP protocol may only be controlled from the site level and the mailbox level but not at the server level.

By default, the protocols that appear in the Protocols container are enabled in all locations. You, as an administrator, may enable and/or disable any of these protocols to configure different functionality. For example, you may configure a protocol to be:

- **Disabled at the site level and enabled on a per-server basis.** This allows clients to connect only to those servers with the protocol enabled.

- **Enabled at the site level and disabled on a per-server basis.** This allows clients to connect only to those servers that do not have the protocol disabled.

- **Enabled at the site level and the server level, but disabled at the mailbox level.** This allows only clients that do not have the protocol disabled to connect to the server.

10

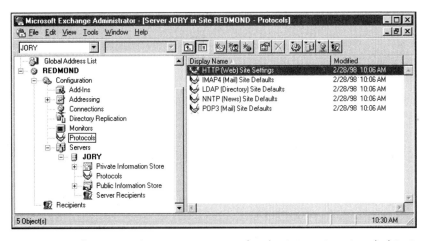

Figure 10.1   The site and server containers for the Internet protocol objects.

If you disable a protocol at the server level, then the mailbox setting has no effect.

The Protocols container has four associated Properties tabs: the General, Permissions, Connections, and MIME Types pages. We cover them briefly in the sections that follow.

The General Properties Page

The General Properties page (see Figure 10.2) is used to set the defaults for all the servers in the site. The options on this tab are as follows:

- **Display Name** This is the name that is displayed in the Microsoft Exchange Administrator program for these protocols. This field can have a maximum of 256 characters.

- **Directory Name** This is a read-only field that is defined during the installation process.

- **Outlook Web Access Server Name** This is where you type in the name of the server.

- **Administrative Note** This area is for any explanatory notes that the administrator deems appropriate.

Within the Internet protocol properties in the Server container, you can select the Use Site Defaults For All Properties checkbox. This will ensure that the configuration made to the protocols in the Site container will be true in the Server container.

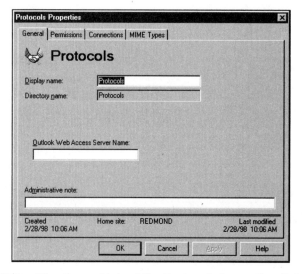

Figure 10.2 The General tab of the Protocols Properties dialog box.

The Permissions Properties Page

The Permissions Properties page is used to specify which objects in the Protocols container a user has access to. You grant permissions to a user (or group) by assigning the user a role. These roles are very similar to those in the recipient objects. You can set permissions on each protocol object in the site and server Protocols container only if you have configured the Exchange Administrator program to display the Permission property pages for all objects.

If you need to use *Secure Sockets Layer (SSL) encryption* with POP3, IMAP4, LDAP, and NNTP, you must grant the Exchange Server service account the Administrator permissions for the local computer.

The Connections Properties Page

The Connections Properties page is used to accept or reject POP3, IMAP4, LDAP, or NNTP access based on a client's IP address. By default, all connections are allowed. Use this page to restrict access to particular protocols, and their related services, on a client-by-client basis.

These settings do not apply to HTTP. To restrict HTTP connections, you must configure the Advanced tab in the Microsoft Internet Information Server Internet Service Manager.

The MIME Types Properties Page

The MIME Types Properties page is used to assign appropriate file extensions for inbound attachments. The Multipurpose Internet Mail Extensions (MIME) content type and the corresponding file extensions are defined in this tab and are used by Microsoft Exchange to assign file extensions to inbound attachments. Duplicate entries are allowed for both content type and file extensions. However, if multiple entries exist, the first occurrence in the list is always used to define the mapping from content type to file extension.

Exchange permits administrators to control protocols not only at the site level, but all protocols (except for LDAP) can also be controlled at the mailbox level. This allows administrators to control individual users who access the Exchange server.

In the sections that follow, you'll take a detailed look at the Internet mail protocols supported in Exchange, and learn how to understand and configure them. We begin with coverage of the Post Office Protocol version 3, also known as POP3, in the section that follows next.

POST OFFICE PROTOCOL VERSION 3 (POP3)

POP3 enables users with a POP3 client to retrieve email messages from the Exchange Inbox. Because Microsoft Exchange uses this standard, any email client application that supports POP3 can be used to connect to a Microsoft Exchange Server and access a user's messages.

 POP3 is known as a *mail-drop service*, which is a service that can hold mail messages until the client requests the messages to be sent.

By default, when you install Microsoft Exchange Server, the POP3 protocol is also installed. This allows POP3 clients to retrieve their email as soon as the server is set up. You must, however, configure the *Internet Mail Service (IMS)* before clients can send email. This is because clients use the POP3 protocol only to retrieve messages, but they use the SMTP protocol to send messages.

The POP3 protocol can be configured at the site, the server, and the mailbox levels:

- **At the site level** These protocol settings are default values that are inherited by all servers in the site.

- **At the server level** These property pages allow you to either use the site defaults or configure different options for each server.

- **At the mailbox level** These property pages allow you to either use the server defaults or configure different options on a mailbox-by-mailbox basis. It is important to note, however, that if you disable POP3 at the server level, then all the mailboxes on that server will be disabled, even if you enable those mailboxes individually.

POP3 SITE AND SERVER PROPERTIES

There are five POP3 Properties tabs that you can configure at the site level. These include General, Permissions, Authentication, Message Format, and Idle Time-out.

The General Properties page (see Figure 10.3) is used to enable or disable the protocol. Also, you can change the display name of the protocol (the name that appears in the Administrator program). The Directory name is displayed in a read-only field.

The Permissions Properties page is where you set user access permissions for the POP3 protocol on the site.

The Authentication Properties page is used to specify the methods of authentication that POP3 clients must use to connect to the Exchange Server.

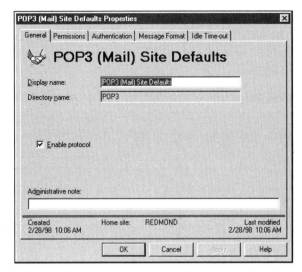

Figure 10.3   The General Properties page of the Site Properties configuration
dialog box.

You can select one of six methods of authentication (or any combination of
them). Table 10.1 describes the six methods.

The Message Format Properties page is used to control the message content
encoding and character set. You can select MIME or UUEncode content
encoding, as well as Rich Text Format.

Table 10.1   POP3 authentication methods.

Option	Description
Basic Authentication (Clear Text)	Uses authentication through an unencrypted username and password. Most POP3 clients support this method of authentication.
Basic Authentication (Clear Text) Using SSL	Uses the SSL protocol to encrypt clear text username and passwords. This method uses port 995.
Windows NT Challenge/ Response Authentication	Uses authentication through Windows NT security and an encrypted password.
Windows NT Challenge/ Response Authentication Using SSL	Uses the SSL protocol to authenticate through Windows NT security. This method uses port 995.
MCIS Membership System	Uses Windows NT security authentication through the Microsoft Commercial Internet Server (MCIS) Membership System.
MCIS Membership System Using SSL	Uses the SSL protocol to authenticate through the Microsoft Commercial Internet Server Membership System using Windows NT security. This method uses port 995.

The Idle Time-out Properties page is used to set the amount of time POP3 needs to be idle before closing a connection. You can select not to close idle connections, or to close idle connections, once a specified amount of time has elapsed (measured in minutes).

You have an extra tab available to you when configuring POP3 at the server level—Diagnostics Logging (shown in Figure 10.4). Diagnostics logging allows you to set logging levels for several Microsoft Exchange Server events.

POP3 MAILBOX CONFIGURATION

You can configure POP3 on a mailbox level by selecting the POP3 protocol and configuring the settings in the Protocol Details Properties page (shown in Figure 10.5) of the mailbox. Any changes you make on this page override the server-level properties, unless this protocol is disabled on the server.

POP3 CLIENT CONFIGURATION

To connect a POP3 client to a Microsoft Exchange Server, you must specify the following information on the client side:

- **POP3 Account Name** The alias name of a Microsoft Exchange Server mailbox that supports POP3.

- **POP3 Email Address** The SMTP email address that Internet users will use to send messages.

- **POP3 Server Name** The computer name of the Microsoft Exchange Server computer that has the POP3 mailbox account on it.

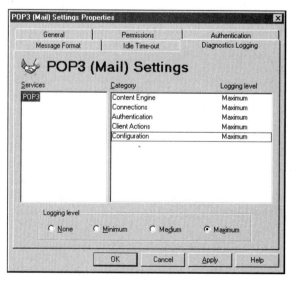

Figure 10.4   The Diagnostics Logging Properties page.

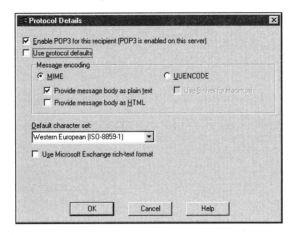

Figure 10.5   The mailbox-level POP3 Protocol Details Properties page.

- **SMTP Server Name** The name of the computer running IMS that provides SMTP services for the POP3 client.

 Because each POP3 client is different, the steps for configuring these clients to connect to a Microsoft Exchange Server POP3 computer are different for each of these clients.

Now that you've covered the elements of POP3 configuration, it's time to turn to the Internet Message Access Protocol, IMAP. This provides the topic for the section that follows next.

INTERNET MESSAGE ACCESS PROTOCOL (IMAP)

IMAP enables users with any IMAP4–compliant client to access email stored in their Exchange Mailbox. Users can also read and post messages to public folders or access other users' mailboxes—if they have been granted the rights to do so.

By default, when you install Microsoft Exchange Server, the IMAP4 protocol is also installed. This allows IMAP4 clients to retrieve their email as soon as the server is set up. You must, however, configure IMS before the clients can send email. This is because the client uses the IMAP4 protocol to retrieve messages, but the SMTP protocol is used to send messages.

The IMAP4 protocol can be configured at the site, server, and mailbox levels:

- **At the site level** These protocol settings are default values that are inherited by the servers.
- **At the server level** These property pages allow you to either use the site defaults or configure different options on each server.

■ **At the mailbox level** These property pages allow you to either use the server defaults or configure different options on a mailbox-by-mailbox basis. It is important to note, however, that if you disable IMAP4 at the server level, all the mailboxes on that server are disabled, even if you enable the mailboxes individually.

IMAP4 SITE AND SERVER PROPERTIES

There are six IMAP4 Properties tabs that you can configure at the site level. These include General, Permissions, Authentication, Anonymous, Message Format, and Idle Time-out.

The General Properties page (see Figure 10.6) is used to enable or disable the protocol. Also, you can change the display name of the protocol (the name that appears in the Administrator program). The directory name is displayed in a read-only field.

The Permissions Properties page is where you set user access permissions for the IMAP4 protocol on the site.

The Authentication Properties page is used to specify the methods of authentication that IMAP4 clients must use to connect to the Exchange Server (these are the same as the methods for POP3 clients). You can select one of six methods of authentication (or any combination of them). Table 10.1 (shown earlier) describes the six methods.

The Anonymous Connections Properties page is used to specify whether IMAP4 clients can connect to the Exchange Server anonymously. Sometimes, it

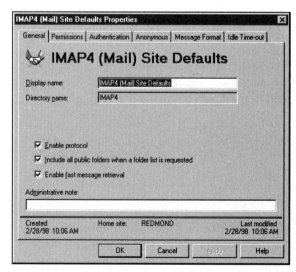

Figure 10.6 The General Properties page of the IMAP4 Site Properties configuration dialog box.

makes sense to allow certain public folders to be accessible to users outside the organization. To make this possible, you can enable anonymous connections. After you enable anonymous access, IMAP4 clients can access information on the Exchange Server without requiring a Windows NT user account.

The Message Format Properties page is used to control the message content encoding and character set. You can select MIME or UUEncode content encoding, as well as Rich Text Format.

The Idle Time-out Properties page is used to set the amount of time IMAP4 needs to be idle before closing a connection. You can select to either not close idle connections or close idle connections after a specified amount of time (measured in minutes).

Similar to the POP3 server-level properties, the IMAP4 server-level configuration has a Diagnostic Logging Properties page. Diagnostic logging allows you to set logging levels for several Microsoft Exchange Server events.

You can configure IMAP4 on a mailbox level by selecting the IMAP4 protocol and configuring the settings in the Protocol Details page of the mailbox (see Figure 10.7). Any changes you make on this page will override the server-level properties, unless the protocol is disabled for the server.

10

IMAP4 Mailbox Configuration

There are additional options available for you to configure in the Mailbox Protocol Details page:

- **Include All Public Folders When A Folder List Is Requested**
  Some IMAP4 clients show poor performance when displaying a large number of public folders. By default, public folders are listed for all

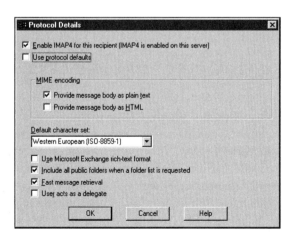

Figure 10.7   The mailbox-level IMAP4 Protocol Details page.

clients. By clearing this option, you can specify that a particular mailbox will not receive the public folder listing to improve client performance.

- **Fast Message Retrieval** This option allows you to specify slow IMAP4 clients so that message headers are sent. The user can then select which messages to download.

- **User Acts As A Delegate** This option allows an IMAP4 to give a user access to another user's mailbox so the personal folders can be viewed.

To connect an IMAP4 client to a Microsoft Exchange Server, you must specify the following information on the client:

- **An IMAP4 Account Name** The alias name of a Microsoft Exchange Server mailbox that supports IMAP4.

- **An IMAP4 Email Address** The SMTP email address that Internet users will use to send messages.

- **An IMAP4 Server Name** The computer name of the Microsoft Exchange Server computer that has the IMAP4 mailbox account on it.

- **SMTP Server Name** The name of the computer running IMS that provides SMTP services for the IMAP4 client.

Because each IMAP4 client is different, the steps for configuring these clients to connect to a Microsoft server IMAP4 computer vary.

Now that you've reviewed the capabilities and properties pages for the IMAP4 protocol in the Exchange environment, it's time to turn your attention to the Lightweight Directory Access Protocol. This topic is addressed in the next section.

LIGHTWEIGHT DIRECTORY ACCESS PROTOCOL (LDAP)

LDAP is an Internet protocol that enables LDAP clients to access directory information on your Microsoft Exchange Server. Given the correct permissions, these clients can browse, read, search, and write directory listing information to the Microsoft Exchange Server directory. Many LDAP clients can access your Microsoft Exchange Server and perform directory queries (including usernames and phone numbers). If you assign the correct permissions, your users can modify Exchange directory information, such as changing their phone numbers.

To configure LDAP, use the Microsoft Exchange Administrator program. The Protocols container includes the configuration parameters for the LDAP object. There are seven LDAP Properties pages that you can configure at the site level. These include General, Permissions, Authentication, Anonymous, Search, Referrals, and Idle Time-out.

The General Properties page (see Figure 10.8) is used to enable or disable the protocol. Also, you can change the display name of the protocol (the name that appears in the Administrator program). The directory name is displayed in a read-only field.

The Permissions Properties page is where you set user access permissions for the LDAP protocol on the site.

Use the Authentication Properties page to specify the methods of authentication that LDAP clients must employ when connecting to the Exchange Server (these are the same as the methods for POP3 and IMAP4 clients). You can select one of six methods of authentication (or any combination of them). Table 10.1 (shown earlier) describes these six methods.

The Anonymous Properties page is used to specify whether LDAP clients can connect to the Exchange Server anonymously.

10

The Search Properties page allows LDAP clients to perform searches on the directory. The LDAP search can perform three types of substring searches:

- **Initial Substring Search** The user specifies an attribute in the directory. The directory then matches the substring to the beginning of

Figure 10.8 The General Properties page of the LDAP Properties page.

the attribute. Initial substring searches tend to be faster than the other types of substring searches.

- **Final Substring Search** The user specifies an attribute in the directory. The directory then matches the substring to the end of the attribute. Final substring searches tend to be slower than initial substring searches.

- **Any Substring Search** The user specifies an attribute in the directory. The directory then matches the substring to any portion of the attribute. Any substring searches are the slowest of the substring searches.

The Referrals Properties page allows you to configure Exchange Server to refer to another server that can fulfill a request. This is allowed because sometimes an LDAP client will request information that your Exchanger Server does not include within its directory database. Be aware that such client requests can only be referred to servers outside the local Exchange organization.

The Idle Time-out Properties page is used to set the amount of time LDAP needs to be idle before closing a connection. You can select to either not close idle connections or close idle connections after a specified amount of time (measured in minutes).

This covers the LDAP settings and configuration properties. In the section that follows, you'll learn about the Network News Transfer Protocol, NNTP, and its capabilities and configuration properties.

NETWORK NEWS TRANSFER PROTOCOL (NNTP) AND NEWSFEEDS

The *Internet News Service* is a method for your organization to connect to a Usenet host to exchange information. The Internet News Service is a Windows NT service based on the Network News Transfer Protocol (NNTP) that allows you to configure both unidirectional (read-only or write-only) and bidirectional (read and write) newsfeeds. This allows your clients to send and receive threaded newsgroup content on the Internet. If you have several Microsoft Exchange Servers in your site, only one of them needs to be configured with the Internet News Service. NNTP clients will still be able to access newsgroup public servers on a server running the Internet News Service.

The Internet News Service integrates tightly with the Information Store to provide newsgroups as public folders. The service connects to Usenet hosts on a scheduled basis, where you set the schedule and frequency of connections. The Internet News Service connects to remote hosts by using either a *push feed* or a *pull feed*. (The different types of newsfeeds are discussed later in this chapter in the section entitled "Newsfeeds.")

The Internet News Service can operate with a dedicated or a dial-up Internet connection. Microsoft Outlook or any other NNTP-compatible client can access all *newsgroup public folders*. As far as third-party newsreaders are concerned, they are communicating with a standard NNTP server, so such newreaders work transparently with Exchange Server as well.

One nice feature of the Internet News Service is its ability to communicate with multiple sources on multiple newsfeeds. It can accommodate such newsfeeds from one or more Microsoft Exchange Server computers.

Newsfeeds

The Internet News Service can use two methods to establish newsfeeds with a remote NNTP host—push feed or pull feed.

With a push feed (shown in Figure 10.9), your provider's host computer initiates a newsfeed to your Exchange Server computer and then "pushes" the news articles to your computer. A push feed is best for a large newsfeed, but it requires you to interact with your newsfeed provider, because the provider controls which newsgroups you receive.

10

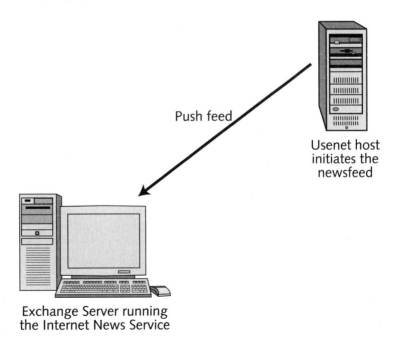

Push feed

Usenet host
initiates the
newsfeed

Exchange Server running
the Internet News Service

Figure 10.9   A push feed.

With a pull feed (shown in Figure 10.10), your Microsoft Exchange Server computer initiates the connection with your provider's NNTP host and delivers any new messages to the host. The pull feed then checks for any updated news messages on the host, and retrieves them. Pull feeds work well when you require only a small feed, or when bandwidth is not in large supply, as when using a dial-up connection.

You can also configure inbound and outbound newsfeeds. An *inbound newsfeed* allows you to pull messages from your provider's NNTP host computer and accept messages that your provider's host pushes to your Exchange Server. An *outbound newsfeed* allows you to push (or send) messages posted by your users to a newsgroup public folder to your provider's host computer. If a remote host computer needs to pull messages from your Exchange Server, you need to configure your computer with only NNTP client support. This allows the host computer to pull messages and act as an NNTP newsreader.

NEWSGROUP PUBLIC FOLDERS

You can designate any public folder in your site as a newsgroup public folder. These folders are accessible to NNTP clients and may be used to send and receive items from a newsfeed. Outlook clients access these newsgroup public folders in the same way that they access any other Exchange public folders. With such newsgroup public folders, your users can exchange information with people all over the world or within your organization.

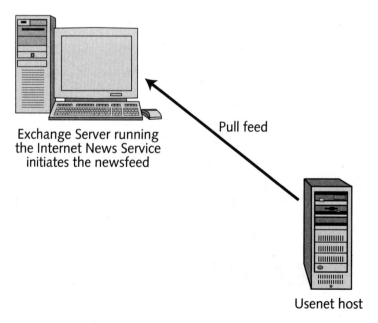

Exchange Server running
the Internet News Service
initiates the newsfeed

Pull feed

Usenet host

Figure 10.10 A pull feed.

By default, when you set up the Internet News Service, it creates a public folder named Internet News. You may rename or move the Internet News public folder, but you may not delete it. Also, you can create other public folders to contain newsgroup public folders.

A newsgroup public folder is just like any other public folder in Microsoft Exchange. You, as the administrator, can set permissions on such public folders to control which users or groups may access the newsgroup. These folders may be replicated within an organization using Exchange public folder replication—just like any other public folders.

You must name your newsgroup public folders carefully. You should assign newsgroup public folders names that are based on their locations in the newsgroup hierarchy. A newsgroup folder inherits a portion of its parent folder. The full newsgroup folder name is the combination of the public folder's name and the name of its parent folder. Each of these names is separated by a period, as with Internet domain names. For example, in Figure 10.11, if the newsgroup public folder named ActiveX is in the microsoft.public hierarchy, then the complete newsgroup name for the ActiveX newsgroup public folder would be microsoft.public.activex.

10

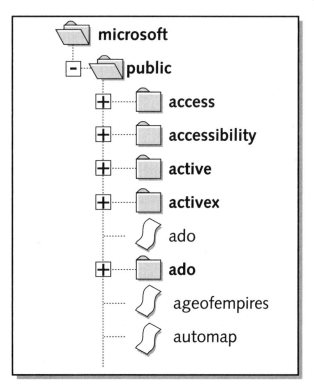

Figure 10.11 Newsgroup public folders hierarchy.

Because periods (.) are used to separate the newsgroup public folder names, you cannot use periods in the name of a public folder. For example, you cannot have a newsgroup public folder named activex.components. If you use an unsupported character (such as a period) in the newsgroup public folder name, then Microsoft Exchange will automatically replace the unsupported character with a hyphen (-). Thus, activex.components would be replaced with activex-components.

Newsgroups can be moderated. When a newsgroup is moderated, all items posted to that newsgroup are first mailed to a designated individual (known as the moderator). The moderator decides whether to accept or reject a posting based on its content. Any messages sent to a moderated newsgroup public folder do not appear in the public folder until the moderator has accepted the posts. To assign a moderator to a newsgroup public folder, use Microsoft Outlook.

CONFIGURING AN NNTP NEWSFEED

To configure the Internet News Service, run the *Newsfeed Configuration Wizard*. The Wizard makes it easy for you to create one or more newsfeeds on an Exchange Server. There are several pieces of information that you need to provide the Wizard. These include:

- The site name of the newsfeed provider that will be supplying your site with the newsfeed. Normally, this is the *fully qualified domain name (FQDN)* of the host computer sending the newsfeed.

- The mailbox name of an administrator that will be able to add and remove newsgroup public folders.

- The name and location of the *active file*—if it will not be downloaded from the newsfeed provider upon installation.

 The active file is a text file that contains all the newsgroups that your newsfeed provider receives at the NNTP host.

To get the active file, you will need to download it from your provider or use the Windows NT Telnet command to create a text file with your provider's active newsgroups. To create the active text file, use the procedure shown in Project 10.2 in this chapter's "Hands-On Projects" section.

A sample active file is shown in the following code:

```
microsoft.public.exchange.admin 42953 27481 y
microsoft.public.exchange.applications 9740 6310 y
```

```
microsoft.public.exchange.clients 24037 18134 y

microsoft.public.exchange.connectivity 24218 16773 y

microsoft.public.exchange.misc 21661 15846 y

microsoft.public.exchange.setup 23771 16560 y

microsoft.public.mail.admin 4030 3041 y

microsoft.public.mail.connectivity 3016 2359 y

microsoft.public.mail.misc 4721 3643 y

microsoft.public.outlook 424 1 y

microsoft.public.outlook.configuration 89 1 y
```

CONFIGURING NEWSFEED PROPERTIES

After a newsfeed is created, you have the option to set additional NNTP properties through the Newsfeed Properties pages. The General Properties page (shown in Figure 10.12) is used to enable the selected newsfeed, specify a display name, and change the Administrator's mailbox.

You can configure the following settings on the General Newsfeed Properties page:

10

- **Display Name** The name displayed in the Exchange Administrator program. This field can be a maximum or 256 alphanumeric characters (which can include spaces and special characters).

- **Directory Name** A read-only field that displays the directory name specified during the installation.

Figure 10.12 The General Properties page.

- **Enable Newsfeed** By selecting this checkbox, you can enable the selected newsfeed to send or receive newsgroup items.
- **Administrator's Mailbox** Use this option to assign an administrator that will have the right to add and remove newsgroup public folders from the selected newsfeed. Click on the Change button to select the mailbox.

The Permissions Properties page is where you set user access permissions for the NNTP protocol on the site.

The Messages Properties page is used to specify the maximum size of all incoming and outgoing messages in the selected newsfeed. You can specify either no limit or a maximum limit (in kilobytes) for both outgoing and incoming messages.

The Hosts Properties page (shown in Figure 10.13) is used to configure the NNTP computers supplied by your newsfeed provider. Normally, you will have an inbound host configured to receive messages and an outbound host configured to send messages. One host can act as both the inbound and outbound host.

If your Microsoft Exchange computer will initiate the connection, you must specify the remote Usenet site and host names. Your Internet News Service can then push messages to the remote site and accept push messages from the site.

You can also configure additional inbound hosts by host names or IP addresses. You will only be required to use this option if your newsfeed provider is pushing messages to you from multiple hosts.

Figure 10.13　The Hosts Properties page.

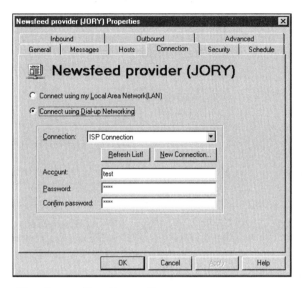

Figure 10.14 The Connection Properties page.

The Connection Properties page (shown in Figure 10.14) is used to specify whether the selected newsfeed is to use a dedicated local area network (LAN) or dial-up connection.

> If you are using a dial-up connection with IMS on the same computer as the Internet News Service, then this connection information can be shared.

You can configure the following settings on the Connection Properties page:

- **Connection** Select an existing RAS Phonebook entry as the dial-up connection you would like to use.

- **Refresh List** By clicking on this button, you can update the Connection drop-down menu with the most current connections.

- **New Connection** Allows you to create a news dial-up connection (RAS Phonebook entry). After adding a new connection, you should choose Refresh List to update the connection list.

- **Account** This is the account name for the dial-up connection. This is an optional field.

- **Password** This is the password for the dial-up connection. This is an optional field. Reenter the password in the Confirm Password field to verify that the password is correct.

By default, security is not enabled for NNTP newsfeeds. Using the Security Properties page (shown in Figure 10.15), however, you can specify that the selected

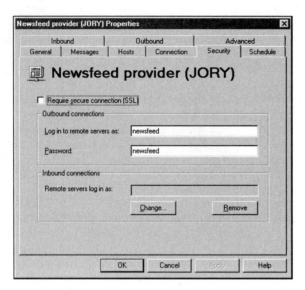

Figure 10.15   The Security Properties page.

newsfeed is to use Secure Sockets Layer (SSL) when connecting to remote servers. This will encrypt all data sent between your Microsoft Exchange Server computer and the remote NNTP host computer. You can also specify the account and password required to log on to the remote NNTP host computer.

You can configure the following settings on the Security Properties page:

- **Require Secure Connection (SSL)** Check this dialog box to enable SSL encryption for message transfer.

- **Outbound Connections** Your Exchange computer will use the username (the Log In To Remote Servers As option) and the password for all outbound host connections. Your newsfeed provider will supply this account name and password to you. These are case-sensitive fields.

- **Inbound Connections** You can specify an Exchange mailbox or custom recipient that your newsfeed provider's host computer will use to log in to your Exchange Server. The password for inbound host connections is a case-sensitive field.

The Schedule Properties page (shown in Figure 10.16) is used to define when your Exchange Server is to connect to your newsfeed provider's remote host to send and receive Usenet messages.

You can specify to connect never, always, or at selected times. If you choose the Selected Times option, then you must also specify when the connections will take place (in 1-hour or 15-minute intervals).

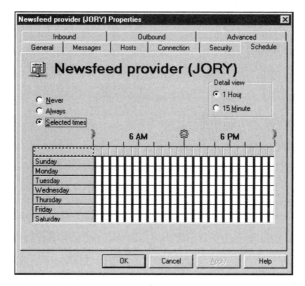

Figure 10.16   The Schedule Properties page.

The Inbound Properties page (shown in Figure 10.17) lists all the newsgroups that are available in the active file. You can configure both pull and push newsfeeds depending on how you configured the newsfeed through the Newsfeed Configuration Wizard.

If your Internet News Service is configured to send outbound newsfeeds to your provider, you can select which newsgroups your Exchange Server will send in the newsfeeds. This is done on the Outbound Properties page (shown in Figure 10.18).

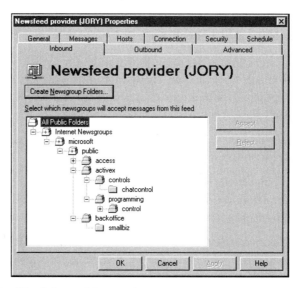

Figure 10.17   The Inbound Properties page.

10

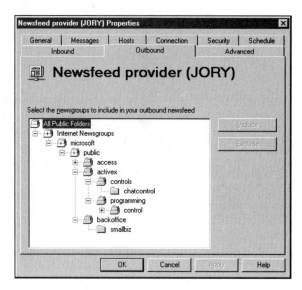

Figure 10.18   The Outbound Properties page.

The Advanced Properties page is used to flush queued messages. By clicking on the Mark All As Delivered button, you flush the queue of messages waiting to be processed. This allows your Exchange Server or another host to catch up on the most recent newsgroup posts.

Setting Up Properties For NNTP

To send and receive Usenet newsfeeds, you must configure the newsfeed and the NNTP properties. You can set the NNTP object properties at both the site and server level. Site-level properties will apply to all the servers in the site, whereas server-level properties will apply to the specified server only.

The General Properties page (shown in Figure 10.19) is used to enable or disable the protocol. Also, you can change the display name of the protocol (the name that appears in the Administrator program). The directory name is displayed in a read-only field. You can also enable or disable client access.

The Permissions Properties page is where you set user access permissions for newsfeeds on the site.

In the Newsfeeds Properties page, you can view the configuration properties of a newsfeed from the site or server level. These configuration properties are covered in the previous section.

The Control Messages Properties page is used to control how new newsgroups are created and how old ones are deleted. All control messages received by the Internet News Service will be queued here until you (as the administrator)

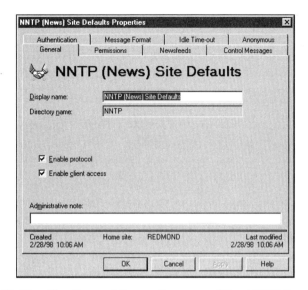

Figure 10.19   The General Properties page of the NNTP Properties page.

10

decide whether to accept or reject the messages. If for some reason you do not trust a particular Usenet host, you can choose to delete the control message without accepting the changes from that host.

The Authentication Properties page is used to specify the methods of authentication that NNTP clients must use to connect to the Exchange Server (these are the same as the methods for POP3, IMAP4, and LDAP clients). You can select one of six methods of authentication (or any combination of them). Table 10.1 (shown earlier) describes the six methods.

The Message Format Properties page is used to control the message content encoding and character set. You can select MIME or UUEncode content encoding, as well as Rich Text Format.

The Idle Time-out Properties page is used to set the amount of time NNTP needs to be idle before closing a connection. You can select either to not close idle connections or close idle connections after a specified amount of time (measured in minutes).

The Anonymous Properties page is used to specify whether NNTP clients can connect to the Exchange Server anonymously.

This concludes your review of NNTP and newsgroup access in Exchange. In the section that follows, you'll change focus from the server to client, as you examine the ins and outs of configuring and managing access to Exchange data over the Web, using Outlook Web Access.

MICROSOFT OUTLOOK WEB ACCESS (OWA)

Microsoft OWA allows users to access data on your Exchange Server using an Internet Web browser from a Macintosh, Unix, or Microsoft Windows-based computer. You can also use it to provide Global Address List (GAL) information and access any public folders you might have on your Exchange Server. Users that have access (a mailbox) to your Exchange Server can log in to their personal accounts to read and send private messages. Users also have the ability to publish information to the Internet without having to convert their documents to the Hypertext Markup Language (HTML) format.

Outlook Web Access works in conjunction with a client's Web browser. The browser communicates with Microsoft Exchange through the Microsoft Internet Information Server (IIS) to provide the interface to the user's mailbox information. Using this feature of Exchange Server, you have the ability to grant your users access to company and personal information from anywhere in the world via the Internet.

OUTLOOK WEB ACCESS INSTALLATION

You have the option to install the Outlook Web Access files during Microsoft Exchange Server setup. OWA uses Active Server Pages (ASP) to provide dynamically changing Web pages, and HTML to provide static Web pages. IIS can be installed on the same Windows NT Server computer as Microsoft Exchange, or it can be installed on a different Microsoft Windows server that can be accessed by the server where OWA is installed. When installing Outlook Web Access and Microsoft Exchange Server on the same computer, you must make sure that the WWW service in IIS is enabled and running.

Internet Information Server (IIS) version 2 can be installed by you when you install Microsoft Windows NT 4. The Active Server Pages component of IIS is only available in IIS version 3 or higher. If you have IIS 2 installed, you must upgrade to IIS 3 or higher for OWA to function. The Active Server Pages component of IIS acts as a connector between Outlook Web Access and a Web browser (such as Microsoft Internet Explorer or Netscape Navigator). Active Server Pages dynamically generate Web pages using a combination of HTML, server-executed scripts, and Remote Procedure Calls (RPCs). You have the option to customize the default ASP files for your organization. For example, you can add your organization's logo to the Outlook Web Access interface.

OUTLOOK WEB ACCESS OPERATIONS

When users want to access their Microsoft Exchange Server computer, they need to start their Web browser and specify the *Universal Resource Locator (URL)* of their Active Server Pages. The Web browser then displays a welcome page (shown in Figure 10.20) that allows the user to log on to the Exchange Server using his mailbox name. Users must enter their Microsoft Exchange Server mailbox alias in the Log On dialog box and either press Enter or click on the Click Here hyperlink.

The Enter Network Password dialog box should appear, prompting users to enter their Windows NT username and password. If logging on to a certain domain, users must type in their domain name and Windows NT username in the Username box in the *Domain\Windows NT username* format, followed by their Windows NT password in the Enter Network Password dialog box (shown in Figure 10.21).

> The user's Exchange Server mailbox alias and Windows NT user account might be different. This is because Windows NT User Manager For Domains and the Exchange Administrator programs allow you to create a differently named mailbox for a single Windows NT account.

AUTHENTICATION

Users can access your Microsoft Exchange Server computer through the Internet using a secure connection to log on as a validated or anonymous user.

10

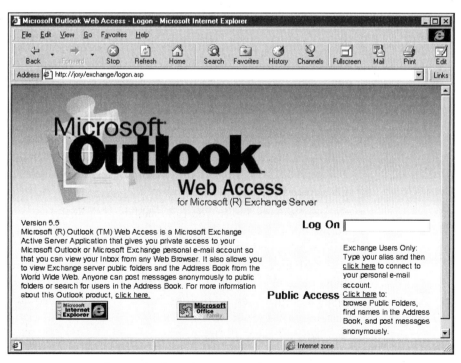

Figure 10.20   The Outlook Web Access welcome page.

Figure 10.21   The Enter Network Password dialog box.

When a user logs on to your Microsoft Exchange Server, a secure and encrypted session is established between the user's Web browser and the IIS computer. Before a user is granted access to his Exchange information, his Windows NT domain account password must be validated with the Windows NT domain. IIS then logs the user on to the Exchange Server computer.

 Remember that it is IIS that authenticates the user in the Windows NT domain, not the Exchange Server. It is also important to note that the different security levels available to you are configured in the Web service of IIS. This is because IIS establishes the secure connection between itself and the user's Web browser.

There are several levels of security available to you for authentication of Internet or intranet users:

- **Basic Authentication** This is the lowest level of security available for Internet and intranet users. When setting up basic authentication, you must also set up the Log On Locally permission on the IIS computer.

- **Windows NT Challenge/Response Authentication** If you have IIS and Microsoft Exchange Server installed on the same computer, you can enable Windows NT Challenge/Response authentication to offer a higher level of security. If IIS is installed on a different computer than Microsoft Exchange Server, then you must disable Windows NT Challenge/Response authentication.

- **Secure Sockets Layer** You can establish additional security by enabling SSL. SSL is used to encrypt all data transferred between the Web browser and IIS. Don't forget that this feature can only be used with Web browsers that support SSL (such as Microsoft Internet Explorer 3.02 and Netscape Navigator 3.01). To enable SSL, you must obtain a security certificate (see Chapter 11 for a detailed discussion of certificates and certificate authorities).

Outlook Web Access uses Windows NT authentication to grant access to a user's mailbox—to validate a user. To be granted access, the user must enter his

Windows NT user account name, password, and mailbox name. After a user has been authenticated successfully, he will have the same permissions as he had when he logged on to the computer directly connected to the network.

An anonymous user is a non-validated user and is not recognized by Microsoft Exchange Server. When users log on to the Microsoft Exchange Server anonymously, they are restricted to viewing and accessing only the published public folders and address lists. You can control which folders and address lists are published using the Exchange Administrator program.

OUTLOOK WEB ACCESS CONFIGURATION

To configure Outlook Web Access, use the Exchange Server Administrator program. You can determine which public folders and GALs anonymous users can view. A public folder that is available to all Internet users is known as a *published public folder* and is configured in the Folders Shortcuts property page. After you have configured Outlook Web Access, the users will access the Outlook Web Access using the following URL: **http://*IIS name*/exchange**.

 For Outlook Web Access to work properly, the user's Web browser must support both JavaScript and frames (in practice this means IE 3.0.2 or higher, or Netscape Navigator 3.0.1 or higher; for both browsers, 4 or higher numbered versions are recommended).

The General Properties page (see Figure 10.22) is used to specify a display name, enable the protocol, and grant anonymous users access to published public folders. You can configure the following settings on the General Properties page:

- **Display Name** The name displayed in the Exchange Administrator program. This field can be a maximum or 256 alphanumeric characters (which can include spaces and special characters).

- **Directory Name** A read-only field that displays the directory name specified during the installation.

- **Enable HTTP** Allows you to enable or disable HTTP access to the site.

The Permissions Properties page is where you set user access permissions for Outlook Web Access on the site.

The Folder Shortcuts tab provides links to the Microsoft Exchange Server published public folders. Use this tab to select which public folders can be accessed by anonymous users when they connect to your Exchange Server from the Internet.

The Advanced Properties page allows you to set the number of Address Book entries that will be returned to the users. The default is set at 50 entries.

Figure 10.22   The General Properties page of the Outlook Web Access Properties page.

CHAPTER SUMMARY

Microsoft Exchange Server has built-in support for the POP3, IMAP4, LDAP, NNTP, and HTTP Internet protocols. This allows a multitude of clients to access the Microsoft Exchange Server to gain access to public folders, private Information Stores, Address Book information, and schedule information.

POP3 enables a user to retrieve email messages from his Inbox. The user can use any POP3 client to gain access to the remote Microsoft Exchange Server.

IMAP4 enables users to retrieve email messages from their Inbox, as well as to retrieve Microsoft Exchange public folder information.

LDAP enables remote Internet users to access the Microsoft Exchange Server directory information. Because LDAP is integrated into the Microsoft Exchange DS, Internet client applications using LDAP can access the Exchange DS.

NNTP allows Microsoft Exchange Server to become a part of Usenet. Microsoft Exchange can both publish and receive Usenet information and newsfeeds. All newsgroups received by the Microsoft Exchange Server are stored as public folders.

HTTP is the main protocol used to communicate between client Web browsers and Internet Web servers. Microsoft Exchange Server, in conjunction with Microsoft Internet Information Server, allows remote clients running any JavaScript- and frames-enabled Web browsers to access mailbox and public folder information on the server, using Outlook Web Access as a lightweight, Web-based email client.

KEY TERMS

- **active file**—A text file that contains a list of all newsgroups available from your newsfeed provider.
- **Basic Authentication**—Provides user authentication through an unencrypted username and password.
- **Basic Authentication Using SSL**—Uses the SSL protocol to encrypt clear text username and passwords.
- **fully qualified domain name (FQDN)**—The full DNS path of an Internet host.
- **Hypertext Markup Language (HTML)**—The language used to create static Web pages.
- **Hypertext Transfer Protocol (HTTP)**—The protocol used to communicate between a Web browser and a Web server (uses HTML).
- **inbound newsfeed**—A newsfeed that is used to receive information from the Usenet through your newsfeed provider.
- **Internet Message Service (IMS)**—A connector used to connect a Microsoft Exchange site to either an SMTP mail system or a remote Microsoft Exchange site.
- **Internet Message Access Protocol version 4 (IMAP4)**—A protocol that allows clients to send and receive messages from their mailbox, and access to public folders.
- **Internet News Service**—A service that uses NNTP to connect the Microsoft Exchange Server to Usenet.
- **Lightweight Directory Access Protocol (LDAP)**—A protocol used to share Exchange Address Book information with external users.
- **mail-drop service**—A service that can hold email messages until the client requests the messages.
- **Microsoft Commercial Internet Service (MCIS) Membership System**—A product that enables an organization to deploy remote application servers anywhere on the Internet and tie them together into a central authentication, authorization, and billing system.
- **Microsoft Commercial Internet Service (MCIS) Membership System Using SSL**—Windows NT security authentication using SSL, which is authenticated through the MCIS Membership System. Uses port 995.
- **Network News Transfer Protocol (NNTP)**—The TCP/IP-based protocol used to distribute, retrieve, inquire about, and post network news, discussion groups, or postings.
- **Newsfeed Configuration Wizard**—A wizard used to configure the Internet News Service for your Microsoft Exchange Server.
- **newsgroup public folder**—An Exchange public folder used with the Internet News Service to store newsgroup information.

10

- **outbound newsfeed**—A newsfeed that is used to send information to Usenet through your newsfeed provider.

- **Outlook Web Access (OWA)**—A program your users can use to access their private mailboxes, schedule information, and Exchange public folders.

- **Post Office Protocol version 3 (POP3)**—A standard Internet mail protocol used to read messages from a mail server.

- **published public folder**—An Exchange folder that is shared to all users. The users log in anonymously through Outlook Web Access.

- **pull feed**—A feed that goes and gets only specified newsgroups from the newsfeed server.

- **push feed**—A feed that "forces" the newsfeed to the destination server. Normally, this means that all newsgroups are pushed to the server.

- **Secure Sockets Layer (SSL) encryption**—A method to encrypt information between hosts.

- **Simple Mail Transfer Protocol (SMTP)**—The mail protocol used to connect two hosts running the TCP/IP protocol.

- **Universal Resource Locator (URL)**—A universal convention to identify a server's name and location on the Internet. For example, **www.microsoft.com**.

- **Windows NT Challenge/Response Authentication**—A protocol that provides user authentication through Windows NT security and an encrypted password.

- **Windows NT Challenge/Response Using SSL**—The same as the Windows NT Challenge/Response authentication, which is a protocol that provides user authentication through NT security. Additionally, the SSL protocol is also used to authenticate users. Uses port 995.

R EVIEW Q UESTIONS

1. Your company upgrades one of your Microsoft Exchange Servers from version 4 to version 5.5. You enable POP3 support on the newly upgraded server. Your users complain that they cannot access their mailbox information using the POP3 protocol. What could be the problem?

   a. The Exchange Service account is set up incorrectly.

   b. POP3 is disabled from the server.

   c. The clients are using the wrong POP3 client.

   d. Windows NT Challenge/Response authentication is disabled.

2. You are migrating from a Unix mail system to Exchange Server. You configure POP3 on the Microsoft Exchange Server and turn off the Unix server. Your users now complain that they can read their messages but can no longer send Internet mail. What could be the problem?

   a. The POP3 service needs to be restarted.

   b. The POP3 service is not running.

   c. IMS is not installed and configured on the Exchange Server.

   d. Exchange cannot act as an Internet mail gateway.

3. What must be done to allow your Exchange Server to share some newsgroups through public folders?

   a. Install a newsreader client on the server and share its data.

   b. Install newsreader client software on each of your user's desktops.

   c. Install and configure the Internet News Service.

   d. This cannot be done with Microsoft Exchange Server.

4. Which of the following is the proper definition of an active file?

   a. A file that contains a list of users who have access to Internet news.

   b. A file that contains a list of all the newsgroups available to Microsoft Exchange from your provider.

   c. A listing of all users who are currently logged on to the Exchange Server.

   d. A list of all Active Server Pages on your Internet Information Server computer.

5. Which of the following components are required to allow users to access your Microsoft Exchange Server through a Web browser? (Choose all that apply.)

   a. Internet Information Server 3 or higher

   b. Outlook Web Access installed and configured on the Microsoft Exchange Server

   c. The IMAP4 protocol

   d. The POP3 protocol

6. IMAP4 and POP3 are just different names for the same protocol. True or False?

7. You want to receive a small number of newsgroups from your newsfeed provider. Which is the best way to configure the newsfeed?

   a. As inbound push

   b. As inbound push, outbound pull

   c. As inbound pull, outbound push

   d. As inbound pull

10

8. You can have IIS running on a different server than Microsoft Exchange Server. True or False?

9. You can use the POP3 protocol to send and receive messages. True or False?

10. Joe uses Microsoft Outlook to access his mailbox when he is in the office. When using a POP3 client from home, he cannot access a message in a folder named Private. What could be the problem?

   a. Any folder named Private is not sent through POP3.

   b. Joe can only access his mailbox using one product, either Outlook or a POP3 client.

   c. The POP3 protocol can only read the user's Inbox, not any subfolders within the Inbox.

   d. Joe must configure Outlook to share the Private folder with his POP3 client.

11. What is the Lightweight Directory Access Protocol (LDAP) used for?

   a. To access public folders through Outlook Web Access.

   b. To access Microsoft Exchange directory information.

   c. To access private mailbox information.

   d. To access private and public folder information.

12. You cannot configure Microsoft Exchange Server to accept both the POP3 and IMAP4 protocols. True or False?

13. One of your sites needs to receive all attachments as MIME, whereas another site needs to receive all attachments as UUEncode. What must you configure to accomplish this?

   a. The SMTP property page

   b. The Encoding property page

   c. The site container

   d. The Internet Mail property page

14. You can use Internet Information Server 2 for Outlook Web Access. True or False?

15. An Exchange Server can receive data from and publish data to Usenet using NNTP. True or False?

16. What is the role of the Active Server?

   a. Dynamically creates Web pages.

   b. Creates and maintains the active list used by the Internet News Service.

   c. Maintains all Windows NT active users.

   d. Is another name for Internet Information Server.

17. Which components would enable a user to send and receive messages through the Internet using a POP3 client? (Choose all that apply.)

    a. POP3

    b. IMAP4

    c. NNTP

    d. SMTP

18. Where would you configure the security level to use with Outlook Web Access?

    a. Internet Service Manager

    b. Exchange Administrator Program

    c. Windows NT Server Manager

    d. Microsoft Outlook client

19. How can you input a list of newsgroups for your Microsoft Exchange Server to receive? (Choose all that apply.)

    a. Manually create the newsgroups using the Newsgroup Configuration Wizard.

    b. Download an active file from your newsfeed provider.

    c. Microsoft Exchange has the default newsgroups configured automatically.

    d. Create the active file, and import it using the Internet News Configuration Wizard.

20. You have a single Microsoft Exchange Server in your organization. Jane complains that she cannot access her Inbox from home using her POP3 application, whereas other employees can. You verify that Jane is entering the correct configuration information into her POP3 application and that other users can access their mailboxes. Jane can access her mailbox at the office using Microsoft Outlook. What is the most likely problem?

    a. POP3 is disabled for the site.

    b. POP3 is disabled for the server.

    c. POP3 is disabled for Jane's mailbox.

    d. Not enough information to find a solution.

HANDS-ON PROJECTS

PROJECT 10.1

To use the Internet News Service Installation Wizard:

    1. To start the Newsfeed Configuration Wizard (shown in Figure 10.23), select the Newsfeed option for the New Other option on the File menu.

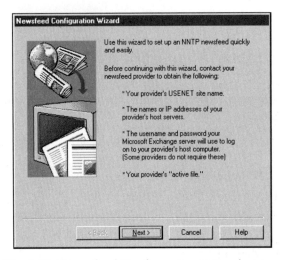

Figure 10.23   The initial Newsfeed Configuration Wizard page.

2. Make sure that you have access to the information requested on the first page (see Figure 10.24) of the Wizard, and click on Next.

3. From the drop-down menu, select the Microsoft Exchange Server computer on which the newsfeed is going to be installed. Next, enter in the Usenet site name for the server. Click on Next, which brings up the newsfeed type selection page (see Figure 10.25).

4. Select the newsfeed type—Inbound And Outbound, Inbound Only, or Outbound Only. Next, select whether you are configuring your Internet News Service with a push- or pull-type of inbound newsfeed. Click on Next, which brings up the connection type selection page (see Figure 10.26).

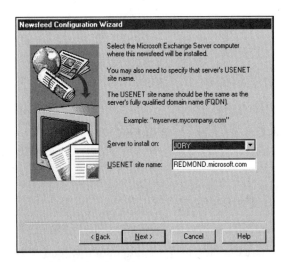

Figure 10.24   The server selection page.

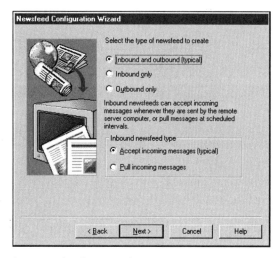

Figure 10.25   The newsfeed type selection page.

5. Select whether you will use a LAN (dedicated) or a dial-up connection. If you select a dial-up connection, you will be required to specify a RAS Phonebook entry, and the account name and password for the entry. Click on Next.

6. From the drop-down menu, select how often the Internet News Service will connect to your newsfeed provider. Your options are: 15 minutes, 1 hour, 3 hours, 6 hours, 12 hours, and 24 hours. Figure 10.27 shows the connection frequency selection page. Click on Next.

7. Enter your provider's Usenet site name. Figure 10.28 shows the provider's Usenet site page. Click on Next.

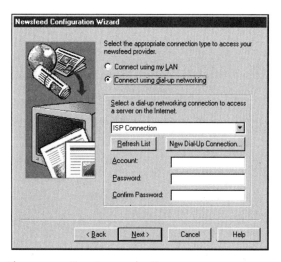

Figure 10.26   The connection type selection page.

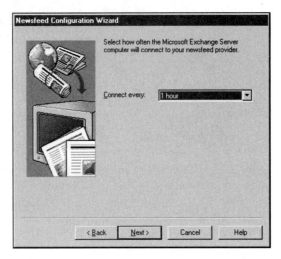

Figure 10.27   The connection frequency selection page.

8. Enter the host name or IP address of your newsfeed provider's host computer. You might also enter any additional newsfeed host names on this page. Figure 10.29 shows the newsfeed provider's host names page. Click on Next.

9. If your newsfeed provider does not require you to use a secure connection, click on Next. If your newsfeed provider requires you to use a secure connection, enter your account name and password. Figure 10.30 shows the login information page. Click on Next.

10. The Newsfeed Configuration Wizard will now install your newsfeed. Figure 10.31 shows the newsfeed installation page. Click on Next.

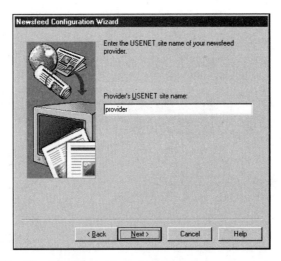

Figure 10.28   The provider's Usenet site page.

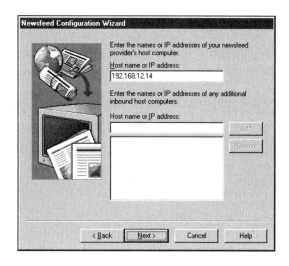

Figure 10.29   The newsfeed provider's host names page.

11. Click on the Change button, and select a mailbox to act as the Internet News administrator. Figure 10.32 shows the Internet news administrator selection page. Click on Next.

12. Select how to generate your active file (import the active file, download it from the newsfeed provider, or configure later). Figure 10.33 shows the active file generation page. Click on Next.

13. Select which newsgroups you would like your Microsoft Exchange Server to receive. Figure 10.34 shows the newsgroup selection page. When done, click on Next.

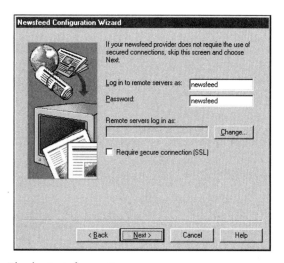

Figure 10.30   The login information page.

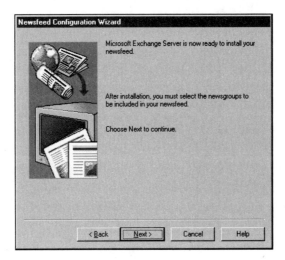

Figure 10.31   The newsfeed installation page.

14. Figure 10.35 shows the final page of the Internet News Configuration Wizard. Click on Finish on this screen to complete the installation.

 PROJECT 10.2

To create an active text file:

  1. On the News Server computer, click on Start, and then click on Run.

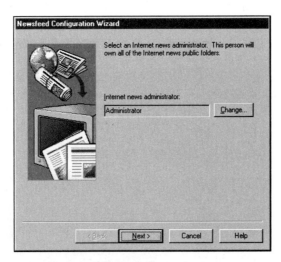

Figure 10.32   Internet News Administrator selection page.

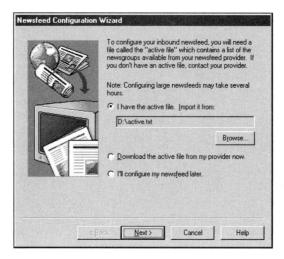

Figure 10.33   Active file generation page.

2. Type "telnet *server_name* 119", where *server_name* is the name of the NNTP server that will be sending you the newsfeed, and 119 is the IP port used by NNTP.

3. In the Telnet application, select Start Logging from the Terminal menu, and then specify a location to store the active file you are creating.

4. From the Terminal menu, select Preferences, and then select the Local Echo checkbox.

5. Type "list active" to capture a list of active newsgroups. Wait for the newsgroup directory list to be completed.

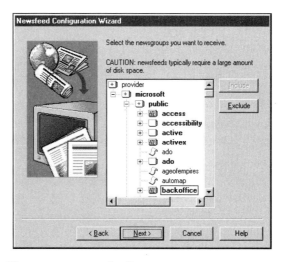

Figure 10.34   The newsgroup selection page.

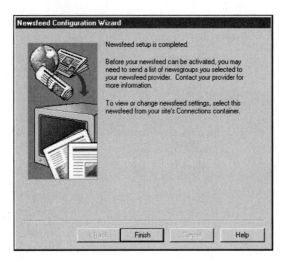

Figure 10.35　The final page of the Internet News Configuration Wizard.

6. From the Terminal menu, select Stop Logging, and exit out of the Telnet application.
7. Using a text editor (such as Notepad), remove the first two lines and the last line (a period). You may also want to remove any newsgroups that you do not want in your newsgroup directory.

CASE PROJECTS

1. You want to connect your Microsoft Exchange Server to the Internet to allow users to access public and private information.

   Required result:

   Allow employees to send and receive messages using Microsoft Outlook Express.

   Optional desired results:

   Allow anonymous users to access specific public folders. Allow Internet users to browse your Address Book.

   Proposed solution:

   Configure the POP3 protocol on Microsoft Exchange Server. Configure and enable the LDAP protocol.

   Which results does this proposed solution provide?

   a. The proposed solution provides the required result and both optional desired results.

b. The proposed solution provides the required result and one optional desired result.

c. The proposed solution provides only the required result.

d. The proposed solution does not provide the required result.

2. You want to connect your Microsoft Exchange Server to the Internet to allow users to access public and private information.

   Required result:

   Allow employees to send and receive messages using Microsoft Outlook Express.

   Optional desired results:

   Allow anonymous users access to specific public folders. Allow Internet users to browse your Address Book.

   Proposed solution:

   Configure the POP3 protocol on Microsoft Exchange Server. Install and configure the Internet Mail Service. Configure and enable the LDAP protocol.

   Which results does the proposed solution provide?

   a. The proposed solution provides the required result and both optional desired results.

   b. The proposed solution provides the required result and one optional desired result.

   c. The proposed solution provides only the required result.

   d. The proposed solution does not provide the required result.

3. You want to connect your Microsoft Exchange Server to the Internet to allow users to access public and private information.

   Required result:

   Allow employees to send and receive messages using Microsoft Outlook Express.

   Optional desired results:

   Allow anonymous users access to specific public folders. Allow Internet users to browse your Address Book.

   Proposed solution:

   Configure the POP3 protocol on Microsoft Exchange Server. Install and configure the Internet Mail Service. Configure Outlook Web Access and specify Public folder shortcuts.

   Which results does the proposed solution provide?

   a. The proposed solution provides the required result and both optional desired results.

10

b. The proposed solution provides the required result and one optional desired result.

c. The proposed solution provides only the required result.

d. The proposed solution does not provide the required result.

CHAPTER ELEVEN

EXCHANGE SERVER SECURITY

One of the most powerful features of Exchange Server is its ability to configure and maintain public folders. Public folders can store all kinds of data, including email messages, word-processing documents, and other files; may even include fill-in forms (for commonly used data acquisition requirements, such as requisitions, purchase orders, travel requests, expense reports, and so forth).

Public folders may also be configured to replicate themselves to other servers within a site or across an entire organization. This allows users anywhere in the organization to access public folder information without having to cross wide area network (WAN) links to communicate with remote servers.

With Exchange Server's advanced security, users may also sign and seal their email messages digitally. This helps maintain security when messages cross public network links, such as the Internet, and helps provide stronger proof that a mailbox ID and the underlying user's identity actually coincide.

AFTER READING THIS CHAPTER AND COMPLETING THE EXERCISES, YOU WILL BE ABLE TO:

- Understand public folder architecture
- Configure public folder replication
- Understand the difference between hierarchy and contents replication
- Understand Exchange advanced security features
- Configure and maintain Key Management Servers

PUBLIC FOLDERS: EXPLORED AND EXPLAINED

Public folders provide an easy way to share information among many users within a site or organization. Public folders can contain several types of information, including:

- Mail messages
- Word processing documents
- Graphic files
- Spreadsheets

A powerful feature in Exchange that combines well with public folders is the ability to create special-purpose applications using custom forms and views. Some examples of such custom applications include:

- Customer tracking systems
- Help desk applications
- Vacation request forms
- Expense forms
- Automated time tracking

Exchange public folders are stored in the public *Information Store*, located in a file called PUB.EDB in the Exchsrvr\Mdbdata directory. You can choose to replicate public folders to one or more remote Exchange Servers.

Public folders are made up of two parts: the public folder hierarchy and the public folder contents. These are explained in the sections that follow next.

PUBLIC FOLDER HIERARCHY

When public folders are created, they take on a tree structure. This structure is similar to that of a directory tree, with root (or top-level) folders at the top of the tree, and subfolders beneath them. This structure is called the *public folder hierarchy*. The public folder hierarchy appears as a series of folders in the Microsoft Outlook client user interface, as shown in Figure 11.1. It must be navigated just like Explorer or the Folder List in Outlook, to select and examine the contents of some particular folder in the hierarchy.

The Information Store on the public folder server supplies whatever information is required to build the hierarchy structure.

 The public folder hierarchy is replicated to all public Information Stores within an organization when public folder replication is configured.

Figure 11.1   The public folder hierarchy.

The highest level in the hierarchy is called the root level or top level. By default, all users can create folders at this level. However, you can use the Exchange Administrator program to modify the list of users who are permitted to create *top-level public folders*.

 If you do not restrict the number of users who can create at the top level, then the hierarchy can become cluttered with everyone's public folders. This makes it difficult to locate specific information, so changing the default is highly recommended.

Subfolders may be created within top-level folders. As with a directory tree, subfolders may be created within subfolders, which may be created within subfolders, and so on. By default, it is a folder's owner (the user who initially creates a folder) who controls user permissions to access and navigate its subfolders. The owner also decides who may create new subfolders as well.

PUBLIC FOLDER CONTENTS

Public folder contents are those messages (made up of the message headers and the bodies with attachments) contained within the public folder hierarchy. The public folder contents are stored in one or more Exchange Server computers (as long as the server has a public Information Store).

It is important to note that although the hierarchy is stored on all public folder servers, the contents are stored only on some of these servers. The location of the content is automatically selected when a user creates a public folder, or the administrator can control this location. For example, if Joe creates a public folder named Joe's Private Folder, and Joe's mailbox resides on the server named Jory, the public folder contents (see Figure 11.2) will automatically be located in Jory's Information Store.

PUBLIC FOLDERS IN THE DIRECTORY

Every public folder created by the users automatically appears in the Exchange directory and can also appear as a recipient. In other words, when a user creates a public folder, the public folder can receive messages just like any other Exchange recipient.

By default, all public folders are hidden recipients and cannot be viewed in the Recipients container in the Exchange Administrator program. To display such hidden recipients, select the Hidden Recipients option from the View menu while in the Recipients container.

You may also force a public folder to appear in the *Global Address List (GAL)* by clearing the Hide From Address Book checkbox in the Advanced property page for that public folder. Figure 11.3 shows how public folders correspond to Exchange directory entries.

DIRECTORY STORE LATENCY PROBLEMS

It is possible that a public folder may appear in the hierarchy for a remote server before the corresponding recipient appears in the Address Book or the Administrator program. This is because replication of the public folder hierarchy sometimes occurs faster than directory replication.

On the flip side, it is possible that a public folder may appear as a recipient in the Administrator program; however, any attempts to obtain its property pages will fail, because the Information Store has not yet replicated that public folder in the hierarchy. This occurs when directory replication takes place faster than the Information Store (and the public folder hierarchy) replication.

!	🗋	▽	0	From	Subject
				Joe Smith	**Picture of the President.tif**
				Joe Smith	**Our Application.zip**
				Joe Smith	**Employee Handbook.doc**
				Joe Smith	**Corporate Logo.bmp**
				Joe Smith	**timesheet template.xls**
				Joe Smith	**timesheet Feb17.xls**
				Joe Smith	**timesheet Feb9.xls**
				Joe Smith	**timesheet Feb22.xls**
				Joe Smith	**timesheet Feb2.xls**
				Joe Smith	**timesheet March1.xls**

Figure 11.2   The public folder contents.

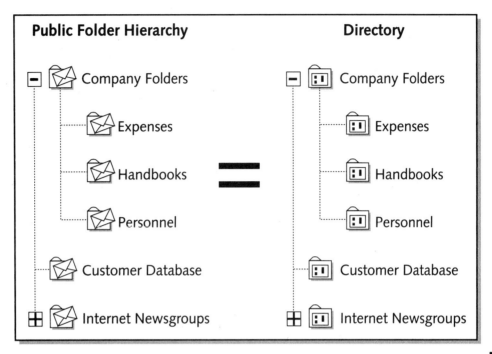

Figure 11.3   How public folders correspond to Exchange Directory entries.

11

These issues lead quite naturally into the configuration details for the various Exchange subsystems involved. In the section that follows, you'll learn what's involved in configuring the Exchange Information Store.

CONFIGURING THE INFORMATION STORE

Using site configuration properties is one way to manage public folders. These properties are controlled through the site configuration object in the Configuration container for the site. Figure 11.4 shows the public Information Store Site Configuration Properties tabs, which include the following elements:

- General tab
- Permissions tab
- Top Level Folder Creation tab
- Storage Warnings tab
- Public Folder Affinity tab

You'll investigate these tabs in the sections that follow.

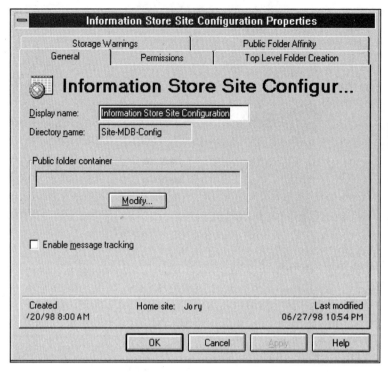

Figure 11.4   The public Information Store Properties tabs.

 For more information about the Information Store Site Configuration Properties tabs, consult the Exchange online help, or you may search the online materials provided with the product; look for "Information Store Site Configuration" in the Index for quickest access to this material.

THE GENERAL TAB

The General tab allows you to configure the following information:

- **Display Name** A name given to the Information Store that will identify it in the Exchange Administrator program. This field can be up to 256 characters in length.

- **Directory Name** A read-only field that displays the directory name.

- **Public Folder Container** Allows you to select where the public folder container will be located.

- **Enable Message Tracking** Allows you to enable or disable message tracking in the Information Store.

TOP-LEVEL FOLDER CREATION TAB

As an Exchange administrator, you have control over who in your organization may create top-level (or root) public folders. By default, all users are allowed to create top-level public folders. Most experts strongly recommend that this default be changed and that only a small subset of users (perhaps one per department), if any, be permitted to create such folders. To configure permissions for creating top-level folders, use the Top Level Folder Creation tab in the Information Store Site Configuration Properties window. The interface looks and works much like the User Manager For Domains utility.

PERMISSIONS TAB

Use the Permissions tab to manage permissions for who's allowed to access and change the entries on the various tabs in the Site Configuration Properties window. In other words, this tab provides controls over who may make what kinds of changes on the tabs that appear in this window.

STORAGE WARNINGS TAB

Use the Storage Warnings tab to specify when notification messages should be sent to mailbox owners or public folder contacts when such folders or mailboxes exceed the storage space assigned to them. Quota limits may be set for public folders in two locations—the General tab for the public Information Store and the Advanced tab for the public folder.

PUBLIC FOLDER SITE AFFINITY TAB

Sometimes, the contents of a public folder are not located on a server within the site, but instead are found on one or more servers in other sites. If this situation occurs, then site affinity must be configured to allow clients access to these folders (or *replicas*) in the remote site. This is known as *public folder site affinity*. The client needs to be able to connect to the server in the remote site using a Remote Procedure Call (RPC) as well as have an affinity value set.

You can use public folder site affinity to specify a preference for one site over another for the client to connect to the remote public folder servers. By default, there is no public folder site affinity set, and it's only necessary when there are folders/replicas located in different remote sites. The client will not connect to a server that contains a replica in a site without having an affinity value. Public folder site affinity is a cost value assigned to a connection between sites, and it's similar to that of the site connector cost value.

 Public folder affinity values may be set only between sites and not between servers within a site or with servers at remote sites.

The site with the lowest affinity value is attempted first. If a connection cannot be established, then the site with the next-lowest affinity value is tried, and so on. For example, if a site can connect to 4 remote sites that have public folder affinity values of 1, 20, 50, and 80 assigned, the site with the affinity value of 1 will be tried first, followed by the site with the next-lowest value (20), and so forth.

As with trust relationships in a Windows NT domain environment, affinity values are one-way only. In other words, if a remote site has an affinity value of 30 to your local site, that does not mean that your local site automatically has an affinity value of 30 to that remote site. You must configure affinity values for the remote site independently.

Now that you've covered the Properties tabs for the Information Store Site Configuration, it's time to change focus and tackle what's involved in creating and managing public folders. Not surprisingly, this serves as the topic for the sections that follow next.

CREATING AND HANDLING PUBLIC FOLDERS

Users with appropriate permissions can access property pages for public folders. They may use these property pages to set general configuration items for public folders, and to define views, permissions, and customized, forms-based applications (such as the travel request and expense report form applications mentioned earlier in this chapter). In the sections that follow, we explain these activities in more detail.

USING THE MICROSOFT OUTLOOK CLIENT TO CREATE A PUBLIC FOLDER

You can create a public folder using Outlook by selecting the Create Subfolder option in the File|Folder menu. A dialog box appears that requests that you enter a folder name and allows you to select the type of folder to create.

PUBLIC FOLDER PERMISSIONS

For users to access a public folder, they must have appropriate permissions. Microsoft Exchange provides you with some predefined permission roles, as an easy way to group required user permissions. There are eight permissions that are set for each role, as shown in Figure 11.5. Table 11.1 describes each permission.

Table 11.2 describes the permissions granted to the following predefined roles:

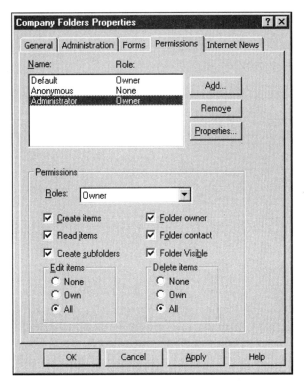

Figure 11.5   The public folder Permissions tab.

Table 11.1   Public folder permissions.

Permission	Description
Create Items	Enables the user to create new items in the folder.
Read Items	Allows the user to open and read items in a folder.
Create Subfolders	Enables the user to create subfolders within a folder.
Edit Items	Enables the user to modify items in a folder.
Folder Owner	Allows the user to perform administrative tasks on the folder as well as change folder permissions.
Folder Contact	Sends the contact any email messages specific to the folder. These notifications might include storage limit notifications or replication conflicts.
Folder Visible	Specifies whether this folder is visible to the user in the public folder hierarchical tree.
Delete Item	Deletes items from a folder.

11

- Owner
- Publishing Editor
- Editor
- Publishing Author
- Author
- Nonediting Author
- Reviewer
- Contributor
- None

 If one of the predefined roles does not meet the needs of your organization, you can grant custom permissions using any combination of permissions.

To prevent users from viewing and reading the contents of a specific public folder (including subfolders), you can remove the Read Items permission. You can remove any name (except the default name and the name of the folder owner) by selecting the name and clicking the Remove button. If you remove the default name or the name of the folder owner, it will reappear the next time the Permissions tab is viewed. This is because a public folder must always have an owner assigned to it.

For a folder that contains private or sensitive information, you can hide it from most users by disabling the Folder Visible checkbox in the Permissions tab of the public folder.

Table 11.2   Pre-defined roles and their corresponding permissions.

Role	Folder Owner	Create Items	Create Subfolders	Edit Items	Delete Items	Read Items	Folder Contact	Folder Visible
Owner	X	X	X	X(all)	X(all)	X	X	X
Publishing Editor		X	X	X(all)	X(all)	X		X
Editor		X		X(own)	X(own)	X		X
Publishing Author		X	X	X(own)	X(own)	X		X
Editor		X		X(own	X(own	X		X
Nonediting Author		X			X(own)	X		X
Reviewer						X		X
Contributor		X						X
None								X

Users can create and use what are called public folder Favorites. Public folder Favorites are links to public folders within the hierarchy and may be used as shortcuts for quick access to these folders. The Favorites are stored in the user's Favorites folders. This link opens the public folder without having to open all the public folders in the hierarchy. This can bypass any permissions you may have set on the top-level folders for the linked folder. To prevent this from happening, change the permissions on all folders and subfolders to those set on the higher-level folders. You can accomplish this by selecting the Propagate These Properties To All Subfolders checkbox in the General tab of the top-level public folders (in the Exchange Administrator program).

Once public folders are defined and permissions have been set, it's imperative to associate names with those folders that will be easy for users to understand. Likewise, it's essential to place those folders within some logical context in the public folder hierarchy, to decide on which server or servers those folders should reside, and so forth. These topics are addressed in the section that follows.

NAMING AND SITUATING PUBLIC FOLDERS

By default (assuming that no public folder replication has been established) the contents of a public folder are stored on a single public folder server. Keeping only one copy of the public folder's contents around has its advantages and disadvantages, as you'll learn in the sections that follow.

11

SINGLE COPY ADVANTAGES

The advantages of maintaining only a single copy of a public folder include the following:

- There is no Exchange Server overhead required to replicate a public folder's contents to other public servers.
- There is no latency (delay) involved in replicating a public folder's contents to another public folder server, because there is no replication.

SINGLE COPY DISADVANTAGES

The disadvantages of maintaining only a single copy of a public folder include the following:

- If many users need access to a folder's contents on a specific public folder server, that server might get overloaded with requests. This could cause delays when accessing such folders.
- If you take a public folder server down for maintenance or the public folder server goes offline unexpectedly, its public folders' contents become unavailable to users.

For most organizations, except small ones, the disadvantages of single copy public folder servers outweigh the advantages. In most cases, convenience alone is enough to mandate multiple copies of public folder data. To that end, you may configure public folders to replicate to other servers within your organization. You may choose to place replicated public folder contents on other servers in the same site, or on servers at remote sites, to cut down on wide area network traffic. You'll learn more about the pros and cons of replication in the sections that follow.

REPLICA ADVANTAGES

Replicating public folder contents to another server on a local network or to a remote site can be most beneficial when you seek to:

- Balance the user access load among several public folder servers within the organization.

- Schedule public folder replication to remote sites to control the use of the available network bandwidth. For example, you might not want users in a remote site to access your local public folder server for content information, because your WAN link is slow or it is billed by the amount of data transferred.

REPLICA DISADVANTAGES

One disadvantage to replicating public folder content to remote public folder servers is that replication adds traffic to a network. This is because the public folder replication sends changes in the form of messages to all remote public folder servers. The key trade-off here is as follows:

- If remote users access public folders regularly, it is less bandwidth consumptive to replicate and provide local access to those users

- If remote users access public folders only seldom, it is less bandwidth intensive to require them to make such access over a wide area link than it is to replicate them.

To make sure you understand the activities involved in replication and the associated overhead, you will learn more about the replication process in the section that follows.

UNDERSTANDING PUBLIC FOLDER REPLICATION

Public folder replication is achieved through two steps: public folder contents replication and public folder hierarchy replication. Each component of the public folders (hierarchy and contents) is replicated and managed separately:

- **Public folder contents replication** Copies of all messages within the public folder that is to be replicated are transferred as email messages to all servers participating in the replication. You can control public folder contents replication on a folder-by-folder basis.

- **Public folder hierarchy replication** Propagates all top-level and subfolder hierarchical information to all servers in the organization as email messages. This process cannot be prevented. This process is designed to deliver a single, consistent view of the public folder hierarchy to all Exchange servers (and clients), whether folders are replicated or not.

Using public folder replication provides you with the following:

- Fault tolerance for your public folder contents should the primary server become unavailable.

- The ability to distribute the workload for those users who access a public folder server, and to improve overall response time when accessing public folder information. The latter may happen because information will be accessed locally rather than remotely, or simply because more servers are available to share the overall load.

- A reduction in the amount of information transferred between your public folder server and your clients over your WAN links.

PUBLIC FOLDER CONTENTS REPLICATION

It is important to know which servers or sites should house a replica, and who will access such replicas. There are numerous issues to consider when you configure public folder contents replication. These include the following:

- Each message with a replica folder is copied to all servers that store that replica.

- You can schedule when replication will occur.

- You must manually assign all servers that are to participate in any specific public folder's replication.

- Setting up replication to remote sites allows clients that do not normally have RPC access to access a public folders server.

Public folder contents replication deals with two levels of *granularity*. Granularity may be defined as the size of the units of data involved in handling some kind of computer activity or feature. For example, the feature could be screen resolution, where size is measured in pixels.

For Exchange, the two levels of granularity are:

- **Granularity of replication** Measured at the message level. Any changes to a message property or to an attachment contained within a message cause the message to be replicated to all other public folder instances.

- **Granularity of configuration** Measured at the folder level. If there are multiple messages to replicate, Exchange Server groups these messages into a single large message and replicates that aggregate message. The size of the combined message is constrained by the maximum message size property.

PUBLIC FOLDER HIERARCHY REPLICATION

The public folder hierarchy is replicated using mail messages to all public folders in the organization. These messages are transferred using the Message Transfer Agent (MTA). The public folder hierarchy is replicated to all public folder servers in the Exchange organization automatically. It is important to note that public folder hierarchy replication cannot be scheduled. Instead, it is replicated at a set interval that is configured in the Windows NT Registry on the affected Exchange Servers.

The default hierarchy replication interval is set to 60 seconds. Therefore, any public folder hierarchy changes are replicated to all public folder servers in the organization every minute. You may control the hierarchy replication interval by changing the following Registry setting (in seconds): HKEY _LOCAL_MACHINE\SYSTEM\CurrentControlSet\Services\MSExchangeIS\ ParametersPublic\Replication Send Folder Tree.

CONFIGURING PUBLIC FOLDER REPLICATION

You configure public folder replication from the Exchange Administrator program. To replicate a specific public folder, you must use the following procedure:

1. Select the public folder to be replicated from the Organization container.

2. Select the Properties option from the File menu.

There are three property tabs that you must access to replicate public folders:

- **Replicas tab** Used to configure which servers within the site or in remote sites will contain the replicas (see Figure 11.6). Any server listed in this tab will have replicas "pushed" to it.

- **Folder Replication Status tab** Displays all public folder servers that receive the replicated folder (see Figure 11.7). By clicking the Columns button, you can specify which columns of information will be displayed in this property page. The different columns that you can specify are:

  - **Server Name** The name of the server to which the folder was replicated.

  - **Last Received Time** The last time the local server received updates from the selected server.

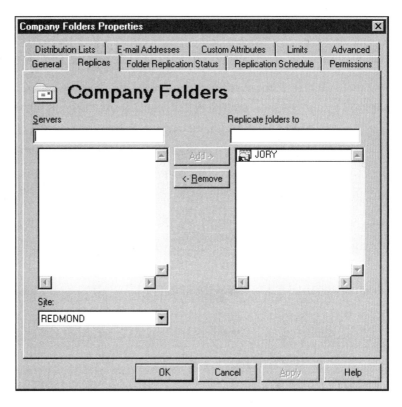

Figure 11.6   The Replicas tab.

- **Average Transmission Time** The average time it takes to update the selected remote server from the local server.

- **Replication Status** The status of the replication. Table 11.3 lists the different status categories.

Table 11.3   Replication status categories.

Status	Description
In Synch	No local public folder has been modified. The remote public folder server is synchronized with the local server.
Local Modified	The local public folder has been modified, but the replicas have not been sent to the remote server.
Last Received Time	The last time the local server received updates from the remote server.
Average Transmission Time	The average time it takes to update the remote server from the local server.
Last Transmission Time	The amount of time it took the last transmission to take place.

- **Replication Schedule tab** Used to configure the intervals at which the public folder will replicate to other public folder servers within the organization (see Figure 11.8). You can specify:

  - **Use Information Store Schedule** This option uses the schedule set in the Replication Schedule tab (discussed in the next section).

  - **Never** This option disables replication for this public folder.

  - **Always** This option replicates the public folder every 15 minutes.

  - **Selected Times** This option allows you to configure specific times to replicate the public folder (in 15-minute or 1-hour intervals).

 If you set a schedule on the folder level for a specific folder, it will override any schedule set at the Information Store level.

Figure 11.7　The Folder Replication Status tab.

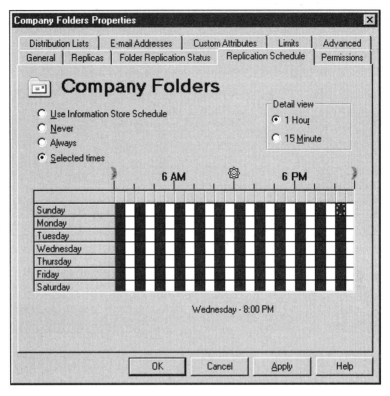

Figure 11.8   The Replication Schedule tab.

CONFIGURING PUBLIC INFORMATION STORE REPLICATION

To control replication of public folders, you must use the Public Information Store Advanced property page. Here's how to access this page:

1. In the Administrator window, choose Servers, and then select a server.

2. Select Public Information Store.

3. From the File menu, choose Properties.

The following property tabs are available to you to configure a public Information Store:

- **Instances tab** Used to configure which replicas of a specified public folder to "pull" to the public Information Store (see Figure 11.9).

- **Replication Schedule tab** Used to set the replication schedule (see Figure 11.10). You can specify the schedule at which this public folder will be replicated to the rest of the public folder servers with the following:

  - **Never** This option disables replication for this public folder.

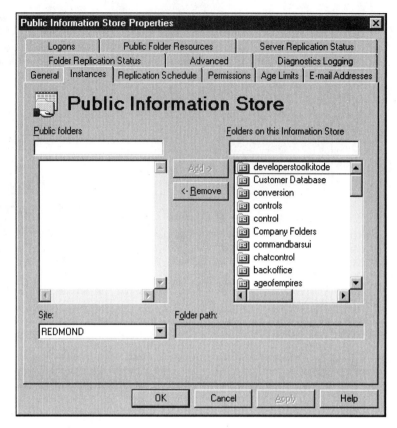

Figure 11.9   The Instances tab.

- **Always** This option replicates the public folder every 15 minutes.
- **Selected Times** This option allows you to configure specific times to replicate the public folder (in 15-minute or 1-hour intervals).
- **Folder Replication Status tab** Displays the public folders that are being replicated and the number of servers to which this folder is being replicated (see Figure 11.11).
- **Advanced tab** Allows you to specify the frequency at which replication of the Information Store will occur and the maximum size of the replication messages.
- **Public Folder Resources tab** Allows you to view the amount of space that is currently being used by the public folders and replicas on this Information Store (see Figure 11.12).
- **Server Replication Status tab** Displays the replication information for all the servers in your organization to which this Information Store is being replicated (see Figure 11.13).

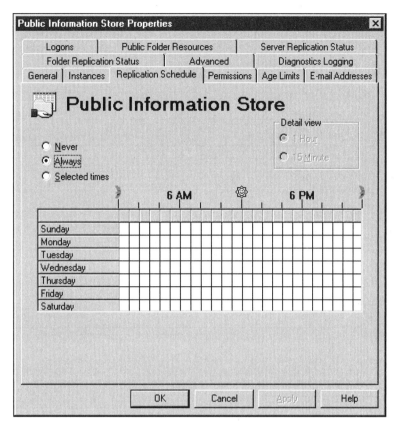

Figure 11.10 The Replication Schedule tab.

REPLICATING PUBLIC FOLDERS

Public folder replication uses the MTA for replication transport. In other words, replication data is packaged in the form of Exchange messages, which the MTA on the sending server addresses to a distribution list of receiving servers. When such messages arrive on the receiving end, they are unpacked and used to update the public folders' contents.

PUBLIC FOLDER REPLICATION AGENT

When more than one instance of a public folder exists, a *Public Folder Replication Agent (PFRA)* monitors all modifications, additions, and deletions to that public folder. The PFRA then sends *change messages* to other Information Stores that store replicated instances.

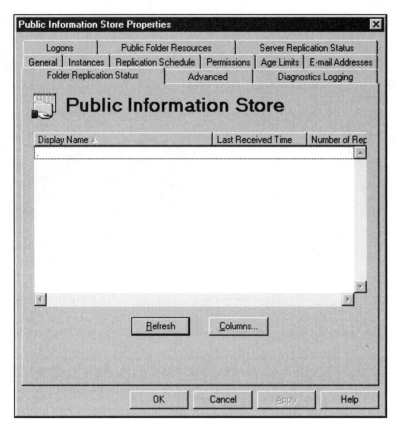

Figure 11.11   The Folder Replication Status tab.

The PFRA uses the following message attributes to ensure that messages are replicated correctly within an organization:

- **Change Number** This is a number that is created using an Information Store identifier/counter that is unique across an entire organization, plus a server-specific change counter. Due to its structure, the change number is Information-Store-specific, and reflects all changes in sequence. A change counter is sequential for all folders and messages in the Information Store but not for a single folder or message.

  When a user changes (adds, modifies, or deletes) a message in any public folder on the server, the change counter is incremented. Following any modification to the public folder contents, the PFRA increments the change counter.

- **Time Stamp** When messages arrive in a public folder, they are assigned a time stamp. When a message is modified, the PFRA assigns a new time stamp using the greater of either the current system time or the old time stamp.

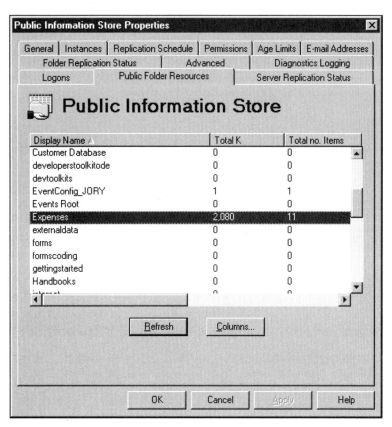

Figure 11.12   The Public Folder Resources tab.

- **Predecessor Change List** The predecessor change list for a specific public folder message is a list of the Information Stores that have made a change with the last change number applied to each Information Store. The predecessor change list is used to help identify and resolve public folder conflicts.

OUT-OF-SYNC PUBLIC FOLDERS AND BACKFILL

It is assumed that messaging transports will deliver any replication message sent by the originating Information Store successfully. There is no way to confirm that a replication message sent between an originating and a receiving Information Stores has completed successfully (other than receiving a non-delivery report). This is because delivery confirmation adds further messaging overhead. If an Information Store sent a confirmation message for every replication message it sent, it would be necessary to add an extra message to each transfer.

If a replication message does not arrive at its intended destination, the Information Store in that location will no longer have an up-to-date copy of the message. Therefore, the public folders on the local and remote computers will no

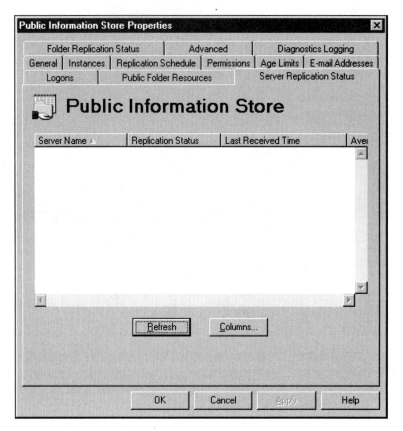

Figure 11.13   The Server Replication Status tab.

longer be synchronized. The originating Information Store assumes that replication has completed successfully, even though this may not always be the case.

To correct this situation if it should occur, public Information Stores also participate in what's called a *backfill* process. A backfill process helps the Information Stores recover from the following scenarios:

- Lost replication messages.
- A public server being restored from a backup.
- A public server that is being shut down and then restarted.

The backfill process occurs as follows:

1. Replication to Information Store 2 fails (see Figure 11.14). Information Store 1 sends out a replication message to Information Store 2 and Information Store 3. Information Store 2 does not receive the replication message. Information Store 1 and Information Store 3 are synchronized, but Information Store 2 has an old version of the message. Information Store 1 and Information Store 3 have a matching change number that is not known to Information Store 2.

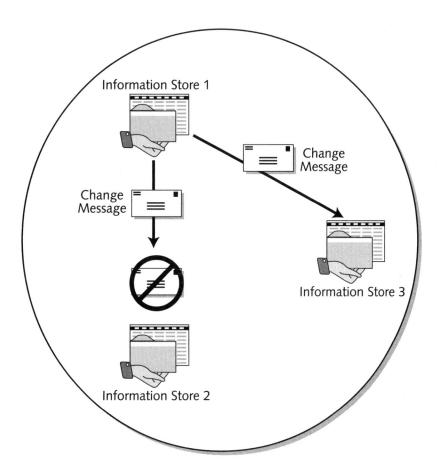

Figure 11.14   Replication to Information Store 2 fails.

2. *Status messages* are sent and analyzed (see Figure 11.15). Information Store 3 sends out a status message to Information Store 1 and Information Store 2. Information Store 2 checks to see if the change numbers are the same as the ones it has recorded. If all change numbers agree, then Information Store 2 and Information Store 3 are synchronized. However, if all change numbers are not the same, Information Store 2 determines if there are any higher change numbers in the list of changes for Information Store 3 that are not in the list of changes for Information Store 2.

3. A *backfill request* is sent (see Figure 11.16). When Information Store 2 finds mismatched change numbers, it creates a backfill request for the changes that it has not yet received. This backfill request is sent as an email message to a preferred public folder server—in this case, Information Store 3.

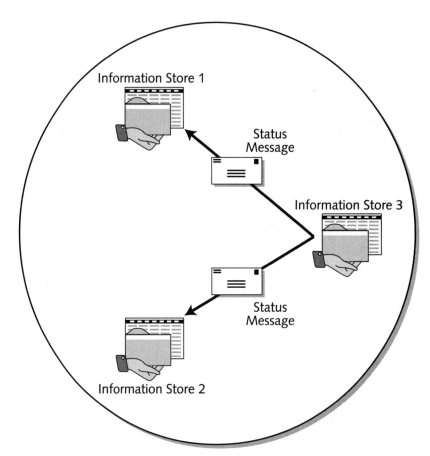

Figure 11.15   Status messages sent and analyzed.

4. The changes are sent (see Figure 11.17). If Information Store 3 does not respond to Information Store 2's backfill request, then another Information Store is selected based on mail transit time and site affinity values. Information Store 2 first attempts to contact all the servers within its own site in the order of average transmission time. If no servers from the local site respond to the backfill request, Information Store 2 uses site affinity values to pick the next site, and then the average transmission time is used to determine an order within the remote site.

In Figure 11.17, Information Store 2 chooses Information Store 3 and sends it the backfill request. Information Store 3 responds to the backfill request by sending the missing changes to Information Store 2, which then modifies its public folders to reflect these changes. Information Store 1, Information Store 2, and Information Store 3 are now synchronized.

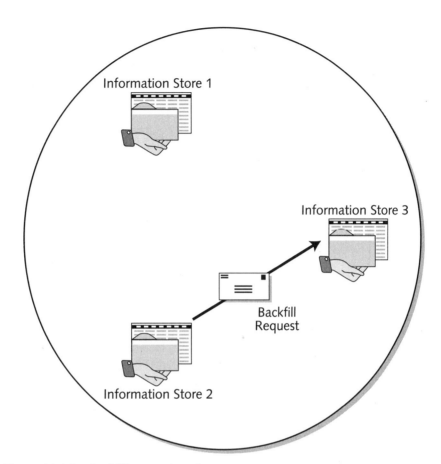

Figure 11.16   Backfill request sent.

CONTENT CONFLICT RESOLUTION

A conflict occurs under the following situation: A user modifies an item in a public folder, and, before those changes can be replicated, another user modifies the same item on another Exchange computer. A conflict occurs as soon as both servers attempt to replicate their changes.

When such a conflict occurs, the public folder contact and the users involved in the conflict receive a notification message about the conflict. The only users that can resolve such a conflict include:

- The public folder contact.
- The public folder owner.
- Any user with the Edit All Item permission to that public folder.

Another conflict can occur when two public folder owners modify a public folder design at the same time. During this type of conflict, the design change that takes place last overwrites previous changes. No messages are displayed in

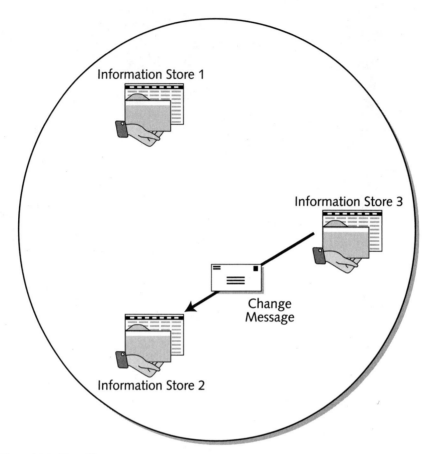

Figure 11.17   Changes sent.

the public folder, but the public folder contact (or the public folder owner) receives notification of the conflict.

This concludes your exploration of public folders and replication. For the remainder of the chapter, you will focus on Exchange Server security and its security-related services and capabilities.

AN ADVANCED SECURITY OVERVIEW

Exchange Server provides your organization with protection and verification of messages. It accomplishes this by using message encryption and key technology.

Exchange Server supports advanced security features when any or all of the following clients are used:

- Microsoft Windows 3.x-based Exchange clients

- Microsoft Windows 95-based Outlook or Exchange clients

- Microsoft Windows NT-based Outlook or Exchange clients

- Macintosh Microsoft Exchange clients

 Exchange Server advanced security is not available if you run the Microsoft MS-DOS-based Exchange client.

Advanced security supports both the *signing* (signatures) and the *sealing* (encryption) of any message generated by either Microsoft Outlook or an Exchange client. With signing, the user places a digital signature on a message. This enables the recipient to verify that a message did indeed originate from its putative user. With sealing, the sender encrypts the message and any attachments, thereby locking its contents. Such a message may only be unsealed (or unlocked) using the correct key.

Within the Exchange environment, advanced security features both for encryption and digital signatures fall under the purview of the *Key Management Server (KM Server)*. This provides the core topic for the sections that follow.

KEYS AND EXCHANGE

To allow users to sign and seal their messages, Exchange Server uses one or two approaches to handling encryption and secure authentication. The first approach relies on an industry-standard encryption technology known as *public/private key* technology. Each mailbox is assigned a key pair. One key is publicly advertised, but only the user knows the other (private) key.

A public key is a fixed-length security string that is made available to all users. The advanced security features of Exchange use two public keys to do the following:

- **Seal the message** One of the public keys is used to encrypt the message, thereby sealing its contents.

- **Verify the message** The other public key is used to verify the identity of the sender of an encrypted (or sealed) message.

With private key encryption, each user keeps an encrypted security file on his computer that contains a fixed-length string. The advanced security features of Exchange use two private keys to perform the following activities, each of which complements one of the preceding public key operations:

- **Sign a message** One of the private keys is used to sign the message, thereby confirming the sender's or receiver's identity.

11

- **Unseal a message** The other private key is used to unseal a sealed message received by a user.

The second approach is called a *secret key* method. This method uses an algorithm based only on a single, secret key to encrypt and decrypt messages. Both sender and recipient use that secret key. This is a more efficient way to encrypt large amounts of data, but requires a secure way for sender and receiver to exchange key information (which is never required in the public/private key approach).

To manage its various security keys, Microsoft Exchange Server uses a service called the Key Management Service (KM Service). This is the topic of the section that follows next.

THE KEY MANAGEMENT SERVICE (KM SERVICE)

To enable and use advanced security features in Microsoft Exchange, you must install the Key Management Service separately.

The Exchange advanced security features use several components to implement its capabilities. Some of these components are server-based, while others are client-based. All these components must be in place to take full advantage of Exchange advanced security.

The server-based components of Exchange Server advanced security must reside on a Windows NT computer running Exchange Server. This computer can be located anywhere in the organization. These server-based components include the following:

- **The Windows NT Key Manager Service** This service is the main component of advanced security. The Key Manager Service allows the machine where it runs, known as the Key Management Server, to function as a certificate authority (CA). A CA creates and assigns keys, maintains a Certification Revocation List (CRL) in the Exchange directory database, and creates and manages the KM database that stores all user public keys.

- **The KM Security DLL** This Dynamic Link Library (SECKM.DLL) supports secure communication between the client and the server. When a client makes a request for a new key, a function in this DLL is called, and the key request is passed on to the KM Service.

- **The KM Database** This database manages advanced security information for an entire Exchange organization.

The person who manages the KM Server is known as the KM administrator. The KM administrator is not necessarily the same person as the Exchange administrator (but in practice, both administrators usually share a common job title, if both roles are not assigned to the same person). The KM administrator must have administrator-level access to the Exchange Administrator program.

 There can only be one KM Server per Exchange organization.

Two other components—the *client security DLL* and a *security administration DLL*—are installed during the KM setup process.

The client security DLL resides on the client computer and is used to sign/verify and seal/unseal advanced security messages. There are two different DLLs involved (depending on your Windows operating system): ETEXCH.DLL and ETEXCH32.DLL. ETEXCH.DLL is used with 16-bit Windows operating systems and ETEXCH32.DLL is used with 32-bit Windows operating systems.

The security administration DLL resides on the Exchange administrator's workstation. It is used by the Exchange Administrator program whenever advanced security is being configured for a user's account.

INSTALLING KM SERVER

Only an administrator can install the KM Server from the Microsoft Exchange Server CD-ROM. The KM Server must be installed onto one of the Exchange Server computers in an organization.

The KM Server setup program performs the following activities:

- Checks for a previous installation of KM Server within the site.
- Checks for a previous installation of KM Server within the organization.
- Copies all necessary files from the CD-ROM.
- Creates the Microsoft Exchange Key Manager Service
- Creates two objects—a certificate authority object and an encryption object—in the directory related to Key Manager Services under the Configuration container for the site.
- Creates a password for the KM Server.

After the setup process is complete, you must start the Microsoft Exchange Key Manager Server service from the Services applet within the Windows NT Control Panel window. Choose that service from the pick list that appears in the window's main pane, and start it with the Start button.

By now, you've probably noticed mention of both a KM Server and a KM Service. This is an important, but vital, distinction to make when trying to understand fully what Key Management means within the Exchange environment. The KM Server is the computer that runs Windows NT Server and Exchange, whereas the KM Server software is also installed. The KM Service is a set of processes that start up automatically when that computer boots, and that make themselves available to any consumers on the network that request such services (as long as the consumers have the proper authorization to do so). Thus, the KM Server is the machine where the software is installed and runs, and the KM Service represents the ability to respond to requests for Key Management Services from clients and administrative utilities elsewhere on the network (or in the case of administrative utilities, even on the same machine).

KM SERVER KEY AND PASSWORD FUNCTIONS

All keys stored within the database are encrypted using a *master encryption key*. This key maintains the security of the information contained within the database itself. This master encryption key is encrypted using passwords from each service that uses the KM Server database.

During the KM Server setup process, a password is created that will be used by the KM Server to do the following:

- **Start the Key Manager Service** This password must be provided at startup, either manually or via a floppy disk.
- **Access the Key Manager database** This password is used to decrypt the lockbox and gain access to the KM database.
- **Restrict password entry** Normally, the startup password is placed in a local file called KMSPWD.INI and is written to a floppy disk. However, you can choose to enter the password manually and not use the floppy disk. Therefore, be aware that the KM Server startup might not be fully automated, because you will have to either supply the password floppy disk or enter it manually. If entering manually, the password is entered in the startup parameters box when the key manager service is started from the services window in the control panel.
- **Encrypt the master encryption key** An additional password is used to encrypt the master key—which becomes a lockbox—for each KM Server administrator.

Different countries in the world have different encryption laws. Owing to this situation, the KM Server is able to provide some control over which encryption algorithm is used to sign and seal messages. All encryption algorithm options are controlled by the encryption object under the Configuration container and are shown in Table 11.4.

Table 11.4   Location-specific encryption algorithms.

Location	Algorithm
North America	CAST-64 (default); DES
International	CAST-40; Plain text (if not using advanced security)

Once the KM Server is running and properly configured, it becomes possible to exploit the KM Server's advanced security capabilities. This provides the topic for the sections that follow.

IMPLEMENTING ADVANCED SECURITY

The creation and management of advanced security, such as public and private signing keys, public and private sealing keys, security tokens, and signing and sealing certificates, take place in two distinct steps:

- The administrator's step
- The client's step

THE ADMINISTRATOR'S STEP

11

The administrator must use the Microsoft Exchange Administrator program to enable advanced security for a specific mailbox or collection of mailboxes. This involves generating and implementing a private and public sealing key and a security token.

The following steps must be completed to enable advanced security for a mailbox. The key management server password will be needed to open the security tab for each user:

1. You select the Enable Advanced Security button under the Advanced Security property page for each user.

2. The security administration DLL retrieves the KM Server location and uses this information to pass the user's name and administrator's password to the KM Service.

3. The KM Service generates a sealing key pair. This key pair is stored in the KM database.

4. The KM Service generates a random 12-character security token and encrypts it using the administrator's password. This token is then passed to the security administration DLL on the administrator's computer.

5. The security administration DLL decrypts the security token and displays it in a dialog box on the administrator's computer.

THE CLIENT STEP

The user submits the security token to the KM Server, which, in turn, issues the sealing keys generated by the administrator back to the client.

The following steps must be completed to enable advanced security on the client side:

1. The KM administrator gives a user an access token using a secure delivery method.

2. The user enables advanced security by selecting Set Up Advanced Security in the Security Properties page. The client enters the security token received in Step 1.

3. The security DLL generates a public and private signing key pair for the user. The public signing key is encrypted (using the security token) and mailed to the hidden mailbox for the Exchange System Attendant.

4. This message is transferred to the Exchange Server computer running the KM Server, and the user is notified of a successful submission.

5. The message is then extracted by the Windows NT System Attendant service and is passed to the KM Service through the KM security DLL.

6. The KM Service decrypts the message, retrieves the public signing key, and places it in the KM database.

7. The KM Service generates two certificates—one for sealing and the other for signing—and generates a message addressed to the user.

8. This message is delivered to the user's mailbox, which prompts the user to enter his password. This password is used to verify the identity of the user.

9. The security DLL extracts the public sealing certificate and submits it to the local directory service for storage and replication.

There are four main storage areas for security information in Exchange Server. These appear in the list that follows next, but where actual certificate authority data resides in each of them appears in Table 11.5 immediately thereafter:

- Directory Store
- Security File
- KM Database
- X.509 Certificate

Table 11.5 Security information storage locations for Microsoft Exchange Server.

Security Information	Directory Store	Security File (.EPF)	KM Database	X.509 Certificate
CA's certificate		X		
CA's directory name				X
CA's signature				X
Certificate expiration date				X
Certificate serial number				X
Private sealing key		X	X	
Private signing key		X		
Public sealing key				X
Public signing key			X	X
Sealing certificate	X	X		
Signing certificate		X		
User's directory name				X

SENDING A SEALED MESSAGE

When sending a sealed message, the following activities occur:

1. The recipient's public key is retrieved from the directory.
2. A bulk encryption key is generated and used to encrypt the contents of the message.
3. A lockbox is created using the public sealing key to encrypt the bulk encryption key.
4. The encrypted message and a lockbox are sent to the Information Store for delivery.

Figure 11.18 shows the icons for sealing and signing email messages.

UNSEALING A SEALED MESSAGE

To unseal a message, the recipient must decrypt the lockbox with his private sealing key. The original bulk encryption key can now be accessed and used to decrypt the message.

SENDING A SIGNED MESSAGE

When a user wants to sign a message, the client uses the sender's private signing key and a technique known as hashing to prevent message tampering. Hashing

11

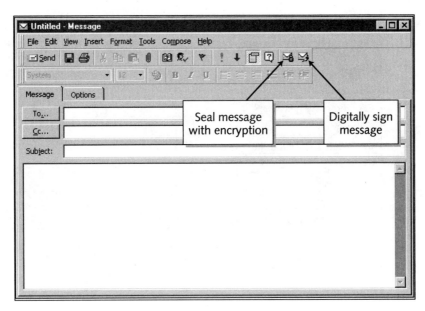

Figure 11.18   Sealing and signing email messages.

reduces a message of any length to a unique 128-bit result known as a message digest. The following activities occur when a message is signed:

1. The original message is hashed to obtain a unique message digest.

2. The user is prompted to enter his security profile password. The encrypted password file (.EPF) is decrypted, and its private signing key is extracted.

3. The message digest is encrypted using its sender's private signing key. This step creates a digital signature.

4. The client sends a copy of the sender's signing certificate, the digital signature, and the message to the Information Store for delivery.

VERIFYING A SIGNED MESSAGE

To verify a message has been sealed, a similar process recalculates the message digest and then verifies that the hash is identical to the hash contained in the message digest included with the message. To that end, the following activities take place:

1. The user displays the message and checks the signature on the message.

2. The client prompts the user for his security profile password.

3. Using the certificate enclosed in the message, the sender's public signing key is extracted and then is used to decrypt the digital signature. The original message digest is then decrypted from the signature.

4. The client performs a hash on the original message.

5. Both digests are compared to ensure that they are identical. If they are, the assumption is that the user's identity is confirmed.

Things really start to get interesting in multisite environments when users from all over an organization need access to key management services. You'll learn more about the issues involved, and the solutions required, in the sections that follow next.

MANAGING MULTIPLE KM SERVERS ACROSS MULTIPLE SITES

There can only be one KM Server in an organization to manage all CA activities. The KM Server setup program, however, needs to be run on one server within each site. This does not actually install another KM Server, but rather, creates an entry that links the directory structure on the machine where this program is run to the KM Server itself.

 You must replicate the existence of the KM Server to a remote site before you can run setup on that site. If replication has not taken place, setup attempts to install a KM Server. Do not let this attempt go forward—cancel it immediately!

11

KEY AND CERTIFICATE MANAGEMENT

Normally, those keys and certificates that are maintained by the KM Server require no management. Sometimes, however, it may become necessary to perform certain management-related duties. As an administrator, you might be required to revoke a user's ability to send signed and sealed messages, or to recover a forgotten or corrupted key pair and certificate. You may occasionally have to update security information that is about to expire as well, particularly if you lease CA information from a third-party provider such as VeriSign.

To revoke advanced security keys and certificates from a mailbox, a KM administrator must use the Exchange Administrator program to perform Step 1 as shown next. The remaining four steps are completed automatically:

1. For each mailbox from which you wish to revoke advanced security, click the Revoke Advanced Security Button on the Security Properties page.

2. The security DLL locates the KM Server and informs it which mailbox is to have its security configuration revoked.

3. The KM Server adds the user's signing and sealing keys to its revocation list.

4. The KM Server tells the Directory Service to add that user's sealing certificate to the Certificate Revocation List (CRL). Once added, that user may no longer sign or seal messages.

5. A dialog box appears to let you know that the task is complete.

Revoking does not delete keys from the KM database. Rather, those keys become unusable for future sealing. However, they may still be used by a KM administrator to unseal any messages that remain signed and sealed by those keys.

If a user forgets a password, or a password becomes corrupt or is accidentally deleted, the KM administrator can perform a recovery. A recovery is similar to enabling advanced security. The KM administrator clicks the Recover Security Key button in the Security Properties page. The KM Server then sends the user a history of the keys associated with the mailbox. The user must then reconfigure advanced security on the computer to create a new EPF file.

New certificates are only valid for 18 months. After this period, a certificate must be renewed, or rolled over. Before a certificate expires, the Exchange client software will send a renewal message.

CHAPTER SUMMARY

Microsoft Exchange public folders are a great way to share data among several people throughout your organization. You can configure different permissions, forms, rules, and views to create folder-based applications. Using Microsoft Outlook, a client can add to, create, or modify existing public folders.

Using public folder replication, you can configure public folder information to appear on different servers within your site or your organization. For example, you can configure a public folder with all employee benefits and handbooks. Updating the information in public folder replicas automatically replicates the changes to all the instances of the public folder.

The Microsoft Exchange Key Management Server allows you to configure advanced security to individual mailboxes. You can create public and private keys for sealing and signing of digital documents. This allows you to securely exchange information without the fear of the data being intercepted or spoofed.

KEY TERMS

- **backfill**—Helps Information Stores recover from lost replication messages, servers restored from a backup, or servers that have been shut down and restarted.

- **backfill request**—A message sent out by the Information Store on one server to request that missing public folder information be sent to it from the remote Information Store.

- **change message**—A message sent out from the Information Store that informs other Information Stores of changes to public folder information.

- **change number**—A number assigned to a public folder modification to allow the different Information Stores to update their databases.

- **client security DLL**—A Dynamic Link Library used to sign/verify and seal/unseal advanced security messages.

- **Global Address List (GAL)**—A global list that contains all the recipient addresses in an organization.

- **granularity**—A computer activity or feature in terms of the size of the units it handles.

- **granularity of configuration**—Granularity measured at the message level.

- **granularity of replication**—Granularity measured at the folder level.

- **Information Store**—A repository of Microsoft Exchange message information.

- **Key Management security DLL**—This Dynamic Link Library responds to any advanced security configuration requests from users and then submits the requests to the Key Manager Service.

- **Key Management Server (KM Server)**—A component of Microsoft Exchange Server that allows an administrator to configure advanced security on individual mailboxes.

- **Key Management Service (KM Service)**—The Windows NT service on a KM Server that responds to user and administrator requests for certificate and key-based services, passwords, and the like.

- **master encryption key**—A key used to encrypt all keys stored within the KM database.

- **permission roles**—A grouping of permissions to allow for easy public folder permission setting.

- **predecessor change list**—A list of the Information Stores that have made changes to the message and the last change number made by each Information Store.

- **private key**—A fixed-length security string that is used to unseal or sign a message.

- **public folder site affinity**—A value given to different sites to control which site is replicated and in which order.

11

- **public folder contents**—The items stored within the public folder hierarchy.

- **public folder contents replication**—The replication process of the public folder contents.

- **public folder hierarchy**—The directory structure of the public folder.

- **public folder hierarchy replication**—The replication process of the public folder hierarchy.

- **public folders**—Shared folders containing email messages, word-processing documents, and other files that can be replicated to remote Exchange Server.

- **Public Folders Replication Agent (PFRA)**—The Microsoft Exchange component responsible for the successful replication of public folder information.

- **public key**—A fixed-length security string that is available to all users. Used to seal or verify a message.

- **replica**—A copy of a public folder on a remote site.

- **sealing**—The sender encrypts the message and any attachments.

- **secret key**—A cryptography key to encrypt or decrypt messages using an algorithm.

- **security administration DLL**—A Dynamic Link Library that is used when advanced security is being configured for a user account.

- **signing**—The sender places a signature on a message to enable the recipient to verify the message's origin and authenticity.

- **status message**—A message sent from one Information Store to another informing it of the current public folder hierarchy and contents status.

- **time stamp**—A time value given to a modification done to a public folder to ease in the tracking of the change.

- **top-level public folders**—The root or highest level in the public folder hierarchy.

REVIEW QUESTIONS

1. What is a predefined group in public folder permissions called?
   - **a.** Groups
   - **b.** Roles
   - **c.** Sets
   - **d.** Clusters

2. What must you do to hide a subfolder from a particular recipient?

   a. Select the Hide From option on the Security Properties page.

   b. Hide the public folder by highlighting it in the Exchange Administrator and clicking the Hide button.

   c. Revoke the Read Items permission from the recipient at the parent folder.

   d. Uncheck the folder visible box on the client permissions page for that recipient.

3. What is a public key?

   a. A cryptography key used to encrypt or decrypt messages using an algorithm.

   b. A fixed-length security string that is used to unseal or sign a message.

   c. A fixed-length security string available from the Exchange Directory that is used to unseal or sign a message.

   d. A 128-bit message digest.

4. What is a private key?

   a. A cryptography key used to encrypt or decrypt messages using an algorithm.

   b. A fixed-length security string that is used to unseal or sign a message.

   c. A fixed-length security string supplied from the KM Service only to a particular user that is used to unseal or sign a message.

   d. A 128-bit message digest.

5. What is a secret key?

   a. A cryptography key used to encrypt or decrypt messages using an algorithm.

   b. A fixed-length security string that is used to unseal or sign a message.

   c. A fixed-length security string shared only between sender and receiver that is used to unseal or sign a message.

   d. A 128-bit message digest.

6. By default, all users can add folders to the top-level folders. True or False?

7. What is the Key Manager security DLL?

   a. A Dynamic Link Library that is used when advanced security is being configured for a user account.

   b. The Microsoft Exchange component responsible for the successful replication of public folder information.

   c. A Dynamic Link Library used to sign/verify and seal/unseal advanced security messages.

   d. A Dynamic Link Library that responds to any advanced security configuration requests from the users and then submits them to the Key Manager Service.

11

8. By default, all public folders are displayed in the GAL. True or False?

9. The CAST-64 encryption algorithm is only for International locations, not North America. True or False?

10. What is the Public Folder Replication Agent?

    a. A Dynamic Link Library that is used when advanced security is being configured for a user account.

    b. The Microsoft Exchange component responsible for the successful replication of public folder information.

    c. A Dynamic Link Library used to sign/verify and seal/unseal advanced security messages.

    d. The Dynamic Link Library that responds to any advanced security configuration requests from the users and then submits them to the Key Manager Service.

11. What is the client security DLL?

    a. A Dynamic Link Library that is used when advanced security is being configured for a user account.

    b. The Microsoft Exchange component responsible for the successful replication of public folder information.

    c. A Dynamic Link Library used to sign/verify and seal/unseal advanced security messages.

    d. The Dynamic Link Library that responds to any advanced security configuration requests from the users and then submits them to the Key Manager Service.

12. You can have multiple Key Management Servers installed. True or False?

13. What is the security administration DLL?

    a. A Dynamic Link Library that is used when advanced security is being configured for a user account.

    b. The Microsoft Exchange component responsible for the successful replication of public folder information.

    c. A Dynamic Link Library used to sign/verify and seal/unseal advanced security messages.

    d. The Dynamic Link Library that responds to any advanced security configuration requests from the users and then submits them to the Key Manager Service.

14. You can have multiple Key Management administrators. True or False?

15. Public folders are created from the client software not from the Exchange Administrator program. True or False?

16. The process that a KM administrator must undertake to restore a missing password or key is called what?

a. Replacement

b. Restitution

c. Recovery

d. Resumption

17. The process used to resolve inconsistencies among public folder contents is called what?

a. Backup and recovery

b. Conflict resolution

c. Backfill

d. Backout

18. What happens when a new certificate becomes 18 months old?

a. Nothing, certificates last indefinitely.

b. A renewal of the certificate lease must be obtained.

c. The certificate must be renewed or rolled over.

d. You must contact the certificate vendor and pay a new lease installment.

19. Of the following, which best represents the distinction between the KM Server and the KM Service?

a. The KM Server is a machine where the KM software is installed, and the KM Service responds to key-related information requests from clients and administrators.

b. The KM Server is a thing, the KM Service is a collection of capabilities.

c. The KM Server resides only in one place, but the KM Service is available to all authorized users on the network.

d. None of the above.

20. Of the following encryption algorithms, which is not supported in Microsoft Exchange Server?

a. CAST-40

b. CAST-64

c. DES

d. RSA BSAFE 4

11

HANDS-ON PROJECTS

In the following projects, you work with various aspects of Exchange security, starting with changing the default permissions on the Exchange top-level (root) folders to something more reasonable. After that, you'll tackle KM Server installation, the source of all advanced Exchange security capabilities.

PROJECT 11.1

To change the top-level permissions:

1. In the Microsoft Exchange Administrator program, expand the site object (in the left pane), and then click the configuration object.

2. In the right pane, double-click the Information Store Site Configuration object. The Properties tabs for the Information Store Site Configuration should appear.

3. Select the Top-Level Folder Creation tab. In this tab, you can specify who can or cannot create public folders at the top-level of the hierarchy.

PROJECT 11.2

To install the Key Manager Server:

1. During the Microsoft Exchange setup (or by running the setup program after Exchange has been installed), you will be prompted to enter the System Attendant account password (see Figure 11.19). Enter the password, and click OK.

2. You will be prompted to either have the password displayed on the screen (this means that you will have to enter in the password at startup) or have the setup program create a floppy disk with the password on it (see Figure 11.20). If you select to have the password displayed, you should write it down and keep it secure (see Figure 11.21). If you select save the password on a floppy, then the setup program will now create it.

Figure 11.19 The Site Services Account page.

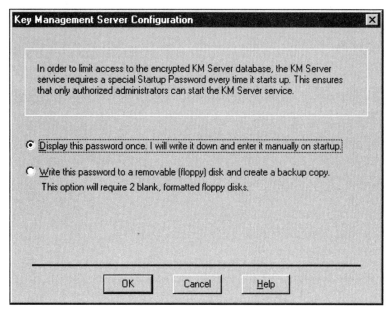

Figure 11.20   The Key Management Server Configuration page.

 CASE PROJECTS

11

1. You have three Microsoft Exchange sites in different parts of the city.

Required result:

Replicate all public folders to your remote site.

Optional desired results:

Allow users in your main site to sign and seal messages. Allow users in your remote sites to sign and seal messages.

Proposed solution:

Configure public folder hierarchy and contents replication. Install Exchange Key Management Server on at least one Exchange computer in each site.

Which results does the proposed solution provide?

Figure 11.21   Displaying the Key Management Server password.

a. The proposed solution provides the required result and both optional desired results.

b. The proposed solution provides the required result and one optional desired result.

c. The proposed solution provides only the required result.

d. The proposed solution does not provide the required result.

2. You have three Microsoft Exchange sites in different parts of the city.

   Required result:

   Replicate all public folder to your remote site.

   Optional desired results:

   Allow users in your main site to sign and seal messages. Allow users in your remote sites to sign and seal messages.

   Proposed solution:

   Configure public folder hierarchy and contents replication. Install Exchange Key Management Server in your main site.

   Which results does the proposed solution provide?

   a. The proposed solution provides the required result and both optional desired results.

   b. The proposed solution provides the required result and one optional desired result.

   c. The proposed solution provides only the required result.

   d. The proposed solution does not provide the required result.

3. You have three Microsoft Exchange sites in different parts of the city.

   Required result:

   Replicate all public folder to your remote site.

   Optional desired results:

   Allow users in your main site to sign and seal messages. Allow users in your remote sites to sign and seal messages.

   Proposed solution:

   Configure public folder hierarchy and contents replication. Install Exchange Key Management Server on an Exchange Server in your main site. Configure the Exchange Servers in the remote sites with the KM Server in your main site.

   Which results does the proposed solution provide?

   a. The proposed solution provides the required result and both optional desired results.

   b. The proposed solution provides the required result and one optional desired result.

   c. The proposed solution provides only the required result.

   d. The proposed solution does not provide the required result.

MONITORING AND MAINTAINING EXCHANGE SERVER

This chapter examines what's involved in maintaining, monitoring, and optimizing Exchange Server's performance. In addition, it explores different data backup and *archiving* options. First, you need to understand the most important maintenance and monitoring tasks that you must undertake to deliver the best level of service to your users. This includes understanding the standard Exchange Server utilities, including MTACHECK, ESEUTIL, and ISINTEG.

From there, using Server Monitors and Link Monitors to monitor an Exchange Server organization is discussed. Using Windows NT Performance Monitor for realtime monitoring of Exchange Server and understanding the key Windows NT and Exchange Server counters are essential to this process. Finally, a variety of data backup and archiving options that work with Exchange, to help preserve its all-important data, are explored.

AFTER READING THIS CHAPTER AND COMPLETING THE EXERCISES, YOU WILL BE ABLE TO:

- Perform maintenance tasks to ensure optimal performance of Microsoft Exchange Server
- Use the standard Microsoft Exchange Server utilities, including MTACHECK, ESEUTIL, and ISINTEG
- Monitor tasks to deliver the best level of service to your users
- Use Server Monitors and Link Monitors to monitor a Microsoft Exchange organization and alert the administrator when problems occur
- Use key Windows NT counters, Microsoft Exchange Server counters, and Microsoft Exchange performance charts
- Apply various data backup and archiving options, including backup creation and verification
- Configure hardware and software to optimize Exchange Server's performance

EXCHANGE SERVER COMPONENTS OVERVIEW

The Exchange Server components may be administered by using the *Exchange Server Administrator* program. Those components that run on the server as *Windows NT* services include the following:

- **Information Store (public and private)** The Information Store is a repository that stores information created by users. IT can store heterogeneous types of data, including email messages, forms, attachments, voice messages, and so on. The Information Store includes two folders: private and public. The private folder stores user mailboxes, and the public folder includes information for all the Exchange clients. You can use the Exchange Server replication engine to replicate public folder data to other servers within a site or across different sites. The MSExchangeIS object represents the Information Store.

 PRIV.EDB and PUB.EDB represent the Information Store private and public databases, respectively. These databases reside within the C:\Exchsrvr\Mdbdata directory on the server.

- **Directory Service** The Exchange Server directory provides a unified view of all users and resources within an organization. You can use the Directory Service to replicate Exchange Server directory databases between different servers within a site and across different sites. Note that the Directory Service is fault tolerant. Therefore, you can synchronize directories even after a hardware failure. The MSExchangeDS object represents the Directory Service.

 Microsoft Exchange Server automatically compacts the Information Store and directory databases without interrupting messaging. DIR.EDB represents the directory database. This database resides within the C:\Exchsrvr\Dsadata directory on the server.

- **Message Transfer Agent (MTA)** The MTA routes data from Exchange Server to other servers. The MSExchangeMTA object represents the MTA.

- **System Attendant** The System Attendant performs the following tasks:
  - Gathers information about each service within a site
  - Logs information about sent messages as they move through the system
  - Generates email addresses for new recipients
  - Monitors links between servers within the same and different sites
  - Builds routing tables

Monitoring Exchange Server includes monitoring the preceding server objects, their associated counters, and the values of these counters, then taking appropriate action based on the values observed. The section entitled "Monitoring Exchange Server" later in this chapter discusses various Exchange Server objects and their counters. That section also discusses what kinds of different performance charts you can use to monitor a server's health.

Files with the .EDB extension represent the Exchange Server databases. These files reside within the \Exchsrvr\Dsadata directory on the server.

Now that you've learned which objects are most worth monitoring in the Exchange environment, you will explore the routines and rituals involved in maintaining one or more Exchange Servers. This provides the topic for the section that follows next.

MAINTAINING EXCHANGE SERVER

When you buy an automobile at a dealership, the dealership includes a maintenance schedule as part of the purchase package. This schedule outlines the kinds of maintenance tasks you must perform at specified intervals to ensure optimal performance from your car. Although Exchange Server is not a car, the idea behind maintaining Exchange Server is no different. To derive the best performance from Exchange Server and to make sure that the server is in optimal condition, you must perform a set of maintenance chores regularly and faithfully.

As you will learn later in this chapter, monitoring a server is different from maintaining one. *Maintenance* involves enacting a predefined set of tasks on a predefined schedule; monitoring means keeping an eye on the server to identify any unusual behavior or activity, then taking appropriate action to remedy any unusual or pathological situations that might occur. The next major section discusses monitoring Exchange Server; the remainder of this section focuses on maintenance.

Maintenance and monitoring responsibilities fall on the shoulders of the Exchange administrator. But Exchange Server provides numerous utilities that, when combined with the *Windows NT Performance Monitor,* can make the life of an Exchange Server administrator easier. Basically, you can classify regular Exchange Server maintenance chores into two categories: general maintenance and specialized maintenance. You'll cover these categories and their constituents in the sections that follow.

12

GENERAL MAINTENANCE CHORES

General maintenance chores are performed within the maintenance window. Therefore, your first task is to identify a *maintenance window*. After the maintenance window is established, you can perform the necessary tasks. General maintenance includes the following items:

- **Identify maintenance windows** A maintenance window is a period of time during which you plan to execute maintenance tasks. A number of such tasks require users to be off the server. Whenever possible, schedule maintenance windows during off or non-peak hours. However, you must also publish this schedule to make all your users aware of the timing. Otherwise, unwary users might create more problems than you want to solve.

- **Apply Service Packs** Although this might seem trivial, you can reduce your headaches by applying the appropriate *Service Pack(s)*. This is critical, because Service Packs include bug fixes that resolve problems you might face with Exchange. Also, be sure to archive each new Service Pack properly should you ever need to reinstall Exchange Server at any point.

- **Install upgrades** *Upgrades* are similar to applying Service Packs. When Microsoft releases upgrades to Exchange Server, plan to install them.

Registered Exchange users receive Service Packs and upgrades automatically. Monitor Microsoft's site at **www.microsoft.com/ exchange** to stay current on the latest news and updates about Exchange Server. Visit **backoffice.microsoft.com/downtrial/ default.asp?product=5** to obtain lists of Service Packs for different versions of Exchange.

- **Defragment the database** This is a simple, everyday task that should be performed to ensure the best performance from Exchange Server. Just as you defragment disk drives to improve disk access, you must also defragment the Exchange database to ensure optimal database access.

- **Check for errors** Check for errors and fix them. These might include errors that occur when applying Service Packs or installing upgrades. If errors occur when applying Service Packs and installing upgrades, make sure you document and communicate those problems to Microsoft. In addition, check the server's error log regularly. Publish information about errors that are fixed or that are in the process of being fixed to keep users aware of the process and to set their expectations.

- **Record configuration changes** Record all changes you make to Windows NT settings, Exchange Server connector configurations, protocol addresses, path information, and so on. Recording such changes often provides the best source of troubleshooting guidance. How many times have you changed the AUTOEXEC.BAT or CONFIG.SYS file on a PC only to realize later that the change you made adversely affected the system? At that point, you probably needed to revert to the original AUTOEXEC.BAT or CONFIG.SYS file so the system could resume normal operations. The same principle applies when making configuration changes to a Windows NT system running Exchange Server.

SPECIALIZED MAINTENANCE CHORES

In addition to general maintenance chores, you will also occasionally need to perform certain specialized maintenance tasks. Specialized maintenance means using a set of standard Exchange Server utilities as part of your regular maintenance schedule, including:

- **ISINTEG** *ISINTEG* checks the consistency of the Information Store database at a database level. You can also direct ISINTEG to fix errors, if any. The following list shows the syntax for using ISINTEG. The ISINTEG file exists within the \Exchsrvr\bin directory. You can run this utility from the command prompt:

```
isinteg -pri|-pub [-fix] [-detailed] [-verbose] [-l
logfilename] -test

testname[[, testname]...]

-pri          check the consistency of the private
              Information Store

-pub

    check the consistency of the public Information Store

-fix

    check and fix the consistency of the Information
    Store

-detailed

    detailed mode (default - non-detailed mode)

-verbose

    generate a verbose report

-l filename

    specify the log file name (default -
    .\isinteg.pri|pub)

-t refdblocation
```

12

```
        reference database location; default is IS location
-test testname
        perform named test on database
EXAMPLES:
Isinteg patch
        repair Information Store after an offline restore
isinteg -pri|-pub -dump [-l logfilename]
        verbose dump of store data
```

- **ESEUTIL** Use *ESEUTIL* to:

  - Check consistency of the Information Store database and directory databases.

  - Defragment the Information Store database and directory databases.

  - Repair any inconsistencies.

  The following list shows the syntax for using ESEUTIL to perform the different database maintenance tasks. The ESEUTIL file exists within the \Exchsrvr\bin directory. You can run this utility from the command prompt:

  - **Defragmentation** ESEUTIL /d *database name* [options]

  - **Recovery** ESEUTIL /r [options]

  - **Integrity** ESEUTIL /g *database name* [options]

  - **Upgrade** ESEUTIL /u *database name* /d *previous .DLL* [options]

  - **File Dump** ESEUTIL /m[mode-modifier] *file name*

  - **Repair** ESEUTIL /p *database name* [options]

- **MTACHECK** *MTACHECK* checks the data the MTA stores within DAT files. This utility also automatically repairs errors, if any. You can find the MTACHECK utility within the \Exchsrvr\mtadata\mtacheck.out directory.

- **Exchange Performance Optimizer** Exchange Performance Optimizer is used to improve the performance of Exchange Server, especially if you upgrade hardware, as when adding more memory to a server.

As mentioned earlier, *monitoring* Exchange Server is the flip side of Exchange's maintaining/monitoring equation. Not only must you create and follow a maintenance schedule, but you must also monitor the server for any unexpected problems or errors. Monitoring provides the topic for the sections that follow.

MONITORING EXCHANGE SERVER

Like maintenance, monitoring also resembles buying a car and regularly checking its operating condition. For example, suppose the hazard lights indicator has been working fine all along, but, all of a sudden, it stops working. You might not be able to detect this problem on a day-to-day basis, because you may not need your hazard lights. But, periodically checking your hazard lights and other seldom-used components in your car should be part of the monitoring process. Obviously, after you discover a problem, you need to alert your mechanic so she can fix the hazard lights (or the indicator, depending on where the problem lies).

Monitoring Exchange Server is quite similar. Exchange Server includes a number of utilities that you can use to monitor each server's operation. You can also configure a server to alert you about any problems, so you can take appropriate action. This is how monitors function: A special software subsystem monitors the server for problems. When a problem occurs, the monitor tries to fix it. If the monitor fails to fix the problem, it notifies the administrator using any of the following methods:

- **Generates a Windows NT alert** The Exchange Server generates and sends a Windows NT alert to a specified computer (for example, a computer at the central monitoring location).

- **Launches a process** The Exchange Server sends a message to the administrator in the event of a problem.

- **Mails a message** The Exchange Server sends a message to the specified user(s).

The method you choose depends on your environment. In some cases, email notification works best, while notification using a combination of methods may work best in other cases. Irrespective of what method you choose, always automate monitoring the server as much as possible.

The key is to benefit from those utilities that are included with Exchange Server and to make your life as an Exchange Server administrator as easy as possible. Two types of monitors make this possible: the Server Monitor and the Link Monitor.

SERVER MONITOR

Use a *Server Monitor* to verify that certain Microsoft Exchange services are running on a specific Microsoft Exchange Server computer. In fact, you can use the Server Monitor to verify any other Windows NT service. To create a Server Monitor, follow these steps:

1. Click Start | Programs | Microsoft Exchange | Microsoft Exchange Administrator.

12

2. Select File | New Other | Server Monitor. The Microsoft Exchange Administrator should display the Properties dialog box for the Server Monitor, as shown in Figure 12.1.

3. Within the General tab's Directory Name text box, specify a name for the monitor.

4. Specify the display name for the monitor within the Display Name text box.

5. Click the Browse button to specify the location of the log file. The log file includes resulting status and notifications.

6. Specify the time intervals for normal and critical polling.

7. Within the Notification dialog box (shown in Figure 12.2), specify the action you'd like the Server Monitor to take.

    To do so, click the New button. Microsoft Exchange Administrator should display the New Notification dialog box, as shown in Figure 12.3. Choose the appropriate action (Launch A Process, Windows NT Alert, or Mail Message).

8. Identify the servers you'd like to monitor within the Servers tab, as shown in Figure 12.4.

9. Within the Actions tab (shown in Figure 12.5), choose an action (Take No Action, Restart The Service, or Restart The Computer) for first attempt, second attempt, and subsequent attempts. You can also specify a restart delay (in seconds) and what message the Server Monitor should display upon a restart.

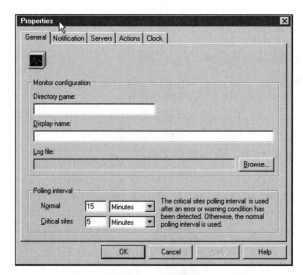

Figure 12.1   The Properties dialog box for the Server Monitor.

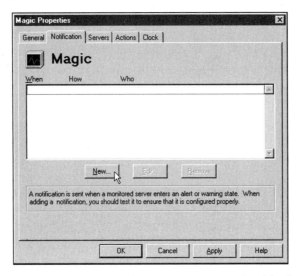

Figure 12.2   Specifying the action the Server Monitor should take.

10. To specify how much the clocks between the monitored servers and the Server Monitor may differ before notification occurs, use the Clock tab (shown in Figure 12.6).

LINK MONITOR

A *Link Monitor* sends messages to specified servers and other email components, such as a MTA when alert conditions trigger a Server Monitor. To create a Link Monitor, follow these steps:

1. Click Start | Programs | Microsoft Exchange | Microsoft Exchange Administrator.

2. Select File | New Other | Link Monitor. Microsoft Exchange Administrator should display the Properties dialog box for the Link Monitor, as shown in Figure 12.7.

3. Within the General tab's Directory Name text box, specify a name for the monitor.

Figure 12.3   The New Notification dialog box.

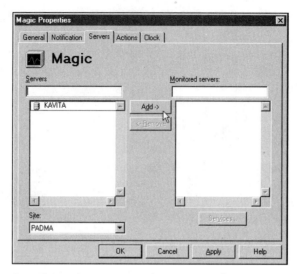

Figure 12.4   Specifying the servers to be monitored.

4. Specify the display name for the monitor within the Display Name text box.

5. Click the Browse button to specify the location of the log file. The log file includes resulting status and notifications.

6. Specify the time intervals for normal and critical polling.

7. Within the Notification dialog box (shown in Figure 12.8), specify the action that you'd like the Link Monitor to take.

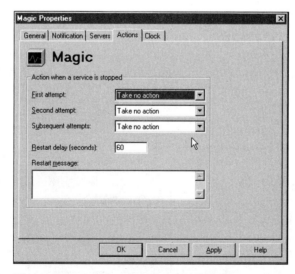

Figure 12.5   The Actions tab for the New Notification Properties dialog box.

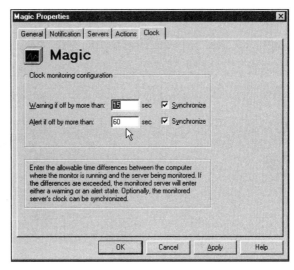

Figure 12.6   The Clock tab for the New Notification Properties dialog box.

To do so, click the New button. Microsoft Exchange Administrator should display the New Notification dialog box, as shown in Figure 12.9. Choose the appropriate action (Launch A Process, Windows NT Alert, or Mail Message).

8. Identify the servers you'd like to monitor within the Servers tab (shown in Figure 12.10).

9. To configure a Link Monitor that checks connections to other organizations or foreign systems, use the Recipients tab (shown in

12

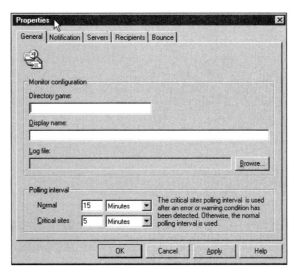

Figure 12.7   The Link Monitor Properties dialog box.

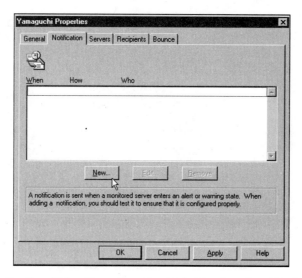

Figure 12.8 Specifying the action the Link Monitor should take.

Figure 12.11). The Link Monitor checks for replies to PING messages sent to the recipients. Based on whether a reply is returned, you can determine whether the link is working correctly.

10. To set the warning and alert durations for each Link Monitor, use the Bounce tab (shown in Figure 12.12). One set of durations applies to all the recipients and servers.

Now that you've learned about Server Monitors and Link Monitors, you'll shift your focus to the object counters in the Windows NT and Exchange Server environments that can shed light on potential and actual performance problems on an Exchange Server.

MONITORING WINDOWS NT COUNTERS

You can monitor a number of *Windows NT counters* to identify potential bottlenecks as well as hardware and software failures. Each counter is associated with a Windows NT object. The counter indicates the object's performance. For

Figure 12.9 The New Notification dialog box.

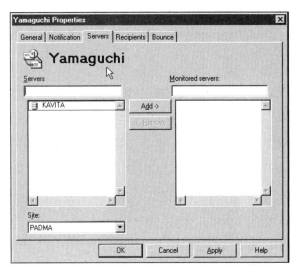

Figure 12.10   Specifying the servers to be monitored.

example, the Bytes Total/sec counter is an attribute of the Redirector object, the Network Errors/sec counter is another attribute of the Redirector object, the %ProcessorTime counter is an attribute of the Processor object, and so on.

The key is to determine if any of the objects shown in Table 12.1 are potential bottlenecks. If they are, they might directly or indirectly affect an Exchange Server's performance.

12

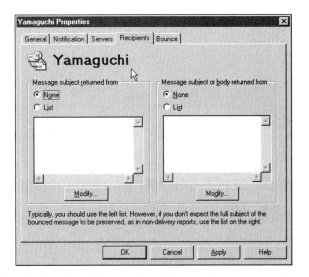

Figure 12.11   Configuring the Link Monitor to check connections to other organizations and foreign systems.

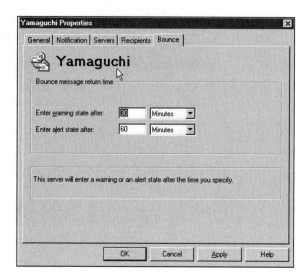

Figure 12.12   Specifying warning and alert durations for a Link Monitor.

The following list explains each of the counters that appears in Table 12.1:

- **%DiskTime (Physical Disk)** This counter measures the percentage of time the disk is reading or writing. Use this counter to determine if the hard drive is a potential bottleneck.

 If the value of the %DiskTime counter is greater than 90 for an extended period of time, the hard drive is indeed a potential bottleneck.

- **pages/sec (Memory)** This counter measures the paging of memory from or to the virtual memory paging file. A high average value of pages/sec indicates that you can improve the Windows NT machine's performance by increasing the RAM.

- **Bytes Total/sec (Network Interface)** This counter measures the total number of bytes the network Redirector sends and receives. This counter helps you determine if the network is a potential bottleneck.

Table 12.1   Key Exchange-related objects and counters.

Object	Counters
Hard Drive	%DiskTime
Memory	pages/sec
Network	Bytes Total/sec, Network Errors/sec
Processor	Elapsed Time, %ProcessorTime

To determine whether the network is a potential bottleneck, compare this value with the network card's maximum throughput value.

- **Network Errors/sec** This counter measures the number of errors the network Redirector receives.

 To determine whether network errors have occurred, check this counter's value. If it's greater than 0, errors have indeed occurred. For details on such network errors, check the system event log.

- **Elapsed Time** This counter measures the number of seconds a process has been running.

- **%ProcessorTime** This counter measures the percentage of time the server's processor is actively engaged in real processing tasks.

 An average value less than 20 percent indicates a server is not heavily used. Because it is an average, a low value might also indicate that key processes are stalled, or that the Exchange Server software is down. A value greater than 90 percent indicates an overloaded processor.

MONITORING EXCHANGE SERVER COUNTERS

In addition to the aforementioned general Windows NT counters, you must also monitor counters that are specific to the Exchange Server. Like Windows NT counters, each *Exchange Server counter* is associated with some Exchange Server object. For example, the Pending Replication Synchronization counter is an attribute of the MSExchangeDS object, the Messages Received counter is an attribute of the MSMI object, the messages/sec counter is an attribute of the MTA object, and so on. The key is to determine if any of the Exchange Server objects are potential bottlenecks.

The Exchange Server objects support a total of 150 Exchange Server counters combined. Table 12.2 describes 53 of the most important objects, out of the total of 150 Exchange Server counters in all.

The following list explains some of the key Exchange Server counters:

- **Average Delivery Time (MS Exchange IS Private)** Measures the average length of time the last 10 messages sent to another server waited before delivery. A high value indicates an MTA performance problem.

- **Average Local Delivery Time (MS Exchange IS Public)** Measures the average length of time the last 10 messages sent on the same server waited before delivery. A high value indicates a performance problem with the Information Store.

Table 12.2   Exchange Server counters.

Object	Counter	Use
MSExchange Internet Protocols	Active Connections	Provides a count of the number of active connections.
MSExchange Internet Protocols	Bytes Received	Provides a count of the number of bytes received from the clients.
MSExchange Internet Protocols	Bytes Sent	Provides a count of the number of bytes sent to the client.
MSExchange Internet Protocols	Incoming Queue Length	Provides the number of outstanding client requests.
MSExchange Internet Protocols	Outgoing Queue Length	Provides the count of the number of buffers waiting to be sent to the clients.
MSExchange Internet Protocols	Outstanding Commands	Provides a count of the number of currently outstanding commands.
MSExchange Internet Protocols	Peak Connections	Provides the maximum number of concurrent client connections.
MSExchange Internet Protocols	Total Commands	Provides a count of the number of total commands executed since the start of the service.
MSExchangeDS	AB Browses/sec	Provides the rate at which the Address Book clients perform the browse operation.
MSExchangeDS	AB Client Sessions	Provides a count of the number of connected Address Book client sessions.
MSExchangeDS	AB Reads/sec	Provides the rate at which the Address Book clients perform read operations.
MSExchangeDS	Access Violations	Provides a count of the number of times the Address Book clients' Write operations failed due to security reasons.
MSExchangeDS	ExDS Client Sessions	Provides a count of the number of connected Extended Directory Service (ExDS) client sessions.

(continued)

Table 12.2 Exchange Server counters *(continued)*.

Object	Counter	Use
MSExchangeDS	ExDS Reads/sec	Provides the rate at which Extended Directory Service (ExDS) clients perform Read operations.
MSExchangeDS	LDAP Searches	Provides a count of the total LDAP searches performed since the Directory Service Agent (SA) started.
MSExchangeES	Average Event Time	Provides the average time spent (in milliseconds) for each event.
MSExchangeES	Average Script Time	Provides the average time spent (in milliseconds) for each executing script.
MSExchangeES	Notify Queue	Provides the queue of stored notifications waiting to be processed.
MSExchangeES	Total Events	Provides a count of the total number of events fired since the start of the service.
MSExchangeES	Total Scripts	Provides a count of the total number of scripts that have been executed since the start of the service.
MSExchangeIMC	Bytes Queued MTS-IN	Provides the size in bytes of the messages that have been converted from Internet Mail and are awaiting the final delivery to the client with Exchange.
MSExchangeIMC	Connections Inbound	Provides the number of SMTP connections to the Internet Mail Service established by the other SMTP hosts.
MSExchangeIMC	Inbound Messages Total	Provides a count of the total number of messages delivered to Exchange.
MSExchangeIMC	NDRs Total Inbound	Provides a count of the total number of non-delivery reports generated for inbound mail.
MSExchangeIMC	Total Messages Queued	Provides a count of the total number of messages waiting in the Internet Mail Service queues.

12

(continued)

Table 12.2   Exchange Server counters *(continued)*.

Object	Counter	Use
MSExchangeIS	Active Anonymous User Count	Provides a count of the number of active anonymous users.
MSExchangeIS	Active User Count	Provides a count of the number of active users who have shown some activity in the last 10 minutes.
MSExchangeIS	Database Session Hit Rate	Provides the rate of reusing database sessions in percent terms.
MSExchangeIS	IMAP Commands Issued	Provides a count of the number of commands issued by the client connected via the IMAP protocol.
MSExchangeIS	Maximum Connections	Provides a count of the number of maximum connections since the start of the service.
MSExchangeIS	Newsfeed Bytes Sent	Provides a count of the number of bytes sent from the Information Store to other NNTP servers by the Internet News Service since the start of the service.
MSExchangeIS	POP3 Commands Issued	Provides a count of the total number of commands issued by the clients connected via the POP3 protocol.
MSExchangeIS	RPC Requests	Provides a count of the total number of client requests that are currently being processed by the Information Store.
MSExchangeIS Private	Active Client Logons	Provides a count of the number of active clients that have shown some activity in the last 10 minutes.
MSExchangeIS Private	Average Delivery Time	Provides an average of the time taken between submission of a message to the Information Store and submission to the message transfer agent in the last 10 minutes.

(continued)

Table 12.2 Exchange Server counters *(continued)*.

Object	Counter	Use
MSExchangeIS Private	Message Opens/sec	Provides the rate at which requests to open messages are submitted to the Information Store.
MSExchangeIS Private	Peak Client Logons	Provides the maximum number of concurrent client logons since the service started.
MSExchangeIS Private	Total Count of Recoverable Items	Provides the total number of items retained for item recovery.
MSExchangeIS Public	Active Client Logons	Provides a count of the number of active clients that have shown some activity in the last 10 minutes.
MSExchangeIS Public	Average Delivery Time	Provides an average of the time taken between delivery of a message to the Information Store and delivery to the MTA in the last 10 minutes.
MSExchangeIS Public	Average Local Delivery Time	Provides an average of the time required for delivery of a local message through the Information Store in the last 10 minutes.
MSExchangeIS Public	Message Opens/sec	Provides the rate at which requests to open messages are submitted to the Information Store.
MSExchangeIS Public	Peak Client Logons	Provides the maximum number of concurrent client logons since the service started.
MSExchangeIS Public	Total Count of Recoverable Items	Provides the total number of items retained for item recovery.
MSExchangeMTA	Adjacent MTA Associations	Provides a count of the total number of open associations this MTA has to other MTA.
MSExchangeMTA	Deferred Delivery Messages	Provides a count of the total number of deferred delivery messages in the MTA.

12

(continued)

Table 12.2 Exchange Server counters *(continued).*

Object	Counter	Use
MSExchangeMTA	Disk File Reads/sec	Provides the rate of Disk File Read operations.
MSExchangeMTA	ExDS Read Calls/sec	Provides the rate of Read Calls to the directory service.
MSExchangeMTA	LAN Receive Bytes/sec	Provides the rate of bytes received over a local area network from the MTA.
MSExchangeMTA Connections	Associations	Provides a count of the total associations between the MTA and the connected entity.
MSExchangeMTA Connections	Cumulative Inbound Associations	Provides a total number of inbound associations with the connected entity.
MSExchangeMTA Connections	Inbound Messages Total	Provides a total number of inbound messages received from the connected entity.
MSExchangeMTA Connections	Total Recipients Inbound Messages	Provides a total number of recipients specified in all messages received from the connected entity.

- **Message Opens/sec (MSExchangeIS Public object)** Measures the total number of messages opened per second within the public folder. Note that this counter does not tell you the name of the person(s) opening the public folder, nor does it tell you which public folder(s) the client(s) opened.

- **Messages Received (MSExchangeMI)** Measures the number of messages received from the Microsoft Mail Connector. An increasing number indicates that the server continues to receive messages. A decreasing number could imply either no mail is transferring or there is a problem transferring mail from the Microsoft Mail Connector to the server.

- **LAN/WAN messages moved/hour ((PC)MTA)** Indicates the performance of Microsoft Mail Connector (PC) MTA. If the counter maintains a constant value, the performance of the connector is okay. A deviation from the normal or constant value indicates a potential problem.

- **messages/sec (MTA)** Measures the number of messages the MTA sends and receives every second.

- **Work Queue Size (MTA)** Indicates the number of messages within the send and receive queue of MTA. A high value indicates there is a performance or server problem.

- **Queue Size (MTA Connections)** Measures the number of seconds a process has been running.

It's important to spend some time with the Performance Monitor utility to learn more about these counters, including how they behave and what they can tell you about actual or pending bottlenecks on your system. In the next section, we explain how to bring some of this information together and use it for diagnostic purposes.

DETERMINING IF YOUR SERVER IS PERFORMING BEYOND ITS CAPABILITIES

A significant part of the monitoring process depends on reviewing an Exchange Server's performance. As an administrator, you are responsible for each server's performance. To make your life easy, Exchange Server comes with a number of *performance charts* you can use to track the server's performance. Table 12.3 lists these charts and their respective update frequencies.

Table 12.3   Performance charts and their update schedules.

Chart	Update Frequency
IMS Queues	1 second
IMS Statistics	30 seconds
IMS Traffic	1 second
Server Health	1 second
Server History	1 minute
Server Load	10 seconds
Server Queues	10 seconds
Server Users	10 seconds

Let's take a closer look at each of these charts:

- **IMS Queues** What does the Internet Mail System's inbound queue look like? How is its outbound queue performing? This is what the IMS Queues chart tells you. The *IMS Queues chart* measures the counters shown in Table 12.4.

Table 12.4   The IMS Queues chart counters and objects.

Counter	Object
Queued Inbound	MSExchangeINC
Queued MTS-IN	MSExchangeINC
Queued MTS-OUT	MSExchangeINC
Queued Outbound	MSExchangeINC

- **IMS Statistics** What kind of email traffic does the Internet generate? What is the total number of inbound messages received since you started the server? What is the total number of outbound messages? This is what you learn from the *IMS Statistics chart*. The IMS Statistics chart measures the counters shown in Table 12.5.

Table 12.5   The IMS Statistics chart counters and objects.

Counter	Object
Inbound Messages	MSExchangeINC
Outbound Messages	MSExchangeINC

- **IMS Traffic** How is the message flow? How many connections exist to or from the server? Get this information from the *IMS Traffic chart*. The IMS Traffic chart measures the counters shown in Table 12.6.

Table 12.6   The IMS Traffic chart counters and objects.

Counter	Object
Messages Entering MTS-IN	MSExchangeINC
Messages Entering MTS-OUT	MSExchangeINC
Messages Leaving MTS-OUT	MSExchangeINC
Connections Inbound	MSExchangeINC
Connections Outbound	MSExchangeINC

- **Server Health** Making sure the server maintains good health at all times is critical to successful access to its services. So, how do you learn more about a server's health? Use the *Server Health chart*. This chart tells you the percentage of processor time each service utilizes. You can determine if any services are overusing the processor and identify those services that may be starved out by other services. The Server Health chart measures the counters shown in Table 12.7.

Table 12.7 The Server Health chart counters and objects.

Counter	Object
% Total Processor Time	System
% Processor Time	Process
% Pages/sec	Memory

- **Server History** How many messages remain outstanding? How many users have a connection to the server? How many pages does the server process per second? You can get all this information from the *Server History chart*. The Server History chart measures the counters shown in Table 12.8.

Table 12.8 The Server History chart counters and objects.

Counter	Object
UserCount	MSExchangeIS
Work Queue Length	MSExchangeITA
Pages/sec	Memory

- **Server Load** How many messages were submitted? How many were actually delivered? To get this type of information, use the *Server Load chart*. The Server Load chart measures the counters shown in Table 12.9.

Table 12.9 The Server Load chart counters and objects.

Counter	Object
Message Recipients Delivered/min	MSExchangeIS Public
Message submitted/min	MSExchangeIS Public
Adjacent MTA Association	MSExchangeMTA
RPC Packets/sec	MSExchangeIS
AB Browses/sec	MSExchangeDS
AB Reads/sec	MSExchangeDS
ExDS Reads/sec	MSExchangeDS
Replication Updates/sec	MSExchangeDS

- **Server Queues** Is the server queue empty? If so, great! Everything is working fine. If not, what is the total number of messages awaiting transmission? Is this number extremely large or small? Determine this by looking at the *Server Queues chart*. The Server Queues chart measures the counters shown in Table 12.10.

Table 12.10   The Server Queues chart counters and objects.

Counter	Object
Work Queue Length	MSExchangeMTA
Send Queue Size	MSExchangeIS Private
Send Queue Size	MSExchangIS Public
Receive Queue Size	MSExchangeIS Private
Receive Queue Size	MSExchangeIS Public

- **Server Users** What is the total number of current users with a connection to the server? The *Server Users chart* tells you this number. The Server Users chart measures the UserCount counter in the MSExchangeIS object.

Nothing beats observing real-live performance for understanding server behavior and bottlenecks, but sometimes it's simply impossible to draw on experience for the information you need. This is especially true when planning for growth of existing servers, or when estimating capacity requirements for new servers. At times like these, simulation tools can come in really handy. Exchange Server includes the Load Simulator, which can help you model message traffic, calculate bandwidth requirements, and more. This provides the topic for the section that follows.

LOAD SIMULATOR

The Load Simulator (LOADSIM.EXE) is a tool that helps you:

- Compare Microsoft Exchange Server performance to other systems.
- Perform tuning exercises (such as the impact of configuration changes on performance) without impacting users.
- Determine the network bandwidth requirements given the varying user behaviors.
- Test the specific server hardware's capacity and performance.

You'll want to experiment with this tool to use it to its best effect. The Load Simulator can be especially helpful in a test lab environment, as you examine system tuning, create potential production machine configurations, and attempt to determine what kind of bandwidth you'll need for your intersite connectors.

This concludes the discussion of the performance and monitoring issues in this chapter. In the sections that follow, you'll shift gears into protective mode, as you examine the requirements and capabilities necessary to back up and restore an Exchange Server.

BACKUP, BACKUP, BACKUP

Three things are for sure in this life: death, taxes, and lost data. The message is simple and clear: Back up or suffer the consequences. If you do not perform regular backups of your data, you might experience a number of problems coupled with tremendous amounts of frustration. Software engineering is an intense task: It takes a lot of concentrated effort to restore any lost data. As the proverb goes, it is better to be safe than sorry. That is why it is absolutely essential to formulate a backup strategy!

In fact, each organization requires its own unique backup strategy. This is because every environment demands a slightly different data backup and *archiving plan*. Any backup strategy must include two basic steps:

1. Create the backups.
2. Verify the backups.

But beyond the basics, numerous other decisions will be needed. You must also decide what else to back up, besides the contents of the server. You must decide where and how to back up the data you wish to preserve and ultimately restore. All this information informs a relatively complete backup strategy, but for a fully complete strategy it's also vital that you formulate some disaster recovery plans as well, in case your place of business (or one of your sites) is rendered inoperable. These topics drive the rest of this section of the chapter, beginning with creating backups, introduced in the next section.

12

CREATING THE BACKUPS

You can create backups in a number of ways, including:

- **Copy** A *copy backup* is simply a snapshot of the databases at any given point in time.

- **Differential** *Differential backups* are normally performed daily, every night of the working week. For any differential backup, you do not back up the entire Information Store and the directory databases. Instead, you back up only a subset of this information. That is, you only back up whatever data has changed since the last complete backup, which Microsoft calls a normal (or full) backup. A differential backup is faster than a normal (full) backup, but not as fast as an incremental backup, because it captures all changes since the last full backup (as the week goes on, the differential backup grows in size). Note that only the log files are backed up but not purged.

- **Incremental** *Incremental backups* are normally performed daily, every night of the working week. For any incremental backup, you do not back up the entire Information Store and directory databases. Instead, you back up only a subset of the data, but use a different approach than with a differential backup. Here, you only back up whatever data has changed since the previous backup was performed, be it a full or an incremental backup (if the recommended schedule is followed, an incremental backup consists of one day's worth of changes to the data). An incremental backup is faster than either a full backup or a differential backup. Note that only the log files are backed up and then purged.

- **Normal (Full)** A *normal backup* means a complete and full backup. You back up everything, including transaction logs, Information Stores, and directory databases. A normal backup can take a long time depending on the amount of information involved. For this reason, such backups usually occur once a week, over the weekend.

Typically, a combination of backup methods is the preferred approach. If for example, you perform a full backup initially, and then perform incremental backups at regular intervals, you need only restore the last full backup, plus all incremental backups that have occurred since that full backup was made to restore your data. With differential backups, you need only restore the last full backup and the most current differential backup to restore the same data.

Once you've backed up your data, how do you know that a backup indeed took place? How do you verify that the backup was successful and that you will not have any problems restoring the data when needed? Here again, it's far better to be safe than sorry. To be sure, you must verify that the backup process was indeed successful. This is the topic of the next section, and is one that is overlooked only at great peril.

VERIFYING BACKUPS

You may verify backups in any number of ways. Microsoft recommends verification at two levels. First, verify that a backup indeed took place by checking the Windows NT event log or using the Backup tool from the *Microsoft BackOffice Resource Kit*. Next, verify the data by restoring it on another server, making sure the data integrity is preserved. The following tasks will help you verify data integrity:

- Test client connectivity to the Information Store and the directory. You can do this with a version of the client software installed on the same computer or by using another client on the network.

- Verify connector and gateway functionality by sending test messages or using a Server Monitor. Several connectors store configuration settings within the Registry. If the backed up data fails to include the Registry files, the connectors may not work.

- Review several mailboxes to ensure that Windows NT domain account associations and permissions are restored correctly.

Both creating and verifying backups should be an integral part of your regular maintenance schedule. You should also make users aware by publishing a schedule for performing backups.

WHAT ELSE SHOULD YOU BACK UP?

So you backed up the Exchange Server transaction logs. Is there anything else you should back up? Indeed, the additional data you must back up includes:

- **Entire Windows NT Server, including the Registry** Create a file-based backup of the entire Windows NT Server. When you do, make sure none of its services is running. This is because any files that are open can prevent the backup process from capturing all data. Also, remember to back up the Windows NT Registry. If you don't, you might run into unexpected problems when restoring the data.

- **Key Management Server and directory synchronization databases** The *Key Management Server database* contains highly sensitive information—all the keys within the database are encrypted using the 64-bit CAST algorithm. Due to the sensitive nature of this information, it's important to back up this database separately, and to maintain high security on this backup. It is also a good idea to back up the directory synchronization database (\Exchsrvr\Dxadata), because it includes information for the directory synchronization process. The recovery process can synchronize directories quickly from a backup, and allow the synchronization process to proceed from the most recent backup forward.

- **Transaction logs** Back up *transaction logs* on a separate disk. If the drive that contains the database fails, the transaction logs will remain intact and available to provide a time-consuming, but complete *restoration* of the Information Store.

BACKUP LOCATIONS

Maintain backups of your data at two separate locations. If one location experiences catastrophic loss, chances are the other location will remain intact. If so, you can restore the data from the backup stored at the other location.

The probability that two separate locations will experience catastrophic loss at the same time is low, although it is still somewhat likely. Depending on your organization's security policy and procedures, a second location may fall within the same organization, or it might be housed at a third-party location. Most large organizations with significant data investments store off-site backups at specially

12

constructed data storage facilities designed to withstand all but the most severe of natural or unnatural disasters.

BACKUP STRATEGY

The following list of elements represents a sample backup strategy:

- **Perform backups on a daily basis** Disable circular logging to perform quick backups. Also, back up your Registry regularly on your domain controllers, occasionally shut down all services, and perform a full file-level backup.

- **Verify backups regularly** In addition, monitor all event and application logs, where you can learn whether or not online backups complete successfully.

- **Set limits on message and mailbox sizes** Setting limits prevents your Information Store and backup and restore times from increasing uncontrollably.

- **Clean mailboxes periodically** It's especially important to monitor the administrator mailbox associated with certain connectors because these can accumulate untoward numbers of junk messages.

- **Separate databases and swap files from the transaction logs** If all these elements are housed on separate drives, this reduces the probability that you will ever lose all of them simultaneously, and boosts performance at the same time (by spreading the disk load over multiple drives).

- **Maintain sufficient free-disk space** Access to adequate free space means you may run the database defragmentation utilities regularly and routinely.

DISASTER RECOVERY PLANNING

Although you cannot totally prevent disasters, you can protect against them by preparing a contingency plan should one ever befall your organization. You can protect the Exchange Server and all the data associated with it in a number of ways. Some of these are outlined in the following sections.

Using Redundant Arrays Of Inexpensive Disks (RAID)

Redundant Arrays of Inexpensive Disks (RAID) provides a high level of fault tolerance. The concept behind RAID is to use an array of inexpensive disks that supports multiple I/O channels in parallel, and significantly improves system throughput and performance.

Depending on the characteristics of your Exchange Server environment, you can choose from the following six common classes of RAID technology:

- **RAID Level 0** RAID Level 0 provides data striping but no data redundancy. The data is striped in small chunks across all the disks within the array. All data reads and writes occur asynchronously.

- **RAID Level 1** RAID Level 1 provides hardware-level disk mirroring but no data striping. As a result, RAID Level 1 provides the highest degree of reliability.

- **RAID Level 2** RAID Level 2 implements a parallel access array. All disks are written and accessed concurrently. However, failure of one disk shuts down the entire array.

- **RAID Level 3** RAID Level 3 also implements a parallel access array. In addition, this level includes a single disk that contains parity information necessary to rebuild a failed device. Level 3 also supports hot swapping of a failed data drive. However, the single disk containing parity information is a potential bottleneck. Failure of the parity disk disables the entire RAID.

- **RAID Level 4** Unlike RAID Level 3, RAID Level 4 is an independent array that does not support a parallel access array. However, this level includes a single disk that contains the parity information necessary to rebuild a failed device. As with RAID Level 3, failure of the parity disk is a potential bottleneck for the entire RAID.

- **RAID Level 5** RAID Level 5 is similar to RAID Level 4, except there is no separate single disk for parity information. The parity information is spread across the other disks within the array.

12

RAID Level 1 and RAID Level 5 are the most commonly used RAID options. Windows NT Server supports both of these levels in the operating system itself, and third-party vendors offer numerous hardware-based implementations as well.

Integrating And Uninterruptible Power Supply (UPS)

An uninterruptible power supply (UPS) provides a second level of fault tolerance for Exchange Server data. The primary level is the database engine. The database engine can self-recover from events that include power outages. Integrating a good UPS with a Windows NT Server provides a second level of safety and security. When a power outage occurs, the UPS lets the server write all unsaved data to the disk and provides a safe and controlled shutdown for the Exchange Server.

Beyond the hardware elements mentioned in the two previous sections, disaster planning consists primarily of making sure your systems can resume operation even if their original site is a smoking ruin. The amount of money, time, and effort that you should be willing to spend on planning for disaster must be proportionate to the value of those systems to your organization.

Some companies go so far as to arrange for hot backup sites, where an administrator need only show up with a set of backup tapes to begin installing them on a set of servers and other *recovery equipment* specifically arranged for their use in an emergency. Other companies have plans to occupy new space on demand, and expect to purchase new equipment. Still others arrange to rent facilities where they can operate temporarily while new, permanent facilities are constructed.

You must think ahead to decide what kind of *recovery servers* will be needed to house your data and applications if your own equipment becomes unavailable. Likewise, it's crucial to think through how much *recovery time* you can allocate to the process of restoring operations. In fact, the costs of lost business are so high for some organizations (online trading companies, for instance) that they maintain their own complete sets of spare equipment that mirror the data on their production sites, ready to take over and begin handling production work at a moment's notice.

Only you and your organization can really know for sure what kind of disaster recovery approach is right for your needs. The important thing is to make that determination, and then to make arrangements to act on it.

CHAPTER SUMMARY

This chapter explored the process of maintaining and monitoring Exchange Server, including using Server Monitors and Link Monitors. This chapter also discussed using Windows NT Performance Monitor for realtime monitoring of Exchange Server, the key Windows NT and Exchange Server counters, and the standard Exchange Server utilities, including MTACHECK, ESEUTIL, and ISINTEG. Finally, this chapter explored a variety of data backup and archiving options, and concluded with a brief discussion of needs for and approaches to disaster recovery planning.

KEY TERMS

- **archiving**—The process of backing up and storing data in a safe place for later use.
- **archiving plan**—The process of devising a plan for backing up and storing data that best suits the environment within your corporation.
- **backup creation**—The process of backing up data for archival and later use.
- **backup cycle**—The period of time between two successive backups.

- **copy backup**—A snapshot of te database at any given point in time.

- **differential backup**—Backing up only a subset of the Information Store and directory databases. A differential backup only backs up the data that has changed since the last normal or incremental backup. Only the log files are backed up but not purged.

- **ESEUTIL**—A Microsoft Exchange Server database utility that you can use to check the consistency of the Information Store database and directory databases, defragment these databases, and repair any inconsistencies.

- **Exchange performance charts**—Charts measuring the various Exchange Server objects and their counters.

- **Exchange Server Administrator**—A Microsoft Exchange Server program that you can use to administer the Exchange Server components, including Information Stores (public and private), Directory Services, System Attendants, and MTAs.

- **Exchange Server counter**—An attribute of an Exchange Server object that you can track to measure the object's performance.

- **IMS Queues chart**—An Exchange Server performance chart that provides Internet Mail Service queue information, such as what the inbound queue looks like, how the outbound queue is performing, and so on.

- **IMS Statistics chart**—An Exchange Server performance chart that provides Internet Mail Service statistics information, such as what kind of email traffic the Internet generates, the total number of inbound messages since you started the server, the total number of outbound messages, and so on.

- **IMS Traffic chart**—An Exchange Server performance chart that provides Internet Mail Service traffic information, such as how the message flow looks, how many connections exist to or from the server, and so on.

- **incremental backup**—Backing up only a subset of the Information Store and directory databases. An incremental backup only backs up the data that has changed since the last normal or incremental backup. Only the log files are backed up and then purged.

- **Internet Protocol (IP)**—The network layer protocol for communication over the Internet.

- **ISINTEG**—A Microsoft Exchange Server database utility that checks the consistency of the Information Store database at the database level. You can also direct ISNTEG to fix errors, if any.

- **Key Management Server database**—A database that contains all the keys within the database encrypted with the 64-bit CAST algorithm.

- **Link Monitor**—An Exchange Server program that sends messages to the specified servers and other email components, such as the MTA.

12

- **maintenance**—The process of maintaining Microsoft servers for generating optimal performance.

- **maintenance window**—A period of time for performing maintenance tasks on the Exchange Server.

- *Microsoft BackOffice Resource Kit*—A toolkit from Microsoft that works with Microsoft server products.

- **monitoring**—The process of identifying a problem or error and making sure everything is working fine.

- **MTACHECK**—An Exchange Server database utility that checks the data the MTA stores within DAT files.

- **normal backup**—A complete and full backup, including transaction logs, Information Stores, and directory databases.

- **recovery equipment**—The equipment required to recover information lost as a result of catastrophic failure.

- **recovery server**—The server that helps in the process of recovering information lost as a result of catastrophic failure.

- **recovery time**—The time the server needs to recover information lost as a result of catastrophic failure.

- **Redundant Array of Inexpensive Disks (RAID)**—An array of inexpensive disks supporting multiple I/Os in parallel.

- **restoration**—The process of making the archived data available for use.

- **Server Health chart**—An Exchange Server performance chart that tells you the percentage of processor time each service uses. You can determine if any services are overusing the processor and identify those services that may be starved out by other services.

- **Server History chart**—An Exchange Server performance chart that provides history information about the server, such as how many messages remain outstanding, how many users have a connection to the server, how many pages the server processes per second, and so on.

- **Server Load chart**—An Exchange Server performance chart that provides server load information, such as how many messages were submitted, how many messages were actually delivered, and so on.

- **Server Monitor**—An Exchange Server program that verifies that specified Microsoft Exchange services are running on a specified Microsoft Exchange Server computer.

- **Server Queues chart**—An Exchange Server performance chart that provides server queue information, such as the total number of messages awaiting transmission, and so on.

- **Server Users chart**—An Exchange Server performance chart that provides user information, such as the total number of current users with a connection to the server.

- **Service Pack**—Patch upgrades to an existing version of software. The patch upgrade includes bug fixes, minor enhancements, and so forth.

- **transaction log**—A record of all transactions.

- **uninterruptible power supply (UPS)**—In the event of a power outage, lets the server write all the data to the disk and provides a safe and controlled shutdown of the server.

- **upgrade**—The process of updating a program from its current version to the vendor's latest release version.

- **Windows NT**—Microsoft's network operating system.

- **Window NT counter**—A Windows NT object's attribute.

- **Windows NT Performance Monitor**—A server program that you can use to monitor the performance of Windows NT and services running under Windows NT, such as Exchange Server.

REVIEW QUESTIONS

1. You have installed Microsoft Exchange on your server, which is a Pentium II dual processor machine. In order to improve the performance on the machine, you decide to add more memory to the server. Having successfully done so, what utility should you run from Microsoft Exchange Server to take advantage of the hardware upgrade?

    a. Run the Microsoft Exchange Setup program.

    b. Reinstall Microsoft Exchange Server.

    c. Run the Microsoft Exchange Administrator program.

    d. Run the Microsoft Exchange Performance Optimizer.

2. If an Information Store is in recovery after a system crash, will Microsoft Exchange duplicate preexisting transactions within the database and only play back uncommitted transactions? Yes or No?

3. What is the default interval of the Exchange public folder hierarchy replication?

    a. 15 seconds

    b. 30 seconds

    c. 45 seconds

    d. 60 seconds

12

4. You recently joined a manufacturing company as its Exchange administrator. A common complaint from some of the users is that several of their contacts complain that their email messages are returned, indicating that the mailbox of the person they try to send an email to has exceeded the allotted space. You are now required to set up a notification system that notifies users when their mailboxes exceed the maximum amount of allocated space. What do you do?

a. Adjust the public object in the applicable Server's container of a site.

b. Adjust the public object in the Configuration container of a site.

c. Adjust the Information Store site configuration object within the site's Configuration container.

d. Adjust the Information Store configuration object in the applicable Server's container of a site.

5. When configuring the replication of public folder contents from the Information Store level, which property page pulls replicas of a specified public folder onto a public Information Store?

a. Public Folder Resources

b. Advanced

c. Instances

d. Scheduling Replication

e. Server Replication Status

f. Folder Replication Status

6. You are the Exchange administrator at XYZ, Inc. One of the users reports that he has forgotten his password for the PST file. What do you tell him?

a. That you, as the administrator, will take ownership of the PST file and reassign a password.

b. The owner of the PST file can take ownership of the PST file and reassign a password.

c. The user can use a third-party decryption utility to recover the data within the PST file.

d. The data within the PST file is lost.

7. An organization has more than 20,000 seats for Exchange Server. Catering to such a huge user base, backing up data is a problem for this organization. You are brought within the organization as a consultant to recommend a daily backup strategy. What do you recommend for a quick but reliable solution?

a. Full daily

b. Full with differential

c. Full with incremental

d. Copy

8. To control the transaction log file's size, you decide to enable circular logging. What events do you expect to occur on the server? (Choose all that apply.)

   a. Fault tolerance is disabled as circular logging is enabled.

   b. After the checkpoint file is updated, the portion of the transaction log written to the database is discarded.

   c. Checkpoints provide fault tolerance.

   d. After the checkpoint file is updated, the portion of the transaction log written to the database is moved to a reserved log.

9. You generally back up your Exchange Server on a tape drive daily. However, the tape drive is not functioning and the hardware rescue team is not available until the next morning. What file should you copy to simulate the backup functionality of Exchange Server?

   a. DLL

   b. EDB

   c. EDP

   d. LOG

   e. SYS

10. You just added a server to your existing site and now you need to verify that there is enough available hard disk space on the server to import the site's directory. What should you do?

   a. Check the size of the EXC.EDB file within the Exchsrvr\Dsadata directory on the server.

   b. Run the Exchange Setup program. A dialog appears if the available hard disk space is not sufficient.

   c. Check the size of the DIR.EDB in the Exchsrvr\Dsadata directory on the server.

   d. Run the Exchange Setup program, then start Exchange.

11. How is data classified within Microsoft Exchange?

   a. Server based

   b. Client based (local)

   c. All of the above

12. Which of the following utilities does not help with administering the Exchange Server?

   a. Microsoft Exchange Administrator

   b. Microsoft Exchange Migration Wizard

   c. Microsoft Exchange Optimizer

   d. Microsoft Exchange Server Health

   e. Microsoft Exchange Server History

   f. Microsoft Exchange Server IMS Queues

12

g. Microsoft Exchange Server IMS Statistics

h. Microsoft Exchange Server IMS Traffic

i. Microsoft Exchange Server Load

j. Microsoft Exchange Server Queues

k. Microsoft Exchange Server Users

13. Executing the command **isinteg –patch** does not run and you receive this error:

```
DS_E_COMMUNICATIONS_ERROR?
```

How do you resolve this problem?

a. Start the Directory Service before executing the command.

b. Shut down Exchange Server before executing the command.

c. Shut down the Directory Service before executing the command.

d. Start Exchange Server before executing the command.

14. What are the different methods to compact the Information Store databases? (Choose all that apply.)

a. Microsoft Exchange Server automatically compacts the Information Store and directory databases without interruption to messaging.

b. Use the Microsoft Exchange Server Compacting utility to compact the Information Store and directory databases.

c. Use the ESEUTIL utility. You can run ESEUTIL with the /d (defragment) option, but you can perform this only after stopping the Information Store service.

d. Whenever you back up the Exchange Server, the server compacts the Information Store and directory databases before backing them up.

15. Which of the following is the key Microsoft Exchange Server counter?

a. Microsoft Exchange MTA Message/Second

b. Microsoft Exchange DA Pending Replication Synchronization

c. Microsoft Exchange MTA Health

d. Microsoft Exchange MSMI Message Received

16. Which performance chart would you use to track the percentage of microprocessor time the core components use?

a. Microsoft Exchange Server Health

b. Microsoft Exchange Server History

c. Microsoft Exchange Server Core Component History

d. Microsoft Exchange IMS Statistics

17. What tool can the client use to repair his PST and OST Files?

    a. ScanDisk utility

    b. Inbox Repair Tool utility

    c. Inbox Recover utility

    d. Exchange Client Recovery utility

18. What is the purpose of a Link Monitor?

    a. To send test messages to designated servers or other email-related components and verify the email connectivity.

    b. To check the link between different Exchange Server sites.

    c. To verify that specified Microsoft Exchange Server services are up and running.

HANDS-ON PROJECTS

These hands-on projects will help you understand the topics discussed throughout this chapter.

PROJECT 12.1

To change the update frequency for the IMS Statistics chart from 30 seconds to 1 second:

1. Click Start|Programs|Microsoft Exchange|Microsoft Exchange Server IMS Statistics.

2. Select Chart from the Options menu. Windows NT Performance Monitor should display the Chart Options dialog box.

3. Specify a different interval (in seconds) within the Periodic Update Time text box.

PROJECT 12.2

To repair the PRIV.EDB database:

1. Click Start|Run|Command, then press Enter.

2. Change to the directory that contains the PRIV.EDB database (C:\Exchsrvr\Mdbdata).

3. Type "C:\winnt\system32\eseutil /p priv.edb".

12

PROJECT 12.3

You can monitor the following Exchange Server counters:

- AB Browses/sec
- AB Reads/sec
- Adjacent MTA Association
- ExDS Reads/sec
- Message Recipients Delivered/min
- Message submitted/min
- Replication Updates/sec
- RPC Packets/sec

To monitor the Exchange Server counters:

1. Click Start | Programs | Microsoft Exchange | Microsoft Exchange Server Load.

 PROJECT 12.4

To create a Server Monitor:

1. Click Start | Programs | Microsoft Exchange | Microsoft Exchange Administrator, then select File | New Other | Server Monitor.

 PROJECT 12.5

To create a Link Monitor:

1. Click Start | Programs | Microsoft Exchange | Microsoft Exchange Administrator, then select File | New Other | Link Monitor.

 CASE PROJECTS

1. You have been flown in to a Seattle-based organization to propose a good backup strategy for the organization's Exchange Server.

   Required result:

   Prepare a checklist of items for the Exchange Server system administrator against a crash.

Optional desired result:

The checklist should also provide a good maintenance procedure for the Exchange Server.

Proposed solution:

- First of all, it is important to perform backups on a daily basis. You might want to disable circular logging to perform quick backups. Also, it is a good idea to back up your Registry regularly on your domain controllers and occasionally shut down the services and perform a full file-level backup.

- Verify your backups regularly. Also, monitor your event and application logs, where you can learn whether your online backups are successful.

- Set limits on the sizes of messages and mailboxes to help prevent your Information Store and your backup and restore time from increasing uncontrollably.

- Periodically clean out mailboxes, especially the administrator mailbox associated with certain connectors.

- Separate databases and swap files from transaction logs. This can significantly reduce the probability that you will ever lose them all simultaneously, and it can improve performance.

- Lastly, maintain sufficient free disk space on your drives, so you can routinely run database-defragmentation utilities.

Which results are provided by the proposed solution?

a. The proposed solution provides the required result and the optional desired result.

b. The proposed solution provides only the required result.

c. The proposed solution does not provide the required result.

2. You are the CIO of a multinational organization that uses Exchange Server for its email needs. The organization has offices in Chicago, London, and Taiwan. The Taiwan site needs to be restored from a backup. You have checked with the IT department within Taiwan, and it confirmed that it has a good backup of the directory and Information Store of the site from which to restore.

Required result:

Restore the Taiwan site from the backup.

Optional desired result:

Because the Taiwan site already existed, it should not be a new site for the other offices.

Proposed solution:

Advise the Taiwan site Exchange administrator to create a new site. You do not want the administrator to Join Existing Site when reinstalling the Exchange Server.

Which results are provided by the proposed solution?

a. The proposed solution provides the required result and the optional desired result.

b. The proposed solution provides only the required result.

c. The proposed solution does not provide the required result.

3. You keep trying to shut down Exchange services, but they keep restarting themselves.

Required result:

You do not want the services to start again once you shut them down.

Optional desired result:

You'd like to automate this task so it does not occur every time you shut down an Exchange service.

Proposed solution:

This is most likely caused by a Server Monitor session configured for the server where you try to shut down the services. By enabling admin /t (maintenance mode) at least one polling interval before stopping the services, Server Monitor is then notified that subsequent polls of the server within maintenance mode do not result in alerts or alarms. You can then stop services and perform maintenance. When completed, run admin /t again to re-enable monitoring.

Which results are provided by the proposed solution?

a. The proposed solution provides the required result and the optional desired result.

b. The proposed solution provides only the required result.

c. The proposed solution does not provide the required result.

4. You want to back up Exchange Server from a Windows NT backup machine that does not have Microsoft Exchange Server or the Exchange Administrator program installed.

Required result:

Make a copy of the physical files that provide a backup copy of the Exchange Server.

Optional desired result:

You have the Exchange Server CD-ROM and can copy some of the files from the CD-ROM to run the NT backup.

Proposed solution:

If you are copying files from an existing Exchange Server, use the following steps:

1. Rename or delete the current WINNT-WINNT-ROOT\ SYSTEM32\NTBACKUP.EXE from the Windows NT backup server.

2. Copy WINNT-WINNT-ROOT\SYSTEM32\NTBACKUP.EXE, EDBBCLI.DLL, and MSVCRT40.DLL from a Microsoft Exchange mail server to the Winnt\System32 subdirectory of the Windows NT backup server.

3. Copy EXCHSRVR\BIN\EDBBACK.DLL from the Microsoft Exchange Server to the Winnt\System32 subdirectory of the Windows NT backup server.

Which results are provided by the proposed solution?

a. The proposed solution provides the required result and the optional desired result.

b. The proposed solution provides only the required result.

c. The proposed solution does not provide the required result.

5. In a company meeting, it is decided that circular logging on the Exchange Server should be disabled. As the system administrator, you find that the server does not have enough disk space to maintain logging all the transactions.

Required result:

You'd like to log all the transactions.

Optional desired result:

You want to have a good transaction log backup that can help you even if there is a hardware failure on the drive that contains the database.

Proposed solution:

Change the physical location of the transaction log to a separate, dedicated disk.

Which results are provided by the proposed solution?

a. The proposed solution provides the required result and the optional desired result.

b. The proposed solution provides only the required result.

c. The proposed solution does not provide the required result.

6. You have tried to restore the database, but, so far, all attempts have failed.

Required result:

You need to restore the database.

Optional desired result:

You do not want to take any risk of deleting the data.

Proposed solution:

Try ESEUTIL /d /r.

Which results are provided by the proposed solution?

a. The proposed solution provides the required result and the optional desired result.

b. The proposed solution provides only the required result.

c. The proposed solution does not provide the required result.

7. You'd like a single mailbox for backup.

Required result:

Perform a single mailbox backup and restore.

Optional desired result:

Your organization requires a separate server online for performing the single mailbox restores if you select Join Existing Site or Create New Site during the installation of Microsoft Exchange server.

Proposed solution:

Do Not Join Site. If you need to maintain a single mailbox restore server, configure the server with the same Org and Site name as the site in which you plan to recover the single mailbox data from; however, Do Not Join Site during install.

Select Create New Site. Be sure to also use a unique computer name when installing Windows NT. If you inadvertently join a site, complete the single mailbox restore procedures. Undesired replication behavior results after running the Directory Service/Information Store consistency adjustment, because you have two sets of mailbox data for the same users within the site after restoring a PRIV.EDB.

Which results are provided by the proposed solution?

a. The proposed solution provides the required result and the optional desired result.

b. The proposed solution provides only the required result.

c. The proposed solution does not provide the required result.

8. Your organization has decided to audit the backup process for the Exchange Server.

Required result:

You are required to take and verify backup of the Exchange Server.

Optional desired result:

Be able to measure the status of the transaction logging process.

Proposed solution:

To view the progress of the transaction log, use Performance Monitor and select the MSExchangeDB object. Configure the following counters:

- Log Bytes Write/sec
- Log Checkpoint Depth

- Log Sessions Waiting

Which results are provided by the proposed solution?

a. The proposed solution provides the required result and the optional desired result.

b. The proposed solution provides only the required result.

c. The proposed solution does not provide the required result.

9. You are the system administrator for an Exchange Server that serves more than 50,000 seats.

Required result:

Recommend a practical backup strategy.

Optional desired result:

Verify the backup process.

Proposed solution:

Take a full with incremental backup. After backing up, view the Windows NT event log for any errors within the backup process.

Which results are provided by the proposed solution?

a. The proposed solution provides the required result and the optional desired result.

b. The proposed solution provides only the required result.

c. The proposed solution does not provide the required result.

10. You'd like to create a maintenance schedule for your Exchange Server.

Required result:

You'd like to make use of the Microsoft Exchange Server utilities to help you automate this task.

Optional desired result:

You want to back up the Exchange Server.

Proposed solution:

Use the following utilities to help you plan for a regular maintenance schedule:

- ESEUTIL
- ISINTEG
- MTACHECK

Which results are provided by the proposed solution?

a. The proposed solution provides the required result and the optional desired result.

b. The proposed solution provides only the required result.

c. The proposed solution does not provide the required result.

11. The system administrator spends a lot of time on tasks such as compacting the Exchange Server database.

12

Required result:

You'd like to automate the process of compacting the Exchange Server database.

Optional desired result:

You'd like to defragment the Information Store and the directory database.

Proposed solution:

Build a custom application that runs a batch file at a user-specified date and time. The batch file, in turn, runs ESEUTIL.

Which results are provided by the proposed solution?

a. The proposed solution provides the required result and the optional desired result.

b. The proposed solution provides only the required result.

c. The proposed solution does not provide the required result.

CHAPTER THIRTEEN

EXCHANGE FORMS

In this chapter, you'll learn how to make Outlook 98 forms work for you. These forms provide the underpinnings that can permit you to create powerful, custom, email-based applications with very little effort.

You'll begin the chapter with a survey of the custom form options that Outlook 98 supports, and then explore those behind-the-scenes Exchange components that make forms-based applications possible. Next, you'll learn how to make efficient use of some of the programming tools available for creating such custom applications, without being forced into becoming a Visual Basic guru. And, finally, you'll learn how to create custom forms and become an efficiency hero without becoming a heavy-duty programmer along the way.

AFTER READING THIS CHAPTER AND COMPLETING THE EXERCISES, YOU WILL BE ABLE TO:

- Use the custom form creation options available to you in Outlook 98
- Describe the components that allow the creation of interactive forms
- Create forms that interact between a server and a client machine
- Understand the roles of permissions
- Modify existing forms to suit your needs
- Create professional and functional forms, without knowing programming

AN ELECTRONIC FORMS OVERVIEW

Before you begin to create your first electronic form, you'll want to take a look at the different types of forms that Exchange and Outlook can support. You'll also want to understand the tools and technologies on which these forms are based. You must also determine whether you want to use Exchange Designer or Outlook forms. You can start with Outlook as the basis for your forms and modify them later to meet your needs. All Outlook-based forms are *32-bit forms*. If you decide to use Exchange forms instead, the next decision that you must make is whether to use 16-bit or 32-bit forms.

It is important to understand the uses for 16-bit forms compared to 32-bit forms. Remember, Windows 3.1 cannot use 32-bit forms. Your users' desktops will therefore exercise a powerful influence on what kinds of forms you choose.

The Exchange client software is expected to become obsolete fairly soon, and Outlook 98 and its successors should take over as the primary client for Exchange Server by the end of 1999. In addition, Microsoft has made it very clear that its testing processes are becoming more dynamic. At the time of this writing, the Exchange exam does not make much mention of Outlook electronic forms, but it's likely that such electronic forms will appear in upcoming versions of this test. This is not only because they are perfect examples of a dynamic technology, but also because forms add so much capability to what Exchange can do for its users. Because this topic is so important to users and administrators alike, this chapter covers Outlook electronic forms and the Exchange client in detail.

EXPLORING SAMPLE FORMS APPLICATIONS

You might wonder what an Exchange form is and how it works. A form is a method to post and gather information using email that might otherwise get lost in a sea of data. Electronic forms are a great alternative to regular types of paperwork, for information that is subject to different security requirements for specific groups or individuals, or (with some development effort) for dramatically streamlining paper trails. A classic example for this last category is a trouble ticket generated for a help desk.

Exchange is capable of handling many different kinds of forms. Some forms are categorized by the content they carry, and include the following types of content:

- **Report forms** These forms are used to automate the creation and sending of reports.

- **Request forms** These forms can ferry almost any kind of request, be it for services, resources, or materiel. For example, a purchase requisition for computer equipment would fit nicely within this kind of form.

- **Survey forms** These forms are handy when collecting information from employees or customers. For example, a public folder might be used to query a Web site visitor on how likely he is to purchase a new widget from your firm.

Other Exchange forms are categorized by the kinds of audiences they can serve. The Exchange forms library contains several types of forms that fit into several of these audience categories. These audiences include the following:

- **Organization forms** These forms are stored on the server, and are accessible by all users. They include elements like personnel profiles, vacation request forms, travel request forms, and other kinds of content that applies to all employees within an organization.

- **Personal forms** This type of form is specific to a certain user and is located in an individual's mailbox. These can include just about any kind of content, and may relate to an individual's job function, technical or topic focus, or other custom needs and requirements.

- **Folder forms** These forms, when they reside in a public folder, can be accessed by everyone. The alternative is to store them on a local drive, which makes them available to the user(s) who shares access to that drive. These may be aimed at a workgroup, a department, or some other functional unit within an organization, where the folder in which they reside helps to identify the intended audience.

13

Now that you've seen the range of form types available, and the kinds of audiences they can serve, you should have some appreciation for what Exchange forms might mean to your organization. But before you can roll them out, it's a good idea to step back and go through some planning exercises. These provide the topic for the section that follows.

PLANNING AND ORGANIZING

Regardless of the final role of a folder, Microsoft gives you 10 guidelines to use as planning principles. Experience will probably teach you to view these guidelines with some respect, because they include some worthwhile recommendations and tips about best practices.

According to Microsoft, here are the top 10 guidelines for creating electronic forms:

- Identify folder users and requirements.

- Create a designer in charge (a lead) who will plan, design, and implement the project folder.

- Formulate a design plan that pinpoints the challenges to be solved and how the folder will overcome those. Be sure to include preliminary graphics of all *views* and windows that will be needed.

- Choose where your design work will take place. If you invite a group to provide input and feedback, be sure to put all such information in a public folder. Early concept and design work may be better off if situated in a personal PST folder or an Outlook mailbox.

- Create or choose a folder design. Choices include creating a new folder, directly modifying an existing folder, or copying a folder design.

- Publish forms in the folder. This may require that you publish a form in either the Standard Forms Library folder or in another folder.

- Design folder views. To assist your users, create folder views with elements such as columns, filters, sorting, and so forth.

- Test the forms folder thoroughly. Be sure to include all views and expressions. Double-check availability, and secure items that should not be changed.

- Copy the folder from its test bed to an appropriate public folder. Test some more, on a limited basis.

- When it's ready, release the form to production use by changing its permissions.

In most cases, your form will be used to communicate information to a group of people. When you are working within a group context, this activity is sometimes called collaboration. Therefore, Microsoft calls developing forms to fill this need collaboration development.

COLLABORATION APPLICATIONS

You've looked at the types of forms you can use, now let's analyze your needs another way. Your needs could mandate realtime interaction, in a synchronous mode (such as in a virtual meeting using NetMeeting), or it might be satisfied with asynchronous collaboration, which may easily be satisfied with an exchange of email messages. One example of the latter kind of interaction occurs when an electronic phone message taken while someone was out to lunch is posted to the recipient's email account. This is the electronic equivalent of a "while you were out" paper message. The major difference is that the office could be in Redmond, WA, while the email recipient might be in Philadelphia, PA.

Whether working in synchronous or asynchronous mode, forms must meet specific information needs. It doesn't matter if such forms relate to a video-based meeting using Microsoft's NetMeeting software, or if they're part of a thread-based discussion running asynchronously. If you collaborate on an Excel spreadsheet, that spreadsheet must reside somewhere that is accessible to all interested parties to make productive collaboration possible. In the section that follows, you'll learn how to manage Exchange forms to facilitate such collaboration.

MANAGING EXCHANGE SERVER FORMS

Let's take a look at some common Exchange components that are needed to support collaboration, regardless of whether such collaboration takes place in realtime or asynchronously. In the sections that follow, you'll learn about Exchange and Outlook elements that can facilitate collaboration, and how forms fit into this picture.

COMPONENTS OF COLLABORATION

In most cases, all forms share the following components:

- **Folders** Without at least a public or a private *folder* to store your data, forms are nothing more than pretty pictures on the screen. It is always a good idea to test any public form from a private folder area to make sure it performs correctly before deploying it across an organization. The failure of a first effort might deter management from extending the use of Exchange forms. Correctly designed public forms greatly improve communication speed and accuracy.

- **Views** Various data elements in a form may represent different things to different users. For example, a help desk form needs to document the trouble a user is reporting, along with who is assigned to the trouble ticket and who sent it. A supervisor only needs an overview of who is working on which tickets to check on workflow and to verify closure of trouble tickets in a timely manner. Help desk supervisors and help desk technicians would therefore benefit from separate views.

- **Fields** A field contains one or more specific data elements. In the trouble ticket system, for example, a data element might supply the name of the individual who's working on the trouble ticket. This field is germane to the trouble ticket's sender, to the individual assigned to the ticket, and to the help desk supervisor.

- **Forms** Forms define how data flows into and out of your Exchange database. If you have ever sent a piece of email, you have used a form. You enter data elements in the To field, the From field is usually filled automatically, and you enter message content into the message field. In fact, all activity within Exchange involves a form of some kind or another.

13

- **Databases** In many cases, Exchange is your database. Using forms, it is possible to link to other databases. Using the Open Database Connectivity (ODBC) Connector, it is also possible to examine the contents of other databases. For example, you could check a SQL database for a part number based on a user's request for that number in a form.

In general, forms provide a means to solicit input from users, and then to manipulate or act on that input to interact with users, or to produce output of some kind in response to a user request. In many cases, a single user interaction will have both effects. For example, filling out a vacation request form could lead to delivery of a message with the specifics to a manager for approval, while at the same time returning a message to the submitter acknowledging receipt of the request and promising a yes/no response by a certain date.

In the section that follows, you will review material originally presented in Chapter 6 that covers how Outlook 98 also supports collaboration.

OUTLOOK INSTANT COLLABORATION

Chapter 6 covered Outlook 98 in detail and discussed its numerous built-in components, which include its Calendar, Tasks, Notes, Contacts, and Journal views. You can use these components to perform instant collaboration between users. Instant collaboration may be accomplished simply by copying a module into a public folder.

If you place the Calendar component into a public folder, users can share, post, and update to this folder. If several projects are active at the same time in your organization, you should create a public folder for each project. Otherwise, our public calendar may become an exercise in confusion and frustration.

The same observation also applies to the Outlook Tasks component. It may be copied into a public folder, where a team could collaborate and demonstrate progress on a task, and a supervisor could track such progress quickly and efficiently. Likewise, the sales staff could use a shared Contacts list in a public folder to obtain customer information quickly and easily.

A public Journal component is another good example of how to use an Exchange form effectively. For example, feedback from a group of product beta testers might revolve around a public journal, where all beta testers could create entries, and members of the development, marketing, and sales teams could share access to that information.

Finally, Notes may also be used publicly as an electronic equal to sticky notes, and Notes may also be sent as messages. A public Notes database could, therefore, become a repository for useful tidbits of information of all kinds, especially if ordinary users were not permitted to make changes directly to that database. In fact, you could use a form to submit suggested changes or additions to the public Notes database in the form of an email message to some administrator. This administrator could review such submissions regularly and post only those items judged to have broad enough impact to be worth including in the database.

Instant collaboration requires putting a public spin on Outlook elements that might otherwise remain purely private, but may be implemented with very little effort. In the section that follows, you'll learn more about a variety of application interfaces available through Exchange that can greatly enhance what forms can do, albeit at the cost of additional planning, effort, and knowledge.

COLLABORATION APPLICATIONS PLATFORM

In large part, Exchange is based on Internet standards. Because these are open standards, you may use Windows 95, Windows 98, and Windows NT to meet your collaboration needs. Because open standards are also open-ended, there is no single right way to plan or execute a rollout of forms that takes advantage of their capabilities. The right way is the way that best fits the requirements for the issues that you are attempting to streamline or address with a forms-based Exchange application.

In our (the authors') case, we use Windows NT Server with Exchange as the database, which, as you learned earlier, can also extend to other databases (such as SQL Server). To make your collaboration as easy as possible, you could also use Internet Information Server (IIS). Keep in mind that Exchange supports the Simple Mail Transfer Protocol (SMTP), Post Office Protocol (POP), Lightweight Directory Access Protocol (LDAP), Network News Transfer Protocol (NNTP), and, finally, public and private folders. These protocols can be used to incorporate collaborative forms.

13

If you use IIS, remember that Index Server is available to your users, which makes locating needed information simple and fast. On the client side, Internet Explorer 4 (IE4) also supports the latest version of the Hypertext Transfer Protocol (HTTP) version 1.1, which includes support for rich media types of many kinds. And last, but certainly not least, with some programming background, you can use Visual Basic scripts to extend the programming power of Active Server Pages (ASP) to create full-blown, interactive applications.

The details involved in building such applications are well beyond the scope of this book, but they may not be beyond the scope of your needs. For more information on the topics mentioned in the preceding paragraphs, visit the Microsoft Web site at **www.microsoft.com** and search on the specific products and technologies mentioned therein. You will also find the Exchange Web site at **www.microsoft.com/exchange** and the Site Builder Web site at **www.microsoft.com/sitebuilder** to be especially informative on these topics.

If you're working in an environment where you can count on a user population that consists entirely of Outlook 98 users, your options for using forms are quite interesting. In the sections that follow, you'll learn more about how Outlook clients can use forms for all kinds of applications.

OUTLOOK COLLABORATION APPLICATIONS ENVIRONMENT

Using Outlook 98 for creating collaboration forms gives you a number of advantages over earlier options. Some benefits include:

- **32-bit forms** Outlook 98 forms are completely 32-bit. Form definitions are less than 15K in size in most cases. This delivers quick performance and fast updates.

- **Rapid Application Development (RAD)** RAD provides the ability to quickly switch back and forth between designing a form and testing it, without recompiling your work between each step.

- **Portable custom forms** Your forms' users can email a form to other users who might not have the form installed. It is also possible to embed a form in other applications.

- **Advanced views and fields** Earlier, in Chapter 6, you saw how easy it is to organize Outlook views. This may be applied to collaboration forms as well. Furthermore, you can include algebraic or other numeric calculations within forms and provide built-in calculations or data checks.

Beyond the advantages that Outlook 98 brings to forms developers when compared to earlier versions, this program also facilitates the development process itself. In the section that follows, you'll learn more about what and how application development is supported in the Outlook 98 environment.

APPLICATION DEVELOPMENT USING OUTLOOK 98

Using Outlook 98 as a design platform greatly enhances your design capabilities when compared to the tools included with Exchange client. Besides having Outlook 98's form designer available, you may also use its Visual Basic scripting tools and the Visual Basic Expression service.

To access the Outlook 98 form designer, select Tools|Forms|Design A Form from the menus, as shown in Figure 13.1. If you have ever used form design before, you'll notice that Outlook 98 uses a different method to get to its forms.

Another change to Outlook 98 is its flexibility in typing form files. Previously, forms were always saved as OFT files. Outlook 98 includes options to save files in Rich Field Text, templates, and other formats, as shown in Figure 13.2.

Figure 13.1 Outlook 98's Design A Form option on the Tools menu.

In addition to its own built-in forms design capabilities, Outlook 98 continues to support a "special relationship" with Visual Basic. Earlier versions of Outlook required knowledge of Visual Basic for forms development; in Outlook 98, this requirement is relaxed, but the relationship persists, partly to support backward compatibility, and partly to permit developers to continue to exploit Visual Basic's capabilities.

Visual Basic

In previous versions of Outlook, when designing a form for collaboration you needed to know something about Visual Basic to perform certain tasks. Although

13

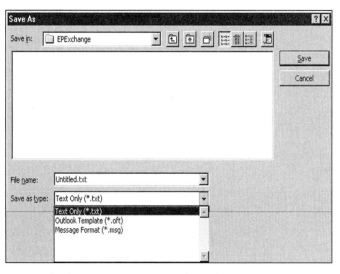

Figure 13.2 Outlook 98's Save As Type drop-down menu.

Visual Basic remains available to you, the forms designer toolbox permits you to create professional-looking forms without using Visual Basic. Notice the toolbox in Figure 13.3. Checkboxes, radio buttons, picture inserts, and more are all available for easy inclusion in forms, and you don't have to know how to use Visual Basic to use these elements.

Beyond the general purpose capabilities of Visual Basic—which is more than just a programming language, but also a reasonably complete programming environment—the Web reaches out to more desktops than Visual Basic can ever access. In the section that follows, you'll learn about key Web-based technologies that can add considerable reach to forms-based applications through Outlook 98, and also through the Outlook Web Assistant.

ACTIVE SERVER AND ACTIVE DESKTOP COMPONENTS

Because of common Web code and tools that are shared between the server and client, both communications and the operation of forms are invisible to end users. Such forms also fit transparently into a Web-based environment. Better still, access to powerful development tools makes it easy for developers to exploit this kind of functionality.

Components that you have at your disposal include:

- **HTML** Because *Hypertext Markup Language (HTML)* can be used with Active Desktop as well as forms, both look the same to the end users. This reduces training time greatly.

- **Scripting** Because ASP supports both *Visual Basic Script* (VBScript) and *JavaScript* (which Microsoft calls JScript), the choice of scripting tools is yours. VBScript currently provides more powerful programming tools, but JavaScript permits you to perform whatever programming

Figure 13.3 Outlook 98's toolbox controls.

tasks are at hand without having to know—or care about—the user's operating system.

- **Components** ASP also allows you to use components developed using other programming languages. Server-side scripting allows users to choose different human languages based on input from the HTML browser.

- **Active Server** This option first became available in IIS version 3. Besides ASP, some of its features include *Transaction Server* and *message queues*. These features help ensure the safety of your data when it must travel across the Internet. In addition, they make sure that a form runs independently from its display information (such as human language).

- **Transaction Server** This component is now a separate product available without charge to authorized NT and IIS users. Transaction Server eliminates a significant amount of required program logic to ensure data accuracy. For example, if you have a form that sells a part from your inventory, Transaction Server will not allow that part to be removed from inventory permanently until the transaction is complete. All you have to know as a developer are two procedure calls—Commit (commits a transaction and changes the data) and Rollback (reverses a transaction, and restores the data to its state before the transaction was committed).

- **Message queues** This is a new component based on transaction messages that keeps outbound messages around until their delivery is confirmed. For example, suppose an Exchange Server is unavailable because AT&T experiences a massive drop of frame relay service. Now, you need to communicate with a server that is not available. Using a message queue, the message destined for the unavailable Exchange Server may be safely stored until AT&T restores your frame relay service. Then, the pending message may be delivered to the Exchange Server.

13

Beyond the software tools used to define fields, solicit input, check values, and deliver input data to databases and other applications, Exchange provides support for numerous other aspects of forms-based applications. Among the most important of these aspects are the folders where forms usually reside; these folders are covered in the section that follows.

CREATING FOLDERS WITH OUTLOOK

Outlook 98 uses these two folder types:

- **File System folders** These folders behave just like a folder created using the Explorer program. This means such folders possess all the properties that any folder created by the operating system (OS) might possess. Likewise, either Outlook 98 or the OS can use these folders.

- **Outlook Item folders** These folders are called Outlook Item folders because they may only be accessed within Outlook 98. You can create a new Outlook Item folder or duplicate and change the design of one of its six predefined folders—Appointments, Contacts, Journal, Message, Post, and Tasks.

You usually create an Outlook 98 Item folder when you don't have a good design to follow or if you want to use the standard options that such folders include. Normally, an Outlook Item folder is used as a discussion folder, a reference folder, or perhaps a tracking folder.

Follow these steps to create a new Outlook 98 Item folder:

1. Right-click the Outlook drop-down menu.
2. Select New Folder. When the dialog box is displayed, name your folder.
3. Notice that Folder Contains is the default selection. This is one of six predefined types of Outlook Item folders.
4. Click where you would like this folder to reside. It can be stored in a top-level folder or in a subfolder.
5. Click OK.
6. Your next choice is whether or not to place a shortcut on the left-most pane for Outlook 98. The default is No. Select No at this time.

Figure 13.4 shows that you cannot only create a subfolder under a subfolder, but you can also adjust the properties for each such folder. Test is a mail folder. The

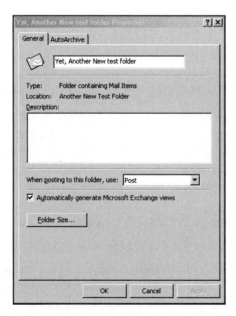

Figure 13.4 Properties of Yet, Another New Test Folder.

Another New Test Folder is for Notes, and the Yet, Another New Test Folder contains mail items.

If forms or other items reside in an Outlook or Exchange folder, the keys to access reside in the permissions associated with that folder. You'll learn more about these in the section that follows.

FOLDER PERMISSIONS

To see the properties for any folder, highlight that folder, right-click, and select Permissions from the pop-up menu that appears. The default for all Exchange users is to read and write to a public folder. This is not the case for a private folder. Private folders deny access to everyone but their owners.

Outlook 98, working in concert with Exchange Server, supplies a collection of predefined permissions. The default permissions for a folder, Author, always apply if that folder has not had its permissions explicitly reset. Table 13.1 shows the standard set of permissions that apply to folders.

Outlook 98 allows one user to assign rights to another. For example, you may assign another user the right to schedule appointments and meetings on your behalf. This is called delegate access. The Delegate Access feature of Outlook 98 only shows up when using Exchange Server. Naturally, this means that you would need a connection to the Exchange Server with the Delegate Access feature installed.

In addition to its abilities to accommodate public and private folders, Exchange also supports a special type of public folder called a moderated folder, which may be used to provide public access to filtered, rather than unfiltered, data and postings. This provides the topic for the section that follows.

13

Table 13.1   The standard set of permissions for a folder.

Role	Rights
Owner	Create, read, modify, and delete all files/items. Allows the creation of subfolders. When creating a subfolder or using an existing folder, the owner can determine who can access the folder.
Publishing Editor	Create, read, modify, and delete all files and items. Can create subfolders.
Editor	Create, read, modify, and delete all files and items.
Author	Create and read files/items. Modify or delete files and items created by the author.
Non-editing Author	Create and read items. No access to editing files/items.
Reviewer	Read files/items only.
Contributor	Create items and files only. The contents of the folder are not shown.
Custom	Whatever the folder owner defines.
None	Cannot open the folder. Equivalent to NT's No Access.

MODERATED FOLDERS

A *moderated folder* is a public folder (or listserv, bulletin board service, and so forth) that does not display messages sent by users until a reviewer chooses to accept a posting. Some lists are lightly moderated, whereas others are heavily moderated. For Exchange, an event service looks for postings to a moderated public folder and transparently forwards such new postings to the Exchange user who has been assigned the role of moderator without modifying its contents. This person then determines the merit of the posting, and, if the message is judged to be suitable, he may post it to the public folder.

To create a moderated folder, right-click the Folder List pane within Outlook, select the New Folder entry from the pop-up menu that appears, and then select Moderated Folder in the pick list in the Folder Contains text entry box, then select the Set Folder As A Moderated Folder checkbox. At this point, the choices on your new folder will be as follows:

- **Forwarding Location** This is where you select the forwarding location to which all postings (other than postings from the moderator) will be forwarded. Any person with a listing, either in the Global Address List (GAL) or the Personal Address Book (PAB), can be a valid moderator. Be careful if you select more than one person as a moderator. If you do, each person gets a copy of every post, which could result in multiple moderators posting the same message. A better idea is to send the message to a secure public folder, available only to the moderators group; once accepted, any moderator can copy the post to the moderated public folder.

- **Send An Automated Reply Message Following A Posting** If you select this option, either a standard or a custom form can be used. The owner of the folder must have Send On Behalf Of turned on. This is required for a custom template reply.

- **Identify The Moderators** When you select the moderator(s) for a folder, you grant a role that allows them to post to the folder.

Once the moderator's *roles* and responsibilities are taken care of, handling a moderated folder is much like handling any other folder, except that two stages of delivery are involved: from the sender to the moderator, and (possibly) from the moderator to the moderated folder. You'll learn more about the details of this message flow in the section that follows.

MESSAGE FLOW

Let's look at how a message works its way through Exchange when a person posting a message is not a moderator:

1. A rule on the folder checks to see if the sender is a moderator.

2. In this example, the sender is not on the list of moderators. Therefore, the message is forwarded to a location selected previously, without any changes to the message.

3. The message is deleted from the folder in which it first landed.

4. If the moderated folder's owner opts to send an auto-responder message to inform the user that the message has been received, such a message is sent to the originator. Remember, moderators who generate messages bypass these rules, so they can post directly.

5. The moderator reviews the message and passes judgment on the validity of the message. If the message fails the standard(s) for the list, the moderator deletes the message. Otherwise, the moderator posts the message to the folder.

For moderated folders, at least two roles apply—that of the user, who posts and reads message traffic, and that of the moderator, who reviews messages and decides what to publish in the moderated folder. To that end, numerous rules are applied to incoming traffic to route it correctly: Ordinary users' postings are directed to an invisible folder where unreviewed messages reside, but also moderator postings are directed straight to the moderated folder itself without any intermediate steps. The roles and rules involved provide the topic for the section that follows.

Roles And Rules

13

The rule for the moderator is found in the list of rules on the folder. Look for <Moderated Folder Rule>, which is found in the Conditions column. Also, check the Actions column for Forward To Moderator and Moderate Message. You need to edit these rules with the Moderated Folder button, which is found in the Administration tab. An owner can rearrange these rules up or down the chain, which affects the order of execution. It is necessary to test your rules carefully and fully before live deployment.

This concludes the discussion of moderated folders. In the section that follows, you'll learn about the level of permissions required to alter Exchange forms, and how to create and change the folders where forms reside.

Cloning And Morphing Folders

Before you begin altering forms, you need owner permissions. If you are not sure of the current status, highlight and right-click the folder. Select Properties, and view the Permissions tab. Also, when working with a folder design, the components of the source folder are merged with the parts of the destination folder.

Only make minor changes to folders that are in use. This prevents you from disrupting users' workflow. Some examples of acceptable changes include adding a view, changing a contact, and updating permissions. Remember that any changes in permissions will not take effect while a user is logged in. The user must log off and log back in for permissions changes to take effect.

When making more serious changes—such as changing rules or modifying forms—copy the design of the folder to a different folder, then make the changes. Test the changes, then copy the modified design back to the original folder. Be sure that you test your changes thoroughly before making them publicly accessible.

Before merging folder designs, you should know that if there are conflicting properties between a source folder and a destination folder, the source folder's properties replace the properties on the destination folder. Double-check which is which. When you merge designs, you bring together permissions, views, forms, rules, and folder descriptions. Be as clear as you can about what you're doing. If necessary, test a copy of the source against a copy of the destination to see what happens.

In the section that follows, you'll learn about personal folders and their potential relationships with private and public Exchange folders.

Personal Folders (PSTs)

Personal folders, or PST files, are located on the user's local hard disk. PSTs usually serve to archive information. Sometimes, however, a clever administrator will use the PST as a temporary storage area to hold a user's data when moving that user's mailbox from one Exchange site to another.

A PST file has the same properties as any other file, which means that it may be renamed, copied, and deleted like any other file. Personal folders support password protection and two levels of encryption. No more than one user at a time can access a PST file.

 Remember that once a PST is in use on a local hard drive, you are no longer backing up the data with the Exchange Server! The burden of backups is moved to the local hard drive. A PST folder can contain the same types of information that are found on the Exchange Server Information Store.

Having explored the variety and capabilities of Exchange and Outlook folders, you may now turn your focus to the details involved in testing a folder before public release, and then releasing that folder once tested. This provides the topic for the section that follows.

TESTING AND RELEASING A FOLDER

By now, you hopefully know the importance of testing. After you are comfortable with the way your folder behaves, ask a few of your users to test your work. When seeking volunteers for such experiments, be sure to include both advanced users (who can easily communicate feedback on a more technical level) and novices (who may become confused more easily).

Be sure to set your permissions to Owners only when you're in a testing phase. When all changes are complete, go to the Folder Properties dialog box, select the Administration tab, and then select the All Users With Access permission. Be sure to remove those who no longer need high-level access from the list that appears. Finally, check this list carefully to be sure that all users have only appropriate access to the folder and its contents.

One important step when deploying a folder for public consumption is to define the rules and views that apply to the folder. This is the topic that is covered in the next section.

CREATING FOLDER RULES AND VIEWS

Rules represent the machinery that makes collaboration work. Rules may be used to customize an engine to reduce workloads, and, when tested thoroughly, can help to eliminate mistakes. On the other hand, rules that are not tested thoroughly can quickly cause multiple errors. Rules may also be used to alert users to messages and to create auto-responder messages.

Views assist in the management or use of folders in ways that benefit their users. Views allow advanced sorting, filtering, and manipulating of a folder's contents. To review some of the advanced features related to the View and Sort features in Outlook, please refer to Chapter 6.

With this overview in mind, let's drill down into the use of rules. You can use rules to:

- Select specific types of items to be returned to the sender automatically.

- Delete unwanted items based on specified conditions. Careful use of a rule can make unwanted mail nothing more than a bad memory.

- Automatically reply to specific types of items using a reply template.

- Manage message handling by machine to forward, copy, or move messages to folders or to route them to other users.

Rules perform their duties based on two fundamental concepts:

- **Conditions** This is the evaluation part of a rule. Choose the simplest form of programming to establish and test for conditions. Such conditions usually test on source address, key words in the header, or other strings that parsing a message can produce.

- **Actions** If a rule is met, some kind of action may be taken. For example, a rule could state that if the From field contains a mail header from the Exchange list, that mail message should be moved to the Exchange List folder.

Figure 13.5 shows a small list of rules in place. Notice the highlighted rule takes any messages from the listserv, in this case an MS-Proxy mailing list, and puts the mail in its own folder. Despite this simple example, rules can become quite complex.

Let's look at how rules are applied. Simply put, rules work in a top-down fashion. Rules are placed using the Inbox Assistant or an Out Of Office Assistant. In Outlook 98, you will find easy assistance with rules under the Tools|Rules Wizard menu entry.

As a message comes in, rules are applied to that message, starting with the rule at the top of the list. If any rule applies, its associated action step is taken. If a rule does not apply, the next rule is invoked and evaluated to see whether that rule applies to the message. Like all well-written tests, each rule must be exact in what it looks for. It is possible to use a rule to take a message from the CEO, for example, and then to copy that message to all department heads. But there are a couple of specific conditions that stop a rule in its tracks. One method is to select the Do Not Process Subsequent Rules option. The other is to delete the message being evaluated using the Delete Rule option.

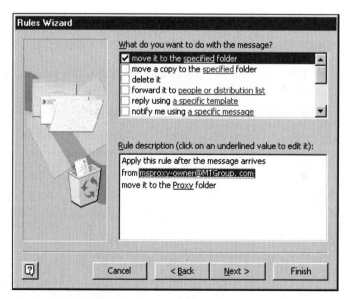

Figure 13.5   The Rules Wizard.

For that reason, if you plan to use the Delete Rule option, be sure to place it last in any rules list. You can make spam a nonissue by applying message filters before forwarding any mail from your Internet Service Provider to your local desktop. Then, use the Rule Wizard to create a rule that forwards mail that does not meet other conditions to a folder intended to capture any leftover spam. Then, before making any permanent deletions from this folder, you can always perform a quick scan of subject and message headers to ensure that you don't accidentally delete any legitimate messages.

When applying rules, creating the correct flow of logic sometimes takes more effort than you might think. Under some circumstances, you might want to impose two sets of behaviors on the same set of circumstances, depending on whether you're at work or at home. For example, you might have administrative alerts set up so that if you have a hard drive failure on a RAID disk subsystem, an SMTP message is created and mailed to you. During working hours, the rules filter incoming mail from your NT system and forward such messages to your desktop with high priority. But on evenings or weekends, other rules route such messages to your home system and call your pager. To create this type of handling, first create both sets of rules separately. Then, aggregate the rules from the two sets so that they are applied in the desired order (you'll probably want to list work hour rules first, and the evening/weekend hours second, because you probably get the bulk of your mail during working hours).

The previous example is only one way to keep you informed. Another approach might be to define a more complex set of conditions. In the preceding example, there is only one condition at work, which may be restated as "if it's from the NT system, track me down." For a rule to function, it must always have at least one condition.

Without a condition, a rule has nothing to evaluate, but it is possible to create sets of rules that include more than one condition. If the first condition is not met, you can add an "or" statement and create another condition. In this case, if either condition is met, the specified action executes. For example, if the message is from the CEO or it is marked with high importance, you can instruct the rule to take some kind of action.

The alternative is to use an "and" statement. Simply changing the "or" to an "and" in the previous example makes a dramatic difference. In this case, the described action will only apply if the message is from the CEO and it is marked at high importance. A high importance message from someone else will not meet this condition. Hopefully this helps illustrate why it is vital to design rules quite carefully.

Of course, you can apply rules to almost any field within a message. You can use the From, Subject, Importance, or any other field. Now that you know what you can evaluate in a message, you can shift your focus to the actions that meeting the conditions in a message can invoke. This is the subject of the section that follows.

13

SPECIFYING AN ACTION

In the previous sections, you were exposed to several rule examples. One was restated as "if it's from the NT system, track me down," others included checking the sender field for the CEO's address and also checking the importance field for the value high. Whenever conditions in a rule are met, association actions may then be performed. The actions shown in Table 13.2 represent the built-in responses that Outlook makes available through its Rules Wizard.

If none of these actions meets your needs for some specific rule, you can create a custom rule that adds to this repertoire. To create a custom rule set, get out the CD-ROMs that contain Microsoft BackOffice, and look for a file named CRARUN. There, you'll find an example of a custom rule. If you follow this example, you should be able to create custom rules of your own.

Having now covered the topic of rules applied to incoming messages, it's now time to turn your attention to how messages and other data may appear within email folders. This provides the subject for the section that follows.

FOLDER VIEWS

Views are simply different ways to see information stored in an Outlook folder. Chapter 6 describes how to change the view for messages, contacts, journal entries, and forms. Every folder in Outlook 98 includes an associated set of standard views. The view type varies with the type of folder that stores the information. To create a new Outlook view, select View | Current View | Define Views.

Now, you can either change an existing view or define a new view by selecting New (see Figure 13.6). Notice the variety of options available to you when creating a new view. The following list details the types of views that you may choose to define:

- **Table** Displays items in a grid of rows and columns. Each row contains one item. A row could be a list of contacts, for example, where each column contains an information field, such as an email address or a phone number, and so forth.

Table 13.2   Rule actions.

Action	Description
Alert	Choose to be notified with sound or a dialog box.
Delete	Delete the item (refer to the previous caution).
Move/Copy To Folder	Move or copy to designated folder. If you have multiple actions, this will take place multiple times.
Forward To	Forward the message to a new recipient.
Reply With/Template	Send an automatic response to the sender.

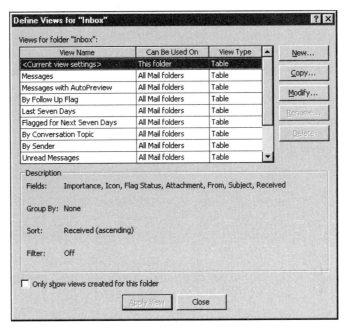

Figure 13.6   Changing an existing view or defining a new view.

- **Timeline** Displays items in chronological order from left to right, oldest to newest. This option is handy if you don't remember the name of an item but you remember that it arrived on some particular date.

- **Card** Displays records as individual cards sorted in some order (this is the default for Contacts, which are sorted by surname).

- **Day/Week/Month** Displays items on the Calendar. Views can range from weekly agendas, to multi-day or monthly formats.

- **Icon** Indicates files and items by icon. This is the default view for Notes.

Custom views can add significant value to Exchange-based applications, particularly when the databases that result from collecting forms input must be made available to a large audience. You should find them quite useful to create just the kind of layout and organization that the data, or your users, require.

In the section that follows, you'll change focus from folder views to the Organizer and Outlook's built-in (and customizable) filters, which can assist you when building forms-based applications, or simply when managing incoming email.

USING THE ORGANIZER AND FILTERS

You can modify or create new fields to view, add custom fields, or select from an almost unlimited variety of options on your existing fields. These features have been available in the past, but, unless users knew where to find them, they remained hidden from most users.

13

With Outlook 98, the Organize button gives end users the ability to access some of these features more easily, even though some functionality seems to have been lost because of the simpler approach that the Organizer uses. The following list includes some of the Organizer's more common productivity boosters:

- **Sorting items** Sorting a view arranges items based on a field or fields, in ascending or descending order. Among other selections, you can sort by subject topic, and by topic and time.

- **Grouping items** Grouping items may be useful for hiding individual items when collapsed into a group. If you arrange items according to a common field, you can get a better overview of an entire database without having to scan all the individual records. Please note that it is not possible to create groups from custom formulas or combination fields.

- **Other views** Sorting and grouping items are common uses, but you can also choose from these views: AutoPreview, Best Fit, Column Alignment, Editable, or Non-editable views.

With Outlook 98, the Office Wizard is standing by to help assist you in your customization efforts. Also, should you or your users become overwhelmed with the sheer volume of data, you can use filters to reduce some of the clutter and drill down from an overview to locate what you seek in a logical manner.

To apply a filter within the Outlook environment, simply click the folder to which you wish to apply a filter, and then follow these steps:

1. On the View menu, point to Current View, and then click Customize Current View.

2. Click Filter.

3. Select the filter options you want. To filter using other criteria such as category or importance level, click the More Choices tab, then select the options you want. To filter using additional or custom fields, click the Advanced tab, then select the options you want.

 For Help on any filter option, click the question mark, then click the option.

If you routinely apply filters to certain message collections, you may want to define a custom view where those filters always apply. Otherwise, you will have to define the filters when you wish to use them, but remove them when they're not needed. A custom view makes it easy to switch back and forth from filtered and unfiltered data. Likewise, if multiple filters are needed, you should define a custom view for each set of filters that you wish to apply.

Beyond the flexibility that the Organizer and filters can provide, you may find it useful to create custom views for certain Outlook databases (which provides a handy way to implement the recommendations in the preceding paragraph). Custom views are the topic of the section that follows.

CUSTOM VIEW OPTIONS

The custom view options can help you create a way to view folders that are organized and arranged to meet your specific needs. These options can also save you from drowning in data. Outlook 98 provides you with several standard views for each folder in the Current View menu, as shown in Figure 13.7.

As you can see in Figure 13.7, you can create or modify forms for this folder. As mentioned earlier, you cannot create groups with combination fields. A combination field is a custom view. For example, you might want to combine two fields, such as First Name and Last Name, or create a list of phone numbers that can be displayed in any order you choose. However, you do not have the ability to use formula functions on combination fields.

Formula functions are used to perform complex functions. A formula editor contains controls for entering the relevant fields and another for pasting arguments and functions. For example, the following formula shows how many days have passed since a particular event:

```
DateValue(Now()-DateValue([Received]) & Day(s)
```

Now that you have learned how to modify existing views and forms, it's time to examine the process of building new forms. This is covered in the sections that follow.

13

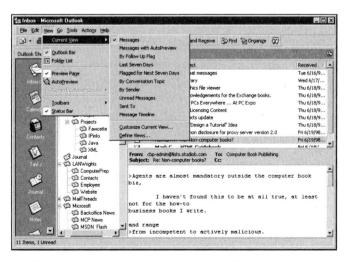

Figure 13.7   The 10 views provided by Outlook 98.

CREATING FORMS

Outlook 98 supplies several basic forms that may be customized. You can modify and extend these forms fairly quickly and easily. They will often provide the best jump-start when starting the process of implementing forms-based Exchange applications. The following sections cover the basic predefined Outlook forms.

MAIL MESSAGE FORMS

You can build forms quite easily to convert routine paperwork into an equivalent system based on electronic messages, but it can sometimes be challenging to choose the recipient for the incoming message flow. But, by combining other features of Exchange, such as distribution lists, you can easily convert a paper-based system into an automated, message-based system that more or less runs itself. Some everyday examples already in widespread use in many organizations include the following:

- **Request forms** These may be used to handle requests of all kinds. Typical implementations include vacation requests, orders for business cards, orders for computer equipment, and so forth.

- **Survey or feedback forms** These may be used to gather information of all kinds. Typical implementations include surveys of employee or customer demographics, market research questionnaires, and the like.

- **Report forms** These are useful for soliciting and distributing routine bits of information. Typical implementations include status reports, travel expense reports, and time sheets.

POST FORMS

Typically, post forms are used for threaded conversations that may or may not be stored in moderated folders. Post forms permit participants in mailing lists or newsgroups to supply their comments, suggestions, and new postings through a simple form that is easy to complete and send. In other words, post forms permit the users to conduct and view online conversations quickly and easily. Any majordomo- or listserv-based mailing list is well-suited for a post form application. Chapter 6 includes a good example of post forms, and how they may be used with Outlook and Exchange.

Other specialized forms may sometimes be necessary in some organizations. In the section that follows, you'll learn how the Microsoft Office suite can be wedded with Outlook and Exchange to handle data associated with one or more Microsoft Office software components.

OFFICE 97 DOCUMENT FORMS

Office 97 Document forms are either posts or messages that are embedded using some Office 97 application, such as Excel, Word, Access, or PowerPoint. Using an Outlook 98 form as a wrapper for an Office 97 document combines the power of the application with an Outlook 98 form.

If, for example, you want to enhance the productivity of your outbound sales force, you could combine an Excel spreadsheet with an expense report form. This would not only simplify things for the sales staff, but would also assist the accounting department as well.

To combine the two technologies, you need to escalate the value of an Excel cell to a view that the spreadsheet can use with Outlook 98. This is known as property promotion. For example, if you have a value in Excel, known as Total, you could link it to a value called Total in an Outlook 98 field. Then, filling in the Excel spreadsheet automatically causes a message containing the expense report data to be transmitted to a list of designated recipients.

Other combinations might include status reports, to bring Word and Outlook forms together, or price lists, to bring Access and Outlook forms together. The relationship between Office components and Outlook forms is bidirectional, too, which means that incoming mail messages can update user's local documents just as changes to local documents can provoke outgoing mail messages to deliver the same information elsewhere.

By now, you should be aware that all Outlook input occurs through some form or another. For example the New Message input window that you use every day to send messages (File|New|Mail Message) is nothing more than a form. As it happens, all the major Outlook components use forms as well. In the next section, you'll learn more about these built-in forms and how they might be used in your own forms-based applications.

BUILT-IN FORMS

Outlook 98 offers considerable built-in functionality, including its Calendar, Contacts, Tasks, Journal, and Notes modules. When building forms-based applications you may elect to customize any of these module's basic forms or add additional forms and controls to their basic layouts and capabilities.

Please note, however, that the first page of any built-in form cannot be modified. This is because certain controls are only available on the first page. One case in point is the Taskpad in the Calendar display (lower right-hand corner of the default pane). In the default Day/Week/Month view, the Taskpad always sits on the first page of the Calendar and must remain in that position.

OUTLOOK STANDARD CONTROLS

Outlook provides a set of standard controls for custom form design, which are available through the Tools|Forms|Design A Form menu. These include a wide variety of customizable layout and formatting tools, and special Insert menu commands that permit files, items, and objects to be freely inserted and manipulated within the context of a screen form. Other special-purpose tools include a spelling checker, an extensible set of actions associated with the type of form in use, and even a customizable set of toolbars when manipulating form layout and content.

In addition, you may customize your form toolbox in Outlook at any time simply by adding ActiveX controls to your system. In the section that follows, you'll narrow your focus from forms in their entirety to the fields where data is solicited and displayed.

FIELDS

Fields act as containers for the values for the items that occupy a form. A quick look at the New Mail Message form in Outlook shows that the form displays four fields, only three of which are labeled:

- **To** This field is where the list of intended recipients for a message must be entered. It is necessary to identify at least one recipient for Outlook to send a message.

- **Cc** This field is where the list of carbon copy recipients may be entered. This is an optional field and no value is required.

- **Subject** This field is where a subject for a message may be entered. This is also an optional field.

- **Message Body** This field is unlabeled and consumes the bulk of the form's display area, and is where the body of a message may be entered or inserted. This, too, is an optional field.

Although numerous predefined fields are available for reuse on forms, especially those that are modified from existing Outlook forms (for example, the Name field in Contacts), you can create custom fields to suit your needs, like an SSN field to capture someone's social security number.

Forms may also contain data that users do not see on screen. The display and behavior of items in a form is set by its properties, which provides the topic of the section that follows.

PROPERTIES

The properties associated with a form, and with items on a form, determine what items a user sees when the form is displayed. All items have associated properties, which may be elicited by right-clicking the field associated with the item while using the Design A Form tool, then selecting Properties from the pop-up menu that appears.

You can change the value of a property when working in design mode on a form. You can change an item's properties either by using the Properties window as described in the preceding paragraph, or using the Advanced Properties section in the Form menu instead. In environments where Exchange is in use, you'll also need sufficient permissions before you may change property values.

The Properties window for a field includes three tabs: Display, Value, and Validation. The Display tab provides access to the properties related to the way a field or a caption appears on screen. The Value tab provides access to field designations, type, format, properties, and value information. It also includes an initialization tool, so you may opt to set some value for the field by default. It also provides a way to associate a formula to the value, if necessary. The Validation tab permits you to specify if a value must be supplied for the field, and also provides a mechanism to require and define a validation check on a field's input value, and even permits you to supply an error message if the validation check fails.

The Display tab properties are worth discussing in additional detail. The display properties associated with fields on a form cover a broad range of attributes that range from the caption associated with the field, to the position and size of the text that may appear within the field. Other values include the fonts in which the text appears, and foreground and background colors for that field. The Properties window also includes a collection of checkboxes for field-related settings as follows:

- **Visible** Controls whether or not the field appears in the on-screen display of the form.

- **Enabled** Controls whether or not the field is enabled (appears in normal colored text with normal colored backgrounds and accepts entry in active fields) or disabled (appears in grayed-out form, accepts no entry in any field).

- **Read only** Controls whether or not the field will accept input, or if values are for display only.

- **Resize with form** Causes the field to be resized if the form is resized on screen.

- **Sunken** Gives controls a 3D appearance.

- **Multiline** Enables input of multiple lines of text in a text box, where the user must hit the Enter key to start each new line.

By using and combining these various properties, you can reposition, reformat, and reset fields to your heart's content. In the section that follows, you'll learn how to extend the capabilities of a form beyond the built-in functions that the Design A Form tool provides inside Outlook.

EXTENDING FORM FUNCTIONALITY

If you are a developer, you can use the following options to customize Outlook even further than its built-in capabilities will allow:

- Outlook provides complete support for the Microsoft Exchange Client extensions interfaces. This means that developers can write C-based extensions to Outlook to perform actions in response to user activities in a form. Such extensions can respond to user requests to open Outlook items, to change item selections, or to specify menu commands or toolbar buttons.

- Outlook also includes a complete Object Linking and Embedding (OLE) Automation object model. Programmers who use Microsoft Visual Basic or Visual Basic for Applications (VBA) can access all Outlook data as objects. Programmers can create, modify, and delete Outlook items, folders, attachments, and so forth. The OLE Automation object model includes more than 30 objects that may be programmatically manipulated.

- As explained earlier in this chapter, Outlook has long enjoyed a special relationship with Microsoft's VBScript. Using Outlook 98, developers can define and use VBScript to respond when users complete actions. These extensions can open, close, send, or change properties for Outlook items. VBScript may be used to add new capabilities to custom forms. Here too, the complete Outlook object model is available to VBScript or Visual Basic programmers.

For those who do wish to write code, the capabilities of Outlook forms-based applications are limitless. But whether or not such extensions are included in an Outlook form, the tool of choice for building forms-based applications is the Outlook forms designer. This invaluable tool provides the subject for the section that follows.

OUTLOOK 98 FORMS DESIGNER

The Outlook 98 forms designer is a 32-bit development tool included with Outlook 98. To get to this tool, click Tools|Forms|Design A Form. The form designer in Outlook 98 supplies a huge selection of forms to help jump-start your custom form designs (see Figure 13.8).

When you edit a form in the forms designer, a special tear-off tool palette called the Field Chooser also appears on screen. The Field Chooser enables you to reuse any of your existing fields quickly by simply dragging and dropping where you want the field you select on the Field Chooser on the form. Figure 13.9 shows

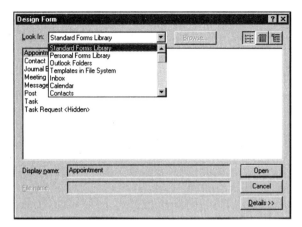

Figure 13.8   Outlook's Design Form provides several categories of forms from which you can draw for your custom work.

the Field Chooser dialog box along with instructions that tell you to drag and drop a field.

The Field Chooser drop-down menu at the top of the box is used to access fields by category. One of your choices is User-Defined Fields In Inbox. These are fields that you have created by selecting the New button at the bottom of the box. Figure 13.10 shows a new yes/no checkbox field named Call Completed?

ADDING CONTROLS TO FORMS

The forms designer also provides a toolbar for forms manipulation that's known as the toolbox. The toolbox is a nice collection of tools that appears above the

13

Figure 13.9   The Field Chooser displays fields already defined in Outlook 98.

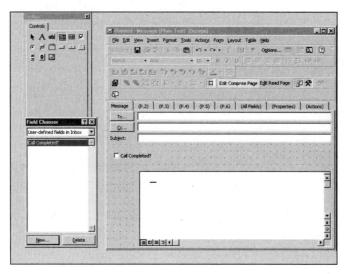

Figure 13.10   A customized form with a new field.

editable area of the form each time you launch the forms designer, and it is quite similar to the toolbars that appear in Outlook itself. You can use the toolbox to create professional forms without requiring any Visual Basic wizardry. But if you are one of those people who has dabbled in Visual Basic (or you know an MCSD), you can even add ActiveX controls to extend the capabilities of your toolbar beyond its built-in tools and controls.

By default, the following tools appear in the Outlook forms designer toolbox (covered in order, from left to right on the toolbar):

- **Publish Form** Makes a form available in a public or private folder once it's been designed and tested.

- **Bring To Front** Brings a graphic, text box, or other display element to the foreground when multiple elements overlap the same display area.

- **Send To Back** Pushes a graphic, text box, or other display element to the bottom of the stack of elements, when multiple elements overlap the same display area.

- **Group** Takes multiple display elements, items, and objects, and groups them as a single object. Permits multiple elements to be moved together to preserve their existing spacing and layout.

- **Ungroup** Takes a grouped element and restores its individual component parts. Use this when you need to edit, alter, or remove one component within a group object.

- **Align Left** Takes one or more selected elements and aligns them on the left boundary of the display area.

- **Align Center** Takes one or more selected elements and aligns them in the center of the display area.

- **Align Right** Takes one or more selected elements and aligns them on the right boundary of the display area.

- **Make Same Width** Takes two or more objects and resizes one or more of them to match the width of the object selected first for this tool.

- **Snap To Grid** Takes one or more selected objects and positions them to align with a background grid. Use this for improved spacing and precise object alignment.

- **Edit Compose Page** Permits editing of the form layout as it appears when it is active for input (in composition mode).

- **Edit Read Mode** Permits editing of the form layout as it appears when it is delivered for review (in read-only mode).

- **Field Chooser** Invokes the Field Chooser floating tool palette.

- **Control Toolbox** Invokes a collection of control elements for forms. The following elements may be quickly dragged and dropped onto a form from this toolbox (from left to right, top to bottom):

  - **Select Objects** Use this to permit objects to be selected on a form.

  - **Label** Use this to associate a label with a form item.

  - **TextBox** Use this to create a text box on a form.

  - **ComboBox** Use this to create a list display that includes column headings.

  - **ListBox** Use this to create a columnar listing of text elements.

  - **CheckBox** Use this to create a checkbox on a form.

  - **OptionButton** Use this to create a radio button on a form (select one or more buttons from two or more selections).

  - **ToggleButton** Use this to create a toggle button (select one button from two selections).

  - **Frame** Use this to draw a frame around a rectangular area on screen.

  - **CommandButton** Use this to drop a command button onto a form (for example a Close, OK, Cancel, or similar button).

  - **TabStrip** Use this to create a set of tabbed pages within a form.

  - **MultiPage** Use this to create a multipage form.

  - **ScrollBar** Use this to place a scroll bar next to a text box or other display area on a form.

13

- **SpinButton** Use this to place a pick list on a form.
- **Image** Use this to position, then insert an image into a form.
- **Properties** Use this to invoke the properties window for the selected field or item on a form.
- **View Code** Use this to view code associated with custom or built-in controls on a form.

This concludes your review of the forms designer. If you choose to take advantage of the kinds of capabilities that this tool can deliver to Outlook users in an Exchange environment, you will no doubt become much more familiar with it as you modify built-in forms and create your own custom forms.

CHAPTER SUMMARY

This chapter took a long, hard look at Outlook 98 forms. It explained how to create forms and how to use rules to make your forms perform automatic functions. In addition, this chapter described how to design and create custom forms that can help to reduce paperwork and streamline collaboration within your organization.

KEY TERMS

- **32-bit forms**—Forms that require a 32-bit operating system and operate with 32 bits of data at one time (as opposed to 16 bits). 32-bit forms are faster and have more features than 16-bit forms.
- **folders**—Used to store data in a logical grouping. Folders may sometimes be called subdirectories.
- **Hypertext Markup Language (HTML)**—The language used to create documents for the World Wide Web.
- **JavaScript (JScript)**—A script or running set of commands, similar to a batch file, but written for the Java language.
- **message queues**—A message equivalent to a freeway onramp. Messages sent are stored in a queue. Here, the message waits its turn to be acted upon. For example, when a message comes in to an Exchange Server, it is placed in a queue, where it is held until it can be handed off to the Information Store.
- **moderated folders**—A public folder (or listserv, Bulletin Board, and so on) that will not display messages sent by users until a reviewer chooses to accept the posting.
- **roles**—A predetermined set of permissions.

- **Transaction Server**—A Microsoft application that provides secure transaction processing as a service to other programs, and thereby eliminates a significant amount of program logic to ensure accurate delivery of data and proper completion of database updates.
- **view**—A template that allows a different way of seeing data from a collection of data. A view can be a summary of data, or it can show a subset of the data.
- **Visual Basic Script (VBScript)**—Similar to JavaScript or a DOS batch file, in that it runs a sequence of events or commands. In the case of VBScript, the command base is Visual Basic in nature.

REVIEW QUESTIONS

1. When Outlook 98 is used to produce an electronic form, what bit-level format is used by default?
   a. 64 bit
   b. 32 bit
   c. 16 bit
   d. 8 bit

2. Which two of the following terms best represent how collaboration may occur in an Exchange environment?
   a. Synchronously
   b. Interactively
   c. Telephonically
   d. Asynchronously

3. Outlook 98 can connect to outside databases using MTAs. True or False?

4. When creating a collaboration form, you can use which Outlook 98 built-in modules? (Choose all that apply.)
   a. Calendar module
   b. Tasks module
   c. Contacts module
   d. Journal module

5. Outlook 98 forms can be extended with which developer tools? (Choose all that apply.)
   a. VBScript
   b. JScript
   c. COBOL
   d. C++

13

6. When designing an application in Outlook 98, you selected a mission-critical application that cannot lose synchronization with the Widgets parts database. To make this possible, what else must you install on the server side?

   a. Message queues

   b. Global Address List

   c. Knowledge Consistency Checker

   d. Transaction Server

7. 32-bit forms are used on Windows 3.x, although they run slowly. You have determined that this is okay for use on a light-use station in an office. True or False?

8. When creating a rule set, two factors come into play. What are they?

   a. Moderators

   b. Wizards

   c. Conditions

   d. Action

9. A form must be created for collaboration. True or False?

10. When creating a form for collaboration, you can switch between development and testing, without the need to recompile the form. True or False?

11. Of the following, which represent steps toward planning the rollout of a custom collaboration form? (Choose all that apply.)

    a. Identify folder users and requirements

    b. Create or choose a folder design

    c. Construct folder icons

    d. Design folder views

12. Of the following choices, which two are parts of an Outlook rule?

    a. Conditions

    b. Choices

    c. Actions

    d. Decisions

13. When setting up a moderated public folder, you must create text for an auto-responder. True or False?

14. What is a field that is made up of several fields?

    a. Custom field

    b. Combination field

    c. Formula field

    d. None of the above

15. Combination fields cannot be grouped in a view. True or False?

16. When merging a collaboration form from a test bed to a live server, the two forms will merge. In which direction will properties flow?

   a. Properties flow from the source folder to the destination folder.

   b. Properties flow from the destination folder to the source folder.

   c. Properties flow from the parent container to the child container.

   d. Properties flow from the child container to the parent container.

17. Custom forms may be adapted from predefined forms in Outlook. True or False?

18. All text input in the Outlook environment occurs through one kind of form or another. True or False?

19. Which of the following are legitimate Outlook forms types? (Choose all that apply.)

   a. Reply forms

   b. Request forms

   c. Post forms

   d. Survey forms

20. Of the following rules, which one causes rule processing to stop as soon as it's encountered?

   a. Check messages when they arrive

   b. Move messages based on content

   c. Assign categories based on content

   d. Stop processing all following rules

13

HANDS-ON PROJECTS

 PROJECT 13.1

For this project, it is assumed that you have Windows NT installed and configured according to the requirements listed in Chapter 2. Furthermore, it is assumed that you have installed Exchange 5.5.

You want to create an instant collaboration application. You will do this by copying a personal folder to the public folder area and creating a new public folder:

1. Choose Start | Programs | Microsoft Outlook.

2. Select Connect To Server (the server to which you wish to connect).

3. Expand the listings in the folder display until you can see the public folders.

4. Create a folder titled TEST.

5. Click OK.

 PROJECT 13.2

Modify the permissions of the public folder you created in Project 13.1:

1. Scroll down (if required) to the folder titled TEST.

2. Right-click TEST.

3. Select Permissions (notice that the default permission is Author—anonymous users have no permissions).

4. In the Name box, verify that Default is selected, then, in the Roles list, click Publishing Editor.

5. Under Name, click Anonymous, then, in the Roles list, select Reviewer.

 PROJECT 13.3

Create and configure a public folder in Outlook:

1. In the left pane, expand Public Folders.

2. Select File|New|Folder, and name the folder. Verify that the folder contains mail items and the location. Click OK.

3. The dialog box asks if you want to add a shortcut to the Outlook Bar. Accept No, which is the default.

4. Verify that Outlook 98 displays the new folder with the name you selected.

 CASE PROJECTS

1. Explain how to create a form for ordering office supplies using Outlook 98. Explain why this form must be available in a public folder so that each department can order supplies. List the kinds of information the form should contain so that supplies can be properly delivered.

2. Explain how you might modify the While You Were Out form that is supplied with Outlook 98. What kinds of fields might you add to assist sorting by the nature of the call?

3. Design a form to replace a paper trouble ticket for your help desk. What fields does it need to accomplish its tasks? Explain how you might create a second view of this database to provide summary data for a help desk

supervisor, assuming that supervisors want to know how many trouble tickets are open, who's assigned to each open ticket, and how many open tickets are assigned to each help desk employee.

4. What are the differences between synchronous and asynchronous applications? Give some examples of each.

13

CHAPTER FOURTEEN

USING EXCHANGE WITH OTHER SYSTEMS

Microsoft Exchange Server is not the only electronic messaging platform in use in the world. Many organizations use other LAN-based email systems besides Exchange, such as Microsoft Mail, Novell GroupWise, Lotus cc:Mail, or Lotus Notes. Host-based systems, such as PROFS and SNADS, also remain widely deployed. In fact, the average large company has an average of five different email systems in place!

It is not realistic to convert an entire company to a new messaging platform all at once—and Microsoft Exchange is no exception. Therefore, a means of communicating with existing messaging systems is required—in the Exchange environment, these software components are called *connectors*. In this chapter, you will learn more about these software components—especially, how to install, configure, and use them.

AFTER READING THIS CHAPTER AND COMPLETING THE EXERCISES, YOU WILL BE ABLE TO:

- Explain the various messaging connectors that are available for use with Microsoft Exchange Server
- Understand how messages flow between Microsoft Exchange Server and other messaging systems
- Install and configure the most popular message connectors

CONNECTOR OVERVIEW

Through a core architecture software component known as a connector, Microsoft Exchange Server is able to communicate with, and transfer to and from, the most popular messaging systems. Once installed and configured properly, these connectors automatically transfer messages between Microsoft Exchange Server and other messaging platforms.

In addition, users of Microsoft Mail For PC Networks, Lotus cc:Mail, Novell GroupWise, Netscape Collabra, PROFS, SNADS, Digital All-in-1, Verimation MEMO, and Unix SendMail gain access to powerful migration utilities that make it easy to migrate users and mail to Microsoft Exchange Server. Migration issues are discussed in further detail in Chapter 15. In the sections that follow, you'll explore the various Exchange connectors, starting with Microsoft Mail for PC Networks.

MICROSOFT MAIL FOR PC NETWORKS CONNECTOR

Messages can be exchanged between Microsoft Exchange Server and one or more *Microsoft Mail (MS Mail) For PC Networks* systems using the *Microsoft Mail Connector*. The two messaging systems can be on the same local area network (LAN), an asynchronous (RAS) connection, or an X.25 connection. This flexibility provides organizations with the ability to seamlessly integrate Microsoft Exchange Server with just about any MS Mail environment. Once the Microsoft Mail Connector is installed and configured, not only can Microsoft Exchange Server and MS Mail messaging systems exchange messages, but they can also synchronize directories.

The Microsoft Mail Connector makes MS Mail 3.x Post Offices appear as Microsoft Exchange Server Post Offices to Microsoft Exchange Server, and it makes Microsoft Exchange Server Post Offices appear like MS Mail Post Offices to MS Mail.

The Microsoft Mail Connector runs as a Windows NT Server service, allowing administrators to monitor the connector using tools such as Performance Monitor and Event Viewer. The Microsoft Mail Connector is multithreaded, which enables higher capacity and quicker response times. The connector uses a polling scheme to exchange messages. This polling scheme can be modified by administrators, and supports flexible scheduling.

There can be more than one Microsoft Mail Connector at each site. However, each Microsoft Exchange Server computer in the site can only have one Mail Connector installed.

The Microsoft Mail Connector has three components that work together to transfer mail between MS Mail Post Offices and Microsoft Exchange Servers. The three components are:

- **Post Office** A temporary information store for inbound and outbound messages. It is also referred to as a gateway Post Office or shadow Post Office. The sole purpose of a Post Office is to transfer messages. So, even though it is referred to as a Post Office, it has no local mailboxes.

- **MTA** *(Message Transfer Agent)* Another Windows NT Server service that connects to and transfers mail between the *Microsoft Mail Connector Post Office* and one or more MS Mail Post Offices. It watches for messages deposited in the Microsoft Mail Connector Post Office (sent to MS Mail recipients from Microsoft Exchange Server users) and then copies the messages to the appropriate MS Mail Post Office. The MTA service must run on a Microsoft Exchange Server computer.

  The MTA serves a dual purpose. It delivers messages from MS Mail users to Microsoft Exchange Server recipients and places them in the Microsoft Mail Connector Post Office.

- **Interchange** A Windows NT Server service that routes and transfers messages between Microsoft Exchange Server and the Microsoft Mail Connector Post Office. When an outbound message is sent from a Microsoft Exchange Server user to an MS Mail recipient, the Microsoft Exchange Server MTA passes the message to *Microsoft Mail Connector Interchange*. Interchange then converts the message to MS Mail format and transfers the message to Microsoft Mail Connector Post Office.

  Interchange also scans the Microsoft Mail Connector Post Office for inbound messages from MS Mail users sent to Microsoft Exchange Server recipients. It transfers these messages to the Microsoft Exchange Server MTA, which then delivers the messages to the appropriate Microsoft Exchange Server recipients.

14

It is not uncommon to have more than one instance of the *Microsoft Mail Connector MTA* in use—in fact, one Microsoft Exchange Server can have up to 10 instances of the Microsoft Mail Connector running at once. Each instance is named and registered as a Windows NT service.

Microsoft recommends that a different instance of the MS Mail Connector be used to service each primary connection type, such as a LAN, asynchronous (RAS), or X.25. Also, MS Mail Post Offices should be grouped together based on the type of connection used. Create a separate instance of the Microsoft Mail Connector MTA to service each such group of Post Offices.

In the sections that follow, you'll learn more about the underpinnings and operation of the MS Mail Connector, and how messages move between Exchange and MS Mail. After that, you'll dig into MS Mail Connector's installation and configuration details.

UNDERSTANDING MESSAGE FLOW BETWEEN MS MAIL AND MICROSOFT EXCHANGE SERVER

When a message is sent to an MS Mail recipient, Microsoft Exchange Server submits the message to the Microsoft Exchange Server MTA. Then, the MTA transfers the message to the Microsoft Mail Connector Interchange. The Microsoft Mail Connector Interchange converts the message to MS Mail format, converts any attachments, and then places the message in the Microsoft Mail Connector Post Office. How a delivery message proceeds from there depends on the physical connection to the MS Mail system.

A message addressed to a mailbox in an MS Mail Post Office that exists on the same LAN connection is retrieved and delivered to the appropriate destination Post Office by the MS Mail Connector MTA.

The MTA component of the Microsoft Mail Connector combines the features of a gateway Post Office and the MS Mail External MTA program—including message delivery and distribution to recipients on MS Mail Post Offices located on the same LAN. It is, therefore, unnecessary to set up the MS Mail External MTA program on LAN-based MS Mail Post Offices.

A message addressed to a mailbox on an MS Mail Post Office over an asynchronous (RAS) or X.25 connection is processed and delivered by the *MS Mail External MTA program*. An instance of the MS Mail External MTA program must be set up at each remote Post Office. This is because the Microsoft Mail Connector MTA can only deliver and distribute a message to an MS Mail Post Office if it is on the same LAN connection.

The MS Mail External MTA program is usually only required for non-LAN environments. In LAN environments, its functionality is performed by the MTA component of the Microsoft Mail Connector. However, there might be situations when it would be wise to continue to use an existing MS Mail External MTA program to perform some of the functions provided by the MTA component of the Microsoft Mail Connector.

For example, when migrating from MS Mail, it might be easier to integrate the Microsoft Mail Connector into the MS Mail system using the existing MS Mail External MTA program. In addition, if there are remote clients within the MS Mail system, the MS Mail External MTA program must continue to be used. This is because all mail transfers between a remote client and an MS Mail Post Office are processed by the MS Mail External MTA program. This functionality cannot be performed by the Microsoft Mail Connector.

When a message that exists on the same LAN connection is addressed to a mailbox on an MS Mail Post Office, the message flow happens as follows:

1. The Exchange Server MTA passes mail to the Microsoft Mail Connector Interchange, which then transfers the mail to the Microsoft Mail Connector Post Office.

2. The Microsoft Mail Connector MTA picks up the mail in the Microsoft Mail Connector Post Office and copies it to the appropriate MS Mail Post Office. The message is now delivered.

When a message is addressed to an MS Mail Post Office over an asynchronous (RAS) or X.25 connection, the message flow happens as follows:

1. The Exchange Server MTA passes mail to the Microsoft Mail Connector Interchange, which then transfers the mail to the Microsoft Mail Connector Post Office.

2. The MS Mail External MTA program picks up the mail in the Microsoft Mail Connector Post Office and delivers it to the appropriate mailbox. The message is now delivered.

Now that you've examined message flow between the Microsoft Mail Connector and MS Mail, it's time to tackle how this connector is installed and configured. This provides the topic for the next section.

INSTALLING AND CONFIGURING THE MICROSOFT MAIL CONNECTOR

14

The Microsoft Mail Connector is installed by default when a Complete installation of Microsoft Exchange Server is performed. If a Custom installation is chosen, the connector is still installed, unless the Microsoft Exchange Server item is selected and the Microsoft Mail Connector is deselected. The Microsoft Mail Connector must be installed before it can be configured.

The Microsoft Mail Connector is configured using the Microsoft Exchange Administrator program. In the Administrator window, choose the site where the Microsoft Mail Connector is installed, choose the Connections container, then double-click the MS Mail Connector. To configure the connector to communicate with MS Mail Post Offices, follow these steps:

1. Configure the Microsoft Mail Connector Interchange.

2. Configure the Microsoft Mail Connector General tab.

3. Set up an MS Mail Post Office connection.

4. Create and configure a Microsoft Mail Connector MTA.

5. Verify Microsoft Mail Connector Post Office configuration.

6. Start the Microsoft Mail Connector MTA service.

7. Configure the MS Mail post office.

8. Test the connection.

Steps 1, 2, and 5 through 8 are the same for LAN, asynchronous (RAS), and X.25 connections. Steps 3 and 4 differ for each connection type. A detailed discussion of each of these steps follows.

Configure The Microsoft Mail Connector Interchange

To configure the Microsoft Mail Connector Interchange, select the Interchange tab on the MS Mail Connector Properties dialog box (shown in Figure 14.1). The Interchange tab must be configured before any other Microsoft Mail Connector tabs can be configured.

This is where the Connector Interchange is configured to move and translate information between Microsoft Exchange Server and the Microsoft Mail Connector. The following must be configured on the MS Mail Connector Properties page:

- **Administrator's Mailbox** Specifies the mailbox that receives delivery status messages. Click the Change button to select a mailbox.

Figure 14.1 The Interchange tab of the MS Mail Connector Properties dialog box.

Consider creating a Postmaster mailbox to receive these and other delivery status messages.

- **Primary Language For Clients** Assigns the primary language used by the majority of Post Offices. This is necessary for interoperability with MS Mail clients that use different languages.

- **Maximize MS Mail 3.x Compatibility** Determines whether MS Mail clients will receive OLE 2 embedded objects from Microsoft Exchange Server users. MS Mail 3.x only supports earlier versions of OLE. To enable such users to view saved or embedded objects sent from Microsoft Exchange Server users, select this option.

This option doubles the size of any OLE message, so select it with caution. If this option is not selected, MS Mail 3.x clients will not be able to view or save embedded objects sent from Microsoft Exchange Server users.

- **Enable Message Tracking** Tracks message movement. It can be applied when troubleshooting message flow through a connector. The progress of a message can be followed as it passes from the Microsoft Exchange Server Information Store to a directly connected MS Mail Post Office.

Configure The MS Mail Connector General Tab

To Configure the MS Mail Connector General tab, select the General tab in the MS Mail Connector Properties dialog box (shown in Figure 14.2).

This is where the basic properties for the Microsoft Mail Connector are defined. The values on this tab are optional. Limits for message size transfer between Microsoft Exchange Server and MS Mail Post Offices can be specified here. The only important settings are in the Message Size frame—the No Limit and Maximum (K) option buttons. If Maximum (K) is selected, the value entered is the maximum size (for both inbound and outbound messages) that can be passed through the connector. Setting a maximum message size can reduce the amount of mail traffic in the network. If the message size is exceeded, the message is returned to the sender in the form of a non-delivery report.

Set Up An MS Mail Post Office Connection

To set up an MS Mail Post Office connection, you must establish a connection to an MS Mail Post Office. To do this, you only need to know the network path to the Post Office directory. The Microsoft Mail Connector extracts the network

14

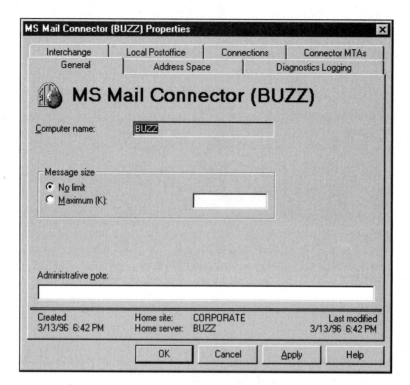

Figure 14.2   The General tab of the MS Mail Connector Properties dialog box.

and Post Office name from the Post Office. Select the Connections tab in the MS Mail Connector Properties dialog box (shown in Figure 14.3).

LAN connections to MS Mail Post Offices are created and viewed in the Connections tab. From that tab, it can optionally be specified whether the Microsoft Mail Connector will indirectly access any MS Mail Post Offices that a LAN-connected MS Mail Post Office exchanges mail with.

 If the MS Mail Post Office resides on a NetWare server, *Gateway Service For NetWare* must be running on the Microsoft Exchange Server.

To create a LAN connection to an MS Mail Post Office, follow these steps:

1. Click the Create button. This should bring up the Create Connection dialog box, shown in Figure 14.4.

2. In the Connection Parameters frame, select LAN. (If Async or X.25 is selected, other relevant connection information will need to be entered.)

3. Click the Change button to specify the MS Mail Post Office path.

Figure 14.3   The Connections tab of the MS Mail Connector Properties dialog box.

4. In the Path text box, type the full path to the server, using UNC format.

Use the uniform naming convention (UNC) format to refer to the Post Office, such as, *servername\sharename\path* for a Windows NT Server, and *servername\\volumnename\path* for a NetWare server.

5. In the Connect As text box, type the network logon name used when connecting to the MS Mail Post Office.

This is only needed if the MS Mail Post Office is in a non-trusted domain or if the Windows NT service account is not a valid user on the server where the Post Office resides.

6. In the Password text box, type the network logon name account password.

7. Click the OK button to return to the Create Connection dialog box.

8. Type a value (from 1 through 99) in the Connection Attempts text box to set the number of attempts to send mail before it is returned to the sender with a non-delivery report.

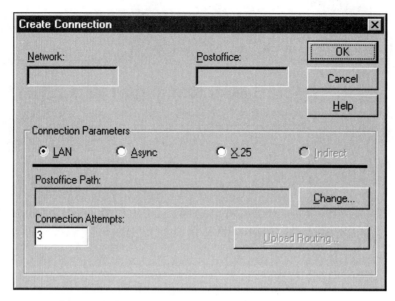

Figure 14.4   The Create Connection dialog box is where LAN connections to MS Mail are configured.

9. Click the Upload Routing button to display a list of any indirect Post Offices connected to the MS Mail Post Office.

Create And Configure A Microsoft Mail Connector MTA

You must create the Microsoft Mail Connector MTA before messages can be transferred between Microsoft Exchange Server and an MS Mail Post Office. The Connector MTAs tab is used to define and configure the Microsoft Mail Connector MTA. More than one Microsoft Mail Connector MTA can be established. Each Microsoft Mail Connector MTA is defined here and becomes a separate Windows NT Server service. Microsoft Mail Connector MTAs can be individually started or stopped using the Control Panel. Select the Connector MTAs tab on the MS Mail Connector Properties dialog box (shown in Figure 14.5).

If the MS Mail Post Office resides on a NetWare server, verify that Windows NT Server is running Gateway Service For NetWare before you create and configure the Microsoft Mail Connector MTA.

To create a Microsoft Mail Connector MTA, follow these steps:

1. Click the New button. This should bring up the New MTA Service dialog box, shown in Figure 14.6.

2. Type in a name for the service. This is the name that will show up in the list of services in the Control Panel.

Figure 14.5   The Connector MTAs tab of the MS Mail Connector Properties dialog box.

3. In the Logging frame, select Log Messages Sent At Services Postoffices to maintain a log of all messages delivered to MS Mail Post Offices. The resulting log file is stored in the \LOG directory of the MS Mail Connector Post Office.

4. In the Logging frame, select Log Messages Received At Serviced Post Offices, to maintain a log of all messages received from MS Mail Post Offices. The resulting log file is stored in the \LOG directory of the connector Post Office.

5. In the Polling Frequency frame's Update Configuration Every text box, specify how often (from 0 through 999 minutes) the Microsoft Mail Connector MTA should check both the connector Post Office and the MS Mail Post Office for updated user and network information.

6. In the Polling Frequency frame's Check For Mail Every text box, specify how often (from 0 through 999 minutes) the Microsoft Mail Connector MTA should check both the MS Mail Connector Post Office and the MS Mail Post Office for mail.

7. In the Connection Parameters frame, select the appropriate connection type.

14

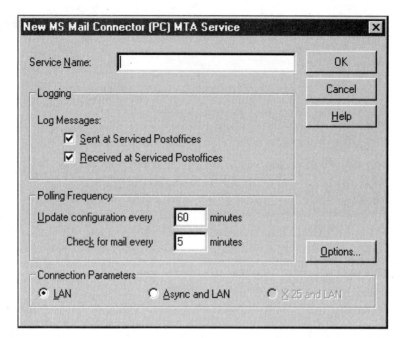

Figure 14.6   The New MTA Service dialog box is where you can create new instances of the MS Mail Connector MTA.

 If Async And LAN or X.25 And LAN is selected for the connection type, additional, relevant connection information will need to be entered.

8. Click the OK button to return to the MS Mail Connector dialog box.

After creating a Microsoft Mail Connector MTA service, additional options can be configured. Options for controlling how the Connector MTA will handle special MS Mail Post Office features—such as Mail Dispatch and *NetBIOS* notification—can be enabled. Also, the Microsoft Mail Connector MTA service can be set to start with system startup or to be started manually.

To access Microsoft Mail Connector MTA options (shown in Figure 14.7):

1. Select the appropriate Microsoft Mail Connector MTA service.

2. Click the Configure button, which brings up the MTA Service dialog box.

3. Click the Options button, which brings up the MTA Options dialog box.

The following can be configured in the MS Mail Connector MTA Options dialog box:

- **Maximum Message Size** Select either No Limit or Size (KB). If Size (KB) is selected, enter the maximum size limit (from 0 through 999999K) for messages delivered (in both directions) through the Microsoft Mail Connector MTA to the Post Offices it serves.

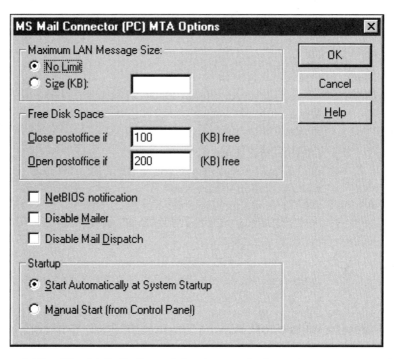

Figure 14.7   The MTA Options dialog box controls maximum message sizes, disk space allocations, and more.

- **Close Postoffice If** Enter the minimum amount of disk space (in kilobytes) that needs to be available on the destination Post Offices that the Microsoft Mail Connector MTA serves before those Post Offices become unavailable. If the amount of free disk space drops below this value, the Microsoft Mail Connector MTA will mark the offending Post Office as unavailable. (If a Post Office becomes unavailable, other available Post Offices served by the Microsoft Mail Connector MTA will not be affected.)

- **Open Postoffice If** Enter the minimum amount of disk space (in kilobytes) that needs to be available on the destination Post Offices that the Microsoft Mail Connector MTA serves before those Post Offices become available again. If the amount of free disk space rises above this value, the Microsoft Mail Connector MTA will mark the offending Post Office as available once again. (If a Post Office becomes available, other unavailable Post Offices served by the Microsoft Mail Connector MTA will not be affected.)

- **NetBIOS Notification** Select this to notify MS Mail users about new mail immediately, using NetBIOS. For notification to occur, both the client computer and the server running the Microsoft Mail

14

Connector MTA must be running the NetBIOS Interface network service. (Only users on the same LAN are notified in this way.)

- **Disable Mailer** Select this to prevent this instance of the Microsoft Mail Connector MTA from distributing messages to users on LAN-connected MS Mail Post Offices it serves. (This does not prevent other Microsoft Mail Connector MTA instances from distributing messages to Post Offices they serve.)

- **Disable Mail Dispatch** Select this to prevent the instance of the Microsoft Mail Connector MTA from delivering directory synchronization messages to LAN-connected Post Offices it serves. (This does not prevent other Microsoft Mail Connector MTA instances from delivering messages to Post Offices they serve.)

- **Start Automatically At System Startup** Select this to make the instance of the Microsoft Mail Connector MTA service start with system services startup. Select Manual Start (from the Control Panel) if the service is to be started manually.

Verify Microsoft Mail Connector Post Office Configuration

The Verify Microsoft Mail Connector Post Office configuration step begins after the Microsoft Mail Connector MTA is set up. You must view (and optionally, change) the Microsoft Mail Connector Post Office (also known as the shadow Post Office). Select the Local Postoffice tab on the MS Mail Connector Properties dialog box, as shown in Figure 14.8.

The information displayed here is needed to configure the real MS Mail Post Offices so they will be able to access the shadow Post Office. This information is used later in the installation process, so you might want to write it down.

Once the service is configured, the next step is to start it and set its runtime characteristics. This is the topic for the section that follows.

Start The Microsoft Mail Connector MTA Service

One of the last steps in configuring the Microsoft Mail Connector is to start the MTA service created earlier. Launch the Services applet from the Control Panel. Scroll down the list to find the new Microsoft Mail Connector MTA service that was created. Change the startup mode to Automatic. Click the Start button to start the service. Also, verify that the MS Mail Connector Interchange service is running.

Once the service is started, you can proceed to configure the MS Mail Post Office on the other side of the connection. This is covered in the section that follows.

Figure 14.8   The Local Postoffice tab of the MS Mail Connector Properties dialog box.

Configure The MS Mail Post Office

Finally, each MS Mail Post Office that was identified in the Microsoft Mail Connector must be configured to access the shadow Post Office. For each MS Mail Post Office, the MS Mail DOS Administrator program is used to create an external Post Office listing for the Microsoft Exchange Server to be communicated with. Use the External|Admin menu option, and create a new entry. You can refer to the notes you took earlier, if you followed our recommendations, to supply the correct Microsoft Mail Connector Post Office address and the network name for the Microsoft Mail Connector from the Local Post Office tab in the Microsoft Mail Connector.

Start the Microsoft Mail Connector MTA service. All that's left now is to test the configuration.

Test The Connection

Send a message from the Exchange Server side to the MS Mail side. Then, send a new message the other way. Until directory synchronization is established, all recipient names must be entered manually—the necessary Exchange address lists will not be populated yet. The following list explains the necessary details:

- **To type in a recipient name manually and send a message from the Exchange or Outlook client** Compose a new message, click the To button, click the New button, select Microsoft Mail Address, then click OK. Fill in the appropriate information, click OK, compose the message, and send it.

- **To type in a recipient name manually and send a message from the MS Mail DOS client** Compose a new message, select the To field, and press Enter, displaying the Postoffice Address List. Press the left arrow key to display the list of available address lists, select the Postoffice Network List, and press Enter. From the network list, select the name of the Microsoft Mail Connector Post Office network, and press Enter. Lastly, type in the name of an Exchange Server mailbox. Proceed to compose the message and send it.

- **To type in a recipient name manually and send a message from the MS Mail Windows client** Compose a new message, choose Address, click the New Address icon, select Custom Address, type the email name and address, then send the message.

If everything has been set up properly, messages should be exchanged between the two mail systems. If the message exchange fails, go back and verify that all of the previous steps have been followed.

MANAGING DIRECTORY SYNCHRONIZATION WITH MS MAIL

If you're using another messaging system in addition to Microsoft Exchange Server, you'll need to maintain another directory. Microsoft Exchange Server uses directory synchronization to maintain address information with other messaging systems. *Directory synchronization* (also known as *DirSync*) is the process of exchanging address information between a Microsoft Exchange Server organization and any other messaging system that uses the MS Mail directory synchronization protocol. The directory synchronization process uses system messages to send address change updates between the messaging systems.

It's helpful to discuss how MS Mail implements directory synchronization, because Microsoft Exchange Server supports a similar implementation. The MS Mail directory synchronization protocol automatically synchronizes the directories on all Post Offices in an MS Mail system—whether the Post Offices that reside on the same LAN are connected asynchronously (RAS) or connected by a gateway. A change or update to an address on one Post Office is automatically sent to other Post Offices in the MS Mail system.

There are two components in the MS Mail directory synchronization protocol:

- **Directory server Post Office** Maintains a central database of directory changes. There can be only one *directory server Post Office*.

- **Directory requestor Post Office** Submits directory changes to the directory server Post Office, and requests directory updates that other *directory requestor Post Offices* have submitted. The directory synchronization agent handles this activity.

Each Post Office in an MS Mail system is either a directory server Post Office or a directory requestor Post Office. One computer in the MS Mail system must be designated as the directory server Post Office. The directory server Post Office records all address updates received from the directory requestor Post Offices.

Directory updates occur at scheduled times. This schedule can be modified as needed. At the scheduled time, the directory requestor Post Office's directory synchronization agent sends any updates to the directory server Post Office. The directory server Post Office combines these changes and, in turn, sends the updates to each requestor Post Office. The MS Mail *DISPATCH.EXE* program processes the updates into the requestor Post Office's address lists.

Microsoft Exchange Server uses a similar but enhanced implementation of the MS Mail directory synchronization protocol. Similar to MS Mail, a Microsoft Exchange Server can be designated as either a directory synchronization requestor or a directory synchronization server. When an MS Mail system is already in place (with one of the Post Offices designated as a directory server), the Microsoft Exchange Server is usually set up as a directory synchronization requestor. Directory synchronization roles are set up using the Microsoft Exchange Server Administrator program.

A Microsoft Exchange Server directory synchronization requestor works just like an MS Mail directory synchronization requestor: Address updates are sent from the directory synchronization requestor to the MS Mail directory server. Then, the MS Mail directory server integrates these changes into its own Global Address List (GAL) and sends recent changes to the Microsoft Exchange Server directory synchronization requestor, which integrates the changes into its own GAL.

14

Alternately, a Microsoft Exchange Server can be set up to be the directory synchronization server instead. In this case, all MS Mail Post Offices need to be set up to be directory synchronization requestors. In addition, each of these MS Mail Post Offices needs to be defined as a remote directory synchronization requestor in the Microsoft Exchange Server Administrator.

Directory synchronization between different Microsoft Exchange Servers is handled via directory replication, not the directory synchronization method described here. In addition, if a Microsoft Exchange Server has been set up as a directory synchronization server, a directory synchronization requestor (remote or otherwise) is not needed. The directory synchronization server handles requestor functions inherently.

Configuring Directory Synchronization With MS Mail

As mentioned earlier, a Microsoft Exchange Server can be set up as either a directory synchronization requestor or a directory synchronization server. Figure 14.9 shows where you create a new directory synchronization requestor.

To install and configure a directory synchronization requestor, choose the Connections container in the Microsoft Exchange Administrator. From the File menu, choose New Other, then choose DirSync Requestor. Select the directory synchronization server from the list of MS Mail Post Offices. In the Microsoft Exchange Administrator again, choose the Connections container and double-click the DirSync requestor. A dialog box with five tabs will be displayed. They are as follows:

- **General** The General tab, shown in Figure 14.9, is where the basic properties for the directory synchronization requestor are set. A display name can be specified, as well as the different address types that should be exchanged during directory synchronization. A DirSync server mailbox can be specified to send and receive system

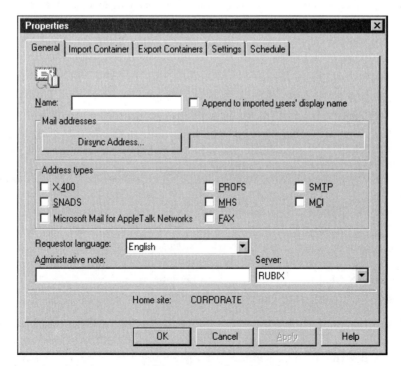

Figure 14.9   Creating a new directory synchronization requestor.

messages. Consider creating a Postmaster mailbox to receive these and other delivery status messages.

- **Import Container** The Import Container tab, shown in Figure 14.10, is where the import container (used to store imported addresses sent from the MS Mail directory server) is specified. A trust level can be assigned to objects being imported. This is an optional field. If no container is specified, addresses will be placed in the GAL. (MS Mail [and other messaging systems] does not have directory objects, nor does it use trust levels. Imported recipient addresses are created with the trust level specified in the import container's trust level value.)

- **Export Container** The Export Containers tab, shown in Figure 14.11, is where the Microsoft Exchange Server recipient containers that should be exported to the MS Mail directory server are specified. By default, the Microsoft Exchange Server directory exchange requestor does not export any recipient containers. A trust level can be specified so that only certain recipients are exported.

- **Settings** The Settings tab, shown in Figure 14.12, provides a means to enter a DirSync password (which must be the same as the DirSync server password). It also provides a means to specify whether

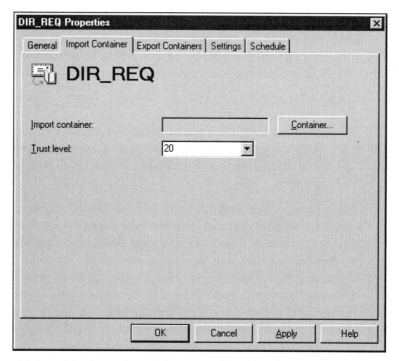

Figure 14.10   The Import Container tab of the New Directory Synchronization Requestor Properties dialog box.

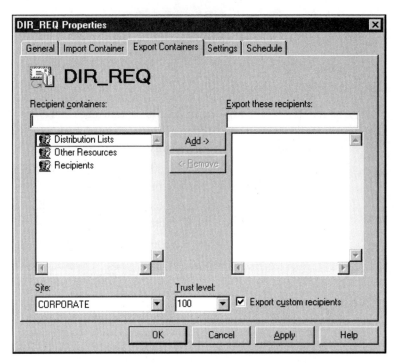

Figure 14.11   The Export Containers tab of the New Directory
Synchronization Requestor Properties dialog box.

the Microsoft Exchange Server DirSync requestor will send and receive
address and template updates.

- **Schedule** The Schedule tab, shown in Figure 14.13, is used to set the
  DirSync requestor schedule so that it coincides with the update
  schedule on the MS Mail directory server. An MS Mail directory server
  only processes directory updates once a day. Updates should be
  scheduled so they are sent to the DirSync server before it processes
  updates.

Configuring the Microsoft Exchange Server DirSync requestor is only half the
battle. The MS Mail directory synchronization server must also be configured so
that it recognizes the Microsoft Exchange Server as a directory requestor. Use
the MS Mail Administrator program to register the Microsoft Exchange Server
DirSync requestor. The Microsoft Mail Connector Post Office network, the Post
Office, and the password will all need to be entered. These can be viewed in the
Microsoft Mail Connector Local Post Office tab. The last step to be performed is
to start the directory synchronization service on the Microsoft Exchange Server
that is serving as the DirSync requestor.

To install and configure a directory synchronization server, choose the
Connections container in the Microsoft Exchange Administrator. From the File

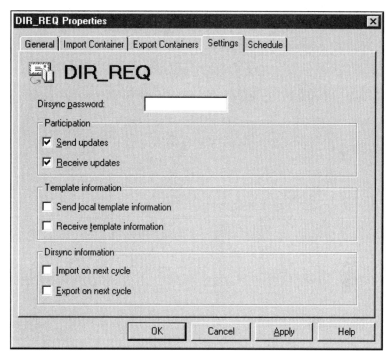

Figure 14.12 The Settings tab of the New Directory Synchronization Requestor Properties dialog box.

menu, choose New Other, then choose DirSync Server. In the Microsoft Exchange Administrator, again choose the Connections container and double-click the DirSync server. A dialog box with the following two tabs should appear:

- **General** The General tab, shown in Figure 14.14, is where the basic directory synchronization server properties are set. A display name as well as a DirSync administrator mailbox to receive copies of incoming and outgoing DirSync system messages can be specified. Consider creating a Postmaster mailbox to receive these and other delivery status messages.

- **Schedule** The Schedule tab, shown in Figure 14.15, is used to specify the time when the Microsoft Exchange Server DirSync server should send master address updates to MS Mail remote DirSync requestors.

Next, you must install and configure a remote directory synchronization requestor. If a Microsoft Exchange Server is set up as a DirSync server, each MS Mail Post Office must be defined as a remote DirSync requestor. In the Microsoft Exchange Administrator, choose the Connections container. From the File menu, choose New Other, then choose *Remote DirSync Requestor*. Select

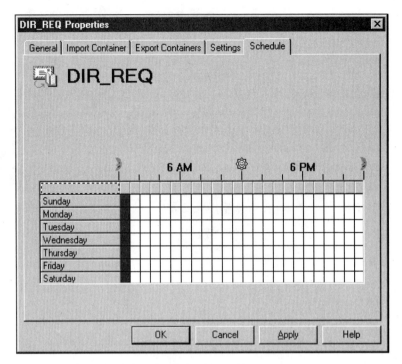

Figure 14.13   The Schedule tab of the New Directory
Synchronization Requestor Properties dialog box.

the directory synchronization requestor from the list of MS Mail Post Offices. In
the Microsoft Exchange Administrator, again choose the Connections container
and double-click the remote DirSync requestor. A dialog box with the following
four tabs should display:

- **General** This is where the primary remote directory synchronization
  requestor properties are set (as shown in Figure 14.16). The following
  can be specified: a display name, a DirSync requestor mailbox (for
  sending and receiving system messages), a password for the remote
  directory requestor, and the requestor address type (*MS* for an MS Mail
  Post Office).

- **Permissions** The Permissions tab is where permissions for the remote
  DirSync requestor object are assigned. Explicit permissions to a user
  (a directory synchronization administrator, for example) for the DirSync
  requestor object can be assigned. For example, a user could be assigned
  Administrator permissions for a remote DirSync requestor object but
  not assigned User permissions for the configuration container. The user
  will have permissions to the remote DirSync requestor only.

- **Import Container** The Import Container tab, shown in
  Figure 14.17, is where the import container (used to store imported

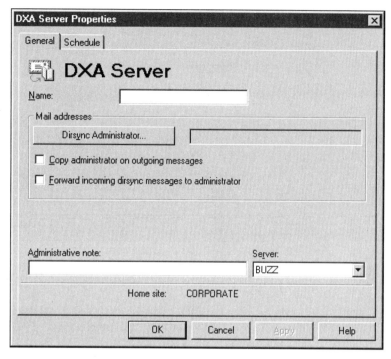

Figure 14.14   The General tab of the New Directory Synchronization Server Properties dialog box.

addresses sent from the MS Mail directory requestor) is specified. A trust level can also be assigned to objects being imported. (MS Mail and other messaging systems do not have directory objects, nor do they use trust levels. Imported recipient addresses are created with the trust level specified in the import container's trust level value.)

- **Export Container** The Export Containers tab, shown in Figure 14.18, is where the Microsoft Exchange Server recipient containers are specified that will be exported to MS Mail directory requestors. By default, the Microsoft Exchange Server directory exchange server does not export any recipient containers. A trust level can be assigned so that only certain recipients are exported.

After installing one or more Microsoft Exchange Server remote directory synchronization requestor Post Offices on the directory synchronization server, the MS Mail directory synchronization requestor Post Office(s) must be configured. Using the MS Mail Administrator program, follow the same process for setting up a directory synchronization requestor as for an MS Mail directory synchronization server.

14

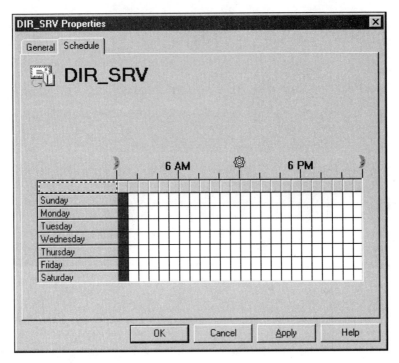

Figure 14.15   The Schedule tab of the New Directory Synchronization Server Properties dialog box.

MICROSOFT SCHEDULE+ FREE/BUSY CONNECTOR

An extension of the Microsoft Mail Connector, the Microsoft Schedule+ *Free/Busy Connector,* lets MS Mail Post Offices and Microsoft Exchange Servers share *Microsoft Schedule+* information. Microsoft Schedule+ is a messaging program that lets users access other users' schedules and reserve meeting times with those users. The program also serves as a tool to manage personal contact information.

Microsoft has replaced most of the functionality of Microsoft Schedule+ with the Microsoft Outlook client. Although the native Microsoft Outlook client stores scheduling data in a different format than Microsoft Schedule+, Microsoft Outlook can be configured to be compatible with Microsoft Schedule+.

Microsoft Schedule+ is compatible with both MS Mail Post Offices and Microsoft Exchange Server, storing scheduling data in hidden folders on both messaging systems. If a company uses both types of messaging systems, scheduling data will need to be shared between those messaging systems—hence the existence of the Microsoft Schedule+ Free/Busy Connector.

The Microsoft Schedule+ Free/Busy Connector is installed when the Microsoft Mail Connector is installed. The Microsoft Schedule+ Free/Busy Connector is only necessary when a working connection to MS Mail Post Offices is required. It is not required for Microsoft Schedule+ if no MS Mail Post Offices are present.

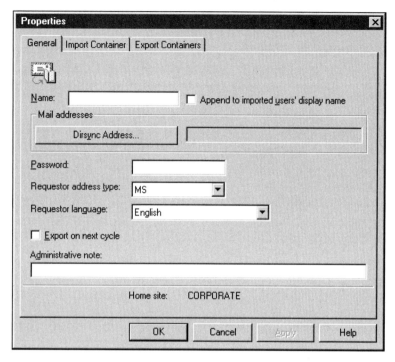

Figure 14.16   The General tab of the New Remote Directory
Synchronization Requestor Properties dialog box.

Configuring The Microsoft Schedule+ Free/Busy Connector

After installing the Microsoft Mail Connector, configuring the Microsoft
Schedule+ Free/Busy Connector to share schedule data between MS Mail and
Microsoft Exchange Server recipients involves the following five steps:

1. Create an *AdminSch* account on all Post Offices that will participate in
   sharing Microsoft Schedule+ data.

   MS Mail and Microsoft Exchange Server use the AdminSch account
   to share Microsoft Schedule+ data. Therefore, every MS Mail Post
   Office and Microsoft Exchange Server that needs to share Microsoft
   Schedule+ data must have an AdminSch account defined. As part of
   the Microsoft Schedule+ Free/Busy Connector installation process,
   an AdminSch account is automatically created on the Microsoft
   Exchange Server computer. Verify that this account exists on all
   applicable MS Mail Post Offices. Once this has been done, run
   directory synchronization between the Microsoft Exchange Server
   and the MS Mail Post Offices to distribute all AdminSch accounts
   across the systems.

14

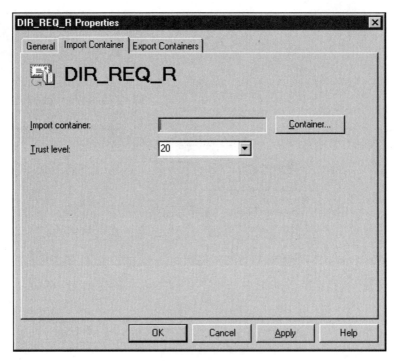

Figure 14.17 The Import Container tab of the New Directory Synchronization Requestor Properties dialog box.

2. Install the Microsoft Schedule+ program files on at least one MS Mail Post Office server, if necessary.

Regardless of Microsoft Exchange Server, if multiple MS Mail Post Offices are in use and Microsoft Schedule+ users need to share schedule data with other MS Mail Post Offices, the Microsoft Schedule+ program files must be installed on at least one of the MS Mail Post Office servers. If there is only one MS Mail Post Office, the program files need not be installed on the Post Office server.

3. Install and configure the Microsoft Schedule+ Administrator program.

After the Administrator program is installed, use it to configure the Microsoft Schedule+ system, specifying schedule storage duration and network schedule-sharing information. The Microsoft Schedule+ Administrator program must be run from a Windows-based computer that is connected to the MS Mail Post Office that contains the Microsoft Schedule+ program files.

4. Configure schedule data distribution.

The MS Mail SCHDIST.EXE program performs the actual schedule data distribution. The program sends users' free and busy times and resources between MS Mail Post Offices and Microsoft Exchange

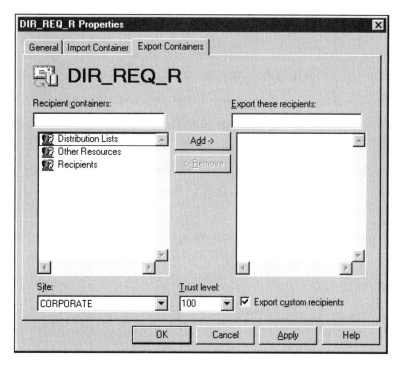

Figure 14.18   The Export Containers tab of the New Directory
Synchronization Requestor Properties dialog box.

Servers. There are a few options in the program that need to be
configured before it will distribute schedule data properly. (See the
MS Mail documentation for more details.)

When the Microsoft Schedule+ Free/Busy Connector is installed,
Microsoft Exchange Server creates an object with the display name
Microsoft Schedule+ Free/Busy Connector (server name). The object
is stored in the Recipients container with an alias name of AdminSch.
Microsoft Schedule+ Free/Busy Connector configuration settings are
changed from this object.

5. Configure the Microsoft Schedule+ Free/Busy Connector.

In the Microsoft Exchange Administrator, choose the site where the
Microsoft Mail Connector is installed, click the Recipients container,
then double-click the Microsoft Schedule+ Free/Busy Connector
(server name). A dialog box with two tabs should display (as shown in
Figure 14.19).

The Schedule+ Free/Busy Connector Options tab is where Microsoft
Exchange Server is configured to exchange Microsoft Schedule+ free

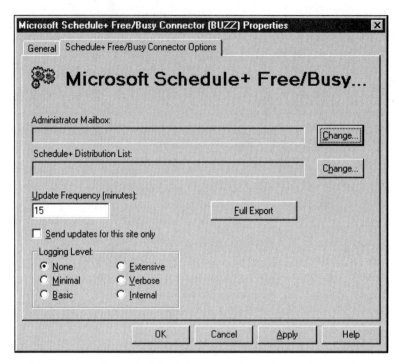

Figure 14.19 The Microsoft Schedule+ Free/Busy Connector Options tab helps coordinate the Exchange Calendar with Schedule+.

and busy information between Microsoft Exchange Server sites and MS Mail Post Offices. The following are found on this tab:

- **Administrator Mailbox** Any mail addressed to the Microsoft Schedule+ Free/Busy Connector that cannot be processed is forwarded to this mailbox. Click the Change button to select a mailbox. This is a required field. Consider creating a Postmaster mailbox to receive these and other delivery-status messages.

- **Schedule+ Distribution List** This is a distribution list containing AdminSch accounts from all the MS Mail Post Offices that share free and busy information with the Microsoft Exchange Server site. Click the Change button to select a distribution list. This is a required field.

- **Full Export** Click this button to export free and busy information for all Microsoft Schedule+ users to Post Offices in the Schedule+ Distribution List. This is necessary when new members have been added to the Schedule+ Distribution List.

- **Update Frequency (Minutes)** Enter a value specifying how often the Microsoft Schedule+ Free/Busy Connector sends free and busy information to MS Mail Post Offices in the Schedule+ Distribution List.

(This value should be equal to the polling interval for the SCHDIST.EXE program in the MS Mail system. Otherwise, the SCHDIST.EXE program might receive new Microsoft Schedule+ updates before it has finished processing older updates.)

- **Send Updates For This Site Only** Select this option if there is more than one Microsoft Schedule+ Free/Busy Connector in the organization and you want to control the sharing of free and busy information. This permits Microsoft Exchange Server sites and MS Mail Post Offices on the Schedule+ Distribution List to exchange Free/Busy information.

- **Logging Level** If problems are being encountered with the Microsoft Schedule+ Free/Busy Connector, specify the logging of events in the Windows NT Server Event Log. Set the logging level appropriate to the problem.

The General tab, shown in Figure 14.20, is where the Microsoft Schedule+ Free/Busy Connector's display name and alias name are specified.

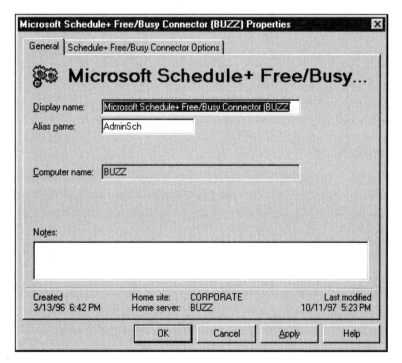

Figure 14.20 The General tab of the Microsoft Schedule+ Free/Busy Connector handles display and alias names, among other attributes.

The following are found on the General tab:

- **Display Name**   This is the name that appears in the Administrator window and in the Address Book. This is a required field.

- **Alias Name**   This is the alias for the Microsoft Schedule+ Free/Busy Connector object. The name must be AdminSch. This is a required field.

 Do not change the Alias Name field! Changes will cause the information flow to stop.

- **Notes**   This is used for recording any information that pertains to the object; however, it is only visible in the Administrator program.

After the previous steps have been performed, Microsoft Schedule+ users should be able to access the schedules of other users—no matter which messaging system (MS Mail or Microsoft Exchange Server) those users' mailboxes are on.

At long last, you've completed the materials on the Microsoft Mail Connector and its many capabilities. You'll shift gears to Lotus cc:Mail in the section that follows.

MICROSOFT EXCHANGE CONNECTOR FOR LOTUS CC:MAIL

Messaging connectivity between Microsoft Exchange Server and *Lotus cc:Mail* is handled by the *Microsoft Exchange Connector For Lotus cc:Mail.* The following two software version combinations of Lotus cc:Mail are supported:

- Lotus cc:Mail Post Office Database version 6 and cc:Mail Import version 5.15 and Export version 5.14

- Lotus cc:Mail Post Office Database version 8 and cc:Mail Import/ Export version 6

Depending on the messaging environment, one or more Lotus cc:Mail connectors can be used to transfer messages and synchronize directories. Each Microsoft Exchange Server can run one instance of the Lotus cc:Mail connector, and the connector can directly service one cc:Mail Post Office. The two messaging systems must be on the same LAN. Like the Microsoft Mail Connector For MS Mail, once the Lotus cc:Mail connector is installed and configured, the Microsoft Exchange Server and Lotus cc:Mail messaging systems will automatically transfer messages and synchronize directories. (Although a Lotus cc:Mail connector can service only one cc:Mail Post Office, other Microsoft Exchange Servers operating separate connector instances can be used to service additional cc:Mail Post Offices.)

The Microsoft Exchange Connector For Lotus cc:Mail runs as a Windows NT Server service. The connector has three components that work together to enable a Lotus cc:Mail Post Office and a Microsoft Exchange Server to communicate. The three components are:

- **Connector For Lotus cc:Mail Service** A Windows NT Server service that performs the actual transferring of messages between Microsoft Exchange Server and Lotus cc:Mail Post Offices. In addition, it also synchronizes a Microsoft Exchange Server GAL with the Lotus cc:Mail directory.

- **Connector For Lotus cc:Mail Store** A group of directories on the Microsoft Exchange Server, used for messages in transit.

- **Lotus cc:Mail Import/Export Programs** Programs used to import Microsoft Exchange Server messages and directory entries into Lotus cc:Mail Post Offices, and to export Lotus cc:Mail messages and directory entries into a Microsoft Exchange Server. The import and export programs come with Lotus cc:Mail. Access to a licensed copy of these programs is required for every Microsoft Exchange Server computer with a Lotus cc:Mail connector installed. Licensed copies of the programs should be copied to a directory in the Microsoft Exchange Server's system path.

Now that you've had the overview, it's time to dive into the details. Starting with an analysis of message flow between Exchange and cc:Mail.

UNDERSTANDING MESSAGE FLOW BETWEEN CC:MAIL AND MICROSOFT EXCHANGE SERVER

14

When a message is sent to a Lotus cc:Mail recipient, Microsoft Exchange Server submits the message to the Microsoft Exchange Server MTA. The MTA then transfers the message to the Connector For cc:Mail Service. The connector proceeds to convert the message to ASCII format, converts any attachments, and finally places the message in the Connector For cc:Mail Store. The Lotus cc:Mail Import program then attempts to deliver the message, and produces a non-delivery report to the sender if the message cannot be delivered.

Sending a message to a Microsoft Exchange Server recipient is similar. The Connector For cc:Mail Service calls the Lotus cc:Mail Export program to export messages to the Connector For cc:Mail Store. The Connector For cc:Mail Service then retrieves the message and passes it on to the Microsoft Exchange Server Information Store.

With message flow explained, you can now tackle installation and configuration issues. These are covered in the following section.

INSTALLING AND CONFIGURING THE MICROSOFT EXCHANGE CONNECTOR FOR LOTUS CC:MAIL

The Microsoft Exchange Connector For Lotus cc:Mail is installed by default when a Complete installation of Microsoft Exchange Server is performed. If a Custom installation is chosen, the connector will still be installed unless the Microsoft Exchange Server item is selected and the Microsoft Exchange Connector For Lotus cc:Mail is deselected. The connector must be installed before it can be configured.

The Microsoft Exchange Server Administrator program is used to configure the Lotus cc:Mail connector. In the Administrator window, choose the site where the Lotus cc:Mail connector is installed, choose the Connections container, and then double-click Connector For cc:Mail. To configure the connector to communicate with cc:Mail Post Offices, follow these steps:

1. Verify that the Import and Export programs are in the system path.

   If they are not already present in the system path, copy *IMPORT.EXE* and *EXPORT.EXE* from the cc:Mail Administrator's directory (\Lotus\CCAdmin, by default) to the \WinNT\System32 directory of the Microsoft Exchange Server where the connector is installed. If using cc:Mail Database version 8 with Import/Export version 6, the file IE.RI must also be present in the system path. If necessary, copy IE.RI from the cc:Mail data directory (\Lotus\CCData, by default) to the \WinNT\System32 directory. To determine the version of Import/Export programs' version numbers, type the program name followed by a **/?** at the MS-DOS prompt (Start|Programs|Command Prompt).

2. Configure the connector's Post Office tab.

   Select the Post Office tab in the Connector For Lotus cc:Mail Properties dialog box. The Post Office tab (shown in Figure 14.21) must be configured before any other Lotus cc:Mail connector tabs can be configured.

   This is where the connector is configured to move and translate information between Microsoft Exchange Server and the Lotus cc:Mail connector. The following can be configured on the tab:

   - **Administrator's Mailbox** Specifies the mailbox that will receive delivery status messages. Click the Change button to select a mailbox. This is a required field. Consider creating a Postmaster mailbox to receive these and other delivery status messages.

   - **Name** Specifies the name of the cc:Mail Post Office with which the connector will communicate.

   - **Password** Specifies the password of the cc:Mail Post Office with which the connector will communicate.

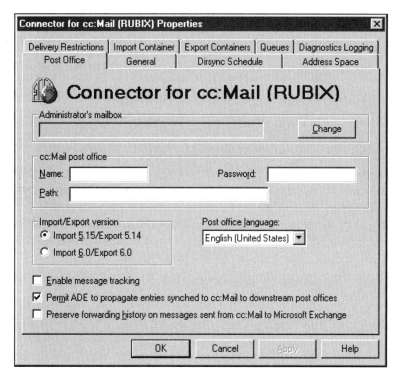

Figure 14.21   The Post Office tab for the Connector For Lotus cc:Mail Properties dialog box is where data transfer and translation are configured.

- **Path**   Specify the network path to the cc:Mail Post Office data directory, in UNC format, here.

A few notes on configuring this option. First, the connector's service account must have read/write permissions in this directory. Second, if the Lotus cc:Mail Post Office resides on a NetWare server, Gateway Service For NetWare must be running on the Microsoft Exchange Server. Third, use the uniform naming convention (UNC) format to refer to the Post Office, such as, *servername**sharename**path* for a Windows NT Server, and *servername**volumename**path* for a NetWare server.

- **Import/Export Version**   Specifies the versions of cc:Mail Import and Export programs that will be used with the connector. These files are used to transfer messages between the connector and the Lotus cc:Mail Post Office.

- **Post Office Language**   Specifies the language to be used for text sent to and from the connector.

14

- **Enable Message Tracking** Enables message tracking for the connector (when selected). This results in the logging of message activities, stored in \ExchSrvr\Tracking.log.

- **Permit ADE To Propagate Entries Synched To cc:Mail To Downstream Post Offices checkbox** When selected, allows directory synchronized entries added to the cc:Mail directory from Microsoft Exchange Server to be generated in cc:Mail Post Offices indirectly connected by Lotus cc:Mail Automatic Directory Exchange.

- **Preserve Forwarding History On Messages Sent From cc:Mail To Microsoft Exchange** When selected, saves the message-forwarding history for messages sent from cc:Mail to Microsoft Exchange Server. The history is stored as a file attached to the message (FORWARD.TXT).

3. Configure the connector's General tab.

   Select the General tab in the MS Mail Connector Properties dialog box. This is where the basic properties for the Lotus cc:Mail connector are defined. The values on this tab are optional. Limits for message size transfer between Microsoft Exchange Server and Lotus cc:Mail Post Offices can be specified here. The only important settings are in the Message Size frame—the No Limit and Maximum (K) option buttons. If Maximum (K) is selected, the value entered is the maximum size (for both inbound and outbound messages) that can be passed through the connector. Setting a maximum message size can reduce the amount of mail traffic in the network. If the message size is exceeded, the message is returned to the sender in the form of a non-delivery report. Regardless of the selection, if the body of a message exceeds 20K, Lotus cc:Mail converts the message body to a text attachment.

4. Configure the connector's Export Containers tab.

   The Export Containers tab is used to specify the Microsoft Exchange Server recipient containers (and, therefore, the recipients themselves) that are to be exported to the cc:Mail Post Office directory. Mailboxes, public folders, distribution lists, and custom recipients can be exported via directory synchronization. By default, Microsoft Exchange Server does not export any recipient containers.

The exported address names are the names generated by the cc:Mail email address generator.

The following can be configured on this tab:

- **Site** Determines which site's recipient containers are displayed.

- **Recipient Containers** Lists the recipient containers that are not currently designated to be exported. To designate a recipient container for export, select the recipient container and click the Add button.

- **Export These Recipients** Lists the recipient containers that are currently designated to be exported. To remove a recipient container for export, select the recipient container and click Remove.

- **Trust Level** Shows the trust level for this connection. Only those recipients with a trust level equal to or lower than the trust level specified will be exported during directory synchronization.

- **Export Custom Recipients** Specifies to also export any custom recipients located in the listed export containers.

5. Configure the connector's Import Containers tab.

   The Import Containers tab is used to specify the Microsoft Exchange Server container where addresses imported from Lotus cc:Mail Post Offices are to be stored. User names, bulletin board names, and mailing lists are imported from cc:Mail to Microsoft Exchange Server. The following can be configured on the Import Containers tab:

   - **Import Container** The recipients container where imported addresses are stored. Click the Container button to select a container.

   - **Filtering** Where importing options are specified. The options are Import All Directory Entries, Only Import Directory Entries Of These Formats, and Do Not Import Directory Entries Of These Formats. If either Only Import Directory Entries Of These Formats or Do Not Import Directory Entries Of These Formats is selected, use the New, Edit, and Remove buttons to edit the list of affected filter formats.

   - **Run DirSync Now** Click this button to launch a manual directory synchronization cycle. This is only required when an immediate update between directories is needed. Otherwise, scheduled directory synchronization is set up on the Schedule tab.

6. Configure the connector's DirSync Schedule tab.

   The DirSync Schedule tab schedules the times when Microsoft Exchange Server and the cc:Mail Post Office will send

14

address list updates to one another. The items to configure on this tab are:

- **Never** Disables directory synchronization.
- **Always** Enables directory synchronization. Updates will be synchronized every 15 minutes.
- **Selected Times** Enables directory synchronization at the specified times in the schedule grid. Use the schedule grid to designate which days and times directory synchronization should occur. The grid can be displayed in either 1 hour or 15-minute intervals, using the Detail View option buttons.

7. Configure the connector's Address Space tab.

The Address Space tab is used to enter information about the addresses that the connector is to process. Use the New, Edit, and Remove buttons to modify the address list. To route all messages through the connector, add an address with type CCMAIL, an asterisk (*) for the address, and a cost of one. The asterisk indicates that all traffic for any cc:Mail Post Office should be routed through this connector. By default, no address types are defined.

8. Start the Connector For cc:Mail Service.

The final step in configuring the Lotus cc:Mail Connector is to start the Connector For cc:Mail Service.

9. Run directory synchronization.

Launch the Services applet from the Control Panel. Scroll down the list to find the service. Change the startup mode to Automatic. Click the Start button to start the service.

10. Test the connection.

The configuration is now ready to be tested. Send a message from a Microsoft Exchange Server recipient to a cc:Mail recipient. To ensure a successful configuration, send a message from a cc:Mail client to a Microsoft Exchange Server recipient.

MANAGING DIRECTORY SYNCHRONIZATION WITH LOTUS CC:MAIL

The directory synchronization used by cc:Mail is not directly compatible with the Microsoft Mail 3.x DirSync protocol. cc:Mail uses similar terms to describe DirSync features, but the process is quite different. Once configured, however, directory synchronization runs as a scheduled process, seamlessly performing appropriate synchronization of the cc:Mail directory with the Microsoft

Exchange Server directory. The Lotus cc:Mail Import and Export programs are utilized by Microsoft Exchange Server, in the following ways:

- **Synchronizing Lotus cc:Mail Addresses To Microsoft Exchange Server** Whether at the scheduled time or when manually initiated, the Connector For Lotus cc:Mail Service launches the cc:Mail Export process (EXPORT.EXE). This extracts all available cc:Mail recipient addresses from the cc:Mail Post Office. The Connector For Lotus cc:Mail Store serves as a temporary storage location for this information. The Connector For Lotus cc:Mail Service next retrieves the information and processes it into the Microsoft Exchange Server directory. The addresses are placed in the Import container that was specified when the connector was configured.

- **Synchronizing Microsoft Exchange Server Addresses To Lotus cc:Mail** Whether at the scheduled time or when manually initiated, the Connector For Lotus cc:Mail Service retrieves all Microsoft Exchange Server recipient information (which has been made available through the specified Export containers) from the Directory Service. Then, it places that information in the Connector For Lotus cc:Mail Store. Next, the connector launches the cc:Mail Import process (IMPORT.EXE) to import this information in the cc:Mail directory.

CONFIGURING DIRECTORY SYNCHRONIZATION WITH LOTUS CC:MAIL

Configuring directory synchronization between Lotus cc:Mail and Microsoft Exchange Server is fairly straightforward; however, there are two things to keep in mind:

- **Trust levels** When Export containers are specified in the Connector For Lotus cc:Mail Service, the specified trust levels are used during directory synchronization. Only those objects in the Microsoft Exchange Server directory with the same, or less, connector's trust level are exported to the cc:Mail Post Office. Interestingly, if an object's trust level increases above the connector's trust level—either by changing the object's trust level or the connector's trust level—the object will automatically be removed from the Lotus cc:Mail directory.

- **Filtering** The Lotus cc:Mail Export process extracts all addresses from the cc:Mail directory. Thus, the Connector For Lotus cc:Mail Service controls which addresses will end up appearing in the Microsoft Exchange Server directory. This is specified using the filtering features on the Import Container tab of the connector.

14

After cc:Mail, NetWare messaging is the most commonly encountered foreign mail system found on most LANs. That's why the NetWare connection is the topic of the section that follows.

UNDERSTANDING EXCHANGE SERVER IN A NETWARE ENVIRONMENT

Microsoft Exchange Server must run on a Windows NT Server computer. However, the rest of the servers and workstations in the network can run other operating systems—including Novell NetWare. In a *NetWare* environment, users can access the Microsoft Exchange Server even if they are on a different LAN.

Microsoft Exchange Server can coexist seamlessly in a NetWare environment, as long as a few items are kept in mind:

- **The SAP agent must be installed** The *Service Access Point (SAP)* agent must be installed and running on the Microsoft Exchange Server for a NetWare client to be able to access it. This agent is not necessary, however, if a NetWare server is on the same LAN as the Microsoft Exchange Server.

- **NetBIOS must be installed** Network Basic Input/Output (NetBIOS) must be supported on the Microsoft Exchange Server. Otherwise, clients will not be able to communicate with the Microsoft Exchange Server.

- **Ethernet frame types must be configured properly** It's not uncommon to configure multiple frame types for the Windows NT NWLink protocol. If this is the case—or if more than one network card is installed in the Microsoft Exchange Server—the internal network number must be set to a unique number greater than zero.

- **File scan must be enabled on appropriate NetWare servers** If users will be storing schedule backups or archives, file scan must be enabled on the NetWare shares where the data is to be stored. Otherwise, Microsoft Outlook information, such as Calendar data, will not be accessible to users. This is because the Microsoft Outlook Calendar does not support certain types of file operations on NetWare servers that have file scan disabled.

- **Gateway Service For NetWare and Client Service For NetWare must be installed** These services should be installed on the Microsoft Exchange Server, to optimize mail delivery performance on servers using the Internetwork Packet Exchange/Sequenced Packet Exchange (IPX/SPX) protocol. Add these services via Network Properties, accessible from the Control Panel.

NetWare Clients And Microsoft Exchange Server

When configured properly, a computer running Windows 95 or Windows NT Workstation that's also using a NetWare client can access a Microsoft Exchange Server without difficulty. In addition to NetWare client software, workstations need to run client software that provides access to the Microsoft Exchange Server—Windows 95 computers use Client For Microsoft Networks, and Windows NT computers use the Windows NT Workstation service.

After domain validation is performed on the Windows network, the computer will be able to access a Microsoft Exchange Server.

Troubleshooting NetWare-Exchange Clients

If set up correctly, there is not much that can prevent NetWare clients from accessing Microsoft Exchange Server. Most problems that arise deal with issues at the Microsoft Exchange Server level. If problems are still encountered, verify the following:

- On Windows 95 clients, in addition to the Client For Novell NetWare, the Client For Microsoft Networks must be installed. On Windows NT clients, in addition to the *Client Service For NetWare*, the Windows NT Workstation service must be installed.

- The NetWare client must be validated on the NT domain on which Microsoft Exchange Server resides.

- The frame type in the Link Driver section of the NET.CFG file on the client must match the frame type on the server.

14

Chapter Summary

Through a core architectural software component known as *connectors*, Microsoft Exchange Server can communicate and transfer messages with a number of other messaging systems.

Messages can be exchanged between Microsoft Exchange Server and MS Mail Post Offices using the Microsoft Mail Connector. The connector has three components: Microsoft Mail Connector Post Office, Microsoft Mail Connector Interchange, and Microsoft Mail Connector MTA. The Microsoft Mail Connector MTA actually delivers the mail if the MS Mail Post Office is on the same LAN. The MS Mail External MTA program actually delivers the mail if the MS Mail Post Office is on a different LAN.

Directory synchronization (DirSync) is the process of using the MS Mail directory synchronization protocol to exchange address information between a Microsoft Exchange Server and another messaging system. In that protocol, each computer must either be a directory synchronization server or a directory synchronization requestor—but only one computer can be designated as the directory synchronization server. If Microsoft Exchange Server is set up to be the directory synchronization server, all MS Mail Post Offices must be set up to be directory synchronization requestors. These MS Mail Post Offices must also be set up in the Microsoft Exchange Server Administrator program as remote DirSync requestors. MS Mail directory synchronization servers and MS Mail remote directory synchronization requestors must be configured to recognize Microsoft Exchange Server as either a directory synchronization requestor or a directory synchronization server.

The Microsoft Schedule+ Free/Busy Connector enables MS Mail Post Offices and Microsoft Exchange Servers to share Microsoft Schedule+ information.

Messaging connectivity between Microsoft Exchange Server and Lotus cc:Mail is accomplished using the Microsoft Exchange Connector For Lotus cc:Mail. The connector has three components: Connector For Lotus cc:Mail Service, Lotus Connector For cc:Mail Store, and Lotus cc:Mail Import/Export Program. The directory synchronization used by cc:Mail is not directly compatible with the Microsoft Mail 3.x DirSync protocol. After directory synchronization is properly configured, synchronization of the cc:Mail directory with the Microsoft Exchange Server directory happens seamlessly. Trust levels and filtering are advanced features that can be utilized when configuring directory synchronization between Lotus cc:Mail and Microsoft Exchange Server.

Microsoft Exchange Server can coexist seamlessly in a NetWare environment, as long as the SAP agent and NetBIOS are installed, Ethernet frame types are configured properly, file scan is enabled on appropriate NetWare servers, and Gateway Service For NetWare and Client Service For NetWare are installed. Windows 95 and Windows NT workstations need to run client software to access the NetWare server as well as the Microsoft Exchange Server. Most communication problems can be traced to Microsoft Exchange Server configuration issues.

KEY TERMS

- **AdminSch**—An NT user account used for sharing Microsoft Schedule+ data between MS Mail and Microsoft Exchange Server.

- **Client Service For NetWare**—A Windows NT service that permits Windows NT computers to access NetWare resources.

- **connector**—The core architecture software component that Microsoft Exchange Server uses to communicate with other messaging systems.

- **Connector For Lotus cc:Mail Service**—A Windows NT Server service that performs the transferring of messages between Microsoft Exchange Server and Lotus cc:Mail Post Offices. It also synchronizes a Microsoft Exchange Server global address list with the Lotus cc:Mail directory.

- **Connector For Lotus cc:Mail Store**—A group of directories on the Microsoft Exchange Server, used for messages in transit.

- **directory requestor Post Office**—Submits directory changes to the directory server Post Office and requests directory updates that other directory requestor Post Offices have submitted; used for directory synchronization.

- **directory server Post Office**—A central database of directory changes that is used for directory synchronization.

- **directory synchronization**—The process of exchanging address information between messaging systems. Also known as DirSync.

- **DISPATCH.EXE**—An application that ships with MS Mail that is used for processing updates into Post Office address lists.

- **EXPORT.EXE**—The Lotus cc:Mail program used to export messages and directory entries from Lotus cc:Mail Post Offices.

- **Gateway Service For NetWare**—A Windows NT Server service that permits domain users of the Windows NT Server to access NetWare resources.

- **IMPORT.EXE**—The Lotus cc:Mail program used to import messages and directory entries into Lotus cc:Mail Post Offices.

- **Lotus cc:Mail**—Lotus's messaging system.

- **Lotus cc:Mail Import/Export programs**—Used to import Microsoft Exchange Server messages and directory entries into Lotus cc:Mail Post Offices, and to export Lotus cc:Mail messages and directory entries into a Microsoft Exchange Server.

- **Microsoft Exchange Connector For Lotus cc:Mail**—The connector that Microsoft Exchange Server uses to communicate with Lotus cc:Mail Post Offices.

- **Microsoft Mail Connector**—The connector that Microsoft Exchange Server uses to communicate with MS Mail.

- **Microsoft Mail Connector Interchange**—A Windows NT Server service that routes and transfers messages between Microsoft Exchange Server and the Microsoft Mail Connector Post Office.

14

- **Microsoft Mail Connector MTA**—A Windows NT Server service that connects to and transfers mail between the Microsoft Mail Connector Post Office and one or more MS Mail Post Offices.

- **Microsoft Mail Connector Post Office**—A temporary information store for MS Mail inbound and outbound messages.

- **Microsoft Mail (MS Mail) For PC Networks**—Microsoft Exchange Server's messaging predecessor.

- **Microsoft Schedule+ Free/Busy Connector**—An Exchange software component that provides the ability to share Microsoft Schedule+ data between MS Mail and Microsoft Exchange Server.

- **MS Mail**—An abbreviated form of the product name Microsoft Mail.

- **MS Mail External MTA**—An application that ships with MS Mail. It delivers mail to other MS Mail Post Offices.

- **NetBIOS**—A communications interface used by applications on a LAN.

- **NetWare**—Novell's network operating system.

- **remote DirSync requestor**—What MS Mail Post Offices are referred to as when Microsoft Exchange Server is set up to be the directory synchronization server.

- **Service Access Point (SAP) agent**—A protocol used by NetWare clients to perform name resolution on NetWare networks.

REVIEW QUESTIONS

1. What are the three primary components of the Microsoft Mail For PC Networks Connector? (Choose all that apply.)

   a. Microsoft Mail Connector Post Office

   b. MS Mail External MTA

   c. Microsoft Mail Connector Interchange

   d. Microsoft Mail Connector MTA

2. MS Mail and Microsoft Exchange Server messaging systems can communicate over which three types of connections? (Choose all that apply.)

   a. LAN

   b. WAN

   c. RAS

   d. X.25

3. There can be more than one Microsoft Mail Connector in each Microsoft Exchange Server site. True or False?

4. Of the following choices, which best defines a shadow Post Office?

   a. A duplicate Post Office that's copied to a remote site to improve responsiveness.

   b. An Exchange component that looks like an MS Mail Post Office to any real MS Mail Post Office.

   c. An MS Mail Post Office that connects to an Exchange Server.

   d. None of the above.

5. What does the Microsoft Mail Connector Interchange do?

   a. Handles message transfer between MS Mail Post Offices.

   b. Converts message formats from MS Mail to Exchange formats, and vice-versa.

   c. A Windows NT Server service that routes and transfers messages between Microsoft Exchange Server and the Microsoft Mail Connector Post Office.

   d. None of the above.

6. When is the MS Mail External MTA required?

   a. For all message transfers between Exchange and MS Mail.

   b. For all message transfers between Exchange and MS Mail where attachments are involved.

   c. Only when Exchange and MS Mail are linked across a LAN.

   d. Only when Exchange and MS Mail are linked across a non-LAN connection.

7. There can be more than one instance of the Microsoft Mail Connector MTA configured in each Microsoft Mail Connector. True or False?

8. Of the following elements, which describe the flow of a message that originates on Microsoft Exchange Server, and is sent to a recipient on an MS Mail Post Office across a LAN connection? (Choose all that apply.)

   a. Exchange Server submits the message to the Microsoft Exchange Server MTA.

   b. MTA transfers the message to the Microsoft Mail Connector Interchange.

   c. Microsoft Mail Connector Interchange converts the message to MS Mail format.

   d. None of the above.

9. What does enabling the Maximize MS Mail 3.x Compatibility option in the Microsoft Mail Connector do?

   a. Performs automatic address and attachment translation between MS Mail and Exchange.

14

    b. Permits MS Mail users on Windows 3.x to access 32-bit Exchange utilities.

    c. Determines whether MS Mail clients will receive OLE 2 embedded objects from Microsoft Exchange Server users.

    d. Permits MS Mail to interoperate with Outlook 98.

10. Which Microsoft Mail Connector component moves mail between the mail connector and MS Mail Post Offices?

    a. The MS Mail Connector MTA

    b. The Maximize MS Mail 3.x Compatibility option

    c. The local Exchange MTA

    d. The Microsoft Mail Connector itself

11. Imported recipient addresses are created with the trust level specified in the import container's trust level value. True or False?

12. An import container must be specified to successfully configure directory synchronization with MS Mail. True or False?

13. The protocol that Microsoft Exchange Server uses for DirSync messages is the same as that used for MS Mail. True or False?

14. By default, how many recipient containers does the DirSync requestor export?

    a. None

    b. All local recipient containers

    c. All remote recipient containers

    d. All recipient containers, whether local or remote.

15. What is the best way to determine if messages sent from the Microsoft Exchange Server to an address on an MS Mail Post Office are being delivered?

    a. Use the logging frame to eliminate all messages that have been delivered.

    b. Watch for non-delivery reports.

    c. Check the Applications log in Event Viewer.

    d. None of the above.

16. The Microsoft Schedule+ Free/Busy Connector is installed separately from the Microsoft Mail Connector. True or False?

17. Which account must be created on all Post Offices that will participate in sharing Microsoft Schedule+ data?

    a. AdminSch

    b. SchShare

    c. SchedAdmin

    d. AdminSched

18. Which versions of Lotus cc:Mail does the Connector For Lotus cc:Mail work with? (Choose all that apply.)

   a. Lotus cc:Mail version 6

   b. Lotus cc:Mail version 7

   c. Lotus cc:Mail version 8

   d. Lotus cc:Mail version 9

19. A single Connector For Lotus cc:Mail can service multiple Lotus cc:Mail Post Offices. True or False?

20. Which Lotus cc:Mail programs are used by the Lotus Connector For cc:Mail Service? (Choose all that apply.)

   a. Connector For Lotus cc:Mail Service

   b. Lotus Connector For cc:Mail Store

   c. Lotus Connector MTA

   d. Lotus cc:Mail Import/Export Program

21. UNCs must be used to refer to both MS Mail and Lotus cc:Mail Post Offices. True or False?

HANDS-ON PROJECTS

To illustrate a successful installation and configuration of the Microsoft Mail Connector, we'll step through the process. To perform these steps, it is necessary to have the Microsoft Exchange Server CD-ROM. It will also be necessary to have access to an MS Mail Post Office and associated utilities.

PROJECT 14.1

To install and configure the Microsoft Mail Connector:

1. Install Microsoft Exchange Server, selecting a Complete installation. If you have already installed Microsoft Exchange Server but didn't install the Microsoft Mail Connector, rerun the installation program, and install the Connector.

2. Log on to the server as Administrator.

3. From the Start menu, select Programs | Microsoft Exchange | Microsoft Exchange Administrator.

4. In the Organizational Hierarchy pane, double-click your site, double-click the Configuration container, then double-click Connections.

14

5. In the right-hand pane, double-click the Microsoft Mail Connector for your server. The Microsoft Mail Connector dialog box should appear.

6. Click the Change button. The Administrator's Mailbox dialog box should appear.

7. Select the mailbox that you want to receive delivery status messages.

8. Select the Connections tab, and click the Create button. The Create Connection dialog box should appear.

9. Verify that the LAN option is selected, then click the Change button.

10. In the Path textbox, type the UNC to your MS Mail Post Office directory, then click the OK button.

11. Verify that the network and Post Office names are correct. Click the OK button.

12. Click the OK button when you are prompted to apply the changes.

13. Click the Yes button when you are prompted to recalculate routing information.

14. Click the OK button when the message appears informing you that the new routing information will take several minutes to take effect.

15. Select the Connector MTAs tab, then click the New button.

16. For Service Name, type "Connector MTA".

17. For Check For Mail Every, type "1 minute".

18. Click the OK button.

19. In the Microsoft Mail Connector dialog box, click the List button. The Serviced LAN Postoffices dialog box should appear.

20. In the Available LAN Postoffices box, select your Post Office, then click the Add button.

21. Click the OK button. This will return you to the Microsoft Mail Connector dialog box.

22. Click the Apply button.

23. Select the Local Postoffice tab, and record the network name and Post Office name.

24. Click the OK button.

25. Use the Services applet in the Control Panel to start the Connector MTA service that was created in Steps 15 through 18.

26. Click the Exit button to close the Services dialog box, then close the Control Panel.

PROJECT 14.2

To configure an MS Mail Post Office to connect to Microsoft Exchange Server:

1. Log on to the MS Mail server as Administrator.
2. Start an MS-DOS session.
3. At the MS-DOS prompt, change to the directory where the MS Mail Post Office executables are located.
4. Type "ADMIN", and press the Enter key.
5. When prompted for a mailbox, type "administrator", and press the Enter key.
6. When prompted for a password, type "password", and press the Enter key. The Administrator screen should appear.
7. Press E to choose External–Admin, then press C to choose Create.
8. Type in the network name from Project 14.1, and press the Enter key.
9. Type in the Post Office name from the prior project, and press the Enter key.
10. Press the Enter key again to select the Direct Route type.
11. Press D to select the MS-DOS Drive option.
12. When prompted to create the entry, press the Enter key.
13. Press the Esc key twice to exit the Administrator program.
14. Press the Enter key when prompted to quit the program.

CASE PROJECTS

1. Suppose the following situation exists:

   You are responsible for your company's MS Mail messaging system. Eventually, your goal is to migrate your messaging system to Microsoft Exchange Server. As a test, you'd like to add a Microsoft Exchange Server to your network and integrate it with your MS Mail messaging system.

   Required result:

   Successfully transfer messages between the two messaging systems.

   Optional desired results:

   Have directory information synchronized between the two messaging systems.

   Be able to share scheduling data between users of both messaging systems.

14

Proposed solution:

Add a Microsoft Exchange Server to your network, with the Microsoft Mail Connector installed. Configure the Microsoft Mail Connector correctly, and establish directory synchronization correctly. Send a message from the Microsoft Exchange client to an MS Mail recipient. Send a return message from the MS Mail Windows client to a Microsoft Exchange client.

Which results does the proposed solution provide?

a. The proposed solution produces the required result and both optional desired results.

b. The proposed solution produces the required result and only one optional desired result.

c. The proposed solution produces only the required result.

d. The proposed solution does not provide the required result.

2. Suppose the following situation exists:

You are the systems administrator for a Novell NetWare network. IPX/SPX is the protocol in use, and Lotus cc:Mail is the messaging system in use. You want to install and implement Microsoft Exchange Server.

Required result:

Successfully integrate Microsoft Exchange Server into your Novell NetWare network.

Optional desired results:

Successfully transfer messages between the two messaging systems.

Optimize message–delivery performance.

Proposed solution:

Add a Microsoft Exchange Server to your network, with the Microsoft Exchange Connector For Lotus cc:Mail installed. Configure the Microsoft Exchange Connector For Lotus cc:Mail correctly. Install both Gateway Service For NetWare and Client Service For NetWare on the Microsoft Exchange Server computer. Send a message from the Microsoft Exchange client to a Lotus cc:Mail recipient. Send a return message from the Lotus cc:Mail client to a Microsoft Exchange client.

Which results does the proposed solution provide?

a. The proposed solution produces the required result and both optional desired results.

b. The proposed solution produces the required result and only one optional desired result.

c. The proposed solution produces only the required result.

d. The proposed solution does not provide the required result.

EXCHANGE SERVER MAINTENANCE, TROUBLESHOOTING, AND PERFORMANCE

To ensure that Microsoft Exchange Server performs optimally and remains reliable, maintenance is required. In addition, troubleshooting might become necessary at certain times. This chapter provides comprehensive information about monitoring activity and troubleshooting problems that might arise. Useful tools for managing and maintaining Exchange Server and Windows NT are also covered.

AFTER READING THIS CHAPTER AND COMPLETING THE EXERCISES, YOU WILL BE ABLE TO:

- Recognize common Microsoft Exchange Server installation and upgrade issues
- Understand the Exchange Server upgrade process
- Maintain the Exchange Server Information Store
- Use Exchange Server tools to resolve problems
- Improve Exchange Server performance
- Migrate users from other messaging systems

MICROSOFT EXCHANGE SERVER INSTALLATION ISSUES

A successful Microsoft Exchange Server installation is dependent foremost on a successful Windows NT Server installation—including the proper NT domain configuration and the establishment of domain trusts (if appropriate). Assuming that Windows NT Server is properly installed and configured, some additional items need to be kept in mind to ensure a successful Exchange Server installation, such as:

- Microsoft Exchange Server 5.5 requires that Windows NT Server 4 (or a later version) is already installed. Service Pack 3 for Windows NT must also be applied before Exchange Server will successfully install.

- You must be logged on to the Microsoft Windows NT domain as a member of the Administrator group to install Exchange Server successfully.

- If you plan on using Microsoft Exchange Server's Internet Mail Service (IMS), the TCP/IP protocol must be installed and configured. Specifically, the steps discussed in the Chapter 9 hands-on project must be followed.

- Microsoft Internet Information Server (IIS) version 3 with *Active Server Pages (ASP)* must be installed if you intend to install *Outlook Web Access (OWA)*. Outlook Web Access is the name given to the portion of Exchange Server that provides Web browser access to mailboxes over the Internet or an intranet. Note that if Active Server Pages are not installed first, a fatal error during Exchange Server installation might be encountered.

- Before Microsoft Exchange Server is installed on a computer, it should have at least 24MB of RAM (32MB is recommended). In addition, there should be enough disk space for your users' email and public folder information. Also, remember that there needs to be sufficient disk space for the Windows NT Server page file. If the computer is being used for other tasks (such as a domain controller, other BackOffice components, and so forth) then more RAM should be installed.

- If you are adding a Microsoft Exchange Server to an existing site, make sure that there is enough space on the new server's hard disk to import the site directory. If this is overlooked, the new server might run out of disk space when directory replication occurs. The size of the site directory can be determined by viewing the properties of the *DIR.EDB* file (located in the \ExchSrvr\DSAData folder) on another server within the site.

- Before installing and configuring Microsoft Exchange Server, it is important to establish the name of your organization, site, and servers. The only way to change this information later is by reinstalling Exchange Server.

- When adding a new site to an organization, make sure you use the same spelling when Microsoft Exchange Server Setup prompts you to type in the organization name. If you use a different spelling, Exchange Server will see this as a new organization/site, preventing the server/site from communication with the real organization.

- Microsoft Exchange Server services start—and periodically perform routine maintenance—using the NT domain service account of your choice. The Exchange Server installation prompts you for this account name and password, using the Administrator account as a default. We recommend using a different, dedicated NT domain account for this— if for no other reason than that, if the Administrator password is changed, the *Exchange Server service account* will still be able to log on as needed. Therefore, create the Exchange Server service account before running Exchange Server Setup. Then, during the Exchange Server Setup, when prompted for the name of the service account, select this service account. For example, you can create an NT account called SrvcExchange, which represents Service-Exchange Server. After selecting the service account, Exchange Server Setup assigns the proper rights and permissions to it.

 The same service account should be used for all Exchange Server computers in a site.

- Make sure that the Windows NT Server Primary Domain Controller (PDC) is running before you install Microsoft Exchange Server. The installation process will need to query the PDC for appropriate data. If it cannot communicate with the PDC, the Exchange Server installation will fail.

- Before installing Microsoft Exchange Server, be sure to shut down any monitors, including Event Viewer, Performance Monitor, Server Monitor, and Link Monitor.

After installing Microsoft Exchange Server, it is wise to verify that the product is working properly. To do this, go to Control Panel, choose Services, and verify that the following services are started (see Figure 15.1):

- Microsoft Exchange System Attendant
- Microsoft Exchange Directory

- Microsoft Exchange Information Store
- Microsoft Exchange Message Transfer Agent

 If any of these services are not running, then Exchange Server is not working properly. See the "Tools And Techniques For Resolving Microsoft Exchange Server Problems" section later in this chapter for a discussion of resolving this problem.

Next to routine troubleshooting, the most predictable form of chaos for an Exchange system is dealing with upgrades and Service Packs. The issues involved with both of these inevitable sources of change are covered in the next section.

MICROSOFT EXCHANGE SERVER UPGRADE ISSUES

Although Microsoft Exchange Server 5.5 can coexist in the same site with version 4 or 5 servers, you'll probably want to upgrade these servers to version 5.5. The Setup program for Microsoft Exchange Server 5.5 upgrades both versions 4 and 5 servers to 5.5. The upgrade process modifies the underlying database structure. The Setup program checks for any Microsoft Exchange Server components that have already been installed on your computer, and it presents you with different options depending on the version already installed. You can determine which version and Service Pack for Exchange Server are currently installed on your computer by viewing the properties of the server object in the Exchange Administrator program.

If you are upgrading to Microsoft Exchange Server 5.5 from a previous version of Exchange Server, here are some items to keep in mind:

- Before upgrading a Microsoft Exchange Server computer, turn off all Server Monitors that include the computer on which Setup is being run.

- If upgrading to Microsoft Exchange Server 5.5 on a computer that has the Chat service installed, stop the Chat service before running Setup.

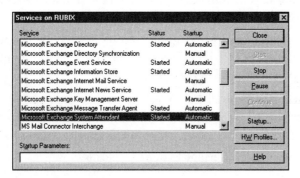

Figure 15.1   The Services applet.

- Don't start the upgrade process unless you have at least as much time as was specified by Setup. Setup estimates the amount of time it will take to upgrade your existing Information Store. Depending on the size of the Information Store, the process can take a long time—even days! You can't suspend the upgrade process and continue it another time.

- If you are upgrading from Exchange Server 4, you must install Service Pack 2 (or greater). There have been reports of data corruption when this step has not been followed. Service Pack 2 can be obtained online from Microsoft (**www.microsoft.com**, search on "Exchange SP2," or through **ftp.microsoft.com**) or from the TechNet CDs. Service Packs may also be ordered directly from Microsoft.

The amount of time required to perform an upgrade depends on the number of messages, the number of folders, and the total size of the Information Store involved. The upgrade time can be reduced by asking users to reduce the amount of mail they keep in their mailboxes prior to installing the upgrade.

How The Upgrade Process Works

During the Microsoft Exchange Server 5.5 upgrade procedure, the existing Information Store (the central storage facility for all Exchange Server messaging data) is converted into a new format—a format optimized for use with Exchange Server 5.5. The conversion process asks for a Database Backup Location in the form of two options:

- **Standard Database Upgrade** Upgrades your Information Store in its current locations. If the conversion process fails, the Information Store must be restored from backup before it can be accessed with the prior version of Microsoft Exchange Server or even before Setup can be run again.

- **Fault-Tolerant Upgrade** Backs up the Information Store to a different, temporary location before upgrading. If the conversion process fails, it's unlikely that you'll need to restore the Information Store. Rather, you can reboot your computer and run Setup again—often successfully.

The Fault-Tolerant Upgrade's alternate location must have at least twice the amount of available disk space as the size of your Information Store. In addition, the alternate location cannot be a network drive.

Despite their names, neither option actually performs a complete backup of your existing Information Store. Therefore, make sure you perform a full backup of your Information Store before performing any upgrades.

15

If you are upgrading from Exchange Server 4, the Fault-Tolerant Upgrade option is not an available option. To perform a Fault-Tolerant Upgrade, the Information Store must first be upgraded to Exchange Server 5 format, using the Microsoft Exchange Server 5 Setup program. Then, the Information Store can be upgraded to Exchange Server 5.5 format.

After the upgrade process has completed, all appropriate Exchange Server services restart, and the Information Store will be immediately available to users. No reboot of Windows NT Server is required.

UPGRADING A MICROSOFT EXCHANGE SERVER 4 IN A MULTISERVER SITE

Because of directory schema changes between Exchange Server 4 and later releases, all Exchange Server computers in a site should first be upgraded to Exchange Server 4, Service Pack 2. Once this step has been completed, all servers in the site can then be upgraded to Exchange Server 5.5.

After you install Exchange Server 5.5 on the first server in the site, the new directory schema must be replicated to all the Exchange Server 4 computers. This happens automatically, but it can take anywhere from a few minutes to a few hours—depending on the number of servers in the site. Use the Windows NT Event Viewer to make sure that directory replication has been completed, then restart all Exchange Server 4 computers. After these steps have been performed, you can upgrade the remaining computers to Exchange Server 5.5.

This concludes the discussion of upgrades and Service Packs. In the section that follows, you'll be the beneficiary of some handy tips and observations about the Exchange Information Store, where all Exchange data ultimately resides. Because of the enormous amount of storage space this can involve, keeping the Information Store cleaned up is extremely important.

INFORMATION STORE MAINTENANCE

The Information Store is the central storage facility for all Microsoft Exchange Server messaging data. It is made up of the private Information Store and the public Information Store. The Exchange Server directory database is an extension of the Information Store. Periodic checks and regular housekeeping of the Information Store will minimize the chances that problems might arise with this vital Exchange asset.

The Microsoft Exchange Administrator program provides a number of tools to check the Exchange Server Information Store. These are covered in the following sections.

CHECKING THE PRIVATE INFORMATION STORE

The Private Information Store Properties dialog box displays the physical resources used by each mailbox on a particular server. You can use this information to determine both current and future disk space needs. The information provided might make it apparent that mailbox storage limits need to be established or that other actions to reduce storage consumption need to be taken.

Follow these steps to access the Private Information Store Properties dialog box to display the physical resources used by each mailbox on a particular server:

1. Open the Microsoft Exchange Administrator program.

2. Select and expand the desired site.

3. Select and expand the Configuration container. The site configuration objects appear in the right-hand pane.

4. Select and expand the Servers container. This displays all the Exchange Servers in the site.

5. Select the server that has the private Information Store you want to view.

6. Select the Private Information Store object. Then, select Properties from the File menu. This will open the Private Information Store Properties dialog box.

7. Select the Mailbox Resources Properties page.

The Mailbox Resources Properties page displays the physical resources used by each mailbox on the server. Pay particular attention to the Total K column, because this indicates the total amount of disk space taken up by the items in each user's mailbox. If disk space on this server becomes an issue, you have a number of options:

- Move one or more mailboxes to another Microsoft Exchange Server within the site. This can help balance disk usage across servers. To move a mailbox to another Exchange Server, follow these steps:

  1. Open the Microsoft Exchange Administrator program.

  2. Select and expand the desired site.

  3. Select and expand the Configuration container. The site configuration objects appear in the right-hand pane.

  4. Select and expand the Servers container. This displays all the Exchange Servers in the site.

  5. Select and expand the server that contains the mailbox you want to move. This displays all the mailboxes on this Exchange Server.

15

6. Select the mailbox you want to move, then select Move Mailbox from the Tools menu. This opens the Move Mailbox dialog box, which displays a list of all Exchange Servers within the site (see Figure 15.2).

7. Select the destination Exchange Server, and click OK. The mailbox will be moved. Depending on the amount of data in the mailbox, it might take a while to finish. Note that when moving a mailbox to a new server, the size of the mailbox contents on the destination server might actually increase. This happens because individual copies of single-instance messages are created for a moved mailbox.

 Moving a mailbox is usually transparent to mailbox users. If the server that a mailbox was moved from remains up until the user logs in, the messaging profile will be automatically updated to reflect the change. If the server that the mailbox was moved from is not up when the user logs in, the user will have to manually update the messaging profile before the user can successfully access the mailbox.

- Cleaning a mailbox deletes the mailbox's contents, increasing the space in the server's private Information Store. You have a good deal of control over what content is actually deleted. To clean a mailbox:

1. Open the Microsoft Exchange Administrator program.

2. Select and expand the desired site.

3. Select and expand the Configuration container. The site configuration objects appear in the right-hand pane.

4. Select and expand the Servers container. This displays all the Exchange Servers in the site.

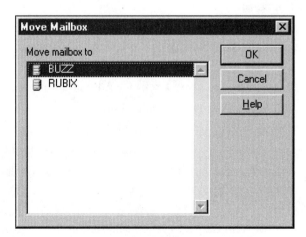

Figure 15.2   The Move Mailbox dialog box.

5. Select and expand the server that contains the mailbox you want to clean. This displays all the mailboxes on this Exchange Server.

6. Select the mailbox you want to clean, then select Clean Mailbox from the Tools menu. This opens the Clean Mailbox dialog box, which provides you with the ability to specify the content you want to delete based on age, size, sensitivity, and read status (see Figure 15.3).

7. Click OK. The content matching the criteria specified will be removed from the mailbox. Depending on what data you choose to remove, this process might take a while to finish.

- Establish mailbox storage limits at either the Information Store level or the individual mailbox level. Information Store level mailbox storage limits are specified via the Information Store Site Configuration Properties dialog box—accessed from the Configuration container for a particular site. Individual mailbox-level storage limits are specified on the individual mailbox properties dialog box, accessed from the Server Recipients container. The Server Recipients container is accessed from the Servers container, which is accessed from the Configuration container for a particular site.

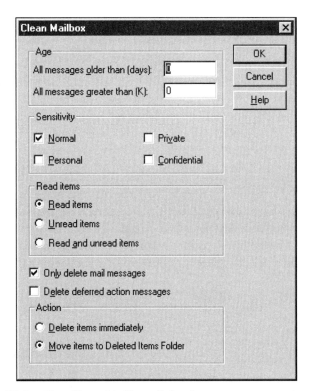

Figure 15.3 The Clean Mailbox dialog box.

CHECKING THE PUBLIC INFORMATION STORE

The Public Information Store Properties dialog box displays the physical resources used by each public folder on a particular server. This information can be used to determine both current and future disk space needs. From checking the public Information Store, you might determine that public folders need to be moved to another server or perhaps even be moderated by a user.

Follow these steps to access the Public Information Store Properties dialog box to display the physical resources used by each public folder on a particular server:

1. Open the Microsoft Exchange Administrator program.

2. Select and expand the desired site.

3. Select and expand the Configuration container. The site configuration objects appear in the right-hand pane.

4. Select and expand the Servers container. This displays all the Exchange Servers in the site.

5. Select the server that has the public folder(s) you want to view.

6. Select the Public Information Store object. Then, select Properties from the File menu. This opens the Public Information Store Properties dialog box.

7. Select the Public Folder Resources tab.

The Public Folder Resources tab displays the physical resources used by each public folder on the server. Again, pay particular attention to the Total K column, because this reveals the total amount of disk space taken up by the items in this public folder. If server disk space becomes an issue, you can move the public folder to another server. You can also choose to establish limits as to who can post new items to the public folder.

To move the public folder to another server, use public folder replication to first copy a public folder to another Microsoft Exchange Server, then remove the public folder from the original Exchange Server. Use the Exchange client or the Outlook client to assign permissions to public folders. Set the permissions such that only selected users have the ability to post new messages to the public folder, whereas all users have the ability to read messages in the public folder.

COMPACTING THE INFORMATION STORE

Over time, Microsoft Exchange Information Stores tend to become fragmented on the disk. This can result in longer response time for users trying to access their mail. Although Exchange Server does a decent job of preventing *defragmentation*, there might be times when you want to defragment the Information Store manually. The Exchange Server *ESEUTIL.EXE* utility (an MS-DOS command-line program) is used to defrag and compact the

Information Store. This utility requires you to stop the Information Store service (if you want to defrag the private and public Information Store) or the directory service (if you want to defrag the Exchange Server directory). Therefore, it is best to run it when users will not need to access their mailboxes. Alternatively, users can be informed in advance that email will be unavailable during a specified time range. Ultimately, you'll want to minimize the inconvenience to users not being able to access their mailboxes.

> Manual defragmentation often becomes necessary when the Microsoft Exchange Server is used for *SMTP (Simple Mail Transport Protocol)* mail.

Before defragging the Information Store, the Microsoft Exchange Information Store service must be stopped. To stop the Information Store service, follow these steps:

1. Go to the Exchange Server with the Information Store you want to defrag.

2. Open the Control Panel, and select the Services icon.

3. Scroll down the list of services, and select Microsoft Exchange Information Store (if you want to defrag the private and public Information Stores) or Microsoft Exchange Directory Service (if you want to defrag the Microsoft Exchange directory).

4. Click the Stop button to stop the selected service.

After the desired service has been stopped, you can proceed to defrag the file using the ESEUTIL.EXE utility.

> The ESEUTIL.EXE utility (known as EDBUTIL.EXE in prior versions of Microsoft Exchange Server) performs functions other than defragmentation. Some of these other functions are covered later in this chapter.

The following is the syntax for using ESEUTIL.EXE to defrag the Information Store:

```
ESEUTIL /d [/ds | /ispriv | /ispub] [/l[<path>]] [/s[<path>]]
[/b<file name>] [/t[<file name>]] [/p] [/o]
```

Table 15.1 shows the options available on ESEUTIL.EXE.

As the defragmentation process proceeds, a rudimentary status bar is displayed. After the file has been defragged, be sure to restart the appropriate Microsoft Exchange service so users can access their mailboxes.

Table 15.1   ESEUTIL.EXE options.

Option	Description
/d	Sets ESEUTIL to defrag mode.
/ds	Defrags the directory store.
/ispriv	Defrags the private Information Store.
/ispub	Defrags the public Information Store.
/l[<path>]	Specifies the location of the log files (default is the current directory).
/s[<path>]	Specifies the location of the system files (default is the current directory).
/b<file name>	Causes a backup copy of the store to be created, using the specified file name.
/t[<file name>]	Sets the temporary database file name (default is TEMPDFRG.EDB).
/p	Leaves the original file uncompacted, and writes compacted file to the temporary database file name.
/o	Suppresses the normally displayed logo.

This concludes the review of Information Store inspection and cleanup tools. In the section that follows, you'll learn about some of the key tools and techniques that should help you to resolve even the most vexing problems with Exchange Server that can sometimes manifest themselves, despite your best maintenance and management efforts.

TOOLS AND TECHNIQUES FOR RESOLVING MICROSOFT EXCHANGE SERVER PROBLEMS

Microsoft Exchange Server ships with a number of built-in tools and resources to make troubleshooting easier. Many of these tools can even be used remotely to diagnose and fix problems throughout your organization.

When a problem with Microsoft Exchange Server arises, solving it usually involves checking more than one source. The recommended strategy is to consult (not necessarily in this order):

- Link Monitor display and logs
- Server Monitor display and logs
- Message tracking and logs
- Diagnostic logs for connectors and services
- Message queues
- Windows NT application event log

In addition, your network topology or routing map will come in handy as these resources are consulted.

LINK MONITORS

Link Monitors are used to verify the efficient routing of test messages. These test messages are called *PING messages*. At the specified polling interval, a PING message is sent to every server and system configured in the Link Monitor. You can use Link Monitors to verify that diagnostic messages sent to other servers in the same site or a different site (or even to foreign systems) are being delivered within a specific amount of time—or if they are being delivered at all. After you create a Link Monitor, it must be started before it can provide the information you'll need to resolve the problem. The originating server is the one you specify when you start the Link Monitor.

If you are alerted to a connection problem, check the Link Monitor display to determine the scope of the problem and which component(s) was affected. Link Monitor configurations are stored in the Exchange Server site directory and are therefore available to all Exchange Servers in the site. To view a Link Monitor display, follow these steps:

1. Open the Microsoft Exchange Administrator program.
2. Select and expand the site in which you suspect the connection problem to be.
3. Select and expand the Configuration container. The site configuration objects appear in the right-hand pane.
4. Select the Monitors container. This displays all the monitors in the site.
5. Double-click the Link Monitor you want to view.

The Link Monitor displays the condition of the connections that were set up to be monitored when the Link Monitor was created. Each line in the Link Monitor display represents one connection. The connections can be sorted by clicking the desired column (shown in Table 15.2).

The Comment column describes the status of the connection based on the thresholds set on the Bounce tab of the Link Monitor Properties page. Table 15.3 displays the comments that can appear in this column.

Double-clicking a connection brings up a Properties page for the connection that contains status information (see Figure 15.4).

Use the Link Monitor information to analyze where the connection problem might be. You can associate the condition of the connections to your network topology map. Using the two resources together can reveal the scope of the problem and point to the source.

15

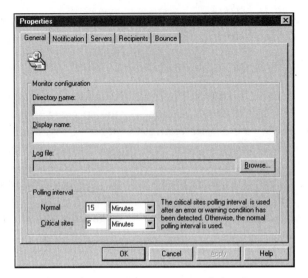

Figure 15.4   The Link Monitor's Properties dialog box.

 If the bounce threshold values are set too low, PING messages on fully operational connections go into warning or alert states.

Link Monitor log files contain written records of recent connection problems. Each Link Monitor can write to one log file only, even if the Link Monitor sends PING messages to more than one server. The log file can be examined even if the Link Monitor is not currently operating. A Link Monitor log includes all information that the Link Monitor displayed, including time stamps, alerts, warnings, notifications, and dates and times when connections started, slowed, or stopped. This information can be a useful addition to the data you are

Table 15.2   Link Monitor columns.

Column	Description
<Symbol>	Connection status. The status can be up, down, warning state, or not yet monitored.
Server	The server the PING message was sent to, from which a return PING is expected.
Last Measurement	The time that the last PING message was sent from the originating server.
Last Change	The time that the status of the connection last changed.
Last Time	The amount of time it took for the last PING message to complete.
Comment	The condition of the connection between the originating and receiving server.

Table 15.3   Link Monitor Comment column values.

Value	Explanation
The Link Is Operational	The PING message was returned within the time specified in the bound threshold.
Bounced Mail Took (Time)	The last PING message was returned, but the bounce time exceeded the warning threshold.
A Message Was Due On (Time)	The last PING message has not returned yet, and the elapsed time has exceeded the warning threshold.
Not Monitored Yet	No PING messages have been returned, and those that were sent are not late yet.

gathering about connection problems. Log file information can be viewed with any text editor. Link Monitor log file names are set in the Link Monitor General tab when the Link Monitor is configured.

Here is an example of a Link Monitor file:

```
3/17/98  2:48 PM SITEA Running The link is operational

3/17/98  2:48 PM SITEB Warning A message was due on 3/17/98  2:45
PM.

3/17/98  2:48 PM Mail Message to

/o=Jones/ou=Company/cn=Recipients/cn=*AUOT01: 'SITEB Warning since

2/17/98  2:48 PM A message was due on 3/17/98  2:45 PM.' -> Send

status: No error.

3/17/98  2:53 PM SITEB Alert A message was due on 3/17/98  2:51 PM.

3/17/98  2:53 PM Launch a Process to C:\\PAGER.EXE SHORT.TXT:SITEB

Alert since 3/17/98 2:51 PM A message was due on 3/17/98 2:51 PM.'
->

Send status: No error.
```

15

If a Link Monitor indicates that a communication problem exists, it is important to note the number of connections that are having problems. If multiple connections are down, check your network topology map for common features of the problem connections, such as a particular server, router, bridge, gateway, or leased line. If just one connection is down, try to determine why the PING message failed to complete within the specified time. You can examine the bounce detail of the PING message in the connection's General tab. A long delay between one hop and the next (or a long delay at the last hop) might indicate a bottleneck or failing connection.

If all PING messages are unsuccessful, you'll need to use other troubleshooting tools to supplement the data from the Link Monitor. All PING messages should return eventually—unless they are being deleted along the route for some reason. If a particular PING message does not return, check the queues in the Message Transfer Agent (MTA) and the Information Stores of the sending and receiving servers. If you have message tracking enabled, the message tracking log can also provide a trace of the PING message.

The Windows NT Event Viewer can also come in handy here. Search the application event logs on the Link Monitor's sending and receiving server. Look for warnings and alerts from the MTA, Information Store, and directory.

Some additional points to keep in mind about Link Monitors:

- Your Link Monitor must be configured correctly to be a useful source of information about network connectivity.

- Configuring and starting Link Monitors are separate processes. Link Monitors are not operational until they are started, and they only function when they are open. If you close the Link Monitor window, the Link Monitor is stopped—it will no longer send or time PING messages, or write to the Link Monitor log.

- Link Monitors assign a status of warnings and alerts based solely on the thresholds you establish on the Link Monitor's Bounce tab. If the threshold is not appropriate for every Link Monitor, the status is not accurate. If one of the routes requires a longer or shorter threshold, create a separate Link Monitor.

- If an Exchange Server's system clock is changed by more than a few minutes, restart the Link Monitor. Otherwise, pending messages will appear to be late, or connections will appear to be down.

SERVER MONITORS

Server Monitors are used to check the condition—including services and clocks—of one or more servers in a site. They use Remote Procedure Calls (RPCs) to do this. Server Monitors can also check servers in other sites if those servers are connected with RPCs. Server Monitors let you specify the actions to take when a service or computer has stopped, including restarting servers and services and resetting clocks.

No special permissions are required to check the state of services on servers in a remote site. However, without the correct permissions on those remote servers, the monitor will not be able to synchronize the clocks or restart services.

After you create a Server Monitor, it must be started before it can provide the information you'll need to resolve any problem. The originating server is the one you specify when you start the Server Monitor.

If you are alerted to a component failure, check the Server Monitor display to determine the scope of the problem and the component(s) affected. Before attempting to interpret the display, examine the configuration of the Server Monitor (using its Properties page, see Figure 15.5) to learn about its configuration. Server Monitor configurations are stored in the Exchange Server site directory and are therefore available to all Exchange Servers in the site. To view a Server Monitor display, follow these steps:

1. Open the Microsoft Exchange Administrator program.

2. Select and expand the site in which you suspect the connection problem to be.

3. Select and expand the Configuration container. The site configuration objects appear in the right-hand pane.

4. Select the Monitors container. This displays all the monitors in the site.

5. Double-click the Server Monitor you want to view.

The Server Monitor displays the status of servers configured to enable them to be monitored when the Server Monitor was created. Each line in the Server

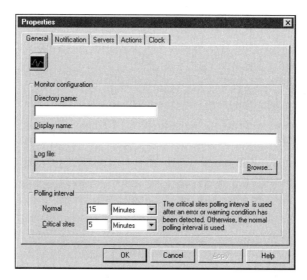

Figure 15.5   The General tab of the Server Monitor's Properties dialog box.

Table 15.4   Server Monitor columns.

Column	Description
\<Symbol\>	Server component status. If any component is down, the server is considered to be down.
Server	The server being monitored.
Last Measurement	The time that the server was polled.
Last Change	The time that the condition of any component of the server changed.
Comment	The condition of the server.

Monitor display represents one server. The servers can be sorted by clicking the desired column (shown in Table 15.4).

Double-clicking a connection will bring up a Properties page containing status information for the connection.

Server Monitor log files contain written records of recent server monitoring events. Each Server Monitor can only write to one log file, even if the Server Monitor monitors multiple servers and/or services. The log file can be examined even if the Server Monitor is not currently operating. A Server Monitor log includes all information that the Server Monitor displayed, including time stamps, alerts, warnings, notifications, and dates and times when server services started or stopped. Log file information can be viewed with any text editor. Server Monitor log file names are set in the Server Monitor General tab when the Server Monitor is configured.

Here is an example of a Server Monitor file:

```
3/17/98 3:37 PM SITEA Alert The service MSExchangeMSMI is
unavailable, its status is Stopped.

3/17/98 3:37 PM Mail Message to

/o=Jones/ou=Company/cn=Recipients/cn=Alig: 'SITEA Alert since 3/17/98

3:37 PM The service MSExchangeMSMI is unavailable, its status is
Stopped.' -> Send status: No error.

3/17/98 3:37 PM Launch a Process to C:\PAGER\PAGE.EXE SERVER.TXT:

'SITEA Alert since 3/17/98 3:37 PM The service MSExchangeMSMI is
unavailable, its status is Stopped.' -> Send status: No error.
```

```
3/17/98 3:37 PM SITEB Repair Set the clock of the remote computer:
No

error.

3/17/98 3:37 PM SITEB Alert Many services (2) are unavailable.

3/17/98 3:37 PM Mail Message to

/o=Jones/ou=Company/cn=Recipients/cn=Alig: 'SITEB Alert since 3/17/
98

3:37 PM Many services (2) are unavailable.' -> Send status: No
error.

3/17/98 3:42 PM SITEA Running The server is running.

3/17/98 3:52 PM SITEB Running The server is running.

3/17/98 3:52 PM Mail Message to

/o=Jones/ou=Company/cn=Recipients/cn=Alig: 'SITEB Running since 9/
15/97

6:00 PM The server is running.' -> Send status: No error.
```

ENABLING MESSAGE TRACKING

Messages sent to and from a Microsoft Exchange Server can be tracked to help resolve mail-delivery problems. With *message tracking*, you can track messages to locate slow or stopped connections, find lost mail, and determine the delay on each segment of a route for link monitoring and performance tuning.

Message tracking must be enabled before it can be used for troubleshooting purposes. Message tracking can be enabled on the MTA, the Information Store, and the MS Mail Connector. When message tracking is enabled, each component handling mail records its activities in a log file. The log file serves as a processing trace of each message as the particular component receives, processes, and delivers the message to the next component. The default for message tracking is off, because excessive logging can affect server performance.

After enabling message tracking, all components must be restarted before writing to the log file will take effect. For example, if you enable message tracking on the Information Store, you must restart all Information Store services in the site.

Enabling Message Tracking On The Information Store Or MTA

To enable message tracking on the Information Store or the MTA, follow these steps:

1. Open the Microsoft Exchange Administrator program.

15

2. Select and expand the site in which you want to enable message tracking.

3. Select and expand the Configuration container. The site configuration objects appear in the right-hand pane.

4. Double-click the Information Store Site Configuration or the MTA Site Configuration on which you want to track messages.

5. Select the General tab.

6. Select Enable Message Tracking.

7. Click OK.

For each server in the site, go to Control Panel | Services applet, and restart the Microsoft Exchange Information Store or the Microsoft Exchange MTA service.

Enabling Message Tracking On MS Mail Connectors

Message tracking must be enabled separately on each MS Mail Connector in the site. To enable message tracking on an MS Mail Connector, follow these steps:

1. Open the Microsoft Exchange Administrator program.

2. Select and expand the site in which you want to enable message tracking.

3. Select and expand the Configuration container. The site configuration objects appear in the right-hand pane.

4. Select and expand the Connections container. The connection objects appear in the right-hand pane.

5. Double-click the MS Mail Connector on which you want to track messages.

6. Select the Interchange tab.

7. Select Enable Message Tracking.

8. Click OK.

9. Go to Control Panel | Services applet, and restart the MS Mail Connector Interchange service.

Enabling Message Tracking On Internet Mail Services

Message tracking must be enabled separately on each Internet Mail Service in the site. If your site has more than one Internet Mail Service, enable message tracking on each. To enable message tracking on the Internet Mail Service, follow these steps:

1. Open the Microsoft Exchange Administrator program.

2. Select and expand the site in which you want to enable message tracking.

3. Select and expand the Configuration container. The site configuration objects appear in the right-hand pane.

4. Select and expand the Connections container. The connection objects appear in the right-hand pane.

5. Double-click the Internet Mail Service on which you want to track messages.

6. Select the Internet Mail tab.

7. Select Enable Message Tracking.

8. Click OK.

9. Go to Control Panel | Services applet, and restart the Microsoft Exchange Internet Mail Service.

PERFORMING MESSAGE TRACKING

After message tracking is enabled, you can use the resources in the Microsoft Exchange Administrator to track individual messages. The Track Message command (available from the Tools menu) initiates the tracing of a message through the network. Daily tracking logs (generated by each component that has message tracking enabled) are searched for any events associated with the specified message. This allows the message to be followed through the logs of all Exchange Server computers on the same physical network. Messages can be selected repeatedly and tracked until the source of the problem has been determined.

To track a message using message tracking, follow these steps:

1. Open the Microsoft Exchange Administrator program.

2. From the Tools menu, choose Message Tracking.

3. Enter the name of the server to which you want to connect. This displays the Select Message To Track dialog box (see Figure 15.6).

 To track a message, you must first connect to a server to locate the message. Select a server that has the sender or recipient of the message in its Global Address List (GAL).

4. Enter the message criteria using the From, Sent To, and Look Back (How Many Days) controls. The From and Sent To buttons display the

15

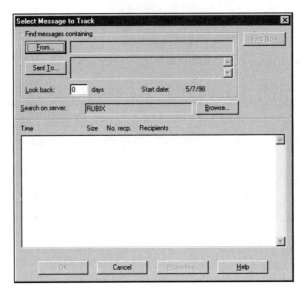

Figure 15.6 The Select Message To Track dialog box.

> GAL, from which you can select the desired mailbox. If zero is entered for the Look Back value, only the current day's logs are searched.

5. Click the Find Now button.

The daily tracking logs are then searched for all references to messages matching your criteria. All message events matching your criteria are displayed in a list below the message criteria information. Table 15.5 shows the matching event's columns.

You can access more detail for each matching message event by clicking the Properties button. This will bring up the Message Properties dialog box, which shows detailed information about the message at the time the event was generated. The Time, Transferred To, and Recipients List information are all

Table 15.5 Matching event's columns.

Column	Description
\<Symbol\>	Event type.
Time	The time and date the message was sent as recorded by the Information Store on the sending server.
Size	The message size, in bytes.
No. Recp.	The number of mailboxes to which the message was sent. (Distribution lists count as one recipient.)
Recipients	The first mailbox in the recipients list. Ellipses (...) indicate that the message was sent to more than one recipient.

particularly useful. Time indicates the time that the message was sent or received. Transferred To documents the Microsoft Exchange Server component that generated this event. The Recipients List itemizes all addresses the message was sent to.

Once a message is found using the Select Message To Track interface, you can trace its path through the network by using the *Message Tracking Center* to trace through the logs of all servers that handled the message. At each step, the process determines which service expected to receive the message next and searches the logs on that server to find related events. The trace is complete when the message leaves the network or is delivered.

You can access the Message Tracking Center from the Select Messages To Track dialog box. Select a message, and click the OK button. The Message Tracking Center dialog box appears, displaying tracking information for the selected message (see Figure 15.7). Click the Track button to activate message tracking. When the search is complete, all matching message tracking events will be displayed in the Tracking History list.

To search for a message in which either the sender or recipient is not in the GAL, or to search for messages originating at gateways, use the Message Tracking Center. To do this, follow these steps:

    1. In the Message Tracking Center, choose Advanced Search. The Advanced Search dialog box appears (see Figure 15.8).

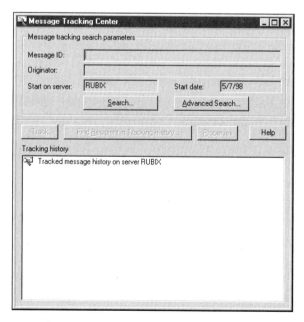

Figure 15.7   The Message Tracking Center dialog box.

15

Figure 15.8   The Message Tracking Center's Advanced Search dialog box.

2. Select Transferred Into This Site, then click OK. The Select Inbound
   Message To Track dialog box appears.

3. Type the email address of the sender, or click the From button to select
   an entry from the GAL.

4. Type the email address of one or more recipients, or click the Sent To
   button to select one or more recipients from the GAL.

5. In the Transferred From pull-down menu, select the connector used to
   transport the message.

6. Modify the Look Back date and server, if appropriate.

7. Click the Find Now button.

The Message Tracking Center displays message tracking results as a hierarchy of
the mail handling events found in the tracking logs. Each line in the list
represents one event, and each level in the hierarchy represents a branch in the
path of a message, some of which might be concurrent. To get more
information, about a particular event:

- Double-click the event to expand or collapse the underlying hierarchy.

- Select an event, and choose Properties to see more detail about the event.

- Click the Find Recipient In Tracking History button to search for
  recipients specified in the message search. Events involving those
  recipients appear in bold.

To try to resolve a problem message, consult the message queues of any affected
components, raise the diagnostics logging level of a component or service,
consult the Windows NT application event log, or change the configuration of a
component.

DIAGNOSTIC LOGGING

Diagnostic logging helps pinpoint messaging problems. Using each component's
Diagnostic Logging Properties page, you can specify the degree of diagnostic

logging you want. Diagnostic logs are recorded in the Windows NT event log, where you can refer to them to try to resolve messaging problems. You can configure diagnostic logging for Microsoft Exchange Server components to record only highly significant events (such as an application failure) or moderately important events (such as receipt of messages across a gateway). By default, only critical events are logged.

Diagnostics logging is available for the following Microsoft Exchange Server components:

- MTA
- Directory
- Information Store
- Internet Mail Service
- MS Mail Connector
- Microsoft Schedule+ Free/Busy Connector
- Microsoft Exchange Connector For Lotus cc:Mail

Diagnostics logging levels are set by category—a category being a group of related functions. Each category of an Exchange Server component has a diagnostics logging level. When a component generates an event that matches or exceeds the logging level, the event is recorded in the Windows NT application event log.

During normal operation, set diagnostics logging to None for every category of every component on every server. Otherwise, you will literally be inundated with diagnostic logging information. With a diagnostic level of None, only error events and critical error messages are written to the log.

Start diagnostics logging if you need to troubleshoot a problem. Also, be selective when you increase a logging level. Increase levels on those aspects of the

15

Table 15.6   Diagnostic logging levels.

Level	Description
None	Only critical and error events are logged. This is the default level.
Minimum	Only high-level events are logged. Use this level to begin troubleshooting a problem.
Medium	Events dealing with the execution of tasks are logged. Use this level when the problem has been narrowed to a component or group of categories.
Maximum	All component operations are logged. Use this level when the problem has been traced to a particular category or categories only. This level logs all events, resulting in a large amount of information—which can have a detrimental effect on performance.

component that you think might be related to the problem only. Table 15.6 shows the diagnostic logging levels.

If you change a diagnostic level, you must stop and restart the respective service for the change to take affect.

MESSAGE QUEUES

The MTA service, Internet Mail Service, and MS Mail Connector message queues can be viewed and modified. Using the Queues tab for each component, you can display the queues, delete messages, and (in some MTA queues) change the order of the messages in the queue.

When messages are not reaching their destinations, examine the queues. Mail is not normally retained in the queues. A backed up queue might indicate:

- A problem with the physical connection between the servers
- A server or MTA configuration error
- An improperly configured connector.

Use the Queues tab to delete any corrupted messages that are blocking the queues.

WINDOWS NT EVENT VIEWER

Windows NT logs events to its system, security, and application log files. This provides you with a means to track significant events, such as server reboots, low disk space messages, and so forth. You can also use the Windows NT Event Viewer to display and search the application event log for Exchange Server-specific problems. You can even set alerts to notify you when problems occur. Because events can differ considerably in their significance, the level of detail of logged events is configured at the component level, using the Diagnostics Logging Properties page (discussed in the section "Diagnostic Logging" earlier in this chapter). Each Exchange Server component generates different types of events, based on the functions it performs. Table 15.7 offers a brief overview of Exchange Server events.

This concludes the discussion of graphical Windows NT and Exchange troubleshooting, monitoring, and diagnostics tools. In the section that follows, you'll learn more about the command line utilities that complement these tools.

OTHER TROUBLESHOOTING TOOLS

Microsoft Exchange Server ships with a number of MS-DOS command-line utilities. Some of these utilities (ESEUTIL, ISINTEG, and MTACHECK) are designed specifically to analyze and repair the Information Store or related

Table 15.7   Exchange Server events overview.

Component	Typical Events
All	Component start, failure to start, and stop.
System Attendant	Routing table calculation problems, errors writing to the tracking log.
MTA	Opening and closing connections to other servers, connection errors.
Directory	Replication requests, success and failure messages, changes to security attributes.
Public Information Store	User logons, replication.
Private Information Store	User logons, sending and receiving of messages.
Administrator program	Configuration of replication features.
Directory import	Import start and finish, import errors and warnings.
Directory synchronization	Any errors.
Security events	Logon, logoff, and privileged use.
Internet Mail Service	Mail connectivity, Internet services, scheduled connection times.

items. There is some overlap among the tools. If you are encountering a problem with Exchange Server, use the tool that seems appropriate for the situation.

ESEUTIL

The Exchange Server ESEUTIL.EXE utility can be used to perform a number of analysis and recovery actions on Exchange Server databases (databases include the Information Store and the directory database). As discussed previously in the section entitled "Compacting The Information Store," ESEUTIL can be used to defragment and reduce the size of the Exchange Information Store. ESEUTIL can also be used (in varying degrees) to:

- Verify the integrity of an Exchange Server database.
- Upgrade a database (created using a previous release of Exchange Server) to the current version.
- Repair a corrupted or damaged database.
- Perform a recovery, bringing all databases to a consistent state.
- Generate formatted output of various database file types (rarely used).

ESEUTIL requires that you stop the Information Store service (if you want to work with the private and public Information Stores) or the directory service (if you want to work with the Exchange Server directory). See the ESEUTIL section for steps to stop the appropriate service.

15

After the appropriate service has been stopped, you can proceed to work on the Information Store or directory using the ESEUTIL.EXE utility.

The following is the syntax for using ESEUTIL.EXE to verify the integrity of an Exchange Server database:

```
ESEUTIL /g [/ds | /ispriv | /ispub] [/t[<file name>]] [/v] [/x] [/o]
```

Table 15.8 shows the ESEUTIL.EXE verify-integrity options.

ESEUTIL in verify-integrity mode performs no recovery (assuming the database is in a consistent state—if this is not the case, an error is returned). As the verify-integrity process proceeds, a simple status bar displays. After the integrity of the file has been verified, be sure to restart the appropriate Microsoft Exchange service so that users can access their mailboxes.

If you need to restore an older Microsoft Exchange Server database from a backup, and the database is in an older database format, you will need to upgrade it to the current version. To upgrade a database to the current version, you will have to provide the appropriate DLL that shipped with that version of Exchange Server. The following is the syntax for using ESEUTIL.EXE to upgrade a database to the current version:

```
ESEUTIL /u <database name> /d<previous .DLL> [/b[<file name>]]
[/t[<file name>]] [/p] [/o]
```

Table 15.9 shows the ESEUTIL.EXE upgrade-database options.

Table 15.8   ESEUTIL.EXE verify-integrity options.

Option	Description
/g	Sets ESEUTIL to integrity-verification mode.
/ds	Verifies the integrity of the directory store.
/ispriv	Verifies the integrity of the private Information Store.
/ispub	Verifies the integrity of the public Information Store.
/t[<file name>]	Sets the temporary database file name (default is INTEG.EDB).
/v	Verbose mode. Provides more feedback on the integrity-verification process.
/x	Provides more information on any error messages encountered.
/o	Suppresses the normally displayed logo.

Table 15.9   ESEUTIL.EXE upgrade-database options.

Option	Description
/u	Sets ESEUTIL to upgrade-database mode.
<database name>	File name of the database to upgrade (for example, PRIV.EDB, PUB.EDB, DIR.EDB).
/d <previous DLL>	File name of the DLL that came with the release of Exchange Server matching the database version.
/b<file name>	Causes a backup copy of the store to be created, using the specified file name.
/t[<file name>]	Sets the temporary database file name (default is TEMPUPGD.EDB).
/p	Leaves the original file unconverted; writes converted file to the temporary database file name.
/o	Suppresses the normally displayed logo.

ESEUTIL in upgrade-database mode should only be used to upgrade a database after an internal database format change has taken place. Before upgrading, the database should be in a consistent state. An error will result if this is not the case. As the verify-integrity process proceeds, a simple status bar displays. After the integrity of the file has been verified, be sure to restart the appropriate Microsoft Exchange service so users can access their mailboxes.

If a message in the Windows NT event log indicates that the Microsoft Exchange Server Information Store is corrupted or damaged, you might be able to resolve the problem by repairing the database. The following is the syntax for using ESEUTIL.EXE to repair a database:

```
ESEUTIL /p [/ds | /ispriv | /ispub] [/t[<file name>]] [/d] [/v]
[/x] [/o]
```

15

Table 15.10 shows the ESEUTIL.EXE repair options.

As the repair database process proceeds, a simple status bar displays. After the database has been repaired, be sure to restart the appropriate Microsoft Exchange service so users can access their mailboxes.

If a message in the Windows NT event log indicates that a Microsoft Exchange Server database is in a consistent state, you might be able to resolve the problem by performing a recovery on the database. The following it the syntax for using ESEUTIL.EXE to perform a recovery on a database:

```
ESEUTIL /r [/ds | /is] [/l[<path>]] [/s[<path>]] [/o]
```

Table 15.10   ESEUTIL.EXE repair options.

Option	Description
/p	Sets ESEUTIL to repair database mode.
/ds	Repairs the directory store.
/ispriv	Repairs the private Information Store.
/ispub	Repairs the public Information Store.
/t[<file name>]	Sets the temporary database file name (default is REPAIR.EDB).
/d	Doesn't repair the database—just scans for errors.
/v	Verbose mode. Provides more feedback on the repair process.
/x	Provides more information on any error messages encountered.
/o	Suppresses the normally displayed logo.

Table 15.11 shows the ESEUTIL.EXE recovery options.

As the recovery process proceeds, a simple status bar displays. After the database has been recovered, be sure to restart the appropriate Microsoft Exchange service so users can access their mailboxes.

ISINTEG

The Exchange Server Information Store Integrity Checker *(ISINTEG.EXE)* finds and eliminates common Information Store database errors. If you cannot start the Information Store service, or users cannot access their mailboxes, use this utility. Also, use this utility after you've recovered an Information Store database with software other than the Windows NT backup utility. ISINTEG.EXE is located in the \ExchSrvr\Bin directory.

Table 15.11   ESEUTIL.EXE recovery options.

Option	Description
/r	Sets ESEUTIL to recovery mode.
/ds	Recovers the directory store.
/is	Recovers the Information Store (both private and public).
/l[<path>]	Location of log files (the default is the current directory).
/s[<path>]	Location of system files (the default is the current directory).
/o	Suppresses the normally displayed logo.

There are three modes of operation for ISINTEG:

- **Check mode** Check mode searches the Information Store databases for table errors, incorrect reference counts, and any objects that are not referenced. ISINTEG displays the results and also writes them to a log file.

- **Check And Fix mode** Check And Fix mode performs the same steps as Check mode, but also attempts to fix any errors it encounters. This mode should only be used when instructed by Microsoft Technical Support. Perform a backup before running this utility.

- **Patch mode** Patch mode repairs Information Stores that will not start after being restored from an offline backup.

ISINTEG must be run separately on the public and private Information Store. It is run from the Windows NT Server command line. The Information Store must be stopped before you run ISINTEG. See the first section titled "Compacting The Information Store," for steps to stop the Information Store service.

By default, ISINTEG examines the Information Store database tables for errors, displays the results, and reports them to a log file. The **–fix** option instructs ISINTEG to attempt to repair the errors it finds. Details of all repairs are recorded in a log file (ISINTEG.PRI or ISINTEG.PUB by default, depending on whether the private or public Information Store was chosen).

The follwoing is the syntax for using ISINTEG.EXE in Check or Check And Fix mode:

```
ISINTEG -pri | -pub [-fix] [-verbose] [-l[<file name>]]
[-test<test name>]
```

Table 15.12 shows the ISINTEG.EXE options.

Table 15.12   ISINTEG.EXE options.

Option	Description
-pri	Works on the private Information Store.
-pub	Works on the public Information Store.
-fix	Specifies that any errors encountered should be fixed.
-verbose	Provides more feedback on the process.
-l[<file name>]	Sets the log file name (default is ISINTEG.PRI or ISINTEG.PUB).
-test<testname>	Performs a specific ISINTEG test. Type "ISINTEG /?" to see a list of available tests.

15

As ISINTEG proceeds, a simple status bar displays. Afterwards, be sure to restart the information service so users can again access their mailboxes.

The Microsoft Exchange Server Information Store will not start if the globally unique identifier (GUID) for the Information Store does not match the GUID stored in the Windows NT Registry and the Exchange Server directory. This can occur if the Information Store is restored from an offline backup. In this situation, use ISINTEG in Patch mode to patch the Information Store.

In Patch mode, ISINTEG records consistent GUID entries in the database, directory, and Registry. This will allow the Information Store service to start again. Note that ISINTEG Patch mode runs on the entire Information Store. It cannot be run on just the public or private Information Store database.

 If the Information Store on your server won't start and Event ID 2084 appears in the Windows NT application event log, you can fix the problem by running ISINTEG in Patch mode.

As with Check and Check And Fix modes, the Information Store service must be stopped before running ISINTEG. The following is the syntax for using ISINTEG.EXE in Patch mode:

```
ISINTEG -patch
```

As ISINTEG proceeds, a simple status bar displays. Afterwards, be sure to restart the information service so users can access their mailboxes. ISINTEG does not perform any database-integrity tests when run in Patch mode. Patch mode and Check mode must be run separately. For that reason, run ISINTEG in Check mode after running it in Patch mode.

MTACHECK

The Message Transfer Agent Check utility *(MTACHECK.EXE)* scans the internal MTA database, looking for objects that are damaged and interfering with queue processing. If messages are not being delivered properly, MTACHECK might be able to resolve the problem. Also, if the Microsoft Exchange MTA service stops and cannot be restarted, MTACHECK can often get it running again. In addition, MTACHECK can be used for routine checks of the integrity of MTA database queues.

MTACHECK places suspect objects from the queues into files, which you can examine. In addition, MTACHECK rebuilds the queues so that the MTA can be restarted and resume processing. Most suspect objects removed from the queue by MTACHECK can be recovered. MTACHECK places all suspect objects it considers to be damaged in DB*.DAT files, in the \ExchSrvr\MTAData\ MTACheck.out directory. You can then examine the objects further and either delete or attempt to repair them.

MTACHECK.EXE is located in the \ExchSrvr\Bin directory. It can only be run from the command line of the Exchange Server with the MTA problem. The MTA service must be stopped before the utility is run. In addition, the MTACheck.out directory (where MTACHECK places suspect objects) must be emptied or deleted. MTACHECK displays progress messages as it progresses. There are numerous options available to alter the actions that MTACHECK takes.

To run MTACHECK, follow these steps:

1. Go to the Exchange Server with the MTA problem (or the one with the queue you want to check).

2. Open Control Panel, and select the Services icon.

3. Scroll down the list of services, and select Microsoft Exchange Message Transfer Agent.

4. Click the Stop button. This stops the MTA service.

5. Use Explorer to empty the \ExchSrvr\MTAData\MTACheck.out folder.

6. At a command prompt, start MTACHECK, with any option switches (shown in Table 15.13).

The following is the syntax for using MTACHECK.EXE:

```
MTACHECK [/V] [/F <file name>] [/RD] [/RP]
```

As MTACHECK proceeds, a simple status bar displays. Afterwards, a message displays indicating the results. Be sure to restart the MTA service so mail is delivered properly again.

15

Table 15.13   MTACHECK.EXE options.

Option	Description
/V	Provides more feedback on the process.
/F <file name>	Saves progress messages to the specified file.
/RD	Repairs database. Useful when data integrity is suspect.
/RP	Repairs post office. Can repair user data, mailboxes, and addresses.

MTACHECK examines each queue in the database. This is known as interpreting MTACHECK output. If MTACHECK finds an error, it reports the name of the queue, the type of error detected, and the number of messages returned to the rebuilt queue. It then proceeds to examine the actual objects in the queues. If an object is found to be in error, it is removed from the queue and placed in a file in \ExchSrvr\MTAData\MTACheck.out. The object ID, error type, queue name, and the MTS-ID of the corrupted message are all reported.

If message tracking is enabled, you can search the log for the offending object by its message ID. By tracing the path of the bad message, you might be able to find the cause of the problem. Keep in mind that you might need to search the logs of more than one site to find the complete path of the message.

Having now reviewed the key Exchange command line utilities, you will next turn your attention to measuring and optimizing Exchange Server performance.

IMPROVING MICROSOFT EXCHANGE SERVER PERFORMANCE

A number of techniques can be used to improve the performance of a Microsoft Exchange Server. Some of these techniques are considered in the following sections.

PERFORMANCE OPTIMIZER

At the end of the installation process, Exchange Server automatically runs *Performance Optimizer*. Performance Optimizer analyzes and optimizes your hardware so that it performs in the most efficient way. The optimizer analyzes the server's logical drives and physical memory. Performance Optimizer can be run at any time. Consider running it on an Exchange Server when you add or remove a connector, change a server's role within a site, change or upgrade any major hardware component, or migrate a large number of users from a non-Exchange system.

For the best performance, before you install Microsoft Exchange Server and run the Performance Optimizer, optimize your disk subsystem. Here is Microsoft's recommended disk configuration for an Exchange Server computer:

- One physical disk for the operating system and the page file.
- One physical disk for the transaction log files. (To increase fault tolerance, mirror this disk.)
- One stripe set consisting of multiple physical disks for all other Exchange Server components. (This allows Exchange Server databases to be accessed in the most efficient manner.)

PERFORMANCE MONITOR

You can monitor the counter values in Windows NT Performance Monitor to determine how Exchange Server is performing or to track any error conditions. The Performance Monitor counters used for showing system conditions fall into two categories—general counters and Microsoft Exchange Server-specific counters.

Table 15.14 lists a number of relevant Windows NT General Performance Monitor counters.

Table 15.15 lists a number of relevant Microsoft Exchange Server Performance Monitor counters (for a complete list of performance monitor counters, see the *Microsoft Exchange Server Resource Kit*).

The only way to truly appreciate the capability of the NT Performance Monitor is to spend some time with this tool, and to explore what its counters and objects can teach you. Although this concludes the discussion of this topic, it should only be the beginning of your continued exploration of this incredibly useful tool.

In the section that follows, you'll explore some of the issues involved when migrating to Exchange from other messaging systems. Because this is an incredibly likely opportunity for problems to occur, it should come as no surprise that this topics is covered in a troubleshooting chapter!

MIGRATING FROM OTHER MESSAGING SYSTEMS

Microsoft Exchange Server includes a Migration Wizard for migrating users from other messaging systems. You can access the Microsoft Exchange Server Migration Wizard from the Microsoft Exchange program group. The Migration Wizard provides the means to migrate users from the following messaging systems:

15

Table 15.14   Relevant Windows NT General Performance Monitor counters.

Object	Counter	Problem Indicated
LogicalDisk	% Disk Time	Sustained value greater than 90 percent indicates that hard drive is a performance bottleneck.
Memory	Pages/sec.	High average value indicates computer needs more memory.
Process	% Process Time	Average value greater than 90 percent indicates that processor is a performance bottleneck.

Table 15.15   Some important Microsoft Exchange Server Performance Monitor counters.

Object	Counter	Problem Indicated
MSExchangeMTA	Work Queue Length	High number indicates a problem with the MTA queue.
MSExchangeISPriv	Avg. Time for Delivery	High value indicates a problem with the private Information Store MTA.
MSExchangeISPub	Avg. Time for Delivery	High value indicates a problem with the public Information Store MTA.
MSExchangeMSMI	Messages Received	If static, might indicate a problem with the MS Mail Connector.
MSExchangePCMTA	File contentions/hour	If high, might indicate that too much traffic is going through that particular shadow Post Office.

- MS Mail For PC Networks
- Lotus cc:Mail
- Novell GroupWise
- Collabra Share

The three steps to the migration process are:

1. Use the Migration Wizard to create a user list.

2. Modify the user list as needed.

3. Use the Migration Wizard to create mailboxes and migrate messages and attachments.

When migrating mailboxes to Microsoft Exchange Server, the Windows NT user account used to log on to Windows NT Server must also have permissions on the Microsoft Exchange Server. If you attempt to migrate post office information and the Windows NT account does not have sufficient permissions on the Exchange Server, the error message "Invalid server specified" appears.

When migrating from MS Mail, the default administrator account (ADMIN) and the Schedule+ administrator account (ADMINSCH) are automatically skipped and are therefore not migrated.

Neither the server nor the post office should be accessed by users during the migration. Also, make sure there is at least twice as much space on the Exchange Server computer as the size of the post office from which you are migrating.

CHAPTER SUMMARY

Before installing Exchange Server, make sure Windows NT 4 Service Pack 3 (or later) is installed, verify the spelling of the organization name, and create and use an Exchange Server service account. Check Exchange Server services to determine if the installation was successful.

If you are upgrading from Microsoft Exchange Server 4 to version 5.5, make sure Service Pack 2 is installed. Give yourself plenty of time for the upgrade to install. Make a backup of the Exchange Server databases before upgrading.

Periodic checking and housekeeping of the Information Store can reduce problems. The Private Information Store Properties dialog box displays the physical resources used by each mailbox on a particular server. You can use this information to determine both current and future disk space needs. If disk space becomes an issue, you can move one or more mailboxes, clean one or more mailboxes, or establish mailbox storage limits. The Public Information Store Properties dialog box displays the physical resources used by each public folder on a particular server. From checking the public Information Store, you might determine that public folders need to be moved to another server or perhaps even be moderated by a user.

ESEUTIL is used to defrag and compact the information and directory stores. ESEUTIL requires that the store service be stopped first.

When an Exchange Server problem arises, consult Link Monitors, Server Monitors, messaging tracking, diagnostic logs, message queues, and the Windows NT application event log.

Link Monitors are used to verify the efficient routing of test messages. Use Link Monitors to verify that diagnostic messages sent—to other servers in the same site or different sites—are being delivered within a specific amount of time. After you create a Link Monitor, it must be started before it can provide the information you'll need to resolve the problem. Link Monitor log files contain written records of recent connection problems.

Server Monitors are used to check the condition of one or more servers in a site. A Server Monitor lets you specify the action(s) to take when a service or a computer has stopped. After you create a Server Monitor, it must be started before it can provide the information you'll need to resolve problems. Server Monitor log files contain written records of recent server monitoring events.

Messages sent to and from an Exchange Server can be tracked to help resolve mail-delivery problems. Message tracking must be enabled before it can be used for troubleshooting purposes. Message tracking can be enabled on the MTA, the Information Store, and the MS Mail Connector. After enabling message tracking,

15

all components must be restarted before writing to the log file will take effect. Once message tracking is enabled, the Track Message command initiates the tracing of a message through the network. Once a message is found using the Select Message To Track interface, you can trace its path through the network by using the Message Tracking Center to trace through the logs of all servers that handled the message.

Diagnostic logging helps pinpoint messaging problems. Diagnostic logs are recorded in the Windows NT event log. You can configure diagnostic logging for Microsoft Exchange Server components to record only highly significant events or moderately important events. By default, only critical events are logged. Be selective when you increase a logging level.

When messages are not reaching their destinations, examine the message queues. Use the Queues tab to delete any corrupted messages that are blocking the queues.

Use the Windows NT Event Viewer to display and search the application event log for Microsoft Exchange Server-specific problems.

ESEUTIL can be used to perform a number of analysis and recovery actions on Exchange Server databases. ISINTEG finds and eliminates common Information Store database errors. MTACHECK scans the internal Message Transfer Agent database, looking for objects that are damaged and interfering with queue processing. MTACHECK places suspect objects from the queues into files, which you can examine.

Performance Optimizer analyzes and optimizes your hardware so that it performs in the most efficient way. Monitor the counter values in Windows NT Performance Monitor to determine how Microsoft Exchange Server is performing or to track any error conditions.

Microsoft Exchange Server includes a migration wizard for migrating users from other messaging systems. The migration wizard provides the means to migrate users from MS Mail For PC Networks, Lotus cc:Mail, Novell GroupWise, and Collabra Share.

KEY TERMS

- **Active Server Pages (ASP)**—A feature of Microsoft Internet Information Server (version 3 and greater) that dynamically creates HTML documents.
- **defragmentation**—A process that eliminates wasted space and improves performance on a hard disk by rearranging large files so that they occupy contiguous areas on the disk's surface.

- **diagnostic logging**—A feature of Exchange Server that helps resolve messaging problems. Entries are written to the Windows NT application event log.

- **DIR.EDB**—The Exchange Server file that contains the directory store.

- **ESEUTIL.EXE**—The Exchange Server utility used to defrag the directory store and the Information Store.

- **Exchange Server service account**—The NT domain account that is used to start and use Exchange Server services.

- **Fault-Tolerant Upgrade**—Backs up the Information Store to a different, temporary location before upgrading.

- **ISINTEG.EXE**—An Exchange Server utility used to find and eliminate common Information Store database errors.

- **Link Monitors**—A feature of Exchange Server used to verify the efficient routing of test messages between servers.

- **message tracking**—A feature of Exchange Server that tracks message events to help resolve communication problems.

- **Message Tracking Center**—An Exchange Server tool used to trace all events for a particular message.

- **MTACHECK.EXE**—An Exchange Server utility used to scan the internal Message Transfer Agent database. MTACHECK looks for objects that are damaged and that are interfering with queue processing.

- **Outlook Web Access (OWA)**—Provides Web browser access to mailboxes over the Internet or an intranet.

- **Performance Optimizer**—An Exchange Server tool that optimizes a server's configuration.

- **PING messages**—Test messages used by Link Monitors to verify efficient routing.

- **Server Monitors**—Used to check the condition of one or more servers in a site.

- **Simple Mail Transport Protocol (SMTP)**—The protocol Microsoft Exchange Server uses to send and receive email over the Internet.

- **Standard Database Upgrade**—Upgrades your Information Store in its current locations.

15

REVIEW QUESTIONS

1. When upgrading from Exchange Server 4 to Exchange Server 5.5 (with no Service Packs applied), which additional step must you perform first?

   a. Upgrade the Internet Mail Connector to the Internet Mail Service.

   b. Upgrade the MS Mail Connector to version 3.5 (or greater).

   c. Install Exchange Server Service Pack 2 (or later).

   d. All of the above.

   e. Nothing, Exchange Server 5.5 can be installed without any additional steps.

2. Which utility may be used to defrag the Information Store?

   a. MTACHECK.EXE

   b. ESEUTIL.EXE

   c. DEFRAG.EXE

   d. ISINTEG.EXE

   e. None of the above

3. How does Microsoft Exchange Server communicate natively with other Exchange Servers?

   a. With RPCs

   b. With named Pipes

   c. With WinSock

   d. With Ethernet

4. Which protocol must be installed for the Internet Mail Service to be able to communicate with the Internet?

   a. NetBEUI

   b. TCP/IP

   c. IPX/SPX

   d. All of the above

5. Active Server Pages must be installed before Outlook Web Access can be installed. True or False?

6. How can you determine if there is enough disk space for the directory on a Microsoft Exchange Server that is about to be added to an existing site?

   a. At least 1GB of free space is always required.

   b. Use the Windows NT Explorer to make sure one drive has at least 50 percent of its space free.

   c. Look at the size of DIR.EDB on another Exchange Server in the site, and make sure there's sufficient free space on the drive.

   d. None of the above.

7. The name of the organization, site, or server can be changed after Microsoft Exchange Server is installed. True or False?

8. Which services should be running to determine if Exchange Server was successfully installed? (Choose all that apply.)

   a. Microsoft Exchange System Attendant

   b. MS Mail Connector Interchange

   c. Microsoft Exchange Directory

   d. Microsoft Exchange Information Store

   e. Microsoft Exchange Message Transfer Agent

9. Which files make up the Information Store? (Choose all that apply.)

   a. DIR.EDB

   b. PRIV.EDB

   c. PUB.EDB

   d. ADDRESS.DLL

   e. All of the above

10. You do not need to back up the Information Store before upgrading to Exchange Server 5.5. True or False?

11. When upgrading multiple Exchange Server 4 servers in a multiserver site to Exchange Server 5.5, you can upgrade all of those servers concurrently. True or False?

12. If an Exchange Server is running low on disk space due to a large private Information Store, what can be done?

    a. Move one or more mailboxes.

    b. Clean one or more mailboxes.

    c. Establish mailbox storage limits.

    d. Compact the private Information Store.

    e. All of the above.

13. Manual defragmentation of the Information Store is unnecessary because Exchange Server performs this maintenance task automatically. True or False?

14. If an Exchange Server is running low on disk space due to a large public Information Store, what should be done? (Choose all that apply.)

    a. Move one or more public folders to another server.

    b. Set permissions such that only selected users can post new messages to the public folders on that server.

    c. Compact the public Information Store.

    d. Run MTACHECK.EXE.

15

15. Whenever a mailbox is moved, the mailbox user will have to manually change the messaging profile. True or False?

16. When a problem arises with Exchange Server, what should be checked? (Choose all that apply.)

    a. Link Monitors

    b. Server Monitors

    c. Disk Administrator

    d. Remote Access Admin

    e. None of the above

17. Diagnostic logging writes events to the Windows NT security event log. True or False?

18. What does a Link Monitor display include? (Choose all that apply.)

    a. The server the PING message was sent to.

    b. The number of physical links between sites.

    c. The condition of the connection.

    d. All of the above.

19. A Link Monitor must be started before it can provide useful diagnostic information. True or False?

20. What can a Server Monitor be used for?

    a. Notification of stopped services.

    b. Resetting server clocks.

    c. Restarting stopped services.

    d. All of the above.

21. Message tracking is only available for locally delivered messages. True or False?

22. The Message Tracking Center is a useful component of the MS Mail Connector. True or False?

23. What might a backed up queue indicate? (Choose all that apply.)

    a. A problem with the physical connection between the servers.

    b. A server or MTA configuration error.

    c. The Message Tracking Center was left open.

    d. An improperly configured connector.

    e. All of the above.

    f. None of the above.

24. By default, where is ISINTEG.EXE located?

    a. In the Windows NT directory.

    b. In the \ExchSrvr directory.

    c. In the root directory.

    d. None of the above.

25. Performance Optimizer should only be run once on each server. True or False?

26. The Microsoft Exchange Server Migration Wizard can help migrate users from which messaging systems? (Choose all that apply.)

   a. MS Mail For PC Networks

   b. Lotus Notes

   c. Novell GroupWise

   d. Collabra Share

HANDS-ON PROJECTS

To illustrate some common Microsoft Exchange Server maintenance situations, you'll step through the processes. You do not need any additional resources to perform these steps.

 PROJECT 15.1

To defrag the private Information Store:

1. Go to the Exchange Server that has the Information Store you want to defrag.

2. Open Control Panel, and select the Services icon.

3. In the Services applet, scroll down the list of services, and select Microsoft Exchange Information Store.

4. Click the Stop button.

5. Open a command-prompt window.

6. Type "ESEUTIL /d /ispriv" and press the Enter key.

7. When the defragmentation is complete, close the command-prompt window, and go back to the Services applet.

8. Make sure the Microsoft Exchange Information Store is still selected.

9. Click the Start button.

10. Close the Services applet.

 PROJECT 15.2

To check the public Information Store database for errors:

1. Go to the Exchange Server that has the Information Store you want to check.

15

2. Open the Control Panel, and select the Services icon.

3. In the Services applet, scroll down the list of services, and select Microsoft Exchange Information Store.

4. Click the Stop button.

5. Open a command-prompt window.

6. Type "ISINTEG -pub" then press the Enter key.

7. When the database check is complete, close the command-prompt window, and go back to the Services applet.

8. Make sure the Microsoft Exchange Information Store is still selected.

9. Click the Start button.

10. Close the Services applet.

 ## PROJECT 15.3

To check the MTA database for corruption:

1. Go to the Exchange Server that has the MTA database you want to check.

2. Open the Control Panel, and select the Services icon.

3. In the Services applet, scroll down the list of services, and select Microsoft Exchange Message Transfer Agent.

4. Click the Stop button.

5. Open Explorer.

6. Navigate to the \ExchSrvr\MTAData\MTACheck.out folder.

7. Delete the contents of the folder, then close Explorer.

8. Open a command-prompt window.

9. Type "MTACHECK" then press the Enter key.

10. When the MTA database check is complete, close the command-prompt window, and go back to the Services applet.

11. Make sure the Microsoft Exchange Message Transfer Agent is still selected.

12. Click the Start button.

13. Close the Services applet.

 ## PROJECT 15.4

To track a message sent to an Internet recipient:

1. Open the Microsoft Exchange Administrator program.

2. Select and expand the site where your Internet Mail Service resides.

3. Select and expand the Configuration container.

4. Select and expand the Connections container.

5. Double-click the Internet Mail Service.

6. Select the Internet Mail tab.

7. Select Enable Message Tracking.

8. Click the OK button.

9. Go to the Control Panel, Services applet, and restart the Microsoft Exchange Internet Mail Service.

10. Use the Exchange or Outlook client to send a message to an Internet recipient.

11. Open the Microsoft Exchange Administrator program.

12. From the Tools menu, choose Message Tracking.

13. Enter the name of the server on which your mailbox resides.

14. In the Select Message To Track dialog box, click the From button, and select your name from the Global Address List.

15. Click the Find Now button.

16. Select your Internet message, and click OK.

17. In the Message Tracking Center, click the Track button.

 CASE PROJECTS

1. You are responsible for your company's Microsoft Exchange Server 4 messaging system. The product was installed about a year ago, and no changes have been made. You recently received Exchange Server 5.5 and would like to upgrade to it. You would also like to set up Internet email and a Link Monitor.

Required result:

Successfully upgrade your Exchange Server 4 to version 5.5.

Optional results:

Be able to send and receive Internet email. Be notified if the Microsoft Exchange Information Store service stops.

Proposed solution:

Install Microsoft Exchange Server 4 Service Pack 2. Make a backup of the Exchange Server databases. Install Exchange Server 5.5. Install the Internet Mail Service, and properly configure it to access your company's T1. Define a Server Monitor that produces an alert if the Microsoft Exchange Information Store service stops. Specify that you should be alerted if the service stops.

15

Which results does the proposed solution provide?

a. The proposed solution produces the required result and both optional results.

b. The proposed solution produces the required result and only one optional result.

c. The proposed solution produces only the required result.

d. The proposed solution does not provide the required result.

2. Your Microsoft Exchange Server is functioning properly, but you determine that it needs more RAM and drive space. You purchase more RAM and another hard drive and plan to install them both on the server. You want Microsoft Exchange Server to fully utilize the additional resources. You also want to enable message tracking to resolve some MS Mail connectivity issues.

Required result:

Improve Exchange Server performance.

Optional results:

Take advantage of additional resources. Establish message tracking on the MS Mail Connector.

Proposed solution:

Shut down the server, and install the additional resources. Enable message tracking on the MS Mail Connector. Stop and restart the MS Mail Connector Interchange.

Which results does the proposed solution provide?

a. The proposed solution produces the required result and both optional results.

b. The proposed solution produces the required result and only one optional result.

c. The proposed solution produces only the required result.

d. The proposed solution does not provide the required result.

KEY EXAM POINTS AND OBJECTIVES

This appendix steps through the key points that you should be aware of before taking the Microsoft Exchange Server certification exam. These key points include planning, installation and configuration, configuring and managing resource access, monitoring and optimization, and troubleshooting.

PLANNING

Planning involves:

- Implementing a strategy for Microsoft Exchange Server.
- Configuring an Exchange Server computer.
- Migrating to Exchange Server 5.5.
- Developing a long term coexistence strategy.
- Installing and integrating Exchange Server clients.
- Devising long-term administration strategies.
- Implementing Exchange Server security strategies.
- Using server-side scripting.

The following sections explore each planning issue.

IMPLEMENTING A STRATEGY FOR MICROSOFT EXCHANGE SERVER

It is important to examine some key issues involved with an Exchange Server implementation. These issues, as they relate to planning, are discussed in detail in this section.

Server Location

Selecting server locations is important; you want to balance the load between your sites. Remember that every Microsoft Exchange site requires at least one Microsoft Exchange Server. You do not want to have user mailboxes residing on an Exchange Server that is in a remote site.

Address Space

The address space represents the paths used by the Exchange connectors to send messages outside the site. Address spaces can be used to balance the messaging load when using multiple connectors. An entry must exist in the address space for every Microsoft Exchange site user who will send mail through the connection.

CONFIGURING AN EXCHANGE SERVER COMPUTER

Before you begin the Exchange Server installation, several issues must be addressed. The most common pre-installation issues include:

- Minimum and recommended hardware requirements
- Software requirements

- NT user permissions necessary for the installation
- Exchange sites and their relationships with NT domains

Minimum And Recommended Hardware Requirements

Table A.1 lists both the minimum and recommended hardware requirements for Exchange Server. Most experienced administrators believe, for good reason, that it's better to have the recommended amounts of resources. The minimum requirements might support an Exchange installation, but it's best to give the system more hardware to work with to run efficiently.

Software Requirements

The software requirements are as follows:

- Windows NT Server 4 or later.
- Service Pack 3 for Windows NT Server 4.
- Transmission Control Protocol/Internet Protocol (TCP/IP) for Windows NT if any Internet protocols are to be used.
- Microsoft Internet Information Server (IIS) version 3 with Active Server Pages (ASP) and a Web-enabled browser. IIS must be installed if Microsoft Outlook Web Access is going to be used.
- Microsoft Certificate Server must be installed if there are plans to use the Key Management Server advanced security.
- Microsoft Cluster Server software must be installed if there are any plans to use a pair of clustered Exchange Servers.

Table A.1   Minimum and recommended hardware requirements.

CPU Minimum Requirements	RAM	Disk Space
Intel Pentium 90MHz or faster	24MB	250MB after Windows NT Server installation, 74MB used for the pagefile.
Digital Alpha 4/275	48MB	300MB after Windows NT Server installation.
Recommended Requirements		
Intel Pentium 166MHz or faster	32MB	Multiple physical drives or a striped drive set, 100MB used for the pagefile.
Digital Alpha 5/500	48MB	Multiple physical drives or a striped drive set, 100MB used for the pagefile.

A

- Windows NT Services For Macintosh must be installed if there are any plans to install the MS Mail Connector to exchange mail with MS Mail for AppleTalk networks.

NT User Permissions

During the installation process, the Setup program grants the currently logged-on user account with Administrator permissions on the Exchange Server computer. This allows the user to grant permissions to administer the Exchange Server to other users. The Windows NT domain or local server administrator must be the currently logged-on user during the installation process. This is due to the services that will be started and the changes that will be made to the *win_root*\SYSTEM32 directory during the installation.

Several of the Exchange Server components run on the NT Server as services. These services (such as the System Attendant and the Directory Service) use an NT user account to log on to the system to operate and function. This account is referred to as the site services account. As such, a service account must be created to successfully complete the installation. The same site services account should be used on all Exchange Server computers within the same site.

Exchange Sites And NT Domains

Because Exchange Server relies so heavily on Windows NT Server for basic functionality and security settings, it is important to understand the relationship between the two. Always double-check the Windows NT permissions and trust relationships between domains to make sure that you have a secure system.

MIGRATING TO EXCHANGE SERVER 5.5

Although Microsoft Exchange Server 5.5 can coexist in the same site with version 4 or 5 servers, you'll probably want to upgrade these servers to version 5.5. The Setup program for Microsoft Exchange Server 5.5 upgrades both versions 4 and 5 to version 5.5. The upgrade process modifies the underlying database structure. The Setup program checks for any previously installed Microsoft Exchange Server components and presents you with different options depending on the version already installed. You can determine which version and Service Pack of Exchange Server are currently installed on your computer by viewing the properties of the server object in the Exchange Administrator program.

If you are upgrading to Microsoft Exchange Server 5.5 from a prior version of Exchange Server, keep the following in mind:

- Before upgrading a Microsoft Exchange Server computer, turn off all Server Monitors that include the computer on which the Setup is being run.

- If upgrading to Microsoft Exchange Server 5.5 on a computer that has the Chat service installed, stop the Chat service before running Setup.

- Setup estimates the amount of time it will take to upgrade your existing Information Store. Depending on the size of the Information Store, the process might take a long time—even days! You can't suspend the upgrade process and continue it another time. Therefore, don't start the upgrade process unless you have at least as much time as specified.

- If you are upgrading from Exchange Server 4, you must install Service Pack 2 (or greater). There have been reports of data corruption when this step has not been followed. Service Pack 2 can be obtained from Microsoft (**www.microsoft.com** or **ftp.microsoft.com**). Service Packs can also be ordered directly from Microsoft.

The amount of time required to perform an upgrade depends on the number of messages and folders, and the total size of the Information Store. The upgrade time can be reduced by asking users to reduce the amount of mail they keep in their mailboxes.

During the Microsoft Exchange Server 5.5 upgrade procedure, the existing Information Store (the central storage facility for all Exchange Server messaging data) is converted into a new format—a format optimized for use with Exchange Server 5.5. The conversion process asks for a database backup location in the form of two options—Standard Database Upgrade and Fault-Tolerant Upgrade. Despite their names, neither option actually performs a complete backup of your existing Information Store. Therefore, make sure you perform a full backup of your Information Store before performing the upgrade. The available upgrade options are as follows:

- **Standard Database Upgrade** Upgrades your Information Store in its current locations. If the conversion process fails, the Information Store must be restored from a backup before it can be accessed with the prior version of Microsoft Exchange Server or even before Setup can be run again.

A

- **Fault–Tolerant Upgrade** Backs up the Information Store to a different, temporary location before upgrading. If the conversion process fails, it's unlikely that you'll need to restore the Information Store. Rather, you can reboot your computer and run Setup again— often successfully. Note that the fault-tolerant upgrade's alternate location must have at least twice the amount of available disk space as the size of your Information Store. In addition, the alternate location cannot be a network drive.

After the upgrade process has completed, all appropriate Exchange Server services will restart, and the Information Store will be immediately available to users. No reboot of Windows NT Server is required (but it is recommended by most experienced administrators).

UNDERSTANDING EXCHANGE SERVER INFRASTRUCTURE

The following list of components all work together to create the Exchange Server infrastructure:

- **Directory Service** The function of the Directory Service is to create and manage the storage of all objects within the organization. The database that stores all the objects within the system is the directory. The directory stores objects in a hierarchical structure. The primary purpose of the directory is to provide a central location for the objects within the system. This allows users and administrators to locate the system's resources easily. The objects stored by the Exchange directory have properties, also called attributes, that are the characteristics of the objects. For example, an object can be a user (such as John Smith) or an entire Exchange organization (Best). Furthermore, objects have permissions, which determine the characteristics of the objects.

- **Information Store** The Information Store is responsible for creating and managing the message database on the Exchange Server. This database stores information such as email messages, electronic forms, spreadsheets, word processor documents, graphics images, audio files, and many other items from almost any application. Users can access the information within the Information Store through their mailboxes and folders in their client applications. The Information Store is comprised of two main databases:

  - **Public Information Store** The public Information Store database is contained in the file PUB.EDB. It contains the public folders on the server. Public folders are containers that can contain documents, messages, forms, and any other information your users want to distribute within the messaging system. Essentially, public folders act like public mailboxes.

  - **Private Information Store** The private Information Store contains the users' mailboxes and private folders. The private Information Store database is contained in the file PRIV.EDB. Exchange uses the integrated security features within Microsoft Windows NT. This means that the user mailboxes and folders will only be accessible by their respective owners and to others who have been given access permission. These folders contain the users' private mailboxes. As such, users can keep private any information they put into these folders and inaccessible by other users.

- **MTA Service** The Message Transfer Agent (MTA) handles the routing of all messages, whether the messages are being routed within the same site, different sites, or to other foreign sites. Additionally, the MTA uses components known as connectors. Connectors manage the actual connection to other systems as well as the transfer of data, whereas the MTA handles all the routing functions. The primary functions of the MTA include originator/recipient addressing, message format translation, and message routing.

  The MTA is modeled after the X.400 standard (which is discussed in the section entitled "X.400 Connector" later in this appendix) and, as such, uses the Originator/Recipient Addressing scheme. If messages are being routed to an X.400 messaging system, the MTA will change the format of the message from the Exchange format, known as the Microsoft Database Exchange Format (MDBEF), to the X.400 format, known as the Interpersonal Message (IPM) format.

  The ability to translate messages allows Exchange clients to exchange mail with X.400 mail users. When the MTA receives a message to be forwarded, it first determines a route for the message to travel to reach its destination. It then examines the message recipient's distinguished name (DN). If this address does not resolve the next route, it then examines the originator/recipient address. The MTA will compare the address with the routing information contained within the Gateway Address Routing Table (GWART). Because there might be several paths available, the administrator can assign values to the different paths. These values are called costs. Costs allow priorities to be assigned to the different routes.

  When the MTA encounters multiple paths, it automatically chooses the path with the lowest cost. In the event that the MTA cannot resolve the specified address, it will send the message originator a report known as a non-delivery report (NDR). An NDR alerts a user or administrator that a message is undeliverable.

- **System Attendant** The System Attendant (SA) is a service that runs in the background. It monitors and logs most of the Exchange Server processes, as well as builds and maintains the routing tables for the site. The SA logs information, such as the tracking information that includes the route the message took and whether the message was received at its destination. The SA also compiles the routing tables for the entire site. This is the table the MTA uses when it is determining which route to take. In addition to these functions, the SA monitors the connection between servers, verifies the connection, and, at the same time, checks the Exchange services running on other servers. It accomplishes this by

A

sending test messages between itself and other servers. Additionally, whenever new user accounts are created, the SA is responsible for generating their email addresses.

INSTALLING AND INTEGRATING EXCHANGE SERVER CLIENTS

The following sections explore some of the more important aspects to consider when installing and integrating Exchange clients.

Schedule+ Interoperability

An extension of the Microsoft Mail Connector, the Microsoft Schedule+ Free/Busy Connector enables MS Mail Post Offices and Microsoft Exchange Servers to share Microsoft Schedule+ information. Microsoft Schedule+ is a messaging-enabled program that lets users access other users' schedules and reserve meeting times with those users. The program also serves as a tool to manage personal contact information.

Microsoft has replaced most of the functionality of Microsoft Schedule+ with the Microsoft Outlook client. Although the native Microsoft Outlook client stores scheduling data in a different format than Microsoft Schedule+, Microsoft Outlook can be configured to be compatible with Microsoft Schedule+.

Microsoft Schedule+ is compatible with both MS Mail Post Offices and Microsoft Exchange Server, storing scheduling data in hidden folders on both messaging systems. If a company uses both types of messaging systems, scheduling data will need to be shared between those messaging systems—hence, the existence of the Microsoft Schedule+ Free/Busy Connector.

The Microsoft Schedule+ Free/Busy Connector is installed when the Microsoft Mail Connector is installed. The Microsoft Schedule+ Free/Busy Connector is only necessary when connectivity to MS Mail Post Offices is required; it is not required for Microsoft Schedule+ if no MS Mail Post Offices are present.

Exchange Forms Interoperability

Exchange is configured to support the following types of forms:

- **Report forms** These forms are used to automate report creation and transfer.

- **Request forms** These forms are useful in the streamlining of a material request. For example, "We need to purchase a new 9GB hard drive, fast! We're using Exchange for so many things we used to do on paper, we're filling the hard drive."

- **Survey forms** These forms are very handy in the collection of information from either employees or customers. For example, a public folder could be used to query Web site visitors on how likely they are to purchase a new widget from your firm.

When planning your forms, the Exchange forms library has several types of forms. These are:

- **Organization forms** These forms are stored on the server and accessible by all users.

- **Personal forms** This type of form is specific to a certain user and is located in the individual's mailbox.

- **Folder forms** These forms can be accessed by everyone when they reside in a public folder. The alternative is to store them on a local drive, which makes them available to the user(s) with access to that drive only.

DEVISING LONG-TERM ADMINISTRATION STRATEGIES

The following sections take a look at some important administrative considerations for your Exchange Server implementation.

A Backup Strategy

Implementing a good backup strategy will save you hours of lost productivity and frustration. There are four types of backups available to you. They are:

- **Full (Normal)** A full backup backs up everything, including transaction logs, Information Stores, and directory databases.

- **Copy** A copy is simply a snapshot of the databases at any given point in time.

- **Differential** A differential backup only backs up the data that has changed since the last full backup. It is faster than a normal backup. Note that only the log files are backed up but not purged. To restore this type of backup, you must first restore your last full backup followed by the differential backup.

- **Incremental** An incremental backup only backs up the data that changed. It is faster than a full backup. Note that only the log files are backed up, then purged. To restore this type of backup, you must first restore your last full backup followed by every incremental backup.

A

A Disaster Recovery Strategy

Along with a good backup strategy, you should implement a disaster recovery strategy. A disaster recovery strategy includes:

- Being prepared for the worst.

- Having a recovery server on standby.

- Having all the necessary software on hand to speed up recovery.
- Having the plan written out and available to all administrators.

Information Store Maintenance

There are two main tools you can use to maintain your Information Stores. They are:

- **ISNTEG** This tool checks the consistency of the Information Store database at a database level. ISNTEG can also be used to fix any errors that might be found in the database.
- **ESEUTIL** This tool can be used to check the consistency of the Information Store and directory databases, defragment these databases, and repair any inconsistencies that might exist within the databases.

Remote Administration

It is usually a good idea to install the Microsoft Exchange Administrator program on your workstation. By doing this, you give yourself the ability to remotely manage all Microsoft Exchange objects without having to go to the server. Often, you will be contacted with a problem or be asked to make a change to the Exchange database. It is much easier for you to accomplish this from your workstation, with the user on the telephone. You can install the Exchange Administrator program by running the Microsoft Exchange Setup program on your workstation, selecting a Custom install, and only specifying the Administrator program.

IMPLEMENTING EXCHANGE SERVER SECURITY STRATEGIES

You must decide which security features of Exchange you will use in your organization. To allow users to sign and seal their messages, Microsoft Exchange Server uses an industry-standard encryption technology known as public/private key technology. Each mailbox is assigned a key pair. One key is publicly known, and only the user knows the other key.

A public key is a fixed-length security string that is made available to all users. The advanced security features of Exchange use two public keys to:

- **Seal the message** This means that one of the public keys is used to encrypt the message, thereby sealing the message.
- **Verify the message** This means that the other public key is used to verify the sender of an encrypted (or sealed) message.

With private key encryption, each user has an encrypted security file on his or her computer that contains a fixed-length string. The advanced security features of Exchange use two private keys to:

- **Sign a message** This means that one of the private keys is used to sign the message, thereby securing it.

- **Unseal a message** This means that the other private key is used to unseal a sealed message that was received by the user.

USING SERVER-SIDE SCRIPTING

Active Server Pages (ASP) provide a server-side scripting environment to create and run dynamic, interactive, high-performance Web server applications. Server-side scripting enables a Web server to perform the work involved in generating customized HTML pages. This gives a developer the opportunity to create a generic Web page that "changes" for each user.

INSTALLATION AND CONFIGURATION

The following list presents a few installation and configuration tips you should follow during and after installing Microsoft Exchange:

- Within a site, all Exchange Servers need the same security context.

- Make a site as large as you can. It is easier to split sites than it is to merge them.

- Replication is more network bandwidth-intensive between servers within a site than between sites.

- The minimum net available bandwidth (NAB) between servers within a site is 64Kbps, with 128Kbps being a more practical minimum.

- The connection to another Exchange site must be permanent, not a dial-up connection.

- Exchange can be installed on a Primary Domain Controller (PDC), Backup Domain Controller (BDC), or a member server. A member server is best, because hardware resources are not consumed while verifying login rights. Understanding NT domains is critical to effectively installing an Exchange organization.

INSTALLING AN EXCHANGE SERVER

To install Exchange Server, perform the following steps:

1. Using an account with administrative privileges, log on to the NT Server.

2. Insert the Exchange CD-ROM into your CD-ROM drive, then launch Windows NT Explorer.

3. Scroll down to i386 or Alpha directories, and click Setup, or enter Setup using the command prompt (Start|Run|CMD.EXE|*X*:\Setup\i386).

4. Accept the licensing agreement, and choose an installation type. Installation types include Typical, Minimum, and Complete/Custom:

   - **Typical** Installs the four Exchange components—Directory Service, System Attendant, Information Store, and MTA—and the Exchange Administrator.

   - **Minimum** Installs the four Exchange components only.

   - **Custom/Complete** Offers the following options:

     - **Default Installation Directory** Allows you to change the default installation directory, and offers the choice of MS Mail Connector, Lotus cc:Mail Connector, X.400 Connector, and Exchange Event Service.

     - **Exchange Administrator** Can be installed on any NT machine for the administration of Exchange. Will not operate with Windows 95.

     - **Books Online** Offers online Exchange documentation. Books Online can be very useful; however, it consumes about 135MB of disk space.

     - **Internet Mail** Will not migrate some routing information.

     - **Outlook Web Access** A lightweight method to gain access via an Exchange client in HTML. Requires IIS version 3 or later.

5. Choose licensing, then click OK.

6. Enter the organization and site information. If this is an initial site, you will be asked, "Are You Sure You Want To Create A New Site?" Choose Yes, if you are creating a new site. Otherwise, choose Join An Existing Site.

7. Enter the information in the Service Account and Password fields. Without a separate service account, Exchange cannot validate and will not run.

8. Confirm that rights have been granted, and click OK.

9. Click OK to begin installation.

CONFIGURING EXCHANGE MESSAGE RECIPIENTS

A recipient is an object that can receive a message. One of the most important roles of an Exchange administrator is the creation and management of these objects. The recipients include mailboxes, distribution lists, custom recipients, and public folders, all of which are discussed in the following sections.

Mailboxes

As a general rule, all users accessing your Microsoft Exchange Server require a mailbox. There are several ways to create mailboxes. You can use the following:

- **User Manager For Domains** When the Microsoft Exchange Server is installed, it installs a User Manager For Domains extension called MAILUMX.DLL. This is a Dynamic Link Library (DLL). It links the Mailbox Properties page of the Exchange Administrator program to the User Manager For Domains. Any time an account is created with User Manager For Domains, a mailbox can also be created. When deleting a user account, the corresponding mailbox can also be deleted.

- **Exchange Administrator program** When you create a new Microsoft Exchange mailbox, you need to associate it with one or more NT user accounts. These accounts can be existing accounts (from the current or a trusted domain) or can be new accounts created by the Exchange Administrator program.

  The Exchange Administrator program has the ability to create NT user accounts by directly accessing the NT domain Security Accounts Manager (SAM) database.

- **The Exchange extraction and import tools** The Exchange extraction and import tools work in tandem to create mailboxes. The extraction tools gather information about the user accounts, and the import tools use this extracted information to create the mailboxes. Exchange Server can import and extract lists from both NetWare and Windows NT, as described in the following:

  - **Extract Windows NT Account List** This tool extracts user account information from existing Windows NT Servers and prepares the data for the creation of Exchange objects. To execute this command, you must be logged into the NT domain from which the user account information is to be extracted. This tool is available from the Administrator program by selecting the Extract Windows NT Account List option from the Tools menu or from the command line.

  - **Extract NetWare Accounts List** This tool extracts user account information from existing Novell NetWare 2.x, 3.x, or 4.x servers (as long as the Novell server is running binary emulation). To use this tool, you must be logged in to the NetWare server with supervisor rights. This tool is available from the Administrator program by selecting the Extract NetWare Account List option from the Tools menu.

A

Distribution Lists

A distribution list is a logical grouping of recipients created to expedite the mass mailing of messages and other information. A message sent to a distribution list will be sent to all members of the distribution list.

Creating a distribution list is easy. In the Microsoft Exchange Administrator program, select the New Distribution List option from the File menu (or press Ctrl+D). This action displays the Properties pages (similar to the ones for mailbox configuration) that you can use to configure a distribution list.

Custom Recipients

A custom recipient is a recipient that resides outside the site, organization, or post office (an example would be an Internet SMTP recipient). When a custom recipient is created, it appears in the Address Book and can receive messages like any other recipient. A custom recipient does not have a mailbox on the local Exchange Server. You can create a custom recipient in one of two ways—you can use the Exchange Administrator program or you can use the directory import feature to import custom recipients from other mail systems.

A custom recipient can be created from the Exchange Administrator program by selecting the New Custom Recipient option from the File menu (or pressing Ctrl+R). You are then prompted to select the type of foreign email address to create and its address. The types of foreign email addresses available are:

- Lotus cc:Mail addresses
- Microsoft Mail addresses
- MacMail addresses
- Internet Mail addresses
- X.400 addresses
- Other addresses

Public Folders

Public folders are used to share information among many users within a site or organization. Public folders can contain several types of information, including:

- Mail messages
- Word processing documents
- Graphic files
- Spreadsheets

A powerful feature of Exchange public folders is the ability to create custom applications using custom forms and views. Some of these custom applications include:

- Customer tracking systems
- Help desk applications
- Vacation time request forms
- Expense forms
- Automated time tracking

CONNECTING EXCHANGE SERVER WITH FOREIGN MAIL SYSTEMS

The following sections take a look at how Exchange Server is able to communicate with other types of mail servers.

X.400 Connector

The X.400 Connector is based on the CCITT X.400 standard. This particular connector can use messaging bridgehead servers to route mail traffic. The X.400 Connector allows you, as the administrator, to restrict times for the connector to be operating and to specify which users can send mail to the remote site.

With an X.400 Connector, each server must pass its information to the messaging bridgehead server. The messaging bridgehead server then connects to its partner bridgehead server in the remote site and transfers the information. Finally, if necessary, the remote messaging bridgehead server passes the information to the final destination.

The X.400 is useful when connecting to sites via a slow network connection or to private or public packet networks. Because all information must be converted to messages before transfer of information can occur, this tends to slow the connector down. Because all mail must flow through the messaging bridgehead servers, messaging bottlenecks can be caused, slowing down intersite communication.

There are some benefits to the X.400 Connector: It is the most generic Exchange connector. It can be used to connect to any X.400 system. The connector allows you to restrict both the size of the message and the users that can access the connector.

An X.400 Connector requires more configuration than the Site Connector. You must perform two steps to install the X.400 Connector: You must install the MTA transport stack and the X.400 Connector.

A

The MTA transport stack configures Microsoft Exchange to use the network transport used by the Windows NT Server. You must first configure one of the appropriate network transports before the connector is configured. The available network transports for the X.400 Connector are:

- **TCP/IP** The Exchange Server uses the Windows NT TCP/IP services. The MTA uses port 102 to communicate.

- **TP4/CLNP** The Exchange Server has an interface that allows it to work with the Windows NT TP4 driver. This interface is used to communicate with remote systems using TP4 for message transport. In CLNP, data is transferred without using a connection request. TP4 is designed for use in a connectionless mode network. The server running the transport stack determines TP4 network address information.

- **TP0/X.25** TP0/X.25 provides both dial-up and direct communication. X.25 network software must be installed and running on the server before installing the MTA transport stack. Multiple X.25 transport stacks can be installed on a server, and you can install multiple X.25 port adapters on one server. Be aware, however, that a separate MTA transport stack is required for each X.25 port on an adapter.

Lotus cc:Mail Connector

The Lotus cc:Mail Connector allows you to integrate Microsoft Exchange with any existing cc:Mail environments. This connector allows you to exchange messages and synchronize directories between Microsoft Exchange and Lotus cc:Mail systems. The Lotus cc:Mail Connector supports both DB6 and DB8 cc:Mail Post Offices. Using this connector, you can migrate users from cc:Mail to Exchange without disrupting regular email services.

Microsoft Mail Connector

The Microsoft Mail Connector allows you to connect to Microsoft Mail For PC Networks, Microsoft Mail For AppleTalk networks, and Microsoft Mail for third-party gateways (such as PROFS, SNADS, and NetWare). The connector uses shadow Post Offices similar to those used in a Microsoft Mail 3.x Post Office.

The Microsoft Mail Connector can be used with the following protocols:

- TCP/IP
- IPX/SPX
- X.25
- NetBEUI
- Remote Access Service (RAS)

CONFIGURING DIRECTORY SYNCHRONIZATION WITH FOREIGN MAIL SYSTEMS

Synchronization is used to synchronize information between Exchange and other systems, such as MS Mail. It is an efficient process because only changed data is handled. Exchange supports this optional step with any system that supports the MS Mail For PC Networks version 3 Directory Synchronization (DirSync) Protocol. This process is most commonly referred to as DirSync. The DirSync process has three steps:

1. DirSync requestors send changes to the DirSync server.

2. The DirSync creates a master copy.

3. The master copy is sent back to the DirSync requestors.

Exchange can be the requestor or the server. In the case of MS Mail, the server should already have a DirSync server running, so Exchange will be a requestor. Keep in mind that MS Mail has an AppleTalk option.

To configure synchronization, perform the following steps:

1. Click File | New Other | DirSync Server.

2. Configure times for the DirSync master copy and the DirSync requestors, and click OK.

3. Click Start | Settings | Control Panel | Services | Start DirSync Service.

4. On the MS Mail Server(s), select File | New Other | DirSync Remote Requestor.

5. While at the MS Mail Post Office, run ADMIN.EXE to send DirSync messages to the shadow Post Office of the Exchange Server.

6. In the Exchange Server, click File | New Other | DirSync Requestor.

7. Set the time for DirSync requestors to send changes to the DirSync server.

8. Click Start | Settings | Control Panel | Services | Start DirSync Service.

DIRECTORY REPLICATION

Replication can be thought of as a cloning process. For example, let's say that you have an address list that is made up of everyone in your multinational company within your Global Address List (GAL). Any time a user in Redmond, WA, wants to find the address of a coworker based in New York, the user would have to go across the network link to find the address. This process might be repeated several times a day, increasing network traffic and costs. If you replicated address lists and other data, such as public folders, the network traffic would drop, reducing costs and increasing performance. You can use the directory replication

A

connector General tab to establish local and remote bridgehead servers. You can also add an administrative note (which are only visible to administrators).

Within a site, directory replication is automatic. Between sites, you can configure directory replication so that only the desired information is replicated to other sites

To set up directory replication between sites, you must create and configure a directory replication connector, which is a bidirectional replication connection between two sites. You must designate and schedule one server in each site to request updated directory information from the other site. At the scheduled times, the local server requests directory updates from the remote server. To configure replication, perform the following steps:

1. Select the Configuration container.

2. Install the directory replication connector.

3. Select File | New Other.

4. Schedule the time that replication should occur.

IMPORTING DATA FROM EXISTING MAIL SYSTEMS

Importing mail can save you a great deal of time and grief. It takes some work to create an import process and to create connections so that you are running two systems while you test your migration. The alternative is to enter the users manually, causing interruptions in mail service to your users. In that light, importing lists of users is a much better choice. The Migration Wizard is available from Exchange. Your other option is to import and kill the old system—choosing this route is not advised.

The Migration Wizard can import from:

- Collabra Share
- Lotus cc:Mail
- MS Mail
- Novell GroupWise

INSTALLING AND CONFIGURING EXCHANGE SERVER CLIENT COMPUTERS

The original Microsoft Exchange client was called the Microsoft Exchange Client. Microsoft has since changed its naming conventions. All server components are now referred to as Exchange, whereas all client components are now referred to as Outlook.

The actual installation of Microsoft Outlook will vary from client to client, but there are several issues you should consider. These include:

- Will users be able to configure their own settings or will you pre-configure, or lock down, the settings?

- How are you going to install Outlook: via CD-ROM, network, or Web download?

- Will Outlook be installed locally or will it be server-based?

USING THE ADMINISTRATOR PROGRAM

The Exchange Administrator program is where you'll spend most of your time configuring Exchange. Be very careful when making changes to your Exchange system. The default is to work at the site level. Exchange uses a container concept, similar to Chinese boxes (boxes within boxes). A change at the organization level will affect the mail for your entire company; a change at the site level affects all servers within the site; and a change at the server level affects only the server.

There are three main sections in the Admin program where you set the permission roles:

- Organization container (top level in the tree)

- Site container

- Configuration container within the site

The organization is the topmost level. Within the organization is the site. A site has configuration data and servers. Another container is the recipients (users). To simplify administration efforts, you can create multiple recipient containers. Pay attention when assigning permissions—permissions follow only as far as a boundary.

MESSAGE TRANSFER AGENT CONFIGURATION

A

Within your configuration container, you will find the Message Transfer Agent (MTA). The MTA allows you to configure simple items, such as Retry and Timeout values. Types of connections include the following:

- **Internet Mail Service (IMS)** Renamed in Exchange 5.5, the IMS was previously called the Internet Mail Connector (IMC). This component was renamed to reflect its additional functionality, such as LDAP and IMAP4.

- **Lotus cc:Mail** The "father" of Notes, Lotus cc:Mail is a popular email system that competed with MS Mail.

- **Lotus Notes** IBM/Lotus's competitor to Exchange.

- **Microsoft Mail** The "father" to Exchange, MS Mail is an older program. You might have to migrate users from MS Mail to Exchange.

- **Remote Access Service (RAS)** RAS is a secure method for dial-up networking. Think of RAS as a way to extend the network, using a very long and very slow network connection from the server to the client.

- **Site Connector** A tool that connects sites within a local area network (LAN) or a wide area network (WAN).

- **X.400** Integrated with the MTA, X.400 can be configured to connect sites within Microsoft Exchange Server or to route messages to foreign X.400 systems. When handling communication between Microsoft Exchange Server and foreign X.400 systems, the connector maps addresses and converts Microsoft Exchange Server messages to native X.400 messages and vice versa.

INTERNET PROTOCOLS AND SERVICES

The following sections explore the various protocols and services that can be added to your Exchange implementation.

Post Office Protocol Version 3 (POP3)

POP3 enables users with a POP3 client to retrieve email messages from the Exchange Inbox. Because Microsoft Exchange uses this standard, any email client application that supports POP3 can be used to connect to a Microsoft Exchange Server and access the user's messages.

By default, when you install Microsoft Exchange Server, the POP3 protocol is also installed. This allows POP3 clients to retrieve their email as soon as the server is set up. You must, however, configure the Internet Mail Service before the clients can send email. This is because the client uses the POP3 protocol to retrieve messages and the SMTP protocol to send messages.

Internet Message Access Protocol Version 4 (IMAP4)

IMAP4 enables users with any IMAP4-compliant client to access email stored in their Exchange mailbox. The users can also read and post messages to public folders or access another user's mailbox—if they have been granted the right to do so.

By default, when you install Microsoft Exchange Server, the IMAP4 protocol is also installed. This allows IMAP4 clients to retrieve their email as soon as the server is set up. However, you must configure the Internet Mail Service before the clients can send email. This is because the client uses the IMAP4 protocol to retrieve messages and the SMTP protocol to send messages.

Active Server

Microsoft Outlook Web Access (OWA) allows users to access data on your Exchange Server using an Internet Web browser from a Macintosh, Unix, or Microsoft Windows-based computer. You can also use it to provide Global Address List information and access any public folders you have on your Exchange Server. Users who have access (a mailbox) to your Exchange Server can log in to their personal accounts to read and send private messages. Users also have the ability to publish information to the Internet without having to convert their documents to the Hypertext Markup Language (HTML) format.

Outlook Web Access works in conjunction with a client's Web browser. The browser communicates with Microsoft Exchange through the Microsoft Internet Information Server (IIS) to provide the interface to the user's mailbox information. Using this feature of Exchange Server, you have the ability to grant your users access to company and personal information from anywhere in the world via the Internet.

You have the option to install the Outlook Web Access files during Microsoft Exchange Server setup. Outlook Web Access uses Active Server Pages (.asp file extension) to provide dynamically changing Web pages as well as HTML to provide static Web pages. The Microsoft Internet Information Server can be installed on the same Windows NT Server computer as Microsoft Exchange, or it can be installed on a different Microsoft Windows server that can be accessed by the server where Outlook Web Access is installed. When installing Outlook Web Access and Microsoft Exchange Server on the same computer, you must make sure that the WWW service in IIS is enabled and running.

You can install Internet Information Server version 2 when you install Microsoft Windows NT Server 4. The ASP component of IIS is only available in Internet Information Server version 3 or higher. If you have IIS 2 installed, you must upgrade it to IIS 3 or higher for Outlook Web Access to function. The Active Server component of IIS acts as a connector between Outlook Web Access and a Web browser (such as Microsoft Internet Explorer or Netscape Navigator). Active Server dynamically generates Web pages using a combination of HTML, server-executed scripts, and Remote Procedure Calls (RPCs). You have the option to customize the default ASP files for your organization. You can, for example, add your organization's logo to Outlook Web Access.

Network News Transfer Protocol (NNTP)

The Internet News Service is a method for your organization to connect to a Usenet host to exchange information with Usenet. The Internet News Service is a Windows NT service that allows you to configure both unidirectional (read-only or write-only) and bidirectional (read and write) newsfeeds using the Network News Transfer Protocol (NNTP). This allows your clients to send messages to and receive messages from the Internet. If you have several Microsoft Exchange Servers in your site, only one of them needs to be configured with Internet News Service. NNTP clients will still be able to access newsgroup public servers on a server running the Internet News Service.

The Internet News Service integrates tightly with the Information Store to provide newsgroups as public folders. The service connects to Usenet hosts on a scheduled basis (one that you set). It connects to the remote hosts by either using a push feed or a pull feed.

The Internet News Service can operate with either a dedicated or a dial-up connection to the Internet. Microsoft Outlook or any other NNTP-compatible client can access the Newsgroup public folders. As far as the third-party newsreaders are concerned, they are communicating with a standard NNTP server.

A nice feature of the Internet News Service is its ability to communicate with multiple sources on multiple newsfeeds. It can perform these newsfeeds from one or more Microsoft Exchange Server computers.

Lightweight Directory Access Protocol (LDAP)

LDAP is an Internet protocol that enables LDAP clients to access directory information on your Microsoft Exchange Server. Given the correct permissions, these clients can browse, read, search, and write directory listing information to the Microsoft Exchange Server directory. Many LDAP clients can access your Microsoft Exchange Server and perform directory queries (including user names and phone numbers). If you assign the correct permissions, then the users can modify Exchange directory information, such as changing your phone number.

MESSAGE TRACKING

Tracking is a critical part of keeping the messages flowing or, sometimes, finding out why they aren't. You use the Exchange Administrator program to configure tracking. Configuration is performed in two areas: the Information Store and the MTA. If a message is bound within a site, it does not leave Exchange, so it is tracked with the Information Store. If a message has a destination outside of the site, it is tracked by the MTA. Message tracking creates a log file, which is stored in the Exchsrvr\tracking subdirectory. This log file is created with the System Attendant. The format is *YYMMDD*.LOG.

MONITORING AND OPTIMIZATION

The following sections explore how you can fine-tune your Exchange Server implementation to get the most out of it.

LINK MONITORS

A Link Monitor is a tool that can be used either to watch for message connections between two Exchange Servers within an Exchange organization, or to test connections between an Exchange system and a foreign mail system.

Link Monitors work by constantly monitoring the requested connection. They do this by sending a test message, also known as a PING (Packet Internet Groper) message, and timing the amount of time it takes for the message to "bounce" back. You can create multiple Exchange Servers or foreign systems to monitor. At a set interval, called the polling interval, a PING message is sent to all Exchange Servers and foreign systems configured in the Link Monitor's Servers tab.

To create a new Link Monitor, follow these steps:

1. Using the Exchange Administrator program, select the appropriate site in your organization.

2. Open the Configuration container by double-clicking on it.

3. Select the Monitors container. The right pane of the Administrator program will display all existing Link (and Server) Monitors for this particular site.

4. From the File menu, under New Other, select Link Monitor. The Link Monitor Properties pages will appear.

The Link Monitor has five tabs that allow you to configure what and how to monitor links between locations. These property pages are:

- **General** This tab allows you to set a directory name for the Link Monitor (this cannot be changed after you create the Link Monitor), a display name (the name that will be displayed in the right pane of the Administrator program), the polling interval, and a log file location (logging to a file is optional).

- **Notification** This tab allows you to configure what event will take place if a faulty message link occurs. You can choose one of three options: Launch A Process, Mail Message, or Windows NT Alert. Launching a program loads an external application (that is, the computer alerts you if something goes wrong). If you select the Mail Message option, the computer will automatically send you (or anyone else you select) an email message stating the problem. Windows NT Alert uses the Windows NT Messenger service to notify a user or group of users of the problem.

- **Servers** This tab allows you to select which Exchange Servers to create a link with.

A

- **Recipients** This tab allows you to configure PING messages for recipients in foreign (non-Exchange) mail systems. Because foreign mail systems do not have the Link Monitor feature like Exchange Server, you will have to create a script that will reply to PING messages. Another option is to send the link messages to a nonexistent account in the foreign system. The Link Monitor will receive the non-delivery message as the PING message. The recipient on the foreign systems must be listed as a custom recipient in the Exchange Directory.

- **Bounce** This tab allows you to configure the amount of time a PING message can take to complete a roundtrip before the server issues a warning or an alert.

SERVER MONITOR

A Server Monitor is a tool that "watches" Windows NT services on remote servers to ensure that they are operating properly. As in a Link Monitor, a polling interval is defined. At each polling interval, the Server Monitor connects to the remote server via a Remote Procedure Call (RPC). It then makes sure that the monitored services are running. The status of the server being monitored is displayed in the right pane of the Administrator program. You also have the ability to start, stop, or pause any service that is being monitored. You do not have to monitor only Exchange-specific services. Any service running on the remote server can be monitored using this tool.

To create a new Server Monitor, follow these steps:

1. Using the Exchange Administrator program, select the appropriate site in your organization.

2. Open the Configuration container by double-clicking on it.

3. Select the Monitors container. The right pane of the Administrator program will display all existing Server (and Link) Monitors for this particular site.

4. From the File menu, under New Other, select Server Monitor. The Server Monitor Properties pages will appear.

The Server Monitor has three tabs that allow you to configure which services to monitor. These tabs are:

- **General** This tab allows you to set a directory name for the Server Monitor (this cannot be changed after you create the Server Monitor), a display name (the name that will be displayed in the right pane of the Administrator program), the polling interval, and a log file location (logging to a file is optional).

- **Notification** This tab allows you to configure what event will take place if the server link notices a problem. You can choose one of three options: Launch A Process, Mail Message, or Windows NT Alert. Launching a program loads an external application (that is, the computer alerts you if something goes wrong). If you select the Mail Message option, the computer will automatically send you (or anyone else you select) an email message stating the problem. Windows NT Alert uses the Windows NT Messenger service to notify a user or group of users of the problem.

- **Servers** This tab allows you to specify which servers are to be monitored by the Server Monitor. By clicking the Service button, you can select any service (or services) to monitor on the remote computer.

After you create a Server Monitor, you must start it so that it can monitor the selected servers. The Server Monitor can be started in two ways: manually or automatically. To start a Server Monitor manually, use the Exchange Administrator window. To start a Server Monitor automatically, use the Windows NT command line. One drawback is that the Server Monitor's windows must be open (or minimized) at all times.

EXCHANGE SERVER OPTIMIZATION

Microsoft Exchange comes with a tool to allow you to easily optimize your installation. This tool is called the Performance Optimizer. It is a utility that analyzes your hardware configuration and then optimizes your server for peak performance. The Performance Optimizer will determine the best place to locate the Exchange files and databases. The Optimizer can change the directory location for the following components and files:

- Information Store
- Directory Service database
- Message Transfer Agent
- Transaction log files

In addition to these changes, the Performance Optimizer can also recommend the amount of memory to be used for caching data from the Information Store and Directory Service.

MONITORING PERFORMANCE USING SNMP AND MADMAN MIB

The Simple Network Management Protocol (SNMP) is the network management protocol of the TCP/IP protocol suite. In SNMP, agents, which can be hardware as well as software, monitor the activity in the various devices on the network and report to a central console. Microsoft Exchange uses the Mail And Directory Management (MADMAN) Management Information Base (MIB) to monitor its messaging infrastructure.

A

EXCHANGE SERVER DISASTER
RECOVERY

This appendix looks at the different options available to you as an Exchange administrator for the backup and recovery of your Exchange Server. The strategies outlined within this appendix should be supplemented with existing online and hard copy documentation. Although Microsoft Exchange is a very stable messaging system robust enough to be used on an enterprise, it is important that you have a plan for restoring the Exchange Servers and data should a disaster occur. Your goal as an administrator is to minimize the downtime to your Exchange infrastructure and to recover lost data as quickly as possible should a failure occur. Don't wait until a disaster occurs before drawing up a recovery plan. Remember that each installation will be different and that this appendix is a general guide to backup and recovery.

Email has become such a critical application for businesses that many companies rely on it on a daily basis. Many corporations would not be able to function efficiently without an email system. With older, shared, file mail systems, backing up was fairly straightforward—you just backed up the shared files and stored the tapes in a safe location. With Exchange being able to handle many users per server and having all messages stored within an active, online database, the rules have changed. With a shared file system, you would simply shut down the mail program and back up the files. In today's world, the Internet has become such a critical part of doing business that its email is a 24-hour, 7-days-a-week, 365-days-a-year operation. You cannot usually shut down Exchange to back up the database. Users are accustomed to accessing email at any time, day or night.

One of Microsoft Exchange's strongest features is how well it operates with Window NT. Exchange uses the Windows NT security model for all its authentication. Due to this fact, it is vitally important that the Windows NT operating system be backed up as well. You must create a backup and recovery plan that includes both the Windows NT operating system and the Microsoft Exchange Server.

Exchange Server was designed to allow you to back up the system without taking the system offline (that is, without shutting down the Exchange services). All the major Exchange components (the Information Store, directory, MTA, and System Attendant) remain active and functioning while the backup is taking place.

DEVELOPING DISASTER RECOVERY STRATEGIES

When you perform routine maintenance on Microsoft Exchange Server, you greatly reduce the need for disaster recovery. Some system administrators would like to believe that they can control nature, but natural disasters continue to occur at the worst possible times. Disasters can range from minor data corruption, to losing critical data due to hard disk failure, right up to losing all your data in a fire or flood.

The following precautions can help you recover from disasters and minimize downtime:

- Perform and verify regular backups.

- Implement and practice a disaster recovery plan.

- Make sure that you have dedicated systems for disaster recovery.

- Train your administrators to implement the disaster recovery plan.

- Consider all server design and configuration information when developing a disaster recovery plan.

The five precautions listed are very important! Make sure that you verify your backups regularly. It is very common to perform a system backup and find out, after a failure, that the backup procedure never backed up key system components. Also, make sure that you (and other administrators) are aware of the disaster recovery plan and know how to implement it. The reasons for having dedicated systems for disaster recovery will become apparent later in this appendix.

You should start creating your disaster recovery plan by documenting your network. The following tables provide a method for you to track hardware (see Table B.1), Windows NT (see Table B.2), and Exchange Server information (see Table B.3).

PERFORMANCE OPTIMIZER

An important utility used to optimize a Microsoft Exchange Server installation is the Microsoft Exchange Performance Optimizer. It is important to run this utility during the recovery process to ensure that the server is tuned properly. The Performance Optimizer tunes the Exchange Server computer based on the following criteria:

Table B.1 Hardware configuration inventory form.

Item	Description
Computer make and model	
Monitor make and model	
Serial numbers	
Motherboard type and revision	
CPU make and model	
Hard disk(s)	
Type and amount of RAM	
Video card make and model	
Network adapter make and model	
SCSI card make and model (if any)	
CD-ROM make and model	
Tape backup make and model	

Table B.2 Windows NT installation configuration inventory form.

Item	Description
Windows NT Server version	
Windows NT Server role	
Domain name	
Computer name	
Installation directory	
Swap file size and location(s)	
Network protocol(s)	
Protocol specific information	
Disk partition information	
Disk file system information	
Special groups	

- The number of users that the server supports and the number of users in your organization.

- The types of activities the server performs.

- The server's hardware resources, including the amount of RAM and the number and type of disks and processors. Microsoft recommends that Exchange Server be allocated its own server. Although this is the ideal situation, it might not always be an acceptable solution.

The Performance Optimizer configures the system based on the following formula:

B

Table B.3   Microsoft Exchange Server installation inventory form.

Item	Description
Organization name	
Site name	
Computer name	
Service account name	
Service account password	
Connectors	

```
# of users  x  type of server  x  # of users in organization  x
Memory usage (MB)
```

Number of users:

- Less than 500
- 500 through 999
- 1,000 through 4,999
- 5,000 through 24,999
- 25,000 through 49,999
- 50,000 or more

Type of server:

- Private store
- Public store
- Connector/directory import
- Multiserver
- POP3/IMAP4/NNTP only

Number of users in the organization:

- Less than 1,000
- 1,001 through 9,999
- 10,000 through 99,999
- 100,000 through 499,999
- 500,000 or more

COMPONENT LOCATIONS

It is also important to note where the Exchange Server components are stored. Table B.4 assumes that Microsoft Exchange Server was installed in the Exchsrvr folder.

Table B.4   Component locations.

Component	Location
Private Information Store	Exchsrvr\Mdbdata
Public Information Store	Exchsrvr\Mdbdata
Information Store logs	Exchsrvr\Mdbdata
Directory Service	Exchsrvr\Dsadata
Directory Service logs	Exchsrvr\Dsadata
Message Transfer Agent	Exchsrvr\Mtadata
Internet Mail Service	Exchsrvr\Imcdata

GENERAL PRACTICES

A successful disaster recovery plan should incorporate the following tasks:

- Creating and verifying daily backups
- Performing periodic file-based backups
- Using standard tape backup formats
- Using a UPS
- Checking the Windows NT Event Logs daily
- Creating a disaster kit
- Creating an Exchange maintenance window
- Calculating downtime costs
- Maintaining offsite tapes and equipment
- Using dedicated recovery equipment
- Keeping all configuration records

Creating And Verifying Daily Backups

Although this is one of the most important tasks you can perform, it is often overlooked by many administrators. The best backup system and planning in the world will not help you if the data you back up is corrupt. Remember that you cannot recover data if your backup is invalid. Most administrators assume that backup tapes are being swapped and that data is being backed up properly. You should make it a daily habit to check and recheck all backup logs. Also, remember that full backups reset and delete transaction logs. This results in more free disk space on your server. If circular logging is not enabled and your full backups are failing, transaction logs will not be deleted and will start to fill the Exchange Server hard drives. Should this occur, you might find your Exchange Server completely shut down!

B

Performing Periodic File-Based Backups

If your Exchange Server resides on your PDC and you back up only your Exchange data, you might find that your data is unusable should you be required to restore your data. Because Microsoft Exchange closely integrates with the Windows NT SAM database, not having the SAM backed up will cause problems. When Windows NT creates a new account, jsmith for example, it assigns the account a Security Identifier (SID). This SID must be unique within a domain. Microsoft Exchange uses this SID to verify the identity of the user accessing a specified mailbox. If these SIDs do not match, the user will not be able to log on to the mailbox. Even if the username is the same, the SIDs are not. For example, if you delete the user jsmith, and then re-create the account using the same name, the SIDs will still be different. The two user accounts are completely different to Windows NT.

Using Standard Tape Backup Formats

Imagine that you create a foolproof disaster-recovery system using a DLT-based tape backup system. Your system runs flawlessly until 4:00 P.M. the Friday before your vacation is to start. By the way, it's December 24—at 4:00 P.M., you lose your Exchange databases due to a power surge. The Exchange Server and all its peripherals, including the tape backup drive, are "fried." No worries, you will stay a few hours longer and recover the information to the recover server you built. You start your recovery process and realize that the recovery server has a DAT drive on it. Good luck trying to fit a DLT tape into a DAT drive. This example illustrates that you need to have a standard tape backup format throughout your organization.

 Remember, nothing is foolproof because fools are so ingenuous.

Using A UPS

Many computer rooms have a UPS but do not use it properly. One time, while on a tour of a client's facility, we were informed that they had spent a great deal of money on their UPS system. They were very proud of the system they had built. As a demonstration, we were asked to press the power kill switch in the room. After doing so, they realized that all the servers were on the UPS except for one. That one server did not start up properly after power was restored.

It is also common to only place the servers on the UPS and not the networking equipment or, more importantly, the monitors. Imagine that all your equipment is on a UPS except for your monitors. Your computer room loses power. Try to do anything on a server without a monitor and you will realize how difficult it is.

Checking The Windows NT Event Logs Daily

This is a good practice to get into for all your servers, not just Microsoft Exchange. By checking the event logs daily, you take a proactive approach rather than a reactive one. This allows you to identify possible problems before they occur.

Creating A Disaster Kit

Your goal is to minimize recovery time. Build a kit that has all the configuration information and software necessary for the recovery. The last thing you want to do when you have a disaster is to go looking for your Windows NT Server installation CD-ROM.

Creating An Exchange Maintenance Window

It is a good idea to schedule regular maintenance of your Exchange Server. This allows you to perform tasks such as Service Pack updates and software and hardware upgrades.

Calculating Downtime Costs

If you calculate the estimated cost for any downtime, it will be easier for you to justify the cost of dedicated disaster-recovery equipment.

Maintaining Off-Site Tapes And Equipment

If your data is critical for the operation of your organization, consider storing your backup tapes off-site. If disaster strikes your organization, such as fire, the hardware might be lost but the data will be intact.

Using Dedicated Recovery Equipment

It is a good idea to have dedicated equipment on standby for a disaster recovery. It is important to maintain this equipment. It is very easy to "borrow" the equipment for a short project because it is not doing anything. If you do this, chances are, you will need the equipment to recover data and it will no longer be available.

B

Keeping All Configuration Records

Keep all your configuration records in a safe and secure location. It is also a good idea to keep several copies of these records should your copy get misplaced. In addition, keep paper copies of the records. Storing the configuration records on the server that has failed will not help you.

WHAT DATA TO BACK UP?

Developing a backup strategy is difficult if you do not know what should be backed up and where it is stored. The type of Exchange data that you should back up can be separated into two areas: user data and configuration data. The user data is the information "seen" by the users. Information such as public folders, mail messages, documents, and so forth. The user data is stored in the public Information Store (PUB.EDB), private Information Store (PRIV.EDB), personal folder files (.pst), offline folder files (.ost), personal address books (.pab), and transaction logs. The configuration data includes information such as the Windows NT Registry and the Exchange Server Directory (DIR.EDB).

By default, Microsoft Exchange Server is installed in the *X*:\Exchsrvr folder, where *X* is a drive letter (C: for example). When you install Exchange Server, you are given the option to change the location of this folder. If you did not accept the defaults during the installation process, then the files will be stored under the folder you specified. For example, if you installed Exchange Server in the C:\Backoffice\Exchange folder, then all the data files (user and configuration) will be stored under the C:\Backoffice\Exchange folder. Table B.5 shows the location of the Exchange Server database files.

PERSONAL MESSAGE STORE

The Personal Message Store (also known as personal folder file) is a file that can contain folders, messages, forms, files, and other items. A user has the ability to create any number of PSTs for use with a single profile. The user can also designate a PST as the delivery location for incoming mail.

Normally, users will store PSTs on their local hard drives. If this is the case, you might not be able to recover from a failure if the user's computer fails. There are several options available for dealing with this problem. The easiest method is to create Home directories on a file server, have the users store their PST files in their designated folder, and back up the file server. The second method is to use a third-party backup software package that installs agents on the client computers and backs their information through the network. It is very easy to recover a PST file from a disaster. First, you need to recover the PST file, you

Table B.5 Exchange Server database file locations.

Information Files	File Location
Private Information Store	Exchsrvr\Mdbdata\Priv.edb
Public Information Store	Exchsrvr\Mdbdata\Pub.edb
Directory	Exchsrvr\Dsadata\Dir.edb
Information Store transaction logs	Exchsrvr\Mdbdata*.log

then place it in the designated folder and add the PST file to an existing profile. All information within the PST file would then be available to the user.

Users have the option to specify a password to protect the PST file from unauthorized access. If a user does this and then forgets the password, there is no way to recover the password or any of the data from within the file (even Microsoft cannot help you with this problem). Make sure that your users know this! It only takes once for a user to forget his password, and he will never forget it again.

OFFLINE MESSAGE STORE

The OST data can be lost when changes are made to the locally stored OST file before it has been replicated to the server. If a client workstation fails, a new OST file can be created on the new workstation, and all the server-based data can be copied to the file via synchronization.

PERSONAL ADDRESS BOOK

The Personal Address Book (PAB) files can be stored either locally or on a server share. The only time the PAB data is at risk is when the files are stored locally and not backed up.

BACKUP TYPES

The following sections take a look at the various available backup types.

ONLINE BACKUPS

An online backup requires that the necessary services (Directory Service or Information Store) are running during the backup process. The backup process does not affect the regular operation of the Microsoft Exchange Server. You should include the Windows NT Registry in your backup.

There are four major types of online backups: full (or normal), copy, incremental, and differential. These are discussed in the following sections.

Full (Normal)

A full, or normal, backup (see Figure B.1) backs up the Exchange database files and then the transaction log files. It then deletes the transaction log files from the directory. Because the backup software deletes the log files, you can have circular logging disabled. If you are performing regular backups, you will not have a problem with your log files filling your hard drive. When you need to restore the data, just restore the last full backup and start the service. Microsoft Exchange will fill in the "blanks."

Copy

A copy backup (also shown in Figure B.1) is very similar to a full backup except that it does not delete the log files on the drive and does not update the backup context in the database files. A copy backup is good if you need to back up the data now, without having to wait for the full backup to take place.

Incremental

An incremental backup (see Figure B.2) only works on the log files; therefore, circular logging must be disabled. Like a full backup, the log files are deleted when the incremental backup is completed. Using an incremental backup is another way to prevent your log files from filling your hard drive space, without having to compromise on your Microsoft Exchange data recoverability. To restore from an incremental backup, you need to first restore your last full backup, which contains the actual database files. You then have to restore *every* incremental backup made after the full backup. This will restore all the log files. Finally, you need to start the Microsoft Exchange services. Microsoft Exchange will then rebuild the database from the log files.

 Make sure that you do not start the Microsoft Exchange services until after you have recovered all the incremental backup sets. If you restart the services before restoring all of the log files, you might lose some of your data.

Differential

A differential backup (see Figure B.3) is similar to an incremental backup in that it also works with the log files. Therefore, you must have circular logging

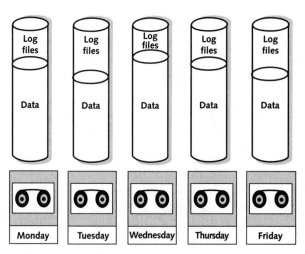

Figure B.1   A normal or copy backup.

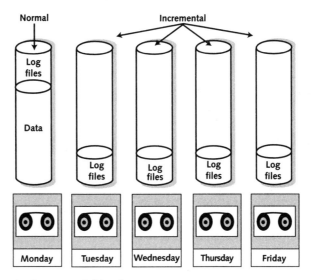

Figure B.2 An incremental backup.

disabled. The differential backup, unlike an incremental backup, does not delete the log files. To restore a differential backup, you must first restore the last full backup and then restore the last differential backup. For example, say you completed a full backup on Monday. On Tuesday, you performed a differential backup, and because a full backup deletes the log files, you backed up the new log files since Monday. On Wednesday, you also perform a differential backup. Because the log files from Tuesday have not been deleted, the log files for both Tuesday and Wednesday are backed up. This continues on Thursday, your differential backup backs up the logs from Tuesday, Wednesday, and Thursday. If your data becomes corrupted on Friday, all that needs to be done to restore the data is to apply the full backup from Monday, and then the differential backup from Thursday. Because the Thursday backup set contains all the information from Tuesday and Wednesday, you do not have to recover these backup sets.

OFFLINE BACKUPS

An offline backup is a backup that is performed when all the services are stopped. You can use any backup software to generate an offline backup. You should, however, be aware that when you restore an offline backup, the backup software does not implement the changes in the log files as it does with online backups. Microsoft does not recommend that you perform offline backups for daily backups.

B

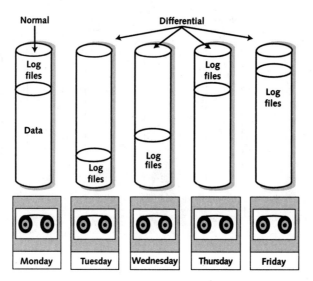

Figure B.3   A differential backup.

COMPLETING THE BACKUP

Windows NT ships with a backup application, named NTBACKUP.EXE. Microsoft Exchange version 4 (the first version Microsoft shipped) arrived on the scene long after Microsoft Windows NT 4 was shipped. The back up program that originally shipped with Windows NT is not Exchange-aware. In other words, it does not know how to back up Exchange or its databases. The new versions of NTBACKUP have the ability to back up "live" data from the Exchange Information Store and directory without having to shut down the messaging system. Table B.6 lists all the versions of NTBACKUP that are available and where they were shipped. Make sure that you are running an Exchange-aware version of the backup program. It is the Dynamic Link Library, EDBBCLI.DLL, that extends the Windows NT NTBACKUP.EXE program.

Don't assume that your version of NTBACKUP is an up-to-date version. Sometimes, when applications are installed, they will install components that are out-of-date without checking first. It is therefore possible that you had the correct version of NTBACKUP installed, but another application installed a non-Exchange-aware version.

BACKING UP MANUALLY

If you want to back up your files manually, you can run the NTBACKUP from the command line. The syntax for the command is:

```
Ntbackup operation path
/a][/v][/r][/d"text"][/b][/hc:{on|off}][/t{option}][/l"file name"]
[/e] [/tape:{n}]
```

Table B.7 defines the switches.

AUTOMATING THE BACKUP

To schedule a backup, use the Windows AT Command Schedule command, WINAT.EXE. WINAT.EXE is located on the Windows NT 4 Resource Kit CD-ROM. The application uses the Windows NT Schedule service to run batch files on specified days and times. Make sure that the schedule service is running before attempting to run the **Winat** command.

 When configuring the schedule service, make sure that you specify its account as a member of the Windows NT Backup Operators group. This will allow a full backup on the information store and directory to take place. Also, configure the batch files (discussed in the upcoming text) as *interactive*, because this is a requirement of the NTBACKUP.EXE program.

The following is a sample batch file that can be used to back up your files while the server remains online, as recommended by Microsoft:

```
ntbackup backup DS \\Jory IS \\Jory /v /d "Jory IS-DS" /b /t Normal
/l c:\winnt\backup.log /e
exit
```

Table B.6   NTBACKUP.EXE versions.

File Name	Size And Version	File Description
NTBACKUP.EXE	675 504 09/23/95 10:57a	Exchange aware, ships with Exchange Server version 4 and higher.
NTBACKUP.EXE	329 777 08/02/96 11:00p	Exchange aware, ships with Exchange Server 4.0a (Service Pack 2).
NTBACKUP.EXE	375 488 03/08/96 4:00a	Not Exchange aware, ships with Windows NT 3.51 Service Pack 4.
NTBACKUP.EXE	716 560 07/15/96 3:30a	Not Exchange aware, ships with Windows NT 4.
NTBACKUP.EXE	716 560 03/08/96 4:00a	Not Exchange aware, ships with Windows NT 3.51.

B

Table B.7 NTBACKUP.EXE switches.

Switch	Definition
Path	The path for the directories to be backed up.
/a	Adds backup sets after the last backup set on the tape. Without this switch, the data that might exist on the tape gets overwritten.
/v	Verifies the operation.
/r	Restricts access.
/d "text"	Specifies a description of the backup contents.
/b	Specifies that the local Registry is to be backed up.
/hc:on or /hc:off	Specifies that hardware compression is on or off.
/t option	Specifies the backup type. The option can be one of the following: normal, copy, incremental, differential, or daily.
Normal	All selected files or Microsoft Exchange Server components are backed up and marked as such on the disk.
Copy	All selected files or Microsoft Exchange Server components are backed up, but they are not marked as such on the disk.
Incremental	Among the selected files or Microsoft Exchange Server components, only those that have been modified are backed up and marked as such on the disk.
Differential	The selected files or Microsoft Exchange Server components that have been modified are backed up, but they are not marked as such on the disk.
Daily	Among the selected files, only those that have been modified the same day are backed up, but they are not marked as such on the disk.
/l "file name"	Specifies the file name for the backup log.
/e	Specifies that the backup log includes exceptions only.
/tape:n	Specifies the tape drive to which the files should be backed up, where n is a number from zero through nine that corresponds to the tape drive number listed in the Registry.

The preceding batch file will cause the NTBACKUP program to back up the directory and Information Store on a server named Jory. It will also run a normal backup.

The following is a sample batch file that can be used to back up your files when the server is offline, as recommended by Microsoft. Remember that this is an example and your installation may be different (different services may be running). In addition, you are not prompted when a service is dependent upon the one you are stopping.

```
echo Stopping Exchange Services...
net stop MSExchangeMSMI
net stop MSExchangePCMTA
net stop MSExchangeFB
net stop MSExchangeDX
net stop MSExchangeIMC
net stop MSExchangeMTA
net stop MSExchangeIS
net stop MSExchangeDS
net stop MSExchangeSA
echo Starting Backup
ntbackup backup c:\ d:\ /a /v /d "Full File Based Backup" /b /l
c:\winnt\backup.log /e
echo Backup Complete... Starting Exchange Services...
net start MSExchangeSA
net start MSExchangeDS
net start MSExchangeIS
net start MSExchangeMTA
net start MSExchangeIMC
net start MSExchangeDX
net start MSExchangeFB
net start MSExchangePCMTA
net start MSExchangeMSMI
```

This batch file will stop all the Exchange services, run a full backup on both the
C: and D: drives, and then restart the Exchange services.

After you have a batch file created, you should test it to make sure that it
performs as intended. When the batch file has been tested successfully, you can
configure the Windows NT Scheduler program. To create a new scheduled task,
select the Add option from the Edit menu. The Add Command dialog box
should appear (see Figure B.4). Enter in the command line for the batch file you
created earlier, select the frequency at which the batch file should be executed,
and select the days and time. Don't forget to check the Interactive checkbox
before clicking OK.

B

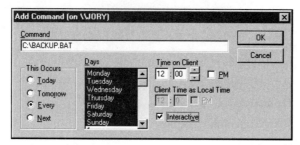

Figure B.4 The Add Command dialog box.

You can configure the Windows NT Scheduler program (shown in Figure B.5) to execute several applications either at the same time or at different times. You can view, edit, or delete currently scheduled applications.

LOG FILES AND CIRCULAR LOGGING

Microsoft Exchange has several databases that it maintains. These files are called stores. One of the main stores, the Information Store, consists of two databases—the private and the public Information Stores. As stated earlier, the private store is located in the PRIV.EDB file, and the public store is located in the PUB.EDB file. Another Exchange store is the directory, which is located in the DIR.EDB file. Microsoft Exchange uses transaction logs to store changes made to these databases.

Microsoft Exchange Server uses a complex technology, called active directory, to maintain the databases and log files. When data in the databases change, Exchange writes them to log files and memory before writing them to the actual databases. The main reasons for this process are performance and recoverability. Because all changes are written to log files sequentially and the changes are written immediately, the changes appear instantaneously to the clients. If you send a message to everyone in the organization, it appears as though the message was sent instantly with no delay.

The Exchange active directory was so well received that Windows NT 5 will use the active directory rather than the "flat" structure used by Windows NT 4.

The Directory Service and Information Stores create the following logs and files:

- Transaction logs
- Previous logs
- Checkpoint files

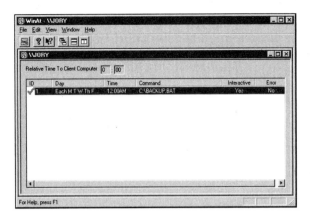

Figure B.5   The Windows NT Scheduler Program, WINAT.EXE.

- Reserved logs
- Patch files

Transaction Logs

The transaction logs and the EDB files can be kept on separate physical drives. By default, the Information Store logs are stored in the Exchsrvr\Mdbdata folder and Directory Service logs are stored in the Exchsrvr\Dsadata folder. Each subfolder contains an EDB.LOG file. This log file is the current transaction log file for that particular service (Information Store or Directory Service). Both the Information Store and the Directory Service maintain different EDB.LOG files. These log files should always be 5,242,800 bytes in size. If they are not this size, then there is a good chance that they are damaged.

Remember that transactions are first written to the EDB.LOG files and then written to the Exchange database. Due to this fact, the actual database is a combination of both the actual EDB database file and the uncommitted transactions in the transaction log file.

Previous Logs

Each transaction is written to the transaction log before being committed to the Exchange database. There is always an inactive part of the transaction log. This inactive portion consists of the transactions in the log files that have already been committed to the database. The rest of the transaction log is referred to as active. The active portion consists of the transactions that have not yet been committed to the Exchange database. When you complete an online backup (full or incremental), the inactive portion of the transaction log is deleted.

B

The transaction log is not a single file but a set of files. Each of these files is exactly 5MB in size. Any new transaction is written to the EDB.LOG file before being committed to the database. As this file becomes full, it is renamed, and a new EDB.LOG file is created. This renamed (or previous) log file is stored in the same folder as the EDB.LOG file, but it's not committed to the database (as this has already occurred). Log files are named using the following format

Edb#####.log

where ##### is a hexadecimal number, such as 00019 and 0001A.

When circular logging is enabled, these previous log files are not maintained and, therefore, are not deleted by the backup operations. When circular logging is enabled, you will not be able to perform an incremental or a differential backup.

When the Microsoft Exchange services are shut down properly, the transactions in the log files are committed to the respective EDB file. You will sometimes notice that it can take a long time to shut down a Microsoft Exchange Server. This is because the transactions need to be committed.

CHECKPOINT FILES

The checkpoint files are used to recover data from transaction logs into EDB files. The checkpoint is a placeholder within the EDB.CHK file that indicates which transactions have been committed to the Exchange database. Both the Information Store and the Directory Service have their own checkpoint files. When data is written to an EDB file from the transaction log, the checkpoint file is updated with information that indicates that the specific transaction has been committed successfully.

RESERVE LOGS

Reserve log files are used when the Information Store or the Directory Service renames its EDB.LOG file and attempts to create a new file without there being enough disk space for the file. This is only used in case of an emergency. Should this occur, an error message is sent to the service. The service then copies any transactions stored in memory that have yet to be written to the transaction log in to the RES1.LOG file and the RES2.LOG file (if necessary). Both the Information Store and the Directory Service have two reserve log files: RES1.LOG and RES2.LOG. These files are stored in the Mdbdata and the Dsadata folders.

Like other log files, the reserve log files are always 5MB in size.

After the transactions stored in memory have been written to the reserve log file(s), the service shuts down and logs an event in the Windows NT event log.

PATCH FILES

Patch files are used when transactions are written to a database during a backup. This allows you to back up the Microsoft Exchange databases without interrupting service to the end users. During the backup operation, data is read from the EDB files. Any transaction made to a section of the EDB file that has been backed up is recorded in the PAT (or patch) file. Any transaction made to a section of the EDB file that has not been backed up is processed and is not written to the PAT file. Each Microsoft Exchange database has its own patch file (PRIV.PAT, PUB.PAT, and DIR.PAT). These files only exist during the backup process.

The online backup operation process is as follows:

1. A PAT file is created for the current database.

2. The backup operation for the current EDB file is started.

3. Transactions that must be written to sections of the EDB file that have already been backed up are recorded in both the EDB and the PAT files.

4. The PAT file is written to the backup tape.

5. The PAT file is deleted from the Mdbdata or Dsadata folder.

RECOVERY SCENARIOS

The following sections cover two main recovery scenarios—single mailbox recovery and full server recovery.

SINGLE MAILBOX RECOVERY

This recovery procedure should not be performed on your production server. As you will see, you need to recover data to a server that is *not* part of your Exchange site. The dedicated recovery server will be installed using the same organization and site name as the production site, but it will be installed by selecting the Create New Site option. The following components are required to accomplish this process:

- A dedicated server with enough hard disk capacity to restore the entire private Information Store database

B

- A back up of the Information Store private database
- The Microsoft Exchange Client software
- The Microsoft Exchange Server software
- Windows NT Server 4
- Windows NT Service Packs

This procedure can be used if a mailbox was accidentally deleted or specific data from within the mailbox was deleted. This assumes that the Deleted Item Retention feature of Microsoft Exchange Server 5.5 has been disabled (the default) or the data being recovered is older than the retention time specified. As you will see, this can be a long process, especially if recovering a very large Information Store, because the entire store needs to be recovered. Your organization will have to decide when this process is to take place. If, for example, your organization has a very large private Information Store on each server, you might only complete this recovery process in very specific cases. Most organizations will only recover mailbox information for upper management (such as the CEO or the COO) and let most of the workforce deal with losing the mail. This is the main reason for the Item Retention feature of Exchange 5.5—it was the feature most requested by administrators to have added to Exchange.

In short, to recover the data you must:

1. Prepare a computer to run Windows NT Server.
2. Install Microsoft Exchange using the same organization and site name as your production site.
3. Restore the entire Information Store from a backup tape.
4. Log on as a Microsoft Exchange Administrator, and assign the Windows NT Administrator ID access to the desired mailbox.
5. Restore the necessary mailbox data to a PST file.
6. Attach the PST file to the desired user profile.

Preparing The Recovery Server

Ideally, for fastest recovery, you should have a server up, running, and available to perform recovery at any time. This server should act only as a recovery server—it should not act as a SQL server or SNA server. You can configure this server as either a PDC, a BDC, or a member server in your domain. You should have Windows NT Server and all necessary Service Packs installed with enough disk space available for a full Information Store recovery. This server should also have a tape drive system that is compatible with the tape drive system available on the production system. You should also test the tape drive system on a regular basis if the computer has not been used.

Remember *not* to join the existing production site during the installation of Microsoft Exchange Server.

After you have Windows NT Server and the Service Packs installed, you should log on to the server as a user with administrator permissions and install Microsoft Exchange using the same site and organization name that was used on the server that you are restoring information from. Remember to perform a Complete Install and to not join the site.

The name of the server you are restoring to does not have to match the name of the production server you are restoring from. This is because you are restoring the Information Store and not the directory. Due to this fact, you can have a server with Windows NT and Exchange already installed. This assumes that you have one server for every site (the site name does matter). If you have one server that is to be used as a recovery server at many sites, you might want to install Windows NT and copy the Exchange installation files from the CD-ROM to speed up the recovery process.

Finally, install Microsoft Outlook on the recovery server.

Restoring The Information Store From Tape

The following procedure assumes that a tape from an online backup is being used to restore information. If an offline tape is used, do not select to start the Exchange services after the restore. Instead, execute the following command:

```
Isinteg - patch
```

Then, start the Directory Service and the Information Store services and perform the DS/IS Consistency Adjustment, as follows:

1. Load the backup tape into the drive.
2. Log on to the recovery server as a user with administrator permissions.
3. From Start, select Backup from the Administrative Tools menu.
4. Select the Microsoft Exchange option from the Operations drop-down menu.
5. Select the tapes icon, and double-click the tape name.
6. Select *Org\Site\Server*\Information Store from the right pane of the Tapes window.
7. Click the Restore button.

B

8. Enter the name of the destination (recovery) server in the Destination Server field on the Restore Information window.

9. Select Erase All Existing Data, Private, Public, Verify After Restore, and Start Service After Restore. Click OK.

10. A dialog box should appear informing you that "You are about to restore Microsoft Exchange components. The Microsoft Exchange services on the destination server will be stopped." Click OK.

11. Click OK when the Verify status window appears.

12. Select the Services applet in the Control Panel, and verify that the Microsoft Exchange Services are running.

Recovering The User Mailbox

To recover the user's mailbox, use the following procedure:

1. Log on to the recovery server using a Windows NT account that has administrative privileges.

2. Run the Microsoft Exchange Administrator application.

3. Run the DS/IS Consistency Adjustment. To do this, click your server name, select Properties from the File menu. In the Advanced tab, select the All Inconsistencies option, and click the Adjust button.

4. Select on the Recipients container, and double-click the desired user's mailbox in the right pane.

5. Click the Primary Windows NT Account button in the General tab.

6. Select the Select An Existing Windows NT Account option, and click OK.

7. Select Administrator, and click the Add button. Click OK.

8. Click OK (in the User Property dialog box).

9. From the Control Panel, double-click the Mail And Fax applet (sometimes this applet only appears as Mail).

10. Configure a profile for the desired user. Make sure that you add a Personal Folder to the profile.

11. Run Microsoft Outlook.

12. Click Mailbox—*Username* in the left pane.

13. Click any message in the right pane.

14. Select the Select All option from the Edit drop-down menu.

15. Select Copy from the File menu.

16. Select the Personal Folder option, and click OK.

17. Copy the PST file to the destination location.

18. Add the PST to the user's profile on the production server and have the user access the necessary messages.

FULL SERVER RECOVERY

This section describes how to restore a Microsoft Exchange Server to a different machine. This process is especially helpful if upgrading Microsoft Exchange to a new, more powerful server. The following components are required to complete a full server recovery:

- A full backup of the Information Store and Exchange directory.

- A second server with the same hardware capacity as the production server.

- Access to the original Windows NT SAM.

- The production server configuration sheet (as outlined at the beginning of this appendix).

- The Microsoft Exchange installation files.

- Windows NT Server installation files.

- Windows NT Service Pack installation files.

Completing a full server recovery is more complex than restoring a single mailbox. Administrators define a full server recovery in different ways, so it is defined here to clarify what a full server recovery means in this appendix:

- A full server recovery is the process of restoring an original production Microsoft Exchange Server so that all the Windows NT configuration and security information, as well as all Microsoft Exchange configuration and data, are recovered.

When a full server recovery is completed, users will be able to log in to their personal mailboxes using their current password.

Recall that when restoring a single mailbox, only the restoration of the Information Store was required. With a full server recovery, both the Information Store and the Exchange Directory need to be restored. Microsoft Exchange Server closely integrates with Windows NT security, so the Security Identifier (SID) is used by Microsoft Exchange to validate users. Two conditions must be met in order for the Directory Service to be recovered successfully; these are:

- You must complete the restore to a Windows NT-based server that has the same site, organization, and server name as the production server.

- You must be able to access the domain which the production server was part of.

B

A full server recovery uses three computers. Two of these computers will be in production and one is a non-production machine. One computer is the Primary Domain Controller, the other is a Backup Domain Controller, and the third computer is the recovery computer. The reasons for requiring all three are due to the way Microsoft Exchange uses the Windows NT SAM database for its authentication of users.

The following procedure can be used to perform a full server recovery using a backup of the Information Store and Directory Service from a production server. When installing Microsoft Exchange, you should note that you will not be joining the site. Instead, you will use the Create New Site option.

Preparing The Recovery Server

Install Windows NT with the same computer name as the production Microsoft Exchange Server you are recovering. If the production server was a BDC, then you should add the recovery server to the production domain as a BDC. Remember that because the production server (the failed computer) and the recovery server name are the same, you will have to remove and then add the computer name to the domain. This process will add the new SID to the domain.

To Create A New Site

The following steps should be performed to create a new site:

1. Log on to the Windows NT recovery server using an account with administrator permissions, and install Microsoft Exchange using the same site and organization name that was used in the production server. Use the **Setup /R** command to allow for the recovery of an existing Microsoft Exchange-based server to new hardware. Make sure that you specify the same service account as that used for the original production server.

2. Run the Microsoft Exchange Performance Optimizer utility to optimize the Microsoft Exchange configuration so that it matches that of the original production server.

3. Install Microsoft Outlook on the recovery server.

Complete The Restore

The following procedure assumes that a tape from an online backup is being used for the restore. If an offline tape is used, do not select to start the Exchange services after the restore. Instead, execute the following command:

```
Isinteg - patch
```

Then, start the Directory Service and the Information Store services, and perform the DS/IS Consistency Adjustment, as follows:

1. Load the backup tape into the drive.

2. Log on to the recovery server as a user with administrator permissions.

3. From Start, select Backup from the Administrative Tools menu.

4. Double-click the Tapes button.

5. Double-click Full Backup Tape. A Catalog Status dialog box should appear informing you that the Catalog is being loaded from tape.

6. In the right pane, select both the directory and the Information Store.

7. Click the Restore button.

8. From the Restore Information dialog box, select Erase All Existing Data, Verify After Restore, Start Services After Restore, and click OK.

9. Click OK.

10. From the Restore Information dialog box, enter the name of the destination server. Select Erase All Existing Data, Verify After Restore, Private, Public, and Start Services After Restore. Click OK.

11. Click OK.

12. When the restore is complete, click OK.

13. Exit the Backup program.

Verify Mailbox And Windows NT Account Associations

After completing the restoration, you need to verify the mailbox and the Windows NT account associations. To do so, perform the following steps:

1. Run the Microsoft Exchange Administrator program.

2. Highlight the Recipients container under the site.

3. Double-click any user.

4. Ensure that the Primary Windows NT Account matches the mailbox.

5. Repeat this procedure for several users.

B

Test User Logon

After verifying the mailbox and the Windows NT account associations, you'll need to make sure your users can log on to the system. To test user log ons, perform the following:

1. Run Microsoft Outlook.

2. Verify that the user password works.

3. Repeat for several users.

GLOSSARY

A

active file A text file that contains a list of all newsgroups available from your newsfeed provider.

Active Server Pages (ASP) A feature of Microsoft Internet Information Server (version 3 and greater) that dynamically creates HTML documents.

address space The path for messages to be sent outside a site.

address space cost A numerical value (from 1 through 100) that is used to assign a cost to a specific address space.

AdminSch An NT user account used to share Microsoft Schedule+ data between MS Mail and Microsoft Exchange Server.

API (application programming interface) A set of instructions that allows one program to invoke the functions of a second program.

archiving The process of backing up and storing data in a safe place for later use.

archiving plan The process of devising a plan for backing up and storing data that best suits the environment within your corporation.

auto-archive The automation of the archiving process.

B

backfill A process that helps Information Stores recover from lost replication messages, servers restored from a backup, or servers that have been shut down and restarted.

backfill request A message sent out by the Information Store on one server to request that missing public folder information be sent to it from the remote Information Store.

BackOffice Resource Kit A toolkit from Microsoft that works with Microsoft server products.

backup creation The process of backing up data for archival and later use.

backup cycle The period of time between two successive backups.

backup verification The process of verifying that a backup was successful by restoring the data on another server and making sure the data integrity is intact.

basic authentication Verification through an unencrypted username and password.

basic authentication using SSL Uses the SSL protocol to encrypt clear text usernames and passwords.

BDC (Backup Domain Controller) A machine within a network that maintains a copy of the entire security accounts database. If the PDC is busy or fails, the BDC takes control and logs on clients.

C

change message A message sent from the Information Store that informs other Information Stores of changes to public folder information.

change number A number assigned to a public folder modification to allow the different Information Stores to update their databases.

child objects Objects that are located within parent objects. The permissions granted to a child object are inherited from its parent.

client security DLL A Dynamic Link Library used to sign/verify and seal/unseal advanced security messages.

Client Service For NetWare A Windows NT service that permits Windows NT computers to access NetWare resources.

connector The core architecture software component that Microsoft Exchange Server uses to communicate with other messaging systems.

connector cost A numerical value (from 1 through 100) that is used to assign a cost to a specific connector.

Connector For Lotus cc:Mail service A Windows NT Server service that performs the transferring of messages between Exchange Server and Lotus cc:Mail Post Offices. It also synchronizes an Exchange Server Global Address List with the Lotus cc:Mail directory.

container An Exchange Server object that holds other objects. Mailbox objects are placed in a recipient's object. This means that the recipient's object is also a container.

copy backup A snapshot of the database at any given point in time.

custom recipient A recipient in a foreign system (non-Exchange) whose address is in the Address Book.

D

defragmentation A process that eliminates wasted space in a file.

deleted message retention The amount of time that deleted messages are kept before being permanently deleted.

diagnostic logging A feature of Exchange Server that helps resolve messaging problems. Entries are written to the Windows NT application event log.

differential backup A backup that backs up only a subset of the Information Store and directory databases (that is, only the data that changed since the last normal or incremental backup).

DIR.EDB The Exchange Server file that contains the directory store.

directory The area that holds information about the organization's resources and users, such as servers, mailboxes, public folders, and distribution lists. The directory and its contents are replicated automatically to all servers within the same site.

directory database The database that contains all the information about the objects in your Exchange Server.

directory replication The process of updating all the Exchange Server directories within a site and between sites, with the same information. Within a site, directory replication is automatic. Between sites, you can configure directory replication so only desired information is replicated to other sites.

Directory Replication Connector A connector used to replicate the Exchange directory between remote sites.

directory requestor Post Office Submits directory changes to the directory server Post Office and requests directory updates that other directory requestor Post Offices have submitted; used for directory synchronization.

directory server Post Office A central database of directory changes; used for directory synchronization.

Directory Service The service that manipulates the information contained within the directory database. This service processes requests from users and applications.

DirSync (directory synchronization) The process of exchanging address information between messaging systems.

DISPATCH.EXE An application that ships with MS Mail. It is used to process updates into Post Office address lists.

distributed processing A computing activity that is distributed on both client and the server computer systems, as clients make requests for services, and servers attempt to satisfy them.

distribution list A logical grouping of recipients created to ease the mass mailing of messages.

DNS (Domain Name System) The hierarchical database of domain name-to-IP address relationships.

domain controller The Windows NT Server computer that maintains the security database of all user accounts in a domain. Windows NT Server domains can have one Primary Domain Controller (PDC) and one or more Backup Domain Controllers (BDCs).

domain name A text identifier of a specific Internet host. During Windows NT installation, you are prompted to assign a domain name to the Internet host on which you are installing NT.

domain name space The DNS database hierarchical tree structure.

Dynamic Link Library (DLL) A library of functions that Windows applications load into memory at runtime.

Dynamic RAS Connector A connector used to connect two remote sites via regular phone lines, ISDN, or X.25.

E

encryption The process of modifying and hiding actual information using a mathematical formula. Only the recipient of the information knows the key to deciphering the information.

enterprise The corporate organization.

ESEUTIL.EXE The Exchange Server utility used to defrag the directory store and the Information Store.

ETRN (Extended Turn) An SMTP extension that causes the remote host to send stored messages.

event logging The process of recording occurrences to a file or database.

Exchange performance chart A chart that measures the various Exchange Server objects and their counters.

Exchange Server Administrator A Microsoft Exchange Server program used to administer the Exchange Server components, including Information Store (public and private), Directory Service, System Attendant, and MTA.

Exchange Server counter An attribute of an Exchange Server object that you can track to measure the object's performance.

Exchange Server service account The NT domain account that is used to start and use Exchange Server services.

expansion server A server used to expand distribution lists.

EXPORT.EXE The Lotus cc:Mail program used to export messages and directory entries from Lotus cc:Mail Post Offices.

F

failover The ability of hardware or software to reroute its functionality to a secondary source in the event of a hardware or software failure.

FAT (File Allocation Table) The file system used by the MS-DOS operating system.

fault-tolerant upgrade A process that backs up the Information Store to a different, temporary location before an upgrade.

FQDN (fully qualified domain name) The full DNS path of an Internet host.

G

GAL (Global Address List) An address book that is generally available to all users. You can restrict what a user can see. The GAL allows views to be sorted by property.

gateway A third-party connector used to move mail out of one type of service into a different one (for example, from Exchange to Lotus Notes).

Gateway Service For NetWare A Windows NT Server service that permits domain users of the Windows NT Server to access NetWare resources.

granularity A computer activity or feature in terms of the size of the units it handles.

granularity of configuration Granularity measured at the message level.

granularity of replication Granularity measured at the folder level.

GWART (Gateway Address Routing Table) A list of the address space information for all the connectors within a site.

H

home server The server where a mailbox is physically located.

HTML (Hypertext Markup Language) The language used to create static Web pages.

HTTP (Hypertext Transfer Protocol) The protocol used to communicate between a Web browser and a Web server.

I

ILS (Internet Locator Server) A server that allows Microsoft NetMeeting users to locate mailboxes to set up online meetings.

IMAP4 (Internet Message Access Protocol version 4) A protocol that enables users with any IMAP4 client (which is compliant with RFC 2060) to access mail in their Microsoft Exchange Server mailbox. IMAP4 can also be used to read and post messages to public folders or to access another user's mailbox, if the proper access rights are granted.

IMPORT.EXE The Lotus cc:Mail program used to import messages and directory entries into Lotus cc:Mail Post Offices.

IMS (Internet Mail Service) A connector used to connect a Microsoft Exchange site to either an SMTP mail system or a remote Microsoft Exchange site.

IMS Queues An Exchange Server performance chart that provides Internet Mail Service queue information, such as what the inbound queue looks like, how the outbound queue is performing, and so on.

IMS Statistics An Exchange Server performance chart that provides Internet Mail Service statistics, such as the type of email traffic the Internet generates, the total number of inbound messages since you started the server, the total number of outbound messages, and so on.

IMS Traffic An Exchange Server performance Chart that provides Internet Mail Service traffic information, such as the status of the message flow, the number of connections that exist to or from the server, and so on.

inbound newsfeed A newsfeed used to receive information from the Usenet through your newsfeed provider.

incremental backup The process of backing up only a subset of the Information Store and directory databases. An incremental backup only backs up the data that changed since the last normal or incremental backup. Only the log files are backed up then purged.

Information Store The area in Exchange that contains the messages in users' mailboxes and public folders. Its two main components are the public Information Store and the private Information Store.

Internet News Service A service that uses NNTP to connect the Microsoft Exchange Server to Usenet.

intersite communication Communication between two Exchange sites.

intrasite communication Communication between two Exchange Servers within a single site.

IP (Internet Protocol) The Network layer protocol for communication over the Internet.

IP address A four-byte number uniquely identifying a machine within the IP internetwork.

ISINTEG.EXE An Exchange Server utility used to find and eliminate common Information Store database errors.

ISP (Internet Service Provider) A third party that offers Internet connectivity to individuals and businesses, usually at a cost.

K

KM (Key Management) security DLL This Dynamic Link Library responds to any advanced security configuration requests from users and then submits the request to the Windows NT Key Manager Service.

KMS (Key Management Server) A component of Microsoft Exchange Server that allows an administrator to configure advanced security on individual mailboxes.

KMS database Contains all the keys within the database encrypted with the 64-bit CAST algorithm.

L

LDAP (Lightweight Directory Access Protocol) An Internet protocol that allows access to directory information. Clients can use LDAP to browse, read, and search directory listings in the Microsoft Exchange Server directory.

Link Monitor An Exchange Server utility that verifies the efficient routing of test messages between servers.

log file A to-do list for Exchange, before messages are committed.

Lotus cc:Mail Lotus's messaging system.

Lotus cc:Mail Import/Export programs The utilities used to import Microsoft Exchange Server messages and directory entries into Lotus cc:Mail Post Offices, and to export Lotus cc:Mail messages and directory entries into a Microsoft Exchange Server.

M

mailbox The location on the Exchange Server to which mail is delivered.

mailbox roles A predefined set of mailbox rights.

mail-drop service A service that can hold email messages until the client requests the messages.

maintenance The process of maintaining Microsoft servers for generating optimal performance.

maintenance window The period of time in which maintenance tasks are performed on the Exchange Server.

MAPI (Messaging Application Programming Interface) A series of APIs designed specifically for messaging.

master encryption key A key used to encrypt all keys stored within the KMS database.

message routing The act of sending messages to remote Exchange sites.

message tracking A feature of Exchange Server that tracks message events to help resolve communication problems.

Message Tracking Center An Exchange Server tool used to trace all events for a particular message.

messaging bridgehead A server that sends messages to remote networks on behalf of the entire Exchange site.

MHTML (MIME HTML) HTML objects in MIME format.

Microsoft Commercial Internet Service (MCIS) Membership System Using SSL Windows NT security authentication using SSL, which is authenticated through the MCIS Membership System. Uses port 995.

Microsoft Exchange Connector For Lotus cc:Mail The connector that Microsoft Exchange Server uses to communicate with Lotus cc:Mail Post Offices.

Microsoft Exchange Server A messaging and groupware server from Microsoft.

Microsoft Mail Connector The connector that Microsoft Exchange Server uses to communicate with MS Mail.

Microsoft Mail Connector Interchange A Windows NT Server service that routes and transfers messages between Microsoft Exchange Server and the Microsoft Mail Connector Post Office.

Microsoft Mail Connector MTA A Windows NT Server service that connects to and transfers mail between the Microsoft Mail Connector Post Office and one or more MS Mail Post Offices.

Microsoft Mail Connector Post Office A temporary Information Store for MS Mail inbound and outbound messages.

Microsoft Outlook A front-end client program from Microsoft for managing emails, contacts, and so on.

Microsoft Schedule+ Free/Busy Connector A utility that provides the ability to share Microsoft Schedule+ data between MS Mail and Exchange Server.

MIME (Multipurpose Internet Mail Extensions) A standard that allows binary, audio, and video data to be transmitted across TCP/IP networks.

monitoring The process of identifying a problem or error and making sure everything is working fine.

MS Mail (Microsoft Mail) Exchange Server's messaging predecessor.

MS Mail External MTA An application that ships with MS Mail. It delivers mail to other MS Mail Post Offices.

MTA (Message Transfer Agent) The component responsible for routing messages to their destinations. The MTA provides addressing and routing information for sending messages.

MTA callback A security feature of the Dynamic RAS connector that forces the remote site to dial the local site back before making a RAS connection.

MTACHECK.EXE An Exchange Server utility used to scan the internal message transfer agent database. MTACHECK looks for damaged objects and objects that are interfering with queue processing.

N

name resolution The process that DNS uses to map a domain name to an IP address.

NDR (non-delivery report) A report sent out to a recipient or distribution list that informs the user or users of message delivery problems.

NetBIOS A network interface that supports the network basic input/output system, a necessary component for communicating on the NetWare network.

NetWare Novell's network operating system.

Newsfeed Configuration Wizard A utility used to configure the Internet News Service for your Exchange Server.

newsgroup public folder An Exchange public folder used with the Internet News Service to store newsgroup information.

NNTP (Network News Transfer Protocol) A format for information via Usenet sites. It is similar to a Bulletin Board System (BBS). One person posts a message that others can read and respond to publicly.

normal backup A complete and full backup, including transaction logs, Information Stores, and directory databases.

O

object A messaging system resource, such as a server, mailbox, public folder, address books, and so forth, that are listed in the directory.

OLE (Object Linking and Embedding) A set of protocols used to place information from one document into another.

online listing information A list of Microsoft NetMeeting users that is used to locate mailboxes to set up online meetings.

organization The largest administrative unit in Microsoft Exchange Server, usually consisting of one or more sites. Organizations provide services for an entire group.

outbound newsfeed A newsfeed that is used to send information to Usenet through your newsfeed provider.

OWA (Outlook Web Access) An option in Exchange that allows users to access their private mailboxes, schedule information, and Exchange public folders.

P

PAB (Personal Address Book) A grouping of contact information, for a person, as opposed to a global or public list.

parent object An object that contains other objects. An object is a parent to all the objects within it.

parent–child relationship The relationship that exists between a parent object and a child object. The relationship is dictated by permissions.

PDC (Primary Domain Controller) A machine within a network that validates the username and password, thus authenticating the logons for clients. The first server within the network must be a PDC.

Performance Optimizer An Exchange Server tool that optimizes a server's configuration.

permission roles A grouping of permissions that allows for easy public folder permission setting.

permissions A set of rules that controls the objects, such as containers within the system. These rules dictate which users can access the object and how those users can manipulate it.

PFRA (public folders replication agent)
The Microsoft Exchange component responsible for the successful replication of public folder information.

PING messages Test messages used by Link Monitors to verify efficient routing.

POP3 (Post Office Protocol version 3) An Internet client protocol used to access mail messages.

predecessor change list A list of the Information Stores that have made changes to the message and the last change number made by each Information Store.

private Information Store The component of the Information Stores that contains user mailboxes and messages.

private key A fixed-length security string that is used to unseal or sign a message.

public folder A repository for many types of information, such as files, that can be shared by many users. Public folders are shared folders that contain email messages, word-processing documents, and so forth, and can be replicated to a remote Exchange Server.

public folder affinity A value given to different sites to control which site is replicated and in what order.

public folder contents The items stored within the public folder hierarchy.

public folder contents replication The replication process of the public folder contents.

public folder hierarchy The directory structure of the public folder.

public folder hierarchy replication The replication process of the public folder hierarchy.

public Information Store The component of the Information Stores that contains public files, folders, and messages.

public key A fixed-length security string that is available with all users. Used to seal or verify a message.

published public folder An Exchange public folder that is shared with all users. The users log in anonymously through Outlook Web Access.

pull feed A feed that retrieves only specified newsgroups from the newsfeed server.

push feed A feed that "forces" the newsfeed to the destination server. Normally, this means that all newsgroups are "pushed" to the server.

R

RAID (Redundant Array of Inexpensive Disks) A standardized method for categorizing fault tolerance storage systems. Windows NT implements Level 0, Level 1, and Level 5 RAID through software, not hardware.

RAS (Remote Access Service) A Windows NT service that allows the server to connect to a remote server using a dial-up connection.

recipient An object in the directory that can receive messages and information. Exchange Server recipients are mailboxes, distribution lists, public folders, and custom recipients.

recovery equipment The equipment required to recover information lost as a result of catastrophic failure.

recovery server The server that helps in the process of recovering information lost as a result of catastrophic failure.

recovery time The time the server needs to recover information lost as a result of catastrophic failure.

remote directory synchronization requestor What MS Mail Post Offices are referred to when Microsoft Exchange Server is set up to be the directory synchronization server.

replica A copy of a public folder on a remote site.

replication bridgehead A server that sends replication messages to remote networks on behalf of the entire Exchange site.

resolver The client software that queries the DNS to convert a domain name to its IP address.

restoration The process of making the archived data available for use.

root domain The top domain in the hierarchical DNS tree (for example, .com or .org).

RPC (Remote Procedure Call) A message-passing facility that allows a distributed application to call services on other machines within the network.

S

SA (System Attendant) A service that must be running for messaging processes to run. The SA is a maintenance service that runs in the background.

SAM (Security Accounts Manager) A component of Windows NT that is responsible for authenticating user accounts. The SAM is a database and can be shared amongst trusted NT domain servers.

SAP (service access point) A protocol used by NetWare clients to perform name resolution on NetWare networks.

SASL (Simple Authentication and Security Layer) authentication A method that uses clear text to authenticate connections.

sealing The sender encrypts the message and any attachments.

secret key A cryptography key to encrypt or decrypt messages using an algorithm.

security administration DLL A Dynamic Link Library that is used when advanced security is being configured for a user account.

Server Health An Exchange Server performance chart that tells you the percentage of processor time each service uses. You can thus determine the services that are overusing the processor and the services that cannot really use the processor as much because of the other services.

Server History An Exchange Server performance chart that provides history information about the server, such as the number of outstanding messages, the number of users connected to the server, the number of pages process by the server per second, and so on.

Server Load An Exchange Server performance chart that provides server load information, such as the number of messages submitted, the number of messages actually delivered, and so on.

Server Monitor An Exchange Server program that verifies that the specified Exchange services are running on the specified Exchange Server computer. Server Monitors are used to check the condition of one or more servers in a site.

Server Queues An Exchange Server performance chart that provides queue information about the server, such as the total number of messages awaiting transmission and so on.

Server Users An Exchange Server performance chart that provides user information, such as the total number of current users with a connection to the server.

service account A Windows NT account used to access Exchange information on the Windows NT Server running Exchange.

Service Pack The program that allows you to apply patch upgrades to an existing version of software. The patch upgrade includes bug fixes, minor enhancements, and so on.

signing When the sender places a signature on a message to enable the recipient to verify the message's origin and authenticity.

simple display name A name used for foreign messaging systems that cannot handle non-ANSI characters.

site One or more Microsoft Exchange Server computers generally corresponding to a single geographical location that share the same directory information (mailboxes, distribution lists, and routing tables). All servers in a site must be able to communicate with each other through synchronous Remote Procedure Calls (RPCs).

Site Connector The most efficient connector available to Microsoft Exchange.

site service account The NT user account that is used by Exchange Server to provide access to system services and functionality.

S/MIME (Secure MIME) Encrypted MIME mail attachments.

SMP (symmetric multiprocessing) The ability of a computer to use more than one microprocessor. SMP allows for a more effective means of multithreading.

SMTP (Simple Mail Transport Protocol) The protocol Microsoft Exchange Server uses to send and receive email over the Internet.

SSL (Secure Sockets Layer) A protocol that creates secure communications using public key cryptography and bulk data encryption.

standard database upgrade Upgrades your Information Store in its current locations.

status message A message sent from one Information Store to another, informing the other Information Store of the current public folder hierarchy and contents status.

subdomain Any domain listed below the top-level, or root domain.

T

target server A server in the remote site that can receive messages from the local site.

target server cost A numerical value (from 1 through 100) that is used to assign a cost to a specific target server.

time stamp A time value given to a modification done to a public folder to ease in the tracking of the change.

top-level domain *See* root domain.

top-level public folders The root, or highest level, in the public folder hierarchy.

transaction log A record of all transactions.

trust level A numerical value assigned to an object to specify whether the object will be replicated during directory synchronization.

U

upgrade A process that changes a program from its current version to a newer release from the vendor.

UPS (uninterruptible power supply) A device that allows a server to write all the data to the disk, in the event of a power failure, and provides a safe and controlled shut down of the server.

URL (Uniform Resource Locator) A universal naming convention used to identify a server's name and location on the Internet (for example, **http://www.lanw.com**).

W

Windows NT Microsoft's network operating system.

Windows NT Challenge/Response authentication A method of authentication and encryption that is available to the Windows NT operating system. Challenge/ Response Authentication provides authentication through Windows NT security and encrypted passwords.

Windows NT Challenge/Response using SSL The same as the Windows NT Challenge/Response authentication, but it uses the SSL protocol to authenticate. Uses port 995.

Window NT counter A Windows NT object's attribute.

Windows NT domain A grouping of network servers and other computers that share common security and user account information. Users log on to the domain, not individual servers in the domain. Once logged on to the domain, the user has access to the network resources within the domain.

Windows NT Performance Monitor A server program used to monitor the performance of Windows NT and services running under Windows NT, such as Exchange Server.

X

X.400 An internationally recognized message-handling system. A Message Transfer Agent is a server-based process in the message-transfer system that is responsible for routing and delivering messages. It is equivalent to a local postal sorting office.

X.500 Defines the standard protocols for a global Directory Service.

GLOSSARY

Index

Special Characters

%DiskTime counter, 356, 507
%ProcessorTime counter, 355, 357, 507
32-bit forms, 418

A

AB Browses/sec counter, 358
AB Client Sessions counter, 358
AB Reads/sec counter, 358
About Microsoft Exchange Server (Exchange Administrator), 182
Accept Connections feature, for IMS, 243
Access, 72, 150
Access Violations counter, 358
Act, importing from, 149
Actions in rules, 404, 406
Active Anonymous User Count counter, 360
Active Client Logons counter, 360, 361
Active Connections counter, 358
Active Desktop, 153, 396–397
Active directory, 560
Active file for newsfeed, 272-273, 285
  creating, 294-296

Active node, 23
Active Server, 153
Active Server Pages (ASP). *See* ASP (Active Server Pages).
Active User Count counter, 360
ActiveX, 153
Add Child permission, 113
Add-Ins object, in hierarchy, 165
Add To Address Book View command (Exchange Administrator), 181
Address book, 24, 117
Address Book View, configuring, 175
Address Book View Container, 175
Address space, 216
  for cc:Mail Connector, 459–460
  for connectors, 197-198, 211
  for IMS (Internet Mail Service), 232-233
  key exam points, 520
  for Site Connector, 203
  for X.400 Connector, 207
Address space cost, 216
Addressing object, in hierarchy, 165
Adjacent MTA Associations counter, 361

D

INDEX

N

O

I
N
D
E
X

INDEX

Transcender Cor
SINGLE-USER LICENS

IMPORTANT. READ THIS LICENSE AGREEMENT (THE "A...MENT") CAREFULLY BEFORE OPENING THE SOFTWARE PACK. YOU AGREE TO BE LEGALLY BOUND BY THE TERMS OF THIS LICENSE AGREEMENT IF YOU EITHER (1) OPEN THE SOFTWARE PACK, OR (2) IF YOU INSTALL, COPY, OR OTHERWISE USE THE ENCLOSED SOFTWARE. IF YOU DO NOT AGREE WITH THESE TERMS, DO NOT OPEN THE SOFTWARE PACK AND DO NOT INSTALL, COPY, OR USE THE SOFTWARE. YOU MAY RETURN THE UNOPENED SOFTWARE TO THE PLACE OF PURCHASE WITHIN FIFTEEN (15) DAYS OF PURCHASE AND RECEIVE A FULL REFUND. NO REFUNDS WILL BE GIVEN FOR SOFTWARE THAT HAS AN OPENED SOFTWARE PACK OR THAT HAS BEEN INSTALLED, USED, ALTERED, OR DAMAGED.

Grant of Single-User License. **YOU ARE THE ONLY PERSON ENTITLED TO USE THIS SOFTWARE.** This is a license agreement between you (an individual) and Transcender Corporation whereby Transcender grants you the non-exclusive and non-transferable license and right to use this software product, updates (if any), and accompanying documentation (collectively the "Software"). ONLY YOU (AND NO ONE ELSE) ARE ENTITLED TO INSTALL, USE, OR COPY THE SOFTWARE. Transcender continues to own the Software, and the Software is protected by copyright and other state and federal intellectual property laws. All rights, title, interest, and all copyrights in and to the Software and any copy made by you remain with Transcender. Unauthorized copying of the Software, or failure to comply with this Agreement will result in automatic termination of this license, and will entitle Transcender to pursue other legal remedies. IMPORTANT, under the terms of this Agreement:

YOU MAY: (a) install and use the Software on only one computer or workstation, and (b) make one (1) copy of the Software for backup purposes only.

YOU MAY NOT: (a) use the Software on more than one computer or workstation; (b) modify, translate, reverse engineer, decompile, decode, decrypt, disassemble, adapt, create a derivative work of, or in any way copy the Software (except one backup); (c) sell, rent, lease, sublicense, or otherwise transfer or distribute the Software to any other person or entity without the prior written consent of Transcender (and any attempt to do so shall be void); (d) allow any other person or entity to use the Software or install the Software on a network of any sort (these require a separate license from Transcender); or (e) remove or cover any proprietary notices, labels, or marks on the Software.

Term. The term of the license granted above shall commence upon the earlier of your opening of the Software, your acceptance of this Agreement or your downloading, installation, copying, or use of the Software; and such license will expire three (3) years thereafter or whenever you discontinue use of the Software, whichever occurs first.

Warranty, Limitation of Remedies and Liability. If applicable, Transcender warrants the media on which the Software is recorded to be free from defects in materials and free from faulty workmanship for a period of thirty (30) days after the date you receive the Software. If, during this 30-day period, the Software media is found to be defective or faulty in workmanship, the media may be returned to Transcender for replacement without charge. YOUR SOLE REMEDY UNDER THIS AGREEMENT SHALL BE THE REPLACEMENT OF DEFECTIVE MEDIA AS SET FORTH ABOVE. EXCEPT AS EXPRESSLY PROVIDED FOR MEDIA ABOVE, TRANSCENDER MAKES NO OTHER OR FURTHER WARRANTIES REGARDING THE SOFTWARE, EITHER EXPRESS OR IMPLIED, INCLUDING THE QUALITY OF THE SOFTWARE, ITS PERFORMANCE, MERCHANTABILITY, OR FITNESS FOR A PARTICULAR PURPOSE. THE SOFTWARE IS LICENSED TO YOU ON AN "AS-IS" BASIS. THE ENTIRE RISK AS TO THE SOFTWARE'S QUALITY AND PERFORMANCE REMAINS SOLELY WITH YOU. TRANSCENDERS EXCLUSIVE AND MAXI-MUM LIABILITY FOR ANY CLAIM BY YOU OR ANYONE CLAIMING THROUGH OR ON BEHALF OF YOU ARISING OUT OF YOUR ORDER, USE, OR INSTALLATION OF THE SOFTWARE SHALL NOT UNDER ANY CIRCUMSTANCE EXCEED THE ACTUAL AMOUNT PAID BY YOU TO TRANSCENDER FOR THE SOFTWARE, AND IN NO EVENT SHALL TRANSCENDER BE LIABLE TO YOU OR ANY PERSON OR ENTITY CLAIMING THROUGH YOU FOR ANY INDIRECT, INCIDENTAL, COLLATERAL, EXEMPLARY, CONSEQUENTIAL, OR SPECIAL DAMAGES OR LOSSES ARISING OUT OF YOUR ORDER, USE, OR INSTAL-LATION OF THE SOFTWARE OR MEDIA DELIVERED TO YOU OR OUT OF THE WARRANTY, INCLUDING WITHOUT LIMITATION, LOSS OF USE, PROFITS, GOODWILL, OR SAVINGS, OR LOSS OF DATA, FILES, OR PROGRAMS STORED BY THE USER. SOME STATES DO NOT ALLOW THE EXCLUSION OR LIMITATION OF INCIDENTAL OR CONSEQUENTIAL DAMAGES, SO THE ABOVE LIMITATIONS MAY NOT APPLY TO YOU.

Restricted Rights. If the Software is acquired by or for the U.S. Government, then it is provided with Restricted Rights. Use, duplication, or disclosure by the U.S. Government is subject to restrictions as set forth in subparagraph (c)(1)(ii) of The Rights in Technical Data and Computer Software clause at DFARS 252.227-7013, or subparagraphs (c)(1) and (2) of the Commercial Computer Software Act—Restricted Rights at 48 CFR 52.227-19, or clause 18-52.227-86(d) of the NASA Supplement to the FAR, as applicable. The contractor/manufacturer is Transcender Corporation, 242 Louise Avenue, Nashville, Tennessee 37203-1812.

General. This Agreement shall be interpreted and governed by the laws of the State of Tennessee without regard to the conflict of laws provisions of such state, and any legal action relating to this Agreement shall be brought in the appropriate state or federal court located in Davidson County, Tennessee, which venue and jurisdiction you agree to submit to, and the prevailing party in any such action shall be entitled to recover reasonable attorney's fees and expenses as part of any judgment or award. This Agreement is the entire Agreement between us and supersedes any other communication, advertisement, or understanding with respect to the Software. If any provision of this Agreement is held invalid or unenforceable, the remainder shall continue in full force and effect. All provisions of this Agreement relating to disclaimers of warranties, limitation of liability, remedies, or damages, and Transcender's ownership of the Software and other proprietary rights shall survive any termination of this Agreement.

Microsoft Certification Exam Objectives
Exam 70-081: Implementing and Supporting
Microsoft Exchange Server 5.5

Planning

Objective	Chapter
Choose an implementation strategy for Microsoft Exchange Server.	Eight, Appendix A
Develop the configuration of an Exchange Server computer.	Seven, Appendix A
Identify strategies for migration from previous versions of Exchange Server to Exchange Server 5.5.	Fifteen, Appendix A
Develop a long-term coexistence strategy for IMAP and LDAP protocols.	Ten
Develop an infrastructure for Exchange Server.	Four, Eight, Nine, Eleven, Thirteen
Choose Microsoft Exchange Client installation and integration strategies.	Three, Thirteen, Fourteen, Appendix A
Develop long-term administration strategies.	Twelve, Appendix A
Develop security strategies.	Eleven, Appendix A
Develop server-side scripting strategies.	Appendix A

Installation and Configuration

Objective	Chapter
Install an Exchange Server computer.	Three, Appendix A
Configure Exchange Server for message recipients.	Three, Five, Eleven, Appendix A
Configure connectivity to a mail system other than Exchange Server.	Three, Seven, Eight, Fourteen, Appendix A
Configure synchronization of directory information between Exchange Server and other mail systems.	Three, Appendix A
Configure directory replication.	Three, Appendix A
Import directory, message, and scheduling data from existing mail systems.	Three, Five, Six, Appendix A
Install and configure Exchange Server client computers.	Six, Appendix A
Configure address lists and accounts by using the Administrator program.	Three, Five, Appendix A
Configure the Message Transfer Agent within a site.	Three, Four, Appendix A
Configure the Message Transfer Agent among sites.	Three, Eight, Appendix A
Configure Internet protocols and services.	Ten, Appendix A
Configure message tracking.	Three, Four, Nine, Appendix A
Configure server locations.	Eleven
Configure security.	Eleven

Configuring and Managing Resource Access

Objective	Chapter	Objective	Chapter
Manage site security.	Eleven	Manage public Information Stores.	Eleven
Manage users.	Five	Manage private Information Stores.	Four, Twelve, Fifteen
Manage distribution lists.	Five	Back up and restore the Exchange Server organization.	Twelve
Manage the directory.	Five, Fourteen	Manage connectivity.	Eight, Fourteen

Monitoring and Optimization

Objective	Chapter
Configure a Link Monitor and a Server Monitor.	Twelve
Optimize Exchange Server.	Seven
Optimize foreign connections and site-to-site connections.	Seven
Monitor and optimize the messaging environment.	Seven
Monitor server performance by using SNMP and MADMAN MIB.	Twelve, Appendix A

Troubleshooting

Objective	Chapter
Diagnose and resolve upgrade problems.	Fifteen
Diagnose and resolve server installation problems.	Fifteen
Diagnose and resolve migration problems.	Fifteen
Diagnose and resolve connectivity problems.	Fifteen
Diagnose and resolve problems with client connectivity.	Fourteen
Diagnose and resolve Information Store problems.	Fifteen
Diagnose and resolve server directory problems.	Fifteen
Diagnose and resolve server resource problems.	Fifteen
Diagnose and resolve message delivery problems.	Fifteen
Diagnose and resolve backup problems and restore problems.	Twelve, Appendix B
Diagnose organization security problems.	Twelve

W

X

I
N
D
E
X